THE GARDENER'S HOME COMPANION

HOW TO RAISE MORE THAN 350 FLOWERS, HERBS, VEGETABLES, SHRUBS, VINES, AND LAWN AND ORNAMENTAL GRASSES

Betty Mackey, Ann Reilly,
Barbara Radcliffe Rogers, Barbara Pleasant,
Diane Bilderback, and Bob Brooke

Gramercy Books
New York

This 2002 edition published by Gramercy Books, an imprint of Random House Value Publishing,
a division of Random House, Inc., 280 Park Avenue, New York, NY 10017, by arrangement with
Macmillan Publishing Company, New York.

Gramercy is a registered trademark and the colophon is a trademark of Random House, Inc.

Designer: Keithley and Associates
Produced by The Philip Lief Group, Inc.

Random House
New York • Toronto • London • Sydney • Auckland
www.randomhouse.com

Printed and bound in the United States of America

Library of Congress Cataloging-in-Publication Data

The gardener's home companion / Betty Mackey ... [et al.].—2002 ed.
        p. cm.
    Originally published: New York : Macmillan Pub. Co., c1991.
    ISBN 0-517-22059-8
        1. Gardening. 2. Gardening—United States. I. Mackey, Betty.

SB453 .G2773 2002
635—dc21
                                                    2001046028

10 9 8 7 6 5 4 3 2 1

THE GARDENER'S HOME COMPANION

THE
CONTRIBUTORS

Betty Mackey, the author of *A Cutting Garden for Florida* and *A Cutting Garden for California,* is the associate editor of *Living Off the Land* and contributes regularly to *Weekend Gardener Journal, Organic Gardening,* and *Horticulture.* She also designed and installed the cutting garden at Leu Botanical Gardens in Orlando, Florida. She now gardens in Pennsylvania.

Ann Reilly, a horticultural writer and photographer, is the author of several books, including *Success with Seeds* and *Step-by-Step Successful Gardening,* both of which were awarded Best Book of the Year by the Garden Writers Association of America. She has also contributed to several gardening books for *Better Homes and Gardens* and is currently working on the Time-Life gardening series. She gardens on Long Island, New York.

Barbara Radcliffe Rogers is a regular contributor to such magazines as *Yankee* and *Country Journal.* She has written three previous books, including *The Encyclopedia of Everlastings.* She gardens in New Hampshire.

Barbara Pleasant is a contributing editor of *Organic Gardening* and a regular columnist for *Progressive Farmer.* She has written for *Flower and Garden, National Gardening,* and *Country Journal,* and is the author of *The Handbook of Southern Vegetable Gardening.* She gardens in Alabama.

Diane Bilderback, who has a degree in botany, is a regional editor of *Organic Gardening* and writes regularly for *National Gardening* and *Family Circle.* She is the coauthor of *Garden Secrets* and *Backyard Fruits and Berries.* She gardens in Montana.

Bob Brooke, a writer and photographer, has written gardening articles for *The Baltimore Sun* and *The Sunday Press,* among others.

HORTICULTURAL
REVIEW BOARD

Dr. Mary Lewnes Albrecht, an associate professor at Kansas State University, specializes in the cultivation and management of ornamental and flowering plants, and teaches courses in floriculture. She has written articles for *Greenhouse Grower* and has contributed to the Brooklyn Botanic Garden's instructional handbook series.

Dr. David W. Davis, professor of horticultural science at the University of Minnesota, specializes in vegetable crops. He has published scientific and popular articles on the breeding, production, and phenology of vegetables, as well as on agricultural development.

Dr. David L. Hensley, associate professor at Kansas State University, specializes in ornamental horticulture. He teaches landscape design, maintenance, and contracting, and is the author of more than a hundred trade and popular press articles in his field. He is currently writing a textbook on landscape management.

Dr. William J. Lamont, Jr., assistant professor of horticulture at Kansas State University, specializes in vegetable research and microclimate modification. He writes for the *Journal of the American Society of Horticultural Science* and *American Vegetable Grower.*

Dr. Jeff L. Nus, a horticultural researcher and educator in turfgrass science, is an assistant professor at Kansas State University. He is a contributor to the New American Society of Agronomy's monograph on turfgrass science, and has authored papers for the International Turfgrass Research Conference.

Dr. Norman E. Pellet, a professor of horticulture at the University of Vermont, researches and writes on ornamental horticulture. He has authored numerous research articles for trade journals.

Dr. Bernadine C. Strik is an assistant professor at Oregon State University and a regional and statewide extension specialist on grape and berry crops. She has published articles in *HortScience* and the *Journal of the American Society of Horticultural Science* and has lectured on viticulture and the culture and physiology of fruit crops.

CONTENTS

INTRODUCTION

HOW TO USE THIS BOOK

As you step up to more ambitious garden plans, your need for information increases. *The Gardener's Home Companion,* a comprehensive, illustrated guide to home gardening, is clear enough for a beginner to understand, yet does not gloss over horticultural complexities. Use it to learn essential gardening principles and techniques, as well as specific practices for growing hundreds of kinds of garden plants.

This easy-to-use reference covers garden planning, preparation, planting, maintenance, and problem solving. There is information on growing plants from seeds and cuttings as well as on purchasing healthy plants. Also helpful are the garden calendars for four general regions of the United States, and the chapters on tools, roses, shrubs, vines, ground covers, ornamental grasses, and lawns.

The plant chapters, however, constitute the heart of this book. You will use them for instant detailed information on the most popular plants for home gardens. Under alphabetized common-name headings such as daylily, basil, raspberry, and tomato, each entry outlines the growing conditions, space requirements, and materials needed to grow plants in the genus or species being discussed. Then, step-by-step instructions are given for all appropriate stages of cultivation, from sowing seed through harvesting. Each entry concludes with a section on available varieties or cultivars. Botanical names are included for greater accuracy.

Within, you will find chapters for flowers (annuals, biennials, and perennials, including wildflowers), vegetables (old and new varieties), herbs, and berries and melons. Like a recipe in a cookbook, the entry-form listing for each plant states exactly what supplies you need and how to accomplish the task at hand (in this case, growing the plant, not cooking it) in an orderly way.

There will be some minor variations in the way information is arranged in each entry—the steps for growing annual vegetables differ from those for growing perennial flowers, for instance. The following sample entry from the flower section shows the kind of information you will find.

SAMPLE ENTRY

Botanical name: The genus (in italics) and family name (in parentheses) according to accepted botanical nomenclature.

Common name(s): A listing of this plant's best-known common names, which may vary from region to region.

PLANT DESCRIPTION: A paragraph or two describing the plant's uses and special features, such as longevity and hardiness, plus handy bits of garden lore, such as the origin of its name.

PLANT TYPE: The category or categories the plant fits into, such as annual, biennial, or perennial. An *annual* plant germinates, grows, blooms, sets seed, and dies in a single season or year. A *biennial* germinates and starts to grow one year, then blooms and dies the next year. A *perennial* lives for more than a year, often for many. Sometimes the same plant behaves differently in different climates. Plants may be *tender* (killed by frost, and harmed by temperatures in the low 30's [F]), *half-hardy* (tolerant of cool but not freezing temperatures), or *hardy* (tolerant of freezing weather).

GROWING RANGE: The plant's tolerance for climate according to the hardiness zones designated by the United States Department of Agriculture. Please refer to the USDA zone map on the endpapers to see which zone you garden in. In this category, upper and lower zone limits (for instance, Zones 3 to 8) are given for each plant.

HARDINESS: The plant's range of tolerance for cold to hot weather, in degrees Fahrenheit where possible.

PLANT HEIGHT: The plant's mature height, or range of height, in feet and inches.

FLOWER COLOR: The range of colors and patterns usually available for this plant.

FLOWER FORM: The blossom's shape, size, and configuration; for example, 3-inch disc and ray flowers on unbranched 8-inch stems, or 5-inch sprays of tiny single blossoms.

SEASON OF BLOOM: The time of year this plant blooms in most regions of the United States. For some plants, different times are given for different regions.

SOIL: The type or types of soil commonly preferred by this plant—moist, dry, sandy, loamy, etc. Sterile soil is emphasized for particularly vulnerable species.

PH: The preferred acidity or alkalinity of soil, on a scale of 0 to 14. A pH under 7 is acidic, 7 is neutral, and over 7 is alkaline.

FERTILIZER: The type of substance preferred or often used to provide nutrients to this kind of plant. It is not necessarily a packaged product—manure and compost also add nutrients and are effective soil improvers. Products with high phosphorus and potassium are sometimes labeled tomato or flower fertilizers. Most plants tolerate nearly any type of fertilizer, though the total amount and proportion of elements needed vary with the species.

WATER: The amount of water usually preferred by mature plants—wet, average, or dry conditions.

EXPOSURE: The amount of sun and wind preferred or tolerated by the plant. *Full sun* means eight or more hours of bright sunlight daily; *partial shade* means filtered sunlight or bright sun for fewer than four hours a day; and *shade* means indirect or filtered sunlight.

SPACING: The preferred spacing for mature plants, in feet and inches. Young plants that will later be transplanted can be more closely spaced.

PROPAGATION: The appropriate means of starting new plants, such as from seed, by tip cuttings, stem cuttings, or division. Most plants can be propagated in several ways.

Method

Step-by-step instructions on when and how to grow this plant, under such subheadings as:

- **Start seeds indoors**

- **Prepare soil outdoors** (for seeds or transplants)

- **Sow seeds outdoors**

- **Thin or transplant** seedlings (Please note that all seedlings may be transplanted, but some require far greater care than others because of their fragility or small size. For these, a warning is usually included. Any seedling grown indoors should be hardened off before transplanting outdoors.)

- **Set plants outdoors**

- **Divide** (It is difficult to give exact instructions for division of perennial plants, for they can be divided at almost any time of the year with expert handling and good conditions. However, some times of the year are more suitable than others, and division is easiest at the time of year suggested in the individual plant entries.)

- **Water**

- **Fertilize**

- **Pests and diseases** (problems and remedies)

- **Mulch** (Mulch, too, is a variable element. Factors such as climate, soil type, and preferred or available mulching materials all come into play. Suggested types and depths are given, but others are also acceptable.)

- **Train, trellis, or stake**

- **Prune, trim, or deadhead** (remove spent blossoms)

- **Protect in winter**

- **Harvest**

- **Dry or store**

- **Yield**

Tips · Special bits of useful information not previously mentioned, on drying, storing, growing, or cooking.

Selected Varieties (naturally occurring varieties) and *Cultivars (cultivated varieties), or Species (subgroups)*

Popular or recommended types of this plant are listed and described by genus (major classified group, such as *Iris*), species (minor classified subgroup such as *I. cristata* or *I. germanica,* and/or variety or cultivar name such as *I. germanica* 'Pink Dream.' The second time the genus name appears in an entry with any species name it is abbreviated to its first initial, as in *I. pumila.* The purpose of this section of the entry is to give you a better idea of the variation among cultivated members of this genus (group), in terms of hardiness, size, color, and taste. Some popular species have hundreds of named cultivars. For these, a cross section of the selections are described.

GENERAL GARDENING SECTION

In this fully illustrated part of *The Gardener's Home Companion,* you will find everything you need to know about creating and maintaining a healthy garden.

You'll find Chapter 1 helpful in planning and placing your garden. What should you plant? What is your garden's function—to be decorative, productive, or recreational? What are its climate and microclimate? How can you assess and manage such growing conditions as sun, shade, soil type, drainage, moisture, topography, and wind exposure? What shape should your garden beds be?

Everything you need to know about tools and equipment can be found in Chapter 2. Here you will learn which tools are most essential and how to select those of the best quality and value—tools for lawn and garden maintenance, pruning gear, watering equipment, and gardening aids for the disabled.

Use Chapter 3 to learn the components, improvement, preparation, and maintenance of your garden soil. How can you test it? What is its pH? What are the major nutrients and trace elements and how do they affect plant growth? The handy diagnostic table on pages 46–47 shows how different nutrient deficiencies affect your plants. What kinds of fertilizers and soil amendments are available? How do you prepare the soil for planting?

Chapter 4 is devoted to planting: how to acquire, propagate, and care for plants. How do you grow them from seed? Do you need a cold frame?

Cold frames, discussed on pages 73–74, provide a climate that is like an indoor one in some ways and an outdoor one in others. Cold frames have seasonal variations in their temperatures, but are warmer than unprotected sites outdoors. Their conditions are also affected by the amount of sun and shade they receive. A cold frame may be used for any plant at any time of year that it provides the right temperatures, even if this is not specifically mentioned in the plant entry.

What are the kinds of beds and borders? How do you grow healthy plants in containers? In window boxes? What about vertical growing? Ground covers and cutting gardens? How can you grow fresh vegetables and herbs? Flowers and shrubs? Climbing roses? How about fruit trees—standard, semidwarf, dwarf, or genetic dwarf? Espaliers? Many common and special techniques are discussed.

In Chapter 5, you'll learn more about garden maintenance—how to care for your plants as they grow. Here are instructions on watering, fertilizing, mulching, weeding, pruning or pinching back, and winter protection. Dividing perennials and bulbs, taking cuttings, layering, deadheading, pruning, crop rotation, and pest and disease control are discussed. You'll find a table on attributes of popular mulching materials and another of organic controls of common garden pests.

Chapter 6, on the gardening year, is a calendar indicating what to do each month in four different U.S. garden regions—Northern (Zones 2 to 5), Central (Zones 6 to 8), Hot Southern (Zones 9 to 11), and Mild West Coast (parts of Zones 9 to 11 with cooler summers). Use this section for a better understanding of which activities to do when, as the seasons pass. Just reading it may give you many ideas about your garden's potential.

In addition to the plant entries and general gardening information, *The Gardener's Home Companion* features sections on shrubs, vines, ground covers, ornamental grasses, and lawn grasses. Each one discusses plant types, placement, selection, acquisition, planting, and maintenance. A detailed chart gives an overview of plant varieties in popular use, plus how and where to grow them.

Trees, because of their size and diversity, have not been included in the entry format. However, some aspects of shade and fruit tree planting and pruning are discussed in Chapter 4.

Finally, the Appendix provides a useful list of nurseries, seed houses, and sellers of garden equipment.

Every part of this book has been edited by a distinguished panel of horticulturists. Its purpose is to give you easy access to the kind of practical information on gardening that takes years of experience and study to gain. All of the contributors hope you will put their experience to work along with your own, and enjoy many years of happy and successful gardening.

THE GARDEN SITE

So, you would like to have a garden. But where? How will it fit into your home landscape? Does your present landscape suit your purposes?

Whether your garden space is large or small, the key to successful gardening is finding the best sites possible, analyzing and improving them, and selecting the most appropriate plants for the varying conditions your landscape offers.

All plants need light for part of the day, soil for support, nutrients, and water. Fruit trees and vegetables require a sunny exposure and well-drained soil with no standing water, but the myriad varieties of flowers, herbs, shrubs, and ground covers you could grow differ as much in their light, water, and temperature requirements as in their appearance.

It is important to know that spots even a few yards away from each other can differ significantly in their exposure to the sun and wind, in soil type, and in drainage. A balcony, small as it is, has several areas with differing conditions called *microclimates* (see the illustration on page 2). A balcony plant in a hanging basket will experience different kinds of air circulation, light, and temperature than one in a pot leaning against the building. Plants on one end of the balcony may receive more shade or wind than those on the other because of the way the building is situated.

The yard of a townhouse or suburban home has even more microclimates and far more potential for diversity. The spacious grounds of a country home offer an array of possibilities that can be somewhat mind boggling, even to an experienced gardener. A fuller discussion of microclimates follows on pages 16–18.

For most garden plants, the best spot for cultivation is one on level or slightly sloping (ideally, south-facing) ground in a sunny spot free from the roots of trees or shrubs. It has rich soil that is easy to till, is well drained, and has a nearby water supply for irrigation.

However, it rarely happens that the portion of property available for gardening is blessed by such perfect conditions. Shade may be cast by large trees or buildings. The soil may be mostly sand, rock, or clay. A steep slope may add to the difficulty of cultivation.

In spite of all this, millions of gardeners manage to grow wonderful gardens by improving their soil and growing conditions however they can, and making the best of what they have.

The plants on this balcony experience different microclimates in spite of their close proximity to one another. The small tree near the wall is sheltered from winds from two directions, but the petunias in the window box are exposed. The fern in the hanging basket is more shaded and sheltered than the other plants.

Partially sheltered microclimate

Sheltered, shaded microclimate

Exposed microclimate

GARDEN PLANNING

Garden planning means striking a balance between what you want from your garden and the possibilities your site can offer. Different garden priorities obviously lead to different garden plans. Here are a few examples of differing objectives:

Gardener One: "I would like to have a large fruit and vegetable garden—away from the house—supplying our table all year long. Because I do a fair amount of entertaining, there should be ornamental and recreational areas surrounding the house, incorporating lawns, ground covers, ornamental grasses, and flowers. I'd especially love a decorative pond with water lilies."

Gardener Two: "I'm home late each day and away some weekends, so I'd like an attractive, easy-care yard with privacy. The colors should be restrained. I don't expect to grow many vegetables, but I'd like to have fresh tomatoes and maybe some salad greens."

Gardener Three: "I'm interested in herbs and fruit. I have a large backyard and would like to work these into the landscape along with ornamental shrubs and flowers."

Gardener Four: "I have always admired those English flower borders with tall, wide clumps of perennial flowers. There should always be something in bloom. I'd like a border like that to be the main feature of my garden, situated near the terrace."

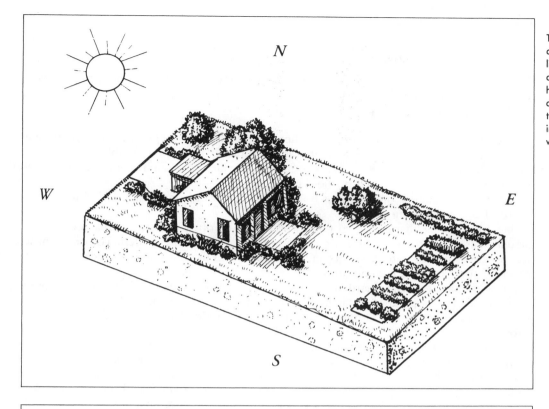

This vegetable garden gets good sunlight and is well drained because it has been placed in a site where no tree or shrub roots interfere with cultivation.

This vegetable garden is in a poor site because it is too close to large trees that block sunlight to the garden and crowd the growing area with their roots. In addition, the steep slope causes erosion of the exposed soil. On the same property, vegetables would grow better if they were mixed among the ornamental plants in the front yard, or else set in terraced beds near the patio in the sunnier portion of the backyard.

Gardener Five: "I want a pretty garden with a wide range of plants. I have time to work in it, and I'd like a nice supply of fruit, herbs, cut flowers, and vegetables as close to the kitchen as possible."

Each gardener has clearly stated his or her main goals. This is a good beginning. It gives direction to garden planning. A new site can be planned, or an older, established landscape modified, with these goals in mind. The same home and its grounds could be developed in a different way to suit each of these gardeners.

What can be done if the site does not offer the growing conditions needed for one or more of the goals in the plan?

Say, for instance, that Gardener One, who entertains often and wants ornamental areas, actually has no room in the yard for an out-of-the-way vegetable garden. To compromise, he can either incorporate the fruits and vegetables into the other gardens near the house or else participate in a community garden away from home.

Suppose that the second gardener, who wants an easy-care garden because she is often away, has a professional landscaper design her yard. If she is clear about her wish for tomatoes and lettuce, the designer will find a way to blend them in with their elegant surroundings.

Gardener Three wants herbs and fruit trees in his large backyard. However, since these plants are sun lovers, they must be planted where the exposure is right. If the exposure is far better in the front yard than the back, Gardener Three will have to decide whether to give up his dream of planting herbs and fruit, or plant them for all the world to see.

Say that the fourth gardener, who wants an English-style perennial flower border, finds that the spot she has chosen slopes down steeply and has thin, gritty soil studded with rocks. These conditions are wrong for the border, but ideal for rock gardening. Most rock garden plants are smaller perennials, neat, low-growing, and boldly flowered. They are demanding and will grow only under the right conditions. Gardener Four would be wise to redirect her enthusiasm rather than take the time and expense to reshape the area, remove the rocks, and bring in a ton of topsoil before she can start gardening.

Gardener Five wants a bit of everything and has to be careful with color and form or the garden will be too messy. He can pick a two-color scheme, perhaps a different one each year or season. The garden might be organized by planting groups of plants in clumps—shorter ones toward the front, taller ones in back. Placement would be guided by exposure and soil in the area's microclimates. Edgings of lettuce or alyssum could help tie it all together. This kind of gardening requires the most expertise and labor.

As you can see, the skills needed for gardening include the art of compromise. Few spaces are ideal. Even for experienced gardeners, it takes time to learn the limits and possibilities of a particular garden spot.

ASSESSING YOUR SITE

Before planning a garden, the site must be studied. It will be helpful to draw a diagram of your house and grounds so you can picture your garden site as it is now and as you would like it to look. Some of its characteristics can be changed, while others are permanent

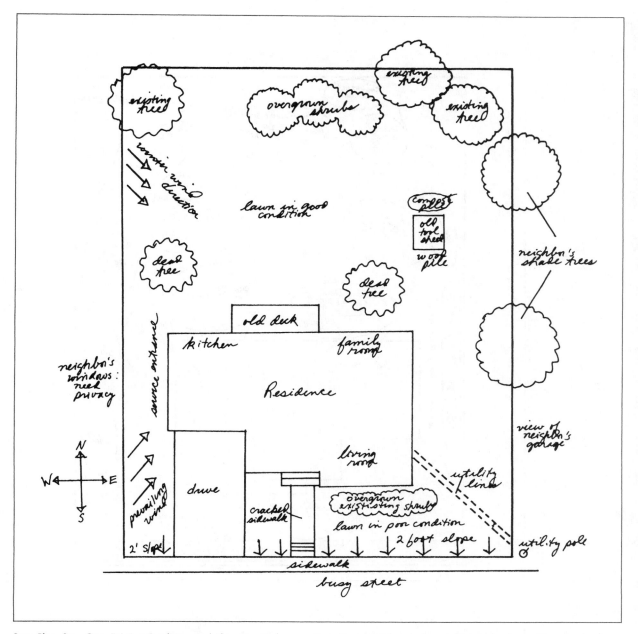

Base Plan, Step One: Existing Conditions and Elements. Study your site in its present form before making a plan for revising your landscape. First, draw a dimensioned site analysis like this one to show existing conditions. Indicate the outer perimeter of the property and any existing buildings, plantings, and pavement. Show their condition wherever it affects landscape planning. Mark features outside the property that should be screened from view. Be sure to mark a compass on the drawing to show the direction of exposure, and indicate prevailing winds with arrows.

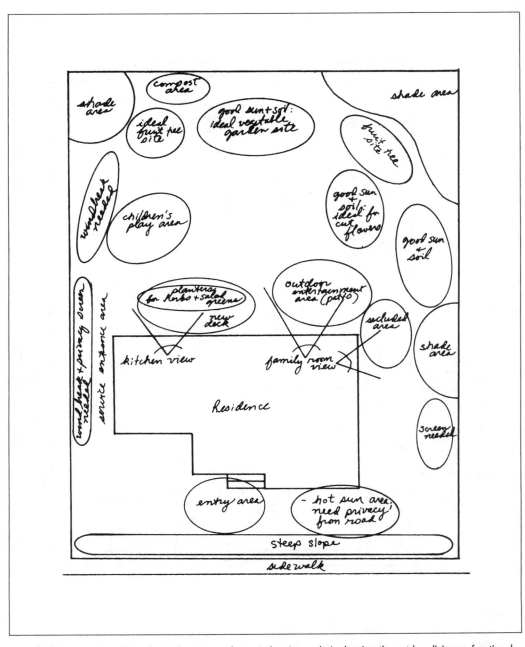

Base Plan, Step Two: Analysis of Needs. Next, make a similar site analysis showing the outdoor living or functional areas desired and the existing growing conditions, such as sun, shade, slope, and soil quality. Be sure to include V-shaped marks to indicate the view from the house, and mark areas in need of correction, such as a spot where a screen or windbreak is needed.

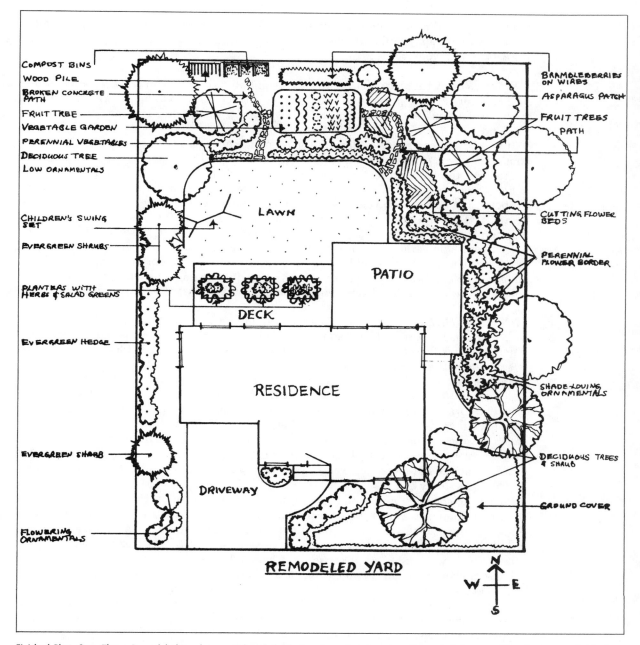

COMPOST BINS
WOOD PILE
BROKEN CONCRETE PATH
FRUIT TREE
VEGETABLE GARDEN
PERENNIAL VEGETABLES
DECIDUOUS TREE
LOW ORNAMENTALS

CHILDREN'S SWING SET
EVERGREEN SHRUBS

PLANTERS WITH HERBS & SALAD GREENS

EVERGREEN HEDGE

EVERGREEN SHRUB

FLOWERING ORNAMENTALS

BRAMBLEBERRIES ON WIRES
ASPARAGUS PATCH
FRUIT TREES
PATH

CUTTING FLOWER BEDS

PERENNIAL FLOWER BORDER

SHADE-LOVING ORNAMENTALS

DECIDUOUS TREES & SHRUB

GROUND COVER

LAWN

PATIO

DECK

RESIDENCE

DRIVEWAY

REMODELED YARD

N
W — E
S

Finished Plan, Step Three: Remodeled Landscape. Take all the factors from your two-step site analysis into consideration in your finished plan. A landscape architect would present you with a plan showing the finished site, something like the one above. It shows the plants, paved areas, decks and patios, and the residence, and their relationship to one another. *Note:* It may take new plantings several years to reach the size shown in the plan.

features that will have to be planned around. Sites vary in exposure, amount and kind of sunshine, topography, soil type, wind, drainage, and climate, and the first thing you should do is take an inventory of each.

EXPOSURE. A flat piece of ground with no buildings or trees has no particular exposure. The exposure of your property is determined by its relationship to buildings, walls, fences, trees, shrubs, and slopes. These affect the way light, wind, frost, and water interact with the land.

If you have a choice of locations for gardening, choose a site sloping down toward the south that is free of roots from trees and shrubs. The southerly exposure will provide your plants with the most protection from freezing weather and catch the sun at a favorable angle. The best spot for vegetables, fruits, and herbs is in the brightest, hottest spot on the property. Do not locate a vegetable garden or flowers needing bright sun just to the west or north of tall trees or buildings; try to place them at least 20 feet away, otherwise you will be plagued with too much shade. A location just to the east, however, is acceptable.

In a vegetable garden, the direction in which you plant your rows will also affect your exposure. The tall plants should not cast too much shade on the shorter ones. To avoid this, tall garden plants, such as fruit trees or corn, should be set on the north side of the garden, and small ones, like rhubarb and spinach, on the south side. Rows should run east to west.

SUN AND SHADE. Seed catalogs and garden references, including this one, mention full sun, light shade, partial shade, and deep shade when giving growing requirements for different plants. Except for an open field, few garden locations are shade-free at all times, but the amount and quality of shade are varied.

Full sun means unobstructed sunlight for the major part of the day, usually for eight hours or longer. *Light shade* refers to the bright dappled shade under or near small-leaved trees or latticework fencing. *Partial shade* means the area has sun part of the day and shade the rest. Then there is the *deep shade* cast by a building or wall through which no direct sunlight passes. As the sun moves, the affected area may change abruptly from deep shade to full sun. An evergreen tree casts shade nearly as deep as a building or deciduous tree, but it is more feathered at the edges. Fences cast varying amounts of shade, depending on their height and solidity.

Given the choice of either morning or afternoon sun for sun-loving plants, it is best to choose morning sun as it is cooler at that time of day and plants are far less likely to wilt. They may need some shade later, during the hotter part of the day. Lawns may be grown in either sun or shade, so long as you choose the species of grass best suited for your conditions. Lawn grasses are discussed in Chapter 15.

How can you judge the amount of shade and sun that falls on your garden site? Looking at a deciduous tree that has dropped its leaves for the winter and trying to guess what kind of shade it will throw when clothed in greenery again will lead to very misleading conclusions. The best time of year to see how much sun and shade a property receives is the end of July. In midsummer the tree leaves are fully expanded and the sun in the Northern Hemisphere is coming in at its high, southern, summer angle (the angle changes as the seasons go by). Sun and shade should be noted in early morning, late morning, noon, early afternoon, late afternoon, and evening. A single large tree will cast shade of varying degrees over a wide area during the course of the day, as the relative position of the sun changes (see Figures A, B, and C on pages 10–11). It is all too easy to underestimate the amount of shade a tree can cast.

Deciduous trees cast different amounts of shade at different times of year and smart gardeners should take advantage of their annual cycle. For instance, areas near or under trees can be planted with early-spring bulbs and ferns that have a relatively low need for moisture. The bulbs need sunlight in late winter and early spring, but not in late spring or summer when the trees are in full leaf. At that point the shade-loving ferns take over.

Trees with small leaves, such as the mimosa or locust, cast very little shade compared to large-leaved trees, such as the maple and oak. Some trees have a high canopy, admitting light when the sun is low in the sky, while other trees and shrubs are leafy all the way to the ground. When selecting and planting trees, you need to take these differences into consideration and estimate the amount of shade that will eventually result when the tree has fully matured. When clearing existing trees to admit sunlight, also think carefully: In some situations, thinning the limbs and raising the canopy by removing all the lower limbs will make the difference to sun-loving plants. In other cases, either the tree will have to go or your garden will be restricted to shade plants.

TOPOGRAPHY. Is your yard on a slope? What direction does it face? Is it on top of a hill, exposed, windy, and dry? Is it at the bottom of a hill, where cold air collects in frost pockets and the soil is boggy because water drainage is poor? The grade of your terrain affects gardening conditions. Land at the top of a slope thaws out earlier in the year than land at the bottom. Why? Because while heat rises, cold air seeks the lowest level and tends to collect at the bottom of a steep hill, where the air circulation is poor. In a hot, dry climate this attribute can be used to advantage, allowing for the planting of more temperate plants, while in colder climates it can be a real problem.

Before siting a garden, try to assess the effects of topography and exposure on your property. Look for places where puddles stand after a rain. Watch to see where snow melts quickly or tends to linger in winter. On the first frosty morning, see which places were struck and which were spared.

Though gardeners try to avoid placing gardens where conditions are unfavorable, sometimes there is no choice. However, there are ways to deal with problems of topography, short of bringing in the bulldozers.

Instead of changing their nature, these and other problem areas can be enhanced with plant colonies perfectly adapted to them. The hilltop, perhaps with the addition of picturesque boulders, might be just the spot for rare alpine plants, and the boggy low area could be transformed into a water lily pool surrounded by Louisiana and Japanese iris, both bog lovers. Many striking and unusual gardens were created in response to "problem" sites.

WIND. Do you have strong winds in summer? In winter? From which direction do they come?

If your garden is near the ocean or in a windy area, you will probably need some form of wind protection. Wind dries plants and soil by increasing the speed of evapotranspiration. Wind also causes erosion, blowing away the smallest and lightest particles of soil—namely, topsoil and dry fertilizer. It leaves sand, gravel, and rock behind, but even these can be blown around if the wind is strong enough. The remaining soil is at best likely to be sandy.

A. In the morning, this leafy tree casts a deep shade that extends several yards to the right.
B. At midday, the shade cast by the same tree is centered below it.
C. In the evening, the shade cast by this tree extends far to the left, quite a few yards from where it fell in the morning. The area of partial shade to the right, below, and to the left of the tree is much larger than the tree's actual canopy size.

Naturally, plants are adversely affected by the resulting soil deficiency, as well as the structural stress caused by the wind blowing on them. It takes plants with a tough, leathery surface to stand up to hard winds. These plants can shield crops, lawns, and tender flowers from some of the force of the wind.

Even fairly moderate winds can cause garden flowers and vegetables to topple over. This is especially likely if plants are leggy or top-heavy as a result of too much shade (in their search for sun, they've been reaching up to the light, sacrificing business for long stems). It can be prevented by staking plants before the need is obvious, and by selecting shorter, stockier plant varieties. Methods of staking garden plants will be discussed in Chapter 5.

In places with cold winters, wind piles snow into drifts in some spots and strips it from others. But deep snow, such a nuisance in some areas, actually serves as a protective blanket over perennial flowers. It keeps them safe from extreme cold and radical temperature changes that alternately freeze and thaw the soil, lifting shallow-rooted plants right out of the ground.

Fences and plants resistant to the wind can be placed in strategic spots to break the force of the wind and protect more tender garden plants. They can enhance the gardener's comfort, too, keeping wind off a terrace or snow off a driveway, for instance. Windbreaks can also protect a home from the effects of the north wind and decrease the amount of fuel needed to heat it in winter.

Before putting in a windbreak, study your property to determine the direction of the prevailing winds. In most areas, winter and summer winds come from different directions. In many parts of the United States, windbreaks are placed across the north and west sides of the property, but this depends on factors unique to each side—slopes, large buildings, and nearby bodies of water.

A windbreak slows down the air approaching it and makes it rise. Eventually the air will fall in a rush of wind, but the protective effect of a 10-foot-tall windbreak extends more than 200 feet beyond it. While wind will not be eliminated by a windbreak, its adverse effect will be greatly decreased. Protection from as little as 10 percent of the force of the wind may be enough to make a nearly unusable area quite acceptable for gardening.

When wind and water carry away soil particles (erosion), the roots of plants, such as those of this large tree, are dangerously exposed, limiting intake of water and nutrients. In addition, badly anchored plants like this one are more likely to be uprooted in a storm.

In order for windbreaks to be effective, they should shield a property from prevailing winds. Here winds from the west are deflected by a dense line of trees.

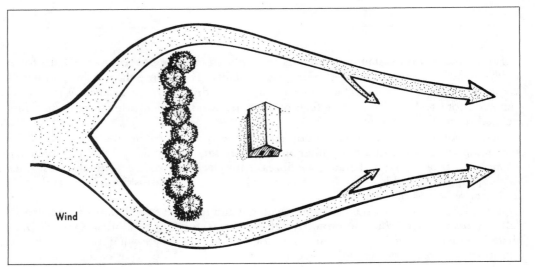

Wind

WINDBREAK AND HEDGE PLANTS

Acacia†	Forsythia	Oak *(Quercus)*
Arborvitae *(Platycladus, Thuja)*	Ginkgo *(Ginkgo biloba)*	Oleander *(Nerium oleander)*†
Ash *(Fraxinus)*	Hemlock *(Tsuga)*	Pine *(Pinus)**
Barberry *(Berberis)*	Holly *(Ilex)*	Pittosporum*†
Bayberry *(Myrica)**	Juniper *(Juniperus)*	Podocarpus*†
Beach Plum *(Prunus maritima)**	Larch *(Larix dedidua)*	Popular *(Populus)**
Beech *(Fagus sylvatica)*	Lilac *(Syringa x chinensis)*	Privet *(Ligustrum)*
Bush honeysuckle *(Lonicera)**	London plane tree *(Platanus acerifolia)*	Rhododendron
Cedar *(Cedrus)**	Loquat†	Rugusa and other roses *(Rosa)**
Cottonwood *(Populus)*	Magnolia†	Smoke tree *(Rhus cotinus)**
Cypress *(Cupressus)*†	Maple *(Acer)*	Spruce *(Picea)*
Dogwood *(Cornus)*	Mountain laurel *(Kalmia latifolia)*	Viburnum
Elm *Ulmus)*	Nandina *(Nandina domestica)*†	Willow *(Salix)*
Fir *(Abies)*		Yew *(Taxus)*

*Recommended near the seashore.
†Recommended in regions with mild winters.

Fences to be used as windbreaks should not be so solid that no wind can get through, or they might be blown down in the force of a gale. Many types of fencing provide protection, yet are open to air passage. Earthen berms—mounds of earth planted with wind-resistant plants or grasses (see the illustration at the top of page 14)—can be used instead of fencing to provide stable and effective wind protection. Berms can be any size, but the proper height-to-width ratio is 2 to 3.

Plants of many kinds can be used in windbreaks, with the appropriate species varying from region to region (see the table above). Any large sturdy hedge plant appropriate to your area will work, as will trees and large shrubs that are native or widely naturalized in your region. Evergreen windbreak plants are effective year-round. Deciduous plants may be used where the windbreak is needed only in summer, although even their bare branches will have some effect in winter.

EROSION. Erosion is hardest to control on steep slopes. There, topsoil is washed or blown away by wind and rain, leaving behind scars and gullies. Bare soil is more vulnerable to erosion than soil with a cover of plants on it because rugged ground covers, grasses, and trees have deep roots that help anchor the soil. Crops, too, will help. So will weeds! Steep inclines should be planted in contoured rows or terraces cutting horizontally across the slope, not vertically. Using sod rather than grass seed for planted slopes helps prevent soil loss while the grass takes hold.

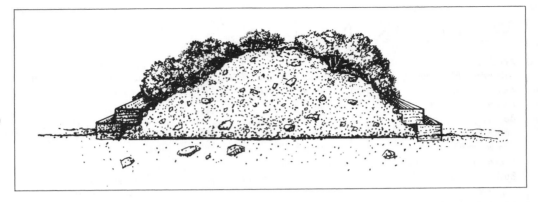

Earthen berms are used in landscaping to serve as windbreaks and provide landscape impact. The ornamental shrubs and railroad ties shown here anchor the soil while adding visual interest.

When grading or reshaping eroded ground, it is important to make changes in small incremental layers (6 to 8 inches of soil at a time) to prevent the formation of large air pockets. Roll or press them with a lawn roller to be sure air pockets are squeezed out. This will prevent soil from settling or shifting months or years later.

Terraces—steplike structures that provide level areas for gardening or farming—effectively prevent most erosion. They break the fall of the water and give it a place to soak into the soil and be used. In elaborate systems, runoff ditches are included for drainage. If you're going to make terraces, very likely some of the topsoil will have to be trucked

Terraces like these add lots of interest to a sloping landscape while reducing or eliminating erosion.

Here an asset was made of a problem slope by converting it into a terraced vegetable garden.

in, an expensive proposition, considering how much you'll need. The walls of terraces may be made of railroad ties, stones, bricks, or soil that has been planted with grass or ivy.

WATER. Is your soil susceptible to flood or drought? Does water settle in puddles when you water your plants or lawn? Does the soil dry out too fast?

The topography and type of soil in your garden affect its capacity to hold water, a substance no plant can live without. Plants absorb nutrients only after the nutrients are dissolved in water. Desert plants that survive months or years without rain have the capacity either to store water or to seek it out with deep taproots, or else they are annuals with seeds that wait long periods for the right growing conditions before germinating.

Most garden plants and lawn grasses need both water and air in their root zone. *Too much water* is just as harmful as too little. Bog plants can grow in standing water because they are adapted for it, but garden vegetables are not. Fortunately, in all but the most extreme areas, it is not difficult to adjust the water level and soil structure enough to suit the plants you wish to grow.

Improving Drainage. As you will read in Chapter 3, soils are composed of mixed particles of sand, silt, clay (small inorganic particles), and humus (decayed organic matter). When soil that is too high in clay gets wet, it becomes sticky because the fine particles retain so much water. You can improve the structure of clay soils by mixing in hay, straw, chopped corn stalks, wood chips, peat moss, or compost. For estimates of amounts, check with your local agricultural extension agent, who can analyze your soil.

Other soils have drainage problems because they are in a flat or low area at the base of a slope, are in a spot with a high underground water table, or rest on a layer of rocky subsoil that holds in water. Drainage can be increased by raising the level of the soil (by putting in raised beds, for instance) and improving its texture as for clay soil. Sometimes the best solution is to add drainpipes or drain tiles to channel excess water away. Call your local soil conservation agent for installation details of these systems.

Conserving Water. A more widespread problem is too light (sandy) a soil that tends to be dry. Sandy soil retains water poorly, and the problem is worsened by a dry climate. It is hard to irrigate sandy soil adequately without first adding organic material to it that will greatly increase its ability to hold water.

You can improve the water-holding capacity of sandy soil by adding plenty of humus (organic matter in the form of compost, leaf mold, peat moss, sawdust, manure, cover crops turned under, seaweed, etc.), and clay. It is not possible to add too much! Try to mix in at least a 12-inch-thick layer of these soil amendments, whichever ones are practical to acquire in bulk.

Mulch is also an effective tool for conserving water. A good layer of mulch (see Chapter 5) keeps the intense rays of the sun from striking the soil and evaporating the water in it. Most mulches keep the soil cool as well, promoting the presence of earthworms. And if the mulch is an organic one, like wood chips or salt hay, it will help improve the soil as it breaks down.

Shade houses—structures made of lath or screen—placed over plants in sunny areas also cut the sun's intensity and prevent up to 50 percent of the evaporation that would otherwise take place. They increase humidity, too, and are widely used by professional nurserymen and growers in hot climates.

Irrigation can be as simple as a garden hose or as technical as an extensive underground watering system controlled by timers. Drip systems conserve water better than overhead spray systems because water is directed where it is needed, on the plants' roots, and less is lost to evaporation. (Watering is discussed more fully in Chapter 5.)

CLIMATE AND MICROCLIMATE. Your climate is the sum of the sunlight, rainfall, wind, and temperatures—regional as well as local—affecting it throughout the year. When books and catalogs refer to "climate" they mean geographically widespread weather patterns: For example, coastal California has a milder climate than the Midwest. *Microclimate* refers to local conditions of a small area. For instance, a flower bed on the south side of a brick building has a hotter, sunnier microclimate than one on its north side.

USDA Plant Hardiness Zones. The United States Department of Agriculture has developed a plant hardiness zone map for the United States. As you can see on the maps on the endpapers, the country is divided into numbered bands representing areas with different average annual minimum temperatures. Each band is assigned a zone number from 1 to 10. For example, Zone 6 has a minimum average temperature range of $-10°$ to $0°F$. It spans the country in a U-shaped arc. Just below it is Zone 7, somewhat warmer with minimum temperatures of $0°$ to $10°F$.

These zones are used as a guide to determine which plants are hardy where. Garden books and seed catalogs often state the hardiness zone range for plants shown. However, other factors of climate and microclimate will affect a particular kind of plant's capacity to survive in a certain zone.

For instance, a mail-order nursery catalog might list *Anemone sylvestris,* a very pretty, white-flowered woodland perennial, as being hardy in Zones 4 to 8. This does not mean that it will thrive in every garden within these zones, or that it will fail in any garden outside them. Zones 4 to 8 are the expected limits of its safe distribution, but local conditions must suit it or it will die. *A. sylvestris* has temperature limits, but it also requires partial shade, a certain level of moisture, and well-drained soil. By providing a favorable environment it is possible to stretch the zone envelope for this plant. There are protected, mulched, or snow-covered spots in Zone 3, and shady areas with cool nights in Zone 9, where *A. sylvestris* can survive.

The hardiness zones are averages and reflect typical conditions. However, weather being what it is, every so often unusually cold weather can be expected. Florida periodically has severe freezes, damaging thousands of acres of orange trees; yet in most years the trees safely survive the winter. Selecting plants at the top or bottom of their temperature range is risky as they can be wiped out in an atypical year, which is sure to come along sooner or later. The risk should be recognized, then accepted as a challenge or rejected as not worth the effort or the loss.

Changing Your Microclimate. Understanding the effects of exposure, light, topography, soil, wind, drainage, and climate on plants is a lifelong study, but here are some tips to help you create a cooler or warmer microclimate right away. As you select and prepare a garden site, keep these points in mind:

- To make a spot warmer, shelter it from north or winter wind with some kind of wall or windbreak. Let it receive as much sunlight as possible, especially in the afternoon. If needed, add sand and gravel to the soil in addition to humus—sandy soils heat up faster. Raise the soil level—cold air flows downhill. Mulch in winter; in spring, do not mulch but let the sun strike the soil directly. The solar energy will heat it faster this way. You may also want to extend the warm season by adding temporary winter protection for the plants such as portable cold frames (glass or plastic-topped boxes—see pages 73–74 for a detailed description).

- To make a spot cooler, give it partial shade. The source of this can be other garden plants, trees, fencing, screening, or lath. Lattice fencing is an attractive source of dappled shade. In some spots, lowering or raising the grade of an adjacent area will help. Water the spot in the evening and also during the heat of the midday sun. For instance, a bed of impatiens can get through a heat wave better if it is cooled off with a 1 P.M. shower in addition to its regular watering. The water, by its evaporative cooling effect in the afternoon, provides relief. The coldest spots in your garden are located in deep shade on the north of a solid wall or building, but few garden plants can thrive in this exposure.

SHAPING AND PLACING GARDEN BEDS

If you are adding a garden bed or gardening for the first time, you will have to figure out where to locate your garden, what shape it will be, how to remove sod, plants, or rocks that may be in the way, and how to prepare and improve the soil.

There are different kinds of landscape spaces for plants. Before digging a bed, consider the homesite as a whole. In smaller or more exposed yards (a corner lot, for instance) it is important to have the whole landscape flow together attractively, whether or not edible plants will be included. Plants in highly visible parts of the landscape should look attractive in all phases of growth. Functional items, such as compost piles, must be screened from view.

In larger sites or sites with portions sheltered from view from the street or house, the appearance of some parts of the garden can take a backseat to their productivity. There is room for cold frames, vegetable gardens, cutting gardens of flowers, compost piles, and other functional areas, in addition to the more ornamental areas and plantings.

Keeping this in mind, along with your assessment of microclimate and exposure on your property, you must decide where to place your garden beds. Remember, they are easily changed back to lawn if you wish, so go ahead fearlessly! If this is your first attempt at gardening, try to keep it simple by finding flat, sunny sites and not creating too large a garden area at first. Be sure there are no tree roots, buried telephone or cable TV wires, or other obstacles in the soil. Most utility companies will locate underground wires for you, free, if you call and ask—so call! Access to water is important, too.

Another factor in the placement of each garden area is its purpose. If you want an herb garden for culinary use, for instance, it makes sense to place it close to the kitchen. If you are interested in ornamentals, place them where they can be seen. If you plan to grow grapes, remember that they usually attract wasps when they ripen, so don't plant them near a doorway or wasps might fly into the house. If you are a shy person, plant your perennial flowers in the backyard so you can work among them in privacy.

SHAPES FOR GARDEN BEDS. A garden may be any size that suits you. A rectangle 5 by 22 feet fits into the outer boundaries of most properties easily and is big enough for eight rows of vegetables, each 5 feet long, with a central path, or a flower border with eight to ten different species or varieties. The growing area is about 100 square feet, a figure often used on fertilizer containers. Typical directions for a powdered fertilizer might say to broadcast it at a rate of 3 pounds per 100 square feet.

Referring back to the diagram of your property, with the house, trees, outbuildings, and pavement locations noted, will aid in planning. It may be worthwhile to call in a professional garden designer or landscape architect before making a major overhaul of the property, even if you plan to do all the labor yourself.

What shapes your beds take is up to you—free-form or geometric. Elliptical island beds, curving flower borders along fences or walkways, and rectangular vegetable gardens are all classics.

In designs for garden beds, as a rule, avoid sharp curves or shapes that are too cramped or extreme. If putting in several beds, make their shapes harmonious with each other, whether your style is formal or informal. Mixing styles is usually a disaster.

Before moving from the drawing pencil to the garden spade, make a preliminary test. Outline curved designs with a garden hose laid on the ground—any curves too small and tight for the hose to conform to should be ruled out. Outline straight lines with lumber, hoses, or lines of lime. These outlines will help you visualize how the beds will fit into the landscape before you dig. They probably will seem larger when filled with plants, the way a room does when furniture is added. Go indoors and look out the windows and doorway. Are the beds at good vantage points? When you look out, what do you see? Would another bed improve the view? Is something needed to screen an unsightly area? Are you taking on too much?

DESIGN AND STRUCTURE WITHIN THE BEDS. As you furnish your beds with growing things, keep in mind that the plants, not the bed shapes, are of most interest. More detail about what to plant in different types of beds is contained in Chapter 4, but these general considerations are helpful in the early planning stages of your design:

The plants in each garden bed must relate to one another harmoniously through the seasons the bed is in use, as well as to the house and landscape in view. Important ornamental areas should contain evergreen material that stays attractive year-round, enhanced, if you like, with plants that leaf out or bloom during their unique peak season. The plant entries in this book will help you determine growth habit and seasonal changes for the most useful garden species. It is usually wise to plan for a particular season of bloom and concentrate on it, to avoid a spotty look from trying to make a bed that will always offer something in flower, whatever the season. Try for a very showy season plus several additional showy plants for other seasons.

Think about vertical space when you design. Although the beds are flat, they offer an opportunity to add height if you wish. Tall or climbing plants fill the eye with color and texture without taking up very much room, adding privacy and blocking unwanted views very efficiently. If you have an attractive vista, however, take care not to block it with tall plants, although you can frame it effectively if it will usually be seen from a particular vantage point such as a terrace or doorway. Before planting vines or climbing plants, set in a sturdy framework (trellis, arch, arbor, or pergola) that will support the height and weight of your plants when they mature, possibly years in the future. Do not worry if the support seems too large at first. Just think, it would be a shame to keep a marvelous clematis vine pruned short because of a support too small for its many potential flowers. Plan ahead!

In larger beds, allow space for walkways or stepping-stones when you design the beds. You will need paths for entering the beds to tend them. Shape smaller beds in a way that lets you reach inside to all areas without stepping in them.

Raised beds can be small or large and don't need to be elaborate to create an area of interest in a garden. This raised bed should be constructed of treated wood to prevent insect damage and rot.

RAISED BEDS. Either for looks, for gardening on slopes, or for improving soil and drainage, garden beds may be raised, anywhere from 6 or 8 inches or several feet above the surrounding soil level. Some gardens are raised enough for gardeners to tend them from a chair or when standing. A bad back is no reason to give up the satisfactions of gardening. Besides, it is very pleasant to see plants at eye level.

Raised beds are like container gardens with no bottoms. They usually have sides or retaining walls to hold in the soil and give them shape, but can simply be mounds of soil. The finished soil level is usually kept 2 or 3 inches lower than the top of the retaining wall, but this varies with slope and soil type. The more subject to erosion the soil is, the higher the retaining wall should be.

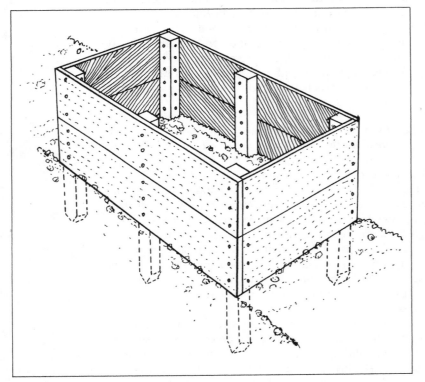

Raised beds are often used for intensive gardening—growing many plants (usually vegetables) in a small space, in very rich soil. Usually the soil is double dug (see pages 53–55) and enriched with compost and manure. Plants are grown in groups rather than rows and sometimes intercropped for best use of space. Soil in intensively planted raised beds does not become compacted if it is enriched with organic matter and not walked on. Plants grow quickly in this environment. Keep in mind that in hot weather the closely spaced plants will need extra water.

Raised beds may be in any shape, provided the interior of the bed can be reached for cultivation. The shape is related to the material used for construction—stone walls lend themselves to rounder shapes than do railroad ties.

When deciding how to construct your beds, keep in mind that wood will break down over the course of time. Though a common sight in raised beds and retaining walls, railroad ties treated with creosote should be avoided because the creosote is poison to plants and will leach out into the soil with the rain. In any event, the creosote ages after a few years and loses its preservative abilities. At this point the ties become an open invitation to termites and carpenter ants. They appear wherever damp wood meets damp soil.

Some wood preservatives are less injurious to plants than creosote, but none are permanent in their protection. Linseed oil is good but must be reapplied often.

Many experienced gardeners prefer dry walls or sides of stone, brick, or cement block because they are more stable and are easy to readjust. Cemented bricks or stones serve well in a sandy soil but tend to crack in a heavy clay soil when the earth they are retaining shifts during wet winters with alternate periods of freezing and thawing. Soil with high sand content minimizes shifts caused by freezing weather, and makes a good home for rock garden plants.

Even with the drawback of having to repair or replace the sides of raised beds from time to time, they offer advantages. They allow more control over soil quality and level than other kinds of garden beds do, give a garden a finished look, and are the basis for many attractive garden designs.

This brick-walled raised bed contains sandy, not clay, soil. Sandy soil drains well and minimizes the motion of alternately freezing and thawing, which expands and contracts the soil. Since water expands when it freezes, an excessively wet soil could exert enough pressure to crack the wall during cold weather.

Garden Decisions

The nice thing about gardening is that it is always changing, always challenging. Every year there will be successes and failures in the garden. As years go on, your control and expertise in managing it increase. Your first garden may be successful, but next year's garden will probably be even better. Each year's garden is a good basis for the next year's improved plan. Reading about gardening is helpful, especially if it is followed by visits to display gardens, comparisons of plants with neighbors and friends, and some practical experience.

A garden must look appropriate in its setting. Plants, whether rare or classic (some might say ordinary), are attractive if they are healthy. Photographs of the garden are helpful in analyzing it. For large borders and garden sites, make panoramic views by joining together a series of photos, overlapping the parts that match. On a property of many acres, an aerial view is also advised.

At the end of the garden season or periodically during its course, make notes on what ideas or plants to keep, and what to change. Jot down combinations of plants that bloom at the same time and look especially nice together. Which vegetables or herbs did the family like best? The next year, expand on the most successful elements of your garden, and try something new besides.

TOOLS AND EQUIPMENT

You may want to glance briefly at this chapter now, and then refer back to it for descriptions of tools and equipment as you read about them in future chapters. However, the information provided here will undoubtedly help to make future chapters more meaningful.

How can you tell when you are using the right tool for the job? The work goes quickly because little motion is wasted. Each tool should fit not only the task, but your body and ability as well. A small person will dig faster with a small short-handled spade than he or she would if struggling with an oversize implement. Good tools are well made and can take the pressure applied during the work. If they have handles, they fit your hands comfortably. If they have wheels, they are sturdy. However, good tools are not necessarily expensive. Shop around and be sure you are paying for workmanship, not for the prestige value of exotic woods or fancy finishes, unless you want to.

ESSENTIAL EQUIPMENT

For any beginning gardener, a few well-made, appropriate tools will suffice. With more experience, gardeners may want to select additional tools for special jobs or purposes.

For hand digging (tilling) gardens, most gardeners need only a spade, trowel, short-handled weeding fork, bow rake, and hoe. For fairly active gardening, or digging in stony soil, a spading fork would also be useful. In a terrace or small garden, only a spade, trowel, and weeding fork are essential. Add garden gloves, a lawn rake, pruning clippers, and a kneeling pad or bench, and you are ready to start. If you have many trees, you might want to invest in a shredder or leaf chopper. Of course, there are many other tools for special chores, but the basic ones usually can serve those purposes.

DIGGING TOOLS. The tools you dig with will bear a great deal of pressure so they must be strong. Carbon steel is an excellent material for spades and hoes because it can be sharpened. Stainless steel is good for the other tools because it is strong, somewhat springy, and stays clean and smooth.

Trowel. For most of us, a trowel is our most frequently used tool: to dig small holes, transplant seedlings and bedding plants, mix potting soil, fill flowerpots, dig up the roots of weeds, and make small seedbeds. Unfortunately, because it is such a small simple implement, it usually gets the least attention. It is worth the effort to find and buy a strong, comfortable trowel that will not cause blisters or crack or bend when digging in heavy soil. Metal-handled trowels are most likely to cause blisters, so look for a sharp stainless-steel blade with a smooth wood or plastic handle, and one-piece metal construction. It is handy to use one with a red or orange handle, to keep it from getting lost when it is set down in the garden. Trowels come in different shapes and widths—typically a trowel is about 12 inches long (including the handle) with a blade 2 or 3 inches wide. A narrow trowel with a deeply cupped blade is good for planting bulbs. Some are marked in inches for convenience when measuring planting depth.

All-purpose garden trowel

Dibble Stick. In well-prepared garden beds, a dibble stick can be used to poke planting holes into the soil. It is good for planting cuttings and bulbs and transplanting seedlings. It is simply a trowel-size, slightly conical wooden or metal stick with a short handle. It is not essential—a trowel may be used instead—but is a highly efficient tool. It is less likely to stab bulbs or the roots of other plants in closely spaced plantings.

Shovel and Spade. Used interchangeably for cutting into soil or sod, shovels and spades are needed for digging garden beds and planting shrubs and trees. Most gardeners use them with both hands and one foot. The blade is set in place nearly perpendicular to the surface of the soil, then pushed down by stepping on top. Shovels are usually rounded and pointed, though shapes vary. Spades have straight sides and a sharp, straight, flat bottom edge that may be slightly rippled. The flat edge can be used for garden edging and trimming chores as well as for digging. You do not need both a spade and shovel. The straight-edged space is more versatile.

The narrow trowel is handy in tight places, especially for planting or digging up bulbs.

Look for a Y-brace handle, a carbon-steel blade, and solid construction. The handle should be made from a strong wood such as ash. The tool should feel well balanced, not too heavy on either end. Avoid cheaper models that have a flimsy neck with a seam where the blade joins the handle. They are likely to split at the seam when heavy pressure is applied.

Digging Fork. Like spades and shovels, digging forks (also called pitchforks) are used to turn over soil. Their sharp tines penetrate soil easily. The spacing and sharpness of the tines vary among the different models—some are needlelike and others are bladelike. Forks with thin, strong tines are dangerous and should be kept away from children. All types are good for digging in rocky soil or near roots that should not be cut. They are also good for lifting potatoes, tilling heavy, dense soil, and distributing straw, compost, or manure, but are useless for tilling light, sandy soil because it falls between the tines. Forks are lighter in weight than spades and shovels, which will make quite a difference after half a day's digging. Springy stainless steel is the best material because it resists snapping under pressure.

Weeding Fork. The short-handled weeding fork, hand cultivator, or scratcher is often sold as a companion to the trowel. It is a handy little item, good for smoothing clods out of small beds or planting areas, gently pulling fallen leaves out of flowering beds without harming them, stirring in topdressings of fertilizer, and raking up weeds or stones. Since not much pressure is put on it, it can be made of any metal. Look for comfort. Small weeding forks with long handles are also available.

Hoe. For real efficiency, it is hard to beat the common garden hoe. A hoe is used to scrape off tiny weeds at the soil line or chop larger ones a bit below it, by pulling the head toward yourself. It is also handy for breaking up clods of garden soil, shaping garden rows, and hilling up soil (making a mound several inches deep) around leeks or other vegetables to be blanched. There are several types of hoes: short-handled ones for window boxes and small flower beds, and several styles of long-handled ones. Some suppliers offer convertible ones that snap into either a short or long handle. The regular square-bladed hoe is excellent, but some people prefer the double-edged scuffle hoe. A weekly hoeing will keep your vegetable garden in great condition. Look for carbon-steel hoe blades and a smooth, comfortable handle. Pointed hoes are less versatile than flat-bottomed ones.

The blunt-ended dibble stick is surprisingly efficient if you work among crowded plants growing in loose, rich soil.

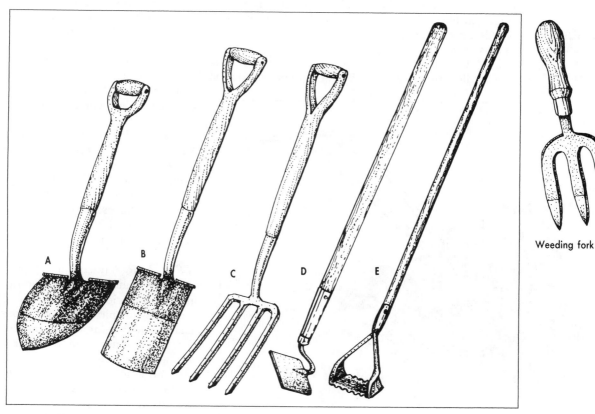

A. Shovel B. Spade C. Digging fork D. Garden hoe E. Scuffle hoe

Weeding fork

Bow Rake. A short-toothed iron bow rake with a long handle is the best finishing tool for garden beds. After the soil has been tilled and clods of earth broken up, raking brings it to a fine finish. The flat top side is sometimes used for shaping beds or wide rows. Rakes come in different sizes. Get one that is not too heavy for you.

Bulb Planter. Long or short handled, a bulb planter has a tin-canlike circular digging blade that lifts out plugs of soil. A good bulb planter is a wonderful convenience tool, especially when you are planting bulbs in your lawn. After the bulb goes in, the soil plug goes back where it came from. Beware of bulb planters made of lightweight metal or aluminum; in heavy soil they will crumple under the pressure of digging. Look for stainless steel instead. Bulbs can be planted without this implement simply by excavating the entire bed, planting the bulbs, and replacing the soil. Use a spade or shovel for large beds, or a trowel for a few single bulbs.

ROTOTILLER. Rototillers are used to till the soil for garden beds and work in soil improvers before planting. Different models have different capabilities of width and depth of digging. Some tillers have rear tines; others have side or front tines. The smallest ones can be used with one hand and are useful (but not essential) in raised beds and intensively tilled gardens, but are less able to handle heavy soil and weeds because tall grasses and weeds get tangled in the tines. A large Rototiller is needed only if crops are grown on an extensive scale.

Look for a model that is easy to start and handle, and does not force you to step on the newly tilled area as you go. Besides gas-powered models, there are easy-to-start, less noisy electric models. Like lawn mowers, Rototillers need annual mechanical care.

For smaller home gardens, a Rototiller can be rented once or twice a year for basic soil preparation, or someone with a Rototiller can be hired to do the job. Local hardware stores, garden centers, or agricultural extension agents can help you find a tiller.

Medium-size Rototiller. Note that the tines of this model are in the rear.

TRACTOR. A tractor pulls plows, mowing blades, and other equipment for agricultural use. Small tractors with plows are not especially practical for home gardeners. It is best not to get one unless you are doing large-scale or farm-size gardening chores. In that case, get a midsize or large model. It would be wise to try one by renting before making a purchase.

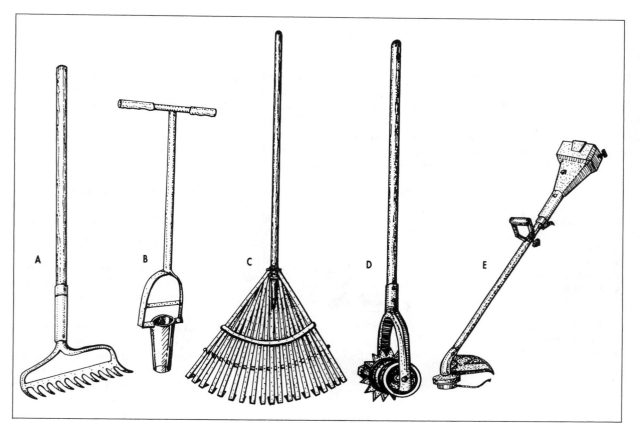

LAWN AND GARDEN MAINTENANCE

Lawn Rake. The fan-shaped, long-handled lawn rake is a useful, ubiquitous gadget for clearing leaves and debris. Lightness is an advantage in this tool, which is one reason for the popularity of bamboo rakes. Avoid cheaper plastics, which break up when used in cold weather, leaving bits all over the yard. Look for a splinter-free handle that fits your hand. Some lawn rakes have adjustable-width tines that can be set for raking out tight places and then adjusted for a broader sweep. There are also special rakes with rubbery tines for cleaning litter from flower beds without harming the plants.

Leaf Blower. Leaf blowers can be electric with long power cords, or cordless, powered by gas or a rechargeable battery. All are useful but not essential for litter cleanup. Blowers are especially appropriate in areas where leaves are swept up at the curb for composting by the municipal cleanup crew. Look for a blower that is not too heavy to carry comfortably.

Edger. Rolling edgers, which seem convenient, actually can get tangled in grass if they are not sharp and well made. A flat-edged spade is a good tool for trimming lawn and garden bed edges. So is the semicircular spadelike lawn edger. Go for a carbon-steel blade so the tool can be sharpened.

String Trimmer. These polelike gadgets whirl a nylon line at high speed to shave off grass and weeds. Most models have to be connected to long power lines, which are a bother. Some types have rechargeable batteries or are gas powered. String trimmers are very handy and safer than other tools of equivalent effectiveness. Do not replace the nylon string with metal or you are risking an injury. Yes, it is a nuisance replacing that line when it wears out during the job. Switch to the heaviest gauge trimmer line that will fit and you will find that replacements are rarely needed.

When choosing a garden shredder, such as this one, select a model large enough to shred most of your garden wastes, then use the chips as mulch. Operate shredders with care, using safety goggles.

Shredder. A clever inventor has made the equivalent of a string trimmer into a leaf shredder by housing the whirling nylon line inside a drum. Leaves go in at the top and come out, finely shredded, through slots at the bottom. This tool is great for quickly reducing leaves to a fine mulch, even when they are wet. It is far safer to operate than metal-bladed shredders, but unfortunately will not handle sticks.

Chippers and shredders come in all sizes and are designed to accommodate different thicknesses of garden clippings. Some tend to jam up when leaves are shredded. Like Rototillers, they can be rented for occasional use or to try out before making the large investment. Unless the amount of wood you have to be chipped is large, you simply can chop branches into bits with long-handled loppers instead (see page 32). Provided that you are not looking for ways to build up your arm muscles, avoid the types of shredders that are cranked by hand.

A power lawn mower can substitute for a shredder—run it over nonwoody garden wastes such as weeds and thin-stemmed brush. Or attach the grass catcher bag and mow your leaf-covered lawn. This way you can mow, clean the lawn, and shred the waste at the same time. Empty the contents of the bag onto the compost pile frequently; the bag fills quickly.

Lawn Mower. There are all sizes and kinds of lawn mowers, from small rotary-cylinder push mowers (human-powered) to tractorlike riding mowers with powerful gasoline engines. In between are various kinds of power mowers without seats. Most are powered by gasoline engines, but some are electric.

If your lawn is very small (under 5000 square feet), you might prefer a push mower. New models are fairly easy to push and have sharp rust-resistant blades. They need little maintenance, are inexpensive, clean, and quiet, and offer the chance for light exercise.

Lawns of medium to large size are usually mowed with some kind of power mower. A ride-on power mower is unsafe on steep hills because of the possibility of its tipping over. It is hard to mow around trees and flower beds with this kind of mower, but it is easy to mow large, flat, open areas of lawn. If this describes your property, look into riding mowers that cut a wide swath at each pass.

A self-propelled power mower that you walk behind (you don't have to push it, just guide it) has some of the ease of use of the ride-on mowers. Its engine turns its wheels as well as its cutting blade. In addition, it is better suited for hills, curves, and mowing in tight places. Because it takes such a large engine to turn the wheels, this type of mower is heavy, in addition to being more complicated and in need of more maintenance than one that is not self-propelled.

A regular power mower rotates its blade for grass cutting as you push and pull it around the lawn. Mowing with it can be a tiring job if the lawn is large.

Mowers of all types can be fitted with grass catcher bags that keep grass clippings off the lawn. They add weight and make it harder to propel the mower, but eliminate the job of raking up the clippings. If you like to gather grass clippings for mulch or compost, the bags are especially useful.

Lawn Sandals. The outrageous-looking lawn sandals are basically a layer of sharp nails embedded in plastic sandals, sharp side down, of course. The sandals strap onto your feet, over your garden shoes. As you walk around your lawn, they not only aerate the soil, but also kill grubs and cutworms below the sod. This sounds strange, but it really works.

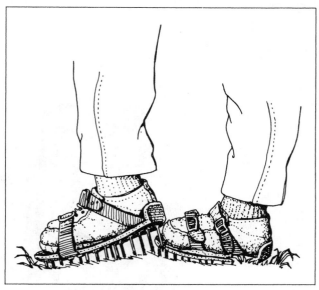

Lawn sandals. Not only do these curious sandals aerate the soil under lawns, they also kill grubs and cutworms lurking beneath the turf.

Wheelbarrow or Garden Cart. Bicycle-wheeled carts help you carry immense loads with very little effort. However, unless your need to tote things around is great, an ordinary wheelbarrow will be sufficient. It is not only smaller, it is cheaper.

Some wheelbarrows have two or three wheels instead of one, to prevent tipping. There are also cloth wheelbarrow extender/liners reinforced with wire to hold the shape, giving you more room for large, lightweight loads such as brush or weeds.

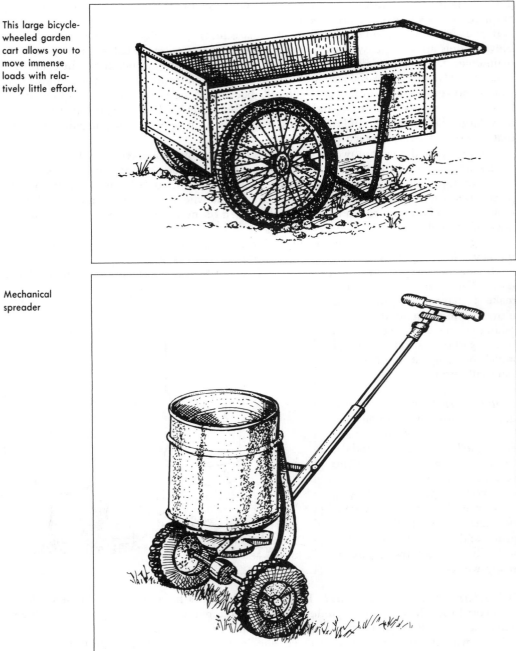

This large bicycle-wheeled garden cart allows you to move immense loads with relatively little effort.

Mechanical spreader

Spreader. For distributing dry fertilizer and lime over a large area evenly, it helps to use a mechanical spreader. It is basically a container on wheels with an oscillating shuttle above an adjustable slot, through which the particles are whirled over the ground at a steady rate. Gravity drop models have problems with fertilizer overlap, while the spray types spread more evenly. Most models are pushed along by hand, but the largest agricultural types are motorized or are attached to a tractor. Machine spreading prevents lawns from getting that patchy look—inevitable when you hand-spread fertilizer.

Sprayer. Insecticides and fertilizers are often applied in a spray. The equipment can be small and simple or large and powerful. A hose-end sprayer is sufficient for most suburban gardens. It is simply a bottle containing a solution of the substance to be sprayed that screws onto the hose. A strawlike tube feeds it to the water supply as it sprays. Some substances come prepacked in a sprayer, with refills available. Others give instructions for quantity and dilution.

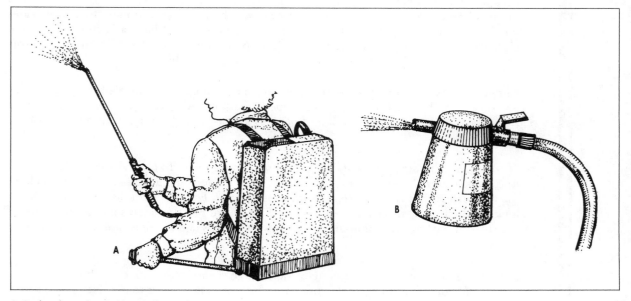

A. Backpack sprayer B. Hose-end sprayer

In areas with less of a need, the old-fashioned bug spritzer is fine—a hand-held, mechanically operated gadget. You push, it sprays. A recycled window cleaner bottle can be used instead if it sprays with a fine mist, not a heavy stream. For home orchards or similar large areas, a battery-operated backpack sprayer is the best. It does a professional, high-pressure, effective spray job. For even larger areas, a power sprayer on wheels is appropriate.

Fruit Picker. Mature, standard-size fruit trees tower over the gardener's head. Fruit harvesting tools prevent some of the ladder work. One of the best is a claw-topped wire

basket on the end of a long pole. Use it to pull off the fruit while catching it in the basket. If the bottom of the basket is not padded, put in a piece of foam rubber to cushion the fruit's fall.

PRUNING GEAR

Clean, sharp cuts are best for plants, whether they are made with saws, knives, clippers, or scissors. Because it is strong and sharp, well-made pruning equipment is a good investment. The middle price range is usually good enough—prices are astronomical on some imported equipment. Avoid the so-called flower-gatherers, scissors that mash the flower's stem. Flowers take water up and last longer if their stems are cut cleanly.

Clippers (secateurs). Scissorlike clippers tend to be the sharpest. Some gardeners avoid the anvil type with a sharp side cutting against a blunt one, but others find it provides stability when clipping larger branches. Small clippers should have a latch to hold them closed and some kind of spring action so they open automatically between cuts. Get a pair of clippers that fits in a leather holster to hang from your belt.

Loppers. A pair of loppers can be a homeowner's primary pruning tool. Giving a lot of leverage, long-handled loppers make a good, sharp cut with very little effort. The blade is small and scissorlike, and the 2-foot handles give a long reach, eliminating some of the ladder work.

Handsaw. Pruning saws of stainless steel with large teeth do a good job. They are easy to clean and remain sharp. Look for a comfortable handle and a blade that is not too long for you—10 inches is a good length for most people. For tree work higher up, there are long-handled saws, also called *pole pruners.* Some have pull-operated snappers to finish off the cut without any tree climbing. Systems with pulleys and ratchets multiply the pruning power.

Hedge Shears. Long-handled, long-bladed hedge shears give a good reach for getting to the top of hedges. Shorter-handled ones are a bit lighter and easier to use. Electric trimmers are a good investment if there is a lot of hedge trimming, but otherwise are not necessary. Those with self-sharpening blades are convenient. Because the interior of hedges should be shaped to let in light, small clippers are needed in addition to hedge shears.

Chain Saw. Most do-it-yourself pruning can be done without power tools. A chain saw tends to make a rougher cut than a handsaw, but when the amount of wood to be cut is large, it gets the job done fast. Consider renting if you would use a chain saw infrequently. Choose a well-balanced model that is not too heavy for comfortable handling, and be sure to keep it clean and well oiled. With chain saws, it is worthwhile to invest in the highest possible quality. Safety features include a hand guard, chain brake, nonslip grip, antikickback device, and antivibration system.

Long-handled fruit picker. Some models have a cushion at the base of the basket to keep the fruit from bruising.

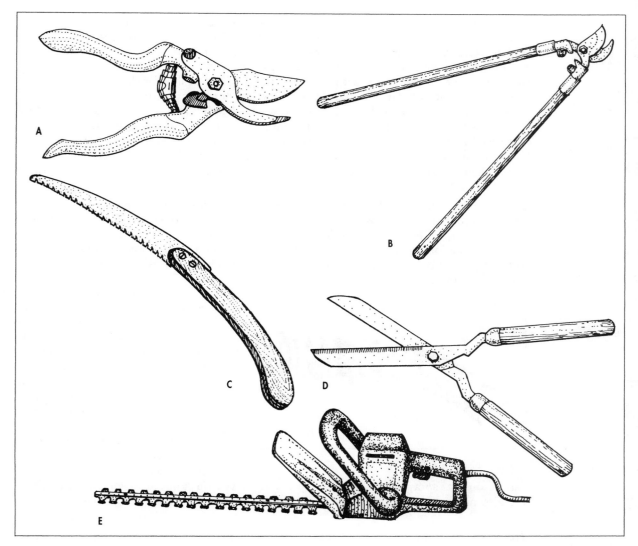

A. Spring-action clippers
B. Long-handled loppers
C. Pruning handsaw
D. Hedge shears
E. Electric hedge trimmer

WATERING EQUIPMENT

Proper watering makes growing healthy plants much easier. Gardeners in dry areas or places with seasonal dry spells often have extensive underground watering systems or else practice xeriscaping—gardening with native and drought-tolerant plants. In areas with steadier or higher rainfall, the only equipment needed may be a hose, sprinkler, and watering can. Watering equipment to meet different levels of need or convenience is discussed here.

Watering Can. For a while it was hard to find old-fashioned galvanized-steel watering cans, but they have made a well-earned comeback. They are less expensive when bought in hardware stores instead of from upscale catalogs, but may have a plastic rose (the round water emitter with holes) instead of a brass one at the end of the spout. Look for a nonclogging rose with fairly large holes. It should be removable for cleaning. The 2-gallon can size is most popular for outdoor watering and fertilizing chores.

Indoor seedlings or small plants must be watered gently but with no misses. One of the best tools for this is an ordinary self-dispensing plastic dish detergent bottle. Rinse it out very well and use it for plain water or dilute liquid fertilizer.

Watering cans come in all sizes and shapes. Not all of them pour their contents out any better than a plastic gallon milk jug, so look for quality, and test before you buy, if possible.

Hose. Hoses differ in style, size, material, price, and ability to withstand extreme weather. Modern polyester fabric hoses are lightweight, collapsible, and easy to store, sometimes on accompanying reels. Standard garden hoses may be made of rubber, vinyl, nylon, or canvas, or a combination of these. Look for well-made hoses and fittings. Avoid cotton canvas—which, in any case, now is hard to find—for it rots. Flexogen™ is especially long lasting, and so is rubber.

Rubber soaker hose

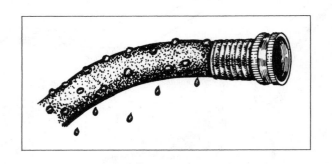

Specialty hoses include rubber soaker hoses, which can be used above the ground or buried. The rubber hose weeps all along its length to permit slow, direct wetting of soil, definitely the most efficient way to water. It does not get clogged the way drip irrigation systems with emitters sometimes do and is very easy to use.

Similar but much cheaper are flat plastic hoses with holes punched all along the sides. These can be used as sprayers at high water pressure or as drip hoses at lower pressure. There are also narrow hose systems that attach to indoor faucets for watering houseplants.

Hose Nozzle. Squirting water with high pressure may be fine for cleaning off the driveway, but it is not recommended for plants. A fine gentle spray is better—otherwise, leaves and stems might be broken or roots disturbed. One of the best types of hose nozzles is fan shaped with a double row of holes. A round hose-end rose is also very good. Either can be attached to a long wand for extension of the hose end. This is especially helpful for watering hanging plants. Some gardeners like a pistol-grip hose nozzle because it can be turned off and on from the far end so easily. The conical brass spray nozzle is also popular for the same reason.

Hose Reel. Some hose reels stay put and others travel with you. Wall-mounted hose reels keep hoses tidily in place during storage. Hose trolleys do the same during use and storage.

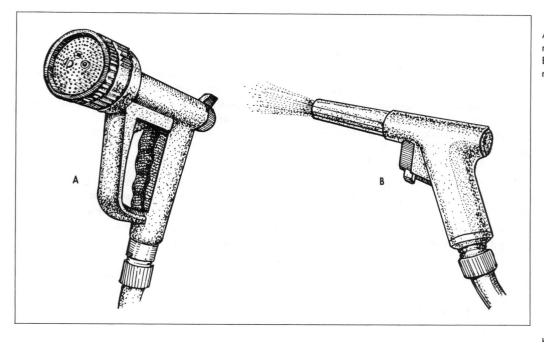

A. Round-end hose nozzle
B. Pistol-grip hose nozzle

Hose trolley

Hose Guides. If you have ever broken off plants while moving a hose around the yard, you understand the need for hose guides. These can be inconspicuous functional guides, such as short, sharp stakes supporting a track for the hose, plain wooden or metal stakes, stones placed at critical points, or decorative, sculpturelike stakes. If you anticipate any friction between your hose and plants, prevent it!

Sprinkler. Water is whirled over our gardens by various kinds of sprinklers. The oscillating sprinklers are good because they give wide, even coverage. Wand sprinklers are easy to move around for coverage where needed. But built-in underground sprinkler systems are the favorite though expensive choice in areas where watering is a frequent chore. Sprinklers tend to waste water—much of it evaporates before it reaches the ground or lands where it is not needed.

Underground Watering System. Underground watering systems offer the maximum convenience. Many are connected to timers for regularly scheduled soakings. However, this can be a very wasteful means of irrigation, especially if the water is applied from pop-up sprayers instead of drip or soaker equipment. If you are choosing a timer, look for one with a manual override system and use it when possible; some timers have built-in locks that prevent an override.

Drip Irrigation System. Drip irrigation systems may be buried below the ground or set on top. They are pipes or hoses with holes (emitters) that release water where it is needed. These systems can be very elaborate and expensive, or considerably simpler. The main drawback is clogging of emitters, which you can prevent by checking and cleaning them from time to time. Moles have been known to eat the emitters.

CONVENIENCES AND SPECIAL ITEMS

Sore knees, blisters, backaches, and sunburn afflict unprotected gardeners at times. Prevention is easy, though, with basic aids such as these (specialty items can be ordered by mail if they are not carried at your local garden center):

Gloves. For cleaner hands and blister protection, wear gloves while gardening. That is easy to say but harder to do. The gloves seem to slide off the hands when doing fine work such as transplanting seedlings. Before you know it, you have switched to digging or pruning without gloves, and it is blister time. This can be prevented by dividing the chores carefully. While wearing heavier gloves, do the heavy work. Before switching to fine handwork, switch to light goatskin gloves that are sensitive enough for the job.

Cotton canvas gloves wear out quickly. Well-made knitted ones are likely to last longer—they have more give. Supple goatskin gloves are long lasting if not used for the heaviest work. They come in lighter or heavier leathers—the thicker goatskin glove is more durable but still has the famous flexibility. Buckskin or pigskin work gloves last and protect well. Plastic-coated cotton gloves offer neither the protection of heavy leather gloves nor the suppleness of light gloves, but are all right for many garden chores anyway.

Hats. It does not matter what kind of hat you prefer, the important thing is to wear one. It is all too easy to forget about a hat when you go out to garden, and then stay out in the sun too long. Hats help prevent sunburn and, more importantly, heat stroke. The farmer is pictured in his straw hat for a reason—it gives portable shade. Keep a cool head and keep your hat on!

Boots and Shoes. Do you have an old pair of sturdy work boots or hiking shoes? Or old but well-made running shoes? They will be good for gardening if there is enough cushioning to protect your feet when you dig. Professional gardeners wear steel-toed work boots for extra protection from accidental contact with garden tools. If you garden with heavy equipment, you might want to follow their example. This is especially important for mowing protection. Rubber overshoes are a help if the ground is wet with dew or rain.

Kneepads. To prevent sore knees, kneepads are tops. Never kneel on a stone terrace without them if you are over eight years old. A plastic-covered foam pad is a fine help. Mark one side so you can be sure to keep the dry side up when you move the pad. Alternatives include tie-on kneepads, which look ridiculous but work, and garden overalls with built-in knee padding. These are great but will get dirty or wet more often than clothes worn with a separate kneepad.

Kneeling Benches and Scooters. There are padded kneeling benches that turn over for use as a seat—very handy! Another possibility is a bench with slots for hand tools and supplies. Even better are three- or four-wheeled garden scooters—buy one if you are too proud to sit on a cast-off child's tricycle. Scooters save you the bother of getting up to move a stationary bench.

SPECIAL GARDENING AIDS FOR THE DISABLED OR ELDERLY

An inability to get around easily does not have to put an end to enjoyable gardening activity. With the aid of appropriate tools and garden design, the garden is still within easy reach. Here are tips for easier gardening. Most are based on information included in *The Easy Path to Gardening* (London: Reader's Digest Association Ltd., 1972). The book was sponsored by Great Britain's Disabled Living Activities Group. Others are gleaned from garden tool catalogs and additional sources.

A wheelchair-bound gardener's access to the garden is increased by laying nonslip paths. Broad paths made of openwork concrete blocks allow grass to grow through the openings, but also support the wheelchair well. A lawn mower glides easily over the blocks for upkeep. Of course, sidewalks and other solid paving are fine, too. Replace steps with ramps that are not too steep. Narrow, not wide, borders may be tended from the chair.

Watering from a wheelchair is easier with a watering wand because it gives a long reach. For small watering jobs, a plastic gallon or half-gallon milk bottle can be used, carried on the person's lap. The screw-on top prevents spills.

A raised garden is easier to tend, especially for those of us in wheelchairs. Short-handled rock gardening tools are recommended. So is a standard hoe with its handle trimmed to 2 feet long. Long-handled, lightweight tools can be used by wheelchair-bound gardeners in ground-level gardens. These can be high-quality children's tools attached to longer handles. Long-handled litter grippers are helpful as well.

For people with a weakened grip, tools with thicker handles are easier to hold. In some cases, Velcro straps are a help. Plastic bicycle handle grips can be added to short- or long-handled tools. Flowerpots and potting soil should be made of lighter weight materials; do not use heavy terra-cotta or dense soils. To avoid fatigue, change jobs and hand motions often.

GUARDING AGAINST INJURY

A. Foot-pedal spade. This unusual garden aid permits you to dig without bending down.
B. Wheeled rake. This device was developed to reduce back strain by permitting you to rake without lifting.
C. Long-handled garden stripper. For picking up leaf litter and other light-weight garden waste without bending over.

To prevent back injury from bending, specialized spades with a foot pedal added to the base of the spade handle are helpful. Long-handled shovels and spades make it possible to dig with less bending. There are leaf rakes with wheels that do not require lifting the rake. Other rakes have handles angled to prevent back strain.

Injuries can be avoided by paying attention to posture when gardening. Keep the angle of handles low when mowing or hoeing. Try not to lean forward. To lift items, do not bend over. Instead, bend down on one knee, keeping the back straight. Support the item from below with one hand, and on the side or top with the other. Hold it close to the body and then straighten the knees. When kneeling for garden tasks, always use a kneepad or kneeling bench. It is easier on the back if you kneel on one knee, not both, and keep the back straight.

Automatic watering systems are a tremendous work saver. So are long-handled watering wands and portable, wheeled hose trolleys. Extensions of hose connections to convenient points in the garden mean that watering can be done with shorter, lighter pieces of hose. Look for easy-to-use snap connector couplings.

A   B   C

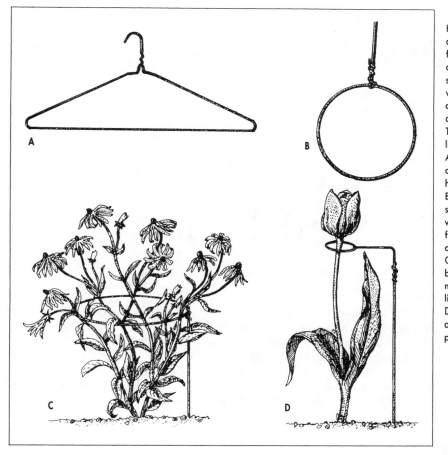

Hooplike stakes are easy to make from coat hangers and are safer than sticklike stakes, which might poke an unwary gardener in the eye. To make a hooplike stake:
A. Start with an ordinary coat hanger.
B. Unfasten it, straighten it out with pliers, and reform a hoop of the desired size.
C. The hoop may be wide, for a multistemmed plant like this rudbeckia.
D. Or narrow, for a single-stemmed plant like this tulip.

Safety Features. Sharp stakes can be extremely dangerous if a gardener slips. Instead, use plants that need no staking or else grow-through types of stakes such as peony hoops. These can be bought or made from coat hangers. Be sure paths and steps are of nonskid materials. Moss-covered stones or bricks are slippery when wet. Steps should have a rise of only 3 inches between levels. Benches and other resting places should be included in the garden.

Maintaining Garden Tools

A place for everything and everything in its place: That is not a cliché, it is garden wisdom. Normally, garden tools are not damaged during use, but rather when they are left outdoors between uses. Keep them in a closet, a toolshed, or the garage. For most tools, just putting them away clean is all the care that is needed. Brush off the soil and, if you like, wipe metal surfaces with machine or mineral oil. Dip rusted tools in cider vinegar and set aside for a few days, then wipe away rust particles. Be sure to oil any moving parts. Sharpen edges and blades with a file or knife sharpener. Treat mowers and Rototillers to clean oil each year and new spark plugs and sharpened blades when needed.

PREPARING
THE SOIL

Good soil is the key to growing beautiful, healthy gardens. Few gardeners are lucky enough to start out with great soil, but gardeners working in any climate, with any soil, can get excellent results by adding soil-improving materials. Many different nutrients are needed for plant growth, and even good soil is often deficient in one or another of them. Corrective treatment for different soil problems is described in this chapter, as well as how to cultivate and dig your garden beds. Improving the soil and making the garden beds are usually done simultaneously.

ABOUT SOIL

Soil is an important but adjustable element of gardening. While correcting some garden problems may take extreme action (for instance, cutting down a large tree to correct for too much shade), poor soil can be improved by mixing in needed elements.

As mentioned in Chapter 1, soil is a mixture of particles of sand, clay, silt, and organic matter (humus or loam), plus air and water. Plants need air, water, a place to anchor their roots deeply, water-soluble nutrients, and light in some amount in order to flourish. All but the light reach the plant through its roots. Water and oxygen react chemically with soil to make nutrients water soluble, thus usable by plants.

If needed substances are not in the soil in usable form, plants will suffer. Because soil is so vital to plant health, do not take chances with it. Before improving or changing the soil in your garden, do a soil test (your garden center or agricultural extension office can help), determine its makeup, and work out a program for its improvement, if necessary.

LAYERS OF SOIL

Soil is found in layers whose thicknesses vary, even in adjacent locations. *Topsoil,* usually browner than the lower levels of soil, has most of the accumulated decomposed organic

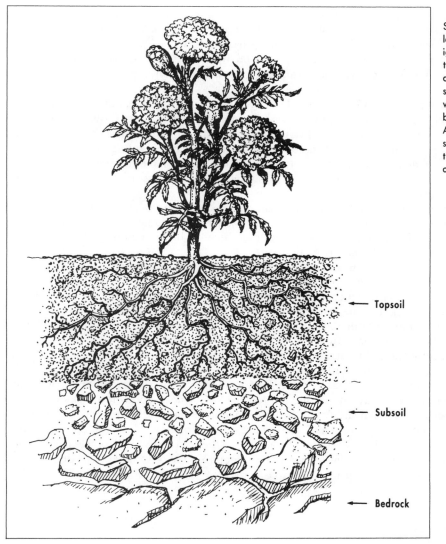

Soil is found in layers. Here a marigold is rooted in topsoil, which rests on dense, rocky subsoil, beneath which is a solid base of bedrock. As bedrock and subsoil weather, they become part of the topsoil.

→ Topsoil

→ Subsoil

→ Bedrock

matter, which is a source of nitrogen. This is the root zone of most plants. Below it is *subsoil,* mainly composed of inorganic compounds such as sand, gravel, stones, clay, or a mixture of them. The type of subsoil affects the pH (see pages 43–45), drainage, and fertility of the soil. Water and minerals are drawn upward from the subsoil as water evaporates from the topsoil. Sandy subsoil drains well, but rocky or clay subsoils usually inhibit drainage. Below the subsoil is *bedrock.* As bedrock ages and breaks down, it becomes part of the subsoil and eventually the topsoil. In some areas the bedrock is limestone, raising the pH of the soil above it. In other areas it may consist of granite or other relatively inert rock of volcanic origin.

The rockiness of the soil and the size of the rocks figure into the kind of gardening you can do. Some sites have little topsoil or subsoil and are mostly solid bedrock. In these, it may be necessary to blast holes for trees and shrubs and fill them with soil. However, a rocky site can be visually exciting and enhanced by setting rock garden plants into the crevices. Other kinds of garden plants can be grown in good soil in tubs on decks or paved areas.

Some sites are more stony than rocky. They are fine for any purpose, but difficult to work. Often, the soil is good and rich, but whenever you dig down, your shovel strikes large stones, which then have to be rooted out before digging can continue—a very frustrating and laborious procedure. Many of the beautiful stone walls of New England were built of rocks and stones cleared by hand from farmers' fields. If you have the time, you can turn your surplus rocks into rock paths, patios, stone walls, or edgings for raised beds, or add them to your gravel driveway.

The topsoil is the layer of most immediate interest to you because most of the soil's fertility is found here. In some areas of the country this layer may be extremely shallow or poor. Some regions, especially in hot, humid climates, have deep soils that are nearly all sand and contain hardly any organic matter.

Sometimes all the good topsoil has been removed, eroded away, or buried. Developers and builders have been known to scrape off the topsoil from a site, load it into dump trucks, and sell it. The new homeowner is then left with subsoil, perhaps concealed by a layer of sod. If you are having a home built, get your builder or developer to agree (preferably in writing) not to remove your topsoil. Do not allow the builder to cover your topsoil with subsoil when the foundation is dug, either. Instead, the topsoil should be bulldozed back, the excavated subsoil spread out, and the topsoil bulldozed or spread back over it for a top layer. Or the subsoil can be hauled away and used for fill elsewhere.

In some places topsoil is several feet deep, especially in valleys or next to rivers or creeks where erosion or floods have deposited silt for years. Consider yourself a lucky gardener if this describes your garden site. Well-cared-for farmland may also have deep, rich topsoil.

To see how deep your topsoil and subsoil are, dig a hole 2 or 3 feet deep in the spot where you expect to make a garden. The layers, if there are any, will be clearly visible. In most areas decent topsoil is at least 8 inches deep. You should be able to dig down 2 or 3 feet before encountering impenetrable bedrock.

SOIL TYPES

Although all soils are mixtures of *sand* (small but easily visible particles), *silt* (fine, barely visible particles), and *clay* (particles so small they are invisible without a microscope), the proportion of the components varies in different kinds of soil. *Loam* is a soil type high in silt. It usually is rich in *humus,* which comes from organic matter and is found in particles of a size classified as silt; this accounts for the partial interchangeability of the terms *silt, loam,* and *humus.* As organic matter decomposes, it helps hold water in the soil and adds valuable fertilizing nutrients.

Although there are many classification systems, widely recognized soil types are named after their predominant component or components; for instance, a sandy soil may be about

85 percent sand with the remaining 15 percent composed of silt and clay. Soil also contains microbes and other organisms that interact with it, constantly affecting its chemistry and composition.

You can see the components in your own soil by performing a simple test. Take a one-quart mayonnaise jar or similar container and fill it halfway with your garden soil. Add tap water until the jar is nearly filled, then cover and shake. The soil components will slowly settle, separating themselves into layers by the weight (and usually the size) of the particles. In a day or two you can look into the side of the undisturbed jar for the results. The sand, being heaviest, will have sunk to the bottom while the other portions remained in suspension. Then the silt will have settled, and finally the clay. The relative proportion of each component tells you how your soil is composed.

LOAM. The best soil for most garden purposes, loam, is a balanced mixture of sand, silt, and clay particles. It contains plentiful organic matter, which enriches the soil while holding water and preventing nutrients from slipping away through the soil. A good loam or sandy loam for gardening should be at least a foot deep, have a somewhat coarse texture, and retain water but not stay soggy. It usually is dark brown, crumbly, but not dense or sticky. It is sometimes compared to chocolate cake! Other soil types are converted into loam by adding organic matter such as compost and manure.

CLAY. Some clays are red, others gray or brown, depending on the geologic features of the area. The particles in clay are so small that, when wet, they make a sticky, muddy soil that holds too much water and excludes air. If rubbed between two fingers, clay feels smooth and slippery, and sticks to the hands until washed off. When wet clay dries out, it makes a hard, bricklike surface, sometimes with cracks. Wet clay soil hurts the survival chances of perennial flowers during the winter. Clay soil is slow to warm up in spring and difficult to work. On the other hand, clay is rich in minerals needed by plants and helps a soil hold the right amount of water if the clay portion is not too high. Garden gypsum (hydrated calcium sulfate) is helpful in aerating and breaking up compacted clay soil, although it tends to make soil more acid (see below for an explanation of pH).

SAND. A sandy soil feels gritty when rubbed between the fingers. Some soils are as sandy as a kid's sandbox and just as inhospitable to garden plants. A pale, sandy soil is likely to contain few nutrients and be too porous to hold water. When fertilizer is applied, it washes out quickly whenever rain falls or the land is irrigated. However, sandy loam is excellent for gardening because the loam helps hold in water and nutrients while the sand allows the soil to drain well and be tilled easily. It is light, airy, and warms up fast in the spring.

SOIL PH: ACID OR ALKALINE?

Soils vary from alkaline (sweet) to acid (sour). This is measured numerically by the pH reading. The scale ranges from 0 to 14 and is a logarithmic scale, meaning that a pH of 2 is ten times more than a pH of 1. A reading of 7 is neutral while above is considered alkaline and below is considered acid. Readings below 4.5 and above 8 are too extreme for the cultivation of garden plants.

The soil's pH balance affects how available the soil's nutrients are to the plants. Having adapted to local soil conditions over the course of thousands of years and retained this adaptation as part of their genetic makeup, different plants prefer different pH levels. Wildflowers and berries from northern parts of the United States favor acid soils. Plants of Mediterranean origin—a large group that includes many of our most popular garden flowers, herbs, fruits, and vegetables—like a neutral soil. Most plants from the American Southwest, such as California poppies and *Phlox drummondii,* grow well in a mildly alkaline soil or are adaptable. More generally, most lawn grasses and flowering or fruiting plants need a slightly acid or neutral pH, from 6.5 to 7. Acid-loving plants such as azaleas and rhododendrons do well from about 5 to 6.5, and plants like beets and perennial baby's-breath prefer a sweet soil, with a pH from 7 to nearly 8. In a rich soil that is too alkaline or acid for a particular species, the plants will show signs of nutrient deficiency as they simply are unable to efficiently utilize the nutrients.

The pH of your garden soil can be measured by your county agricultural extension agent, a pH meter, or soil test kit (the latter two are sold in garden centers and by mail-order seed companies). A fuller discussion of soil testing follows on page 49.

To estimate the pH of your soil without a test, see which plants grow well on it. The presence of flourishing wild rhododendrons, mountain laurel, moss, blueberries, and wild strawberries indicates acidic soil. In the Southwest, soils generally tend to be alkaline because of salts left behind by evaporation, but there are many exceptions. The presence of sagebrush and cacti hints at alkaline soil.

Changing the pH Reading

The pH of soil can be raised or lowered. Over time, corrected soil will tend to return to its original pH unless treatment is continued. In some areas sweetening the soil (making it more alkaline) with a yearly application of lime is routine. Changing pH is most practical if the amount of change needed is one pH point or less, or the area to be changed is not too large. For ornamental gardens, it may not be necessary to change pH if you select plants naturally suited to the pH you have. Herbs and vegetables are more specific in their pH preferences, so corrections are more likely to be needed when growing them. If changing the pH of a large area is not practical, smaller pockets of soil can be treated, or plants may be grown in containers filled with the right type of soil.

To Raise pH (make soil less acid). Add agricultural limestone. The results of a professional soil test usually come with recommendations for the amount of amendment needed to improve the soil. For a typical clay soil, about 5 pounds of limestone are needed for each 100 square feet to raise the pH one point. For large areas, it is practical to use a mechanical spreader (see page 31) to do this. Limestone, which also helps improve the texture of a clay soil, is tilled in along with fertilizer, compost, and other additives.

To Lower pH (make soil less alkaline). Ground sulfur, aluminum sulfate, peat moss, and garden gypsum can be used. The amounts will be determined by soil test results and recommendations. It may take several tests and adjustments to get the pH right.

When organic matter breaks down, the pH of the residue is nearly neutral. Compost is usually about 6.5, a little on the acid side. Improving soil by composting leaves and other plant residues tends to neutralize your soil's pH if it is extremely high or low. If it is neutral, compost will make it slightly acidic.

NUTRIENT CONTENT AND FERTILIZERS

The chief nutrients that plants require in soil are nitrogen, which is important for photosynthesis; phosphorus, which is needed for the development of roots, flowers, seeds, and fruits; and potassium, which is important for healthy stems and disease resistance. Many kinds of organic and inorganic substances referred to as "fertilizer" add these three basic nutrients and others. Manure and compost are organic fertilizers. Though less concentrated than inorganic chemical fertilizers, they offer trace nutrients (see below) and beneficial soil bacteria, and physically build the soil. Sometimes manure and compost are used as fertilizer, other times just to improve soil structure, but usually they are brought in to do both jobs simultaneously.

A hundred years ago there were no bagged or bottled chemical fertilizers. Compost, cover crops tilled in, wood ashes, and animal manure were used and gardens looked fine. Now you have a choice of packaged, commercial inorganic and organic fertilizer products. Many chemical (inorganic) fertilizer products are effective and convenient, although adherents of organic gardening claim that they leave salt residues that damage the soil. Most gardeners can see the need for both types of fertilizers at once, especially for transitional soils that are poor but are being improved in stages. It can take heavy work for several years to perfect soil using organic amendments. In the meantime, give your crops a boost with other nutrients. Plants take up almost all nutrients in inorganic form, regardless of the source.

Bagged or boxed commercial fertilizers contain the three basic nutrients in different proportions. The numbers on the fertilizer container (whether the contents are organic or inorganic) represent the nutrients in a standard order referred to as the NPK number—nitrogen (N), phosphorus (phosphoric acid, or P), and potash (potassium or K). A 6-6-6 fertilizer has equal amounts of N, P, and K, and a 12-4-8 is high in nitrogen, low in phosphorus, and intermediate in potash. The higher the number, the more concentrated the fertilizer. Amounts of other components are also listed.

Some plants are harmed ("burned") by too much fertilizer, whether from a natural substance like fresh manure or a powdered or liquid chemical. Be especially cautious around clematis, wildflowers, begonias, ferns, poppies, seedling vegetables, alpine plants, and rock garden plants.

Usually, lawn fertilizer has a superabundance of nitrogen. When used on other plants, it promotes growth of leaves at the expense of flowers. Do not use such a fertilizer on any hardy plants at the end of the growing season, when they are getting ready to go into winter dormancy. The new leaves it stimulates to grow will be killed by cold weather. For most garden purposes, including late-season use, high-phosphorus fertilizers with an N-P-K number of 10-20-20—often labeled "blossom boosters"—are best, but it depends on the soil's natural fertility as well. Low-nitrogen formulations especially for acid-loving plants (Holly-Tone™, for instance) are useful when applied at the start of cooler weather.

SOIL NUTRIENTS, SOURCES AND EFFECTS*

NUTRIENT	SOURCES	FUNCTION	SYMPTOMS OF DEFICIENCY
Boron	Composted melon plants, clover, borax (add only if prescribed), granite dust	Vital to plant growth	Rare slow growth, dieback from terminal buds, internal cork of apples, cracked stem in celery, heart rot and girdle of beets
Calcium	Limestone, lime, gypsum, calcite, eggshells, fish meal, wood ashes	Cell division, flowering, fruiting, building plant proteins	Blossom end rot, cavities in tomatoes, black heart, black roots, pale leaf margins, deformed terminal leaves
Chlorine	All green plants, water	—	Rare, supplied in rainfall
Copper	Manure, rock powders, copper sulfate (use cautiously), composted dandelions, grass clippings, sawdust	Plant growth, utilization of iron	(Sometimes found in peat or muck soils) slow or stopped growth, growth tip dieback, citrus dieback, lack of leaf development in citrus
Iodine	Fish emulsion fertilizer, seaweed, fish meal	Not known to be necessary to plants	Plants are healthy but are less nutritious to people and animals
Iron	Humus, manure, compost, blood meal, N.J. greensand	Plant growth, chlorophyll and carbohydrate production	Chlorosis—spotted, colorless areas on leaves, leaves yellowed at tips (symptoms also may be caused by soil that is too alkaline for plant species)
Magnesium	All green plants, talc, dolomitic limestone, manure, N.J. greensand	Develops plant strength	(Widespread in sandy soils) poor quality of flowers and fruit, yellowing between green veins of leaves, oddly colored leaves, premature defoliation

*Table compiled from information in *The Encyclopedia of Organic Gardening* (Emmaus, Pa.: Rodale Press, 1978) and other sources.

Domesticated flowering and fruiting plants, as a rule, are heavy feeders, as are lawn grasses. Even light feeders like wildflowers need additional nutrients each year, preferably from soil enriched with leaf mold or compost so they will not be burned by excess nitrogen.

For garden crops, it is customary to add compost or manure, granular fertilizer, and possibly lime and ashes before plowing and planting. Minimum tillage methods can also be used. A layer of mulch keeps the soil soft, attracts earthworms, and eliminates much of the need for plowing. Manure and compost can be tucked under the mulch, where they will soon break down and become part of the soil. Do not let plants come in direct contact with fresh manure.

NUTRIENT	SOURCES	FUNCTION	SYMPTOMS OF DEFICIENCY
Manganese	Oak leaves, leaf mold, carrot tops, alfalfa	Growth and maturation of all plants	Plants are slow to grow, late to mature, areas between leaf veins become yellow, then brown
Nitrogen	Manure, cottonseed meal, fish meal, bonemeal, blood meal, composted legumes (peas, beans, peanuts), ammonium sulfate or nitrate	Green, leafy growth, constituent of chlorophyll and protein	Chlorosis—yellowing of leaves; slow growth, thin stems, lack of vigor, stunted growth
Phosphorus	Bonemeal, phosphate rock, N.J. greensand	Disease resistance, strong growth, root development, fruit development	Premature fruit drop, slow growth, deformed corn ears, reddish color under leaves and on stems
Potassium	Wood ashes, potash rock, manure, granite dust, N.J. greensand, fish meal, potassium sulfate or nitrate	Root development, good cell wall structure, moisture conservation, promotion of photosynthesis	Poor root systems, susceptibility to frost and wind damage, susceptibility to wilting and wilt diseases, leaf curl, leaf bronzing, uneven ripening of tomatoes, misshapen, flavorless carrots
Sulfur	Gypsum, composted legumes, composted cabbage leaves	Healthy growth	(Very rare)
Zinc	Manure, composted corn, ragweed, vetch	Fruit development	(Occurs in peat and alkaline soils) abnormally long, narrow leaves, mottled, yellowed leaves, poor fruiting, dieback

Flower beds need fertilizer, too. Even when the soil is improved organically it is helpful to add a high-phosphorus, high-potassium, slow-release fertilizer to promote flowering. Several popular products are formed into round beads of slow-release fertilizer that will last several months. They help keep growth steady and do not wash out of the soil as easily as other kinds. Not so long ago, slow-release fertilizer beads were available only to commercial growers, but now are sold at retail garden shops and even grocery stores.

Plants need trace amounts of boron, manganese, zinc, copper, iron, sulfur, molybdenum, chlorine, calcium, and magnesium in addition to the three major nutrients. Trace elements are found in most soils, especially those high in organic content. The last two, calcium and magnesium, are supplied in agricultural lime, called dolomitic limestone.

FERTILIZERS

TYPE OF PRODUCT	DESCRIPTION	METHOD OF APPLICATION	PURPOSE
Bagged granular dry fertilizer (chemical)	Dry granules, predominantly white or gray, in different formulations for various purposes, especially as lawn food. Highly soluble—runoff may pollute ponds and streams.	Spread a measured amount with a mechanical spreader or by hand from cup or container. Scratch or till into soil.	This product provides basic nutrients quickly and conveniently to plants of all kinds. It is often used and sold as lawn food.
Boxed granular dry fertilizer (chemical)	Same as above, in smaller quantities. Often called rose food, blossom booster, tomato food, etc., depending on the formulation.	Spread by hand by shaking onto the ground from the container, then till in.	Same as above.
Bagged or boxed dry fertilizer (organic)	Often made from seaweed, fish, manure, or treated sewage by-products. Brown or dark in color. May become malodorous when wet.	Spread a measured amount with a mechanical spreader or dispense by hand from container, then till in.	Provides basic and trace nutrients for fast yet sustained soil improvement for all kinds of plants.
"Instant" soluble powdered fertilizer (chemical)	Often sold in tins or small plastic tubs, it looks like blue or green sandy crystals. Many formulations are available.	Mix into irrigation water as directed. Dilute further for seedling plants or tender species to prevent burning.	Liquids provide a quick fertilizer boost, especially useful for plants in outdoor containers. Use with caution on tender species and seedlings.
Liquid fertilizer (chemical)	A dark or thick liquid, usually bottled, it sometimes comes with eyedropper applicator. Many formulations are available.	Same as above, unless the product warns that it might clog sprayers.	Same as above.

Some soils are deficient in one or several needed minerals. Nutrient deficiencies are revealed by characteristic plant disorders. The table on pages 46–47 shows the symptoms of deficiencies and organic sources of the nutrient needed to correct the problem. The recommended amount can be determined by soil tests.

TYPE OF PRODUCT	DESCRIPTION	METHOD OF APPLICATION	PURPOSE
Liquid fertilizer (organic)	This thick, dark liquid, often made from fish or seaweed, is usually sold in bottles. Major and trace nutrients are supplied in various formulations.	Apply according to product directions, usually by diluting in water and watering by hand.	Same as above, with added benefit of trace nutrients.
Timed-release chemical fertilizer	This product is sold as beads, pellets, tablets, sticks, or tree spikes. Composition and time release period vary by product.	Spread fine-grained or beaded types by hand or machine. Place tablets, sticks, and spikes by hand according to directions.	This broad group of products provides a long-term or season-long supply of nutrients, which is an aid in growing plants in poor soil or confined conditions.
Greensand	This naturally occurring marine substance contains phosphorus and potassium, plus many valuable trace minerals. It appears sandy or granular, and is sold bagged or in bulk.	Spread the recommended amount with a mechanical spreader or dispense it from the container by hand, then till it in.	Greensand lastingly improves soil fertility and texture, and adds to its ability to hold water.
Rock powders (dusts)	Dusty to granular milled-rock fertilizer is sold bagged or in bulk. Granite rock yields potassium, phosphate rock gives phosphorus, and basalt and other rocks yield many minerals, but no nitrogen.	Same as above.	Benefitting the soil for five to ten years, rock powders improve both fertility and texture. Supplement them with nitrogen and fast-acting fertilizers.
Cottonseed meal	Processed, this is an oily brown meal sold in bags or in bulk. Typically it yields 6/1/1 NPK.	Same as above.	This cotton by-product is used to provide high levels of nitrogen in a long-lasting form.

Continued

SOIL TESTING

No two garden experts agree on the formula for perfect soil, but all suggest you begin by having the soil tested. This is good advice. Tests from county agricultural extension offices and garden centers not only show what kind of soil you have, they are accompanied by

FERTILIZERS *(Continued)*

TYPE OF PRODUCT	DESCRIPTION	METHOD OF APPLICATION	PURPOSE
Manure (dried)	Usually sold in large bags, this product is usually composed of dark granules that look something like soil. Often high in nitrogen, manures vary in nutrient content.	Spread and till in by hand or machine.	Manures of all types provide for long-term supply of basic and trace minerals in addition to improving the texture of the soil.
Manure (composted)	Sometimes sold bagged, but also sold from farms in large quantities, composted manure varies in nutrient content. It may contain straw or wood chips in addition to the manure.	Spread and till in by hand or machine. Handle quantities of damp composted manure with a spading fork.	Same as above, with even greater improvement of soil texture.
Bonemeal (steamed)	Usually packaged in boxes or bags, this is a dry, whitish gray powder containing high phosphorus, low nitrogen, and lime. Typically the product yields 4/12/0 NPK.	Spread the recommended amount with a mechanical spreader or dispense it from the container by hand where it is needed, then till it in.	Bonemeal releases nutrients slowly but effectively for long-term soil enrichment. Apply it near bulbs and shrubs at planting time.
Hoof and horn meal	Processed into grayish or brownish granules, this product is sometimes sold in bulk at garden stores. Though high in nitrogen and phosphorus, it contains no potassium.	Same as above.	This is an old-fashioned, all-purpose fertilizer that is slowly released into the soil. Supplement it with potassium, which is present in wood ashes.

recommendations for improving it as well. A complete test covers pH, soil type, and available amounts of major and minor nutrients.

PROFESSIONAL TESTING. Inexpensive soil test kits can be requested from agricultural extension offices in counties all over the United States. These "Ag" offices are "extensions" of land grant colleges and universities, meant to extend research to the state's farmers and gardeners. The kit arrives in the mail and you return it by mail, with a plastic sack filled with your garden soil. To collect a sample for testing, use a clean trowel and extract soil from several inches below the surface in different parts of the same garden. Drop scoops of soil into a covered plastic container and shake well. Use part of this mixture for the soil test. If you have several garden spots with different soil conditions, have a test done on each one.

Precise instructions on how much soil to include and where to collect it should accompany the kit. It may take several weeks to obtain results if your request comes during the busiest part of spring, so plan ahead. In many states, results are sent as a computer printout of findings and recommendations.

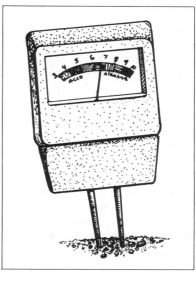

This soil test meter is great for home use, giving you as many pH readings as you like.

HOME TESTING. For obtaining results quickly at home, soil test meters that need no batteries are very convenient and give repeated readings. Seed catalogs and local garden centers are good sources for these. However, as with other measuring devices (the bathroom scale, for instance), the calibration may become less accurate after a while. Some meters can be recalibrated, others cannot. One of the advantages of a professional test is that presumably the calibration of the test equipment is correct.

It is wise to have soil tested, or test it yourself, in the fall. In areas with mild winters, test in summer, before the fall gardening season begins. This allows time to receive test results and make improvements to the soil before planting time arrives.

CULTIVATING AND DIGGING GARDEN BEDS

After you decide where your garden beds are to be located and what shape they will have, they must be cleared and dug. The basic principles and techniques you will need are included here. Refer back to Chapter 2 for detailed descriptions of garden tools.

CLEARING THE SOIL. Soil for new garden beds can be cleared of rocks, sod, weeds, and garden plants at any time of year when the soil is not frozen. If you are digging by hand, try to avoid working during the hottest part of the year for your own health and comfort. In areas with freezing winters (Zone 8 and above), autumn is the best but not the only time to make a new garden bed. The soil does not have to be worked as finely then because clods of earth will weather and break down during the winter. By spring planting time, the overturned sod and the added soil amendments such as compost and manure will have become part of the soil.

Begin by marking the outline of the bed to be cleared with lime or sticks and string. Visible rocks and garden plants inside the boundaries should be removed. Plants such as shrubs, ground covers, and perennials may be moved to other spots in the garden. Dig them up with as big a root and soil ball as possible, replant them elsewhere immediately, and keep them well watered until they are reestablished. Any that are to go back into the new bed can be dug, watered, put in the shade, and covered with damp cloth or paper until they can be replanted. Prune back about one-third of the tops of shrubs before you move them. Ideally, no roots of woody plants will remain in the new garden.

In many cases, you will want to dig the garden bed out of part of the lawn. The grass can either be moved, plowed in or dug under deeply, or killed. Landscapers use sod-stripping machines to clear large areas and are able to shape them precisely. You can dig up the sod by hand by cutting strips about a foot wide and 3 or 4 inches deep with a flat spade. If the grass sod is healthy and weed-free, you may plant it elsewhere. Or if turned under and covered with enough soil, the sod will decompose, and improve the soil's structure and fertility. However, if you have a lot of sod to clear and no use for it elsewhere, digging will be easier if you kill the sod first. Do not use herbicides (weed killers) because these chemicals will drift and cause damage to ornamental trees and shrubs as well as fruit trees and berries. Instead, sod can be killed by smothering it under a solid layer of mulch that will keep light from reaching the grass. This is most effective during hot summer weather.

A mulch of your own grass clippings, if you have them, is effective for killing sod. They, too, should be free of herbicides. Lay 6 to 8 inches of fresh green clippings on the entire surface of the future garden bed. No live grass should poke through. After four to six weeks of warm weather, the grass below should be thoroughly rotted. The heat from the decomposing clippings and the lack of light will have combined to kill it. If the grass below is merely yellow, that means it is weak but still alive and will grow again if given light, so it should be recovered with mulch.

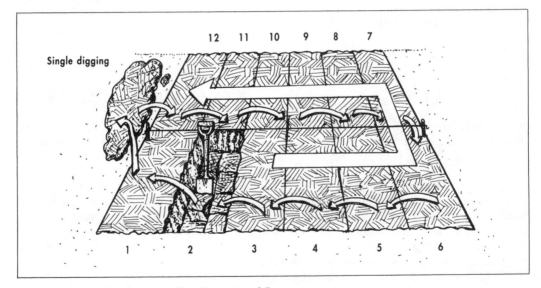

The easiest way to dig a large area like this one is as follows:

1. Begin by dividing the plot in half, marking it with a string.

2. Spread soil improvers such as fertilizer, manure, and compost in an even layer over the plot.

3. Go to one end (trench #1) and dig a trench about 1 foot deep and 2 feet wide. Place the soil in a wheelbarrow or in a pile outside the garden bed (preferably near trench #12).

4. Dig a second trench next to the edge of the first and put the soil and soil improvers from the second trench into the empty trench (#1).

5. Work each trench in this way, following the direction shown by the broad white arrow. (The smaller arrows indicate the soil placement.)

A sheet of black plastic mulch, weighted down by stones, will also smother and kill sod. This is helpful in killing certain pests while clearing garden sites. The high temperature produced by solar energy under the mulch helps to fumigate the soil, killing some weed seeds and helping to eliminate root-knot nematodes, microscopic worms that attack roots. They can be a serious problem in southern areas.

Certain weeds, such as nut and quack grass or crabgrass, have rhizomes (knobby roots) that can regrow new plants from a surprising depth. They should be removed as thoroughly as possible and discarded before making garden beds. Many gardeners wish that their Kentucky bluegrass lawns were as hardy as these weeds!

SINGLE DIGGING. The depth to which your garden bed should be dug depends on the soil type, the purpose of the garden, and the energy of you, the gardener. Single digging rather than double digging is sufficient for most kinds of gardens. For areas larger than 20 by 20 feet, you might want to hire professionals to do the job for you.

Single digging, by hand, means turning and mixing the soil and soil improvers to the depth a spade reaches in one solid stroke. In areas where the sod has been cleared, the soil is good, ivy or other rugged ground covers will be planted, or the garden will be deeply mulched, single digging is sufficient.

To begin, spread recommended soil improvers (see pages 55–56) in an even layer over the cleared bed. Go to one end and, with a shovel or spade, dig a trench 1 foot deep and 2 feet wide. After the first spadeful, make each new slice about 4 inches back from the hole and lift it out. Place the soil in a container or pile it up outside the garden bed, then dig a second trench next to the edge of the first. Put this soil into the first trench, soil improvers and all, mixing the different elements together. This soil has now been worked, and a new trench to fill has been created next to it. Repeat this in progression through the garden. Put the soil removed from the first trench into the last empty trench. Working a double row of trenches will save you from carrying soil a long distance. Hoe lumps of soil and rake them smooth. If the garden will rest over the winter before being planted, save the hoeing and raking for spring. Mulching the area will help keep soil loose and light. Do not underestimate the exercise level required. There is no need to do the whole job in one day.

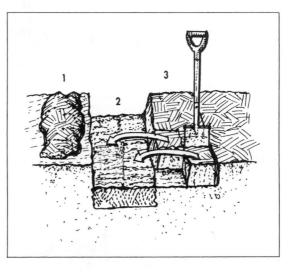

The soil from each trench is turned over and used to fill the preceding trench.

DOUBLE DIGGING. Problem soils and intensive gardens, where plants are grown very closely together, should be double dug, although many consider it too ambitious a task to do themselves. It is not necessary to remove sod before digging because it will be deeply buried. This method is used to reclaim badly compacted soils with little air and poor

Double digging is a laborious, three-step process used to reclaim problem soils.

A. Dig the first trench about 2 feet wide and 2 feet deep, setting the soil aside.

B. Put the top foot of soil from what will be the next trench into the first trench and mix in soil improvers. Dig the lower foot of soil from the same trench, mix it with soil improvers, and put it into the first trench as well.

C. Repeat the process progressively around the garden. The last trench is filled with soil taken out of the first one.

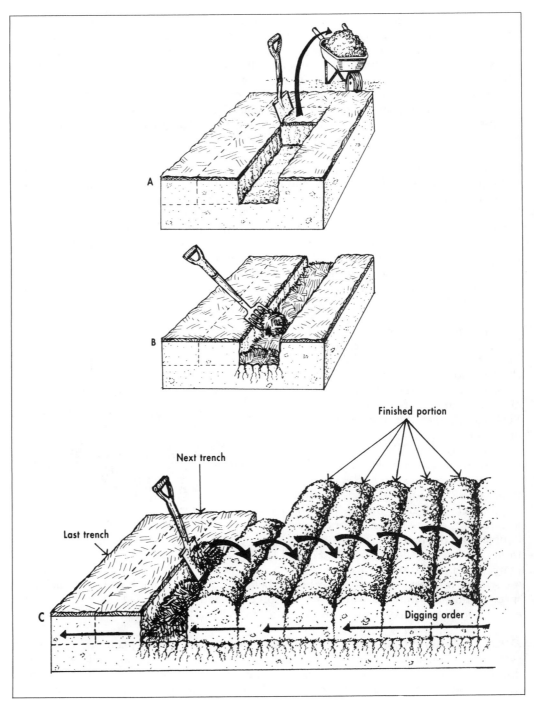

A

B

Finished portion

Next trench

Last trench

C

Digging order

drainage, and is good for quickly improving a barren, infertile soil. At least twice as much of the recommended soil improvers are mixed in. Laborious double digging is not the only way to correct soil problems, but it is the fastest.

Double digging is like single digging, only the plot is more deeply dug. This is a three-step rather than a two-step process. Dig the first trench 2 feet wide and 20 to 24 inches deep, setting the soil aside. Put the top layer (10 or 12 inches) of what will be the next trench into the first, grass, weeds, and all. Mix in the recommended soil improvers. Dig the next layer of the adjacent trench, along with soil improvers, and put it into the first one as well. The process is repeated progressively around the garden. The last trench is filled with soil taken out of the first one.

ROTOTILLING AND PLOWING. Established gardens and new beds without heavy, compacted soil may be rototilled rather than dug by hand. There are individual contractors who do custom rototilling. In advertisements, tillers tend to sound easier to use than they actually are. Most cannot be forced to bite into heavy soils or sod, but will work well on soil that is sandy or in good shape.

For large vegetable gardens, it may be possible to contract for someone with a plow to prepare the area. A heavy plow will be able to work just about any soil. Plows are too big to be practical for making moderate or small flower beds and vegetable gardens.

CONDITIONING AND IMPROVING SOIL

Soil-building substances range from seaweed to bonemeal. Some help restructure soil, some add nutrients, and some do both. Every gardener has his or her favorite soil fixer—compost, peat moss, horse or cow manure, oak leaves, wood ashes, leaf mold, vermiculite, perlite, fish meal, phosphate, sand, clay-based (clean) kitty litter, lime, garden gypsum, sawdust, rock powders, peanut hulls, ground oyster shells, blood meal, and processed Zoo Doo, to name a few. Many are available by mail or at garden centers, but others are commercial by-products or must be gathered in the neighborhood. There is no one right answer, or right component. It depends on what is wrong with your soil and what soil-building materials are at hand. If you live in Ohio next to a dairy farm, seaweed is not going to be as practical for you as is another time-tested, soil-boosting substance within sniffing distance. Adding several different kinds of improvers adds more minerals and structure to the soil than adding just one. It is hard to add too much, but soil test results should help you figure out just how much to add. Repeat the tests after making the additions, and each year afterward if you wish. The healthy or unhealthy condition of your garden plants will also indicate whether your soil still needs adjustment.

IMPROVING SANDY SOIL. Sandy soil needs greater water retentiveness and fertility because water tends to pass right through it, carrying off nutrients as it goes. All the additives mentioned, except for perlite, will improve it. If you add woody or leafy matter, add extra nitrogen (in the form of manure, blood meal, or some other high-nitrogen source—see the soil nutrient table on pages 46–47) to help it break down. Clay is very helpful, too. It takes a surprisingly large amount of aged or dried manure, compost, peat moss, grass clippings, sawdust, leaves, and so on, tilled in, to upgrade sandy soil significantly. Until the soil is improved to a good depth—1 ½ to 2 feet—it will continue to lose nutrients rapidly. The alternative to building up the soil is the constant application of increasing amounts of chemical fertilizer and water. Slow-release fertilizers are particularly useful in sandy soil. For a further discussion of fertilizers, see pages 45–48.

Digging in a 10-inch-deep layer of various mixed soil improvers over the entire garden area is a good starter for Florida residents and others who must contend with dry white sand. The sand is virtually inert. If your sandy site is near the beach, gathering seaweed and burying it in the garden, composted or uncomposted, is helpful and inexpensive. Do not lay it on top, for it will dry out and blow away, and don't wash it off. For environmental protection, don't remove live seaweed from the water—after a storm pick up what washes ashore in areas where this is permitted.

IMPROVING CLAY SOIL. Clay soil is harder to dig up but more easily improved than sandy soil. It usually has accessible nutrients, but may have a poor structure that holds water too long and keeps out air. Clay can be improved by lightening it with compost, composted manure, and vegetable matter, plus sand, garden gypsum, lime, and perlite. It takes the addition of at least 4 to 6 inches of improvers over the entire area to make any difference. There is no way to add too much compost, although it is possible to overfertilize or add too much lime. Beware of soil that is clay mixed with sand, without organic matter. When it dries, you'll have a good substitute for brick.

Work improvers into clay soil during the fall so the garden will be ready for spring planting. Clay soil should not be tilled or dug when it is very wet because it becomes badly compacted.

YEARLY MAINTENANCE OF SOIL. Each year soil must be renewed to replace elements used up by garden plants or lost by leaching through soil. Whether or not you use chemical fertilizers, it is important to maintain good soil structure by adding compost or manure. In most regions, unmulched vegetable and annual flower gardens should be tilled in fall, incorporating compost, grass clippings, and crop residues. This will make the garden ready for planting earlier the following spring.

You can renew the soil without disturbing the roots of trees, shrubs, herbs, and perennial flowers and ornamental grasses. One way to do this is to apply a side-dressing of fertilizer during the growing season, according to package directions. Organic gardeners often mulch each plant with a nutritious mixture such as this:

Mix together two parts compost, two parts garden soil, two parts premoistened peat moss, and one part composted manure. Add a 2-inch layer of this to the top of the soil around each shrub and cover the entire perennial bed with it. The action of the rain, irrigation, and earthworms will bring the nutrients to the plants. For fruit trees, place a ring of this nutritious mixture several inches away from the trunks to keep from giving shelter to mice. Spread the mulch out to the width of a tree's leaf canopy if possible.

Additional mulch materials such as pine needles, salt hay, chopped leaves, and grass clippings may also be used, though their appearance is less tidy. If using these, the peat moss is not needed. Mulched gardens need less soil enrichment because the mulch renews the soil. As old layers of mulch work their way into the soil, new layers are applied above them.

COMPOST

A lot has been said about compost in these pages. It is a variable but always enriching substance made from decomposed organic matter, which resembles rich potting soil. Compost can be made at home or purchased in bags, ready to use. In some communities, fallen leaves are gathered, made into compost, and then either sold or distributed free.

Compost is made of vegetable table scraps, leaves, weeds, crop residues, eggshells, grass clippings, and such things, piled up to decompose in a heap at least several feet wide. The vegetable matter should be mixed or layered with manure or soil, or both. Microorganisms and earthworms digest the "food" and turn it into superenriched, soillike compost containing all the major and minor nutrients. The compost pile will heat up as a result of this microbial digestion. Nitrogen, found in green leaves and manures, will make the pile more biologically active. You can make perfectly good compost without manure if you use enough fresh green grass clippings or leaves.

Do not include animal matter in your compost or you may attract rodents to the pile. For neatness, compost is often made in large plastic, wood, or wire-framed containers. Some setups have several bins, one for each stage of compost development, in an out-of-the-way utility area.

Anything derived from vegetable matter can be put into a compost pile, except diseased plants. The smaller the pieces, the sooner the compost will be finished, because of the greater exposed surface area. Shredded leaves are closer to being fully composted months before whole ones are. Compost should be mixed and turned with a garden fork several times while it is being made. Keeping the pile moist but not flooded will also help speed things up. Fast compost can be made from small shredded bits of organic matter in a few weeks; rougher, unshredded vegetation will take from a few months to a year.

When the compost is finished, it is dark brown and its ingredients are no longer recognizable. Spread it with a shovel or trowel. You can remove finished compost from the bottom of the pile and still add new material to the top. It can be used as a mulch, in potting soil, as a fertilizer, or as a soil-building ingredient, and is beneficial for all plants and all types of soil.

COVER CROPS

If you must improve soil on many acres or a large area, you can do it most efficiently and economically by planting cover crops—crops whose main purpose is to be plowed under for soil enrichment. Their roots help loosen the soil, and later, when plowed under, the decomposing plants add large quantities of humus and nutrients. Sometimes referred to as "green manure," cover crops are meadowlike plantings of clover, rye, buckwheat, alfalfa, soybeans, vetch, or other plants that are used as living compost. Some but not all cover crops (soybeans, for instance) have a second use as a harvestable crop. For best results, till and fertilize the field before planting cover crops so you get more growth. Grassy cover crops are usually plowed in when nearly mature, when their nutrient value is highest; others at any time from partial to complete maturity. Allow about two weeks between plowing under a cover crop and planting your garden in the same spot. Coarse or tall cover crops should be mowed before they are tilled in.

Most plants used as cover crops, especially legumes like clover and soybeans, add extra nitrogen to the soil. However, for best garden crops, you may need to add supplemental nitrogen to the soil after you plow in cover crops for the first time. The decomposition of the cover crops takes nitrogen out of the soil as part of the chemical process, but will eventually return it later in the cycle.

Even in small areas, patches of cover crops such as clover can be useful. Although their main use is as a rotation crop on farmland, cover crops can be planted by home gardeners to improve soil for vegetable gardens, mini-orchards, and future lawns. In smaller gardens they are generally considered too unsightly to be much used.

In areas with warm summers and freezing winters, cover crops can be sown in spring, summer, or fall, depending on the species and circumstances. Most often, a cover crop is planted in late summer or early fall where another crop was harvested, and left to grow and stabilize the soil until it is time to plow and plant a new crop in the spring. However, some cover crops, such as soybeans and peanuts, are planted in late spring, harvested in early fall (these two offer a crop in addition to acting as a soil builder), and then plowed under. Sweet clover, white clover, red clover, alfalfa, annual ryegrass, buckwheat, oats, and hairy vetch are used.

In southern areas with mild winters and hot summers, cover crops are usually planted in late spring after the garden season ends, to grow through the hot season and then be plowed in when planting resumes in the fall. Cowpeas, peanuts, amaranth, buckwheat, annual ryegrass, sorghum, and soybeans are used.

The diversity of soil types and measures to improve them prevents giving exact formulas here. Soil is the life-support system of plants—its importance cannot be overstated. After you prepare the soil for your plants, observe their growth and health for clues to fine-tuning the system. In nature, deep, fertile soils may take hundreds of years to build. In your backyard, with some attention, soil can be brought into excellent condition in just a year or two, and continue to be improved as the seasons pass.

PLANTING TECHNIQUES

T he soil looks inviting after you have prepared the garden. Like a stretched canvas, it is ready for the picture. Now that the heavy work is done, which plants would you like to grow? How will you get them? When? Where will they be planted?

CHOOSING PLANTS ADAPTED TO YOUR GROWING AREA

Chapter 1 discussed climate and the other characteristics of every garden site, such as exposure, sun and shade, and topography. Understanding the growing conditions offered by your garden will help you choose plants that are best suited for it.

Climate is one of the most important influences on plant growth and the one you can do the least to change. Climate includes such factors as winter and summer day length, average lowest winter temperature, average daytime summer temperatures, number of frost-free days, and number of winter hours below 45°F. Day length will often influence when many plants flower or form bulbs. For example, spinach and many varieties of lettuce will "bolt" (form flower stalks instead of leafy heads) when day lengths are more than fourteen hours. Gardeners in the northern part of the country must grow these plants in the early spring, before the longest days in June, or in the late fall, when day lengths are shorter. The average lowest winter temperature is most important when it comes to choosing varieties of perennial flowers, ornamental shrubs, fruit trees, and berries because it would be a waste of time and money to plant species or varieties of species that couldn't survive normal winter low temperatures. The average daytime summer temperatures will affect whether you grow, for example, a cold-tolerant variety of tomato or flower rather than a variety that thrives in the heat.

Many fruit trees, berries, ornamentals, and shade trees are deciduous. By losing their leaves, they are better able to withstand the colder winter temperatures. These plants need a certain number of cold days (those below 45°F) in the winter, during their dormant period, before they will begin to leaf out or grow in the spring; this is called *chill requirement.* Plants with a high chill requirement do well in the northern parts of the United States, where winters are cool or where winter temperatures fluctuate between warm and cool. If not for their high chill requirement, they would break dormancy and begin growing during a winter warm spell, after which they would be killed by the next normal cold winter weather. But if these plants were planted in the Deep South, where they wouldn't receive enough cold hours, they would be very slow to leaf out in the summer and in some areas wouldn't leaf out at all.

In the Deep South, where there are fewer winter hours below 45°F, plants have adapted to a much lower chill requirement, making them leaf out earlier. However, if, for example, you planted a low chill variety of blueberry or flowering shrub in the North, it would likely lose *hardiness* (a chemical state that helps protect the plant from freezing) and be killed in the next freezing weather.

Each individual plant entry in this book features categories such as hardiness, growing range, and chill requirement, where appropriate, to help you choose plants that are suited to your garden. Other sources of information about which species and varieties of species will be most appropriate for your climate are your local extension office, public gardens, arboreta, and experienced gardeners in your area.

BOTANICAL NOMENCLATURE

The common names for many garden plants vary from one place to the next, so it helps to learn, or at least be aware of, the proper botanical name of plants that you wish to buy or grow.

In the plant entries in this book, each plant is identified by its common names and the botanical names of its genus, species, and family. In botanical nomenclature, the first word in the plant's Latinized botanical name is the genus name, and the second word indicates the species. Plants in the same genus share similar characteristics up to a point. For instance, the botanical name for potato is *Solanum tuberosum,* and that of eggplant is *Solanum melongena.* These two crops belong to the same genus; they have similar flower shapes and share a few other characteristics. However, they differ significantly, so they are given different species names.

Related plants belonging to different genera (plural of genus) are grouped together in families. The tomato is related to both the potato and eggplant, all of which belong to the Solanaceae family, which is called the tomato, or nightshade, family. Plants in the same family grouping often will be plagued by similar plant pests or diseases, and should be rotated with plants of other families every year (see plant rotation on page 130). In the plant entries each plant's family name is identified after the genus and species, and is in parentheses.

Many garden catalogs list their plants by variety or cultivar (short for *cultivated varieties).* For instance, 'Burpee's Big Boy' and 'Oregon Spring' are varieties of tomato, *Lycopersicon esculentum.* Although they are both tomatoes, they have very different growing characteristics. 'Burpee's Big Boy' grows well in hot, long-growing climates, and 'Oregon Spring' matures early in cool growing climates. A good reference for botanical nomenclature is *Hortus Third,* a dictionary of plants published by Macmillan Publishing Company and carried in most public libraries.

PLANT AVAILABILITY

You can set grown plants in your garden or grow your own from seeds or cuttings. Seeds, seedlings, or more mature specimens can be purchased from local stores or by mail, or collected, in the form of seeds, transplants, cuttings, or divisions, from other gardeners—a generous group of people. (Expressing your admiration for someone's garden often inspires a gift of cuttings.) Sometimes you can collect seeds or transplants of wild plants yourself, if they are not endangered species and you have owners' permission, or if they are going to be destroyed in the process of construction.

NURSERY PLANTS. At nurseries and garden centers, most bedding plants are sold in six-packs with 2-inch cups and in 4-inch pots. Select annual flowers, herbs, and vegetables while they are young and healthy. Older bedding plants in full flower or fruit may be permanently stunted if they have been forced to bloom too long in tiny pots with their roots

The six-pack of marigolds on the left may, at first, look like the better choice, but notice how tall and leggy the flowers are. They have not been given enough room to grow, and have matured too quickly with too little leaf growth. The younger, leafier marigolds on the right are a better choice, promising more and better flowers and new growth in your garden.

The tomato plant on the left has outgrown its pot and is too tall and leggy, indicating that it was grown under crowded conditions, possibly under poor lighting. The plant on the right shows signs of even, healthy growth, and is more likely to continue to grow quickly.

The impatiens on the left has overcrowded roots that are growing out of the drainage holes of the pot. Also, the top growth is thin and rangy. Although its appearance might eventually improve if it were given a larger pot or placed in the garden, the stocky plant on the right is a better choice. Its healthy growth should continue at a steady pace in your garden.

crowded. Avoid aged annuals, especially if their leaves are yellowed; they never will catch up. Look for flowering bedding annuals that are just beginning to bloom. Annuals grown in larger pots are usually healthier, but more expensive per plant. However, if the ones in the six-packs are small, young, and healthy, they are a better buy, for they will make up for their small size by growing quickly.

Perennial plants should look crisp and green when in active growth. It is better to buy most types before they flower, but if they are growing in large pots it does not make much difference. Groundcover plants in flats should be healthy and well rooted.

It is fun to select flowering trees while they are in bloom, and fortunately that is the best time to do so, except when buying bare-root plants. Trees and shrubs are sold either with their roots bare of soil or else growing in soil (usually in a container). Soilless, bare-root plants should be dormant, with buds but with no leaves or flowers showing. Do not buy them if they are already leafy. You can tell when dormant plants are healthy because the stems feel springy and flexible, not brittle. Trees or shrubs that must be dug up should be dormant or just starting their new growth. Those growing in containers may be bought and planted at any time, whether they are dormant or not.

Bulbs and bulblike corms are sold a little ahead of and during planting time in your area. They should feel sound and firm, not flaky or squishy. Watch out for packages of warm-weather types like dahlias and lilies if they have already sprouted. If the sprouts have twisted inside the packaging, the plants might not grow straight.

Many eagle-eyed gardeners will be out there scanning the garden centers for ideal plants. In some areas, all the white impatiens are sold the first week, leaving behind less popular colors. It helps to be early. When you see what you want, get it. Trust the markers telling the color of flowers that have not bloomed. If you wait for the buds to open before buying, the ones you want may be gone. If you are planting large areas and need specific colors or varieties, call nurseries or growers and place an order. You may find one to custom-grow and deliver your selections.

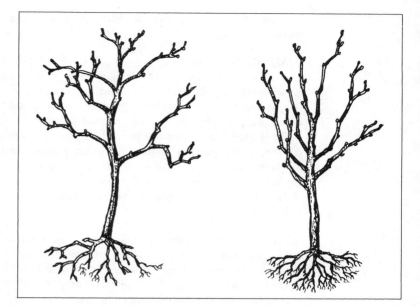

Bare-rooted trees. Although the tree on the left is well branched, its root system has been damaged and lacks the smaller root hairs. The tree on the right appears to be in better condition, and would be a safer choice at the nursery.

FACTORS AFFECTING PLANTING

PERMANENCE OF PLANTING.

If you are not sure what to plant, you can include lots of annuals the first year, since they last only one season. Most are extremely floriferous, or productive. Biennial plants are planted from seed one year, bloom and go to seed the next year, and then die. New plants grow from the seeds if allowed to. Perennial plants live for many years. Most garden perennials have outstanding blooms for a few weeks each year as well as attractive foliage. Some make good ground covers. In each category (annual, bien-

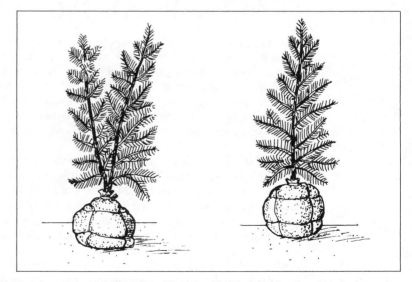

These two young trees are offered for sale with soil and roots wrapped in burlap and tied with string. The plant on the left has lost its leader (central growth point). Two branches have taken its place, forming a weak V-shaped crotch that is likely to split when the plant is mature. The plant on the right is well shaped and healthy, and is clearly a much better choice.

nial, or perennial) there are flowers, grasses, vegetables, and herbs. Of course, shrubs and trees live and grow for many years.

TIMING. Your own experience is one of the best guides to the time of planting, which varies by both region and the hardiness of each plant. Keeping notes on your garden activities is helpful, and so are your local county agent and garden columnists. Chapter 6 is a month-by-month regional guide to planting and garden chores; specific plant preferences are provided in the individual entries.

Plant hardy, cool-weather plants like peas and pansies a few weeks or months earlier than tender, warm-weather plants such as eggplants and zinnias. Follow these with late-season crops that grow in the cooler weather of autumn. Annual plants are especially affected by the date of planting. They will perform poorly if planted at the wrong time of year. Since shrubs and perennials live for years in spite of changeable weather, they are more adaptable.

SPACING. Like people, plants prefer elbow room. Overcrowded plants will not be as attractive or productive as those with room enough for leaves and roots to grow well. But if there is too much space between plants, weeds will fill in. Also, water will evaporate faster from the exposed soil. Each plant's entry includes recommended spacing. In especially fertile soils (as found in intensive beds), plants may be spaced a bit closer than is indicated.

GROWING PLANTS FROM SEED

You can grow outstanding plants from seeds at home, whether they are popular favorites or rare exotics. Some types are easier or grow faster than others. Seeds are sown indoors or out: in the house or greenhouse under bright lighting, in a cold frame or protected spot outdoors, or outdoors in the open ground. Which ones go where? It depends on the type of seed and the growing conditions you can provide. There are many ways to grow the same kind of plant successfully. Though there are various hazards, seeds are primed to grow. In nature, self-sown seedlings thrive with no help from gardeners.

SEED SOURCES. Mail-order suppliers often have extensive catalogs and well-tested supplies. Thousands of varieties are available, the results of a great deal of research. Local garden centers sell seeds, too. Members of horticultural groups such as the American Rock Garden Society swap rare seeds by mail. Many collectors of older plant varieties exchange heritage seeds. You can also grow home-saved seed if you do not mind variation among the offspring. For a selection of seed sources, see the Appendix.

LABELING. It really helps to label each container or row of seeds as soon as you plant it. Labels usually are made of plastic, metal, or wood. Inexpensive, durable plastic labels come in long strips that pull apart. Some wooden labels such as Popsicle sticks darken and rot after a few months; cedar labels are better; metal ones are fairly permanent. A fine-point, indelible marking pen (one that will mark laundry or write on aluminum foil) will make labels that last. In vegetable gardens, the traditional label is the seed packet on a stick—open the packet from the bottom so it will be right side up.

On each label, write the species and variety name, the planting date, and, if you like to be thorough, the source of the seed. A label might read, "Lettuce 'Selma Lollo,' 3/1/90, Park Seed." Put one in each container or near each row. These labels may not seem necessary on planting day, but several weeks later you will be glad you made them. By then you may have to decide where to set seedlings (now what were they?) ready for transplanting, or be wondering whether the third row in the flat will ever germinate.

GERMINATION. Keep the soil moisture for seeds at a happy medium. Seeds that are germinating will die if they dry out, but might rot in soggy, wet soil.

Usually, over 90 percent of freshly packed seeds of popular garden varieties will sprout. The germination time of seeds varies from a few days to many months, but each species or variety has a typical germination time and preferred temperature. Some seeds will remain dormant until they freeze and thaw as if they were outdoors in a cold climate. You can imitate nature by holding the seeds in your freezer for several weeks, then planting them the usual way. Most annual flowers and vegetables germinate within ten days of planting if temperature and moisture are right. Some perennials (alstroemeria, for one) have seeds that germinate sporadically. Sprouts appear months apart even within a single batch of seeds. It is wise to wait patiently for some kinds of seeds to germinate. Alpine plant collectors often hold on to no-show seeds a long time. They continue to care for the planted seeds (in their containers) for up to three years before giving up. Sometimes they are rewarded by the late appearance of a rare plant.

VARIATION IN SEED SIZE. Some plants are large-seeded, like squash, with ½-inch-long seeds that are easy to see and pick up. Others, like begonias, have dustlike, nearly invisible seeds. Seeds of most garden plants are somewhere in between. Grow the smallest seeds indoors, and the rest either indoors or out.

DEPTH AND SPACING. Cover seeds with a layer of soil about twice the diameter of the seed. Plant a little deeper in sandy soil, more shallowly in clay soil. There is more danger in planting too deeply. Seeds are usually planted closer than plants would be and later thinned to the correct spacing. As seeds become more expensive, gardeners tend to space them farther apart to minimize waste. Depth and spacing are given in the individual plant entries as well as on seed packets.

PREGERMINATION. Usually, dry seeds are planted in soil, but you can presprout (pregerminate) them in damp conditions before you plant them if you wish. This speeds germination and increases success with medium or large seeds. The sprouts then can be set indoors or out. As long as they are large enough to handle, you can pregerminate seeds that normally germinate within a few weeks; others are too likely to rot.

Soak large seeds like beans or peas in water at room temperature to presprout them. In a jar, cover a layer of seeds with three times its volume of water. After a few hours or overnight, rinse the seeds and change the water—most of it will have been absorbed. From now on, barely cover the plump seeds with water and keep the jar in a dark place. Change

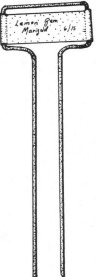

Plant labels may be made of plastic, metal, or wood. Metal labels are the most permanent.

the water twice daily. When small white sprouts appear, usually in less than three days, plant the seeds in soil.

Pregerminate smaller but easily seen seeds, such as those for pansies and basil, on moist paper. Moisten a piece of paper toweling and spread a few seeds on it so that they do not touch each other. Carefully roll the towel up with seeds inside, folding the ends over. Wrap the packet in plastic wrap, label it, and set it aside. Do not let the paper dry out. Soon the seeds will germinate. Plant them immediately in pots or in the ground. The tiny seeds may be lifted off the paper with tweezers, or left on the paper, instead, and then buried just under the soil's surface. The paper will soon disintegrate. Long planting strips may be prespaced and germinated this way. Be sure to plant germinated seeds promptly or they will grow crookedly.

TIME OF PLANTING. You want your seeds to get a safe start outdoors when the weather is right. You want the ones you grow indoors to be healthy transplants. Time of planting depends on the germination time of the seeds, the quality of the indoor environment you offer, and the outdoor garden's climate. In low indoor light, plants will grow tall with thin stems and leaves adapted to low light, making them easily damaged by the wind and sun when moved to the garden.

If you plant seeds too early indoors, their growth may become stunted by cramped conditions, and if planted too late, they may not be large enough to transplant into the garden when the weather is right. In most cases, plant hardy flowers and vegetables indoors about eight to twelve weeks before your last expected frost, tender ones three to nine weeks before frost ends. Though individual preferences vary, most seeds will germinate and grow at temperatures from 60° to 80°F, and many cold-hardy types can be grown in temperatures fluctuating between freezing and over 60°F.

Sow the seed for most cold-hardy plants, such as peas and spinach, outdoors when the soil has thawed in spring, or in winter in frost-free areas. The seed for tender plants may be sown after the danger of freezing passes.

STARTING SEEDS INDOORS. It is easy to grow seeds indoors because of the controlled climate and lack of pests. You can use ordinary potting soil, a sterile growing medium such as milled sphagnum moss, a mixture of sand with peat or sawdust and sterilized compost, or commercial seed starting mixes, often sold by the bag. Some media contain plant food but others, such as sphagnum moss, do not, so seedlings will need fertilizer as most seeds contain only enough nutrients to support germination.

Many kinds of containers may be used—plastic or terra-cotta pots, peat pots, or flats. Or you can use preformed plugs of peat moss or preformed soil cubes, which are sold with matching plastic liners. There are also seed starting kits and containers sized to fit on windowsills. Recycled six-packs or other containers may be used if they are washed in soapy water mixed with some chlorine bleach.

In greenhouses and where space allows, flats make good seed nurseries. They may be made of wood or plastic and are filled with the growing medium. A popular size is 10 inches wide and 20 inches long, with sides 3 inches high. Flats and pots should have holes for drainage and will need waterproof liners of any sort to protect windowsills and furniture.

Moisten the growing medium with lukewarm water and then fill the containers to within ½ inch of the top before planting seeds. Plant large seeds one or two to a small pot (2

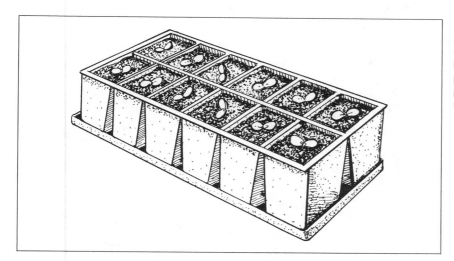

Seedlings grow well in containers like this, with pockets filled with pasteurized potting soil.

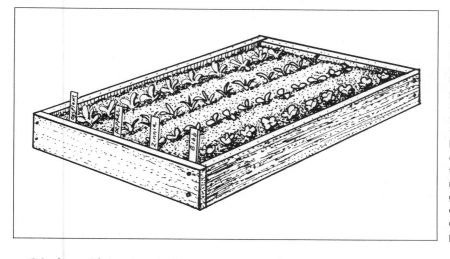

Wooden seed flats are great for growing quantities of seedlings, if you have the right place for them. Since water seeps through the container and good lighting is needed over the wide surface area, flats are most often used in greenhouses and cold frames, and on lined, lighted plant shelves.

to 5 inches wide), or an inch or two apart in flats. Cover them with ¼ to ½ inch of soil (the general rule is to plant seeds at a depth twice their width) and water sparingly. A few days after germination, thin or move the seedlings so there is one to a pot. Once they germinate, they will quickly outgrow flats and six-pack pockets, and will need to grow in larger pots or the garden outdoors.

Plant medium-size or small seeds closer together and grow them a while longer before thinning or transplanting. In flats, make furrows (rows) about ½ inch deep and 3 inches apart. Carefully place the seeds in the rows about ½ inch apart. Cover with ⅛ inch of soil, sprinkled on top and patted down. (The shallow furrow that results will hold the moisture better and will allow you to see where you planted.) Water just enough to moisten the seeds—the growing medium is already dampened. Plant small seeds in six-packs or small pots the same way, but put two seeds in the center of each cell, about ½ inch apart. If both

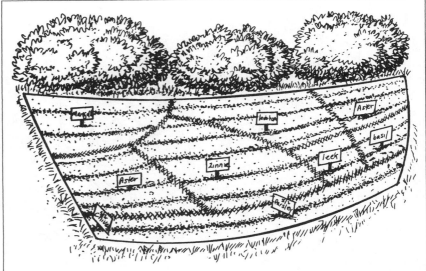

This newly planted seedbed is arranged in traditional straight lines—an aid in distinguishing your seedlings from weed seedlings and assisting in plant identification later.

germinate, thin to the strongest plant by pinching off the other one or transplanting it within days of its appearance. If seed is scarcer than space, put just one seed in each cell.

Plant very small or dustlike seeds in flats or small pots. They are hard to handle, so mix them in a cup with a spoonful of fine, dry sand and then sprinkle the mixture thinly onto the soil's surface to help space the seeds evenly. Pat the seeds in place, but do not cover them with soil as these seeds usually require sunlight for germination. Mist them with a fine spray of water containing a soluble fungicide, such as Captan, to prevent the possibility of damping off—succumbing to a fungus that attacks seedlings. Cover the container with a piece of glass or plastic to keep the soil moist and create a humid environment, very helpful during and just after germination because such tiny plantlets are so easily dehydrated.

STARTING SEEDS OUTDOORS. Of course you may want to plant seeds directly in the garden rather than indoors. For many popular species, outdoor planting is the fastest and most practical way to grow large numbers of plants. Some plants like an outdoor climate or do not transplant easily and are best grown from seed in their permanent spots. The drawbacks of and obstacles to outdoor planting include damage from pests, washouts of seed during stormy weather, a long period before growth is attractive, and growing seasons too short to permit plants to mature.

Prepare and till the garden, then plant your seeds at the appropriate depth and spacing indicated in the plant entries. If you plant in rows, it is easier to tell your plants from weeds. Label each row. Plant more than you need because some will not germinate or survive pests. Thin plants later, after they have begun to grow well. In fields, farmers sow seeds at the correct spacing to save the work of thinning them—a few vacant spaces do not matter to them. Keep the seedbed moist until the seeds germinate. In some areas, especially those with sandy soil, seedbeds should be watered daily. After plants appear, water slightly less frequently; this will force the plants to send their roots deeper underground.

Sowing seeds outdoors is covered more fully in the sections on flowers and vegetables (see pages 76–85 and 85–88) and in the individual plant entries.

Care of Seedlings

No matter where they are grown, new seedlings need the correct amount of light, good soil, protection from pests, basic nutrients, and water. For the first few days after germination, seedlings are so delicate that they are easily dehydrated or overfertilized. Because new seedlings are soft and succulent, they are tempting to pests but sensitive to pesticides. They are so small that one bite from a cutworm will finish them off. Even with careful pest prevention (see Chapter 5) some seedlings will probably be lost, so do not thin them too soon.

INDOOR SEEDLINGS. Give your indoor seedlings bright light for straight, strong growth. Vegetables and ornamentals that grow in full sun need more light than others. If you do not have a greenhouse or sunroom, use a sunny windowsill and turn the containers around once or twice a day to promote even growth.

You may want to use fluorescent lights, either in combination with natural light or in its place. Seedlings should be placed just a few inches below the light fixtures. Many garden shops and catalogs sell plant shelves with built-in plant lights, or you can fix up your own growing area with the kind of fluorescent lighting fixtures used for workshops, or easy-to-install sticklike fixtures. The bulbs do not have to be special plant lights, but it helps to combine one warm and one cool fluorescent bulb in each fixture. For an easy alternative

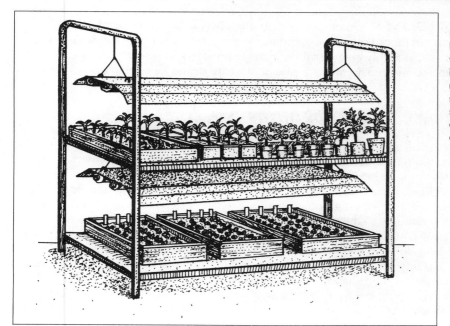

Plant shelves with lights are available for growing seeds in areas where natural light is insufficient. In some setups, the lights are connected to automatic timers.

to shelves and lights, anchor a fluorescent light fixture to a board and place it over a box holding the planted seedlings. This can be set up anywhere, even in a dark closet. To increase light, line the box with aluminum foil.

Most plants, especially annuals, are sensitive to day length—the number of hours of light per day. In northern areas, day length increases dramatically as winter ends and spring progresses toward summer. You can stimulate plants to grow faster by increasing day length to twelve hours with artificial light. Start seeds with ten hours of light per day and gradually increase the amount to fourteen or sixteen hours daily over the next few weeks.

Once seeds have germinated, they can grow at cooler or more variable temperatures than they needed for germination. The new seedlings will need fertilizer if the planting medium you used did not include it. A gentle diluted liquid or a slow-release fertilizer at half the recommended strength will give them a good start. Increase the fertilizer to its full pre-scribed level when your plants start to grow vigorously. Keep their water supply steady. Young plants with leaves that have a reddish color underneath need more phosphorus; those with yellow leaves need more nitrogen.

If they were covered, give your seedlings ventilation by propping up or opening the covers. Gradually increase the amount of fresh air the plants get. When the seedlings have adjusted to lower humidity, remove the covers but be sure to check the soil moisture daily.

The main danger to indoor seedlings is a fungus disease known as damping off, which causes them to wilt at the soil line and keel over. It is more of a threat to plants from tiny seeds than to plants from large ones. Prevent damping off by using sterile growing media or treating the growing media with a mild fungicide, as mentioned on page 68, and maintaining the correct moisture level—not too wet. Sometimes damping off can be stopped by increasing the lighting and ventilation and administering another dose of fungicide.

OUTDOOR SEEDLINGS. Outdoor seedlings already have the fertilizer they need in the soil, and there is not much you can do about the weather except for laying down emergency covers during unseasonably cold weather. Your main job is to monitor the soil moisture and water plants as necessary. More is said about care in the next chapter.

Thinning and Transplanting Seedlings

Your seeds are growing, some indoors, some in the garden. If you have not had serious pest problems, the seedlings are crowded. Maybe you have too many. Now what?

When the young plants have two or four true leaves (those that resemble what the mature leaves will look like), you can move them from crowded flats, pots, or garden rows to give them more space. Before you dig out any plants, prepare the spots into which they will be moved. If they go straight to the garden, make sure the soil has been tilled, then make small holes for the plants, at the necessary spacing. If they are to be moved into larger pots, fill the pots with damp soil and make a small hole in the center of each with a pencil—the best tool for handling tiny seedlings. In either case, holding the plantlet by a leaf (the stem is squashed too easily) with one hand, pry out the root carefully with the pencil point. Replant immediately by dropping the root into the waiting hole, then firming the plant into place and watering. Seedlings grow into good bedding plants or transplants when they develop one to a pot or six-pack pocket.

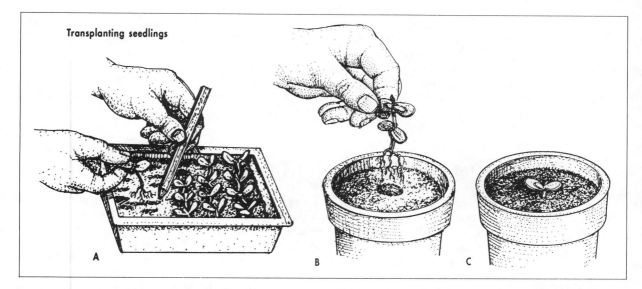

Transplanting seedlings

A. A pencil is a good tool for removing seedlings from flats. Hold the seedlings by the leaves, not the stems.

B. Replant seedlings immediately, in a prefilled pot with a small hole dug for the roots. If the seedlings are leggy, plant them a little deeper than they grew, right up to the bottom two leaves.

C. Replanted seedlings, whether they were leggy or not, should look something like this after they are settled into their new pots.

Seedlings grown indoors have been pampered, so they need a transition period of "hardening off" before you can safely transplant them to their outdoor positions. They need time to adjust to the direct sunlight, wind, arid air, and drier growing conditions of the outdoors. As they harden off in stages, their stems and leaves become firmer, thicker, and less succulent.

When the young plants are large enough to transplant (usually when they have four to six true leaves), take them outdoors in their original containers and place them in a shaded, windless area for about three hours the first day. For the next several days, set them outside again for periods of four to five hours, bringing them back inside after each airing. Gradually increase their exposure to brighter sunlight and wind. Give them plenty of water during this procedure—daily, in most cases. Then increase the time bit by bit. After about a week (the time varies with the conditions and species), leave them outdoors for twenty-four hours (still in their containers). If they do not wilt, they are ready to plant in the garden; otherwise, continue to harden them off in stages until they can safely spend the entire length of the day outside.

If you prefer, harden off seedlings under some kind of shelter, so they won't need to be carried back and forth. A shaded, ventilated cold frame is ideal for this—if it is in too much sunshine, shade it with lath strips, shade cloth, row covers, or several layers of white cheesecloth. Over the course of about a week, gradually permit more light and air to reach the tender plants, making sure water is always adequate. Alternatively, harden off seedlings outdoors under floating row covers rather than inside a constructed shelter. The cloth alone is sufficient to reduce the light and wind. Remove it when plants have adjusted to outdoor conditions. This method is especially practical when you handle large quantities.

If your seedlings are already in the right spot, but are too crowded, you have to decide whether or not to transplant the extras. Is it worthwhile to disturb the roots? If you have too many plants, you can thin them just by pinching off unwanted ones at the soil line, leaving the chosen ones (the strongest) undisturbed.

Sometimes seedlings grown in too little light are too tall, or leggy, which makes them weaker. If yours are, pry them out carefully, as explained above, and plant them deeper than they grew when you move them to larger pots or to the garden so they can grow correctly. You may safely bury stems of single-stemmed plants up to their first true leaves. Multistemmed plants may be buried up to their crown, the place where the leaves and stems come out from the base of the plant. Extra soil may be placed around the stems of seedlings as they grow, up to the crown or true leaves, for stronger plants.

HANDLING BEDDING PLANTS

Bedding-size plants have many leaves and a large well-branched root. If you need to step them up into larger pots, add enough potting soil to the bottom of the new container so that the plant stands at about the same distance from the lip of the pot. Surround the root ball with soil and fill the pot nearly to the top with more potting soil. If the plants are to be transplanted outdoors, harden them off, then dig holes in prepared garden soil, set in the plants, firm the soil around them, and water.

To take a bedding-size plant out of its container, lay the plant sideways on a table or the ground, with newspaper below to catch soil, and tap on the pot with a trowel to loosen

A. To remove bedding plants from their containers, lay them down on their sides and tap the pot gently with a trowel to loosen the roots from the sides of the pot.
B. With experience, gardeners learn to support the plant that is being repotted with one hand while loosening the roots from the sides of the pot with the other. A slap or two should do the job.

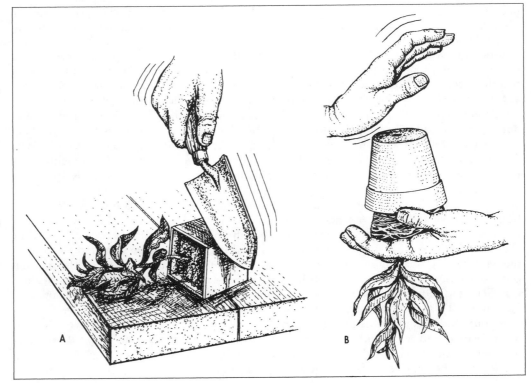

it. Experienced gardeners will turn a plant upside down, holding its main stem between their fingers at the soil line with one hand, and thump on the overturned bottom of the pot with the other to jar it loose. The pot lifts off easily; the plant is already in hand and ready to plant. If the plant is so pot-bound that its roots hold the shape of its pot, untangle them and fan them out before replanting it.

To transplant bedding-size plants already growing in the garden, dig them up with a trowel or spade with as much of the root system and surrounding soil as possible. Save this job for an overcast day to minimize the plants' water loss from evaporation, and replant your transplants immediately.

COLD FRAMES

A cold frame is a miniature greenhouse. Usually it is an outdoor, bottomless wooden or cinderblock box, partially buried in garden soil. Window sashes or sheets of Plexiglas make the top, either hinged to the frame or simply resting upon it. A good-size cold frame is 3 by 6 feet, with walls 1 to 3 feet high. However, there are many designs and sizes for cold frames. You can make your own, or buy them in kits or prefabricated and ready to set out. Many of the newer frames are transparent on their sides as well as their tops.

Use a cold frame for growing plants from seed; hardening off seedlings grown indoors; rooting cuttings; forcing tulips, crocus, and other bulbs for winter blossoming; growing cold-hardy crops like lettuce late into fall or through winter, and giving winter protection to semihardy plants. Under a cold frame, seedlings have the advantage of good outdoor light plus protection from cold, rain, snow, wind, and hailstones. A cold frame adds 10° to 25°F to the outdoor temperature, depending on the weather and the type of frame, and extends the growing season a month to six weeks in both spring and fall. In areas that get just a few frosts, a cold frame can maintain a frost-free environment.

You should sow seedlings four to six weeks earlier in spring in a cold frame than in open ground. Garden plants in cold frames grow somewhat more slowly but are stronger than those grown in greenhouses because of the bright natural light and fluctuating temperatures.

If you are going to set plants directly into the soil of your cold frame, you need to prepare the soil in an area larger than that to be occupied by the cold frame in the same way as for a garden bed, then set the cold frame on top. Like a garden, the cold frame soil will need tilling and replacement soil builders each season. If you use your cold frame only for container plants, the cold frame may be placed on cleared, level soil or a paved surface.

For the best exposure, place a cold frame in full sun with its front facing south. A building, wall, or windbreak at its back will provide wind protection. If you want to root cuttings in your cold frame, put it in the shade or shade it with lath strips. Some kinds of cold frames are portable, so they can be moved and used for different purposes at different times of the year.

Cold frames collect solar energy for heat. During parts of the year when the weather is warm and bright, they overheat quickly, so venting is needed to provide both fresh air and temperature control. Some cold frames come with, or can be fitted with, an automatic venting device. One type that needs no electricity is a thermally operated gadget consisting of coiled wires. When the weather is warm, the wires expand and push open a vent. When it gets cold, wires contract and close it. Cold frames also may be vented manually.

For greater warmth, underground electric heating cables or old-fashioned hotbeds (heat-generating layers of fresh manure or compost and soil) are topped with a cold frame. Double-walled glass or plastic tops give more insulation than single-walled ones. Cold frames may be topped with blankets or a layer of straw on cold nights for extra protection.

One inexpensive substitute for a cold frame is a clear plastic molded dome that is placed over a cellar window well. It gets heat from solar buildup plus indoor heat escaping through the window. It lacks ventilation and must be vented manually in sunny weather. Other substitutes are insulating cloths known as floating row covers, which admit light and protect plants from light frosts (27°F), and transparent plastic covers, which are held up by wire supports to make tunnellike plant shelters. In addition, plastic tunnels made from bubble plastic protect plants from hard frosts (20°F), and a water-filled tepee sold under the brand name Wall-O-Water protects plants down to 10°F.

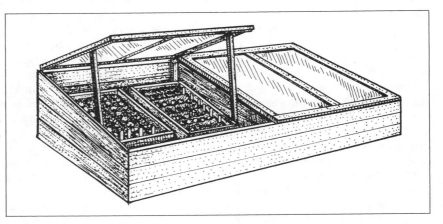

Cold frames like this one topped with window sashes can be made at home, sometimes with scrap materials. Some of the newer prefabricated models have transparent glass or plastic on the sides as well as the top, plus automatic venting.

Cinder block can be topped with glass window sashes for a long-lasting cold frame.

Just one of many means of giving coldframelike protection, tunnels of plastic held up with wire frames provide plants with shelter from cold or wet weather.

GROWING PLANTS IN CONTAINERS OUTDOORS

One of the easiest ways to make more room for gardening is to use planters and containers for mature outdoor plants—ornamental, food-bearing, or both. The containers can be set anywhere and serve as long-lasting or permanent growing places.

The soil used for container gardening should be rich in humus and nutrients because plant roots are not free to roam and forage for themselves. It should also hold water well.

There are many soil variations, depending on plant preferences and substances at hand, but a good all-purpose potting soil formula is one part sand, two parts leaf mold or roughly sifted compost, and one part vermiculite. Be careful; if the soil is too finely milled, it will harden in the pots when it dries out. Bagged potting soils are convenient but expensive.

You can pasteurize ordinary garden soil and compost at home for use in pots by "cooking" the soil to eliminate insects and some soil-borne weeds and diseases. To do this, moisten and spread a 2-inch-thick layer of soil in a disposable baking pan, which can be saved and reused to cook more soil. Preheat the oven to 200°F, then bake the soil for 25 minutes. Soil may also be microwaved in small batches for several minutes (do not use aluminum containers in the microwave).

Fertilize soil in containers appropriately for the plants being grown. The combination of slow-release dry fertilizer with occasional boosts of liquid fertilizer works well for most potted plants. Because of this soil enrichment, plants in pots may be spaced closer together than plants in regular beds.

Plants may be grown from seeds or bulbs in their pots, or set in as seedlings or larger plants. In any case, use containers that have holes for drainage. Then crock the pots—put a layer of stones or chips of flowerpots on the bottom to further improve drainage and prevent your soil from flowing out the drainage hole. Then add a few inches of moistened potting soil. Set plants in and fill the pots with soil to about 1/2 inch from the top. For seeds or bulbs, fill the containers to about 1/2 inch from the top, plant them, pat down the soil, and water.

Plants that grow in containers outdoors lose a great deal of moisture on hot, sunny days, but very little on cool, cloudy ones. In hot, dry areas, you may have to water plants in terra-cotta pots twice a day. Plastic pots hold water longer, but do not keep the roots as cool. The smaller the pot, the more often it must be watered, and the faster the roots overheat on warm days. For this reason, plants in large pots are easier to tend than plants in small ones. In cold areas, do not leave clay (especially terra-cotta) pots filled with soil and plants outside during the winter—when the soil freezes, it expands and is likely to crack the pots. For permanent outdoor plantings, use more giving planters, such as wooden tubs.

More on container gardens is found in the sections on ornamentals, herbs, vegetables, shrubs, etc., later in this chapter.

PLANTING ORNAMENTALS AND FLOWERS

Colorful flowers, dramatic ornamental grasses, and varied leafy plants accent the garden. The effect can be bold or subtle, as you wish.

More diversity exists among ornamental and flowering plants than among edible plants. Some ornamentals are suited to practically any environment—hot, cold, sunny, shady, wet, or dry. The growing conditions needed for the cultivation of over one hundred favorite flowering species, and their cultivars, are included in the individual flower entries. Similar information on vines, ornamental grasses, and ground covers can be found in each of those sections as well.

Planning has a greater role in decorative than in edible plantings because so many factors are at work. Different kinds of plants are grouped together for reasons such as similar soil and exposure requirements, coordinated time of bloom, coordinated height, color, and showiness, and aesthetics.

Like vegetables, most annual flowers grow best in a well-balanced, rich soil. This is not true for all ornamental plants: Most wildflowers, ferns, alpine plants, and desert plants will do better in less fertile soils. Some species need a strongly acidic soil, whereas others prefer a sweet (alkaline) soil.

Flowers and other ornamentals are customarily planted in borders—rectangular or free-form beds, often bordering a path, terrace, or wall. The border may be a small spot a few feet long or a large landscape feature several hundred feet long. The space may be filled with many identical plants (only pink wax begonias, for instance) or with several or many different kinds of plants—a mixed border. Usually a mass planting of just a couple of plant varieties seems more formal than a mixed border. Seeds of fast-growing plants are sometimes planted in a border, but more often it is filled with bedding plants, sizable transplants, and perennials.

Beds and borders should have a neatly cut edge where they meet the lawn, or they may be edged with a row of bricks, railroad ties, a walkway, a partly buried edging strip of wood or plastic, or, for large spaces, a curb of molded concrete.

English gardeners are famous for their mixed borders of contrasting patches of different kinds of flowers, grasses, and herbs, including many kinds of perennials. They became popular when nineteenth-century plant explorers sent their finds back to be planted in England, where those receiving them did not know what the new plants would look like or how large they would grow. By planting in patches, with the taller plants set behind lower-growing kinds, you can accommodate many kinds of plants, and let their textures and

colors contrast in interesting ways. Some patches bloom while others are in leaf, making for constantly changing combinations. You can easily move plants to refine the effect of the design.

Attention is drawn to the portions of the border that are in bloom and away from those that are less showy at the moment. In a moderate-size border, each patch of plants should be roughly 3 feet long and 2 feet wide, with some a bit larger and others a bit smaller. Large wide borders often have a backdrop of shrubs for the flowers to play off.

Some mixed borders consist of mass plantings of several species in a carefully arranged design, and others are organized according to flower or leaf color. Here are some of the more popular color schemes: a border composed of different types of white flowers (at night, white flowers are showier than colored ones), a border including only blue and gold flowers, or a border of pale pink, lilac, and white flowers with green or gray leaves. Mixed borders may contain plant collections, such as different forms of succulents, hostas, or irises. Other borders are mixed collections of shrubs, perennials, and annuals, and still others include just one of these categories.

It may take several years of observant gardening before you develop your mixed border to your total satisfaction. Even when borders look marvelous in their first year, they tend to evolve. As you notice particularly successful plants and combinations of plants, give them a greater share of the space.

After you decide where to locate a mixed border, assess the area's soil type and the amount of sunshine it receives before selecting plants. Dig the bed and improve the soil, as outlined in the previous chapter.

In an English-style mixed flower border, the plants are arranged in contrasting clumps, with taller types toward the back and shorter types in front.

Before choosing your plants, visit display gardens in your region and see what your neighbors have planted. This way you can see what professional and experienced gardeners have planted in sites that are similar to yours. Once you decide what you want to grow, in most gardens you should put in at least three of each kind of plant; less than that and your specimens are likely to get lost in the border. The larger the garden, the more plants go in each patch of each kind of flower. When laying out the patches, make them somewhat wedge shaped or linear rather than round or square. This will make the portion of the border that is in bloom seem more prominent, because a flowering plant fills more space and is showier at the height of its bloom, but can be trimmed back and made less obvious after blooming.

ISLAND BEDS. Island beds are ornamental plantings either cut from the lawn or surrounded by pavement. Borders usually have a front and a back side, but island beds are approached or seen from all directions. Their shapes are frequently geometric—circles, squares, rectangles, and so on—but can be wavy free-form shapes instead.

Filled with bedding plants, neatly arranged, island beds are often used in landscapes of hotels, parks, cemeteries, shopping centers, country clubs, and large private estates, planted

This island flower bed surrounded by lawn looks attractive when seen from any direction.

and tended by professional gardeners. This kind of bed requires a high degree of soil enrichment and maintenance.

Island beds in home landscapes should match the formality or informality of the home, or they will look out of place. Less formal island beds, like the one on the opposite page, are used in the same way as mixed borders, the main difference being that the tallest plants are placed in the center of an island bed. The beds may be filled with perennial flowers, a selection of annuals, tall ornamental grasses, canna lilies, ground covers, daylilies, or whatever you like—perhaps an island bed of mixed meadow flowers, growing closely together. As with mixed borders, a color scheme or plant theme for the garden can be very successful.

GROUND COVER. These rugged plants cover the ground in a way that takes the place of lawns or flower beds. They hold the soil in place and grow so close together that weeds have trouble getting through. Like mulch, they hold water in the soil.

Ground covers are usually evergreen and tidy looking, and some carry blossoms or berries for part of the year. Ground covers are used for beds and borders of quiet design, as a substitute for a lawn, as a transition between the lawn and shrubs or trees, and as a cover for slopes or other spots that are hard to mow. Some ground covers will grow in spots too shady or filled with tree roots for lawns and gardens to thrive.

It takes time and effort to establish beds of ground cover, but they can be maintained with just a little yearly care. There are different plants for different exposures and climates. Some of the most popular ground covers are ivy, pachysandra, liriope, fern, myrtle, lamium, ajuga, cotoneaster, and creeping juniper. Ground covers can be perennial plants, vines, or low-growing shrubs, which are covered in Chapter 14.

Be careful; plants such as English ivy can be very invasive for the same reasons that make them such effective ground covers. Friends with lots of ivy will probably be glad to share. Do not mix different types of viny groundcover plants together or you will soon have extra work keeping them from overrunning each other. However, you may underplant myrtle and other less dense ground covers with spring-flowering bulbs.

Planting Ground Cover. After you decide where to put a ground cover and which one it will be, prepare the soil by single digging (see page 53), adding fertilizer at the same time. On a cloudy day, if possible, set in the plants or cuttings at the necessary spacing—if you use unrooted cuttings, shade them with a layer of burlap or salt hay until they root. Your ground cover will look finished sooner if it is closely planted. Water often until plants are established.

After the plants take hold, they will continue to grow and spread. If some areas grow thicker than others, respace some of the plants. Trim the outer edges of the bed for a neat shape and weed it several times a year. In a few years, the bed will be so dense you will have plenty of cuttings or plants to give to friends.

CUTTING GARDENS. It is great to have loads of cut flowers. Whereas most flower beds are planned for their landscape value, cutting gardens are used as production areas of flowers for indoor bouquets. Herbs may be grown here, too. Ideally, cutting gardens are hidden from view or in a background position because they are more like vegetable gardens than flower beds in their purpose. In fact, the vegetable garden is a good location for several rows of flowers for cutting.

Garden centers usually concentrate more on flowers for bedding than for cutting. As a rule, flowers for cutting are taller, have longer stems, and are not as neat in the garden. Their season of bloom may be shorter or more sporadic. Some good choices for a cutting garden are annual or perennial baby's-breath, statice, zinnias, poppies, delphinium, asters, butterfly weed, strawflowers, shasta daisies, feverfew, rudbeckias, cosmos, ornamental grasses, and narcissi. When choosing for your cutting garden, keep in mind your flowers' ultimate destination. If bouquets are needed for a blue dining room, for instance, plant flowers in compatible colors.

A cutting garden is also a good place to experiment. Try growing packets of mixed seed of flowers for bouquets, or a wildflower mix. Plant several successive sowings from the same packet. When the surprise mixture blooms, you will have good material for bouquets. You may also get some ideas for plants to use in more conspicuous flower beds, and the best time of year to plant them.

GROWING FLOWERS IN CONTAINERS. You can grow all kinds of flowering or ornamental plants very easily in containers. Even where garden space is limited, containers make it possible to add color and interest where you want it while permitting custom soil mixes for plants with special needs. You can grow potted plants in a nursery area and bring them to the terrace or indoors when they are at the peak of bloom, then take them away when the show is over.

The size of the pot will affect the health and size of the plant. Although petunias will bloom in those little six-pack pockets when forced with lots of fertilizer and water, they won't stay healthy for long. They need larger pots. They will grow well for months when you plant them in clay pots 8 inches wide and 8 inches deep—each such pot will accommodate three healthy plants. They will grow even better in larger, deeper pots, which hold water longer and do not blow over as easily on windy days. Small pots cramp roots and stunt growth—the principle behind Oriental bonsai, or miniaturized trees.

Wide Choice of Containers. Flowerpots should be of subdued color and design, in order that they enhance, not compete with, the colors and textures of the plants in them. Pots and containers to be used in the same area should harmonize. Plastic pots can be slipped into pottery, wood, or basketry planters or liners for a more natural look. Pottery crocks serve well as covers for plastic flowerpots, but watch that water does not build up in the bottom. It is hard to go wrong with terra-cotta (red clay) pots in classic shapes. Fiberglass containers mimic antique lead, stone, or terra-cotta, without the weight. Whiskey or wine barrels, cut in half, make good, deep planters. Some gardeners create their own stonelike troughs by molding them of concrete mixed with garden soil and pebbles—a nice container for miniature arrangements of alpine plants and succulents. Some pots, such as strawberry jars, have planting pockets along the sides as well as on top. These can look very strange if planted with tall flowers; if in doubt about what to use in them, stick to strawberries and sempervivums.

Flowerpots and containers may be planted with a single plant, several plants of the same variety, or a combination of plants. Formal entryways often feature a matched pair of planters filled with identical plants. Groupings of potted plants, like mixed borders, look

Garden centers usually stock flowerpots and containers of wood, terra-cotta, and fiberglass in many shapes and sizes.

best with taller types behind lower growing ones, and some kind of organizing theme. Plan before you buy, with attention to color.

Foliage houseplants are often repotted and set outside when the weather is right for them—summer in the North, fall and spring in the far South. Their new pots should be about 2 inches wider and deeper than the old.

Window Boxes. Window boxes may be custom built or purchased ready-to-hang from the windowsill. Wooden window boxes are traditional, and plastic and fiberglass have the advantage of lighter weight, but any window box will be heavy when filled with plants and soil. Window boxes must be of sound construction and securely attached to a wall or sill, particularly if it is above the ground floor. Have window boxes installed by a professional or test them rigorously.

Window boxes are usually tended from the inside of the building, but their showiest flowers and leaves face outward toward the light. Some boxes are given permanent or long-term plantings, whereas others are given a fresh design for every season. For these, bedding plants may be kept in their pots and plugged into holes in the soil. Before designing the contents of a window box, check the vantage point: Will the box be seen from below or at eye level? Or perhaps from above? Choose plants accordingly.

By design, a windowbox planting is usually limited to one, two, or three kinds of plants. For harmony, every window box mounted on the house should be given the same design of container and planting. A design with trailing plants like ivy topped by more upright plants such as geraniums looks very nice.

Windowbox plants vary from region to region. In most exposures they must withstand more heat, cold, and wind than garden plants in the same geographic area. Use plants with a long flowering season. Some choices for use in summer window boxes in Zones 3 to 8 include upright plants such as salvia, geraniums, marigolds, ageratum, multiflora and grandiflora petunias, dwarf dahlias, dwarf snapdragons, dusty miller, wax begonias, dianthus, caladiums, vinca, dwarf celosia, and (in shade) impatiens. Trailing plants include verbena, lobelia, ivy, browallia, ivy geraniums, *Thunbergia alata,* alyssum, and cascade petunias.

This attractive window flower box has ivy spilling gracefully over the sides and geraniums for color and height.

Spring and fall window boxes in Zones 3 to 8 may include crocus and other seasonal bulbs, pansies, violas, petunias, ivy, dianthus, and other cold-tolerant plants. These may be used in Zones 9, 10, and 11 in winter. In these southern zones, unshaded window boxes dry out very quickly in summer and suffer a great deal of heat buildup, except in areas cooled by ocean breezes, so they are rarely used during the hotter part of the year.

For the least disturbance of the plants, hang the boxes before putting in the plants. Half-fill the boxes with rich potting soil, then place the plants into the box, with trailing plants to the front and sides, and more upright plants behind them. Leave at least an inch or two of empty space around each plant for filling with potting soil. This gives roots room to grow. Check the arrangement—be sure there is room for plants to spread and grow. When you're satisfied, fill the box with soil, pat it down, and water thoroughly. During hot sunny weather the window boxes may have to be watered daily. Always check soil moisture level before adding more water.

Hanging Baskets. Cascading or drooping plants look better in hanging baskets than upright ones because we usually see the baskets from below. Some flowers that look especially nice are abutilon, achimenes, alyssum, browallia, cascade petunia, cascading begonia, dwarf sweet pea, forget-me-not *(Myosotis),* fuchsia, hoya, impatiens, ivy geranium, lantana, lobelia, morning glory, nasturtium, oxalis, portulaca, sanvitalia, *Thunbergia alata,* torenia, verbena, and viola. Usually several plants of the same type share container space. You can buy plants already in hanging baskets or plant your own, the second method usually being the less expensive of the two.

Flowering plants in hanging baskets need water frequently and grow more luxuriantly when soluble plant food is added to their water. Feed and water plants more often in warm, sunny weather, less often in the shade or during cold weather.

Hanging containers for plants are usually made of plastic because it is cheap, holds water well, and does not add weight. However, there is really no excuse for the ugliness of some of these containers. It is practically impossible to conceal a white plastic hanging "basket" that is seen from below, no matter how luxuriant the plant, so why use it? Green or brown plastic, though not much better looking, at least blends in. The plants and soil in hanging baskets are already so heavy that the additional weight of a clay pot is manageable. Wall brackets or ceiling supports should be firmly anchored and strong enough to carry the weight.

Wire hanging baskets are lighter-weight alternatives. They should be lined with sphagnum moss (see figure A) and filled with potting soil. Not only can the plants be set in at the top, they also may be poked into the sides and the bottom (see figure B). When well grown, plants in wire baskets cover the containers completely, creating a showy sphere of flowers or foliage (see figure C). They drip when watered, however, and, even more than other hanging containers, prefer high humidity and must be watered frequently. This is not a problem in greenhouses or most outdoor sites. Dripping can be minimized by lining the moss with plastic film. You can make a small slit in the plastic when you insert rooted cuttings into the bottom and sides of the container.

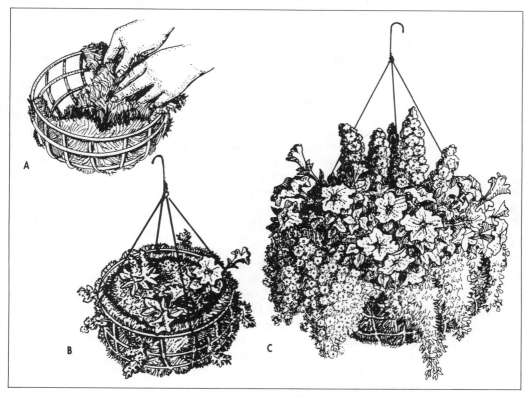

A. Line the basket with dampened sphagnum moss and fill it with potting soil that has been mixed with timed-release fertilizer granules. Dripping can be minimized by setting a layer of plastic film between the moss and the soil, but this slows drainage.
B. Set rooted cuttings or small plants into the sides as well as the top of the container, making slits through the moss and plastic film where necessary for insertion of plants into the soil.
C. When complete, a successful hanging basket grows into a sphere of lush foliage and flowers.

WILDFLOWER MEADOWS

Instead of making a lawn or a garden, you can turn a portion of your property (where permitted or appropriate) into a wildflower meadow, or keep it as one. Many products of varying quality and effectiveness are on the market for this purpose. Some imply that all you have to do is shake a canful of seeds onto the spot for instant results. Although it is not quite that simple, it is not too difficult, either.

So-called wildflowers are not always native plants, and it is not necessary to use exclusively natives in wildflower meadows. Other flowers naturalize well, too—for instance, gaillardia, oxeye daisies, scarlet poppies, and blue cornflowers. All combine well with native plants without being too invasive. In shady areas, foxgloves and columbines self-sow for an easily grown wild garden. Planting native wildflowers such as black-eyed Susans and New England asters assures plentiful flowering from hardy perennials. There are different flowers for northern, southern, eastern, western, and prairie areas. Select a wildflower seed mix that has been especially formulated for your geographic region by a good supplier, or gather your own seeds locally.

Starting a meadowful of wildflowers involves growing flowers from seeds and clearing areas to plant them in. Before you dig up an area that is in its natural state, take a careful look at what is already there. An open field in the Northeast, for instance, might look empty in March to the untrained eye. However, under the strawy residue of last year's "weeds" may be the perennial roots and small green leaves of attractive wild or naturalized flowers such as New England aster, oxeye daisy, butter-and-eggs, daylily, yarrow, goldenrod, Queen Anne's lace, trout lily, bluet, blue-eyed grass, violet, knapweed, butterfly weed, wild geranium, and wild bergamot—the very flowers you are trying to grow. If you do not recognize the plants, either call in an expert or leave the area alone for a year to observe it and learn about them. If you have wildflowers already, you need only clear the field of ragweed and other undesirable weeds and seedlings of woody plants, such as maples. Without disturbing existing flowering plants, clear and turn the soil here and there so you can plant seeds. In early spring, you may divide and transplant perennial wildflowers growing on your land. Of course, if you are converting a lawn to a meadow, you have to provide all the wildflowers. Have the area of lawn plowed before you plant it.

All the information on growing flower seeds in ordinary garden conditions is relevant to meadow flowers. They, too, need a start in tilled soil that lets them take root without too much competition, soil improvers to correct for soil problems, and regular watering until small plants grow stronger and more deeply rooted. Plant most wildflower seeds at a time of year when the weather is cool but not bitterly cold—in northern and central states, about six weeks before the frost-free date. In Zones 9 and 10, November through February are the best months to plant most varieties. Scratch the seeds into the soil very shallowly, fertilize lightly, and give them a covering of straw or grass clippings less than ¼ inch thick, so the soil shows through in places. This helps keep the soil from drying out during the plants' germination. If you plant perennial wildflowers, they will bloom very little the first year but make a grand show the next. Annuals will bloom the first year, and some will reseed themselves.

Each fall (or later in Zones 9 to 11), after the flowers have bloomed and their seeds have ripened, gather the seeds and sprinkle them in areas that are still bare. Then mow the meadow (6 to 12 inches above the ground) once a year to keep seedling trees from overtaking it. In spring, divide and move some of the perennial plants to cover more of the area, and, again, remove weeds and plant more flowers. In time, the desired plants will dominate your lovely, nearly carefree meadow garden.

PLANTING HERBS AND VEGETABLES

If you enjoy fresh vegetables and herbs, it is fun to grow your own. Depending on the kind of garden space you have, you can either grow them in their own separate gardens or blend them in with ornamental plantings.

Traditional herb gardens are highly designed, very formal and geometric, with perennial species employed as edgings. But herbs can be grown less elaborately in mixed borders, in containers, or in garden rows, like vegetables. Most herbs, wherever they are grown, need sunshine and well-drained soil, which does not have to be especially fertile. Individual plant species and their needs are covered in the herb entries starting on page 394.

Vegetables, too, can be grown in either decorative or functional ways, and grow best in full sun and very fertile soil.

SPACING. It is important to space plants for productivity; the exact distance depends on soil fertility, plant type, and row configuration. Plants may be grown in straight rows, single or double, or in groups with the plants evenly spaced. Sometimes several species share space in the same row, container, or area.

Single Rows. In rural areas with plentiful garden space, herbs and vegetables are often grown in straight, single rows in rectangular plots. Usually, each row contains one kind of plant—you might plant one row of parsley, one row of radishes, four rows of lettuce, and ten rows of sweet corn. There are paths between the rows to allow space for walking or garden machinery. In very large gardens, the spacing between the rows allows a Rototiller or tractor to pass for cultivation and weeding. In smaller gardens, there is just a foot or two between rows—enough space for a gardener with a hoe.

After you have tilled the entire garden plot or a sizable portion of it as explained in Chapter 3, measure and make the rows. This is easy if you use two movable stakes with a string the length of the planned row tied between them (see the illustration on page 86). Insert the stakes where you want to make a row. Then, using the string as a guide, drag the corner of a garden hoe or some other cultivating tool along in a straight line, making a furrow about 2 inches deep. Some Rototillers have attachments for making rows by machine. After making each row, move the stakes and string to the next spot. You can plant seeds or set in plants the same day, or a few days later, if no rain is in the forecast to aid in germination.

Double Rows, Wide Bands. Some vegetables are more productive when grown in double rows or wide bands. This is especially true of root vegetables, peas, and quick crops like bush beans. Legumes such as peas and beans benefit from being planted with their seeds close together, so that nitrogen-fixing bacteria on the roots work for the whole group of

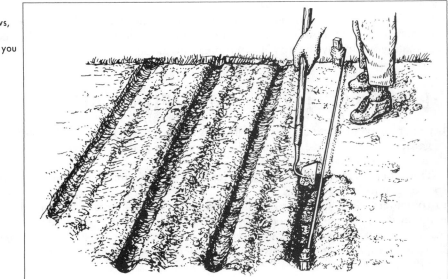

For straight rows, use stakes and string to guide you as you hoe.

plants. Other plants should be spaced the usual distance apart. Herbs should not be overcrowded.

Make double rows 5 or 6 inches apart, with paths on the outside. In the rows, you can combine a quick crop with a slow one, plant the same crop in both rows, or pair an herb with a vegetable.

To make a wide-band planting, prepare an area 2 or 3 feet wide and as long as you like. You should be able to reach into all parts of the bands while standing on the paths between them. Fill the wide bands with seeds or plants spaced at their recommended distances. Space bands at least 2 feet apart.

Equidistant Planting. The technique of equidistant planting allows you to use your garden space efficiently or to include vegetables and herbs attractively in ornamental gardens of any shape and size. In this method of planting, the edible plants are not necessarily set out in rows or any geometric arrangement, but, instead, plants of the same type are grown together, equally spaced from one another. The edible plants are treated like the bedding plants in mixed ornamental borders, planted where their color and texture show up the best.

You can edge flower beds with leaf lettuce, put in nice-looking vegetables, like red peppers, eggplants, scallions, and kale, and include herb plants among flowering ones, usually in groups of three or more of a kind. As you learn how they will look as they grow, you will be able to place them to their best advantage.

Hilling. Vining plants such as squash that spread out and need a large growing area are best planted in hills. A hill is a group of seeds planted together rather than in a row. Sow about six seeds per hill, and thin to the three strongest plants. Hills can be anywhere from 2 to 3 feet apart, depending on the eventual size of the plants grown there.

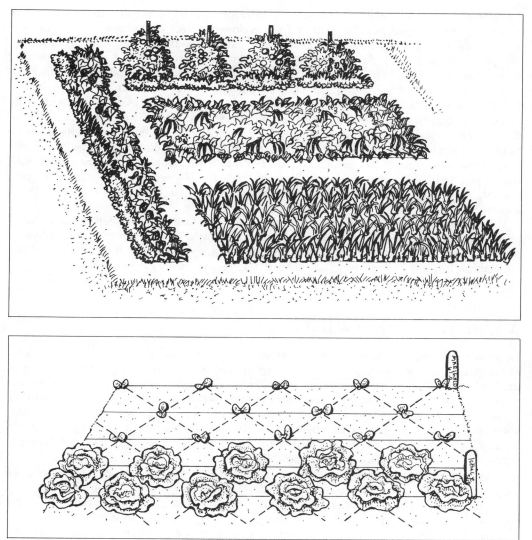

Vegetables and herbs may be planted in wide rows instead of narrow ones to maximize use of space.

Equidistant planting permits good use of space and looks attractive in any bed shape.

Spacing in Intensive Beds. As mentioned in Chapter 3, intensive gardens permit the closer spacing of plants and result in greater production in a small space. The fertile, airy soil must never be walked on—that would compact it and inhibit plant growth. Plants are spaced so that when mature, their leaves brush against one another, making a complete covering of the soil. When plants are young they may be spaced twice as close and then thinned or transplanted. Good use of space includes planting edges and corners—these can be used to grow seedlings that will be moved to other rows or blocks when the plants in them are harvested. Mats of low-growing herbs can surround taller central plants, such as peppers and eggplants.

VEGETABLES AND HERBS IN CONTAINERS. Growing edibles in containers is becoming increasingly popular. Either for decorative effect or because of soil or site problems, a terrace, deck, rooftop, or windowsill can be a source of flavors and fragrances. The pots must be appropriate to the size of the plant being grown. You'll need a large tub, such as half a whiskey barrel, to grow strawberry popcorn, but 8-inch pots will be fine for peppers or parsley. It is better for pots to be too large than too small.

All herbs and most vegetables will look very nice in pots. Herbs are often grown in rectangular planters, with trailing ones spilling over the edges and upright ones behind them. Some vegetables with good shapes for pots are peppers, eggplants, lettuce, bush beans, onion sets, chard, kale, collard greens, bush squashes, and cucumbers, as well as patio tomatoes and melons. Some especially attractive herbs for containers are the tiny-leaved basil 'Spicy Globe' *(Ocimum basilicum),* chives, rosemary, thyme, oregano, coriander, and chervil. Vegetables, flowers, and herbs may be combined with each other in large tubs or containers.

Vegetables in containers need exceptionally fertile soil. Use plenty of well-rotted manure or a vegetable fertilizer according to directions. It is important to water well and often—sometimes twice a day in hot, dry weather. Herbs can grow in a less fertile potting soil than vegetables, but need richer soil and more water than herbs in garden beds.

VERTICAL GROWING

Large vertical supports, like trellises and fences, help you control and support viny plants of all types. And by growing your garden up instead of out, you can produce more in a smaller area. Grapes, roses, jasmine, peas, pole beans, cucumbers, tomatoes, vining squashes, kiwis, morning glories, and other tall, sprawling, or viny plants may be grown in this way, trained onto supports as formal as a pergola or as casual as the posts supporting a wooden deck. Some plants climb by twisting around the supports or grasping them with tendrils, whereas others have to be tied to the supports. More about tying plants to their supports is discussed in Staking on pages 107–10.

Select supports that are sturdy enough to do the job. A bearing grapevine or kiwi puts a lot of weight on its support—use 4- by 4-inch posts 8 or more feet tall, with interconnecting strong wood or wire crossbars. Flowering annuals like nasturtiums or morning glories grow well on smaller and lighter supports.

Bury the bottom of the support several feet deep. If the posts are not buried deeply enough, they will lean toward the center of the row or collapse. If the posts are too thin, they may break. If they are too short, they will not give the plants all the support they need. Tie or train the plants to the supports as they grow; do not wait until the need is obvious, for by then it is difficult to adjust the plants without breaking their stems.

Here are some of the most popular climbing or viny vegetables and their supports:

BEANS. Climbing beans (pole beans) include some types of string beans, shell beans, Italian broad beans, lima beans, Oriental beans, hyacinth beans, cranberry beans, and scarlet runner beans. Although usually sold as flowers, scarlet runner beans are edible—delicious, in fact. All these varieties grow 6 to 10 feet tall or more. They may be twined onto lower supports if there is enough horizontal space for them to spread. They have no tendrils but climb by wrapping their growing stems around the supports. Bush beans need no support.

Beans climb well on mesh fences, 6- or 8-foot wooden tomato stakes buried at least 2 feet deep, trellises made of stakes and strings, netting, or other similar supports. In rural areas, saplings are sometimes cut and used as stakes. The most decorative climbing bean plants are cranberry beans, hyacinth beans (strangely flavored, some say), and scarlet runner beans, which are all used like snap beans in their early stages before the pods get fibrous; when mature they are harvested like shell beans.

An A-frame support with strings makes a tidy pea trellis.

PEAS. This group includes snow peas, snap peas, and green peas. English peas, as they are called in the South, have tendrils and are good climbers. Even the shorter types should be supported by brush (pieces of twiggy branches) or stakes and strings for better growth. Three feet is tall enough for the short types, which sometimes are advertised as needing no support. Climbing types such as 'Sugar Snap' easily grow taller than 6 feet. As the growing season for peas is short, temporary, portable A-frame trellises with strings for vines to climb on (see the illustration to the right) are excellent for supporting peas. After the peas finish bearing, you can either remove the trellises or use them for hot-weather annual vines such as morning glories, beans, or cucumbers.

GRAPES. Grapes can be grown on many different types of trellis. Gardeners often like to use the commercially available wood lattice trellises made for growing roses, placing it up against the house or framing a gateway, and training the vine over the structure. Others may simply plant and train the vine to cover an already existing fence for landscape interest. Another method for warm climates is to plant the vine next to a deck or patio area and train the vine up overhead into an arbor so that during the growing season it shades the area (see the illustration on page 90). (Use a wooden lattice to help support the vines or strong metal wires strung 2 feet apart.) However, although these trellising methods add visual excitement to your yard, they aren't the most productive methods for growing grapes. In the grape entry on pages 546–53, you will find two recommended methods: the Geneva Double Curtain (GDC) form of trellising for American grapes, and the verticle hedgerow, or two-cane Kniffin system, for European grapes, along with illustrations for each.

SQUASHES AND OTHER CUCURBITS. Bush squashes and bush cucumbers need no support. You can give vining winter squashes, cucumbers, pumpkins, melons, and other

A classic grape arbor provides an inviting garden entranceway.

cucurbits the support of posts, stakes, trellises, arbors, or fences, or else leave them to sprawl on the ground. Field-grown runners of these plants can easily exceed 20 feet in length because some of them root as they grow. You will limit plant size if you support the plants without giving them a place to put down extra roots; this is often desirable. In smaller gardens, you probably will want to provide them with vertical support, which improves the appearance of the garden, saves space, and helps in pest control by making it harder for pests to hide and keeping the crop out of reach of tunneling wire worms and other pests that live in the soil. For this reason, cucumbers grown vertically have fewer blemishes. Winter squash and pumpkin plants can be very heavy, so if they are to be supported, tie them to strong 4- by 4- or 2- by 4-inch posts or sturdy fences, supporting the crop in individual slings if necessary, as shown in the illustrations at the top of page 91.

ROSES. Shrub and hybrid tea roses need no support, but the long-lived climbing and rambler roses grow well on trellises, arbors, fences, walls, lattices, and pergolas of many shapes and sizes. The canes (stems) of the climbing types range from a few to well over 15 feet tall. Different rose varieties reach different heights, so check when you acquire a new one.

Climbing roses send strong, flexible, asparaguslike new shoots up from hardy roots. In just one growing season, these will become woody branches that bloom in their second year and for many years afterward. The shoots from an older plant are thicker and will grow taller—sometimes more than 10 feet in one year—than those from a young plant. To train a climbing or rambler rose, tie or train the young shoot onto the desired support as it grows; rose tacks or vine supports are useful for this. Aim for an arched shape, with the shoot growing straight up for about half its ultimate length and then curving out sideways, as shown to the right.

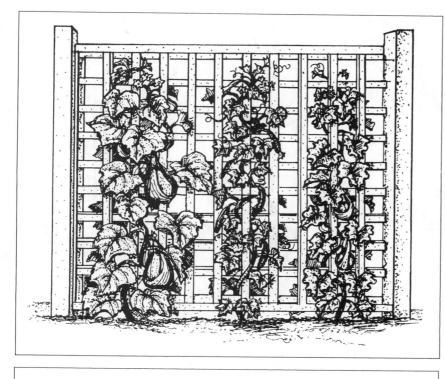

When looks are important and space is limited, grow cucurbits like squashes, cucumbers, and melons on a trellis.

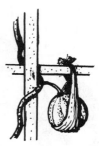

Support heavy melons and squashes in cloth slings tied to the trellis.

A rose on a trellis makes great use of a sunny wall.

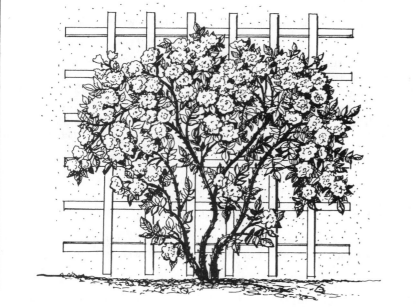

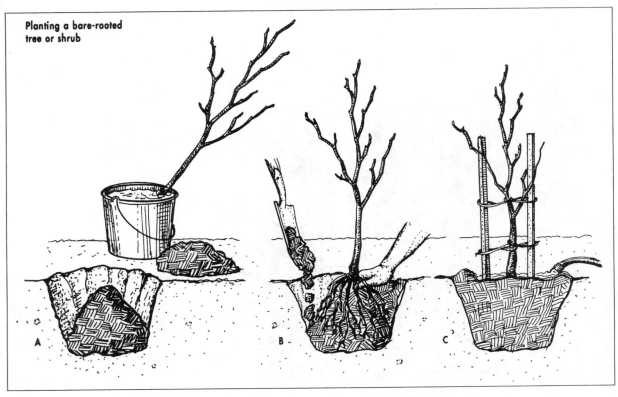

Planting a bare-rooted tree or shrub

A. Unwrap the tree and soak it overnight in a bucket of water to prevent the roots from drying out.

B. Mix soil from the hole with recommended soil amendments. Make a cone of improved soil at the base of the hole and spread the roots over it. Cover the roots with more of the improved soil and lightly tamp the soil down to remove air pockets. Make sure the tree's graft joint is above the surface of the soil.

C. Fill in the hole with the remaining improved soil, shaping the top like a shallow basin to catch water. Water well, mulch, and, if necessary, stake and tie the tree, especially larger trees.

Climbing roses need little pruning (see page 578), just enough to remove the dead wood and keep the canes from becoming overcrowded. In regions where winter temperatures dip to 10°F or below frequently, tie climbing roses to their supports rather than intertwine them. In fall, for protection from cold winter weather, untie them and let them rest on the ground, covered with a layer of mulch, if you don't receive enough snow cover to protect them. In early spring, uncover them gradually and retie them to their supports before their new leaves develop.

PLANTING TREES AND SHRUBS

You can easily plant trees and shrubs yourself if your plants are not too big to handle without special equipment and your soil is not too rocky. Otherwise, you might prefer to have the nursery staff do the job.

The trees, shrubs, vines, and small berry plants you purchase from mail-order companies usually arrive well wrapped, but with the plant roots bare of soil. Such plants are held in cold storage and shipped while still dormant. Once they arrive, keep their roots moist at all times and either plant them immediately or, if you just don't have the time to do that, heel them in—cover the roots and part of the stems with damp soil or wet sawdust—until they can be planted properly. The same goes for freshly dug or bare-root trees from local nurseries, but you can take your time if your plants arrive in containers full of soil. Smart northern gardeners prepare planting holes in autumn for trees that will arrive in spring to avoid having to dig in half-frozen or muddy soil.

Dig a hole at least a foot wider and deeper than the root ball of the plant—2 or 3 feet wider and deeper for large trees and shrubs. Mix the soil you removed with fertilizer and soil amendments, like compost and peat moss, which are suited to the type of soil you have (see Chapter 3) and the needs of the plant. If your soil is already good, you do not have to alter it much or dig as large a hole. Give the shrub or tree a good start, but do not pamper it so much that it refuses to stretch its roots beyond the original planting hole.

Place a thick layer of amended soil in the hole, then set the plant in at the depth it grew, spreading its roots out and covering them with the rest of the amended soil. With grafted trees (see below), the graft union (you can find it by searching for the bumps or scars near the base of the trunk) should be several inches above the soil line, or else the upper part of the tree will root and lose the effect of the graft. After you plant, shape the soil to catch water by centering a depression around the trunk or center of the plant and making a raised rim of soil around it. This "dish" might be about 3 feet wide for a 4-foot shrub.

If you are planting a single-stemmed tree, set in two to four 4-foot stakes around it at the same time. Tie the trunk to each stake (separately). This will stabilize the tree while it roots. After planting, water the tree often until new roots and leaves have begun to grow well.

PLANTING FRUIT

Well-tended fruit looks as good as it tastes and is integrated often into ornamental garden areas. Plantings of fruiting trees, shrubs, canes, vines, and nonwoody (herbaceous) plants can be used in place of landscape trees or be cultivated in home orchards. The immense productivity of mature fruiting plants can sometimes be surprising. A mature dwarf apple tree can produce several bushels of fruit a season. A standard tree will yield many bushels.

Plant most fruits in the same way as ornamental shrubs or trees of similar size and type. They need full or nearly full sun. Fruit and nut trees usually prefer rich soil because of the nutritional demands of setting and growing a large crop. Manure, compost, and mulches are beneficial additives to the soil.

You can usually buy fruit plants from local nurseries, whose staffers should know which ones do well in your area. Other sources are rare fruit clubs and specialty mail-order nurseries. Most named fruit tree cultivars have been grafted onto a different root, called the rootstock. This way you get the fruit variety you want, and any of a number of valuable overall plant characteristics from the rootstock, including resistance to disease, hardiness, vigor, and/or dwarf height. Local experts can tell you which of these grafted cultivars are best for your area.

Fruit trees grown from seeds bear fruit several years later than those grafted onto rootstock, and usually grow inconveniently tall. The fruit yield and quality of these trees are unpredictable but usually substandard, though there are always exceptions to the rule.

Planting a container-grown tree or shrub

A. Remove the plant from its container. Sometimes the container must be slit on one or two sides.

B. If the roots are tightly wrapped around the ball, loosen them so they will grow outward into the soil.

C. Mound improved soil at the base of a large planting hole and set the tree in place, spreading the roots outward as much as possible. Fill the hole with the remaining improved soil and tamp it down to fill in pockets of air. Shape the top of the soil like a shallow basin to catch water. Water well, and add a layer of mulch.

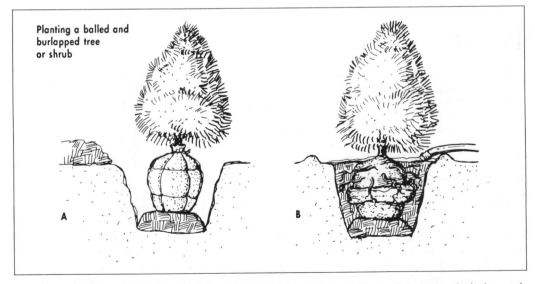

Planting a balled and burlapped tree or shrub

A. Set the tree in place on a mound of improved soil at the base of the large planting hole. Loosen the burlap, peel it back as much as possible without destroying the root ball, and pull branches of the root outward. *Note:* If the cloth wrapping is plastic, it is not biodegradable. Remove it entirely as you plant the tree.

B. Fill the hole with the remaining improved soil and tamp down to fill in pockets of air. Shape the top of the soil like a shallow basin to catch water. Water well, and add a layer of mulch.

You can use these seed-grown plants as rootstocks, budding or grafting compatible standard varieties to them.

STANDARD, SEMIDWARF, AND DWARF FRUIT TREES. Standard-size fruit trees may be 25 or more feet tall and have spreads 20 feet at maturity. Fruits are borne high on the trees, so you will have to use a ladder for pruning and harvesting. Each tree needs full sun, so ample room is needed, up to 20 to 25 feet between trees.

Fortunately, some fruit trees are considerably smaller at maturity, usually produced, as already mentioned, by using a size-controlling (dwarfing) rootstock. Semidwarf trees grow 12 to 18 feet tall and should be spaced 15 to 20 feet apart; dwarf fruit trees, which grow about 8 to 12 feet tall, are usually spaced from 8 to 15 feet apart. If espaliered (see below), they may be planted much closer together. The smallest fruit trees are genetic dwarfs. Most types do not exceed 10 feet in height and may be kept shorter very easily by pruning. They may be grown in large kegs, tubs, and pots at least 20 inches wide and 18 inches high, always in rich soil. In northern areas, the containers must be flexible enough to withstand alternate freezing and thawing. In addition to needing less space than standard fruit trees, semidwarf and dwarf trees are easier to prune, spray, and harvest, making them ideal for most home gardens.

ESPALIER. The time-honored way to incorporate fruit trees into small spaces in ornamental gardens is espalier. Dwarf trees, either genetic or grafted, may be grown this way. They are pruned severely and trained to grow flat against a wall or as a freestanding narrow

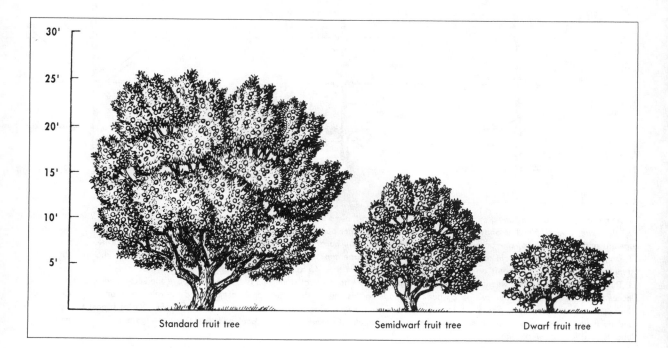

Standard fruit tree   Semidwarf fruit tree   Dwarf fruit tree

hedge, in a decorative geometric or free-form pattern. Fruits on espaliered trees are especially large and attractive because they receive more than the usual share of sun and nutrients. Because they have fewer fruits, leaves, and branches, they need less space and fertilizer than trees with full, round shapes.

Espaliered trees may be used as a hedge, a screen for privacy, or the backdrop for an herb or flower garden. If espaliered trees are to be trained against a wall, carefully consider the possible effects of the wall's exposure, as exposure strongly affects these trees because of their lack of protective leaves and branches. A southern exposure may be so hot it cooks the fruit; an eastern or western exposure may be better.

It takes several years to train a young tree to grow into an attractive espalier. To avoid this awkward training phase, you can buy trees already trained by professionals. However, it is not too difficult to create your own espaliers if you faithfully attend to the bending, tying, and pruning needed several times a year.

The tree to be trained is tied to a wooden or metal frame that stays with it until it is planted in its permanent position while it is still growing in a container. Selected buds and nodes along the tree's trunk and branches are allowed to grow so the plant will conform to the pattern. Branches are bent and trained as they grow, and all unwanted sprouts or suckers are trimmed off. The short, stubby spurs that hold the fruit and leaves are left on.

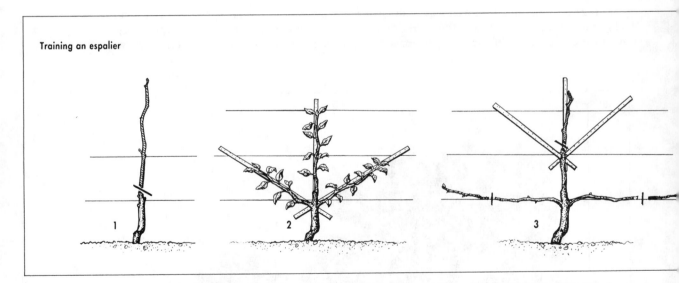

Training an espalier

1. At planting time before new growth begins (first winter), cut the main stem of a one-year-old tree or vine back to a bud 2 inches above the first wire, about 15 inches above the ground. Retain three other buds, as shown, to form branches in the future. The top bud will grow upward and the other two, one on each side of the stem, will form horizontal branches. Rub off the other buds and shoots.

2. During the first summer, train the new growth by tying the uppermost shoot or cane to a vertical wooden support, in line with the main stem or trunk. Tie the side shoots or canes to wooden supports set at a 45° angle, as shown.

3. During the second winter, when the plant is dormant, cut back the central stem to a bud 2 inches above the second wire, about 30 inches above the ground. Again, rub off all but three buds on this central stem, the uppermost bud and the other two, one on each side of the upper main stem or trunk. These will form branches during the growing season. Unfasten and lower the first tier of branches (leaders) and tie them to the wire with string so they will grow horizontally. Cut them back to about half their length—slightly more for strong leaders, and less for weak ones.

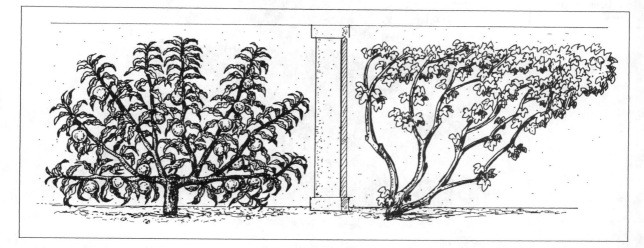

This nectarine tree (left) has been pruned and trained as a fan-shaped espalier. This grapevine (right) makes an attractive free-form espalier. It is invisibly supported against the wall with rose tacks.

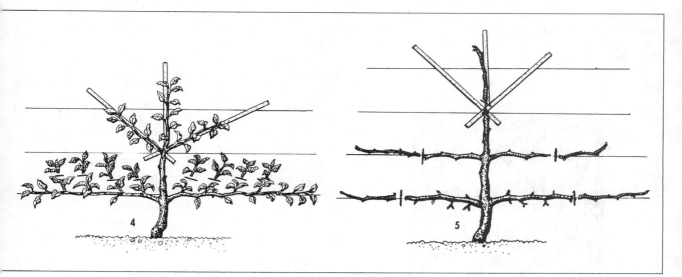

4. During the second summer, fasten the new canes or branches in the same manner as in step 3, so that the central shoot is trained upward and the lateral branches are supported at a 45° angle. Cut back unwanted growth of mature laterals on the lower tier, as shown.
5. During the third winter, form a new tier by the same procedure used in the first and third steps. Train the lateral branches to the wires horizontally, and prune them to approximately half their length. Continue in this manner until the espalier reaches the size and shape desired. *Note:* Raising the angle of a lateral branch will speed its growth, and lowering it will slow growth down.

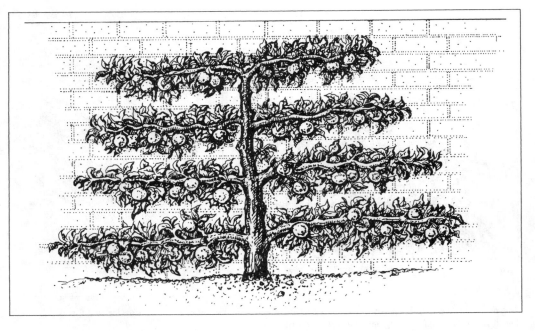

New growth along the trunk and branches is usually confined to 2 to 6 inches in length. The major pruning should be done in late winter at the end of the plant's dormant period, and light trimming may be done in summer. A tree that has already been trained must be maintained by regular pruning or it will grow out of shape.

The crisscrossing branches of three apple trees shape this Belgian fence espalier.

The easiest shape for an espalier is free-form and informal. The tree should please the eye and stay flat against the wall or supports to which it is tied. A fan shape, which is similar, is especially well suited to cherries, gooseberries, plums, peaches, nectarines, citrus, loquat, and cane fruits like raspberries and blackberries.

Cordons have horizontal arms and are often used for grapes, apples, and pears. The central growing tip is pinched or clipped off and the desired side shoots are trained as arms (called *leaders*), supported by wires or tied to a wall. Leaders may be allowed to grow quite long to fill a horizontal space.

The beautiful Belgian fence is trained similarly, but the selected branches are interwoven as a lattice. Three or more trees are planted in a line. The two trees on the ends are pruned so that they have branches on only one side of their trunks, the side going into the lattice. Their central growing tip may be tied and bent to make the top of the fence. The inner tree, or trees, ordinarily have just two branches that make a Y, with one arm going left, the other to the right.

CARING FOR PLANTS AS THEY GROW

W hile preparing soil is heavy work and selecting plants is a challenge, caring for your garden is easy and satisfying. The continuing care of a garden, which so many people enjoy, is more like "puttering around" than real work. Just the same, caring for your garden is necessary for your plants to look their best, bear fruit, remain healthy, and increase in size and quantity.

WATERING

Every plant, even a cactus, needs water to live, although some species are adapted to bogs, others to normal soil, and still others to dry soil. Water is needed for both plant nutrition and temperature control. Water in the soil dissolves dry fertilizers so that they can be absorbed through plant roots. It is the main component of sap, which circulates in plants carrying vital nutrients in suspension (plants are mostly water, in fact). Water evaporates as stomates, pores in a plant's leaves, open for gas exchange. Much water is lost this way and from the soil on hot, bright, or windy days, and must be replaced by rain or irrigation.

Irrigation is also used to heat and cool plants during extreme weather. A five-minute spray will refresh wilting bedding plants during hot weather above 90°F, even when the soil is already moist. A spray of water is sometimes used to protect cold-sensitive plants during spring frosts. When water freezes it gives off heat and keeps the plant from frost damage.

Soil type (discussed in Chapter 3) affects your garden's need for water. A water-retentive soil that is partly clay and humus may hold water for over two weeks without rain. A porous, sandy soil may need watering every day or every other day during hot weather. A layer of mulch on the soil prevents quick evaporation of the moisture in the soil (see pages 103–106 for a discussion of mulching).

HOW MUCH SHOULD YOU WATER? Soil should be watered deeply, but not too often. For most plants, the soil should feel slightly damp but not wet. The top crust may be nearly dry except where seeds, small seedlings, and salad vegetables are planted. These must never dry out. If there is damp soil ½ inch below the surface, mature plants will get the water they need. The dry surface will help keep down weed growth. However, intensively planted beds, in which plants are grown closely together (see page 87), need more water than other gardens and should be watered to capacity, never drying out more than ½ inch deep.

Learn to recognize water stress symptoms and water thoroughly if they appear. Plants show their need for water with dull, drooping, or wilted foliage. Try to prevent this from happening because it can set back plant growth and make salad crops bitter.

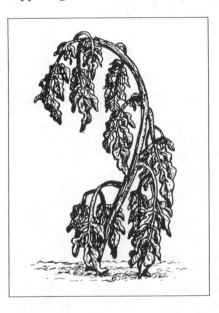

This wilted tomato plant shows unmistakable signs of water stress, but will recover if watered immediately.

Too much water can be harmful, too. In spots with slow or poor drainage, overwatering quickly results in waterlogged soil with no air pockets and plants in a very vulnerable state. Roots rot and plants die suddenly, with no advance warning. Check for soggy or muddy soil, especially if you use an automatic watering system.

HOW SHOULD YOU WATER? AND WHEN? Gardeners debate the ideal time of day and means of watering. You should water early in the morning or late in the evening to keep water from evaporating before it soaks in. Water plants that are likely to get fungus diseases, such as mildew or black spot, in the morning so their leaves will dry off before dark. After a dry period, apply water slowly at first to prevent runoff; it will take the soil a few minutes to begin absorbing the water. Water deeply into the root zone, usually a foot or more for most garden plants. Sandy soils need more frequent but lighter watering than loams or clays because they cannot retain the water. Remember to water with a fine mist or gentle spray, not a hard stream; this will lessen the likelihood of runoff and damage to your plants.

Automatic Underground Sprinkling Systems. Systems that pop up to spray broad areas of lawn and garden are becoming popular throughout the United States but are expensive to install. In hot or dry climates some gardeners consider them necessities. However, they use a great deal of water, which goes to all plants whether they need it or not. If you water this way, you should test your system to be sure water goes where it is needed and does not strike plants with too much force. Automatic timers for these systems are convenient but waste water when they are not adjusted to suit the weather. You often see sprinklers operating during rainstorms in some parts of the country!

Drip (or Trickle) Irrigation Systems. These use a network of small tubes or punctured plastic or rubber pipes that drip water directly into the root zone of plants. These systems

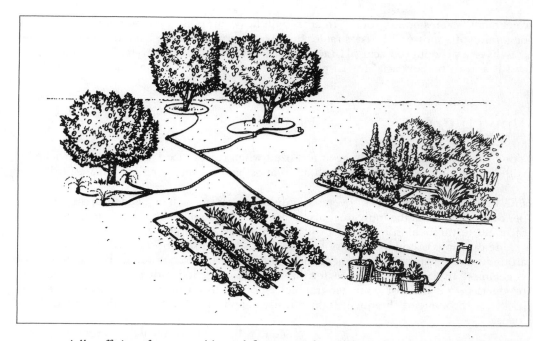

An aboveground drip irrigation system like this one makes quick work of your watering chores.

are especially efficient for vegetable and flower gardens. Their drawbacks are that a clean water source is required since they can become clogged if not properly maintained and animals such as gophers may eat them.

Watering with Hand-held Containers or Hoses. These methods are not wasteful, but are so time consuming that they tend to encourage underwatering. Try to water well enough to soak the lower layers of soil, so roots will grow downward, not stay too close to the surface. This gives plants more ability to withstand drought. Inexpensive, portable hose-end sprinklers are practical, for they can be left on long enough to do the job right, without much attention from you. To prevent overwatering, use an inexpensive timer that will shut off automatically when a set amount of water has been used.

Water Restrictions. In some areas, water use on gardens is limited by law, especially during droughts. During times when watering is restricted, you can still irrigate with gray water—water used once for household purposes such as bathing and dishwashing—if there are no laws against recycling it. Never use water contaminated with sewage, for it might spread disease. Even if gray water is prohibited, there is always clean water that may be caught and used, for instance, the cool water that would otherwise go down the drain while you wait for tap water to heat up. Water from cooking (if not salted) can be used, too—it is beneficial for plants because it contains traces of nitrogen and nutrients. Cool it off before using it on house or garden plants. When you use recycled water you will have to water by hand unless you are very clever with siphons or pumps.

Rainwater may be collected in barrels under house gutters or in open buckets or pots outdoors. Some homes in areas with a rainy season followed by a dry season have rainwater catchment systems underground. In areas with heavy air pollution, the rainwater from the beginning of a shower is not desirable. In the northern half of the United States, rainwater may have a pronounced acid pH (acid rain). However, most rainwater is clean and pure and is said to be beneficial for all plants, especially delicate seedlings and cuttings.

FERTILIZING

Your garden bed should have been fertilized when it was made. Ideally, you enriched it with long-lasting soil improvers such as compost and manure, or slow-release fertilizer.

FERTILIZING METHODS. Even so, additional fertilizer will be needed by some plants, per our directions in the individual plant entries in this book and on product labels. A dose of liquid fertilizer high in phosphorus for transplants is helpful.

Side-dressings or topdressings of fertilizer—doses of fertilizer scratched into soil near or around mature plants—may be needed for plants bearing a continuing crop of flowers or vegetables. In sandy soil, where fertilizer leaches out, it is advisable to fertilize with products formulated for your geographic region or to fertilize a little more often than packages recommend. Frequent light fertilizer applications are better than single heavy feeds.

Fertilizer spikes give large plants a steady supply of timed-release nutrients.

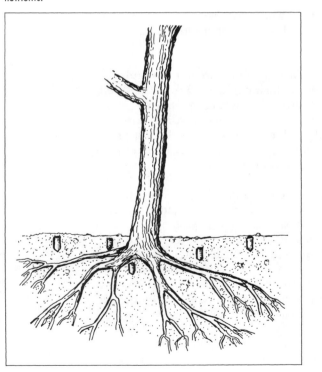

You will need to fertilize perennial plants, shrubs, and trees in a way that does not disturb their roots. Adding a 3-inch layer of compost and the recommended amount of fertilizer to the top of the soil each year will give good results—you will conserve soil moisture and provide a nutrient supply. A liquid fertilizer boost can be applied when flower buds appear and as fruits and vegetables develop.

Fertilizer spikes are available for shrubs and trees. These are plugs of fertilizer, in solid form (see the figure to the left) that you bury beneath the soil near the plant. For a large tree, several are used in a ring around the trunk. They break down slowly for long-lasting effect and are convenient. They do not replace proper soil preparation and maintenance, but are a useful supplement, especially in areas with infertile, porous soils that quickly lose liquid or granular fertilizers. In rich clay soils, they have far less value.

HOW MUCH TO FERTILIZE. Fertilizer needs vary with the plant species and variety. Garden fruits and vegetables have been bred for productivity and so require highly fertile soils, in most cases. Annual flowers usually need more fertilizer than perennial flowers, ornamental grasses, or herbs. Wildflowers and herbs can be harmed by the level of fertilizer it takes to grow a tomato plant properly. Grasses usually need a higher proportion of nitrogen in the fertilizer than flowers do. Trees and shrubs have deep roots to seek nutrients with; they can manage well for themselves where the soil is good, but require a great deal of fertilizer where soil is poor.

WHEN TO FERTILIZE. Each year beds where annual flowers and vegetables were grown the year before will have been somewhat depleted by the demands of the last crop. In northern and central parts of the United States, turn the soil under roughly along with compost, shredded leaves, grass clippings, and manure at the end of the garden season in fall. By spring, these additives will have become part of a much improved soil. The first few years this is done, you may notice that plants seem to need additional nitrogen (indicated by pale or yellow foliage). Nitrogen is chemically "borrowed" during the decomposition of the additives, but is returned at the end of the cycle. A spring application of fertilizer high in nitrogen (grass food type but containing no weed killers or additives) will compensate until the soil improves.

In the South, improve soil similarly a month or two before the next planting season. Because soil organisms are more active in warmer weather, the soil will be ready in a shorter time than in the North. In Florida and other Zones 9, 10, and 11 areas, whether in the East or West, an August soil treatment will get things ready for early October sowing.

MULCHING

There are true believers in the incredible benefits of mulching, and others who claim that it leads to insect problems. Both groups are absolutely correct.

Mulch is a layer, usually of organic matter of some kind, but sometimes of plastic or stone, that covers the soil like a blanket. Most mulches are spread 2 to 6 inches deep, but mulch can be a thin layer of plastic or a thick layer of straw piled over a foot deep. Like other garden procedures, mulching can be done in many ways. The effect varies with the local conditions and materials used.

Mulching prevents water from evaporating out of the soil. It keeps plant roots moist and smothers emerging weeds. It promotes fast, steady, uninterrupted growth. Organic mulches add nutrients to the soil when they decompose. Mulches that include clover or other legumes add nitrogen. Some mulches, such as pine bark chips, look neat enough for ornamental areas but others, such as layers of shredded newspaper, are strictly functional. It is easier to use mulch around grown plants than around seedlings. You want to surround plants with mulch to smother weeds, but not inadvertently smother the garden plants.

PROS AND CONS. Know your soil before adding mulch. Mulch will keep sandy, porous soils moister, but may slow needed drainage in a wet, boggy clay. Different mulches have their advantages and disadvantages. The table on pages 104–105 shows attributes of some of the most widely used mulches. Mulch is also discussed under winter protection on pages 134–35. Using the right mulch in the right spot will make your gardening chores much easier.

ATTRIBUTES OF POPULAR MULCHING MATERIALS

MULCH	MULCH DEPTH	CHARACTERISTICS
Bark chips	3–6"	Nice appearance. Available in different sizes.
Black plastic sheeting		Warms cold soil in the early spring. Prevents weeds from growing. Doesn't add any organic material. Careful watering is needed in hot weather.
Clear plastic sheeting		Warms cold soil in the early spring. Doesn't prevent weeds from growing. Doesn't add any organic material. Careful watering is needed in hot weather.
Compost	2–8"	Nice appearance. May be made at home. Enriches soil.
Evergreen boughs	8–24"	Good winter protection for hardy perennials in cold climates. Remove gradually when new shoots start to come up in spring.
Grass clippings	2–6"	Good mulch for vegetable gardens. Use them green. Add extra nitrogen to garden to compensate for nitrogen lost as grass breaks down. Do not use herbicide-treated grass until a month or two after cutting.
Hay, salt hay	6–12"	Good in vegetable gardens or as winter protection for hardy perennials. Salt hay has fewer weed seeds than other hay.
Leaves	2–5" (shredded) 5–12" (whole)	Shredded leaves are a good all-purpose mulch. Whole leaves blow away easily unless weighted down or contained by fence, and are too coarse for delicate plants. Leaves tend to be acid, but vary with species. Avoid leaves of black walnut trees—they kill other plant species.

MULCH	MULCH DEPTH	CHARACTERISTICS
Mushroom soil compost	1–4"	Attractive soil layer, rich in nutrients. Contains gypsum and is alkaline.
Newspapers	½–2"	May be shredded or used whole. Appropriate in large vegetable gardens. Unattractive unless covered by bark, pine needles, stones, or other natural substance. Must be weighted to prevent its blowing away. Avoid colored pages because of toxic inks.
Peat moss	2–4"	Attractive in flower beds. Should be wetted down and mixed with sand, vermiculite, and soil to prevent its blowing away. Somewhat acidic. May be mixed with lime to counteract acidity.
Pebbles	3–6" or more	Good mulch for dry gardens. Available in various sizes and colors. Edgings of stone or brick keep them in place. Large quantities are available from building supply companies.
Pine needles	3–6"	Slightly acidic, good for azaleas, rhododendrons, and blueberries, etc. Attractive, stable mulch. May be used shredded or unshredded.
Straw	4–12"	Tends to look messy, but is effective. Appropriate in vegetable gardens. Add extra nitrogen to compensate for nitrogen lost when straw breaks down.
Wood chips	3–8" (more in sandy soil)	Good for building up sandy soil. Add extra nitrogen to compensate for nitrogen lost as chips break down. May harbor termites or slugs.

On the downside, it is true that slugs, snails, sow bugs, earwigs, and other pests hide under mulch and creep out to attack plants. However, they can be kept under control with measures discussed later in this chapter.

CHOOSING THE RIGHT MULCH. Some mulching materials are better insulators than others. Light-colored mulches tend to keep the soil and plant roots below them cool. Black plastic or fabric mulch and dark-colored stones or bark chips absorb solar energy and heat up the soil. Clear plastic acts as a heat trap and gets even hotter than black plastic, but weeds will grow underneath it because the sun's rays do filter through.

In cool weather, black or clear plastic mulch can be used to give an early start to heat-loving plants such as peppers, squashes, and eggplant, after danger of frost is past. It can be used even earlier for frost-hardy plants like lettuce and peas. To create even warmer conditions, use it in combination with floating row covers, which add frost protection (see page 75). Lay out the mulch and make X-shaped slits for the seeds or plants at the desired spacing—nothing will grow through plastic unless it has holes in it.

Most kinds of mulch are used during hot, dry weather rather than in cool, humid weather. Organic mulch such as straw, applied too early in the year, when weather is still cold, will delay the rise in soil temperature needed for good seed germination and plant growth. Plant cool-weather crops such as peas and lettuce in bare soil (you can pull back existing mulch) and wait until the weather warms up before you replace the mulch. Small-seeded plants should be allowed to grow at least an inch or two before being mulched, but large-seeded types like peas can easily grow right through a light covering of organic mulch. If you use plastic mulch, check the soil often to make sure that it is moist enough for good plant growth.

WEEDING

Even the best-prepared and -mulched plot of earth will have weeds. Unmulched, open soil beds must be weeded often. Like other plants, weeds start small and quickly grow to imposing sizes, especially in well-made, fertile garden beds. If unchecked, they will out-grow your flowers and vegetables, which are not bred for competition in the wild. A light scuffle with a hoe throughout your garden each week will keep weeds under control. The most important time to weed is early in the gardening season when weeds can easily stunt the growth of young seedlings.

IDENTIFYING THE WEEDS. To weed well, you must be able to distinguish between the weeds and the wanted plants while they are still immature. Planting carefully in rows or at exactly spaced intervals will help, even if your desired plants are new and unfamiliar to you. Look closely at the plantlets. The weeds will be all through the garden—usually the same few types, which are easily learned. Your emerging seedlings will be different from row to row.

WEEDING METHODS. For the fastest weeding, a long-handled hoe is best. In tight spaces you can use a short-handled hoe or weeding fork. Go up and down the rows, or all through the bed, scraping off the weed seedlings near the top of the soil (see the illustration below). Unless they are really out of control, weeds come up easily, especially in soft, well-prepared garden beds.

In vegetable gardens, where appearance isn't necessarily important, you can leave weeds where they fall. On a warm sunny day they will dry out and die completely in a few hours, becoming part of the mulch or soil. The exceptions are larger seed-bearing weeds and certain fleshy or succulent species such as purslane. They can reroot from each broken piece, so remove them from the garden. Remove dandelions and thistles, too, for they have a long taproot that will regrow if you do not get it all out. A long, pronged metal digging stick is useful for prying them up, but any hand trowel will do the job.

The old-fashioned garden hoe scrapes weeds away with ease.

To pull up midsize weeds, scratch under their roots with a small garden fork in one hand and hold the weed, giving a sharp pull, with the other. It may take heavy work with a spade if weeds are permitted to get waist high, but light hoeing, forking, and hand pulling each week will keep garden weeds under tight control.

Weeds have long roots that bring up nutrients from the subsoil layer. For this reason they are a wonderful addition to the compost pile. Think of a large weed as a compost opportunity. Incidentally, many of the most common weeds are as edible as the vegetables we plant. Dandelion, sorrel, purslane, lamb's-quarters, and chickweed are delicious examples. Their younger, more tender leaves may be eaten raw in salad or cooked in casseroles or soups. However, some other common weeds such as jimsonweed and inkberry are poisonous. Use a guide to wild edibles, preferably one illustrated with photographs rather than drawings, for reference before experimenting. Even then, eat a very small portion the first time in case of an allergic reaction.

For information on controlling weeds, see herbicides on pages 131–34.

STAKING

Staking plants is a matter of training as well as supporting them. For best results, stake garden plants before the need is obvious. When your tall dahlias are lush with flowers, when your tomatoes are loaded with fruit, it is already too late to stake them properly. The bending and tying might crack their brittle stems. However, even that is better than having promising plants flattened by wind or rain.

Stakes are props of wood or metal that hold plants upright and keep heavy flowers or fruits from bending toward the ground or breaking the stems. Most stakes are sticks of some

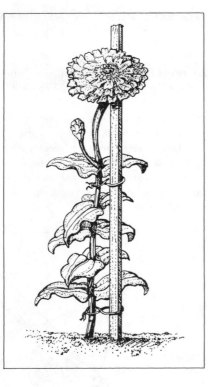

Stake your plants before the need is obvious, since they will need the support as they grow.

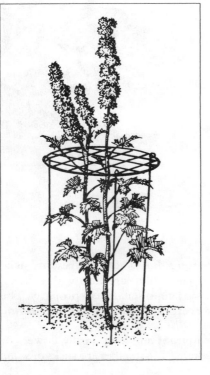

Several stems of delphiniums grow through the same peony hoop. Train them as they grow so the flowers will be supported before they open. This prevents damage when they are in their prime.

kind, either purchased or made from twigs, branches, or small trees (saplings). They can be any size and shape that will support the plant adequately. In ornamental gardens, they should be as inconspicuous as possible. The ties should always be soft, not sharp. String, yarn, or wire covered with plastic or rubber (to keep its sharpness from damaging stems) all work very well. Brown, tan, or green ties are less conspicuous than white or brightly colored ones.

A plant with a single main stem should be tied loosely to a stake set next to it. The ties go at intervals along the main stem, not binding leaves or side branches. More ties are added as the plant grows. Tie the string or bit of yarn around the stake and knot it. Then make a generous loop for the plant stem and tie it again. A plant pinched back for bushiness may grow with an extra heavy load of flowers or fruit, and have even more need for staking.

Plants that grow with many main stems may be trained to grow up through peony hoops or groups of four stakes tied together, encircling the clump. Peony hoops and linking stakes come in several sizes and forms, but all are attractive and inconspicuous—also expensive. A very pretty substitute can be made out of grapevines wound into wreathlike hoops and used with ordinary sticks or stakes.

Vertical supports for taller plants (over 4 feet) are discussed in Chapter 4 on pages 88–92.

Set stakes in about a fourth as deep as their height—a stake 4 feet tall is buried a foot deep, leaving 3 feet for holding up the plant. You should try to set stakes in when you plant or while plants are still small to prevent your accidentally stabbing the roots or bulbs when putting stakes in later. If the stakes are too conspicuous after perennial plants finish blooming or fruiting, remove them and replace them with short pegs to mark the spots. Next year put the old stakes back in the same places with no danger to plant roots or bulbs.

FLOWERS AND HERBS. Low-growing types of flowers, such as alyssum and ageratum, never need staking, while flowers a foot or two tall sometimes need assistance. They can be staked with inconspicuous, 1- to 2-foot-long twigs or bamboo stakes about ½ inch in diameter. Taller flowers, such as lilies, zinnias, dahlias, and cosmos, often need staking. Wooden stakes should be at least an inch in diameter for heavier flowers, such as dahlias and peonies.

You will find that the need for staking depends partly on the growing conditions of your plants. In full sun they grow stockier and have less need for staking than in shade. If you put a sun-loving flower in partial shade, it may grow attractively but lack strength in its stems, which you can make up for with supports. Also, just to make things confusing, some cultivated varieties (cultivars) have naturally stronger stems than others of the same species, so you will have to use your own judgment. It is better to stake unnecessarily than fail to stake plants in time. Special needs for staking are noted in the individual flower entries later in the book.

Wildflowers hardly ever need staking because breeders have not increased the size of the flowers beyond the plants' ability to hold them up, as has happened with domesticated flowers. It is rare for herbs or ornamental grasses to need staking. Many are low, mat-forming plants, and the others tend to have balanced, not top-heavy growth.

VEGETABLES. Many vegetables benefit from staking and other supports, especially when being grown in windy areas or where space is limited. Wooden stakes an inch in diameter and 2 or 3 feet tall are good for peppers and eggplants, one stake per plant. Tomato plants may be tied to stout stakes at least an inch thick and 2 inches wide, and up to 8 feet tall, depending on the variety. Tomatoes can also be grown inside "cages" of wire mesh held up by stakes, with large holes here and there for reaching in and harvesting,

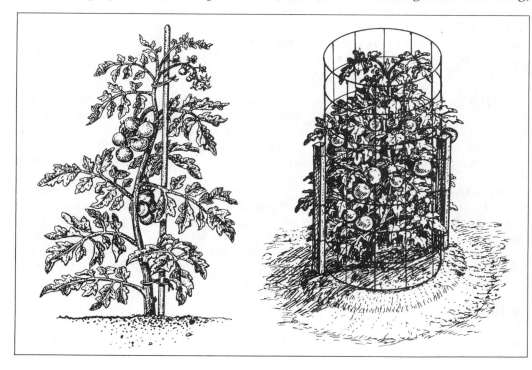

Far left: Tomato plants may be staked with wooden sticks to keep the tomatoes from touching the ground.
Left: Bushy tomato plants are self-supporting in wire cages. Some types of cages have convenient windows cut into the mesh for harvesting.

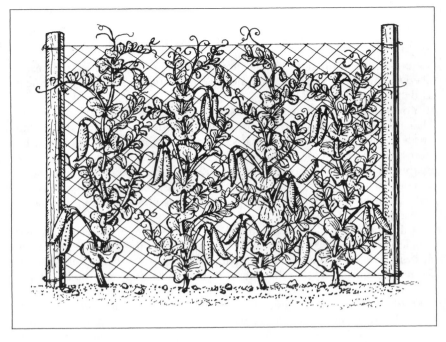

Peas climb on a nylon mesh fence, which is easy to remove or set up, as needed.

or you can encircle them with heavy-gauge wire frames or several wooden stakes tied together. Peas, even bush varieties, do well if they have something to climb on. A piece of chicken wire or nylon netting, held up by strong stakes about 6 feet apart, will make a good lightweight support. You can also save brush—branches cut off from trees and shrubs—when you prune and stick the pieces in along the row for peas to climb on. Beans are even heavier than peas; climbing types are discussed under vertical growing in Chapter 4, and bush varieties do not need staking. Most leafy or root-crop vegetables need no staking.

FRUIT, TREES, AND VINES. Fruit plants often need staking. Cane fruits such as raspberry and blackberry (as well as the trailing varieties of blackberry) can be staked or trellised. For detailed instructions, as well as illustrations, see the individual plant entries. Sometimes fruit tree limbs bear such heavy crops that they need to be supported temporarily—stout pieces of lumber or saplings are used for this (see the illustration on the next page).

Young trees of all types (fruit, nut, shade, or flowering) should be staked when they are planted (see the illustrations on page 92). This helps keep them from blowing in the wind and losing their roothold. At the same time it trains them to grow upright. The stakes may be removed after a year or two. Shrubs may also be staked but it is rarely necessary.

Vines and climbing rosebushes need more than stakes; they need trellises, fences, arches, arbors, or pergolas, which are discussed in the section on vertical growing in Chapter 4.

VEGETATIVE PROPAGATION

As you cultivate garden plants that live for more than a year, you will find that plant care goes hand in hand with propagation. Each plant must be provided with room to grow but

Propping up branches heavily laden with fruit will prevent the weight of the fruit from pulling the branches away from the trunk.

also have its size kept in check, which can be done by making divisions and pruning. With the pieces you have divided or pruned off, you can grow many more plants, each one genetically identical to its parent. Using portions of live plants to start new ones is called vegetative propagation, an alternative to growing plants from seed.

In some cases, you are not allowed to propagate a plant vegetatively because the breeder has obtained plant patent protection. This allows the breeder solely to profit from his or her "invention," which may have taken years of research to produce. Such plants are sold with warning tags. Some sellers interpret this protection very narrowly as meaning it is illegal to propagate the variety at all, even for home use. Others interpret it more liberally, believing it should prevent the sale of patented plants propagated vegetatively without permission, but not home use.

The fact is, it is very easy to propagate plants by dividing crowded clumps, by taking and rooting vegetative cuttings, and by rooting offshoots or branches attached to the parent plant. Most perennials increase rapidly, unassisted, when grown in good conditions. Some plants, like peonies, are very stable and may be left undisturbed, increasing slowly, for five to ten years. Clumps are known to last a hundred years and more. Others, like strawberries with runners, spread aggressively and must be controlled annually. Most are somewhere in between. The individual plant entries include guidelines on when and how to propagate the particular plant.

DIVIDING PERENNIALS. You will need to divide herbaceous (leafy, not woody) perennial flowers, herbs, fruits, and vegetables from time to time because new plants form at the base of the old ones each year. There is not enough room for all to grow healthily unless some are moved. These divisions are excellent sources of new plants exactly like the parent plant. You can use them to make large attractive groups of identical plants or new colonies of the plants in a different part of the landscape. Divisions are also nice to give to friends or trade at plant swaps sponsored by horticultural organizations.

Dividing Clump-forming or Stoloniferous Perennials. Many plants spread by growing underground or ground-level rooted offshoots (stolons) in a circle around the main plant. Some are more far-reaching than others: Ajuga and strawberries send runners out in new directions, with plantlets rooting in chained progression at distances many inches away from the main plant. Others, like chrysanthemums, keep the offspring close to the original stem, forming a crowded clump. Perennials of either type are easy to divide because the offshoots are rooted plantlets, ready to live separate lives when cut from the clump and planted by themselves. Do not divide a clump unless you are sure that it is composed of many different plants, not just one large one with many branches. The way to tell is by checking for rooted offshoots at the soil line.

Plants forming a cluster of rooted stems, like this clump of chrysanthemums, are easy to dig up, divide, and replant at improved spacing.

The safest times of the year to divide plants, in most cases, are early spring after new growth begins but before the plant is more than 3 inches tall, and again after the heat of summer passes, in early or late autumn, depending on geography. Most plants with rooted offshoots can be divided at any time during the growing season if you work carefully and follow up by watering frequently.

With some species, such as goatsbeard *(Aruncus dioicus),* the parent plant at the center of a clump of offshoots dies each year, with a ring of young offspring crowded around it. The decayed center should be discarded and the new plants respaced and planted.

Do your dividing and replanting on cloudy or misty days, if possible. This will keep plants from dehydrating while becoming reestablished. Begin by taking a close look at the clump to be divided. How many divisions will there be? Where will they grow? Will you want to pot some of them to give away or trade? Prepare the soil (see Chapters 3 and 4) in the bed or pots the divisions will be moved into ahead of time. This helps minimize the time the plants will spend out of the ground.

Assemble your tools—spade, trowel, knife, pruning clippers, cloth or newspaper to hold plants, and, if needed, a wheelbarrow. Dig up the clump to be divided by circling it with spade or trowel cuts as deep as its roots grow and lifting it up. Set it on the cloth or newspaper and decide how to take it apart with the least damage to the roots. Most perennials can be pulled apart easily with little problem. Use clippers to cut the connections to the main plant, and separate the smaller plants by hand. Some clumps are very tough and matted. If you cannot separate the plants by pulling them apart gently, cut the clump in half or into large planting pieces with a sharp knife. Plant immediately at the same depth at which they are growing, or up to the crown. Water especially well until growth resumes. Potted divisions should be grown in a sheltered area or greenhouse until they have become established.

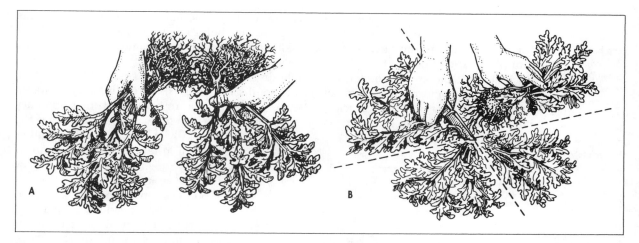

Dividing Hardy Bulbs. If you plant a single daffodil bulb, you will have one or two flowers the next spring. The year after, you may have a small cluster of flowers. Where there was one bulb, now there are several. The year after that, there will be even more, but their size will probably decrease. If undivided, they will continue to multiply but will diminish in quality because the crowded bulbs have too much competition. Eventually most will stop blooming.

A. Dividing clump-forming perennials by hand does very little damage to the fragile roots. B. Use a knife to divide clumps of perennials if they are very dense, fibrous, or otherwise too woody to divide by hand.

This can be prevented by digging up the clump every few years, dividing the bulbs, and replanting them in well-prepared soil at the appropriate spacing. Use the same tools and techniques just described for dump-forming perennials.

Hardy bulbs and corms, such as daffodils, snowdrops, crocus, tulips, scilla, and hyacinths, can be lifted, separated, and replanted at several different stages of their growth. Since they grow and bloom only once a year, the time of bloom is an important factor in identifying and moving them. For most of the year, their bulbs are underground and cannot be seen.

Some gardeners prefer to divide bulbs "in the green." In this method, bulbs are carefully dug up, the roots disturbed as little as possible, and teased apart just before, during, or just after flowering, while the leaves are green, and then replanted where they are wanted, foliage intact. Tiny plants such as snowdrops are especially easy to move this way. (If moved while flowering, some of their beauty may be lost, but the plants will survive.) This can also be done with daffodils and hyacinths, but not as easily because of their size and deeper planting depth. It is not advised for tulips, which will be more shocked by such a move. The advantage of moving bulbs "in the green" is that the results are seen and checked immediately, not the next year. No great feats of labeling or memory are needed.

More often, spring-flowering bulbs are lifted and divided a few weeks after they finish blooming, when their foliage begins to turn yellow. Their growth is complete for the year and they are becoming dormant. After they are dug and divided, they may be replanted in refreshed beds at proper spacing, or dried in the sun for a week or two to prevent rot, and then stored indoors (leaves and roots removed) in paper bags in a dry place such as a closet until fall planting time. Be careful about labeling them. The smaller bulbs (grape hyacinths, snowdrops, crocus) tend to overdry in storage more readily than larger ones such as tulips—you may want to replant them right away if they show signs of dehydration.

Snowdrop bulbs can be dug up and divided "in the green," even while in full bloom, if you are careful to dig up the entire root system and replant the clumps immediately.

If their locations have been marked carefully, spring-blooming bulbs may also be dug up, divided, and replanted in the fall when similar bulbs appear in garden stores. Take special care not to stab them—they are hidden underground and can easily be injured by misplaced digging.

Lilies that bloom in summer are usually divided after their stems turn yellow—fall in northern and central areas, summer farther south. They must be carefully, deeply dug up and replanted at improved spacing. They are difficult to store because of their tendency to sprout too soon, so it is best to dig and replant immediately. Flakes that break off the main bulb may be replanted and grown. They will develop fully in a few years. Tiny bulbils sometimes form in leaf axils on lily stems. If planted about ½ inch deep, each will grow into a new plant in a few years.

Tender bulbs, corms, and tubers, such as dahlias, anemones, caladiums, gladioli, freesia, amaryllis, crinum lilies, agapanthus, cannas, and callas, are usually divided when they go dormant at the end of the growing season—in areas with little or no winter frost, when flowers fade and leaves turn yellow.

In Zones 9 to 11, dig up crowded plants that grow from corms, tubers, rhizomes, and bulbs while they are dormant. Trim off most of the foliage, divide them gently, and plant them directly in their new places. The canna lily is an exception, for it is tropical and under warm conditions does not have a dormant period. Divide its rhizomes during warm, moist weather whenever plants become crowded, and replant immediately in well-irrigated fertile soil.

To cause the least damage to the bulbs being divided, tease the plants apart without cutting either the bulbs or the roots. Although these snowdrops may be divided while still in bloom, most bulbs should be moved after flowers fade and leaves start to yellow.

Flakes from the main bulb may be used to propagate lilies vegetatively. Break off several of them in spring or fall.

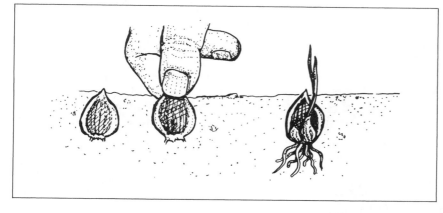

Plant the bulb flakes in pots or nursery beds so that the uppermost tip barely shows above the surface of the soil. In about a year, the small but developed plantlet may be moved to the garden.

In places with cold winters (Zone 8 and above), dig up and divide tender bulbs, corms, tubers, and rhizomes immediately after the first fall frost damages the leaves. After digging, wash off the clumps and trim off all but the bottom 2 inches of foliage. Some species, such as gladiolus and freesia, have relatively firm, dry corms that can be stored in drier conditions than other species that grow from fleshy tubers, rhizomes, or bulbs. Check individual plant entries for more specific directions. However, as a rule, dry out gladioli and similar corms for several weeks and then store them in an airy, cool (near 50°F) place on screens, shelves, or trays—with labels telling the type and color. When fully dry, they may be packed in paper bags. They tolerate a fairly wide range of temperatures and are normally preserved successfully until planting time the next year unless they freeze or get wet.

Dahlias and other plants from fleshy tubers, rhizomes, and bulbs are harder to store, for they need moisture but must not be allowed to contract fungus diseases and rot—which is all too likely except under unusually good conditions. After you dig, clean, trim leaves, and separate intertwined root portions, you should dust the plants with fungicide and let them dry out for a few days in a frost-free, airy place. Then store them in a cool basement inside boxes of moist sand (like carrots) or in plastic packets of slightly dampened sphagnum moss or vermiculite until it is time to replant them the following spring.

TAKING CUTTINGS. Plants grown from cuttings are genetically identical to the parent plant, but usually are stockier than those from seed. Cuttings may be taken from different portions of the plant:

Tip cuttings are taken from branch ends and may be taken from last year's growth (hardwood cuttings) or fresh new growth (softwood cuttings). *Stem cuttings* are portions of the stem, without the tip. A branch or trunk may be cut into several stem cuttings. *Root cuttings* are taken from thickened, fleshy parts of the root, not the fine root hairs. *Leaf cuttings* are taken from pieces of a leaf or are composed of the entire leaf. They are sometimes used to propagate begonias and other tropical plants. If these plant cuttings are given a hospitable rooting medium and a humid environment that is not too hot or cold, they will form roots and make new plants. Plant species have individual preferences among available methods of propagation, which are included in their individual entries.

Except for members of the lily family and some kinds of annual flowers and vegetables, most plants may be grown from cuttings. Flowers, herbs, fruits, nut trees, and shrubs are often grown this way. Some annuals, like basil, tomatoes, scarlet sage, marigolds, and petunias, will grow roots from cuttings, but usually are grown from seed for convenience or to prevent disease. Fungi and diseases can remain viable (even when invisible) on live green plants, but are much less able to persist on dry seeds.

A single plant such as this young geranium can be made into several types of cuttings.

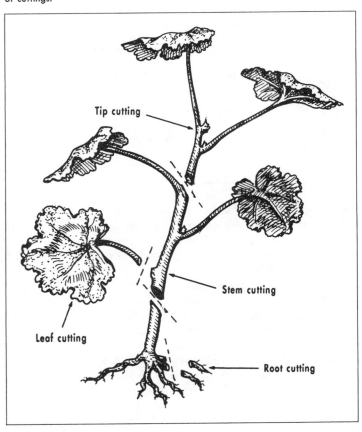

Tip cutting

Stem cutting

Leaf cutting

Root cutting

Rooting Cuttings in Water. Some types of plants are far easier to propagate from cuttings than others. The most easily rooted plants may be propagated simply by keeping a tip, stem, or (rarely) leaf cutting in a glass of water. Root development of some of these is a bit better in soil, but the water-rooted cuttings will catch up when they are planted. Some plants that may be cultivated in this way are wax begonias, ivy, pachysandra, impatiens, allamanda, marigolds, pussy willows, grapevines, geraniums *(Pelargonium),* coleus, wandering Jew *(Tradescantia),* and scarlet sage. For these, take stem or tip cuttings 6 to 8 inches long, remove the bottom leaves and all flowers and seedpods, and put them in water in groups of three or four. Keep the bottom

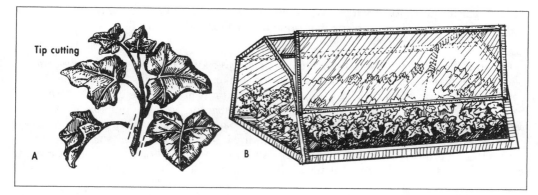

A. Tip cuttings are taken from the ends of stems or branches, such as this piece of ivy. To prepare cuttings for rooting, make the stem cut at an angle. Remove the lower leaves and dust the cut ends with rooting hormone if you wish. Set the stem in moist but well-drained soil (rooting medium), to a depth of roughly half its length.
B. Tip cuttings root best under controlled, humid conditions in partial shade. This cold frame provides an excellent environment for cuttings to root in if heat is not permitted to build up. Inside protective cold frames like this one, cuttings can be rooted in flats, individual pots, or directly in the soil.

half of the cuttings covered with water and set in a bright place but out of direct sunlight. Change the water once a week and discard rotted or yellowed but not wilted leaves. Cuttings may wilt before they root and recover afterward. Hardwoods, such as grapevines, forsythia, and pussy willows, root fast if cut in late winter while they are dormant, but less easily later in their annual cycle. Others will root at any time.

Roots usually show up in two or three weeks, sometimes less. New cuttings seem to root faster when put in with rooted cuttings of the same variety. When the roots are about 2 inches long, pot the plants or move them to the garden, keeping their soil very moist for a few weeks until they adjust to the new growing medium.

Rooting Cuttings in Soil. Most plants that grow from cuttings are rooted in potting soil. It is important to provide soil that is clean, disease- and bug-free, and suited to the type of plant you are growing. Premixed, packaged potting or rooting media, as sold by garden stores, are fine for this purpose. Some other favorite rooting mixtures are:

- **⅓ peat, ⅓ sand, ⅓ humus.**
  Good for acid-loving plants like blueberries and rhododendrons.

- **½ perlite, ½ vermiculite.**
  Good for houseplants and others that root quickly, such as impatiens and sweet potato cuttings, in a soil that stays damp.
  Water-rooted cuttings with liquid fertilizer diluted to half the recommended strength.

- **⅔ perlite, ⅓ humus or vermiculite.**
  Good for plants that root slowly—hardwoods, for instance. This well-drained soil discourages rotting.

- Water-rooted cuttings with liquid fertilizer diluted to half the recommended strength.

· Rich garden soil mixed with sawdust and coarse sand in equal amounts. Good for all plants rooted outdoors in the open ground under shading such as lath or screen, or under trees.

Cuttings that have not rooted or have just begun to root need a protected environment, one that is shaded and moist. The lack of roots makes them unable to survive in drying conditions, such as wind or bright sun. Indoors, cuttings may be rooted in flowerpots or flats that are misted frequently, or in closed, transparent propagating boxes similar to terrariums, which hold in moisture. Jars or plastic bags serve the same purpose. In closed containers it is particularly important to use a disease-free propagating soil or medium.

Outdoors, cuttings may be rooted in pots, flats, or propagating boxes set in shady, humid, protected areas. A cold frame set up in the shade is ideal. They may also be rooted in

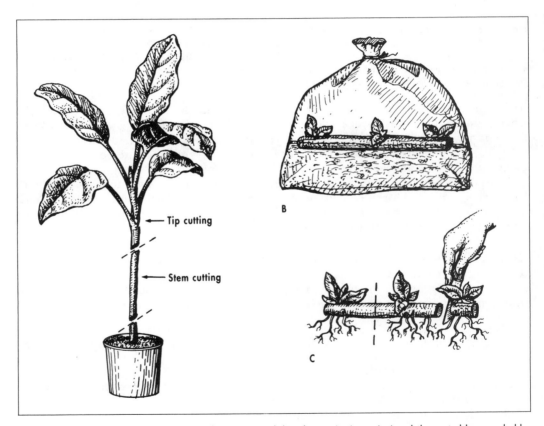

All three portions of this dieffenbachia may be propagated, but the top (a tip cutting) and the rooted base probably will produce only one new plant apiece. The stem cutting can be the source of several new plants—one per node. Lay the stem cutting on its side in a moist, clean rooting medium (B). Nick the bark slightly near each node where the stem touches the soil. Root the cuttings under humid conditions inside a plastic bag, cold frame, or greenhouse, and make sure that there's partial shade to prevent heat buildup. Leaves and roots will emerge from each node and the rooted stem can be cut up to create several new plants (C).

Propagating African violets from leaf cuttings.
A. Cut off a healthy, full-grown leaf near the crown of the plant.
B. With the stem end down, set each leaf into a rooting medium up to the leaf base. Several leaves can be rooted in the same pot. Keep cuttings in humid conditions, away from drafts and bright sunlight.
C. When roots form and a healthy offshoot develops, cuttings may be transplanted to individual pots.

propagating beds in the ground. The soil can be a mix of sand or perlite, vermiculite, and humus such as sawdust or compost-rich soil. The mixture can be made in different ways, as long as it is light enough to allow root growth and is moisture retentive. The beds should be placed in the shade or shaded with lath strips or screening.

Use only pest- and disease-free plants for propagation. Take soft cuttings with a sharp knife or snap them off cleanly to minimize damage to cells. Use pruning clippers for woody cuttings. The cut end or parts may be dipped in a rooting hormone or mix of rooting hormone and fungicide such as Rootone, to promote faster, more reliable root growth.

Get the pots, flats, or beds ready for the cuttings by filling them with one of the moist rooting media described on pages 117–18. Several cuttings may be rooted together in the same pot and separated later when roots have formed. In flats or beds, line up the cuttings in rows, with many cuttings in each one. A ruler or marked planting stick will help keep rows straight and evenly spaced. Generally, cuttings are closely spaced, with their leaves touching or nearly touching.

Tip cuttings should be 4 to 8 inches long for most plants, although vines and tropical plants may be started from longer ones. Trim the leaves off the lower third of each stem, and remove flowers and flower buds. If the cuttings are not woody, make holes in the rooting medium with a pencil or similar object, rather than poking the stems in directly. They should be covered to about half their length, then firmed in by hand and watered before leaving them in their sheltered spot to root. Water the soil if it becomes dry, but do not wiggle the cuttings around to test them until at least several weeks pass. Such jostling will inhibit root growth.

Treat stem cuttings similarly, although they are usually shorter than tip cuttings. Bury half or all of the stem either on a slant, upright, or horizontally, depending on the plant variety (check the individual entries). Cover horizontally set cuttings with soil about twice the depth of the diameter of the cutting. Each piece of stem should have at least one leaf node (bud) on it so a new plant can grow.

Leaf cuttings are somewhat more difficult to handle than stem or tip cuttings. They are used to propagate certain plants mainly from tropical or semitropical areas. A few plants, such as African violets, will root from a single, entire leaf placed in a glass of water or in a propagating medium. Others, such as rex begonias, will root from a leaf buried flat under about an inch of propagating medium. In either case, just score the leaf with small cuts through main veins at several points, and plantlets with roots will originate near the cuts. When they are large enough to handle easily, they may be moved into individual pots. You can also root 2-inch pieces cut from begonia leaves if you bury them halfway, perpendicular to the soil surface.

Root cuttings should be several inches long. Sometimes a portion of stem is attached. If so, it can be allowed to poke through. Many hardy perennial flowers and some tropical plants are propagated this way. To root these cuttings, cover them shallowly but completely with soil.

Allow all cuttings to grow a healthy crop of new roots before removing them from their sheltered nursery areas, and then treat them like seedling plants (see pages 69–72) until they are stronger. Harden them off gradually for about three weeks by improving ventilation and lighting in stages.

A word to beginners: Not even the most experienced professional nurseryman or -woman expects every single cutting to take root, even when all have received identical treatment. Nature has her mysteries. If your cuttings fail, just try again. In most cases, some of the batch will take hold and others will fade away—this is to be expected. Woody plants, such as certain blueberry varieties, are often hard to root. Many gardeners are convinced that the phase of the moon affects the rooting of cuttings, causing better results for cuttings planted during the waning of the moon.

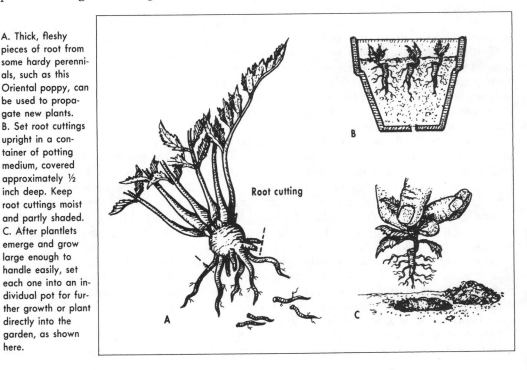

A. Thick, fleshy pieces of root from some hardy perennials, such as this Oriental poppy, can be used to propagate new plants.
B. Set root cuttings upright in a container of potting medium, covered approximately ½ inch deep. Keep root cuttings moist and partly shaded.
C. After plantlets emerge and grow large enough to handle easily, set each one into an individual pot for further growth or plant directly into the garden, as shown here.

Root cutting

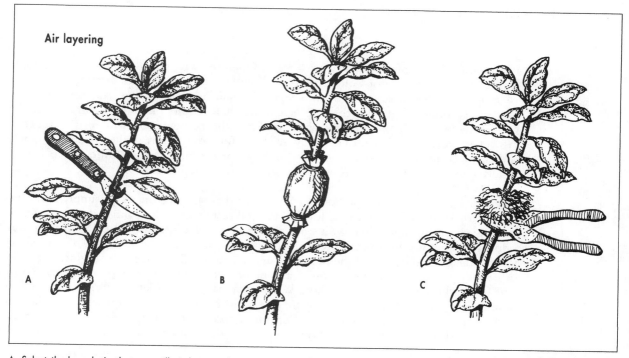

Air layering

A. Select the branch tip that you will air layer and score it about 8 inches from the tip by scraping away the bark halfway around the stem.

B. Wrap the scored part of the branch with a dampened rooting medium, such as sphagnum moss. Cover this with a layer of plastic, sealing it with string or tape so that no water can get in or out.

C. After healthy roots form, clip the rooted stem free just below the root mass. Plant the rooted cutting immediately in a nursery pot or in its place in the garden. Keep it moist and shaded until it is firmly established.

LAYERING. A similar means of vegetative propagation is called layering. It is used for hard-to-root plants because it permits plants to root offshoots that are still attached to the parent plant, providing a reliable life-support system during the most chancy phase of propagation.

Layering may be used for any plant that will grow from cuttings, but is most commonly used for rhododendrons, roses, azaleas, and other hard- or slow-to-root woody plants. Conifers such as pines and cedars are not effectively layered, in most cases.

To layer a plant, a portion of a branch's bark is nicked (scraped away) or scored part of the way around, but not sliced through entirely. It is then put in contact with a rooting medium or soil in one of several ways:

Air Layering. This refers to a way of rooting parts of branches without moving them from their original positions. Choose a branch portion, usually about 10 to 12 inches from the branch tip, and scrape away a thin line of bark halfway around the stem. Cover it with a wad of moist sphagnum or peat moss (not too wet) or a rooting medium several inches thick, wrapped in a sheet of brown or black plastic and taped to the branch above and below the cut. Using horticultural or electrical tape, seal the packet carefully so that no water can get in or out. Yes, this is somewhat unsightly, but can be done to less visible parts of the plant in most cases. With northern hardwood plants, this is often done in the early spring when crocus bloom. After a few weeks or months, you will probably find that the rooting medium inside the plastic is filled with roots. Open the wrappings and take a quick look, then reseal if roots are not well developed. (Some plants such as lilacs may take up to two years.) At this point, if root growth is vigorous, you can remove the wrappings and clip the layered branch free an inch or so below the roots. Prune off about a third of the top part of the branch to minimize the amount of growth the new roots will need to support. However, be sure to leave one or several buds for growth tips. Either plant the newly rooted piece in its permanent position or in a pot for later transplanting. Keep it well watered and shaded until its roots are large and well established.

Regular Layering. This method is even easier than air layering. You simply bend the branch to be layered down to the level of the soil or to a pot filled with soil. Score or nick the branch on the side where you want roots to form. Do not cut the bark on the other side—you do not want to cut off circulation of nutrients. The cut should be about half as long as the circumference of the branch. Bury the cut portion under several inches of soil or a rooting medium and weight it with a stone or brick to keep it from popping out. Roots will form where the bark was nicked. When they have grown large enough, after a few months to a year later, clip the new plant free an inch below the root growth, trim the top back by roughly a third, and replant it. Currants, gooseberries, clematis, grapevines, rhodo-dendrons, tropical plants, sage, thyme, sedums and succulents, myrtle, and rosebushes,

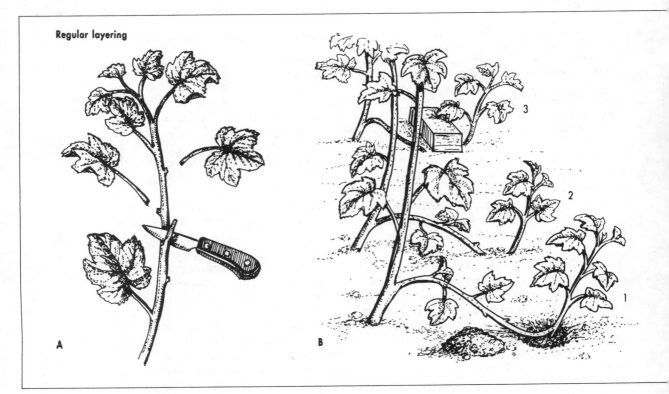

Regular layering

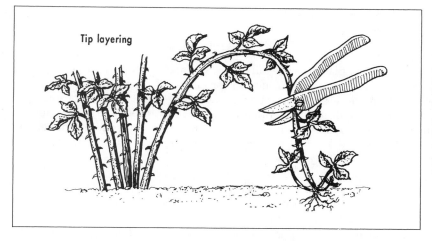

Tip layering

Cane fruits like this blackberry often take root by way of tip layering. New roots form where the branch tip touches the ground. The new plant can then be cut free and re-planted where you want it to grow.

among others, are often propagated this way. It will work with any plant that can be grown from tip or stem cuttings.

Tip Layering. This method is similar to regular layering, but in this case only the tip of the branch or offshoot touches the soil. Many plants with invasive tendencies, particularly blackberries and other berries that grow on canes, grow tip layers unassisted. Roots form where the arching canes touch the ground. Strawberries, gooseberries, ivy, myrtle, and

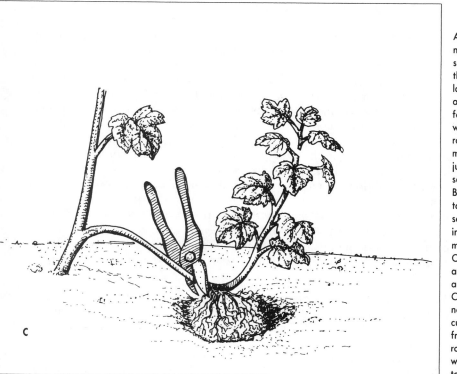

C

A. In spring, after new leaves appear, score the bark of the branch to be layered halfway around its circum-ference, where you would like new roots to grow. Re-move several leaves just above the scored portion.
B. Bend the branch to the ground and set the scored area into a damp rooting medium or soil. Cover it shallowly and anchor it with a rock or brick.
C. After healthy new roots develop, cut the new plant free just below the roots and plant it where you want it to grow.

forsythia are other examples of plants that readily grow tip layers. If you wish to propagate plants this way, bend shoots down to the ground in spring or fall. Make a nick on the side of the shoot where roots should grow and anchor the tip under about 4 inches of soil. This can be done in containers of soil, for convenient transplants, or directly in the ground in tilled soil. Several months later, when sturdy roots are a few inches long, cut the connection to the parent plant. After a week or so to recuperate, the new plant may be set in its permanent position.

TIMING OF PROPAGATION. Timing is crucial to your success with vegetative propagation. Different species take root more easily at different times of year. The individual plant entries give recommended methods and times.

In general, tropical or warm-weather plants are propagated (as well as divided or transplanted) most successfully during warm, moist weather between 75° and 85°F. Hardy plants are propagated, divided, or transplanted more easily in early spring when the sap is rising and the year's new growth begins after a winter of dormancy. Their powerful generative action at this time of year is most impressive. Often, a tip cutting of grapevine, pussy willow, rose, or hardy hydrangea will take root if simply stuck into moist soil when its leaf buds begin to fatten but before they open.

TRAINING AND PRUNING

A helping hand is needed to shape and control many of our favorite garden plants. Rosebushes, fruit trees, hedges, shrubs, grapevines, shade trees, and even flowering annuals need a pinch or a clip at the right time if they are to attain their optimal shape, health, and productivity. Training involves cutting and placing or bending branches to shape a young plant, and pruning (cutting) is done to keep a mature plant in this proper form. Done correctly, training and pruning also increase the amount of flowers and fruit and/or their size. Each should be done in gentle stages every year as the plant develops, not in a drastic way after years of neglect.

Training is partly a matter of style, or even personality. Some gardeners like a close-clipped, controlled finish on their plants; others like a freer, more natural look. Constructive, healthy training may be done in either style, and is more likely to be consistent and attractive if the same person supervises or performs all the training on the property.

Style aside, there are right and wrong ways to train and prune. Study well-formed plants in display and botanical gardens and practice on your garden plants at home with sensitivity to their growth patterns. A pruning manual will explain the procedures in far more detail, but here are some guidelines that will help you make pruning and training decisions more easily:

- Since you will make open cuts on plants when you prune, do it in a way that will help them heal over quickly and completely. Use sharp equipment to minimize mashing the stems. Scissor-type clippers, long-handled lopping shears, and a variety of saws are often used (see Pruning Gear, page 32).

    Where possible, make cuts flush with the branch or trunk; do not leave stubs, which will rot, providing an entry for bugs and diseases. If you are pruning branches back, but not all the way to the main branch or trunk, make cuts just above a bud that faces toward the outside of the plant (this will direct new growth outward). Make the cut at a 45° angle across the branch with the higher edge just above the bud.

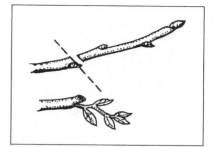

- Remove dead, broken, or infected portions of any plant, clipping all the way back to healthy wood. After clipping diseased or dead branches, clean your equipment with a rag soaked in chlorine bleach, or your clippers might spread the disease to healthy plants. Discard diseased cuttings by burning them or getting rid of them in the trash—do not use them in the compost pile.

- Where branches cross and rub each other, cut one away. Anticipate future crosses and shape plants to prevent them. Remove tangled growth. Remove shoots growing straight up (called suckers or water sprouts) from the centers of shrubs or trees, unless they will be trained as replacement main branches.

- Remove spindly or overcrowded growth, but give room to healthy new growth. Some newly formed branches are conspicuously fatter and healthier than others. Climbing roses, for instance, usually have several strong new canes coming up above the graft (the bump on the lower stem) in spring, somewhat like spears of asparagus. These are the ones to encourage and train for flowers the following year. Other new growth comes

Prune to an outward-facing bud, clipping slantwise behind the bud as shown. When the bud develops, the resulting branch will grow outward in the right direction, not inward where it would crowd growth in the shrub's interior.

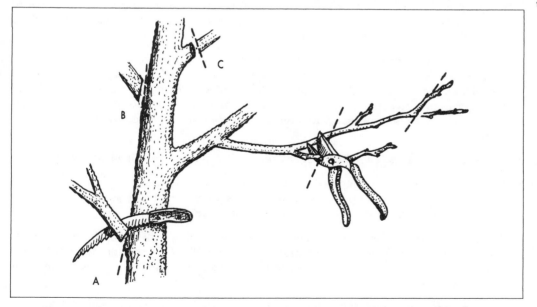

Prune branches off cleanly, flush with the trunk. The cut on the bottom left (A) is slightly incorrect because the slanted stub of the branch looks messy and is also more vulnerable to pests and diseases. The cut above it on the left (B) is the best of the three, since it removes the branch with the least possible leftover tissue and the smallest opening. The cut on the top right (C) is incorrect, because it leaves a conspicuous stub that is an invitation to pests and diseases.

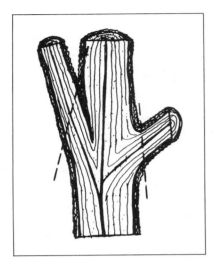

The branch on the left should be eliminated, since it is growing at an unhealthy angle. The deeply V-shaped crotch becomes weaker as the tree grows because of the bark entering the tree trunk area. The greater angle of the branch on the right will allow both the trunk and the branch to grow in diameter as the tree matures.

up very small and weak, and should be removed at ground level or flush with the stem it grows from. The best of the new growth will be an asset to a plant.

- Prune early-blooming plants, such as forsythia and azalea, immediately after they bloom. Their new growth after pruning will have flower buds for bloom the following year. Prune climbing roses after they bloom, and only where necessary because of weak wood. Prune hybrid tea roses before they bloom, when forsythia and crocus begin to flower.

- Train shade trees from their early days. A branch on a trunk will always be the same distance from the ground, even when the tree grows tall. It is much healthier for the tree if its unwanted branches are removed while they are the thickness of pencils, not baseball bats. Do not permit low branches to grow on trees that will have a high crown if you want people to be able to walk beneath them.

- Train trees to promote strong lateral branches. The angle of growth affects whether the branch will split from the trunk in a storm. A V-shaped crotch is much weaker than a 60° crotch because the layers of wood and bark are too narrow when squeezed together this way. Stress from wind or snow easily causes splits. If choosing which branches to leave and which to eliminate, leave the ones growing at better angles. Cut away the others flush with the trunk or main branch.

- Prune fruit trees at the end of their dormancy period, just before new growth begins. Encourage lateral branching. Get rid of perpendicular growth such as water sprouts and suckers. Do not let branches reach the ground, but encourage low branches so fruit will be easier to pick. Keep the tree open so sun can penetrate the interior. On large trees, clip branch tips back a few inches to limit tree size. Burn them to get rid of possible insect eggs.

- Cut wood, not leaves. There is never any reason to clip leaves in half when hand pruning.

- For bushier evergreens, pinch back half of each candle, or spindle of new growth, in spring while it is soft. You may start doing this when the tree is still small. If heavy pruning is needed, do it from midsummer to late summer.

- Study the growth pattern of each plant and train in keeping with it. For instance, azaleas have fan-shaped branches and look highly unnatural when clipped into tight balls. Just prune to control the overall shape by cutting off unwanted branches flush with the stems they grow from.

- Pinch back for bushiness. When the leader (the central stem or main branch) is cut, new growth will emerge from side buds. Promote bushiness in annual flowers, chrysanthemums, and other plants by pinching out central leader buds or tips. This can be done with branching vegetables, such as peppers, with certain flowering perennials if you want several side stems rather than a central stem of flowers (do not do this with members

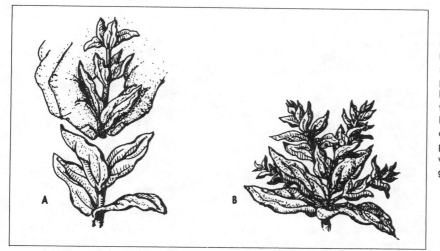

A. Pinch off the central growth tip (as shown with this zinnia seedling) to promote lateral branches and more flowers.
B. Several weeks after pinching, the plant responds with bushy new growth.

of the lily or iris family or bush tomato varieties, though), and with shrubs. Most trees grow better if the central leader is not disturbed.

- Hedges need training from their earliest days. They should be wider at the base than at the top—wedge shaped. Interior clipping lets in light for healthy growth throughout the hedge, not just on the outside edge. Even when they are regularly sheared for neatness, hedges need hand clipping to eliminate crossed branches and provide for renewed growth.

- When cutting large branches, use a saw. A long heavy branch can be removed in two stages to prevent any ragged tears in the bark. First, make a cut 1 foot away from the trunk, under the branch, cutting halfway through. Then cut down from above to meet the cut on the underside. The branch will fall. Next, for the second stage, cut the foot-long stub off cleanly, flush with the trunk. Use paint or pruning sealant on a large wound if you wish, to help keep it from being infected. However, a clean cut will heal better by itself in most cases.

DEADHEADING

Removal of spent flowers and ripening seedpods is called deadheading. There are times you may want to leave seedpods on, but usually you will want to remove them.

VEGETABLES. In most cases, flowers are the first stage of the harvest and should be left on so fruit can ripen. However, squashes, melons, and other members of the cucurbit family are unusual in that they have separate male and female flowers. Only the female flowers, the ones with the visible fruit-shaped ovary behind the flower, will grow into fruits. The others may be removed after they bloom to eliminate mildew or insects. The appearance of flowers on root or leaf crops such as turnips, radishes, and lettuce is a sign that the whole

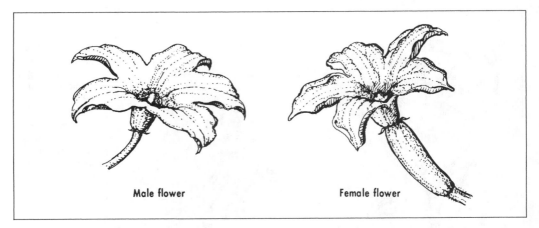

Male flower   Female flower

The male squash flower provides pollen, but contains no ovary to develop into the fruit of the plant. Squash plants usually produce more male than female flowers. The female squash flower shows the ovary behind the flower. If fertilized with pollen, it will develop into the fruit of the squash plant. If it is not fertilized, it will wither and fall off the plant without growing.

plant is past its prime, although young green seedpods of radishes and cole crops are edible. Unless the seeds are wanted, just pull up the whole plant and put it on the compost pile.

HERBS. Flowers and seedpods of branching herbs may be pinched off to promote bushiness, or they may be left on to let seeds ripen. Flowers of chives and other flowering members of the onion family may be left on for decoration or seed, or removed to promote bulb growth.

Anatomy of a flower

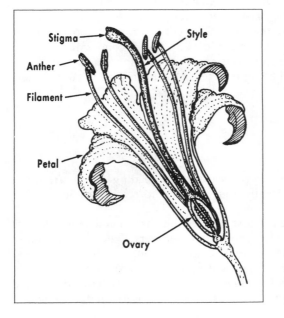

Stigma
Anther
Filament
Style
Petal
Ovary

ANNUAL FLOWERS. The aim in life of an annual flowering plant is to grow seed for the next generation. They develop in an ovary behind or under the petals. When the plant's mission is complete, it is likely to wither and die. To keep flowers blooming many more weeks, prevent the seeds from ripening by removing flowers in their prime for bouquets or just after they fade. A few can be left to set seed if you want to save and grow them. Multiflowering plants such as alyssum may be sheared back if they become too seedy and weedy looking.

BIENNIAL FLOWERS. Most biennial flowers begin as a small plantlet one year, then bloom, set seed, and die the next. The show of bloom is spectacular but short-lived, so deadheading is of little use. On the other hand, most biennials grow very well from their own self-sown or hand-saved seeds, so you may want to leave them on to ripen.

PERENNIAL FLOWERS. Some perennials will continue to bloom for a long period if spent flowers are removed, but others will bloom only once. In most cases, plants look much better when flowers are removed after they bloom. The energy that the plant would have spent on seeds goes into roots, bulbs, or leaves instead, promoting a greater show of flowers the next year. In some cases, seed is wanted, so the flower head may be left on the plant to ripen.

SHRUBS AND TREES. Spent flowers may be picked off to prevent the growth of seedpods on shrubs such as rhododendrons and roses, but it is not absolutely necessary. It improves their neatness and leaf growth, but makes very little difference in plant health. Trees are not normally deadheaded. If you do remove clusters of seedpods from trees or shrubs, do so carefully so that new green shoots are not disturbed. If seeds or pods are ornamental, leave them on. Some roses have especially attractive hips (pods) that add color to the landscape in autumn. Many of them are fine natural food for wildlife.

PEST AND DISEASE CONTROL

There is no part of garden care as heatedly debated as pest and disease control. Organic gardeners oppose all chemical treatment for pests of any kind. Chemical remedies exist for many problems, but can be quite toxic to people, animals, fish, earthworms, and even plants, especially when used carelessly. Yet some gardeners, lawn care companies, and farmers use them liberally at the least sign of trouble or as a preventative. Pests can develop resistance to pesticides, and pesticides can build up in the soil to a dangerous level of toxicity. Another group of gardeners sensibly keeps chemical pesticides and herbicides in reserve, rarely used, resorted to only for serious infestations that have not been controlled by earlier attempts with safer methods. Dormant oil sprays, pyrethrum, rotenone, diatomaceous earth, and biological controls are effective but do not harm the environment.

A clean, healthy garden is the gardener's first defense against harmful insects, fungus, viral or bacterial infection, and weeds. It prevents the appearance of some problems and the spread of others. Healthy, fast-growing plants are generally more resistant to pests than are weaker plants. (An exception to this rule is the disease fire blight, which affects fast-growing trees such as apple, pear, and some ornamentals.)

Most garden problems start small and then spread. Check under leaves for the eggs of harmful insects. The underside of outer leaves is a favored location. The tip of new shoots is another. Remove the first or second generation of pests early in the season and more may never appear. For positive identification of garden insects and diseases and the remedies for them, most local garden stores can help. County agricultural extension agents, local horticultural societies, and Master Gardeners—volunteers trained in horticulture by extension agents—are also glad to provide expert assistance.

Harmful insects and disease organisms are harbored in garden litter such as piles of weeds, wormy fallen fruit, fallen leaves that succumbed to insects or disease, and hollow stems. If a plant is badly infested with disease or an insidious pest, such as leaf miners, remove and discard it entirely, or at a minimum the part that is even lightly affected. Do not add infested plant matter to the compost pile; instead, burn it or throw it out with your trash. This way the colony of harmful operators can be eliminated before they multiply.

Hoe or pull weeds while they are very small, before they go to seed or make hiding places for pests. When piles of weeds, prunings, discarded plants, or other organic matter are added to the compost pile, shred or chop it into smaller pieces. It packs down for a heated pile that will kill pests and weed seeds better. It will break down into soil faster this way, too.

A watchful gardener can eliminate problems before they reach epidemic proportions. In the table on pages 132–33 are environmentally safe, organic remedies for common garden pests. Some are home remedies, most are available from local garden stores, and the rest are available from mail-order garden suppliers.

PLANT ROTATION. Another way to prevent soil-borne disease and pest problems is to rotate or change the place where you plant your annual flowers, vegetables, berries, and melons each year so that you don't plant crops from the same family in the same place two years in a row (for an explanation of plant families, see pages 60–61). For instance, if you grew tomato-family vegetables such as eggplants, tomatoes, peppers, or potatoes in one end of your vegetable garden, you should plant corn, onions, or other vegetables from other families in that portion of the garden the next year. For annual flowers, if you grew petunias (part of the tomato family) in your bed one year, you should plant marigolds or other annual flowers from a different family in the same spot the next year. This kind of rotation keeps soil-borne diseases specific to certain plant families from flourishing year to year.

Organic Pesticides

BOTANICAL CONTROLS. Some plants have the ability to kill or discourage insect and animal pests. Many pests are repelled by strong-smelling herbs and flowers such as tansy, nasturtiums, marigolds, mint, basil, and savory, which may be interplanted in any kind of garden or orchard. Onions, chives, and garlic repel many bugs including Japanese beetles and grasshoppers as well as deer, squirrels, rabbits, and other garden-browsing mammals. Daffodils are repellent to deer (also, keep in mind if you have small children that daffodil bulbs and foliage are toxic). Soapy water applied to leaves slows down caterpillars and aphids.

A very effective spray can be made in the blender by mixing 2 cups water, 2 garlic cloves, a spoonful of liquid dish detergent, a teaspoon or two of salad oil, and a tablespoon of cayenne pepper. Puree briefly, and spray and sprinkle on any garden plant up to several days before harvest. This inhibits chewing critters great and small. Be sure to wash off flowers or edible plants sprayed with this before using them, not because it is toxic but because of the smell and taste. Diatomaceous earth, a powderlike substance composed of the glassy, microscopic shells of sea creatures, kills sucking and chewing insects when it is dusted on the leaves on which they feed.

Strong botanical controls such as rotenone and pyrethrum, which are made from plants, kill beneficial insects along with harmful ones, but are effective for only a short time and will not cause lasting environmental damage the way inorganic pesticides often do. Still, they are more drastic than the other remedies and should be used as a last resort. When buying pyrethrum or rotenone powders, take care to read the label to see what other chemicals have been added.

BIOLOGICAL CONTROLS. These are beneficial animals, insects, or microorganisms that help gardeners by attacking the insects that harm plants. Some are microorganisms, such as *Bacillus thuringiensis* (Bt, sold as Dipel and Thuricide) and *Bacillus popilliae* (milky spore disease), which attack by causing disease in the target insects. They can be bought as sprays, pellets, or powders. Others are insects or other creatures that eat harmful insects. The praying mantis, lacewing fly, and ladybug eat plant-chewing pests such as aphids. Some kinds of wasps kill caterpillars by laying their eggs in them. Moles are beneficial because they eat underground grubs, but their tunnels are so unsightly that the creatures are considered pests. To get rid of the moles, get rid of the grubs.

Birds are natural pest controllers. Though some birds steal cherry tomatoes and peck fruit, they also eat many harmful insects and weed seeds. Birds can be encouraged by planting wild fruits such as chokecherries and trees and shrubs that produce ornamental berries such as pyracantha, dogwood, and hawthorn. They often seem to prefer these to the less flavorful domestic fruits—fortunately.

PHYSICAL BARRIERS. Mammals are the worst pests, as anyone knows who gardens where deer, rabbits, squirrels, mice, raccoons, opossums, and groundhogs have the run of the garden. Fencing is the best way to keep most of them out. The holes in the fencing should be small enough to keep young rabbits out—less than 2 inches in diameter—and buried at least a foot below ground level to prevent their burrowing under it. It takes a fence over 8 feet high to discourage deer, which are becoming ever more destructive in suburban areas because of the lack of natural (and human) predators. Some farmers and gardeners have turned to electrified fencing, which is beyond the scope of this book. Check with the agricultural extension agent in your area for recommendations. In suburban areas, local police forces sometimes include animal control officers who will assist with the removal of raccoons, opossums, deer, dogs, and other relatively large mammals.

Many insects are repelled by painting a mixture of one part lime, one part wood ashes, and five parts water to leaf surfaces. Repellents such as noisemakers, scarecrows, plastic snakes and owls, human hair, and similar devices are sometimes successful in keeping animals or birds away from gardens, but the effects wear off as the creatures get used to them. The garlic/soap/cayenne pepper spray is a good way to keep squirrels away from nut trees, sunflowers, and other goodies, but must be reapplied every few days or after each rain.

Inorganic Pesticides and Herbicides.

Sometimes natural remedies are not strong enough to eliminate severe garden problems, and you may have to turn to chemical remedies. Captan is a widely accepted all-purpose fungicide that can be used at home if necessary. The chemicals malathion and Sevin are both effective against a wide spectrum of insects. However, they harm bees and earthworms, which are beneficial to plants. If you use any of these chemicals, do so sparingly, follow package directions carefully, and store the packages out of reach of children.

ORGANIC CONTROLS OF GARDEN PESTS

PEST	CONTROL
Aphid	Diatomaceous earth, pyrethrum, soapy water, wood ashes, ladybugs, lacewing flies, hosing bugs off plants with water, garlic/cayenne/soap/water spray
Asparagus beetle	Rotenone
Bagworm	Handpicking and burning brown cocoons
Bean beetle	Handpicking bugs and eggs, rotenone, pyrethrum, insecticidal soap, praying mantis, ash/lime/water paint on leaves, diatomaceous earth
Cabbage looper Cabbage mother	Trichogramma wasps, *Bacillus thuringiensis* (Bt), handpicking bugs, rotenone, pyrethrum, diatomaceous earth, wiping leaves with soapy water
Carrot weevil	Rotenone, repelling with rosemary
Codling moth	Wettable sulfur, trichogramma wasps, coating tree base with ash/lime/water paint
Corn borer Corn earworm	Rotenone, trichogramma wasps, probing with wire, mineral oil on tassel, garlic/cayenne/soap/water spray
Cucumber beetle (striped, spotted)	Handpicking bugs and eggs, rotenone, repelling by planting with radishes and tansy or with ash/lime/water paint on leaves
Cutworm	Cutworm collars, *Bacillus thuringiensis*, rotenone, turning soil over so birds find and eat pests, spiked lawn sandals (see page 29)
Earwig	Trapping in hollow plant stems or paper tubes, then killing in soapy water or burning
Flea beetle	Rotenone, garlic/cayenne/soap/water spray, pyrethrum, ash/lime/water paint on leaves
Grasshopper	Tilling garden beds after harvest, garlic/cayenne/soap/water spray

See pages 130–31 for directions and explanations of remedies.
Table compiled from firsthand experience, research from Rodale Press *(Organic Gardening),* and other sources.

PEST	CONTROL
Japanese beetle	Milky spore disease, traps, rotenone
Leaf miner	Removing affected leaves with characteristic winding trails, eliminating host weeds
Maggot (cabbage)	Wood ashes, black plastic mulch
Nematode	Cultivating soil frequently to expose larvae to sunshine, adding compost—organisms in it attack nematodes, rotating crops
Potato beetle	Handpicking bugs and eggs, rotenone circling plants with wood ashes
Scale insects	Dormant oil or soapy water spray, dabbing with soapy water or alcohol
Slugs Snails	Trapping and drowning in shallow pans of beer, trapping under damp cardboard or cabbage leaves, then destroying them, repelling with lime, sand, and diatomaceous earth
Sowbugs	Repelling with wood ashes, trapping and destroying like slugs or earwigs
Squash borer	Rotenone, killing borer by stabbing it with a lengthwise (not crosswise) slit through stem, repelling with ashes, rock powders, tansy
Squash bug	Rotenone dust, handpicking bugs and egg cases, trapping bugs under boards, then destroying them
Webworm, tent caterpillar	Pruning out and burning infested branches, sticky traps and tree wraps, and soapy water sprays that tear through webs
Whitefly	Pyrethrum, rotenone, soap spray, oil spray
Wireworm	Trapping under damp cardboard and destroying

The highly toxic chemical Vapam® is widely used against nematodes living in the soil. These microscopic worms attack the roots of plants, and are a serious and widespread problem, particularly for southern gardeners. An organic alternative to this toxic treatment is to cultivate and solarize the soil as described on page 153.

Herbicides such as broadleaf weed killers are effective garden aids, but, unfortunately, they tend to drift into areas set aside for growing vegetables, herbs, fruits, and flowers, damaging them along with the weeds. If weed killer is used for lawns, do not compost or use the clippings for a month or so afterward, to keep from getting the chemicals on your garden. Remember that rain will wash herbicides into nearby garden beds, so use them sparingly or do without them. Weed killers eliminate some maintenance chores, but they contaminate groundwater, streams, and lakes in areas where runoff from treated areas reaches them or water percolates through soil easily. Rather than treating a large area with few weeds, use a spot applicator to kill individual persistent weeds.

WINTER PROTECTION

Safety measures will prepare your plants for colder winter weather, which reaches all parts of the United States, even up to Zone 10. Plants need protection from the cold and, sometimes, help in adjusting to the seasonal change.

NORTHERN REGIONS. In areas with freezing winters, deciduous plants lose their leaves and go into dormancy. Do not delay the protective dormant phase by fertilizing heavily just before cold weather comes. This will stimulate new growth that will not survive the winter. However, do not hesitate to water moderately if the autumn is dry. The combination of freezing and drying is very hard on plants.

The hardiest plants will need little or no attention, but plants that are of borderline hardiness in your zone may need to be sheltered behind snow fences or burlap wraps. Garden litter should be cleared away and either plowed in or composted. This will help eliminate insect pests that are using it to get through the winter.

In areas with clay or damp soils, prepare the garden beds in fall to facilitate cool-weather planting in early spring. Otherwise, the soil will be too wet to work in and may prohibit the spring planting of peas, poppies, and other early plants.

Mulch is used to protect the roots of perennial flowers and herbs during the weather changes of winter by insulating the ground and keeping it frozen hard. Attributes and recommended depths for different mulching materials are given in the table on pages 104–105. If unmulched, the action of soil alternately freezing and thawing as the weather changes will push roots and bulbs out of the ground, where they might die. If a part of your garden was not mulched, apply mulch for winter protection. After cold weather arrives, lay a mulch such as bark chips, straw, or small evergreen branches under each plant's crown of leaves, but tight against the plant. Beds of spring-blooming bulbs should be covered completely with a thick but loose layer of mulch. Evergreen boughs are good. Ideally, do this after the ground is frozen, to keep it that way until spring, but earlier applications are also helpful. In areas where snow falls early and remains on the ground all winter, the snow will serve the same purpose as a mulch and will offer additional insulation from very cold weather.

When the weather begins to warm in early spring, remove the mulch gradually, not all at once, in case the weather turns very cold again. If bulbs have emerged and are being stunted or yellowed by heavy mulch, be sure to get it out of the way in time for their new growth, which occurs months before T-shirt weather arrives.

SOUTHERN REGIONS. In areas where frost occurs rarely, it is always a shock to plants when it comes. Gardeners in the warmest zones can hardly help pushing their luck with plants that are too tropical for the region. For a really carefree landscape, native plants are best. They are already adapted to the weather and its occasional spells of frost.

To give tender plants such as orange trees and tropicals the help they need, do not fertilize them just before cold weather because it will delay the plants' natural semidormancy and encourage vulnerable new growth. Temporary wind shelters help keep cold air from blowing onto plants. Blankets, sheets, layers of cloth, large cardboard boxes, plastic bubble cloth, and inverted trash cans can cover shrubs overnight for severe cold snaps, but will be effective only if the ground itself is covered. In Florida, it is not surprising to see a treasured plant wrapped and tied snugly inside in a quilt for protection in a freeze. Potted plants may be hauled indoors. Screened areas may be given a protective layer of plastic for makeshift greenhouse protection of plants within. Plant leaves should not touch the plastic or they may be damaged by the cold.

Many tropical plants such as mangoes will regrow from the roots if the top of the plant is killed. For this reason, mulch will help protect the underground parts of the plant even when nothing can be done to save the top.

Appropriate planting will save much labor by eliminating the need for drastic measures during cold spells. Alternatively, tropical plants may be grown in subtropical areas by taking cuttings each fall, rooting them indoors, and setting them out each spring—a clever way to avoid the perils of winter.

THE GARDENING YEAR

B asic gardening chores are very much the same in all parts of the country. However, their timing is an important element of successful gardening. Different kinds of plants have their own preferences for the time of year to be sown, divided, or pruned. For instance, in New York, spring planting of lettuce is an April chore. In southern Florida, lettuce for early spring can be sown in the mild weather of November. Some annuals prefer cool weather, others like warmer temperatures. Hardy plants develop in response to the weather. An azalea cultivar that blooms in May in Pennsylvania might bloom in March in Georgia. Except in timing, the care of azaleas is similar in the two states, and elsewhere.

Not only does temperature vary by region, so does the amount of sunlight per day. The farther north you are, the more change there is. On a given date, a northern garden is darker in winter and brighter in summer than a southern one. In the North, more light is added each day as the season progresses toward spring and summer. By June, daylight lasts several hours longer in Boston than it does in Miami. Some plants are especially sensitive to day length and grow amazingly quickly during the North's long summer days.

This chapter is done as a calender to guide you through the gardening year in different regions of the United States. It is roughly divided into four climate zones: *Northern* (United States Department of Agriculture [USDA] Zones 2 to 5), *Central* (USDA Zones 6 to 8), *Hot Southern* (USDA Zones 9 to 11), and *Mild West Coast* (USDA Zones 9 to 11 in areas with cooler summers).

There are additional notations for specific areas. Factors such as temperature, rainfall, soil type, altitude, exposure, and unusual weather patterns affect what each gardener should do when. Some types of plants are more forgiving than others and will succeed under a broader range of conditions. Even in the same location, weather conditions vary from year to year.

These guidelines should be useful as you plan your garden calendar, but are no substitute for your own observation of local conditions. Keep a garden diary of what you do when, and the results. Record plant heights and duration of bloom of different cultivars and species for future planning. Mark the date of your first and last frosts and signs of the passing seasons, such as the date of the first forsythia blooms, the leafing out of maple trees, or the arrival of orange blossoms. With experience, these will become cues for seasonal garden chores.

Local agricultural extension offices offer expertise in the timing of garden practices for your county or area. They can also tell you which USDA zone you are in and how many frost-free days to expect in an average year.

Gardening Calendar for Northern U.S. Regions (Zones 2 to 5)

JANUARY. Map and plan your garden. Before making your seed order, you might want to go through old seed packets and test the seeds to see if they are still viable (alive and able to grow). Wrap a few of the seeds in a moist paper towel, label, and keep at room temperature inside a plastic bag. Most kinds of seeds should sprout in under a week; the seedlings either may be transplanted to indoor pots or discarded if it is too early for this variety to be started indoors. Discard packets of seeds too old to germinate. Send orders for new seeds now, for best selection.

Fertilize indoor plants lightly every two weeks. Spray houseplants with water several times a week or use a humidifier to counteract dry indoor air.

Outdoors, shovel snow over perennials and berry plants to prevent their freezing and thawing. Order fruit and nut trees that should arrive while still dormant. If you planned ahead, you prepared their planting holes last fall. Save wood ashes in waterproof containers to use on the garden later. Spray fruit and hemlock trees with dormant oil if the temperature is predicted to rise above 40°F for several days, for control of scale and other insects. Provide food and water for birds, which also feed on overwintering pests.

Cut long stems of pussy willow, witch hazel, flowering quince, or forsythia and soak them in a tub overnight. Then arrange them in vases of water and watch them open in the indoor light and warmth. If they root while in the water, they may be kept there after bloom and planted outdoors in April or May.

FEBRUARY. Order ornamental trees, shrubs, and perennials by mail, plus fruit and nut trees if you did not get to it in January. Tap maple trees for syrup. Repot and fertilize houseplants. Complete repairs and maintenance of garden equipment. If you were not able to spray fruit and hemlock trees in January, do it now, weather permitting.

MARCH. Prune fruit trees and berries. Spray fruit and trees with dormant oil spray if the temperature will be above 40°F for several days—and hemlocks, too, if they have not already been sprayed more than once.

Indoors, start caladium bulbs and begonia tubers. Start seeds of slower-growing warm-weather vegetables and flowers such as peppers, celery, eggplants, dahlias, nicotiana, impatiens, ageratum, scarlet sage, and petunias. Plant seeds of perennial flowers and herbs. Move these plants to a frost-free cold frame or greenhouse as soon as they have germinated, or grow them in the house in bright lighting a few inches below fluorescent fixtures.

In the middle of the month, sow seeds indoors for early starts of cool-weather vegetables and flowers: lettuce, onion, alyssum, stock, annual baby's-breath, calendula, bachelor's button, sweet pea, delphinium and everlastings like acroclinium, strawflower, statice, and ornamental annual grasses. All do well during cool weather and may be set out by the middle of May if they have been hardened off (see page 71). Start tomatoes indoors the last week of March to the first week of April. Move all of these plants to a frost-free cold frame or greenhouse as soon as they have germinated, if possible, or to bright lighting a few inches below fluorescent fixtures. Loosen mulches over spring bulbs, uncovering their growing tips but leaving 2 or 3 inches around the plants. Check perennials and tuck mulch around but not over the crowns. If any start to come out of the soil, tuck them back in.

At the end of the month, turn cover crops under if the snow has melted and the ground is workable (in many colder areas of these zones, this may not occur until May). Till compost or rotted manure into vegetable gardens. Sprinkle ground potash rock on beds for extra potassium. Weed and spread rotted manure or compost around the base of fruit trees, berries, and perennial flowers.

APRIL. Transplant tomato, eggplant, and pepper seedlings to 6-inch pots. If you are growing them in a cold frame, open it on warm days to allow them to adjust to full sunlight. As soon as the soil can be worked, plant peas, radishes, parsnips, parsley, dill, sorrel, early beets, chard, and early carrots, covering with row covers for faster harvests. Plant or prune grapevines and rosebushes. Thin and divide older strawberry beds or plant new beds. Plant shade and fruit trees, berries, vines, and perennial herbs. Bed out (set out) pansies, violas, calendula, and alyssum. Acquire new perennial flowers and ornamental grasses early, while selection is at its best. Divide perennials such as shasta daisies, daylilies, coreopsis, and chrysanthemums when their new growth begins to appear. Make new beds of ground cover with ivy myrtle (periwinkle) or pachysandra thinnings and trimmings; they take root quickly as spring arrives. Make new beds for flowers and vegetables, or refresh and shape old ones. This is a good time to make drywall edgings for raised beds by piling up rocks pulled from soil you are tilling. They will be in place before plants start to grow over them.

From the middle to the end of April, start cole crops such as broccoli, cauliflower, cabbage, and Brussels sprouts indoors for transplanting to the garden in May. As soon as they have germinated, move them to a frost-free cold frame or greenhouse. Sow seed of cold-tolerant flowers such as wildflower mixtures, shasta daisies, dianthus, larkspur, columbine, Shirley poppies, stock, alyssum, sweet peas, and baby's-breath directly into the beds. Give them protection under floating row covers or other shelter in colder regions until the weather improves. Try growing rhubarb (a perennial) from seed; it's not hard and some kinds bear the first year they are planted. Dig up and divide horseradish roots—plant the top 4 or 5 inches of the root. Clean and grate the rest, mix it with vinegar, and refrigerate it in jars.

MAY. In colder areas, continue direct outdoor plantings as mentioned for April except spinach (it will bolt if planted now—wait until July to replant for a fall crop). Harden off cole crops so that they can be transplanted to the garden after the middle of the month. Early in the month, plant seed of fast-growing summer annuals such as cosmos, morning glories, balsam, marigolds, and dwarf zinnias indoors and move to a frost-free cold frame or greenhouse as soon as they have germinated. Early May is a good time to tend the lawn.

Aerate it with nail-spiked lawn sandals, which also stab and kill underground grubs, then apply fertilizer and grass seed. For instant lawn, especially on a slope, purchase and roll out grass sod after tilling the top few inches and fertilizing the ground lightly.

From the second to third week of May, start zucchini, cucumbers, squashes, and pumpkins indoors for transplanting to the garden in June. Transplant cole crops to the garden and harden off all other indoor-grown seedlings. This is a good time to start biennials such as sweet William and Iceland poppy from seed. Pinch back chrysanthemums to promote bushiness. There's still time to sow seed of late crops of cole, beets, chard, carrots, bolt-resistant lettuce, and peas outdoors. Plant potatoes and sweet corn in the last half of May. Beans need warm soils and so should not be planted until the very last week of May at the earliest.

Control pests such as slugs, which become especially active during cool, moist spring days. Spray fruit trees for codling moth, plum curculio, and apple maggot at intervals through spring and summer. Sticky traps such as Tanglefoot will control apple maggots. Check Chapter 5 for more on pest control.

JUNE. This month usually brings balmy weather, ideal for most gardening activities. Set out large well-rooted tomato and pepper plants for earliest fruits. Keep plants well watered and fertilized—northerners must get the most out of every frost-free day. In northernmost areas, frost can occur unexpectedly on clear nights, so be prepared to cover frost-sensitive plants with cloth or other insulation when warnings are forecast.

Outdoors, continue to plant seeds of fast-growing plants such as marigolds, nasturtiums, zucchini, and beans. Continue to set out warm-weather bedding plants, both flowers and vegetables, and to move plants from the cold frame to the garden. Impatiens is easy and will grow in sun or shade. Dianthus is fairly reliable but needs full sun. Put summer vegetables in the sunniest places. In colder areas, mulch tomatoes, squashes, and peppers with black plastic to collect solar heat. For even more solar heat, use floating row covers in addition to the black mulch.

Prune azaleas after bloom is finished. Thin fruit on apple, pear, and peach trees, if necessary. If too many flowers on a branch set fruit, it will cause fruit size to decrease. Weed and stake garden plants as needed—both weeds and garden plants grow very fast at this time of year. Houseplants may be brought outdoors to spend the summer in light shade.

JULY. Cut flowers and grasses for drying and hang in bunches indoors. Harvest herbs and dry them just before they flower. Prune climbing roses after they bloom. Cut out dead wood and thin twiggy canes. Do not cut new main shoots from the ground, but train them as they grow. For garden ideas, visit botanical or display gardens while they are at their peak.

Water and mulch gardens to keep them growing steadily. Continue to stake and support plants as they grow, especially lilies, gladioli, dahlias, and climbers. Early in the month, pinch back chrysanthemums one last time. Prowl for harmful insects and eggs, and destroy those you find (see Chapter 5). Trap Japanese beetles as they emerge from their underground larval stage. Trap and drown slugs in pans of beer. Recycled cottage cheese containers, set into holes in the garden, are just the right size.

This is the last chance for short-season gardeners to plant fast-growing summer vegetables such as zucchini and beans. Outdoors, continue to plant seeds of biennials such as pansies, hollyhocks, sweet Williams, and foxgloves for bloom next year. Seeds of perennial flowers may be sown outdoors, too. After bloom is finished, dig up and divide irises, lilies of the valley, bleeding hearts, daylilies, and Oriental poppies if they are overcrowded. Replant them in beds enriched with compost and bonemeal. Collect seeds of columbine (especially the native *Aquilegia canadensis*) and strew them in semishaded areas to naturalize them. Plant seeds for fall vegetables and flowers like cabbage, kale, lettuce, and calendulas indoors toward the end of the month.

Evergreens and hedge plants may be pruned. Look for holes of borers in young fruit trees and berry canes. Destroy them in trees by finding the holes and sticking in a wire to kill the pests. Cut off and burn infested canes. Begin to make hardwood cuttings from flowering trees and shrubs.

AUGUST. Enjoy your own garden and visit others. Freeze, can, or make preserves with the wonderful summer produce. Continue to harvest flowers and pods for dried bouquets. Pick and dry herbs. Harvest zucchini and other summer squashes while small and tender. Check your plants often. They say that if you leave your car unlocked in Maine, someone will come along and fill it with giant zucchini.

If the first frost is not expected until the middle of September, there is still time to sow late outdoor crops of lettuce, kale, spinach, Chinese cabbage, and turnips. Harvest onions if the tops are starting to topple over. Dry them in a single layer in the sun for several days before storing them in a cool place. They keep best when maintained at close to 32°F.

Fertilize late-summer and fall flowers, especially chrysanthemums. Keep the garden watered well through hot, dry weather. Make especially sure fruit and nut trees have enough water, or they may drop part of the crop. Reseed bare spots in the lawn. Order spring-flowering bulbs. Bring in all houseplants before cold weather returns.

Plant seeds of perennials and biennials indoors or out, and move them to a cold frame in a few weeks when weather gets cooler. Divide perennials that grow offshoots this time of year—for example, ajuga and some types of campanula. Let your strawberry runners grow where they are wanted, but remove them from other spots before they become too invasive. Cut back raspberry canes that bore fruit this year (except fall-bearing types) to get strong new offshoots for next year's crop.

SEPTEMBER. Clear garden debris and weeds. Chop the litter into small pieces with a rotary lawn mower or a chipper/shredder before composting them. Plant cover crops in cleared garden beds. Refurbish flower beds with bedding plants of ornamental kale, pansy, chrysanthemum, and Nippon daisy for frostproof fall color. Neaten groundcover beds and enlarge them or start new ones with offshoots and cuttings. Clear beds for fall planting of spring-flowering bulbs. Complete pruning of all shrubs and vines. In coldest areas, plant bulbs for spring bloom before the month ends. Where frost is not expected until October or later, you have another month or so for planting bulbs. Harvest apples and pears for indoor storage before they are fully ripe so they will stay fresh in storage longer. Store them in the refrigerator or in a cool (50°F) basement on shelves. For eating out of hand, let them ripen on the trees.

Fall vegetables may still be planted in cold frames, but it is too late for most types to grow out of doors. However, you might be able to get a late planting of turnips through the winter under snow for an early crop next spring. Fresh turnips taste far better than most people imagine. Harvest all remaining squashes, onions, tomatoes, peppers, potatoes, and beans before the first freeze. Tomatoes and peppers will continue to ripen indoors. Gather pods and grasses to dry for bouquets. Pick remaining basil and frost-sensitive herbs. Take cuttings of impatiens, ivy, nasturtiums, and begonias, and root them in water or damp soil for potting up indoors in sunny areas. Continue to seed bare lawn with grass seed or transplant sod. Dig and enrich new beds or enlarge old ones for the following year. Roughly turned soil will weather for easy tilling next spring. Make planting holes for shrubs to be planted early next spring. Divide peonies. Lift bulbs and corms of dahlia, *Anemone coronaria,* gladiolus, begonia, canna, caladium, and other tender bulbs. Cure them in the sun for a day or two before storing them—longer for gladiolus. A cool basement makes a good storage site for cold-tolerant dahlia, gladiolus, and anemone tubers and corms, if they are dusted with fungicide and wrapped in slightly damp vermiculite or sphagnum moss inside plastic bags (see pages 114–16). Old houses sometimes have root cellars that are ideal for overwintering summer bulb flowers.

Save most planting of trees (especially hollies), shrubs, and perennials for next spring—why not let the growers have the risk of winter kill? Exceptions are peonies, evergreens, and rugged shrubs such as privet, which get a healthier start if planted in the fall.

Cover chrysanthemums, pansies, and fall vegetables if a hard frost (under 28°F) is expected. Put cloths on nightly and remove them during the day, or leave bubbled plastic insulation or spun-bonded floating row covers in place day and night. Gather black walnuts before the squirrels find them all. Let them sit in a shed or garage to cure for a few weeks, then remove the husks, watching out for stains that will not wash off skin or clothing easily. Shell the nuts and use right away or freeze.

Try propagating roses from cuttings the way our grandmothers did. Take stem cuttings about 10 inches long. Bury each one 5 inches deep in garden soil, labeled, and cover it with a one-quart glass mayonnaise jar. By April, some (but probably not all) will have rooted successfully. This works best with climbing or rugosa roses that grow on their own roots, not grafted to a rootstock.

OCTOBER. Pick the last fall crop of spinach, lettuce, cabbage, and other garden vegetables. Dig up and pot some parsley and chives for the windowsill. Clear debris such as weeds and plant stems. Shred or compost fallen leaves and debris for garden enrichment, and dig it into the garden. Chipped garden debris also makes good mulch. Be sure to mulch under the leaves of perennial flowers. Do not smother them. Mulch beds of bulbs after watering them well.

Harvest any remaining apples and pears, and Oriental persimmons. Let native persimmons freeze once before picking them—this improves their flavor. Crab apples are sour but edible and can be used to make delicious jam. Cut and condition chrysanthemums by soaking them overnight in a bucket or tall container of cool water mixed with a spoonful of bleach, up to the flower heads. Change the water and then, in the same container, refrigerate them or keep them in a cool, dark place. They will stay fresh for up to several weeks, giving you a source for bouquets after the outdoor flowers are gone.

Leaves, manure, and rough compost may be dug into the soil this fall for breakdown by spring. Complete the garden cleanup and eliminate ways for pests to get through the winter. Store garden produce in a root cellar, refrigerator, or cool area. Winter squashes and potatoes may be stored at about 55°F. Cole (cabbage family) crops keep better at close to 32°F. Complete your notes for your garden diary before the triumphs and disasters of the season are forgotten. Send away for seed and plant catalogs for happy winter browsing ahead—they are a wealth of information, and many are free for the asking. The companies advertise them in garden magazines.

Outdoors, privet, lilac, evergreens, leucothoe, and other hardy shrubs may be planted or transplanted wherever soil is workable. Water and mulch them thoroughly. Finish planting spring flowering bulbs, watering and mulching before you leave them to nature's care for the winter. Finish planting spring bulbs by the first of the month. Cover newly planted tulips and daffodils with 4 to 6 inches of mulch.

If you plan to have a live Christmas tree, dig a planting hole for it now, before the soil freezes. Do the same for fruit trees, canes, shrubs, and vines that will be planted at the end of winter. Deeply cover or mulch the soil that will go back in the holes to try to keep it from freezing solid.

Bring in any remaining stakes, trellises, and tomato cages for indoor storage over winter. Shut off outdoor faucets so the pipes will not freeze during the winter. If hoses are not yet indoors, bring them in now and store them in a frost-free area. Bring all clay pots indoors. Those filled with soil and plants might freeze and crack outdoors.

Tie perennial vines to supports in order to prevent them from being whipped around and damaged by winter wind. Make a thorough check of lawn and garden beds. Grass will die if smothered under a thick layer of leaves. Clean and sweep the lawn, and make sure perennial plants are surrounded by mulch, but not smothered under it.

NOVEMBER. Let everyone know which garden books you would like to receive for the holidays. Make wreaths and bouquets with the dried leaves, flowers, and pods you saved in the summer and fall. Check perennials and shrubs to be sure they are mulched and ready for the next growing season.

DECEMBER. Very little outdoor work remains. Remember that snow is one of the best insulators for biennial and perennial plants trying to survive the winter, so shovel it onto flower beds and strawberry patches for a thick permanent cover. If there is no snow, a light covering of salt hay over other mulch will protect the crowns from cold, dry wind without smothering them.

Use December leisure time for garden reading and research. As you study by the fireplace, save your wood ashes in a sealed container for use on the spring garden. Learn as much as possible about plants for your area. Review your notes and then investigate plant species that you found most successful: If your shady yard was right for hostas (shade-tolerant, leafy perennials), for instance, you could acquire special cultivars in differing colors, textures, and sizes. You can be sure that they are not a risky investment because of last year's results.

December is a good time to get supplies ready for indoor planting. Order pots and soil or growing media. If you plan to spray, get your sprayer and dormant oil ready now. When perfect spraying weather comes along in February or March, you will not have to waste time going to the store. Clean recycled pots and six-packs in a dishpanful of sudsy water that includes a cup of chlorine bleach for antiseptic action. Clean window boxes and planters, and repaint those that need it. Check indoor plant lights and replace bulbs in fluorescent fixtures if necessary. They go dim long before they blow out.

Indoors, plant amaryllis, calla, Madonna lily, and paperwhite narcissus bulbs, and lily of the valley pips. If ordering them by mail, be sure that they will be handled properly, not left on a doorstep to freeze. Mist houseplants frequently to counteract the dryness of heated indoor air. In cool but bright indoor conditions (about 50°F), petunia seed may be planted this month, along with other slow starters such as salpiglossis, lisianthus, cactus, and hardy succulents. They may also be grown in warmer conditions (above 65°F), along with seeds of browallia, begonias, tropical plants, and 'Patio' or other tomatoes for indoor pots.

Outdoors in a cold frame, seeds of many rock garden, native, or herbaceous perennial plants can be planted to freeze and thaw, then germinate in early spring. Pots of bulbs in the cold frame may be brought indoors as they begin to sprout. Do not water heavily until growth is several inches tall, or plants may rot.

GARDENING CALENDAR FOR CENTRAL U.S. REGIONS (ZONES 6 TO 8)

Though the garden plants and methods here are similar to those in northern regions of the country, the growing season is much longer, allowing you more flexibility in timing garden activities. There is more time for succession planting, too, so soil enrichment is especially important here in gardens where one crop follows another immediately. Because the climate is warmer, but still has a well-defined winter season, more kinds of plants may be grown than in areas that are either colder or warmer.

JANUARY. Fertilize indoor plants lightly every two weeks. Map and plan your garden. Before you make your seed order, you might want to go through seed packets left over from previous years and test the seeds to see if they are still viable (alive and able to grow). Wrap a few seeds from a packet in a moist paper towel, label, and keep at room temperature inside a plastic bag. Most kinds of seeds normally sprout in under a week. If they should but do not, discard the packet and replace it when you make your order. Sprouts may be transplanted to pots or discarded if it is too early to start this type indoors. Send in your seed orders now, for best selection. Get the cold frame ready for February planting.

Spray fruit and hemlock trees for scale and other insects with dormant oil if temperatures are expected to stay above 40°F for several days. Prune grapes if wood is not frozen.

Provide food and water for birds, which also eat overwintering pests. Spread rotted manure on asparagus and peony beds if you did not do so last fall, but do not manure beds of spring bulbs—it is too strong for them. Order fruit and nut trees. Save ashes in sealed containers for use on the garden in spring and summer.

Water new outdoor plantings if they are dry. Check mulches and refresh them if they have been disturbed by wind or rain. Check bulbs and corms being stored indoors, discarding any that are rotten.

Cut 2- or 3-foot-long stems of pussy willow, witch hazel, grapevine, flowering quince, or forsythia and soak them in a tub overnight. Then arrange them in vases of water and watch them open in the indoor light and warmth. If they root while in the water, they may be kept and planted outdoors in April.

FEBRUARY. Loosen mulch over spring bulbs, uncovering their growing tips but leaving 2 or 3 inches around the plants. Check perennials and tuck mulch around but not over crowns. If any plants start to come out of the soil, tuck them back in. Plant and prune grapevines early in the month, but not while they are frozen.

Turn cover crops under as soon as the ground is workable. Dig in compost and sprinkle ground potash rock on beds for extra potassium. Have soil samples tested before the spring rush.

Indoors in a cool room or outdoors under a cold frame, start seeds of cold-hardy flowers, herbs, and vegetables such as alyssum, cornflowers, stock, calendulas, coreopsis, baby's-breath, delphinium, sweet peas, celery, parsley, chives, dill, lettuce, onions, cabbage, and broccoli. Slower-growing heat lovers such as dahlias, eggplants, peppers, and tomatoes can be planted indoors, too. If there is not enough room, start them in March after the cold-hardy types go outside. Also indoors or under cold frames, grow seedlings for everlastings such as acroclinium, strawflowers, statice, and ornamental grasses. All do well during cool weather and may be planted outside a few weeks before the last expected frost. Indoors, start caladium bulbs and begonia tubers.

Prune apple and pear trees. Spray fruit trees again with dormant oil spray if the temperature is expected to be above 40°F for several days, especially if you were not able to last month. Order ornamental trees, shrubs, and perennials by mail.

MARCH. Complete the pruning of all fruit trees early in the month. Weed and fertilize them. Continue planting and spraying them. Prune tea roses but not climbers. Fertilize trees, shrubs, perennials, and roses. Plant bare-rooted nursery stock in March or April.

Indoors or in the cold frame, plant seeds of summer plants such as tomatoes, cosmos, dahlias, and scarlet sage. Plant seed of perennial flowers and herbs. Pot up some or all of the stored bulbs, corms, and tubers of summer flowers such as dahlias, tuberous begonias, and canna lilies, to grow indoors until you transplant them outside when the danger of frost has passed.

Step up seedlings planted earlier to larger pots if necessary. It is not too late to start seeds of lettuce, broccoli, and other cool-weather vegetables. Wait a while longer before sprouting squashes, marigolds, and other large or fast-growing types that must have heat so they will not be pot-bound or overcrowded. Repot and fertilize houseplants. Complete repairs and maintenance of garden equipment.

Continue to remove mulch from over early spring flowers such as snowdrops, narcissi, crocus, and primroses, so their growth will not be blocked. Bed out calendulas, pansies, and violas among them. Divide perennials such as shasta daisies, daylilies, coreopsis, ornamental grasses, and chrysanthemums when their new growth begins to appear. Make new beds of ground cover with ivy, myrtle (periwinkle), or pachysandra thinnings and trimmings. They take root quickly as spring arrives. Make new beds for flowers and vegetables, or refresh, shape, and edge old ones. Sow cold-tolerant flowers such as larkspur, columbine, Shirley poppies, stock, sweet peas, and baby's-breath directly in the beds.

Fertilize and till vegetable gardens. Sow the seeds of peas, lettuce, spinach, onions (from seed or sets), celery, parsley, dill, beets, and cabbage family plants directly into outdoor beds. Fresh chives are easily grown from seed and are perennial. Shape herb gardens and transplant or divide perennial herbs when new growth begins.

For indoor bloom, stems of flowering quince and dogwood may be forced in vases.

APRIL. Early in the month, set out bedding-size plants of calendula, stock, alyssum, pansies, and violas. Add snapdragons later in the month. These will not be harmed by light frost and are good bedding or windowbox plants. Continue direct outdoor planting as mentioned for March. Stake or trellis peas and sweet peas. Balsam, nasturtium, dianthus, cleome, rudbeckia, and many other flowers may be sown. It is interesting to sow mixtures of meadow flower, wildflower, or cutting flower seed as a test for flowers naturally suited to your garden conditions.

As early in the month as possible, finish planting lettuce, onions, carrots, parsnips, parsley, sorrel, dill, peas, beets, rhubarb, and other cool-weather vegetables and herbs.

It is not hard to grow rhubarb (a perennial) from seed. Some kinds bear the first year they are planted. Dig up and divide horseradish roots—plant the top 4 or 5 inches of the root. Clean and grate the rest, mix it with vinegar, and refrigerate it in jars.

Thin and divide strawberry plants and perennial herbs. Finish dividing and fertilizing perennials. Divide and transplant ferns before new growth gets too large.

Try layering clematis for new plants. Find stems that can be bent down to the ground, score them slightly, and cover the scored part with earth without separating it from the parent plant. Roots and shoots will follow before summer arrives. When they are sturdy, cut the new plant free and transplant it to its permanent position (see pages 121–24 for more about layering).

Indoors, transplant tomato seedlings to larger pots. Plant marigold, zinnia, and aster seed outdoors. Plant scarlet runner beans indoors or out after, soaking the seeds in water overnight. The climbing vines have red flowers that attract hummingbirds, and the plants bear edible green beans whose dark red seeds, when ripe, may be dried and stored for winter.

Harden off indoor-grown hardy seedlings gradually and transplant them to the garden. Frost-sensitive plants still need shelter indoors or in a cold frame. Step them up to larger pots as needed.

Early April is time to tend the lawn. Aerate it with nail-spiked lawn sandals, which also stab and kill underground grubs, then apply fertilizer and grass seed. For instant lawn, especially on a slope, purchase and roll out grass sod after tilling the top few inches and fertilizing the ground lightly.

Start zucchini, cucumbers, squashes, and pumpkins indoors in mid-April or late April. Be sure to plant them outside before they are pot-bound, but after the frost-free date. By late April, plant morning glories outdoors or give them a quick, fast start indoors. They grow quickly.

Control pests such as slugs, which become especially active during cool, moist spring days. Spray fruit trees for codling moth, plum curculio, and apple maggot at intervals through spring and summer. Sticky traps such as Tanglefoot will control apple maggots. Check Chapter 5 for more on pest control.

MAY. After the frost-free date, set out petunias, zinnias, dahlias, gladioli, ageratum, marigolds, and many other summer garden flowers. Impatiens are easy and will grow in sun or shade. Fast-growing zinnias and marigolds may be grown from seed sown now. Thin seedlings and pinch back those that need early shaping. Pinch chrysanthemums to promote bushiness. Harvest everlasting flowers of acroclinium and hang them upside down in bunches to dry.

The middle of the month usually brings balmy weather, ideal for most gardening activities. Set out large, well-rooted tomato plants for earliest fruits. Keep plants well watered and fertilized. In northernmost areas, frost can still occur. Cover frost-sensitive plants with sheets or floating row covers when warnings are forecast.

Outdoors, plant seeds of fast-growing summer plants such as basil, zucchini, and beans. Continue to sow or set out warm-weather plants. Plant summer vegetables such as corn in the sunniest places. Summer lettuce will stand more heat if it is grown in partial shade. Mulch heat-loving tomatoes, okra, squashes, and peppers with black plastic, which collects solar heat but keeps roots moist.

Prune azaleas after they bloom. Weed and stake garden plants as needed. Grow-through hoops or rings are good for peonies and other clump-forming flowers. Houseplants may be brought outdoors to spend the summer in light shade.

JUNE. Container-grown nursery stock, even fruit trees, may still be planted, though it is too late for bare-rooted plants. Look for holes of borers in young fruit trees and berry canes. Destroy them in trees by stabbing the pests with a wire stuck in their holes. Cut off and burn infested canes. Thin fruit on apple, pear, and peach trees if necessary, for larger fruit size. If too many flowers on a branch set fruit, it will cause fruit size to decrease.

Continue to plant warm-weather flowers, vegetables, and herbs. Basil and tomatoes seem to grow well together—maybe each repels the pests that go after the other. Plant seeds of sweet William and other biennials for bloom next year. Finish moving plants from the cold frame to the garden. After it is empty, it can be shaded and used to root cuttings during the summer.

Finish pruning ornamental trees, shrubs, and hedges. Follow up hedge pruning with a light shearing whenever edges look ragged with new growth, but do not shave off all the new growth. Prune dead wood, stray twigs, and unwanted branches from climbing roses after they bloom. Do not cut down older canes if they are healthy and well placed. Train new growth upward and outward.

Keep the garden well cultivated or mulched because weeds are growing at a feverish pace. So are your garden plants. Stake lilies, dahlias, tall annuals, and tall perennials. Climbing beans, flowering vines, tomatoes, cucumbers, and squashes should be trellised, caged, or staked before they get too large, and trained as they grow. Pinch tall annual flowers and chrysanthemums for shape. Deadhead flowers.

If temperatures are above 85°F by the end of the month, put a layer of grass clippings or straw on top of black plastic mulch to moderate the heat buildup. Check squash vines for borers and destroy any you find with a knife or wire. Keep after insect and animal pests (see Chapter 5).

JULY. Cut flowers and grasses, and hang in bunches indoors to dry. Harvest herbs and dry them before they bloom. For garden ideas, visit botanical or display gardens while they are at their peak.

Water and mulch gardens to keep them growing steadily. Continue to stake and support plants as they grow, especially lilies, gladioli, dahlias, and climbers. Pinch back chrysanthemums one last time before letting the flower buds develop. Fertilize shrubs, trees, and berries one last time—later fertilization promotes new growth that will not harden off in time for winter.

Prowl for harmful insects and eggs, and destroy those you find. Trap Japanese beetles as they emerge. If beetles are a major and unavoidable problem, disbud (cut flower buds off) your roses for two or three weeks. Your roses will come back strong with new flowers after the beetles have gone on their way. Trap and drown slugs in pans of beer. Recycled cottage cheese containers, set into holes in the garden, are just the right size. Check Chapter 5 and your local agricultural extension agent for other pest controls.

Plant fast-growing summer vegetables such as zucchini and beans in spots that open up in the garden when early crops are finished. Choose short-season varieties. Turn and fertilize the soil before planting the next crop.

After bloom is finished, dig and divide irises, lilies of the valley, bleeding hearts, day-lilies, and Oriental poppies if they are overcrowded. Replant them in beds enriched with compost and bonemeal. Collect seeds of columbine (especially the native *Aquilegia canadensis*) and strew them in semishaded areas to naturalize them.

AUGUST. Enjoy your own garden and visit others. Freeze, can, or make preserves with bountiful garden produce. Continue to harvest flowers and pods for dried bouquets. Pick and dry herbs. Harvest summer squashes and cucumbers often, while they are small and tender. For sustained productivity, keep your tomato plants well watered and fertilized throughout August.

There is still time for sowing late outdoor crops of bush beans, lettuce, kale, spinach, Chinese cabbage, and turnips. Harvest onions if the tops are starting to topple over. Dry them for several days before storing them. They keep best when maintained at close to 32°F.

Fertilize late-summer and fall flowers, especially chrysanthemums. Continue to deadhead annuals and perennials. Keep flowers, lawns, and rosebushes watered well through hot, dry weather. Make sure fruit and nut trees have enough water, or they may drop part of the crop. Prune small suckers, or water sprouts, from fruit trees.

Order spring-flowering bulbs. Plant seeds of biennials and perennials indoors, and move them to a cold frame when the weather is cooler, or grow them outdoors. Dig up and divide perennials that grow offshoots this time of year, like oenothera, ajuga, and campanula. Let plantlets from strawberry runners grow where they are wanted, but remove them from other spots before they become too invasive. Cut back raspberry canes that bore fruit this year (except fall-bearing types) to encourage strong new growth for next year's crop. Remove fallen fruit and mulch from around fruit trees—this will also remove insect pests.

SEPTEMBER. Bring in all houseplants before cold weather arrives, after checking them for pests. Harvest herbs for drying and storing indoors. Harvest apples and pears for indoor storage before they are fully ripe. They will stay fresh longer. Store them in the refrigerator or in a cool (50°F) basement on shelves. For eating out of hand, let them ripen on the trees.

Outdoors, plant seeds for hardy fall vegetables such as cabbage, kale, turnips, and lettuce. Seeds of perennial flowers may be sown outdoors, too. They germinate better after the August heat lessens. Seedlings started late will grow better if given protection under floating row covers during cold spells.

Get rid of lawn weeds and reseed or sod bare spots in the lawn before the autumn leaves fall. This is a good time of year to repair an old lawn or start a new one (see pages 632–34). Trim beds of ground cover and enlarge them if necessary with cuttings and divisions of ivy, ajuga, pachysandra, myrtle, and lamium. Plant evergreens and hardy shrubs. Clear beds for fall planting of spring-flowering bulbs.

OCTOBER. Refurbish flower beds with bedding plants of ornamental cabbage and kale, pansies, chrysanthemums, and Nippon daisies for frostproof fall color. Complete pruning of all shrubs and vines. In colder areas, plant spring bulbs such as crocus, tulip, grape hyacinth, and narcissus before the month ends. Where hard frost is not expected until November or later, you have another month or so for planting bulbs. This is also a good time of year to plant true lilies, which establish themselves in the winter and bloom in late spring or summer.

Hardy fall vegetables may still be planted in cold frames, but not in open beds except at the southernmost edge of this region. Harvest all remaining squashes, onions, potatoes, and beans before the first freeze. Store garden produce in a root cellar, refrigerator, or cool area. Winter squashes and potatoes may be stored at about 55°F. Cole (cabbage family) crops keep better at close to 32°F. Take cuttings of impatiens, ivy, nasturtiums, and begonias, and root them in water or damp soil for potting up indoors in sunny areas.

Prepare new garden beds or enlarge old ones for the following year. Roughly turned soil that has been enriched with compost, leaves, and manure will weather for easy tilling next spring. Sow cover crops to build up soil. Divide peonies if they are overgrown.

Lift (dig up) bulbs and corms of dahlias, *Anemone coronaria,* gladioli, begonias, cannas, caladiums, and other tender bulbs. Those of you with a spare refrigerator will find that it makes a good storage site for them if they are dusted with fungicide and wrapped in slightly damp vermiculite inside plastic bags. Root cellars are also ideal for overwintering summer bulb flowers.

Shred or compost fallen leaves for garden enrichment. Chipped garden debris makes good mulch. Be sure to mulch around but under the leaves of perennial flowers and herbs. Mulch beds of bulbs after watering them well.

NOVEMBER. Let everyone know which garden books you would like to receive for the holidays. Make wreaths and bouquets with the dried leaves, flowers, and pods you saved. Check perennials and shrubs to be sure they are mulched and ready for the next growing season.

Indoors, pot up amaryllis and paperwhite narcissus. Outdoors, finish planting spring-blooming bulbs. Put a few in pots in a cold frame. They can be forced into bloom early if brought indoors in December or January.

Complete the garden cleanup, which helps eliminate ways for pests to get through the winter. Bring in stakes, temporary trellises, tomato cages, flowerpots, and other garden equipment, and put them away for next year. Shut off outdoor faucets so the pipes will not freeze during the winter. If hoses are not yet indoors, bring them in now and store them in a frost-free area.

Make planting holes now for shrubs and trees—including one for the live Christmas tree if that's the way you celebrate the holiday—to be planted early next year.

Cover chrysanthemums, calendulas, pansies, and fall vegetables if a hard frost (under 28°F) is threatened. Either cover with cloths nightly, or leave bubbled plastic insulation or spun-bonded floating row covers in place day and night. You may get several extra weeks of gardening in before a killing cold ends it.

Tie perennial vines to supports in order to prevent damage from wind whipping. Clean and sweep the lawn, and make sure perennial plants are surrounded by mulch but not smothered under it.

In your garden diary, note the triumphs and disasters of the past season. Send for seed and plant catalogs for happy winter browsing—free catalogs are advertised in garden magazines.

DECEMBER. Very little outdoor work remains. Snow is one of the best insulators for biennial and perennial plants trying to survive the winter, so pile it on them if it is available. Although it will not make a permanent cover, it will help plants get through some of the coldest days. A thick covering of salt hay is helpful, too.

Use December leisure time for garden reading and research. Learn more about plants for your area. Review your notes and then look up plant species that were most successful: If your shady yard was right for shade-loving, perennial astilbe, you might want to acquire special cultivars in differing colors, shapes, and sizes. You can be sure that they are not a risky investment. As you study by the fireplace, save your wood ashes in a sealed container for use on the spring garden.

December is a good time to get supplies ready for indoor planting. Order pots and soil. Clean recycled pots and six-packs in a dishpanful of sudsy water that includes a cup of chlorine bleach for antiseptic action. Clean window boxes and planters, and repaint those that need it. Check indoor plant lights and replace bulbs in fluorescent fixtures if necessary. They become dim long before they blow out.

Indoors, plant calla and madonna lilies and pips of lily of the valley. If ordering them by mail, be sure that they will not be left on a doorstep to freeze. Mist houseplants frequently to counteract the dryness of heated indoor air. In cool indoor conditions, petunia seed may be planted this month, along with other slow starters such as salpiglossis, lisianthus, and succulents. They may also be grown in warmer (above 65°F) conditions, as may browallia, begonias, tropical plants, and tomatoes.

Outdoors in a cold frame, seeds of some kinds of rock garden, native, and herbaceous perennial plants can be planted to freeze and thaw, then germinate in early spring. By December's end, pots of spring bulbs in the cold frame may be brought indoors as they begin to sprout.

GARDENING CALENDAR FOR HOT SOUTHERN U.S. REGIONS (PARTS OF ZONES 9, 10, AND 11, WITH VERY HOT SUMMERS)

In this book, Zones 9 and 10 are divided into two regions, Hot Southern and Mild West Coast, because summer temperatures differ in places where the winter temperatures (on which the USDA bases the zones) are similar. If you live in a part of Zone 9 or 10 where temperatures often rise above 90°F during long hot summers, this calendar is meant for you. In Zone 10, which is nearly tropical, there is a chance of frost in winter, but it does not occur every year. In Zone 9, occasional light to heavy winter freezes are the norm.

Winter days in the South are warm and pleasant between cold spells. When weather reports threaten a freeze, gardeners here cover tender tropical plants with cloths, quilts, bubbled plastic sheeting, cardboard boxes, floating row covers, overturned trash cans, and whatever else they can find until the cold snap passes. Here, unheated cold frames are almost always frost-free. Those gardeners who choose to grow only native and cold-hardy plants, not tropical ones, have less to worry about in winter, but miss out on some of the special plants that may be grown here with extra protection (see below).

JANUARY. The changeable days of January in the South parallel early-spring days in the North. Plants sense the coming growing season and are getting ready. Some plants grow best during the cool weather you usually have this month. Outdoors, you can plant the seeds of frost-hardy herbs, flowers, and vegetables, such as peas, sweet peas, alyssum, baby's-breath, stock, delphinium, lettuce, spinach, broccoli, dill, chives, and onions. Outdoors in warmer areas, or under cold frames, grow seedlings for everlastings such as acroclinium, strawflowers, statice, and ornamental grasses. All do well during cool weather and may be planted outside a few weeks before the last expected frost.

Set out cold-tolerant bedding flowers such as dianthus, petunias, calendulas, snapdragons, alyssum, stock, and pansies in Zone 10 and lower parts of Zone 9. Also set out plants of cool-weather herbs and vegetables.

Water outdoor plantings if they are dry. Check perennials and tuck mulch around but not over crowns so they will have protection but will not smother. In the North, mulch insulates roots and keeps them frozen solid, but here it protects them from frost.

Plant and prune grapevines, fruit trees, and nut trees. Spray fruit and nut trees with dormant oil if the temperature will be above 40°F for several days to prevent an infestation of scale or other insects. Prune crape myrtle for shape and to stimulate the growth of new wood, which bears the flowers. The cuttings are not hard to propagate (see Chapter 5).

Indoors, start seedlings of cosmos, scarlet sage, marigolds, peppers, eggplants, tomatoes, and, farther south, summer squash for a jump on the coming spring season. Fertilize indoor plants lightly every two weeks.

Purchase and start bulbs and tubers of gloriosa lilies, crinum lilies, dahlias, caladiums, begonias, calla lilies, amaryllis, and freesia. Grow them indoors if freezing weather is likely, or outdoors if it is safe. Freesias and amaryllis naturalize well outdoors in Zones 9 and 10.

FEBRUARY. Plant your holiday poinsettia outside in bright semishade after the danger of frost passes. In much of the South, it will grow into an attractive shrub. Even in places where it freezes now and then, a well-mulched poinsettia will come back from the roots, blooming brightly once each year.

Plant and fertilize your amaryllis, gloriosa lilies, ismene, glads, and other tender perennial bulbs if frosts are past. Toward the end of the month, it is usually safe to set out plants of dianthus, petunias, stock, pansies, cool-weather or perennial herbs, and cool-weather vegetables—even in upper Zone 9. Plant perennials and hardy annuals in all parts of the South. Prune tea roses, but wait until after the main bloom is finished to prune climbers. Prune oleander and crape myrtle if it was not done last month. In southern parts of the region, it is safe to plant most kinds of flowers, vegetables, and herbs. Do it early in the month to give a good start during cooler weather.

Select and plant flowering trees and shrubs such as camellia while they are in bloom.

Plant fruit trees and woody plants for landscaping. Fertilize trees, shrubs, perennials, and roses. Prune trees and shrubs. In Zone 10, divide perennials.

Step up seedlings you started earlier to larger pots if necessary, or plant them outdoors. Repot and fertilize houseplants. Divide perennials such as shasta daisies, daylilies, coreopsis, and chrysanthemums when their new growth appears. Make new beds of ground cover with ivy, ferns, periwinkle, or liriope. They can be bought at local garden centers or started with thinnings from other beds. Zone 9 gardeners can easily grow leather fern, used in florists' bouquets, in shade as a ground cover.

MARCH. Continue to sow or set out cold-hardy annuals, vegetables, and herbs in Zone 9, but it is already too late in Zone 10. Stake or trellis peas and sweet peas. Plant balsam, nasturtiums, dianthus, cleomes, rudbeckias, and many other flowers from seed. It is interesting to sow mixtures of meadow flower, wildflower, or cutting flower seed as a test for flowers naturally suited to your garden conditions.

In Zone 10, plant warm-weather annuals and vegetables now, either from seed or plants. Try sweet potatoes under mulch for bigger crops. It is perennial in this climate. Calabaza squash (well known in Puerto Rico) is heat tolerant and extremely productive, if you have space for the pumpkinlike vines. Pinch the growing tips of citrus trees to promote bushiness. Plant exotic tropicals such as ginger, bougainvillea, bird of paradise, mahoe, bauhinia, jasmine, and heliconia.

In Zone 9, finish dividing perennials. Divide and transplant ferns before new growth gets too large. Harden off indoor-grown hardy seedlings gradually and transplant them to the garden. Frost-sensitive plants still need shelter indoors or in a cold frame.

In all parts of the region, it is time to tend the lawn. Fertilize lawns and gardens for this important growth season with a product formulated for your area (available at local garden centers). Aerate the lawn with nail-spiked lawn sandals, which also stab and kill underground grubs, then apply fertilizer and grass seed. For an instant lawn, especially on a slope, purchase and roll out grass sod after tilling the top few inches and fertilizing the ground lightly. In sandy areas, add humus to the soil before laying sod. Check with local experts about the best type of grass to use in your area. For more information on growing and caring for lawns, see Chapter 15.

Prune and mulch azaleas, which need acid soil, after they bloom. Pine needles, whole or shredded, are ideal for mulching them because they help make the soil more acid. Weed and stake garden plants as needed. Grow-through hoops or rings are good for clump-forming flowers such as shasta daisies. Pinch tall annual flowers for a fuller shape. Remove withered flowers.

Houseplants may be brought outdoors to spend the summer in light shade. They do well inside screened enclosures, which keep bugs away and cut the intensity of the sunlight.

Look for holes of borers in young fruit trees and berry canes. Destroy them in trees by probing the pests with a wire. Cut off and burn infested canes. Thin fruit on apple, pear, and peach trees, if necessary, for larger fruit size.

APRIL. Your plants grow amazingly fast this month. If you plant them where they will grow, zinnias and marigolds go from seed to bloom in as little as six weeks. Plant all kinds of warm-weather flowers, herbs, melons, and vegetables. Start zucchini, cucumbers, squashes, beans, peanuts, field peas, and pumpkins outdoors right away, before the weather gets too hot. Grow sunflowers if there is room—the small-flowered types make good cut flowers.

Container-grown nursery stock may still be planted, but avoid bare-rooted plants this time of year—it is too hot for them. Fertilize fruit trees. Buy hibiscus plants in bloom so you can see the flower size and color.

Control active pests such as slugs and emerging grasshoppers. Spray fruit trees. Sticky traps such as Tanglefoot will control apple maggots.

Prune and fertilize ornamental trees, shrubs, and hedges. Follow up hedge pruning with a light shearing wherever edges look ragged, but do not shave off all the new growth. Prune away dead wood, stray twigs, and unwanted branches from climbing roses after they bloom. Do not cut down older canes if they are healthy and well placed. Train new growth upward and outward.

If temperatures are above 85°F by the end of the month, put a layer of grass clippings or straw on top of black plastic mulch, if you have used it, to moderate the heat buildup. Check squash vines for borers and destroy any you find. Keep after insect and animal pests (see Chapter 5).

MAY. Pick and dry herbs. Harvest summer squashes and cucumbers often, while they are small and tender. For sustained productivity, keep your tomato plants well mulched, watered, and fertilized. Remove faded flowers from annuals and perennials. Keep flowers, lawns, and rosebushes well watered through hot, dry weather. Water in the morning or evening, not the hottest part of the day, so the water will not evaporate before soaking into the ground. Make sure fruit and nut trees have enough water, or they may drop part of the crop. Prune small suckers, or water sprouts, from fruit trees.

After their bloom is finished, dig up and divide irises, lilies of the valley, daylilies, and Oriental poppies if they are overcrowded. Replant them in beds enriched with compost and bonemeal.

Cultivate the garden often because weeds are growing at a feverish pace. So are your garden plants. Keep everything well watered. Place stakes near lilies, dahlias, tall annuals, and tall perennials. Climbing beans, flowering vines, tomatoes, cucumbers, and squashes should be trellised, caged, or staked before they get too large, and trained as they grow.

JUNE. Especially toward the southernmost end of this region, garden chores are slowing down because of the arrival of hot weather. This is a good time of year to study heat-tolerant plants that will make your southern garden easier to care for. Native plants and trees will thrive with less water, get through the heat, and survive sporadic freezes in winter. Other heat lovers include gazania, salvia, African daisies, marigolds, impatiens, torenia (Florida pansies), Boston ferns (used as a ground cover in Zone 9), snake plants, croton, mahoe, hibiscus, bougainvillea, allamanda, thunbergia, poinsettia, tropical fruits, sweet potatoes, and peppers. In cooler parts of Zone 9, follow garden directions for June and July in the preceding section, written for residents of the Central Region.

JULY. If you must garden during this very hot month, do it early in the morning while it is cooler, and be sure to wear a hat. In semitropical zones, most gardeners take a vacation from heavy chores, keeping the garden watered and neat, but waiting until the weather cools off a little in September or October before planting new beds or doing anything too ambitious. In fact, most garden centers in Florida do not sell seeds during the summer months.

Lounging near a swimming pool, if possible, or inside where it is air conditioned, make plans for next fall's garden. Send for seed and garden catalogs. Before you make your seed order, you might want to go through seed packets from previous years. Test their viability (ability to live and grow) if you are in doubt—wrap a few of the seeds in pieces of moist paper towel, label them, and keep them inside a plastic bag at room temperature. Most kinds of seeds should sprout in under a week. If they do not, discard the packet and order new seeds. If it is the right time of year and you have the space, you can pot and grow the sprouts rather than discard them.

Water and mulch gardens to keep them at their peak. Thin melons to two or three to a vine, and place a piece of cardboard under each one to help keep the bottom of the melon clean and free from underground pests.

AUGUST. Farther south, continue your July activities, or lack of them. Toward the end of the month, treat garden beds for root-knot nematodes if they are prevalent in your area—and they probably are. If your smaller plants grow poorly and have knobby roots, you have them. These minute worms damage roots and stunt the growth of plants, especially shallow-rooted annuals. Although Vapam® can be used to fumigate the soil for ornamentals, it is so toxic that it is prohibited in some areas. Another way nematodes can be reduced is by "soil solarization." Clear and till the soil in your afflicted garden beds. Expose it to sunlight for a few days, which will kill some of the pests. Turn it over again and cover the bed with clear plastic. It will absorb enough solar heat to raise the soil temperature and eliminate many pests—weeds as well as nematodes. Leave the plastic in place for about three weeks before removing it and planting the area. Also keep in mind that improved soil is less likely to harbor the pests. It also helps to use plant varieties that resist nematodes, and larger plants whose roots grow down below the surface area nematodes predominantly inhabit.

In some Zone 9 areas, especially in those with a relatively high altitude, August is an active gardening time. If temperatures are below 90°F, sow fall crops of everything from arugula to zucchini. Choose varieties developed for short seasons because plants grow more slowly now that the days are becoming shorter. If it is still too hot to consider working outdoors, wait a few more weeks. Start lettuce and cole (cabbage family) crops indoors where it is cooler and transplant the seedlings outside when the weather improves.

August is a good time to root cuttings from poinsettias and other tropical plants (see Chapter 4). In general, this group roots very readily. Tip cuttings of allamanda, a gorgeous viny shrub with large golden flowers, will root in a glass of water on the windowsill.

SEPTEMBER. Continue to make and plant garden beds for fall and winter. In warm, coastal areas this is the right time to plant most annual flowers, vegetables, and herbs: Even tomatoes and peppers grow now if you set out plants rather than seeds. They set fruit better now that the hottest days are past. Plant seeds or plants of peas, sweet peas, broccoli, Chinese cabbage, dill, calendulas, and other fall annuals.

In the upper southern regions, plant the seeds of biennial flowers such as sweet Williams and Iceland poppies now. They will sprout quickly at this time of year and bloom very well next spring. It is worth taking a chance with those hardy annuals that often make it through the winter: Shirley poppies, California poppies, coreopsis, bachelor's buttons, snapdragons, statice, violas, delphinium, stock, *Phlox drummondii,* and alyssum. Perennials such as rudbeckia and gaillardia may be planted now, too. These diverse flowers can be grown as meadow plants or in garden beds. Those that survive winter (and most are likely to) will be larger and stronger than those planted next spring. They will have built up great root systems during the mild days of fall and winter, and enough cold tolerance to withstand heavy frost. In the warmer parts of the South, their chances of survival are even better. Plant them in October or November during cooler weather.

OCTOBER. Buy and plant fruit trees, including citrus, if appropriate for your area. There are varieties of apple, pear, and plum bred for areas with warm winters—most types need more chilling. Continue to plant seeds for hardy fall vegetables such as cabbage, kale, turnips, and lettuce. Seeds of hardy annual, biennial, and perennial flowers may be sown outdoors, too. They germinate better after heat moderates. In some areas, late starters will need protection during cold spells.

Get rid of lawn weeds and reseed or sod bare spots in the lawn. This is a good time of year to repair an old lawn or start a new one. Trim beds of ground cover and enlarge them if necessary. Plant evergreens and hardy shrubs. In colder areas, plant spring bulbs such as crocus, tulip, grape hyacinth, and narcissus. This is a good time of year to plant true lilies.

NOVEMBER. Bring in all houseplants before the onset of cold weather, after checking them for pests. Harvest all remaining squashes, onions, tomatoes, potatoes, and beans before the first freeze. Take cuttings of impatiens, ivy, and begonias. Root them in water or damp soil for potting up indoors in sunny areas.

In areas with the least amount of frost, mulch established bulbs and corms of dahlia, *Anemone coronaria,* amaryllis, paperwhite narcissus, sparaxis, freesia, gladiolus, begonia, canna, and caladium, to protect them through winter. Gardeners in colder parts of the region should dig up and store the bulbs indoors.

Shred or compost fallen leaves for garden enrichment. Chipped garden debris makes good mulch. Be sure to mulch around but under the leaves of perennial flowers and herbs.

DECEMBER. Frost-free or nearly frost-free areas differ dramatically from nearby areas that expect temperatures to go five or more degrees below the freezing point. Subtropic plants such as citrus can tolerate a few degrees of frost without damage, but are severely damaged or killed by slightly colder weather. Some plants have a certain amount of frost tolerance, whereas others readily freeze and die back to ground level but grow again from bulbs, stems, and roots below the soil's frostline. Amaryllis is a good example. If the frost goes deep into the soil, amaryllis bulbs will be killed. (A layer of mulch helps prevent this.) If only the foliage is frozen, the bulbs will grow new foliage and bloom again in late winter.

In southern areas expecting heavy or frequent frosts, you can still grow the most cold-hardy annual vegetables and flowers such as collards, Brussels sprouts, alyssum, calendulas, and pansies, especially if you cover them on the coldest nights of the year. Rye or other cover crops may be used as a green manure on bare parts of the garden.

In areas with little or no frost, December is perfect gardening weather. Almost anything may be planted at this time of year. Seeds planted in December will grow in the cool, mild days ahead. Since your region is affected by heat in the 90's or over 100°F in the late spring, summer, and into fall, the period from November to April is the most enjoyable time of year for gardening—it usually takes newcomers a few years to learn to understand the South's garden calendar. Salad vegetables, herbs, hardy annuals, biennials, and exotic bulbs may be planted all throughout Zone 10 and in the warmer half of Zone 9. Zone 10 gardeners can also plant warm-weather vegetables (by northern standards), herbs, and flowers such as zucchini, corn, tomatoes, beans, coriander, dill, basil, impatiens, violas, dianthus, snapdragons, petunias, nasturtiums—in fact, just about any annual can be grown because it is neither too hot nor too cold. This is the best time of the year for planting citrus trees, fruit and nut trees, evergreens, vines, shrubs, and perennials. Make and repair beds of ground cover because cuttings and transplants root very easily now. Thin and divide strawberry plants and perennial flowers and herbs now, for the same reason.

Frost-free areas should plant tender perennial bulbs now through February. Sparaxis, freesia, calla lily, tuberose, gloriosa lily, and many others are wonderful in the garden. December to March is a good time of year to buy orchids in bloom.

If you must have the northern spring flowers, plant prechilled tulip, narcissus, and hyacinth bulbs now. Many southern gardeners who cannot grow tulips and daffodils without help from their refrigerators find that paperwhite narcissus grows well for them. It is native to the Mediterranean area and naturalizes very well, spreading and blooming year after year. Plant paperwhites in well-drained soil under deciduous trees if possible. After they bloom, let the foliage start to turn yellow before you cut it down.

GARDENING CALENDAR FOR THE MILD WEST COAST (ZONES 9, 10, AND 11, WITH MILD SUMMERS)

The West Coast tends to have cool, wet winters and mild but dry summers. If you live here, you are in a garden spot that supplies the rest of us with seeds and supermarket produce. Because your growing season never really ends, naturally you have a lot of flexibility in timing your garden activities.

Under the balmy influence of the Pacific Ocean, the western coastal areas are milder than places at the same latitude a few miles farther east. While coastal areas stay cool in summer and warm in winter, farther inland the climate is more extreme, turning into desert in some areas if you go far enough. This section of the book is for you if you garden in the mild, foggy parts of the West Coast. If you are near but outside this area, turn to one of the other sections, Northern, Central, or Hot Southern, whichever is most appropriate.

JANUARY. January is cool and mild, but unpredictable. Watch out for frosty nights and protect tender plants as described at the end of Chapter 5. With luck and attention, they can come through the winter unharmed.

In all coastal areas, fertilize gardens for the growing period just ahead. Plant seeds of wildflowers, sweet peas, alyssum, phlox, coneflowers, California poppies, baby's-breath, delphinium, lupines, and penstemons. Plant peas, onions, chives, dill, lettuce, broccoli, spinach, radishes, carrots, beets, cabbage, kohlrabi, shallots, and other cool-weather vegetables. Set out hardy plants of calendula, alyssum, viola, stock, pansy, Iceland poppy, and flowering cabbage. Plants of cabbage, kale, cauliflower, broccoli, and Brussels sprouts may be bedded out.

Plant perennials, trees, and shrubs, including bare-rooted stock. Start artichoke beds. Plant bulbs, tubers, and corms of freesia, rain lilies, alstroemeria, anemone, and ranunculus. Prune and fertilize grapes, fruit and nut trees, tea roses, and hydrangea. Climbing roses should be pruned after they bloom.

In frost-free areas, plant tender perennial bulbs during the cool weather: caladiums, dahlias, tigridia, ixia, montbretia, callas, cannas, gladioli, ismene, sparaxis, amaryllis, crinum, and begonias. Plant seeds of dianthus, carnations, toadflax, morning glories, nasturtiums, balsam, geraniums, petunias, primroses, calceolaria, cineraria, salvia, and roses. Go ahead with seeds of spring and summer vegetables. Fertilize your garden beds before planting.

Indoors, in cooler areas, sow seeds of ageratum, nigella, nasturtiums, celosia, four-o'clocks, cosmos, zinnias, sunflowers, thunbergia, stock, nicotiana, marigolds, dianthus, tomatoes, peppers, and salvia. Fertilize indoor plants lightly every two weeks.

Southernmost residents should choose types of fruits, including kiwi, that do not need much winter chilling. Try to get trees and shrubs in the ground now—you can plant interesting ones such as olive, sweet bay, date, bird of paradise, citrus, ginger, Surinam cherry, loquat, poinciana, cassia, tamarind, pomegranate, lychee, almond, avocado, and pistachio.

FEBRUARY. Days lengthen noticeably, and plants respond. Divide perennials as new growth begins to appear. Stake or trellis peas and sweet peas. Select and plant native plants and flowering trees while they are in bloom. Continue to set out ornamentals such as violas, lobelia, mimulis, calceolaria, sweet peas, Iceland poppies, nasturtiums, snapdragons, petunias, salvia, alyssum, fuchsia, ranunculus, primroses, geraniums, nemesia, clarkia, calendulas, wildflowers, and, where the frost is past, all kinds of begonias.

Finish pruning and fertilizing. On dry days, spray peaches with lime sulfur to control peach leaf curl. Put in cane fruits and strawberries.

Plant seeds of flowers for drier months such as California poppy, gaillardia, coreopsis, coneflower, wild penstemon, gloriosa daisy (rudbeckia), and ornamental grasses. Plant spinach, potatoes, cole (cabbage family) crops, peas, celery, turnips, beets, parsley, coriander, lettuce, radishes, onions, and so on. In warmer zones, go ahead with beans, corn, squashes, melons, and other hot-weather crops.

For the terrace, pot up large containers with combinations of small citrus trees, such as key lime, lemon, or calamondin, with creeping herbs, alyssum, nasturtiums, or houseleeks (sempervivum). Train ivy topiary onto shaped supports fashioned from stakes and wires.

In cooler areas, it is safe to plant most kinds of flowers, grasses, bulbs, vegetables, and herbs by the end of the month.

In warmer areas, plant your holiday poinsettia outside in bright semishade. In much of the South, it grows into an attractive shrub, blooming wildly once each year. Even in places where it freezes now and then, a well-mulched poinsettia will grow back from the roots.

Step up seedlings to larger pots if necessary, or plant them outdoors. Repot and fertilize houseplants. After they adjust, set them outside in semishade if you like.

MARCH. Finish planting what you grow from seeds. Balsam, nasturtium, dianthus, cleome, rudbeckia, cosmos, impatiens, and many other flowers may be sown. It is interesting to sow mixtures of meadow flower, wildflower, or cutting flower seed as a test for flowers naturally suited to your garden conditions. Continue to plant herbs, ornamental grasses, and wildflowers for the dry season ahead. Get weeds out now while they are small and tender. It is not too late to plant trees and shrubs.

In warmer areas, pinch back the growing tips of citrus trees to promote bushiness. Plant exotic tropicals such as ginger, bougainvillea, bird of paradise, and heliconia. This is your last chance for cool-weather crops—choose short-season varieties, and give them more shade.

Most parts of the region stay mild, so, here, continue to plant cool-weather crops. Be sure to plant celery, head lettuce, peas, and herbs. Fertilize soil for everything. Keep watering, and add mulch. Do not let flowers and fruits dry out during this important growth period.

Prune and mulch azaleas after they bloom. Pine needles and bark chips are ideal as they help make the soil acid. Weed and stake garden plants as needed. Grow-through hoops or rings are good for clump-forming flowers.

Thin fruit on apple, pear, and peach trees if necessary, for better fruit size. Prune deadwood winter-freeze damage from citrus and avocado.

APRIL. Get mulches in place (see Chapter 5) for the dry period ahead. There is still time to go ahead with most planting. Plant lettuce such as 'Black-Seeded Simpson,' which are reliable and slow to bolt. This pale green one is attractive for bed edgings and grows very fast. In cooler areas, you can still plant head lettuce.

In all areas, plant fast-growing warm-weather flowers, herbs, melons, and vegetables. Zinnias and marigolds go from seed to bloom in as little as six weeks. Start zucchini, cucumbers, squashes, beans, peanuts, field peas, and pumpkins outdoors if your summers are warm and sunny. Keep watering garlic as bulbs enlarge. Plant gladioli. Grow sunflowers if there is room—the small-flowered types make good cut flowers. If pinched back for bushiness, they look nice in flower borders.

Container-grown nursery stock may still be bought and planted, but avoid bare-rooted plants this time of year because it is too warm. Fertilize fruit trees.

Control active pests such as slugs and snails (see Chapter 5). *Bacillus thuringiensis* (Bt) kills green worms and white grubs. Spray fruit trees. Sticky traps such as Tanglefoot will control apple maggots. Dusting plants with diatomaceous earth (found in swimming-pool supply stores) kills chewing insects without chemicals. Use the soapy water cure for aphids.

Feed everything again this month to carry it through summer. Prune deadwood from citrus, avocados, azaleas, camellias, and rhododendrons. Marguerites and chrysanthemums grow quickly now from softwood cuttings.

Prune and fertilize ornamental trees, shrubs, and hedges. Follow up hedge pruning with a light shearing wherever edges look ragged, but do not shave off all the new growth. Prune deadwood, stray twigs, and unwanted branches from climbing roses after they bloom. Do not cut down older canes if they are healthy and well placed. Train new growth upward and outward

MAY. For sustained productivity, keep your warm-weather plants, especially melon and tomato plants, well mulched, watered, and fertilized. Continue to remove faded flowers from annuals and perennials. Pinch back annuals and chrysanthemums. Remove spent annuals. Keep flowers, lawns, and rosebushes well watered through hot, dry weather. Make sure fruit and nut trees have enough water, or they may drop part of the crop. Prune small suckers, or water sprouts, from fruit trees. Clean up fallen fruit. With irrigation and partial shade, mild areas can still grow lettuce for some of the best crops of the year.

Plant seeds or plants of drought-resistant coreopsis, hollyhock, cosmos, bee balm, rudbeckia, coneflower, and verbena. After bloom is finished, dig and divide irises, lilies of the valley, daylilies, coralbells, and Oriental poppies if they are overcrowded. Replant them in beds enriched with compost and bonemeal.

Cultivate the garden often because weeds are growing wildly. So are your garden plants. Keep everything well watered. Place stakes near lilies, dahlias, tall annuals, and tall perennials. Climbing beans, flowering vines, tomatoes, cucumbers, and squashes should be trellised, caged, or staked before they get too large, and trained as they grow.

JUNE. If the weather is dry, harvest garlic and shallot bulbs and let them dry about two weeks to cure. Put in more peppers, eggplants, tomatoes, corn, squashes, cucumbers, melons, and okra. It is possible to grow cool-weather plants under screen or lath in hot areas. Mulch and irrigate plants, especially fruit and nut trees, camellias, azaleas, and rhododendrons, which are from wetter climates. Make a point of planting native plants that need less nurturing. Set out hibiscus, chrysanthemums, and asters for fall color. Also, set out the vines thunbergia, morning glory, allamanda, and *Mandevilla splendens*—they are great for color at summer's end. Refresh ornamental beds with seeds or plants of heat-resistant bedding annuals: salvia, marigolds, zinnias, and cosmos, to name a few.

Harvest herbs and dry them. Pick and dry everlasting flowers, grasses, and pods for bouquets and wreaths. Take advantage of dry days to harvest ripe shell beans, fruits, sunflower heads, and nuts.

JULY. Plant colchicum, *Crocus sativus* (saffron), spider lilies, and other fall-blooming bulbs. Milder areas can get an early start on fall peas, salad greens, and perennial flowers from seed, as well as other seed-grown plants. Try dahlias from seed.

In hotter areas, use shaded, well-watered beds to propagate cuttings from tropical plants. This is not a favorable time for sowing small seeds outdoors—the seedbeds overheat. Instead, start seedlings indoors and transplant them outside after they reach bedding size.

Continue to protect trees from drought. Keep garden litter cleaned up, and really go after garden pests again. Probe sticky holes on fruit tree trunks with wire to destroy borers. Use *Bacillus thuringiensis* to eliminate budworms.

AUGUST. Continue to root cuttings from poinsettia and other tropical plants. In general, this group roots readily. Tip cuttings of allamanda, a gorgeous viny shrub with large golden flowers, will root in a glass of water on the windowsill.

You should begin to plant fall vegetables, herbs, and flowers if it is not too hot to work outdoors comfortably. The long autumn growing season is ahead. Plants grow steadily for months, but not as quickly as they do in spring because there is less light. Some kinds of cole crops and lettuce are less likely to bolt to seed.

SEPTEMBER. Make and plant garden beds for fall and winter. Fill empty spots with vinca for carefree color. In warm, coastal areas, this is the right time of year to plant most annual flowers, vegetables, and herbs: Even tomatoes and peppers grow now in Zone 10 if you set out plants rather than seeds. Plant peas, sweet peas, broccoli, Chinese cabbage, calendulas, and other fall annuals. Propagate rosemary cuttings. Try planting a packet of mesclun, a seed mixture that includes French lettuce and other salad vegetables. Plant endive, raddichio, chicory, fennel, dill, coriander, and endive for late-winter harvests.

If it is not too hot, plant seeds of biennial and perennial flowers such as sweet William, hesperis, lunaria, rudbeckia, shasta daisy, gaillardia, penstemon, cheiranthus, Iceland poppy, foxglove, coneflower, and aubrieta now. They will sprout quickly at this time of year and bloom very well next spring. Try planting alstroemeria where you want it to grow—it resists transplanting. Grow the hardy annuals that make it through the winter: Shirley poppy, coreopsis, bachelor's button, dianthus, toadflax, snapdragon, stock, statice, viola, pansy, delphinium, godetia, and alyssum. These diverse flowers can be grown as meadow plants or in garden beds. They will be larger and stronger than those planted next spring, as they will have built up great root systems during fall and winter, and enough cold tolerance to withstand frost.

OCTOBER. Buy and plant container-grown ornamental and fruit trees, including citrus, if appropriate in your area. Plant container-grown perennials such as geum, daylilies, sedum, sempervivum, hardy herbs, and coralbells. Prickly pear—if you want it—will root quickly from half-buried cactus pads. Plant garlic cloves, shallots, and onion seeds or sets of short day-length varieties. Continue to plant seeds for hardy fall vegetables such as cabbage, kale, turnips, and lettuce. Seeds of hardy annual, biennial, and perennial flowers may be sown outdoors, too. They will germinate better after the heat moderates. In some areas, late starters will need protection during cold spells.

Get rid of lawn weeds and reseed or sod bare spots in the lawn. This is a good time of year to repair an old lawn or start a new one. Trim beds of ground cover and enlarge them if necessary. Plant evergreens and hardy shrubs. In colder areas, plant spring bulbs such as crocus, tulip, grape hyacinth, and narcissus. Choose the smaller-flowered types, which are closer to the Mediterranean natives and well suited to a California climate. However, try to be sure that the plants you buy were not stripped from natural sites in Turkey or Afghanistan. Nursery-grown bulbs are larger and, unlike the ones gathered in the wild, are free from nicks and scratches. This is also a good time of year to plant true lilies.

NOVEMBER. In colder areas, bring in all houseplants before the onset of cold weather, after checking them for pests. Harvest all remaining squashes, onions, tomatoes, potatoes, and beans before the first freeze. Take cuttings of impatiens, ivy, and begonias. Root them in water or damp soil for potting up indoors in sunny areas.

Send for seed catalogs and drop hints for holiday garden books.

In areas with the least frost, mulch established bulbs and corms of dahlia, *Anemone coronaria,* amaryllis, paperwhite narcissus, sparaxis, freesia, gladiolus, begonia, canna, and caladium, to protect them through winter. Gardeners in cold or very wet parts of the region should dig up the plants and store the bulbs indoors, instead.

Shred or compost fallen leaves for garden enrichment. Chipped garden debris makes good mulch. Be sure to mulch around but under the leaves of perennial flowers and herbs.

DECEMBER. Map and plan next year's garden. Test seed viability (ability to live) if in doubt—wrap a few seeds from each old packet in moist paper towel, labeled, inside a plastic bag, and hold at room temperature. Check them in a few days—most types should sprout in under a week. If some types of seeds are too old to germinate, discard and replace the packets and reorder fresh seeds. Go over notes from last year's garden and plan for more of the plants that performed best. Try exotic cultivars of the same species you had luck with. Send in your seed and plant orders. Improve your future garden with long-term plantings of trees and shrubs.

Frost-free or nearly frost-free areas differ dramatically from nearby areas that expect temperatures to go five or more degrees below the freezing point. Subtropic plants such as citrus can tolerate a few degrees of frost without damage, but are severely damaged or killed by slightly colder weather.

In areas with little or no frost, December is perfect gardening weather. Almost anything may be planted at this time of year. Seeds planted in December will grow on in the cool, mild days ahead. Salad vegetables, herbs, hardy annuals, biennials, and exotic bulbs may be planted. Here, this is the best time of the year for planting citrus trees, garlic, fruit and nut trees, evergreens, vines, shrubs, and perennials. Make and repair beds of ground cover because cuttings and transplants root very easily now. Thin and divide strawberry plants and perennial flowers and herbs for the same reason.

Frost-free areas should make good use of tender perennial bulbs now through February. Sparaxis, freesia, crinum, calla lily, tuberose, caladium, gloriosa lily, and many others are wonderful in the garden (see January). December to March is also a good time of year to buy orchids in bloom.

Even the colder areas of this region are too warm for some northern spring bulbs. However, cold-weather annual flowers and vegetables usually grown in spring in the North and that tolerate light frost will thrive in this region during the winter.

For northern spring flowers, plant prechilled tulip, narcissus, and hyacinth bulbs now. Many southern gardeners who cannot grow tulips and daffodils outdoors grow paperwhite narcissus outside instead, not indoors the way northern gardeners do. A Mediterranean native, the paperwhite naturalizes well in mild areas, spreading and blooming year after year. Plant them in well-drained soil under deciduous trees if possible. After they bloom, let the foliage start to turn yellow before you cut it down.

FLOWERS

ACANTHUS

Botanical name: *Acanthus* (Acanthaceae)
Other common name: Bear's breech

A rugged perennial with an imposing appearance, acanthus is a heat-loving plant from the Mediterranean region. Its leaves, symbolizing heaven, were used as a motif on Corinthian columns and are still sometimes used on Italian terra-cotta pots. Its long-lasting flowers bloom, snapdragonlike, on impressive spires, and its huge, deeply cut dark leaves are a glossy grayish green. It makes a good focal plant with its architectural qualities, but looks somewhat somber. It is often used in large-scale perennial flower borders and for fresh cut flowers. Since it takes several years to grow from seed, most gardeners buy plants.

PLANT TYPE: Tender perennial.
GROWING RANGE: Zones 6 to 10.
HARDINESS: Heat tolerant, but killed by deeply frozen ground.
PLANT HEIGHT: 2 to over 5 feet.
FLOWER COLOR: White to grayish rose-lilac.
FLOWER FORM: Tubular flowers on long spires.
SEASON OF BLOOM: Early summer.
SOIL: Well-drained, good garden loam, sandy if possible.
PH: Near 7 (neutral).
FERTILIZER: Well-rotted manure, compost, bonemeal, and/or all-purpose fertilizer.
WATER: Prefers moist soil.
EXPOSURE: Full sun or, in hot climates, light shade. In the northern part of its range, shelter plants next to south-facing walls.
SPACING: 3 to 4 feet.
PROPAGATION: Seed or division.

Method

- **Start seeds indoors.** Acanthus takes several years to flower from seed—most gardeners buy plants. Indoors, start seed eight to ten weeks before the last frost. Germination is variable. Plant two seeds in each small pot or six-pack pocket, ¼ inch deep, and later thin to the better seedling. Water and keep containers at 60°F until the seeds germinate, then grow seedlings in a sunny area or a few inches below a fluorescent light.

- **Transplant** them to larger pots whenever their roots become crowded.

- **Prepare soil outdoors** by deeply digging the bed and turning in compost and fertilizer. Improve drainage with sand if needed.

- **Sow seeds outdoors** ¼ inch deep in individual containers when spring weather is warm (after the danger of frost has passed) or later when seeds ripen naturally. Do not let seedlings dry out.

- **Set plants outdoors** in late winter (Zones 9 and 10) or early spring when the weather is warm, in nursery rows in light shade. Keep seedlings in pots for their first two years unless they can grow to full size in their permanent positions—these plants are deeply rooted and difficult to transplant.

- **Divide** mature plants in late winter to early spring, after the danger of heavy frost has passed, when new growth begins.

- **Water** frequently if needed.

- **Fertilize** at planting time. Side-dress with flower fertilizer in late spring and summer.

- **Pests and diseases** are few. When young, plants are prey to slugs—dust the ground with lime and ashes or diatomaceous earth, or trap slugs in partly submerged pans of beer.

- **Mulch** with several inches of bark chips or other clean mulch in hot and dry areas.

- **Trim** flower stalks after blooms fade.

Selected Species and Cultivars

Acanthus mollis (Artist's acanthus). Considered the best garden type, this may exceed 5 feet in good growing conditions. *A. mollis* 'Latifolius' is a cultivar said to be somewhat hardier than most.

A. spinosa. Similar to but smaller than *A. mollis,* this type has leaves that are finely cut and covered by sharp spines. Less cold tolerant, it is grown in Zones 8 to 10.

AGERATUM

Botanical name: *Ageratum houstonianum* (Compositae)
Other common name: Floss flower

With fuzzy, wide flower heads, ageratum is a popular annual for edgings, borders, window boxes, and planters. Most plants are low growing and spreading, sturdy and well branched, and remain in bloom for many months. There are tall types for cutting, too. Ageratum is easy to combine with other flowers. Many gardeners purchase bedding plants each year rather than grow them from seed. At garden centers, look for young plants just starting to bloom.

PLANT TYPE: Hardy annual.
GROWING RANGE: All zones.
HARDINESS: Killed by frost, good tolerance of weather from cool to hot.
PLANT HEIGHT: 6 to 18 inches.
FLOWER COLOR: Pale to deep blue, white, pink, violet.
FLOWER FORM: Small heads of fuzzy florets, in wide, flat bunches.
SEASON OF BLOOM: Summer in most areas, any time in frost-free areas.
SOIL: Any good garden soil.
PH: 6.5 to 7.5.
FERTILIZER: Well-rotted manure, all-purpose or flower fertilizer.
WATER: Average moisture.
EXPOSURE: Full sun; pink- and white-colored cultivars should receive afternoon shade to prevent scorching blossoms.
SPACING: 6 to 8 inches.
PROPAGATION: Usually from seed, though cuttings will root.

Method

· **Start seeds indoors** six or eight weeks before the last frost in flats or six-packs in potting soil, 1/8 inch deep and at least 1/2 inch apart. Seeds usually germinate in ten to fourteen days. Water and keep containers in a warm (65° to 75°F) place in bright sunlight or a few inches below a fluorescent light fixture.

· **Prepare soil outdoors** by digging the bed and turning in compost, fertilizer, and other soil amendments, as needed.

· **Sow seeds outdoors** after the danger of frost has passed, in nursery rows or their permanent places. In Zones 10 and 11, sow in winter. In a smoothly prepared and fertilized bed, make seed drills (rows) about 2 inches deep. Plant seeds an inch or two apart and cover with 1/8 inch of soil. Do not let the seedbed dry out.

· **Thin or transplant** seedlings (indoor or outdoor-grown) when they are large enough to handle, if they are crowded. Step them up from the flats to small pots when they are 2 or 3 inches tall. In outdoor rows, thin or transplant them to their permanent spots by the time they are 3 inches tall.

· **Set plants outdoors** (whether purchased or grown at home indoors) at any time after the danger of frost has passed, after hardening them off outdoors in shade for several days.

· **Water** frequently to keep plants from wilting.

· **Fertilize** at planting time and steadily during growth. Timed-release flower fertilizers or frequent liquid feedings give good results.

- **Pests and diseases** are rarely a problem after the seedling stage.

- **Mulch** plants with several inches of small bark chips or other mulch in dry areas.

- **Deadhead** spent blossoms frequently.

Selected Cultivars

'Blue Danube,' an F$_1$ hybrid, uniform and early blooming, with pretty lavender-blue flowers on plants 6 to 8 inches tall;

'Blue Mink,' a spreading type, 9 to 12 inches tall, with powder blue flowers and a neat appearance;

'Blue Ribbon,' with bright blue, long-lasting, early flowers, growing 7 inches tall and a foot wide;

'North Sea,' with deep blue flowers on long-lasting 8-inch plants;

'Pink Powderpuffs,' compact plants 6 inches tall with deep rose-pink flowers;

'Southern Cross,' an unusual bicolored plant with blue and white flowers and an attractive "hazy" appearance, growing 8 to 12 inches tall; and

'Wonder' and 'Wonder White,' two long-stemmed types for cutting, growing 18 inches tall.

AJUGA

Botanical name: *Ajuga* (Labiatae)
Other common name: Bugleweed

This easy-to-grow, fast-spreading perennial in the mint family is extremely floriferous for several weeks in spring, attracting honeybees from all around. After its tiny flowers bloom on short spires, ajuga makes a neat mat of small basal rosettes. When well established, it is so thick it is practically weedproof—but it is considered a weed itself by many gardeners. Runners quickly fill the spaces between plants, making it useful as a ground cover where there is room for its spread, or where physical boundaries limit it. It is a great ground cover for difficult damp areas. The plant's appearance is also fine for rock gardens and low borders, but its invasiveness is a problem. Usually evergreen in Zones 8 and 9, ajuga dies back in winter farther north but reappears early in the year.

PLANT TYPE: Hardy perennial.
GROWING RANGE: Zones 3 to 9.
HARDINESS: Resistant to both cold and heat.
PLANT HEIGHT: 6 to 10 inches in bloom; 3 inches in leaf only.
FLOWER COLOR: Usually blue; also pink, violet, white.
FLOWER FORM: Bugle-shaped flowers ¼ inch long on masses of spires several inches tall.
SEASON OF BLOOM: Late winter in frost-free areas, spring elsewhere.
SOIL: Any good garden soil (tolerates wet soil).
PH: 6.5 to over 7.
FERTILIZER: Flower or all-purpose fertilizer.
WATER: Wet or dry conditions.

EXPOSURE: Full sun to partial shade. Provide midday shade in Zones 8 and 9.
SPACING: 8 to 10 inches.
PROPAGATION: Almost always by division, also from seed.

Method

- **Start seeds indoors** in bright light, in flats or six-packs filled with sterile potting soil at least ½ inch apart. Cover seeds with ⅛ inch of soil or finely milled vermiculite. When plants are large enough to handle, shift to one plant per six-pack pocket. Set plants outdoors any time after the danger of frost has passed. They usually bloom in their second year.

- **Prepare soil outdoors** before planting, incorporating soil improvers and fertilizer if needed.

- **Sow seeds outdoors** after the danger of frost has passed in finely tilled beds. Plant seeds an inch apart, in rows, and cover with ⅛ inch of soil. Keep soil evenly moist until plants germinate.

- **Thin or transplant** seedlings or plants whenever they become crowded. When seedlings are an inch wide, thin to 3 inches apart.

- **Set out plants** any time after the danger of frost from spring through fall.

- **Divide** plants by transplanting offshoots. In spring (before the bees appear!) or summer, dig up small rosettes and replant where wanted. Each year after plants bloom, check on their spread and remove extras.

- **Water** young or newly divided plants often. Established plantings will tolerate wet or dry soil.

- **Fertilize** plants before they bloom, and again in midsummer. Very little fertilizer is needed if the soil is good.

- **Pests and diseases** seldom are problems.

- **Remove** flower stalks after blooming is finished.

Selected Species and Cultivars

Ajuga genevensis. 'Pink Beauty' is an unusual cultivar with shiny green mats of foliage topped by small spires of delicate pink flowers in late spring. It grows in sun or shade. There are white-blooming cultivars, too. Plant them 12 inches apart.

A. pyramidalis. This type is less invasive than *A. reptans* because it does not increase with stolons. It has 10-inch blue flower spikes on low, somewhat bushy plants.

A. reptans (Blue bugle plant). This familiar spreading species is a weed to some, and a useful ground cover to others, for it is extremely vigorous. Some interesting cultivars include:

'Alba,' a white-flowered form with dark green leaves and white flowers on 6-inch spires;

'Atropurpurea,' with bronze leaves and purple flowers;

'Burgundy Glow,' with burgundy leaves marked with white streaks when mature. The 6-inch flower stalks bear blue blossoms;

'Jungle Green,' with jumbo-size glossy green leaves and blue flowers; and

'Variegata,' with blue flowers and green leaves mottled with creamy white streaks.

ALLIUM

Botanical name: *Allium* (Amaryllidaceae)
Other common name: Ornamental onion

The alliums, comprising several hundred species, are a large group of flowers related to garlic. They grow from bulbs or bulblike rhizomes. The rhizome-rooted types need room to spread. Some alliums are hardy, others not. American plant dealers usually sell hardy types. Though the leaves smell garlicky if cut or bruised, many of the flowers are exceptionally sweet smelling. Typically, they look like chive blossoms, with each round flower cluster held on a single, straight stem. Use small sorts in flower beds and rock gardens. Tall varieties are good in perennial borders or as accent plants.

PLANT TYPE: Hardy or tender bulb.
GROWING RANGE: Zones 4 to 9 for most popular types.
HARDINESS: Varies by species; some are tender, many are hardy.
PLANT HEIGHT: 6 inches to over 4 feet.
FLOWER COLOR: Yellow, white, cream, purple, pink, red, violet-blue.
FLOWER FORM: Tiny, lily-shaped flowers in rounded clusters.
SEASON OF BLOOM: Spring or summer for most. The blooming period is relatively
  short.
SOIL: Any well-drained soil.
PH: Near 7 (neutral).
FERTILIZER: Moderate. Well-rotted manure, bonemeal, and slow-release fertilizer,
  applied lightly.
WATER: Moderate, not too wet.
EXPOSURE: Sun or dappled shade under deciduous trees.
SPACING: From 2 or 3 inches apart and deep to 12 inches apart, 8 inches deep,
  depending on type.
PROPAGATION: Usually from bulbs, also from seed.

Method

· **Start seeds indoors** in late winter to early spring. Plant ⅛ inch deep, ½ inch apart, in flats or one per pocket in six-packs in bright light at about 60°F. The potting mix should be a third to a half sand. Seeds usually germinate in ten to thirty days. Some types need a freeze to break dormancy and may take up to a year to germinate. Plants are delicate at first, then gain strength.

· **Prepare soil outdoors** by digging the bed and turning in compost, fertilizer, sand (for drainage), and other soil amendments, as needed.

- **Sow seeds outdoors** a few weeks before the frost-free date or plant them in summer when seeds ripen. For some types, plant in fall in cold frames. Plant ⅛ inch deep, 1 inch apart, in finely tilled soil, in rows.

- **Thin or transplant.** When indoor-grown seedlings are a few inches tall, shift them to one plant per pocket of six-packs or to outdoor nursery beds. When seedlings grown outdoors become crowded, thin or transplant them to permanent positions. Most types flower in their second year.

- **Set out bulbs.** Alliums are most often grown from bulbs purchased and planted in fall. Plant according to package directions in the places where they will bloom. Most types should be planted 3 to 5 inches deep. In specialty nurseries, alliums may sometimes be purchased in bloom, in pots. Plant them immediately.

- **Dig and separate** crowded plants after they bloom, when foliage starts to yellow, being careful not to cut into the bulbs. After lifting a clump with a spade, tease the bulbs apart by hand. With special care, you can also move small, shallowly planted types in spring before they bloom or even while blooming (only if necessary!).

- **Water** if needed while plants have green foliage. Do not overwater or bulbs will rot.

- **Fertilize** during active growth with bonemeal and all-purpose bulb or flower fertilizer.

- **Pests and diseases** rarely trouble the oniony alliums. If slugs are a problem, dust the ground with ashes and lime or diatomaceous earth, or trap the slugs in partly submerged pans of beer.

- **Weed** the bed in spring before plants come up.

- **Stake** large, tall types, if necessary, by tying each one to a slim bamboo stick.

- **Remove** flower heads and stems after bloom is finished, unless seed is wanted. Let leaves disappear by themselves, or remove them when they yellow. Mark the spot, for plants do not show while dormant.

- **Protect in winter.** In areas with freezing winters, dig and store bulbs of any alliums that are not cold hardy. Refrigerate them in plastic bags filled with barely moistened peat until the danger of freezing weather has passed. Most types sold in the United States are hardy and need no winter care.

Selected Species

Allium aflatunense. This large-flowered type may grow 2 to 4 feet tall, depending on the cultivar. Large, globelike, violet-purple flowers on strong stems appear once a year, in late spring. Stake taller types.

A. cernuum (Nodding onion, Lady's leek). From straight stems, clusters of small purple to pink flowers droop gracefully. Attractive seed heads follow the flowers on 1-foot plants.

A. christophii, formerly *A. albopilosum* (Stars of Persia). Huge, showy round umbels of starry, amethyst-colored flowers, 12 inches across, on strong stems up to 2 feet tall, bloom in late spring. These are also beautiful when dried. Plant bulbs 4 to 5 inches deep, 10 inches apart.

A. giganteum (Giant ornamental onion). These giants grow up to 4 feet tall with flower heads 5 or more inches wide in summer. Each bloom must be staked. Flowers bloom the second year from seed started in spring. Blooms are long lasting on the plants or when cut. Plant bulbs 8 inches deep, 1 foot apart.

A. moly (Lily leek). Small yellow flowers grow in 2-inch-wide, globe-shaped clusters on 10- to 15-inch stems. This type was called golden garlic by ancient Greeks and is supposed to bring good fortune. It blooms about the same time as late tulips. Plant bulbs 4 inches deep, 4 inches apart.

A. neapolitanum (Daffodil garlic). White, with good form and sweet scent, this type grows to about 18 inches and naturalizes easily. Plant bulbs in clumps, 3 inches deep, 3 inches apart, and let plants self-sow.

A. ostrowskianum. This reddish allium from Turkestan grows 10 inches tall with nice blooms. Plant bulbs 5 inches deep, 10 inches apart in Zones 3 to 9.

A. sphaerocephalum (Drumstick allium). The 15- to 30-inch-tall stems bear cone-shaped, densely filled, red-purple flower heads in late spring or summer. Follow general planting instructions.

ALSTROEMERIA

Botanical name: *Alstroemeria* (Alstroemeriaceae)
Other common name: Peruvian lily

Florists love to work with these exotic, long-lasting flowers, but they remain rare in American home gardens outside California. Originally from Chile, Peruvian lilies can be grown only in warm climates. The vividly colored, bearded flowers open over a period of several weeks.

PLANT TYPE: Tender tuberous perennial.
GROWING RANGE: Zones 7 to 9.
HARDINESS: Cannot tolerate frozen soil and likes hot weather.
PLANT HEIGHT: 3 feet.
FLOWER COLOR: Orange, yellow, red, pink, often in combination.
FLOWER FORM: 2-inch blossoms in clusters.
SEASON OF BLOOM: Early summer to midsummer.
SOIL: Deep, well drained, with high organic matter content.
PH: 6 to 6.5.
FERTILIZER: Well-rotted manure and bonemeal added to planting site.
WATER: Above average spring through summer; little required at other times of year.
EXPOSURE: Full sun.
SPACING: 1 foot.
PROPAGATION: Seed or division.

Method

- **Sow seeds outdoors** in early spring, ¼ inch deep, 1 inch apart, in containers in a protected place, like a cold frame. To speed germination, soak the seeds in water overnight before planting. Plants started from seed require two years to reach maturity and produce flowers.

- **Prepare soil outdoors** by cultivating thoroughly to a depth of 15 inches. Mix in one part rotted manure to three parts soil, and ½ cup bonemeal per foot of row. If the soil is not of a sandy nature, sand may be added to improve drainage.

- **Set plants outdoors,** purchased as brittle, dormant roots, in early spring when soil can be worked. Plant them 5 inches deep. Set out homegrown seedlings at the beginning of their second spring.

- **Mulch** with a 2-inch layer of straw or grass clippings in early summer to control weeds and help retain soil moisture.

- **Divide** permanent plantings by digging up a section of the root mass in early spring, leaving the rest intact. Replant the excavated roots immediately, as outlined above and avoid bruising them.

- **Water** frequently and deeply in early summer while the plants are growing rapidly. Weekly watering may be needed during extremely dry periods.

- **Fertilize** the planting site with manure (to condition the soil and provide nitrogen) and bonemeal (a good source of slow-release phosphorus).

- **Pests** may include mice, which like seeds and small seedlings. Use screens to keep them away from the plants. Diseases are not a problem.

- **Winter protection** is important in Zone 7, where the ground must be kept from freezing. In fall, place a 6-inch layer of leaves, branches, or other mulch over the planting, and leave it in place until the danger of frost has passed. Then remove most of it in gradual stages.

Tip · Avoid digging or moving mature alstroemerias. Once planted, they like to stay in one place.

Selected Species

Alstroemeria aurantiaca 'Moerheim Orange' grows to nearly 4 feet, with vibrant orange and yellow blooms. It is one of the hardiest forms of this plant.

A. ligtu, originally from Chile, is a vigorous grower with primarily red flowers. Hybrid forms are available.

A. pelegrina (Lily of the Incas). Try this plant, with spotted lilac-and-red flowers or white ones, where good winter hardiness is not required.

ALYSSUM (PERENNIAL)

Botanical names: *Alyssum, Aurinia* (Cruciferae)

Perennial alyssums are wonderful wall, slope, and rock garden plants. They require good drainage but otherwise are easy to grow. Most varieties make an outstanding display in spring at about the time of daffodils and tulips. Plants are long lived and improve in appearance over the years. Plants are not hard to grow from seeds and bloom the year after they are planted.

PLANT TYPE: Hardy perennial.
GROWING RANGE: Zones 3 to 9.
HARDINESS: Hardy in cold (some types to −30°F) or hot (90°F and above) weather.
PLANT HEIGHT: 4 to over 12 inches.
FLOWER COLOR: Pale, bright, or greenish yellow.
FLOWER FORM: Carpetlike masses of tiny flat blossoms, sometimes in sprays.
SEASON OF BLOOM: Spring or summer.
SOIL: Any good, well-drained garden soil.
PH: 6 to 7.
FERTILIZER: All-purpose or flower fertilizer.
WATER: Average conditions.
EXPOSURE: Full sun or partial shade, more shade in the South.
SPACING: 6 to 12 inches.
PROPAGATION: Usually by tip cuttings and division, also from seed.

🌱 *Method*

- **Start seeds indoors** in spring or summer in flats (sprinkle evenly over entire flat, 1 inch apart) or small pots filled with damp growing medium, covering the seed no more than ⅛ inch deep. Water and keep in a brightly lit place at 65° to 80°F until seeds germinate, then grow in bright sunlight or a few inches below a fluorescent light fixture.

- **Prepare soil outdoors** in beds by tilling in soil amendments such as fertilizer, lime, and compost, as needed.

- **Sow seeds outdoors** where they will grow or in nursery areas, when ripe or in summer in most zones, fall in Zone 9. Plant seeds 3 or more inches apart and cover with ⅛ inch of soil, pressed down. Do not let seedbed dry out. Seedlings appear in about four weeks.

- **Thin and transplant** seedlings when they are 2 or 3 inches high, if they are crowded. Shift those growing indoors to individual pots. Those growing outdoors may be set in nursery spacing about 6 inches apart the first year and moved to permanent spacing the next.

- **Set plants outdoors** when daffodils bloom or later, if they were grown indoors, after hardening them off outdoors in shade.

- **Divide** plants in spring when new growth begins, if they are crowded. Replant divisions immediately.

- **Root cuttings** of soft, new growth when it is about 4 inches long in a dampened mixture of sand and compost, not too acid (add lime if it is), under mist or high humidity. Temperatures should range between 50° and 80°F.

- **Water** frequently if needed until plants are 3 to 4 inches tall. Water if plants seem wilted or listless. Alyssum tolerates drought, but grows faster in moist soil.

- **Fertilize** steadily but lightly during active growth. Side-dress plants with light applications of low-nitrogen, high-phosphorus and -potassium fertilizer ("blossom booster" or "tomato" fertilizer) when plants start to form buds.

- **Mulch** plants with grass clippings or small bark chips to keep soil moist, in very dry regions.

- **Pests and diseases** rarely are problems.

- **Trim** plants after they bloom to keep them neat, in good condition, and encourage basal branching.

- **Protect in winter** by lightly mulching around and over plants with evergreen boughs or hay north of Zone 6. Remove mulch in early spring.

Selected Species and Cultivars

Alyssum montanum (Madwort). This type grows 6 inches tall and 12 inches wide. Its fragrant yellow flowers appear in spring above tufted grayish-green foliage and last several months. It is most at home in rock gardens or as a ground cover.

Aurinia saxatilis, formerly *Alyssum saxatile* (Basket-of-gold, Golden tuft). This spring-blooming perennial is stunning in full bloom on rock walls, or anywhere that its greenish-gold tones are set off well. Available varieties include:

'Argenteum,' with bright yellow flowers in late spring. Plants are a foot tall and extremely well branched and bushy;

'Citrinum,' growing 9 to 12 inches tall and 12 inches wide. Abundant yellow flowers with a greenish cast make a brilliant show;

'Compactum,' a low-growing dwarf form resembling 'Citrinum'; and

'Golden Queen,' growing 9 to 12 inches tall and 12 inches wide. Gray foliage hugs the ground and once a year is topped by masses of bright yellow flower clusters.

ALYSSUM, SWEET

Botanical name: *Lobularia maritima* (Cruciferae)

Sweet alyssum is most treasured for its long-blooming, mossy-looking mats of white flowers, though there are other colors as well. In full bloom, tiny petals of flowers in clusters cover the ground like snow. Alyssum looks best in crowded masses, not a narrow line. Use it for the front of borders, in mixed flowerpots and window boxes, as accent plants tucked into crevices in stone walls, on slopes, and in rock gardens. Shallow rooted and tenacious, annual alyssum serves as a living mulch around and between taller flowers. The following year, self-sown plants are plentiful, blending with whatever grows nearby. Unwanted seedlings are easily removed.

PLANT TYPE: Hardy annual.
GROWING RANGE: All zones.
HARDINESS: Tolerates light frost without damage to leaves or flowers, but is killed by hard frost and prolonged temperatures in the upper 90's (F).

PLANT HEIGHT: 3 to 6 inches.
FLOWER COLOR: White, pink, rose, violet.
FLOWER FORM: Carpetlike masses of tiny flat blossoms in rounded heads.
SEASON OF BLOOM: Summer in most areas, most or all of year in Zones 9 to 11.
SOIL: Any good garden soil.
PH: 6 to 7.
FERTILIZER: All-purpose or flower fertilizer.
WATER: Average conditions.
EXPOSURE: Full sun to partial shade, more shade in hot regions.
SPACING: 4 to 6 inches.
PROPAGATION: Usually seed or tip cuttings.

Method

- **Start seeds indoors** six or eight weeks before the last frost. Grow in flats (sprinkle evenly about ½ inch apart over the entire flat) or small pots filled with damp growing medium, covering the seed no more than ⅛ inch deep. Water and keep in a warm (65° to 75°F) place until the seeds germinate, then grow in cooler temperatures in bright sunlight or a few inches below a fluorescent light fixture.

- **Prepare soil outdoors** in beds by tilling in soil amendments such as fertilizer, lime, and compost, as needed.

- **Sow seeds outdoors** where they will grow about a month before the last expected frost (at about the same time as lettuce) or a few weeks later. A late-March planting will usually yield flowers from late May onward. Plant seeds an inch or more apart and cover with ⅛ inch of soil, pressed down. Do not let seedbed dry out. Make several successive sowings a few weeks apart for a continued supply of plants.

- **Thin and transplant** seedlings when they are 2 inches high. Those growing indoors in flats may be shifted to individual pots. However, several plants may grow together, even in a small pot, but will develop best if grown one to a pot. Those growing outdoors may be set in permanent spacing. Thinnings transplant easily if dug carefully and buried a little deeper than they grew, then watered well until established—usually in less than a week.

- **Set plants outdoors** when daffodils bloom or later, if they were grown indoors, after hardening them off outdoors in the shade. In areas with mild winters (a few light frosts), sow and set out alyssum at any time of year except when temperatures regularly exceed 94°F.

- **Root cuttings** 4 to 6 inches long in a dampened mixture of sand and compost, not too acid (add lime if it is), under mist or high humidity. Temperatures should range between 50° and 70°F.

- **Water** frequently if needed until plants are 3 to 4 inches tall. By then roots are deeper. Water if plants seem wilted or listless. Alyssum tolerates drought, but grows faster in moist soil.

- **Fertilize** steadily during active growth. Side-dress plants with light applications of low-nitrogen, high-phosphorus, and -potassium fertilizer ("blossom booster" or "tomato" fertilizer) when plants start to form buds.
- **Mulch** plants with grass clippings or small bark chips to keep soil moist.
- **Shear off tops** of plants if they become too straggly, to stimulate a new crop of flowers.
- **Pests and diseases** rarely are problems.

Selected Cultivars

'Carpet of Snow,' 4 inches tall and a foot or more wide at maturity, a spreading carpet of tiny white flowers, in clusters;

'Rosie O'Day,' 4 inches tall, a widely spreading carpet of rosy-colored blooms, long lasting as well as early blooming;

'Royal Carpet,' with violet flowers on 3-inch-tall plants with a 10-inch spread;

'Sweet White,' an old-fashioned, sweet-smelling type; and

'Wonderland,' a boldly colored strain forming dense, wide mats of flowers 4 inches tall, in rosy red, purple, or white.

AMARYLLIS

Botanical name: *Hippeastrum* (Amaryllidaceae)

As an indoor or outdoor plant, amaryllis provides stunning large blossoms for maximum visual impact. Flowers may be wider than 8 inches each, with two or four per stalk. In Zones 8 to 10, where this tender perennial bulb is hardy, amaryllis is grown outdoors as a spring-blooming bulb—a southerner's answer to tulips and daffodils. In cooler areas, amaryllis may be grown outdoors if the bulbs are brought indoors each winter, but more commonly it is grown as a showy pot plant that is sold for Christmas blooming. The green, straplike leaves are attractive most of the year. The huge flowers last up to two weeks, and sometimes are used as cut flowers in bold, vibrant bouquets.

PLANT TYPE: Tender bulb.
GROWING RANGE: Zones 8 to 11 (outdoors).
HARDINESS: Withstands heat, killed by hard frost.
PLANT HEIGHT: 1 to 2 feet.
FLOWER COLOR: Red, burgundy, orange, peach, pink, or white, sometimes bicolored.
FLOWER FORM: Broad, lilylike, trumpet-shaped, single flowers from 5 to 10 inches wide, 2 or 4 per tall, leafless stalk.
SEASON OF BLOOM: Once a year in late winter or early spring.
SOIL: Rich, well drained.
PH: 5.5 to 6.5.
FERTILIZER: High-phosphorus flower fertilizer.
WATER: Average conditions during growth, drought during dormancy.

EXPOSURE: Bright partial shade outdoors, full sun or bright light indoors.

SPACING: 1 to 2 feet outdoors, one bulb per 5-inch pot indoors.

PROPAGATION: Bulb offsets or seed. Most gardeners purchase large bulbs that bloom in several weeks, as seeds and offsets may take years to bloom.

Method

- **Start seeds indoors** if you wish, remembering that it will probably take five to eight years for them to begin to flower. Plant them in small pots filled with moist potting soil, one or two seeds per pot, covering ⅛ inch deep. Water and keep at 70°F until seeds germinate. Keep seedlings in a sunny area or a few inches below a fluorescent light fixture.

- **Prepare soil outdoors** before planting by tilling in fertilizer, sand, compost, and other soil improvers, as needed.

- **Sow seeds outdoors** in nursery beds in warm spring weather, around 70°F, or as soon as they ripen on the plants. Plant them ⅛ inch deep and about 4 inches apart. Do not let them dry out.

- **Thin and transplant** seedlings growing indoors to individual pots or 2- to 4-inch spacing when they are a few inches tall, to allow room for bulb development.

- **Set bulbs outdoors** in Zones 9 to 11 in winter. Plant them in early spring in Zone 8. From Zone 7 north, plant bulbs indoors in winter in a sunny area about 60° or 70°F. The top third of the bulb should be above the soil line. The plants will shoot up and bloom in just a few weeks. Later on, set out plants either still in their pots or directly into the garden after the danger of frost has passed, to promote good bulb and leaf growth. This helps restore the strength in the bulb for healthy flowers the next year.

- **Divide** established plants if they are overcrowded by digging up and separating bulbs during their dormant period in late summer or fall. Do not cut or harm the individual bulbs. Bulbs may be dried and stored indoors for several months. Replant bulbs immediately or at the start of the growing season in well-prepared soil. Plants do not mind staying in the same pot until they become crowded. Repot every three or four years.

- **Water** plants during active growth whenever the soil feels dry. Stop watering plants growing indoors at the end of summer and remove the foliage as it withers. Leave the bulbs in their containers but keep them dry and in a shaded place. Put them back into the light and water them again after a few months of rest, or as soon as new growth appears spontaneously.

- **Fertilize** at planting time and weekly during active growth, to support growth of large healthy bulbs. Withhold fertilizer at the end of the growing season.

- **Pests and diseases** seldom are problems.

- **Mulch** plants growing outdoors in dry weather with 2 inches of pine straw or other mulch.

- **Remove** spent blossoms unless seed is wanted. Cut down the bloom stalk after it starts to wither.

- **Protect in winter** outdoors in Zones 8 and 9 by mulching over and around bulbs with several inches of dense mulch. Pull back the mulch after the danger of frost ends so new leaves can come up.

Tip · Outdoor-grown bulbs may be dried and stored at the end of summer. Keep them in paper bags in a cool closet, and plant outside again after the danger of frost passes.

Selected Species and Cultivars

Hippeastrum hybrids, known as giant amaryllis, are popular as pot plants in all areas, and as outdoor perennials in Zones 8 to 11.

The 'Ludwig' cultivars, from Holland, usually have 8-inch flowers in clusters of four. Named cultivars in this series include 'Appleblossom,' white with pink stripes; 'Carousel,' red with a white star; 'La Forest Morton,' clear deep rose; 'Ludwig's Goliath,' fire-engine red; 'Maria Goretti,' white; and 'Royal Velvet,' intense wine red.

Other *Hippeastrum* hybrids include 'Picotee Petticoat,' white with a red picotee edging, and 'Apricot Sensation,' with huge peachy apricot flowers 8 to 9 inches wide, four per stem, as well as many others.

H. papilio (Butterfly amaryllis). This South American species has large greenish flowers elegantly striped with burgundy markings, two blossoms per 2-foot stem.

ANAPHALIS

Botanical name: *Anaphalis* (Compositae)
Other common name: Pearly everlasting

This delightful everlasting is hardy, perennial, and carefree. Its clusters of small blooms appear white in the garden, but at close range their pearly texture can be seen. Profusely blooming on woolly, upright stems, this native plant is well suited to gardens in less than ideal soil. Its linear foliage is green with a silvery underside. Fresh or dry, this is an important plant for flower arrangers. Anaphalis also makes a good plant for borders—place several clumps together. It also may be naturalized in perennial meadows, where it self-sows. Male and female flowers grow on separate plants, so, for plants to set seed, both must be present.

PLANT TYPE: Hardy perennial.
GROWING RANGE: Zones 3 to 8.
HARDINESS: Cold hardy, but harmed by hot, muggy summers.
PLANT HEIGHT: 8 inches to 3 feet.
FLOWER COLOR: Pearly white.
FLOWER FORM: Flat clusters of small, double, starlike blossoms.

SEASON OF BLOOM: Summer.
SOIL: Well drained, poor to average.
PH: 6.5 to 7.5.
FERTILIZER: Bonemeal, all-purpose fertilizer.
WATER: Moderate.
EXPOSURE: Sun or light dappled shade.
SPACING: 1 foot.
PROPAGATION: Seed or division.

Method

- **Start seeds indoors** at almost any time, planting ⅛ inch deep and 1 inch apart in flats or six-packs (one per pocket) in bright light at 55° to 60°F. Seedlings usually germinate in four to eight weeks. In cold frames, sow in spring eight weeks before the last expected frost, or in autumn.

- **Prepare soil outdoors** before planting by tilling in compost, fertilizer, sand, and other soil amendments, if needed.

- **Sow seeds outdoors** in summer, ⅛ inch deep and 2 inches apart in finely tilled soil.

- **Thin or transplant** seedlings if they are crowded. When container-grown plants are a few inches tall, shift them to individual 4-inch pots. When outdoor-grown seedlings are 4 inches high, thin them to 6 inches apart, transplanting the extras if you wish. When they become crowded again, thin or transplant them to permanent positions in the garden, but only during cool, moist weather.

- **Set out plants** from indoor plantings or the garden center in spring after the danger of hard frost passes. Harden them off in shade for several days before planting them.

- **Divide** plants in early spring when new growth begins.

- **Water** young or new plants frequently, though established plants tolerate dry soil.

- **Fertilize** lightly at planting time and early each spring. Do not overfertilize.

- **Pests and diseases** rarely are problems.

- **Mulch** with 2 inches of bark chips or shredded leaves in dry areas.

- **Stake** tall plants if necessary.

- **Dry** flowers by picking long-stemmed clusters before flowers open fully. Tie them in small bunches and hang them upside down in a cool, dry place.

Selected Species

Anaphalis margaritacea (Pearly everlasting). This widespread native plant grows 1½ to 3 feet tall, with clusters of everlasting white or silvery flowers. Seedsmen usually sell shorter, stockier strains, which need no staking.

A. triplinervis. Growing 8 inches tall and a foot wide, this is a neat, bushy plant with fluffy clusters of everlasting flowers. It is very cold hardy because it is from the alpine Himalayas, but is difficult to grow in areas with hot summers.

ANEMONE

Botanical name: *Anemone* (Ranunculaceae)
Other common name: Windflower

Anemones are widespread in differing habitats throughout the world, in the wild and as garden flowers. The genus includes numerous species of varying hardiness and size. Most anemones have daisylike or poppylike flowers with a short season of bloom. Although they can be grown from seed, home gardeners usually buy tubers, rhizomes, or plants. The florist's type, a variant of *Anemone coronaria,* is a tender tuber that is easily grown indoors in bright light, or outdoors in balmy temperatures. For most hardy types, it takes at least two years from when seed is sown to blooming time. Tender types usually take one year. Grow anemones in rock gardens, flower beds, and containers, and for cut flowers.

PLANT TYPE: Tender or hardy perennial.
GROWING RANGE: Zones 4 to 10, varying with the species.
HARDINESS: Varies greatly by species (see selected species on page 178–79).
PLANT HEIGHT: 3 inches to over 3 feet.
FLOWER COLOR: White, yellow, pink, red, violet-blue, lavender, or rose. Some types have black centers, others yellow.
FLOWER FORM: Colorful sepals of daisylike or poppylike form.
SEASON OF BLOOM: Usually spring, but this varies with species and climate.
SOIL: Well-drained, average to good garden soil on the light side (sandy).
PH: Near 7 (neutral) for most species, but this varies.
FERTILIZER: Decayed manure and bonemeal, plus flower fertilizer for *A. coronaria.*
WATER: Moderate—tubers and rhizomes will rot if soil is too wet.
EXPOSURE: Light shade for most types.
SPACING: Set small varieties 4 inches apart, others 8 or more inches apart.
PROPAGATION: Seed, tuber, or division of rhizomes.

Method

· **Start seeds indoors** as soon as they are received or gathered, for they do not remain viable for long. Indoors, *A. coronaria* germinates best at 60°F, in five to six weeks. Other types are more variable. Sprinkle seeds sparingly over the entire flat (1 or 2 inches apart) or grow in six-packs, several seeds per pocket, in sterile germinating soil, covering no more than 1/8 inch. Water moderately. After germination, grow in a sunny area or a few inches below a fluorescent light at 60° to 70°F.

· **Prepare soil outdoors** at planting time by tilling in compost, fertilizer, and coarse grit or sand (for drainage), if needed.

- **Sow seeds outdoors.** Plant *A. blanda* and other small or perennial types outdoors where they will grow when seeds ripen. Dig and smooth areas near the parent plants and spread seeds or let them fall on the spots. Their germination is irregular, but some may germinate the first year and bloom the next. Also, you can sow seeds of any anemone species in a cold frame in early spring.

- **Thin or transplant.** When indoor-grown seedlings are over an inch tall, step them up to larger pots or containers if they are crowded. Thin or transplant outdoor-grown seedlings if they are crowded, moving them to permanent locations when they are large enough to handle and the weather is settled, but cool and damp.

- **Set plants outdoors** after the threat of frost has passed in spring after hardening them off in shade. Set out *A. coronaria* in large pots or in permanent garden places after the danger of heavy frost passes, or grow plants in a greenhouse or brightly lit indoor area.

- **Plant tubers.** Presoak tubers of *A. coronaria* overnight and plant them 1 inch deep outdoors in spring after the danger of heavy frost passes, with the visible stem scar pointing up. Plant them in winter in frost-free areas. Presoak tubers of *A. blanda* for 2 hours and plant in the fall, 3 inches deep.

- **Divide** types with running roots (rhizomes) in early spring or fall. Divide other perennial types in early spring.

- **Water** moderately if needed.

- **Fertilize** all anemones at planting time. Side-dress *A. hupehensis* and *A. coronaria* with light applications of all-purpose flower fertilizer before flowers appear. Use gentle or organic fertilizers on all other species, which are easily burned by an overdose of nitrogen.

- **Pests and diseases** are few. Plants are sometimes affected by leaf rollers and aphids; if so, dust them with rotenone.

- **Remove** faded flowers and yellowed leaves. Cut off flowering stems of fall-blooming anemones after blossoms finish.

- **Protect in winter.** North of Zone 8, *A. coronaria* tubers must be lifted, dried, and stored indoors. Dig them after the foliage yellows in early summer, dry them, and store them in plastic bags containing about a cup of vermiculite per dozen or two of tubers in a cool basement or the refrigerator. Replant the tubers in the spring. Even with this effort, it is hard to keep them for many years, but it is easy to buy fresh tubers. In Zones 8 to 10, mulch plants in winter to protect tubers from frost. Where the climate is right, plants increase from year to year.

Selected Species

Anemone blanda. Petite, daisylike windflowers 3 to 6 inches tall that grow in Zones 4 to 8. Plants have ferny low foliage and bloom with daffodils in blue, white, or pink tones. Leaves disappear in summer. This type is best grown in large patches under deciduous trees or in the open. Soak purchased tubers for two hours before planting them in fall. They may be difficult to establish but those that take will spread and self-sow, particularly the large-flowered 'White Splendor' cultivar. This species prefers light sandy soil and a sunny exposure.

A. canadensis. Rapidly spreading, 2-foot plants have showy, white 2-inch flowers in early summer that close at night. Rhizomes form good-size colonies and are easily divided in early spring. Grow this in Zones 4 to 8.

A. coronaria (Poppy-flowered anemone). This is the large, poppylike, dark-centered florist's type, a tender perennial. Presoak dried tubers overnight and plant in sandy garden loam a few weeks before the frost-free date. 'De Caan' and 'St. Brigid' are the most popular strains. This species may be naturalized in cooler parts of Zones 8, 9, and 10.

A. deltoidea (Wood anemone). From the evergreen forests of the western United States comes this beautiful variety with 2-inch white blooms held on 6-inch stems. It needs humusy soil in partial shade and will not survive in areas with hot, muggy summers. Purchase plants or seeds of this rhizome-rooted type and grow it in Zones 4 to 8.

A. x *fulgens.* Highly recommended, this hardy scarlet windflower resembling the single strain of *A. coronaria* is easy to grow in Zones 5 to 8. Grown from tubers, it blooms in late spring on plants 6 to 12 inches tall. *A. pavonina* hybrids are similar.

A. hupehensis, A. japonica (Japanese anemone). With exceptionally pretty clusters of pink, white, or rose flowers on 20-inch stems in autumn, this species may be grown in woodland areas or semishaded gardens in Zones 5 to 8. It grows from rhizomelike roots. Blossoms resemble single roses. Mulch plants during the winter. Use this in borders or as cut flowers, removing stems after blooms are finished.

A. nemerosa (European wood anemone). Rhizome rooted, this spreading type thrives in humusy soil. Six-inch-tall plants bloom in spring. They are excellent in masses under deciduous trees in Zones 4 to 8. *A. n.* 'Alba Flore-pleno' is a large-blooming, double white cultivar. 'Vestal' is a double white, and 'Blue Bonnet' is a lovely deep blue with golden centers.

A. pulsatilla (Pasque flower). With red, white, or violet flowers in spring, this type grows about 6 inches tall. Its silvery, feathery seed heads are often used in dried arrangements. If they are left on the plants they eventually scatter and self-sow. Plants are hardy in Zones 4 to 8.

A. ranunculoides (Yellow wood anemone). Similar in size, appearance, and needs to *A. nemerosa* and a good companion for it, this rhizome-rooted type grows in semishade in Zones 4 to 8.

A. sylvestris (Snowdrop anemone). This stoloniferous type blooms for several weeks in spring or early summer. It is 1 foot tall while in bloom with clusters of pretty white and gold flowers held above ferny leaves. Grow it in light shade in Zones 4 to 8.

A. vitifolia (Grapeleaf anemone). From the Himalayas, this hardy anemone blooms from late summer through fall in Zones 4 to 8, and is similar to *A. hupehensis.* It is nearly 3 feet tall while in bloom. Stake if necessary.

ARTEMISIA

Botanical name: *Artemisia* (Compositae)
Other common names: Wormwood, Sagebrush

Members of this group of rugged, hardy perennials usually have finely divided leaves of pale silvery gray. Artemisia is attractive in the garden from spring to fall. Small types are best suited to rock gardens, while taller varieties need room to spread. Some plants spread by stolons and must be controlled in smaller gardens or they will take over. Foliage is easily dried for everlasting bouquets and wreaths.

PLANT TYPE: Hardy perennial.
GROWING RANGE: Zones 2 to 9.
HARDINESS: Varies with species; most types resist cold and heat.
PLANT HEIGHT: 4 inches to over 3 feet.
FLOWER COLOR: Yellow.
FLOWER FORM: Daisylike, small, and inconspicuous.
SEASON OF BLOOM: Late summer.
SOIL: Good drainage, any soil.
PH: 6.5 to 7.5.
FERTILIZER: Well-rotted manure, bonemeal, and slow-release fertilizer.
WATER: Low to average. Drought tolerant.
EXPOSURE: Full sun or light dappled shade. May become leggy if too shaded.
SPACING: 3 inches to 3 feet.
PROPAGATION: Division, cuttings, or seed.

Method

- **Start seeds indoors** almost any time. Plant ⅛ inch deep in flats or six-packs in bright light at 60° to 75°F. Seeds germinate in four to eight weeks. When plants are a few inches tall, shift to 4-inch pots for optimum root growth.

- **Prepare soil** in flower bed with compost and fertilizer, and, if needed, add sand or gravel for drainage.

- **Sow seeds outdoors** in late spring or summer. Plant ⅛ inch deep, 1 inch apart, in finely tilled soil.

- **Thin or transplant** crowded seedlings to their permanent positions when they are large enough to handle easily, after the threat of frost has passed.

- **Set plants outdoors** in spring or, south of Zone 6, in fall.

- **Divide** plants in early spring. Root cuttings during late spring and summer in Zones 2 to 8, in fall and winter in Zone 9.

- **Water** until plants are established, then decrease irrigation. Grow in well-drained areas if possible.

- **Fertilize** lightly; overfertilization results in excessive growth and mounds spreading open in the middle.

- **Pests and diseases** are seldom a problem.

- **Trim** plants if they look weedy.

Selected Species

Artemisia absinthium (Absinthe, Common wormwood). Discussed at greater length on pages 457–58.

   A. frigida (Fringed sage). This plant creates spreading, 1-foot-wide mats of silver-gray foliage and yellow flowers. It should be pruned for shape and grown in a dry climate.

   A. ludoviciana (Southernwood). Also known as white sage, 'Silver King' and other cultivars grow into 3-foot, rounded clumps of silvery foliage. It grows best in Zones 5 to 9.

   A. schmidtiana. Cultivars such as 'Silver Mound' and 'Silver Frost' are very low-growing, fine-textured perennials about a foot tall. This highly desirable variety is most suited to Zones 4 to 8.

   A. spicata 'Genipi.' This grows in cushion-shaped mounds only 4 to 6 inches tall. It works nicely for rock gardens or edgings in Zones 5 to 9.

ASCLEPIAS

Botanical name: *Asclepias* (Asclepiadaceae)
Other common name: Milkweed

This butterfly weed is a carefree, showy, native perennial wildflower that is tolerant of extremes of climate. Loved by butterflies and hummingbirds, it is a form of milkweed. Some types have been hybridized for wider color range and better form. Sprays of bright, waxy flowers grow on stout stems. Because it is not invasive, it makes a good border plant. It is slow to reach full size, so you might want to fill spaces between asclepias plants with annuals until they mature enough to occupy all the space—usually by the second or third year. Plants also may be naturalized in perennial meadows if they will not be plowed under.

   PLANT TYPE: Hardy perennial.
   GROWING RANGE: Zones 2 to 10.
   HARDINESS: Resistant to cold and heat.
   PLANT HEIGHT: 1 to 3 feet.
   FLOWER COLOR: Bright orange, yellow, scarlet, pink, or cream, with waxy green leaves.
   FLOWER FORM: Umbels of small, starlike, waxy flowers in showy profusion.
   SEASON OF BLOOM: Most or all of summer.
   SOIL: Any garden soil.
   PH: 6.5 to 7.5.
   FERTILIZER: Flower or all-purpose fertilizer, such as well-rotted manure.
   WATER: Wet to dry conditions.
   EXPOSURE: Full sun.
   SPACING: 2 feet.
   PROPAGATION: Seed, division, or root cuttings.

Method

- **Sow seeds indoors** in bright light 1 inch apart in flats or one per pocket in six-packs filled with sterile potting soil. Cover seeds with ⅛ inch of soil or finely milled vermiculite. When plants are large enough to handle, shift to one plant per six-pack pocket. Plants usually bloom in their second year, but sometimes the first if they are started early.

- **Prepare soil outdoors** by tilling in fertilizer, compost, and other soil amendments, as needed.

- **Sow seeds outdoors** after the danger of frost passes. Summer is a good time in most areas, but early spring and fall are better in Zones 9 and 10. Make seed drills (rows) 2 inches deep. Plant seeds an inch or two apart and cover them with ⅛ inch of soil, keeping the soil moist until seeds germinate. The plants' roots will develop before the tops do.

- **Thin or transplant** seedlings when they are large enough to handle, about 3 inches tall, if they are crowded. Indoors, step them up to 4-inch pots. Outdoors, thin them to at least 4 inches apart. When young plants are 6 to 8 inches tall, move them to permanent positions in the garden or to larger pots.

- **Set out plants** at the depth at which they grew any time from spring through fall in most places, and also in winter in frost-free areas.

- **Divide** plants in early spring when new growth begins, if they are crowded, digging deeply and carefully. Disturb plants as little as possible. The deep taproot makes division or movement difficult, so it helps to grow young plants in pots until they can be put in their permanent positions.

- **Take cuttings** 2 inches long in spring, from the fleshy, thick portion of the root. Plant them in moist soil in semishade until new plants develop.

- **Water** new plants often until they are established. Mature plants are drought tolerant.

- **Fertilize** with composted manure or all-purpose organic fertilizer at planting time and each year in spring.

- **Pests and diseases** rarely are problems.

- **Save seeds** in a dry place after they ripen on the plant.

- **Remove** stalks of flowers after blooming and seed formation are finished.

- **Protect in winter.** First-year or potted plants should be mulched in winter, the latter dug, pot and all, into the soil. Mature plants growing in beds need no winter care.

- **Label** plants carefully in the fall, for they are late to break dormancy and show up in spring. Otherwise, it is all too easy to damage the plants by cultivating the area where they are growing.

Tip · To use milkweed as cut flowers, seal the milky sap in the stems by searing the cut part with a match.

Selected Species

Asclepias physocarpa (Swan plant). This type from South Africa is somewhat less hardy than *A. tuberosa,* growing best in Zones 5 to 9. It has white blooms and attractive round, prickly seedpods about 2 inches long.

A. tuberosa (Butterfly weed). This native plant has wide, well-filled, brilliant orange flower heads. It grows on tuberous taproots, and is extremely hardy and carefree. A domesticated strain, called 'Bright Butterflies,' is a hybrid seed mixture offering large, wide flower heads in the full range of vivid colors.

ASTER

Botanical name: *Aster* (Compositae)
Other common names: Hardy aster, Michaelmas daisy

Most types of true asters are carefree, dependably hardy perennials with rhizomatous roots. Many of the species are native to North America or were bred from U.S. natives. These are valued for their ability to grow in damp clay soils and bloom in northern gardens after frost in the fall. They are used for borders, edgings, rock gardens, and cut flowers. Another genus, *Callistephus,* also goes by the common name *aster,* but is discussed under the heading China Aster, pages 219–20.

PLANT TYPES: Hardy perennial, annual, or biennial.
GROWING RANGE: Zones 4 to 9.
HARDINESS: Hardy in cold and hot weather.
PLANT HEIGHT: 6 inches to over 5 feet.
FLOWER COLOR: Red, pink, white, violet, mauve, or purple, with golden centers.
FLOWER FORM: Disc and ray flowers, usually small individually but found in large
    showy clusters.
SEASON OF BLOOM: Midsummer to late fall.
SOIL: Average to rich, thrives in clay soil.
PH: 5.5 to 7.
FERTILIZER: Well-rotted manure, compost, all-purpose fertilizer.
WATER: Average to high soil moisture.
EXPOSURE: Full sun to light shade.
SPACING: 8 inches to 3 feet.
PROPAGATION: Seed or division.

Method

· **Start seeds indoors** in spring 1 inch apart in flats or one per pocket in six-packs filled with sterile seed starting medium. Cover seeds ⅛ inch deep, water, and keep at 65° to

75°F. Seeds germinate in two to four weeks. Grow seedlings in bright sunlight or a few inches below a fluorescent light fixture.

- **Prepare soil outdoors** by tilling in compost, fertilizer, and other soil amendments, if needed.

- **Sow seeds outdoors** in smoothly prepared and fertilized beds in early summer or when temperatures are about 70°F. Make seed drills (rows) about 1 inch deep. Plant seeds an inch apart and barely cover with ⅛ inch of soil. Do not let the seedbed dry out.

- **Thin and transplant** indoor-grown seedlings to individual small pots or six-pack pockets when they are about 2 inches tall. Thin or transplant outdoor-grown seedlings to 3 inches apart when they are 3 or 4 inches high. A month or two later, thin or transplant them to permanent positions.

- **Set plants outdoors** in permanent places any time from spring through fall, after hardening them off if necessary. When grown from seed, most types will bloom the following year.

- **Divide** large clumps in half or thirds when new growth begins in early spring; divisions should bloom the same year.

- **Water** frequently enough to keep the soil evenly moist.

- **Fertilize** lightly at planting time and keep plants steadily but not excessively fertilized.

- **Pests and diseases** include slugs (trap in partly submerged pans of beer or prevent by dusting the ground with wood ashes or diatomaceous earth), powdery mildew (set plants in well-ventilated areas and/or use fungicide), and wilt (discard affected plants and the soil they grew in).

- **Mulch** with composted leaves or small bark chips to help keep moisture in the soil.

- **Pinch back** tall types for bushiness early in the summer in most areas.

- **Stake** asters instead of pinching them back in Zone 4 and northward. They will be less compact, but they will have time to bloom before cold weather sets in. Stake taller varieties before their first flower buds open by tying them to 4-foot bamboo stakes or propping them up with brush or inside peony hoops.

- **Trim back** the tops after they turn brown, for neatness. New plants often grow from self-sown seeds.

- **Protect in winter** by mulching plants in places where the ground freezes and thaws repeatedly.

Selected Species and Cultivars

Aster alpinus. Dwarf, easy-to-grow, and hardy, these perennial plants grow in compact mounds with white, pink, or blue daisylike flowers and golden centers.

A. amellus (Italian aster). Very hardy 2-foot-tall perennials, these asters have hairy leaves and relatively large violet flowers. The most popular of this type is *A.* x *frikartii,* a long-blooming, perennial purple aster with flowers about 2 inches wide. It is easy to grow and daintily showy, as well as pest-free.

A. cordifolius (Bluewood aster). Growing to 6 feet tall, this aster has tiny blue flowers in large loose bunches.

A. ericoides (Heath aster). This aster has very hardy white, blue, violet, or pink sprays of flowers. They grow on 3-foot stems that come from woody crowns.

A. novae-angliae (New England aster). Usually a deep purple, these native perennial asters are hardy and tall—up to 6 feet. There are many related cultivated types, including the compact 'Benary's Composition Formula Mix,' with pink, white, rose, red, purple, or violet clusters of flowers borne on plants about 2½ feet high.

A. tanacetifolius, now *Machaeranthera tanacetifolia* (Tahoka daisy). This popular sun-loving annual with blue flowers for cutting grows 1½ feet tall and may be started from seed indoors or out.

A. tongolensis. These attractive, mat-forming rock garden perennials have flowers over 2 inches wide once a year, borne on 1-foot stems. The centers are orange and the petals lilac-blue. 'Bergarten' is a larger cultivar growing over 1½ feet tall.

ASTILBE

Botanical name: *Astilbe* (Saxifragaceae)
Other common name: False spirea

One of the mainstays of perennial gardens, astilbe provides graceful, showy plumes of flowers for several weeks each summer, and attractive foliage from late spring until after frost. One- to three-foot-long sprays of leaves are rich green or bronze, deeply cut and ferny. Blossoms, usually in pastel colors, rise above them. Flowers will be brighter and maintain their color better if grown in partial shade rather than full sun. Astilbe is noninvasive, very good in all kinds of flower beds, and especially nice looking in groups of three. Mass plants for ground cover in moist, shady spots—they look stunning!

For dried bouquets, cut plumes of astilbe when the lower flowers begin to open. More will open as they dry. Hang them upside down in small bunches until they are firm.

PLANT TYPE: Hardy perennial.
GROWING RANGE: Zones 3 to 9 (best growth in Zones 4 to 8).
HARDINESS: Cold hardy, but not happy in prolonged high heat in the mid-90's (F).
PLANT HEIGHT: 1 to 3 feet.
FLOWER COLOR: White, pale pink, rose and red shades, lilac, red-purple.
FLOWER FORM: Feathery but substantial tall plumes of small flowers.
SEASON OF BLOOM: Several weeks in midsummer or late summer.
SOIL: At least 1 foot deep, rich and humusy.
PH: 6.5 to 7.
FERTILIZER: Flower or all-purpose fertilizer such as well-rotted manure.
WATER: Keep soil moist, though some varieties have been bred for drought tolerance.
EXPOSURE: Light shade to full sun, more shade in the South and areas of excessive heat (mid-90's to high 90's).

SPACING: 1 to 2 feet.

PROPAGATION: Usually by division, also from seed.

Method

- **Start seeds indoors** in spring or summer an inch apart in flats or one per pocket in six-packs filled with sterile potting soil. Seeds germinate in six to eight weeks at 65°F in bright light. Cover seeds with ⅛ inch of soil or finely milled vermiculite. When plants are large enough to handle, shift them to one plant per six-pack pocket.

- **Prepare soil outdoors** by tilling it deeply, incorporating fertilizer and soil amendments and adding extra humus such as compost or peat moss.

- **Sow seeds outdoors** in shaded beds in the summer. In rows, plant seeds an inch apart and cover with ⅛ inch of soil. Keep the seedbed moist until plants germinate.

- **Thin or transplant** seedlings when they are about 4 inches tall. Thin those growing in beds to nursery spacing at least 6 inches apart. Early the next spring move them to their permanent positions or to nursery spacing 1 foot apart. Thin or transplant those growing in containers by moving them to individual 4- to 6-inch pots. If potted outdoors, submerge the containers in soil to keep the roots cool.

- **Set plants outdoors** after the danger of frost passes, in early spring. Potted plants may be set out from spring through fall, or in winter in frost-free areas. Plants usually bloom during their second year.

- **Divide** plants in early spring when new growth begins, if they are crowded. Dig deeply and carefully to disturb the roots as little as possible. Use a sharp pruning knife to cut through the woody root. Replant divisions immediately.

- **Water** plants frequently, especially while they are young.

- **Fertilize** lightly but steadily. Apply composted manure or all-purpose flower fertilizer in spring.

- **Pests and diseases** seldom are problems.

- **Mulch** plants with several inches of compost or bark chips to keep roots cool and retain moisture.

- **Remove** flower stalks when they turn brown after blooming. This will prevent self-sown seedlings. However, if you prefer, leave them on for winter texture in the garden.

- **Protect in winter** in cold areas by mulching around and over crowns of plants. Remove any mulch on top of the crowns in early spring when growth resumes.

Selected Species and Cultivars

Astilbe x *arendsii.* Many cultivars are available in this popular species, a cross of several others. They range from 2 to 4 feet tall and bear showy, 12- to 20-inch-long, narrow flower panicles above shiny dark foliage. Cultivars include 'Avalanche' (white), 'Bridal Veil' (a tall, white late bloomer), 'Europa' (pink), 'Fanal' (carmine with bronze foliage), 'Ostrich Plume' (salmon pink), 'Peach Blossom' (light rose), and 'Rheinland' (carmine-pink).

A. chinensis. 'Finale' is an especially good cultivar with graceful, feathery plumes in silvery pink. Also available in a range of attractive pastel shades.

A. chinensis pumila. Less than a foot tall, this variety is dwarf with matlike foliage. Its plumes are rounded and less feathery than other types.

A. taqueti. Tall and upright, this type has flower spikes reaching 4 feet. Blooming late in season, 'Superba' is a strong pink cultivar with red stems.

BABY'S-BREATH (ANNUAL)

Botanical name: *Gypsophila elegans* (Caryophyllaceae)

Annual baby's-breath, so lovely in bouquets, is an easily grown hardy annual. An early-April planting outdoors will bloom in June. Time of planting is important—plants perform best in cool to warm weather, not too hot. Seedlings pass through light frosts unharmed. Successive sowings will keep fresh supplies coming. Use baby's-breath with its clouds of ¼- to ½-inch pastel flowers borne on minutely branched, angled stems in flower beds, cutting gardens, or large containers. Plants show up well in groups of a dozen or more. Generous quantities are needed because they are so subtle and filmy. If garden pests make it hard to grow baby's-breath, try some in a large tub on the patio, alone or combined with other plants.

PLANT TYPE: Hardy annual.
GROWING RANGE: All zones.
HARDINESS: Killed by hard frost and prolonged heat in the 90's (F).
PLANT HEIGHT: 1½ to 2½ feet.
FLOWER COLOR: White, pink, rose.
FLOWER FORM: Many ¼-inch flowers, single or double, on branched stems about a
     foot long.
SEASON OF BLOOM: Spring and early summer in most zones, earlier and for a longer
     time in Zones 9 to 11. Each plant blooms for about 6 weeks.
SOIL: Any good garden soil, well drained.
PH: 7.
FERTILIZER: Flower or all-purpose fertilizer.
WATER: Keep soil moist, not soggy.
EXPOSURE: Full sun in most areas, partial shade where temperatures exceed 90°F.
SPACING: 6 to 10 inches.
PROPAGATION: Seed.

Method

- **Start seeds indoors** or in cold frames four to eight weeks before the last frost in flats or small pots. In Zones 9 to 11, sow in late fall or winter. Water and keep at 60° to 70°F until seedlings germinate in about a week. Grow them at temperatures from 50° to 80°F, ideally 70°F, in bright sunlight or just below a fluorescent light fixture.

- **Prepare soil outdoors** where plants will grow by thoroughly tilling fertilizer, compost, lime, and other soil amendments, as needed, into the soil.

- **Sow seeds outdoors** where plants will remain, six weeks before the last expected frost and at intervals for about six weeks. Place seeds 3 inches apart, ⅛ inch deep. In Zones 9 and 10, sow in late fall for early-spring bloom.

- **Thin or transplant** seedlings when they are about 3 inches tall. Those growing indoors should be moved to individual 4-inch pots or to their positions in the garden. Those growing outdoors are harder to transplant, so just thin them to the desired spacing.

- **Set out plants** grown indoors or from garden centers from two weeks before to two weeks after the last expected frost, after hardening them off in shade.

- **Water** plants often enough to keep soil evenly moist but not soggy, so growth will be steady. A daily shower helps keep plants cool during hot, dry weather in southern regions.

- **Fertilize** at planting time and use liquid fertilizer when flower buds appear and during hot weather.

- **Pests** include caterpillars, sow bugs, leaf miners, and slugs. Prevent slug damage by dusting the ground and plants with diatomaceous earth, lime, or wood ashes, and treat other insect pests with rotenone or pyrethrum.

- **Mulch** plants with small bark chips or other nonacid mulch in hot, dry areas.

- **Pinch back** tips when plants are 6 to 8 inches tall to stimulate side branch growth.

- **Stake** plants inconspicuously by propping them up with twiggy branches.

- **Remove** spent branches after flowers fade, or cut fresh flowers to stimulate new growth. Discard plants when they become unsightly after several weeks of bloom.

Tip · For fresh arrangements, cut when blooms begin to open. Plunge stems into cool water immediately. Condition in deep water (up to the lower flowers) for several hours before recutting and arranging.

Selected Cultivars

'Covent Garden,' the classic type, well branched and graceful, growing 18 inches tall with pure white flowers;
    'Giant White,' similar to 'Covent Garden,' but with flowers 15 to 25 percent larger;
    'Kermesina,' with deep rose flowers on strong plants 2½ feet tall; and
    'Shell Pink,' a lovely color on plants 15 inches tall.

BABY'S-BREATH (PERENNIAL)

Botanical name: *Gypsophila* (Caryophyllaceae)

A "must" for flower arrangers, perennial baby's-breath is an easily grown, shrublike plant bearing minutely branched wiry stems starred with small flowers. It is long lived if the growing conditions are right, needing sweet (alkaline) soil. A too-acid soil is a common cause of failure. Gypsophila may be grown in corrected soil in large tubs—this is the easiest way in regions where the soil is naturally too acid. Use gypsophila in flower beds, cutting gardens, and large containers. Usually, it looks best in groups of three or more. Dwarf types, massed, make good ground cover.

PLANT TYPE: Hardy perennial.
GROWING RANGE: Zones 3 to 9.
HARDINESS: Hardy to −30°F and in heat into the 90's.
PLANT HEIGHT: 6 inches to 4 feet.
FLOWER COLOR: White, pink, rosy red.
FLOWER FORM: Many ¼-inch flowers, single or double, in loose clusters on branched, spreading stems.
SEASON OF BLOOM: Summer in most zones, February to May in areas with warm winters, longer in the cool, mild climate of much of the Pacific Coast.
SOIL: Any good, well-drained garden soil. Plants like sand and gravel.
PH: 7 to 7.5 (neutral to alkaline).
FERTILIZER: Flower or all-purpose fertilizer and well-rotted manure.
WATER: Average, not too wet. Good drainage is important.
EXPOSURE: 8 or more hours of bright sunlight per day, partial shade in the South.
SPACING: 1 to over 3 feet.
PROPAGATION: Seed or stem cuttings.

Method

- **Start seeds indoors** or in cold frames four to eight weeks before the last frost 1 to 2 inches apart in flats or small pots, one or two seeds per pot. Cover with ⅛ inch of soil. Water and keep at 60° to 70°F until seedlings germinate, in about two weeks. Grow in bright sunlight or just below a fluorescent light fixture.

- **Prepare soil outdoors** where plants will grow by turning it under thoroughly, adding fertilizer, gravel, and lime if needed. Plants like a sweet, gravelly soil. Some gardeners find terra-cotta chips helpful.

- **Sow seeds outdoors** after the last frost, in finely tilled soil. Plant seeds 3 or more inches apart and cover them with ⅛ inch of soil. Do not let the seedbed dry out.

- **Thin or transplant** seedlings when they are 3 or 4 inches tall, large enough to handle easily. Shift those growing indoors or in containers to individual 4-inch pots for optimum root growth. When growth fills these, shift plants to gallon or 6-inch standard pots. Thin and transplant those growing outdoors to nursery spacing, 8 to 12 inches apart. Thin them to permanent spacing when they become crowded.

- **Set out plants** purchased with bare roots in early spring while they are still dormant. Move one-year-old seedlings or cuttings grown outdoors at this time, too. Potted plants grown indoors or out can be set out in spring or summer. Do not disturb roots at any time of year unless necessary.

- **Take cuttings** 8 inches long after flowers bloom. Dip ends in rooting hormone (such as Rootone), and set them in a shaded bed in moist, sandy soil or a vermiculite/perlite mix for several months or the winter. Keep cuttings misted or under high humidity. Do not move them until they are well rooted, then put them in pots or nursery beds.

- **Water** young plants well, but do not keep them too wet, so growth will be steady. Keep mature plants on the dry side.

- **Fertilize** plants by enriching poorer soils with manure, peat, and compost. Side-dress plants with all-purpose fertilizer before blooming and again in summer. Mature plants need more fertilizer than young ones. Liquid fertilizer (diluted) is helpful in hot weather.

- **Pests and diseases** include armyworms, leaf miners, crown gall, and red spider mites. They can be controlled with rotenone and pyrethrum sprays. Pick off and discard leaves showing the trails of leaf miners.

- **Mulch** plants in hot, dry areas, to keep soil cool and moist.

- **Prune** and clip plants for shape after they bloom, but do not cut them all the way to the ground.

- **Protect in winter** with several inches of mulch around the crowns of plants in Zone 6 and above.

Tips · For fresh flower arrangements, cut long stems of gypsophila with sharp snippers when blooms begin to open. Plunge the stems into cool water immediately. Condition them in water for several hours before recutting and arranging.
· For dried bouquets, hang small bunches upside down to dry.

Selected Cultivars

Gypsophila paniculata. Popular varieties of this include:
   'Bristol Fairy' and 'Double White' with dainty double white flowers. Both cultivars grow 3 feet tall;
   'Double Snowflake,' which is especially early to bloom and has extra double, pure white flowers on 3-foot plants; and
   'Pacifica,' a pink form, 3 feet tall.
   G. repens. This species is a dwarf growing only 6 inches tall but spreading several feet wide in time. Flowers are pink or white. It makes an excellent perennial ground cover where soil is not acid. Because it has a cascading habit, it is especially effective above a wall or ledge.

BAPTISIA

Botanical name: *Baptisia* (Leguminosae)
Other common names: Wild indigo, False indigo

Baptisia offers showy, lupinelike flowers on long racemes or in small bunches. Native to the eastern states, it is a long-lived, attractive garden perennial that seldom needs division. It makes a good border plant in groups of three or more, and may be naturalized easily in perennial meadows. Baptisia takes a while to become established, needing attention in its early stages of growth, but is exceptionally self-reliant when it matures.

PLANT TYPE: Hardy perennial.
GROWING RANGE: Zones 3 to 9.
HARDINESS: Cold hardy and heat resistant.
PLANT HEIGHT: 2 to 6 feet.
FLOWER COLOR: Blue shades (especially indigo), yellow, white.
FLOWER FORM: Pealike flowers, usually on tall spires.
SEASON OF BLOOM: Summer.
SOIL: Any garden soil.
PH: 6.5 to 7.5.
FERTILIZER: Well-rotted manure or flower fertilizer.
WATER: Average moisture preferred, dry conditions tolerated.
EXPOSURE: Full sun.
SPACING: 1 to 3 feet.
PROPAGATION: Seed or division.

Method

- **Sow seeds indoors.** In late winter, chill the dry seeds in the refrigerator for a few weeks. Then, to speed germination, presoak seeds overnight in water, or wrap them in a moist paper towel and keep them inside a covered container for a few days at room temperature, or break the seed coat with an emery board. Start seeds in flats or small pots filled with sterile potting soil, planting them ¼ inch deep. Germination time varies from ten to thirty days.

- **Prepare soil outdoors** at planting time by tilling in fertilizer and soil amendments, as needed.

- **Sow seeds outdoors** at almost any time. Plant them at least 2 inches apart and cover ¼ inch deep. Seeds sown in fall usually germinate the following spring, but may remain dormant another year.

- **Thin and transplant** seedlings when they are 4 inches tall, if they are crowded. In the garden, thin them to nursery positions 6 inches apart. Step up container-grown plants to 4- to 6-inch pots. When plants are over 8 inches tall, move them to permanent positions or larger pots.

- **Set out plants** grown indoors in the spring when the danger of frost passes.

- **Lift and divide** plants once every three years if necessary, in spring when new growth begins.

- **Water** small plants often, mature plants moderately.

- **Fertilize** lightly at planting time and side-dress plants with composted manure or all-purpose fertilizer each spring.

- **Pests and diseases** seldom are problems. If slugs go after young plants, surround them with wood ashes or diatomaceous earth.

- **Deadhead** plants before seeds ripen, for freer flowering. However, seed may be useful; it can be gathered and planted when ripe in fall. Pods are often used in dried bouquets. Remove stalks of flowers after blooming and seed formation. Cut back plants during winter.

- **Protect in winter** north of Zone 7 by mulching plants with 2 inches of small bark chips or other mulch, removing it when growth resumes in spring. Seedling plants in pots should be submerged in soil and mulched well.

Selected Species

Baptisia alba. This species is grown for its tall white flower spikes on erect plants 3 feet tall. Plant it any time.

B. australis (Blue false indigo, Plains false indigo). This species with showy spikes of indigo blue flowers deserves to be more widely grown, for it is the showiest variety, forming huge clumps 3 to 6 feet tall.

B. leucantha (Prairie false indigo, White false indigo). A long-lived perennial with white flowers, sometimes tinged purple, this species is 3 to 5 feet tall while in bloom, outstanding in a sunny border.

B. tinctoria (Yellow wild indigo). This U.S. native is not as showy as *B. australis,* but it is truly drought tolerant, blooming in summer with plentiful small clusters of pealike flowers. It is also known as horsefly weed, for it is said to repel horseflies when a sprig is stuck behind the horse's ear—or one's own. This is a good plant for carefree perennial meadows.

B. viridis. This species grows 2 to 4 feet tall and is very hardy. Its yellow sweetpealike flowers are followed by marble-size pods that are used for dried arrangements.

BEGONIA

Botanical name: *Begonia* (Begoniaceae)

Begonias are well loved for their lush flowers borne on attractive plants with succulent or fleshy leaves and stems. Colors and forms vary. Over a thousand species have been bred into over ten thousand registered cultivars. They are tender perennials, most often grown as annuals. Several main types mentioned here are most widely used for outdoor gardens. Small-flowered, fibrous-rooted ones are fine for bedding and patio containers, as are tuberous and other large-flowered types. Pendulous varieties are used in hanging baskets.

PLANT TYPE: Tender perennial, often grown as an annual.

GROWING RANGE: All zones as an annual. Zones 10 and 11 as a perennial.

HARDINESS: Most types prefer temperatures from 60° to 80°F and are killed by frost. Fibrous-rooted wax begonias tolerate more heat.

PLANT HEIGHT: 3 inches to over 4 feet.

FLOWER COLOR: Yellow, white, pink, rose, red, orange, or peach, with many bicolors.

FLOWER FORM: Single or double flowers, borne in clusters or singly, from ¼ to 6 inches wide. Male flowers are showier than females.

SEASON OF BLOOM: Fibrous-rooted bedding types are in constant bloom. Tuberous begonias bloom four or five months after planting. Most begonias bloom in summer, but some flower in winter.

SOIL: Light, humusy, with good drainage.

PH: 6 to 7.

FERTILIZER: Osmocote slow-release fertilizer, supplemented with light liquid feedings. Also well-rotted manure, compost, and oak leaf mold. Some growers suggest a superphosphate boost.

WATER: Damp but well-drained soil, high humidity.

EXPOSURE: Partial or filtered shade, especially at midday. Protect from strong wind and sun. Full shade in hot areas (highs regularly in the 90's).

SPACING: 4 inches to 2 feet.

PROPAGATION: Stem, tip, or leaf cuttings; tubers; air layering, or (with difficulty) seed.

Method

- **Start seeds indoors** while temperatures can be kept between 60° and 80°F. For fibrous begonias, start in December or January for May planting to the garden in areas with late frosts. In clean or nearly sterile conditions, fill flat with a light, finely milled, moistened potting medium. It should consist of one-third sand for good drainage. Press soil down gently. Mix seed with a spoonful of fine dry sand and sprinkle it evenly over the top. Mist lightly. Cover with a fitted, plastic top and keep in a shady place, over bottom heat if night temperatures are cool, until seeds germinate, in about three weeks. Gradually bring seedlings out into more light—eventually into bright light but not direct sun. Water only if needed, adding liquid fertilizer at one-fourth the recommended strength. Increase strength of fertilizer when seedlings are larger.

- **Prepare soil outdoors** in flower bed or containers with average to rich soil, tilling in soil amendments such as compost, sand, and fertilizer, if needed. Part-clay soil helps encourage stronger, less succulent plants, which are somewhat slower growing.

- **Do not grow** seed outdoors (under most conditions).

- **Thin or transplant** seedlings or cuttings to larger pots whenever they become crowded. When they outgrow these pots, step them up to larger sizes or plant them in garden positions.

- **Plant tubers,** without covering the tops with soil, in early spring, convex side down, in individual pots or 5 inches apart in flats indoors. Leave one, two, or at the most three sprouts on each tuber; pinch off any extras and either discard or root them. Grow plants in potting mixture recommended above.

- **Set out plants** after the danger of frost passes, first hardening them off in shade for several days.

- **Divide** fibrous-rooted begonias with many stems during warm weather.

- **Take cuttings.** Fibrous-rooted begonias can also be propagated from stem or tip cuttings at any time temperatures are above 65°F, simply by planting pieces in desired spots and watering well for a few weeks. They also root in glasses of rainwater. In good conditions, cuttings root fast and remain in bloom.

  Cuttings from tuberous and other types of begonias are usually rooted indoors in a sandy potting medium, under high humidity. They root from stem, tip, or leaf cuttings.

- **Air layer** difficult plants in spring for summer bloom.

- **Water** until plants are established, then decrease irrigation somewhat. Mist and water often during dry weather.

- **Fertilize** plants steadily but not heavily. Slow-release fertilizers low in nitrogen are recommended.

- **Pests and diseases** rarely are problems. Seedlings sometimes develop damping off fungus, which is best treated by transplanting flowers when they are large enough to handle, taking care not to overwater them.

- **Stake** if necessary.

- **Pinch off** the first few flower buds as soon as they appear, to encourage better plant growth. Fibrous-rooted begonias, especially semperflorens types used in bedding, need little or no care. If they become straggly, clip them back into shape. The trimmings may be planted for additional plants—they root quickly.

- **Protect in winter** by overwintering tubers indoors (in areas where the growing season is long enough for them to develop fully); they may be regrown the following year. At the end of the season, or after frost, dig out the plants and let them dry. Remove all foliage, bit by bit, as it yellows, over the course of several weeks. Be sure to remove the bottom of the stem, over the stem scar. Store in plastic bags filled with vermiculite and a bit of fungicide, in a cool, dark place. Do not let freeze.

- **Pot** fibrous-rooted begonias before cold weather arrives and bring them indoors to bloom in fall and winter, although this may give pests a trip inside. For bug-free (but less attractive, at first) plants, take cuttings, wash them, and pot them.

Selected Species

Begonia rex (Rex begonia, Beefsteak begonia). Leaves are large and showy, but flowers rarely appear and are usually inconspicuous. The damp shade of trees and ferns, in mild, balmy temperatures, is the natural environment for these plants, which are outstanding in beds with the right conditions.

B. x *semperflorens* (Wax begonia). This fibrous-rooted variety has green leaves mottled with white, or bronze. Its tiny clustered flowers, white, pink, or red, maintain their bloom and are found in flower beds everywhere. They are easy to grow and heat tolerant. The red-flowered, bronze-leaved strains are most weather resistant.

B. x *tuberhybrida* (Tuberous begonia). Beautiful and dramatic, tuberous begonias have large camellialike flowers up to 6 inches in diameter, in all the colors and forms of begonias. Although easy to grow in coastal California, they are difficult outdoors in most parts of the United States because of summer heat or too short a summer season. In moist, shaded locations they sometimes do well. Plants are upright, but often need staking. New hybrids are smaller and bloom earlier.

Home gardeners usually grow them from tubers or buy plants, but some of the new hybrids bloom in only four or five months from seed instead of the usual year or more.

Some forms of this variety are perfect for hanging baskets. Called trailing begonias, they have a graceful, pendulous shape. As with other tuberous begonias, outdoor weather is a problem for these in most regions, but if kept in shade and watered well they may perform beautifully.

BERGENIA

Botanical name: *Bergenia* (Saxifragaceae)

Bergenia is a rugged, old-fashioned perennial that is among the earliest to bloom each year. It must appeal to the child in us all—in some regions, it is nicknamed pig squeak (from the sound made if you pull a leaf between your thumb and forefinger) and elephant's ears. In Great Britain and in mild Pacific Coast climates, where it is evergreen, it may bloom in December or January. In colder areas, its leaves die back in the winter, but it reappears early in spring and blooms with the crocus or daffodils. Its dense stands of large, round, leathery/waxy leaves make it a valuable ground cover, though it can be invasive. It also makes a good border or container plant. Bergenia leaves and flowers are exceptionally nice in flower arrangements, staying fresh for weeks.

PLANT TYPE: Hardy perennial.
GROWING RANGE: Zones 3 to 9.
HARDINESS: Very cold tolerant, harmed by prolonged heat in the 90's (F).
PLANT HEIGHT: 8 to 24 inches.
FLOWER COLOR: White, pink, rose, lavender, peach.
FLOWER FORM: Spikes of clustered small, flaring, bell-like or starlike blossoms that are waxy and substantial.
SEASON OF BLOOM: Late winter or early spring.
SOIL: Well-drained sandy or gravelly loam.
PH: 6.5 to 7.
FERTILIZER: Flower fertilizer, well-rotted manure.
WATER: Keep somewhat moist, not too wet.
EXPOSURE: Full sun to heavy shade (more shade in the South and in hot regions), blooming better in more light.

SPACING: 10 to 20 inches.

PROPAGATION: Seed, division, or tip cuttings.

Method

- **Start seeds indoors** in winter or early spring, at 60° to 70°F, about an inch apart. Press ⅛ inch deep into a sterile potting mix, one-third to one-half sand. Cover flats with glass or plastic (an inch or so above soil level) until germination occurs, in one to six months.

- **Prepare soil outdoors** by tilling in compost, fertilizer, sand, gravel, and other soil amendments, as needed.

- **Sow seeds outdoors** or in a cold frame in early spring while soil is still cool, ⅛ inch deep and at least ½ inch apart, in fine-textured sandy soil. Mark rows or pots well. It may germinate in a month or two, or any time up to a year later.

- **Thin and transplant** seedlings when they are 3 to 4 inches high, if they are crowded. In the garden, thin them to nursery positions 6 inches apart. Step up container-grown plants (indoors or out) to 4- to 6-inch pots. When they grow enough to become crowded again, thin or transplant them to their permanent positions outdoors, or to larger pots.

- **Set out plants** grown indoors after the danger of frost passes, after hardening them off in shade. Set plants growing outdoors into their places in the garden at any time the soil can be worked.

- **Divide** plants in early spring, replanting divisions immediately. The rootstock is very thick.

- **Take cuttings** with several inches of stem in spring. Root them in moist, sandy soil in shade directly in the garden or in pots or flats.

- **Water** often enough to keep soil moist but not soggy.

- **Fertilize** moderately at planting time and each spring with low-nitrogen, high-phosphorus and -potassium fertilizer.

- **Pests and diseases** rarely disturb these rugged plants.

- **Remove** spent flower stalks and damaged leaves.

- **Mulch** with evergreen boughs where ground freezes deeply in winter, but remove mulch in early spring. In hot, dry regions, mulch with bark chips to help keep roots cool and soil moist.

Selected Species and Cultivars

Bergenia ciliata (Winter bergenia). This species has sturdy, round, 8-inch-long leaves, in rosettes. Flower spikes 12 inches tall appear in early spring. There may be several stems of pink or white flowers on each rosette.

B. cordifolia (Heartleaf bergenia). This is an evergreen perennial from Siberia with large, glossy, heart-shaped leaves up to 1 foot tall, in rosettes. Flower spikes may be 12 to 16 inches tall in shades of pink, white, or lavender.

Hybrid cultivars of mixed heritage include:

'Bressingham Salmon,' which holds compact spikes of salmon pink flowers above rosettes of 9- to 12-inch-long leaves. The broad green leaves are tinged pink or purple in winter. It blooms later than 'Bressingham White'; and

'Bressingham White,' a vigorous plant up to 24 inches tall while in bloom. It has very showy, pure white flower spikes in spring, and attractive, leathery, green leaves. It blooms earlier than some of the pink types.

BROWALLIA

Botanical name: *Browallia* (Solanaceae)
Other common name: Bush violet

Browallia is a tender perennial most often grown as an annual. It is delicate looking without being dull—plants are well covered with blue or white star-shaped flowers for many months. Most types trail attractively in hanging baskets. It is also useful in the front edges of borders, in pots and window boxes, and, in frost-free areas, as shrublike foundation plants. Browallia will self-sow under the right conditions, is easy to grow, and is less prone to heat prostration than impatiens or tuberous begonias. Plants may become established as perennials in Zones 10 and 11.

PLANT TYPE: Tender perennial, usually grown as an annual.
GROWING RANGE: All zones as an annual, Zones 10 and 11 as a perennial.
HARDINESS: Easily frozen but tolerant of heat in the 90's (F). Plants are overchilled when exposed to temperatures under 60°F and may drop buds, lose leaf color, and die.
PLANT HEIGHT: 8 inches to 5 feet, depending on variety. Most are under 18 inches tall.
FLOWER COLOR: Deep violet-blue, medium blue, or white, against rich green foliage.
FLOWER FORM: Flat, outward-facing star-shaped flowers up to 1½ inches wide. They appear singly or in small clusters at stem ends and in leaf axils.
SEASON OF BLOOM: Summer in most areas, most or all of year in frost-free areas.
SOIL: Any good garden soil.
PH: 6.5 to 7.
FERTILIZER: Any flower fertilizer.
WATER: Water often enough to keep plants from wilting—keep soil moist.
EXPOSURE: Bright partial shade. Protect from late-afternoon sun. If plants become too leggy, put in brighter light.
SPACING: 8 inches to 3 feet.
PROPAGATION: Seed or stem cuttings.

❧ *Method*

· **Start seeds indoors** in fall or winter for spring bloom. Grow in flats (sprinkle seeds evenly over flat) or one or two per six-pack pocket in potting soil. Cover seed with no more than ⅛ inch of soil. Water and keep in a warm (65° to 75°F) place until seeds germinate. Then keep plants between 60° and 85°F, in bright sunlight or a few inches below a fluorescent light fixture. If grown as annuals, seedlings should have twelve to fourteen hours of light per day; as perennials, at least ten.

- **Prepare soil outdoors** in flower bed by tilling in compost, fertilizer, and other soil amendments, as needed.

- **Sow seeds outdoors** where they will grow after any danger of frost has passed. Results are usually better indoors.

- **Thin and transplant** indoor-grown seedlings whenever they become crowded. Indoor- or outdoor-grown plants may be set in their permanent locations when they are 4 to 6 inches high.

- **Set plants outdoors** after all danger of freezing weather passes, after hardening off in the shade. Plant five or six together in hanging baskets.

- **Root cuttings** in a mix of sand and compost, under mist or high humidity and in shade. Temperatures should range between about 65° and 80°F.

- **Water** often enough to keep soil slightly moist but not soggy. Plants are easily damaged by overwatering.

- **Fertilize** when plants start to form buds by side-dressing with a light application of low-nitrogen, high-phosphorus and -potassium fertilizer ("blossom booster" or "tomato" fertilizer). Keep the level constant throughout the blooming season. Overfeeding will stimulate too much foliage, at the expense of flowers.

- **Pests and diseases** are rare outdoors, but browallia may be affected by whiteflies and other common greenhouse pests indoors. Combat them with a spray of rotenone or insecticidal soap.

- **Pinch back** tips for bushiness when plants are 5 inches tall, and again once or twice a few weeks later.

- **Mulch** with grass clippings or small bark chips to keep soil moist.

- **Trim** if plants become straggly.

- **Protect in winter** in mild climates by mulching with several inches of bark chips. In cold climates, plants may survive winter indoors as houseplants.

Selected Species and Cultivars

Browallia speciosa. Cultivars for hanging baskets include:
  'Blue Bells,' in rich violet-blue, growing 14 inches tall with 2-inch flowers and a branching habit;
  'Dawn Blue,' a very showy variety. Its 2-inch flowers are pale blue with darker veins and are borne on 18-inch-tall plants;
  'Powder Blue,' a medium light blue variety growing 14 inches tall with 2-inch flowers; and
  'Silver Bells,' the white version of 'Blue Bells.'

For bedding, potting, or hanging baskets, dwarf cultivars under 10 inches tall include:
'Blue Troll,' with deep blue-violet flowers; and
'White Troll,' with large white flowers and a bushy habit.

BRUNNERA

Botanical name: *Brunnera* (Boraginaceae)
Other common name: Bugloss

With flowers resembling forget-me-nots, brunnera is hardy in most of the United States and into Canada. It has somewhat hairy, deep green, heart-shaped leaves, topped by bright blue flowers in spring. Mass plants in woodlands or shaded flower beds. Although this plant self-sows readily, it is difficult to grow indoors, partly because seed must be fresh.

PLANT TYPE: Hardy perennial.
GROWING RANGE: Zones 3 to 8.
HARDINESS: Very cold hardy, tolerating temperatures below −30°F, but killed by high heat.
PLANT HEIGHT: 1 to 1½ feet.
FLOWER COLOR: Blue with yellow eyes.
FLOWER FORM: Cymes or sprays of ¼-inch single blossoms.
SEASON OF BLOOM: Mid-spring to late spring.
SOIL: Humusy, rich.
PH: 6.5 to 7.
FERTILIZER: Well-rotted manure, all-purpose fertilizer.
WATER: Moist conditions.
EXPOSURE: Semishade or woodland conditions.
SPACING: 1 foot.
PROPAGATION: Division, seed, or root cuttings.

Method

- **Prepare soil outdoors** before planting time by tilling in aged manure, leaf mold, compost, and other soil amendments, as needed.

- **Sow seeds outdoors** after the danger of frost has passed. Plant seeds while fresh, spacing them an inch or more apart and covering with ⅛ inch of soil. Keep moist.

- **Thin and transplant** seedlings when they become crowded, to 6 inches apart or grow in 4-inch pots, working on an overcast day if possible to minimize drying out. Move plants to permanent positions or larger pots when they are 8 to 10 inches tall.

- **Set out** bare-root or field-grown plants in early spring before the last frost. Set out potted plants in spring or summer after the danger of frost passes.

- **Divide** plants in early spring when growth begins.

- **Take cuttings** from thick portions of root in fall and propagate them in a cold frame over winter, planted 2 or 3 inches deep.

- **Water** plants well, especially during hot weather.
- **Fertilize** lightly in early and late spring with aged manure and all-purpose fertilizer.
- **Pests and diseases** rarely are problems.
- **Mulch** plants with a 2-inch layer of humusy compost.
- **Remove** stalks of flowers after they bloom if seeds are not wanted. Trim off brown leaves.
- **Protect in winter** by mulching plants with 3 inches of bark chips or 6 inches of salt hay in regions where ground freezes hard. Dig potted plants into soil and mulch them before cold weather arrives. Remove salt hay in spring when new growth begins; make sure bark chips or other permanent mulches are around but not over crowns.

Selected Species

Brunnera macrophylla, formerly *Anchusa myosotidiflora* (Siberian bugloss). This is the most popular garden brunnera. Bunches of tiny blue, yellow-centered flowers contrast well with forest-green leaves on plants 1 to 1 ½ feet high.

CALCEOLARIA

Botanical name: *Calceolaria* (Scrophulariaceae)
Other common names: Pocketbook flower, Slipper flower

With its clusters of gaily colored, balloonlike blossoms, annual calceolaria is a popular potted greenhouse plant. It is also striking in flower beds where summers are not too hot for it—in England and parts of the Pacific Coast, for instance. There are several hundred species of calceolaria and many hybrids. Most are annuals but a few are hardy or tender perennials. Use calceolaria in pots, for bedding, or in rock gardens.

PLANT TYPES: Annual, or hardy or tender perennial.
GROWING RANGE: All zones.
HARDINESS: Most annuals are easily killed by temperatures under 35° or over 90°F. Perennials are less tender but their tolerance varies with the species.
PLANT HEIGHT: 4 to 20 inches for popular annual types. Some hardy perennials are subshrubs reaching 6 feet; others grow to just a few inches.
FLOWER COLOR: Yellow, rose, red, or orange. Some blooms are bicolored red and white or red and yellow. Many are dotted or spotted.
FLOWER FORM: Balloonlike or slipperlike blossoms. Annual plants hold blooms in dense clusters.
SEASON OF BLOOM: Annuals most often bloom in late winter or early spring. Perennials bloom in spring or summer.
SOIL: Light, well drained, sandy or gritty.
PH: 6.5 to 7.
FERTILIZER: Annuals should receive slow-release flower fertilizer such as Osmocote. Perennials should be given well-rotted manure and a light dose of all-purpose fertilizer.

WATER: Keep soil slightly moist but not too wet.
EXPOSURE: Full sun in cold weather, semishade in warm weather.
SPACING: Varies with type, from a few inches to several feet.
PROPAGATION: Seed (annuals and, rarely, perennials) or division (perennials).

Method

- **Start seeds indoors** (annuals) in September or October for bloom in spring. Sow in small pots or flats in moistened, finely milled soil made up of one-third vermiculite. Do not cover seed. Germination takes up to ten days at 65°F. Damping off is often a problem; treat soil with fungicide before planting seed. Transplant seedlings one to a six-pack pocket when they are large enough to handle.

- **Prepare soil outdoors** incorporating leaf mold, compost, and sand or fine grit if needed for improved drainage.

- **Sow seeds outdoors** if you live in the mild climate of the Pacific Northwest. Soil should be very finely tilled and hoed into shallow rows. Mix seeds with a small amount of dry sand and sprinkle sparingly on rows. Do not cover. Irrigate frequently but gently, so the soil surface never dries out.

- **Thin or transplant** indoor- and outdoor-grown seedlings if they are crowded. Plant annual types individually in 4- to 6-inch pots or space them about 10 inches apart outdoors. Perennials may be grown in nursery beds for a season before being moved to their permanent positions.

- **Set out plants** of annual types during cool weather in winter or spring, when temperature will remain above freezing but under 60°F. Few parts of the United States have the right climate. Set out hardy perennials in early spring, after they are hardened off, when new growth begins, a few weeks before the danger of frost ends, or later, but before hot weather arrives.

- **Divide and reset** perennial calceolarias occasionally, only if needed, in early spring when new growth begins.

- **Water** plants often enough to keep soil somewhat moist. Mist plants during hot weather.

- **Fertilize** annuals steadily. Supplement slow-release fertilizer with light liquid feedings when plants begin to bud. Provide a light, constant level of fertilizer to perennials through soil enrichment with well-rotted manure and compost.

- **Pests** include whiteflies, aphids, mites, and damping off fungus. Prevent the insects with insecticidal soap and rotenone, and use fungicide and good ventilation to control damping off.

- **Remove** spent flowers and brown leaves. Discard annual plants when they finish blooming.

- **Protect in winter** by keeping pots of annual calceolarias indoors at cool temperatures near 50°F. Perennials should be sheltered or mulched with bark chips 2 or 3 inches deep.

Selected Species and Cultivars

Calceolaria biflora. Long stems are topped with delicate golden pouches. This 6-inch-tall perennial grows well in semishade only in a cool climate, as in parts of Zones 5 to 8. 'Goldcrest' is a cultivar that has somewhat larger flowers and grows 8 inches tall.

C. crenatiflora, formerly *C. herbeohybrida.* These hybrids for greenhouse conditions are available in grandiflora and multiflora types, both standard and dwarf. Cultivars recommended for home greenhouses include:

'Anytime,' which is less sensitive to heat and day length and may be sown at any time of year indoors for attractive pot plants about four months later. Grow at 50° to 70°F in bright light. Plants bloom when about 5 inches tall. The series includes clear rose, rose and white, red and yellow, bronze, yellow spotted, and red shades; and

'Jewel Cluster,' about 1 foot tall, blooming in late winter or spring from a fall planting. Keep temperatures under 60°F. Many colors, heavily speckled, are included.

C. darwinii. For cool, damp rock garden sites in partial shade, this is a beautiful, slipper-like perennial flower. Blooms are gold and mahogany with a white bar across the lip. It grows about 5 inches tall and 9 inches wide in Zones 5 to 8.

C. integrifolia. This half-hardy perennial becomes shrublike in places where the climate permits its survival—cool parts of Zones 8 to 10. Large golden pouches bloom in clusters for many weeks, weather permitting. It usually grows 1 to 2 feet tall and may be discarded at the end of the flowering season. 'Sunshine,' 'Midas,' and 'Golden Bunch' are cultivars.

CALENDULA

Botanical name: *Calendula* (Compositae)
Other common names: English marigold, Pot marigold

When planted at the right time of year, calendulas are among the easiest of the hardy annuals to grow from seed. The large seeds develop quickly into striking flowering plants in sunny colors. Because stems are strong and flowers last well, they are popular for cutting. Use them as colorful herbs, as bedding plants, and in containers, too. In areas where calendulas thrive, they self-sow and naturalize themselves readily.

Most calendulas dislike heat but thrive in cold, even freezing weather. New hybrids with better heat tolerance have been developed. The calendula is a cottage garden plant with practical as well as aesthetic uses. Petals are used to garnish soups, salads, and hors d'oeuvres. They are cooked with rice as a substitute for saffron, but impart color only, no flavor or scent. Calendula leaves had a reputation in ancient herbal lore for curing small warts.

> PLANT TYPE: Hardy annual, sometimes grown as a biennial.
> GROWING RANGE: All zones.
> HARDINESS: Survives light to moderate freezes, but does not thrive in prolonged heat in the 90's (F), especially if weather is humid.
> PLANT HEIGHT: 8 to 30 inches.
> FLOWER COLOR: Orange, cream, lemon-yellow, gold, shrimp, peach, or rusty orange. Some have chocolate-brown centers.

FLOWER FORM: Round, fluffy disc and ray flowers 1½ to 3 inches wide. Some are extremely double, and some are quilled, incurved, or crested. Flowers close at night and on cloudy days.

SEASON OF BLOOM: Summer and fall in most areas; fall, winter, and spring in places with mild winters; year-round in mild Pacific Coast climates.

SOIL: Any good garden soil, well drained.

PH: 6.5 to 7.

FERTILIZER: Flower fertilizer high in phosphorus and potassium.

WATER: Keep soil slightly moist.

EXPOSURE: Full sun or bright partial shade, more shade in areas where temperatures are consistently in the 90's.

SPACING: 8 to 12 inches.

PROPAGATION: Seed.

Method

- **Start seeds indoors** in flats, small pots, or six-packs filled with moistened potting soil. Plant one seed per pot, or space 1 inch apart. Plant ⅛ to ¼ inch deep—they need darkness to germinate. Starting seeds in individual pots saves having to transplant them. Germinate seeds at about 65° to 75°F. After germination (in about 8 to 10 days) they can be grown in temperatures from about 50° to 80°F. In northern and central areas, sow seeds in February to put out in April, or sow them in early August to bloom outside in autumn. In areas with mild winters, start seeds in fall or early winter. In mild Pacific Coast areas, start seeds at any time.

- **Prepare soil outdoors** by tilling in fertilizer and soil amendments to a depth of 1 foot.

- **Sow seeds outdoors** where they will grow four weeks before frost-free date or during warm weather at the same time of year as indoor-grown seedlings are set outdoors. Sow in rows with seeds spaced 2 or more inches apart. Germination percentage is usually excellent.

- **Thin or transplant** indoor- or outdoor-grown seedlings to permanent spacing when they are 4 to 6 inches tall.

- **Set plants outdoors** during cool times of year—spring in northern and central states, winter in Zones 9 to 11. When indoor-grown plants are about 4 inches tall, harden them off outdoors. You can set them out even if light frosts are possible, but protect them from temperatures below 28°F.

- **Water** often enough to keep soil moist but not soggy.

- **Fertilize** steadily during growth. Side-dress with a light application of low-nitrogen, high-phosphorus and -potassium fertilizer ("blossom booster" or "tomato" fertilizer) when plants start to form buds.

- **Pests and diseases** are few. Nematodes in soil deter gardeners from growing calendulas in Florida and other southern locations, for they are one of the most susceptible plants. In nematode-prone areas, grow calendulas in containers of sterile soil, not in the ground.

Slugs and snails are less of a problem, and can be treated or prevented by dusting the ground with wood ashes or diatomaceous earth, setting out traps of shallow pans of beer, or with slug and snail bait.

- **Pinch back** tips for bushiness when plants are 6 inches tall.

- **Mulch** plants in dry areas with grass clippings or small bark chips.

- **Remove** spent flower heads (unless seed is wanted) and trim plants if they become straggly. Remove and replace them when they are too unsightly.

- **Protect in winter** in mild-winter areas by covering plants with cloths or cardboard boxes whenever a hard freeze (26°F or colder) is predicted, and uncover them the next day or when the weather warms sufficiently. In other areas, plants may be grown easily in cool greenhouses or sunrooms in winter, but cannot live outdoors.

- **Harvest** flowers to be used as herbs as soon as they are fully open. Petals may be used fresh or dried.

- **Dry** flowers on a screen in a warm, airy, dry place. The petals may be removed from the flower head either before or after drying.

- **Store** dried petals in an airtight container.

Tip · **In the muggy summer weather of the central East Coast and Midwest, it is difficult to grow most calendulas well. Try the new heat-tolerant types like 'Bon Bon' or plant standard types in late summer for fall bloom. Both flowers and leaves of calendula survive light frost easily. Although seed packets suggest planting calendula in early spring, hot weather often comes so early that plants do not have time to reach their peak. Fall may be better!**

Selected Species and Cultivars

Calendula officinalis (Pot marigold). The old-fashioned pot marigold is often included in herb gardens. Plants are usually about 12 inches tall, but sometimes reach 24 inches. They are more delicate and have smaller flowers than the hybrid bedding types.

Calendula hybrids, primarily related to *C. officinalis,* are available in an array of forms and sizes. Flowers are large and showy, sometimes more than 3 inches wide. Tall varieties range from 18 to 30 inches in height, dwarf types from 8 to 18 inches. Some notable cultivars are:

'Apricot Sherbet,' a heat-resistant, early-blooming, easily grown strain. It grows 15 inches tall and has peachy flowers up to 3 inches wide;

'Bon Bon,' bred to continue blooming in spite of hot weather. It is early blooming and a compact 12 inches in height. Flowers are about 2½ inches wide. Colors include yellow, orange, and apricot;

'Geisha Girl,' 24 inches tall, with orange, incurved petals resembling football chrysanthemums;

'Kablouna,' 20 inches tall, with large crested flowers in a range of colors;

'Pacific Beauty,' which can be obtained in mixed or individual colors in the full range available among calendulas. Robust plants grow to 20 inches tall; and

'Radio Extra Selected,' with quilled petals like a cactus dahlia. It has large, bright orange blooms and grows 18 to 20 inches tall.

CALIFORNIA POPPY

Botanical name: *Eschscholzia californica* (Papaveraceae)

California poppy, the state flower of California, is a popular member of the poppy family with silky, four-petaled, cup-shaped flowers. Flowers may be single or double and often have a crinkled texture; leaves are blue-green and finely divided. The blossoms close at night and on cloudy days, but provide color for many months in sunlight. California poppy, a hardy annual, is used in wildflower gardens, on slopes, in borders and massed plantings. It is also tolerant of salt spray and grows well by the seashore. It is not propagated vegetatively.

PLANT TYPE: Hardy annual.
GROWING RANGE: All zones.
HARDINESS: Heat tolerant, sensitive to frost.
PLANT HEIGHT: 12 to 24 inches.
FLOWER COLOR: Yellow, orange, pink, red.
FLOWER FORM: Single or double flowers 2 to 3 inches across.
SEASON OF BLOOM: Spring and summer.
SOIL: Light, sandy, well drained, not too rich.
PH: 6 to 7.5.
FERTILIZER: Well-rotted manure, compost, or all-purpose fertilizer.
WATER: Average to dry conditions.
EXPOSURE: Full sun.
SPACING: 6 to 8 inches.
PROPAGATION: Seed.

Method

- **Start seeds indoors** six to eight weeks before outdoor planting time in small pots filled with sterile seed starting medium. Plant seeds ⅛ inch deep, water, and keep in a cool (55° to 60°F) place until they germinate in ten to twelve days. Grow seedlings in bright sunlight or a few inches below a fluorescent light fixture.

- **Prepare soil outdoors** before planting by tilling in fertilizer and a light amount of compost or other organic soil improvers, as needed.

- **Sow seeds outdoors** in smoothly prepared and fertilized beds in early spring as soon as the soil can be worked. Plant seeds 12 inches apart and ⅛ inch deep. Do not let the seedbed dry out. Where frost does not occur in winter, sow in fall for early-spring bloom.

- **Thin** outdoor-grown seedlings to their permanent spacing when they are 4 inches high.

- **Set plants outdoors** in midspring after they have been hardened off. Transplant carefully as California poppy roots do not like to be disturbed.

- **Water** when the soil dries out. California poppy is very drought tolerant.

- **Fertilize** at planting time; no further feeding is necessary.

- **Pests** are not a problem; **diseases** include mildew and root rots, which can be controlled by improving air circulation between plants and by improving drainage.

Tips · California poppy readily self-sows where winter temperatures do not fall below freezing.
   · Keep faded flowers picked off to extend the blooming period further into the summer.

Selected Cultivars

Several cultivars of the California poppy have been developed. These include 'Aurantiaca,' a glowing rich orange; 'Ballerina,' a mixture of double and semidouble flowers in many colors (sometimes bicolored); and 'Mission Bells,' which comes in a bright range of colors with semidouble flowers.

CALLA LILY

Botanical name: *Zantedeschia* (Araceae)
Other common names: Arum lily, Lily of the Nile

The beautiful calla lily of California poster fame is a tender perennial that grows from a rhizome. Its large flowers are side-wrapped, flaring trumpets stretched to a dramatic point. Stylized and tropical looking, it comes from Africa. Its bold heart- or arrow-shaped leaves are fleshy and substantial, yet graceful. Use calla lilies as container, bedding, and accent plants with a bold, tropical look, and as cut flowers. Plants show well in groups of three or more. In colder areas, they are kept indoors over winter.

PLANT TYPE: Tender perennial.
GROWING RANGE: Zones 9 to 11. Must be brought indoors in zones north of 9.
HARDINESS: Easily chilled or frozen, but tolerant of heat in the high 90's (F).
PLANT HEIGHT: 1 to 3 feet.
FLOWER COLOR: White, yellow, pink, peach, rose tones.
FLOWER FORM: 3- to 6-inch-long flowers are showy, flaring, trumpetlike spathes with a central spadix.
SEASON OF BLOOM: Summer in northern and central states; most of the year, particularly spring, in areas with mild winters.
SOIL: Rich, loamy sand, well drained.
PH: 6.5 to 7.
FERTILIZER: Slow-release flower fertilizer and liquid feeding supplement.

WATER: Keep soil somewhat moist but do not allow it to remain too wet, or rhizomes may rot.

EXPOSURE: Bright partial shade. Plants need 8 or more hours of filtered sunlight per day. Brighter sunlight is safe if temperatures are cool (in the 60° to 70°F range).

SPACING: 1 to 3 feet.

PROPAGATION: Seed, division, or rhizome cuttings.

Method

- **Sow seeds indoors** ¼ inch deep, one or two seeds per pot, in moist, sandy potting soil in 4-inch pots where the temperature range is from 65° to 80°F. Do not let potting medium dry out. They will germinate in one to three months. When seedlings appear, grow them in bright light at temperatures between 55° and 80°F. Step them up to larger pots when roots fill growing space.

- **Prepare soil outdoors** in flower beds, adding fine grit or sand for improved drainage if it is needed, along with other soil amendments.

- **Sow seeds outdoors** only where there is a long, warm, frost-free period (above 60°F for at least five months), as in Zones 7 to 11, and protection from harsh weather and pests. When weather is warm and settled, prepare a finely tilled, weed-free area and plant seeds 4 inches apart in shallow rows 2 or 3 inches deep. Cover with about ¼ inch of soil. Soil surface must not dry out.

- **Grow rhizomes and plants** indoors or out. Treat rhizomes with fungicide or dust them with Rootone F (which contains fungicide) before planting. Indoors, set them into large pots of rich soil with the top third of the rhizome exposed, as with irises. Grow them in bright light at about 65° to 75°F. A tub 15 inches in diameter is large enough to grow three rhizomes of a large variety or seven of a small type to maturity. They may be started indoors in smaller pots and moved outside to larger pots or the flower bed when the weather is warm enough—this works best in most areas.

  Outdoors, set rhizomes or plants where they are wanted when the temperature has stabilized in the 65° to 85°F range.

- **Divide** plants in borders every few years, if necessary, dusting cuts with fungicide. If potted, crowded plants may be shifted to larger containers.

- **Root cuttings** of rhizomes in a mix of sand and compost, under mist or high humidity, in shade. Allow cuts to heal over for twenty-four hours in open air and dust the entire piece with fungicide before planting. Temperatures should range between 65° and 80°F.

- **Water** often enough to keep soil slightly moist but not soggy. Plants tend to rot when overwatered. Mist plants if humidity is low.

- **Fertilize** plants steadily with slow-release and liquid fertilizers. Healthy plants are heavy feeders during periods of active growth.

- **Pests and diseases** are few, though calla lilies are prone to various kinds of fungi. Always plant them in clean soil and keep soil from becoming overly sodden. Dust or treat rhizomes with fungicide before planting.

- **Rest** rhizomes of calla lilies for a required dormant period, which occurs at different times of the year in different locations or with different schedules. In northern and central states, callas are either grown indoors in fall, winter, and spring and rested in summer, or else started indoors in spring and grown outdoors in summer and early fall, then rested for the remainder of fall and winter. In southern or mild-winter areas (Zones 8 to 10), plants are usually rested during the hottest part of summer and left to regrow during cooler weather. Plants will become dormant if water is withheld. Leaves should be removed with a gentle pull when they turn yellow or drop.

- **Protect in winter** in mild-winter areas with 2 or 3 inches of bark chips or other mulch to shield them from cold spells. If soil is excessively wet during the dormant period, dig the rhizomes and store them indoors. In areas with freezing winters, rhizomes are either dug and stored in cool conditions (like dahlia tubers) for winter or grown indoors. All parts of calla lilies must be protected from heavy frost.

Tip · A plant called Monarch of the East is sometimes lumped with calla lilies in catalogs. This is not a true calla, but *Sauromatum guttatum,* with an entirely different flower and leaf. Its brownish flowers are large but strange looking, appearing before the leaves. Its umbrellalike leaves are very tropical and attractive. Unless the gardener is expecting this appearance and not *Zantedeschia,* there is bound to be some disappointment.

Selected Species and Cultivars

Zantedeschia aethiopica (White calla). This type grows 2½ to 3 feet tall and has a very large, white, flaring, cone-shaped flower with a prominent yellow spadix. Flowers are often 6 inches long and leaves broad and graceful. It is customary to group several plants together for effect. 'Giant White' is a good popular cultivar.

Elliottiana (Golden or Yellow calla). Plants grow about 18 inches tall. Flowers are smaller and narrower—3 or 4 inches long—than those of *Z. aethiopica* and leaves also are sometimes relatively narrow. They may be flecked with white dots.

Z. rehmannii (Pink calla). Somewhat smaller than *Z. elliottiana,* this type has a soft, lovely, rosy flower color.

Zantedeschia hybrids. Several strains of hybrids bloom in a range of colors from cream through yellow, peach, and pink. 'New Zealand' hybrids and 'Sunrise' are examples. These plants are smaller than *Z. aethiopica* and do not include true whites, but are very pretty.

CAMPANULA

Botanical Name: *Campanula* (Campanulaceae)
Other common name: Bellflower

Campanulas come in so many forms that one can be chosen to fit practically any garden situation. Some tiny perennials thrive in the cracks in a garden wall, while bigger, more robust species respond to pampering in a fertile cultivated bed. All campanulas produce dainty blossoms over a period of several weeks.

PLANT TYPES: Hardy perennial, biennial, or annual.
GROWING RANGE: Zones 3 to 8 as perennials, Zones 3 to 9 as biennials and annuals.
HARDINESS: Cold hardy, but not tolerant of extreme summer heat.
PLANT HEIGHT: 5 to 48 inches.
FLOWER COLOR: Blue, purple, muted pink, white.
FLOWER FORM: Varies with species. Bell-shaped flowers common.
SEASON OF BLOOM: Spring through summer, depending on species.
SOIL: Fertile, gritty garden loam with good drainage, except for species suited to rock garden sites.
PH: 5.5 to 7.
FERTILIZER: Add well-rotted manure or compost to planting site. Light feedings with a liquid fertilizer, like fish emulsion, may be made every few weeks in spring.
WATER: Average. Plants should receive water once a week in spring and summer.
EXPOSURE: Full sun to half-day shade.
SPACING: 5 to 24 inches, depending on species.
PROPAGATION: Seed or division.

Method

- **Sow seeds indoors** in early spring (for perennials and annuals) or early fall (for perennials and biennials). Sow them thinly over a premoistened flat, and barely cover with soil. Keep in a warm (70°F) place until seeds germinate, about two weeks.

- **Prepare soil outdoors** by digging a 2-inch layer of rotted manure into the planting site. Add coarse sand to clay soil to improve drainage; add peat moss to sandy soil to help it retain moisture.

- **Sow seeds outdoors** of vigorous perennial varieties in early spring or early fall. Direct-seed only species known to thrive in your area.

- **Thin** seedlings (indoor and outdoor grown) to 3 inches apart when the first true leaves appear. Move the flat to the cold frame or other protected place for about three weeks before setting out plants.

- **Set plants outdoors** when they have four or five true leaves. Transplant perennials in late spring or fall. Biennials may be set out from late summer to fall, until two weeks before the first hard freeze is expected.

- **Divide** established perennial plants by digging clusters of rooted stems from the outside of the clump in early spring or fall, and transplanting them immediately.

- **Water** immediately after planting, and during dry periods in spring and summer. Water until the plants are thoroughly soaked.

- **Fertilize** lightly with a liquid fertilizer two weeks after transplanting. In spring, apply a weak solution of fish emulsion or manure tea every two to three weeks. Rock garden species require less fertilizer than larger cultivated varieties.

- **Pests and diseases** include aphids, which can be controlled by spraying the plants with soapy water. Crown rot may develop because of overwatering and/or poor drainage.

- **Winter protection** consists of a 5-inch layer of mulch spread around the plants' crowns in fall. Allow a little green growth to poke through the mulch, especially when growing a biennial species.

Tips • Just prior to flowering, tall varieties may require staking to keep them from falling over.
  • The biennial species of campanula help fill in the "flower gap" between spring-flowering bulbs and summer annuals.

Selected Species

Campanula carpatica, C. collina, and *C. raineri* (Carpathian harebell, Tussock bellflower) are good perennial rock garden species under 9 inches tall.

C. glomerata (Clustered bellflower). This showy perennial produces short flowering spikes topped by clusters of vibrant purple blossoms. Plant it in beds.

C. medium (Canterbury bells) is one of the showiest of all biennial flowers, growing 2½ to 4 feet tall. Plant seed in late summer or fall in temperatures around 70°F, 4 inches apart. Transplant to permanent position in early spring when new growth begins. Some double-flowered varieties are available.

C. persicifolia (Peach-bells, Willow bellflower) is an easy-to-grow 3-foot-tall perennial species for informal borders. Space mature plants 24 inches apart.

CANDYTUFT

Botanical name: *Iberis* (Cruciferae)

Candytuft, from Crete (formerly known as Candia), is an easy-care plant that makes low-growing bright spots. Myriads of tiny flowers bloom in flat or rounded clusters. The annual types are popular bedding plants, and the perennials are long lived and attractive. The leaves stay green in winter. In spring, when the tulips bloom, they provide dazzling white cascades of flowers over walls or in rock gardens, or can be massed as a ground cover or near the front in mixed borders. Seeds of candytuft are said to have been used for mustard in ancient Egypt.

PLANT TYPES: Hardy annual or perennial.
GROWING RANGE: All zones as annuals. Zones 3 to 9 as perennials.
HARDINESS: Annuals tolerate light frost but not heavy frost or high heat. Perennials are hardy to −30°F and tolerate summer heat in the low 90's (F).
PLANT HEIGHT: 4 to 15 inches.
FLOWER COLOR: Annuals, white, pink, rosy red, scarlet, violet, purple; perennials, white.
FLOWER FORM: Clusters of many tiny flat, single blossoms, creating a carpetlike effect.

SEASON OF BLOOM: Annuals, late spring through summer in most areas, February to May in Zones 9 and 10; perennials, early to late spring.

SOIL: Any good garden soil, well drained.

PH: 5.5 to 7.

FERTILIZER: Flower or all-purpose fertilizer.

WATER: Not too wet. Good drainage is important.

EXPOSURE: 8 or more hours of sunlight per day, with midday shade in hot climates.

SPACING: Annuals, 6 to 10 inches; perennials, 1 foot, sometimes more for established plants.

PROPAGATION: Annuals from seed, perennials by division or stem cuttings, or from seed.

Method

- **Start seeds indoors** an inch apart in flats or one or two seeds per six-pack pocket, in sterile potting soil about eight weeks before the last expected frost (in cold frames, six weeks before the last frost). In Zones 9 to 11, sow seeds in fall or winter. Cover with ⅛ inch of soil. Seeds of annuals germinate in less than two weeks, but perennials may take two months. Grow seedlings in bright sunlight or a few inches below a fluorescent light fixture, at temperatures between 50° and 75°F.

- **Prepare soil outdoors** by turning it thoroughly, mixing in fertilizer, compost, sand, gravel, or other soil amendments, if necessary.

- **Sow seeds outdoors** in tilled, fertilized beds, 2 or more inches apart, covered ⅛ inch deep. Plant annuals in spring, after the danger of heavy frost has passed, a few weeks before the last expected frost. Make two or three successive sowings several weeks apart. Plant perennials in late spring or early summer, when seeds ripen.

- **Thin or transplant** seedlings when they are large enough to handle easily, if they are crowded. Shift indoor-grown plants to 4-inch pots for optimum root growth, or set them outdoors, weather permitting. Thin but do not transplant annuals growing outdoors. Thin and transplant perennials growing outdoors to permanent positions at the end of their first summer or early the following spring.

- **Set out plants** grown indoors at the frost-free date, or a bit earlier.

- **Divide** perennial plants in early spring when new growth begins only if they are rooted in several places. Do not cut those having only one main stem.

- **Take cuttings** 6 inches long from perennials right after flowers bloom. Dip cut ends in rooting hormone, and insert them 2 inches apart in a shaded bed in a mix of sand, vermiculite, perlite, and peat moss, or your usual rooting mix. Keep cuttings moist and do not move them until they are well rooted, then put them in pots or nursery beds, 6 inches apart.

- **Fertilize** annual and perennial plants with all-purpose fertilizer just before they bloom. Fertilize perennials again in midsummer.

- **Pests and diseases** rarely are problems. Slugs, which like young seedlings, are the worst pests. Dust the ground with diatomaceous earth, lime, or wood ashes to deter them.

- **Prune** perennials for shape after they bloom. Shear tips off mature plants to stimulate new growth.

- **Protect in winter** north of Zone 6 by mulching around but not over plants with several inches of lightweight mulch such as salt hay; remove mulch when crocus bloom.

Selected Species and Cultivars

Iberis sempervirens (Hardy candytuft). Solidly covered with white umbels of flowers on evergreen, spreading, low-growing, shrublike foliage, perennial candytuft is dramatic in bloom. Usually about 6 inches tall, mature plants may spread to a width of 2 feet or more. Plants grown from seed bloom in their second year. Good cultivars include:

'Autumn Snow,' 9 inches tall, which reblooms in autumn;

'Purity,' a clear white, 7 inches tall;

'Pygmea,' a dwarf variety growing 4 inches tall; and

'Snowflake,' a cultivar 9 inches tall with a 24-inch spread. Unlike some, this comes true from seed.

I. umbellata (Annual candytuft). This species usually likes cooler weather, but heat-tolerant strains are being developed. Easy to grow from seed in the right climate, this comes in various heights and colors, for instance:

'Brilliant,' offering 10-inch plants in a wide color range, with brightly colored blooms on nice stems;

'Dwarf Fairy,' a compact, profuse bloomer in pink, rose, carmine, crimson, lavender, purple, or white;

'Flash,' showy plants, all red or in mixed colors, 9 to 12 inches tall; and

'Hyacinth Flowered,' with spires of white flowers on plants 15 to 20 inches tall. This good variety for cutting blooms well for many weeks if cut frequently.

CANNA

Botanical name: *Canna* (Cannaceae)

Canna lilies are showy tropical plants that were especially popular in the Victorian era. With their large oval leaves and orchidlike flowers, they have plenty of visual impact as bedding plants—some would say too much! Shorter types are easy to use in mixed borders, greenhouses, and tubs. Tall types are often used in island beds. Since they like wet soil, they do especially well near lakes and streams. Cannas spread aggressively on rhizomes in Zones 9 to 11, but need protection to survive winter in other areas. In northern regions (Zone 7 and north), the rhizomes must be dug up and stored inside for the winter. The plants are evergreen except where frost kills the leaves. Foliage is usually glossy green, but in some varieties it is bronze or streaked with pale yellow-green.

PLANT TYPE: Tender bulb.
GROWING RANGE: All zones.
HARDINESS: Killed by hard frost but tolerant of high heat.
PLANT HEIGHT: 2 to over 8 feet.
FLOWER COLOR: Red, pink, cream, peach, yellow, orange, or rust, sometimes spotted or streaked.

FLOWER FORM: Plumes of tubular, flaring flowers with several petals held above ornamental foliage.

SEASON OF BLOOM: Summer in Zone 8 and north, any time in frost-free areas.

SOIL: Rich.

PH: 6 to 8.

FERTILIZER: Well-rotted manure or compost and all-purpose or slow-release bedding plant fertilizer (14-14-14).

WATER: Average to plentiful, preferring high humidity.

EXPOSURE: Full sun.

SPACING: 1 to 2½ feet.

PROPAGATION: Usually by division of rhizomes, sometimes from seed.

Method

- **Sow seeds indoors** by nicking the seed coat and soaking the pealike seeds in water overnight. Start seed any time in flats or six-packs filled with clean seed starting medium. Cover seeds ½ inch deep, water, and grow at 70°F or above. Seeds germinate sporadically, usually taking many weeks. Grow seedlings in bright sunlight or a few inches below a fluorescent light fixture.

- **Prepare soil outdoors** in beds 2 feet deep when the danger of frost is past, incorporating a 3-inch layer of aged manure, if possible.

- **Sow seeds outdoors** by planting nicked, soaked seeds in smoothly prepared and fertilized beds after all danger of frost passes, at least 3 inches apart and covered ½ inch deep—slightly deeper if it is sandy. Do not let the seedbed dry out.

- **Thin or transplant** indoor-grown seedlings to individual 4-inch pots when they are about 2 inches tall. A few weeks later, when they are sturdy, harden them off and plant them outdoors in their permanent places in garden beds or a bit closer together in nursery beds. Thin and transplant 4-inch-tall, outdoor-grown seedlings either to their permanent places or to 8 inches apart in nursery beds, thinning or transplanting them again to their permanent positions before they get crowded.

- **Set rhizomes or plants outdoors** in permanent places if the weather is warm and steady, with no danger of frost, in spring or summer in most places, but any time in Zones 9 to 11. Cover rhizomes with 3 or 4 inches of soil, but set plants out at the same depth at which they grew.

- **Divide** cannas by digging up clumps. In cold-winter areas (Zone 7 and above), do this just before the arrival of frost, replanting the rhizomes the following spring or summer. In frost-free areas, divide cannas whenever weather is warm and steady. Choose a portion of root several inches long with at least one eye or sprout attached, and separate it from the parent plant with a sharp spade. Replant it immediately in enriched soil. In Zones 10 and 11, cannas growing in rich soil should be divided at least once each year, in some cases twice. If the weather is warm and wet, they can be dug (deeply) and moved while in bloom and will not even stop blooming. Make sure they are watered often until new roots grow in a few weeks.

- **Water** cannas frequently enough to keep the soil evenly moist and also for added humidity when the weather is dry.

- **Fertilize** at planting time and steadily during growth.

- **Pests and diseases** rarely cause problems. If caterpillars attack, treat plants with rotenone or pyrethrum.

- **Mulch** plants with several inches of composted leaves or bark chips to keep moisture in the soil.

- **Remove** seedpods and spent flowers, but do not pinch plants back for bushiness.

- **Protect in winter** where heavy freezes are likely by digging up plants in fall. Wash off the plants, cut off the stem above the rhizome, and let the fleshy rhizomes dry in the sun for a few days. Store them indoors in a cool basement, either wrapped in plastic or in boxes of barely dampened sand.

  In frost-free areas, just keep your cannas in the ground with no special winter care.

  In Zones 8 and 9, cannas may stay in the ground if they are protected from frost. In November or December, cut off the leaves and cover plants with a 5- or 6-inch layer of a dense, heavy mulch such as wood chips. Remove it in February or when the danger of frost has passed. If you prefer, dig plants up and store them indoors, as in northern areas.

Selected Cultivars

Canna x *hybrida* or *Canna* x *generalis.* The parentage of ornamental cannas is mixed, so they generally go by these names. There are dwarf, medium, and tall varieties. Some types are grown more for their ornamental, exotic-looking leaves, but others, usually the shorter types, have very full, showy flowers as their outstanding attribute. Some popular cultivars include:

'Garbo,' with luscious salmon pink flowers and red leaves. It grows less than 2 feet tall;

'King Humbert,' the old-fashioned tall type. It exceeds 7 feet in height and is topped by scarlet flowers. It is used for shrublike stands of foliage;

'Nirvana,' from India, 2 feet tall, with red buds opening to rich yellow with a white central stripe. The foliage is bright green striped with golden yellow; and

'Pfitzer's Dwarf,' developed by a German hybridizer, Wilhelm Pfitzer. These 30-inch-tall cannas with especially large, full flowers may be coral, yellow, pink, or red.

CARNATION

Botanical name: *Dianthus* (Caryophyllaceae)

Carnations are best known as cut flowers. Short-lived perennials, they are specially bred mixtures of dianthus species, most often grown in cool greenhouses. Several types may be grown in outdoor pots and flower borders, and are discussed here. Even among these, hardiness varies. Generally these flower on shorter, bushier plants and are not nearly as large as florist types, but they are quite attractive with frilled double flowers with a clovelike scent. Foliage is linear, somewhat waxy and whitened, and sometimes bluish green. There are new hybrids that flower in five months from seed. Greenhouse types may take two years. Plants grow well in light, fertile, sandy soil. Mass carnations in large bands or groups in the flower border as well as in tubs and large planters. The dwarf types are nice in window boxes, where they may be combined with ivy and alyssum.

PLANT TYPE: Hardy perennial, sometimes grown as an annual.
GROWING RANGE: All zones, varying with the species.
HARDINESS: Some are not reliably cold hardy. Prolonged heat in the 90's (F) is a problem for most, for they prefer cool, moist weather.
PLANT HEIGHT: 6 inches to 4 feet.
FLOWER COLOR: Red, pink, shrimp, yellow, purple, maroon, or white; sometimes bicolored, streaked, or tipped.
FLOWER FORM: Fat, pointed buds open into frilled, round double blossoms, typically 2 to 3 inches wide. Petal edges range from smooth to frilled and deeply fringed. Stems may bear just one flower or a bouquetlike cluster.
SEASON OF BLOOM: Summer in most regions, year-round in frost-free areas. Many greenhouse types bloom in winter.
SOIL: Well-drained garden soil, preferably sandy.
PH: 6 to 7.
FERTILIZER: Slow-release flower fertilizer.
WATER: Keep plants moist but well drained.
EXPOSURE: Full sun or bright partial shade. Shield from harsh midday sun.
SPACING: 6 inches to over 1 foot, depending on the species.
PROPAGATION: Seed or stem cuttings.

Method

- **Start seeds indoors** eight to twelve weeks before the last frost, about an inch apart, in flats or six-packs, shifting individual seedlings to 4-inch pots for optimum root growth. In cold frames, sow six weeks before the last frost. In frost-free areas, sow plants during cool times of the year. Cover with 1/8 inch of soil. Water and keep in a warm (65° to 75°F) place. Seeds germinate in about two weeks, sometimes less. Grow seedlings in bright sunlight or a few inches below a fluorescent light fixture. Harden them off outdoors.

- **Prepare soil outdoors** in beds before planting by tilling in sand, fertilizer, compost, and other soil improvers, as needed.

- **Sow seeds outdoors** only in mild areas, after the danger of frost passes. In tilled, fertilized beds, plant seeds 2 inches apart and cover with 1/8 inch of soil. Keep seedbed evenly moist.

- **Thin** seedlings grown outdoors when they are 3 or 4 inches high, or whenever they become crowded, to permanent positions.

- **Set plants outdoors** after the danger of frost passes, when they are several inches tall.

- **Divide** perennial types in early spring when new growth begins, if they are crowded. Replant immediately.

- **Water** when soil becomes dry, more frequently at first.

- **Fertilize** lightly at planting time and periodically during growth with slow-release blossom booster fertilizer.

- **Pests** include cutworms and slugs. Protect plants from cutworms by sprinkling the ground with wood ashes and setting up cutworm collars—rings of cardboard 3 inches tall, set in 1 inch deep around the stems of a young plant. Kill or repel slugs by sprinkling the ground with diatomaceous earth or wood ashes or by putting out slug and snail bait and/or partly submerged pans of beer. **Diseases** are seldom a problem.

- **Propagate cuttings** about 5 inches long (cut between joints) by rooting in sandy soil in a cold frame or shaded area. Cuttings taken in summer will root over winter. In mild-winter areas, take cuttings in autumn after weather begins to cool. Plant out to permanent places in spring after the danger of frost passes.

- **Mulch** with 2 or 3 inches of shredded leaves or bark chips in dry areas.

- **Pinch back** seedlings when 4 inches tall to promote bushiness, if desired, and remove side buds when very small if you want to produce larger flowers.

- **Stake** tall plants, especially in windy areas.

- **Remove** spent blooms, or cut flowers for bouquets, to promote new growth.

- **Protect in winter** by cutting back plants in early fall and then mulching them with a layer of evergreen boughs or other cover when the ground freezes. Remove mulch in early spring. Alternatively, keep plants in a cool greenhouse or cold frame through the winter.

Selected Cultivars

Dianthus hybrids. All carnations are hybrids. Some have *D. plumarius* in their ancestry, but are derived mainly from *D. caryophyllus* crosses. Carnation cultivars for outdoor gardens include:

'Bambino,' a dwarf, fragrant carnation easily grown from seed, available in all carnation colors. The 8-inch plants are good for bedding and pots;

'Dwarf Grenadin,' very hardy and floriferous, 15 inches high, available in a wide color range;

'Giant Chabaud,' with fringed flowers on 24-inch plants and a nice scent; grows in six months from seed, available in all colors;

'Grenadin,' a hardy perennial, 2 feet tall, with large double flowers in many colors;

'Knight,' offering strong, stemmed double flowers on 12-inch-tall plants with a 12-inch spread from seed in five months. Grow as an annual;

'Lilliput,' only 6 to 8 inches tall, with large flowers (2½ inches wide) on short, strong stems. This everbloomer grows from seed in four and a half months as an annual; and

'Mini Skirt,' a tall but compact, free-flowering type. In most areas, sow in summer and winter plants over indoors for spring pot and bedding plants.

CELOSIA

Botanical name: *Celosia cristata* (Amaranthaceae)
Other common names: Cockscomb, Woolflower

Silky plumed or rippled (crested) flower heads are the outstanding feature of celosia, more often called cockscomb, especially if it is the rippled rather than the plumed type. An easy-care, heat-loving flower, it performs twice—once in the garden and again in dried flower arrangements indoors. Cockscomb is used for bedding, in containers, for cut flowers fresh or dry, and in the greenhouse. The small bushy plants grow with linear green or bronze leaves.

PLANT TYPE: Tender annual.
GROWING RANGE: All zones.
HARDINESS: Killed by frost, tolerates high heat.
PLANT HEIGHT: 1 to over 3 feet.
FLOWER COLOR: Red, pink, peach, yellow, orange, rust, burgundy.
FLOWER FORM: Plumes or fan-shaped "cockscombs" composed of thousands of tiny silky florets. Rippled or crested forms look like brains!
SEASON OF BLOOM: Summer in most areas, any time in frost-free areas.
SOIL: Average to rich.
PH: 6 to 7.
FERTILIZER: Well-rotted manure, compost, all-purpose fertilizer, or slow-release bedding plant fertilizer (14-14-14).
WATER: Average to plentiful.
EXPOSURE: Full sun.
SPACING: 1 to 2 feet.
PROPAGATION: Seed.

Method

· **Start seeds indoors** six weeks before the last frost 1 inch apart in flats or one per six-pack pocket filled with sterile seed starting medium. Cover seeds ⅛ inch deep, water, and grow at 70°F or above. Seeds germinate in about a week. Grow seedlings in bright sunlight or a few inches below a fluorescent light.

· **Prepare soil outdoors** in beds deeply, adding fertilizer and organic matter for more water retention.

· **Sow seeds outdoors** in smoothly prepared and fertilized beds after all danger of frost passes and soil warms up. Plant seeds 3 or more inches apart and cover with ¼ inch of soil—a little more if it is sandy. Do not let the seedbed dry out.

· **Thin or transplant** seedlings growing indoors to individual six-pack pockets or 4-inch pots when they are about 2 inches tall. Thin and transplant seedlings growing outdoors to their garden positions when they are 3 or 4 inches tall, before they become crowded.

· **Set plants outdoors** after hardening them off in shade for several days. Plant them in permanent places when the weather is warm and steady, with no danger of frost, at the same depth at which they grew or an inch or two deeper.

- **Water** frequently enough to keep the soil evenly moist.

- **Fertilize** at planting time and keep plants steadily fertilized during growth.

- **Pests and diseases** rarely attack celosia, but at times caterpillars eat leaves (treat with pyrethrum or rotenone) or root-knot nematodes permanently stunt growth (next time you plant, add manure and compost to garden soil, or grow plants in sterilized soil in containers). Discard but do not compost nematode-infested plants.

- **Mulch** around growing plants with 2 inches of composted leaves, bark chips, or other mulch, to keep soil moist.

- **Pinch back** plants only if you prefer branched plants to those with large plumes or crests. It is especially important to leave crested types unpinched.

- **Dry** celosia for winter bouquets by hanging cut stems upside down in bunches in well-ventilated spots indoors. Colors will darken somewhat. Harvest stems as they begin to bloom.

Tips · **When making mixed dried bouquets, break the large dried plumes or crests of celosia into smaller pieces and, with florists' tape, tape each one onto florist wire before making an arrangement, if you want a more delicate effect.**
· **The small black seeds from mature plumes or crests may be shaken out of them and grown, but the offspring will not necessarily resemble their parents. It's best to plant new seed every year for consistent results.**

Selected Cultivars

Celosia has been a popular garden flower for many years, and has been bred into varied sizes and forms. Though they are of the same species, some types are crested, others are plumed. Here are some of the many named cultivars in current seed catalogs:

Crested types

'Chief,' a 3½-foot-tall type for bouquets; and
   'Treasure Chest' and 'Jewel Box,' with large combs on 8- to 10-inch-tall plants, for bedding.

Plumed types

'Apricot Brandy,' an early-blooming plant of medium height (20 inches) with feathery orange plumes;
   'Century,' available in a mix of colors on plants 20 to 24 inches tall, blooming in less than six weeks from seed under good growing conditions; and
   'New Look,' with brilliant scarlet plumes on bronze foliage, only 10 inches tall, ideal for pots and bedding.

CHINA ASTER

Botanical name: *Callistephus chinensis* (Compositae)
Other common name: Aster

Sweet-scented China asters are grown everywhere for their large fluffy flowers, long lasting both on the plants and in bouquets. Their botanical name means "most beautiful crown." China asters, which are tender annuals, are grown from seed at home or purchased as bedding plants. They are well suited for beds or containers; compact types are popular for edgings and in window boxes.

PLANT TYPE: Tender annual.
GROWING RANGE: All zones.
HARDINESS: Killed by frost, sensitive to high heat.
PLANT HEIGHT: 6 inches to over 3 feet.
FLOWER COLOR: Red, pink, peach, yellow, wine, white, violet, mauve, or purple, sometimes with golden centers and/or bicolored petals.
FLOWER FORM: Individual disc and ray flowers, 2 to 5 inches wide, on long stems, single or double.
SEASON OF BLOOM: Summer in most areas, any time in frost-free areas.
SOIL: Rich, well drained.
PH: 6 to 7.5.
FERTILIZER: Well-rotted manure or compost plus all-purpose or slow-release bedding plant fertilizer (14-14-14).
WATER: Average.
EXPOSURE: Full sun. Provide shelter from strong wind.
SPACING: 1 to 3 feet.
PROPAGATION: Seed.

Method

- **Start seeds indoors** six weeks before the last expected frost an inch apart in flats or one per six-pack pocket filled with sterile seed starting medium. Cover seeds ⅛ inch deep, water, and keep at 65° to 75°F. Seeds germinate in one to two weeks. Grow seedlings in bright sunlight or a few inches below a fluorescent light fixture.

- **Prepare soil outdoors** at planting time by tilling in compost, fertilizer, sand, and other soil amendments, if needed.

- **Sow seeds outdoors** after the danger of frost has passed, in smoothly prepared and fertilized beds. Plant seeds 2 or more inches apart and cover with ⅛ inch of soil. Do not let the seedbed dry out.

- **Thin or transplant** indoor-grown seedlings to individual 2½- to 4-inch pots or to six-pack pockets when they are about 2 inches tall. Thin or transplant 4-inch, outdoor-grown seedlings either to their permanent places or to 6 or more inches apart, thinning or transplanting them again to their permanent positions before they get crowded.

- **Set out plants** grown indoors in their permanent places outdoors if the weather is warm and steady, with no danger of frost, after hardening them off in their shade for several days.

- **Water** frequently enough to keep the soil evenly moist.

- **Fertilize** lightly at planting time and keep plants steadily fertilized.

- **Diseases** include wilt and aster yellows. Choose wilt-resistant varieties and rotate them in the garden—that is, grow China asters in different spots from year to year so they are not infected with overwintering fungi from last year's plants. Aster yellows is a disease transmitted by leafhoppers. Plants will yellow and wilt. Destroy infected plants and control leafhoppers with rotenone to minimize the problem.

- **Mulch** shallow-rooted China asters with 2 to 3 inches of composted leaves or small bark chips or other mulch to help keep moisture in the soil.

- **Pinch back** plants for bushiness early in the summer.

- **Stake** taller varieties before their first flower buds open by tying plants to 3-foot-tall bamboo stakes or use peony hoops.

- **Remove** the spent flowers or cut the flowers for fresh bouquets to prolong the blooming period.

Selected Cultivars

China asters have been bred into many forms, colors, and heights. The main types are dwarf (6 to 12 inches tall), medium (12 to 18 inches), or tall (18 to 36 inches). Petals may be single or double, shorter or longer, curved or straight, quilled or flat. Some interesting cultivars include:

'Famil Silvery Blue,' with fluffy, incurved white blossoms touched with lavender-blue, 2½ inches wide. This type grows on strong stems and is ideal for cutting. Plants grow 3 feet tall;

'Giant Single Andrella,' a mix featuring single flowers for cutting or borders in shades of wine, rose, blue, and purple and white, each centered with a golden disc, growing 2 feet tall;

'Matsumoto Mix,' a heat-tolerant type available in all colors, with contrasting golden centers, 16 inches tall. This type is very productive for cut flowers and is also a good border plant;

'Pinocchio,' a spreading, 6-inch-tall dwarf type that comes into bloom fairly early. This is a showy border plant for weeks. It comes in clear shades of yellow, white, rose, pink, and lavender, and is resistant to wilt; and

'Totem Pole,' with double flowers between 4 and 5 inches wide growing on sturdy, 2-foot-tall stems. This midseason mix includes rich shades of blue, scarlet, cherry red, and white.

CHRYSANTHEMUM

Botanical name: *Chrysanthemum* (Compositae)
Other common name: Daisy

With their sunny charm, chrysanthemums and daisies number among our most treasured garden assets. There are types to bloom from spring to fall in temperate climates and all year in the semitropics and greenhouses. Though species differ, they all share the ability to blossom generously.

Members of the chrysanthemum tribe resist most pests. One, *Chrysanthemum coccineum* (pyrethrum), has flowers that are dried, powdered, and used as an insecticide, but it is also grown as an ornamental border plant. Most perennial chrysanthemums form stoloniferous clumps, so they are very easy to increase vegetatively while the annual and biennial types are not hard to grow from seed.

Use chrysanthemums of different types in garden beds, especially for fall color in the North, in containers, as nonevergreen ground covers, and for cut flowers.

PLANT TYPES: Hardy annual, biennial, or perennial.

GROWING RANGE: All zones.

HARDINESS: Withstands heat and cold to varying degrees, according to the species.

PLANT HEIGHT: Under 6 inches to over 4 feet.

FLOWER COLOR: Many shades of red, orange, rust, yellow, white, cream, rose, or lavender-pink, with some bicolors.

FLOWER FORM: Daisylike single or double flowers. Petals may be flat, curved, quilled, or spoon-shaped. Flowers from ½ to 6 inches wide grow in clusters or singly, usually on long stems.

SEASON OF BLOOM: Best known for fall bloom, but year-round bloom is possible in warm-weather regions.

SOIL: Rich, well drained, any type.

PH: 6.5 to 7.5.

FERTILIZER: Well-rotted manure, all-purpose or high-phosphorus fertilizer.

WATER: Average conditions.

EXPOSURE: Full or nearly full sun in most areas; bright, dappled shade in Zones 8 to 11.

SPACING: 1 to 3 feet for most types.

PROPAGATION: Division or seed.

Method

- **Start seeds indoors** individually in small pots or an inch or two apart in flats filled with moist potting soil, covering seeds ⅛ inch deep. Water and keep at 60° to 70°F until seeds germinate, in about a week. Annuals should be started about six weeks before the last expected frost, perennials in spring or summer, or in late fall in Zones 9 to 11. Grow seedlings in a sunny area or a few inches below a fluorescent light fixture. When they get crowded, shift them to larger or separate pots.

- **Prepare soil outdoors** in beds before planting by tilling in fertilizer, compost, and other soil improvers, as needed.

- **Sow seeds outdoors** in nursery beds in summer (for perennials or biennials) or spring (for annuals), 3 inches apart and ⅛ inch deep. Do not let seedbed dry out.

- **Thin or transplant** seedlings grown outdoors to their permanent spacing when they are sturdy plantlets several inches tall. Self-sown seedlings of feverfew and other daisies are easily moved to desired places.

- **Set indoor-grown seedlings** with four to six true leaves outdoors when the weather is warm and settled, a week or two after the last frost, after hardening them off in shade for several days.

- **Divide** established perennial plants each year when new growth begins in spring. Dig up crowded clumps, gently separate the individual stems (each is rooted), and replant them immediately in rich soil. Plants will flower well later the same year.

- **Water** plants whenever the soil starts to dry out.

- **Fertilize** lightly at planting time and periodically during the growing season. Boost blossoms by applying a low-nitrogen, high-phosphorus and -potassium fertilizer when plants are about 6 inches tall.

- **Pests and diseases** seldom are problems.

- **Mulch** plants in dry weather with several inches of bark chips, salt hay, shredded leaves, or other mulch.

- **Pinch back** tips of *C.* x *morifolium* (garden chrysanthemum) several times for bushiness, until ten weeks before the first frost or expected time of bloom. Disbud them (remove side buds near a central bud) for larger flowers if you wish, before buds are ¼ inch wide. Pinch back annual and biennial chrysanthemums once or twice if you wish.

- **Remove** spent blossoms unless seed is wanted.

- **Stake** tall varieties by letting the shoots grow through peony hoops or tying them to thin wooden or bamboo sticks. In full sun, plants are less likely to need staking.

- **Protect in winter** by mulching perennial and biennial plants as outlined above. Pull back the mulch in spring, after the danger of heavy frost is past, so new shoots can come up unchecked.

Selected Species

Here are some of the popular species of chrysanthemums and their kin. Because there are so many species, space prevents the listing of named cultivars.

Chrysanthemum carinatum (Rainbow daisy). This is one of the annual chrysanthemums, with multicolored 2-inch-wide, daisylike flowers on plants 2 to 3 feet tall. This one does better in cool regions such as Pacific Coast areas where temperatures rarely exceed the 80's (F).

C. coccineum (Pyrethrum, Painted daisy). These are ornamental perennials, 2 to 3 feet tall, perfect for the border. Plants have thin, ferny leaves with daisy flowers of white, red, lilac, or magenta, with golden discs; they flower in summer in most regions, spring in Zones 9 and 10. Plants need well-drained soil, especially in winter. Mulch plants in winter north of Washington, D.C. The plants do not grow and bloom as thickly as other chrysanthemums. 'Roseum' is grown for its use as an insecticide.

C. x *morifolium* (Mum, Garden chrysanthemum, Florist's chrysanthemum). This popular hardy chrysanthemum is probably of Chinese origin. It is the best-known chrysanthemum, blooming in fall in northern and central states, and, sometimes, in both fall and spring in warm-winter areas. Clusters of large flowers make the maximum visual impact in all the chrysanthemum colors such as white, yellow, red, violet, and bronze. Stems are strong and will branch well if pinched back. They have the unusual ability to survive being transplanted while in full bloom. In the most northern states (Zones 3 to 5), plants should be overwintered in a cold frame or under heavy mulch, but in most areas they are perfectly hardy. Petals may be long, short, curved, straight, or quilled, resulting in buttonlike, spiderlike, spoonlike, or daisylike flowers. The so-called football mum and some other large-flowered Japanese chrysanthemums usually are not hardy and grow best in the greenhouse.

C. nipponicum (Nippon daisy). This looks like a shasta daisy *(C.* x *superbum)* when in flower, but a closer look will reveal a plant with fat, succulent leaves and stronger stems. Plants are showy with 3-inch-wide blooms, opening at the same time as the last of the hardy chrysanthemums. Nippon daisies are not stoloniferous, but have woody stems ringed by buds of new shoots in spring. In mild spring weather, the old main stem and its roots may be split into two or three perpendicular sections as long as there are new buds and old roots on each one. Each piece should be replanted immediately, either where it will grow or in gallon pots. This is a good plant for Zones 5 to 8 and cooler parts of 9. Pinch it for bushiness in warmer areas, but leave it unpinched for earlier bloom where summers are short.

C. parthenium (Feverfew). As its common name suggests, this little daisy was found useful as medicine, but these days its ornamental virtues are more appreciated. Available in cultivars ranging from several inches to several feet tall, it is a biennial with perennial tendencies, though it is hard to tell because the plants self-sow freely. They will grow practically anywhere. In hot climates, plant seeds in the late fall, but in places with short summers, plant them at the end of spring. Flowers are usually white, although yellow types are available. The blooms may be daisy, button, or pompon shaped and appear spring through fall.

C. x *superbum* (Shasta daisy). The shasta, popular perennial daisy often sold as a cut flower, was developed by Luther Burbank near Mt. Shasta in California. The gold-centered white flowers may be single or double, and are available in various sizes up to about 3 inches wide, on plants from 1 to 3 feet tall. Plants are easily grown from seed, sometimes blooming the first year, unlike most other perennials. They bloom in the spring in southern zones, summer in northern zones. Divide established plants every other year. In Zone 5 and northward, give plants protection in a cold frame or under heavy mulch. Cultivars vary in hardiness, but some will grow well as far south as Zone 9 and cooler parts of Zones 10 and 11.

CIMICIFUGA

Botanical name: *Cimicifuga* (Ranunculaceae)
Other common names: Bugbane, Cohosh, Snakeroot

Cimicifuga species, some native of Asia and others North America, are dependably hardy perennials ideal for difficult damp, shady spots with acid soil. Choice plants for woodland gardens, the white spires of cimicifuga are among the last flowers to bloom in autumn, adding interest late in the year. The flowers show up well against a dark hedge, fence, or evergreen tree. Use cimicifuga in woodland gardens and flower borders.

PLANT TYPE: Hardy perennial.
GROWING RANGE: Zones 4 to 8.
HARDINESS: Hardy in cold and hot weather, winter chilling needed.
PLANT HEIGHT: 2 to 8 feet.
FLOWER COLOR: Ivory white or greenish white.
FLOWER FORM: Groups of long, slim spires of pale, frothy flowers that rise above ferny foliage.
SEASON OF BLOOM: Late summer to late fall.
SOIL: Moist, humusy, rich in leaf mold.
PH: 5 to 6 (acidic).
FERTILIZER: Well-rotted manure, compost, all-purpose fertilizer.
WATER: Average to high soil moisture.
EXPOSURE: Light shade, but if soil is right, plants will grow in full sun or deep shade, with more shade needed in hot areas.
SPACING: 1½ to 3 feet.
PROPAGATION: Usually by division, also from seed.

Method

- **Prepare soil outdoors** in fall to permit planting early in spring. Till in peat moss, compost, and leaf mold for an acidic, water-retentive soil.

- **Sow seeds outdoors** in fall, as soon as they are ripe, in a cold frame or a smoothly prepared and fertilized shady bed, for germination the following spring. Make rows about 1 inch deep and plant seeds an inch apart, barely covering them with ⅛ inch of soil. Do not let the seedbed dry out—mulch it with 3 inches of salt hay in winter, but remove it when the crocus bloom so seedlings can germinate and grow. Plants sometimes self-sow; it is difficult to grow cimicifuga from seed indoors.

- **Thin or transplant** seedlings to 6 inches apart when they are 3 or 4 inches high. A month or two later, thin or transplant them to permanent positions.

- **Set store-bought plants outdoors** in their permanent places in early spring.

- **Divide** large clumps in half or thirds when new growth begins in early spring if they are crowded and you want to propagate more plants; however, they may be left undisturbed indefinitely.

- **Water** frequently enough to keep the soil evenly moist.

- **Fertilize** lightly at planting time and keep plants steadily but not excessively fertilized.

- **Pests** are few, as hinted at in the common name, bugbane.

- **Mulch** plants with several inches of composted leaves or small bark chips to help keep moisture in the soil. Do not cover crowns.

- **Do not pinch** plants back because it will delay blooming.

- **Maintain in winter** by trimming back browned stems and leaves for neatness.

Selected Species

Cimicifuga americana (American bugbane, Mountain bugbane, Summer cohosh). Native to eastern areas from Pennsylvania to Georgia, and westward to Tennessee, this pretty white wildflower is about 4 feet tall when in bloom.

   C. racemosa (Black snakeroot, Cohosh bugbane). Used as a medication for rheumatism in folk medicine, this 5- to 7-foot species from Virginia and Tennessee has long, showy greenish-white flower spikes and does well in perennial borders.

   C. simplex (Kamchatka bugbane). From the Orient, this summer-blooming bugbane is more compact than the others, usually growing 2 or 3 feet tall, but has the showiest flowers. 'White Pearl' is one of several named cultivars.

CINERARIA, FLORIST'S

Botanical name: *Senecio* x *hybridus* (Compositae)

There are two main groups of plants known as cinerarias, the flowering house and patio plants with their showy, daisylike flowers, and the silver-leaved dusty millers, valued for their foliage, described in more depth on pages 258–60.

   Flowering cinerarias offer a generous, wide cluster of brilliantly colored flowers surrounded by large, green, rounded leaves in a neat mound. Tender perennials, they are grown as annuals or biennials, taking many months to grow from seed. They are most particular about moisture, lighting, and temperature, so they are usually grown by florists under controlled conditions, sold as patio, sunroom, or indoor holiday plants while they are in bloom, and then discarded. In areas where the climate is not hot or dry, they make a nice but temporary addition to the landscape. In some moist, mild parts of coastal California, they are so easy to grow that they self-sow readily.

   PLANT TYPE: Tender perennial, usually grown as an annual.
   GROWING RANGE: All zones as an annual, in cool western portions of Zones 9 and 10 as a perennial.
   HARDINESS: Killed by frost and high heat (above 90°F).
   PLANT HEIGHT: 8 to 36 inches.
   FLOWER COLOR: Purple, pink, rosy red, magenta, blue, or white, sometimes bicolored.

FLOWER FORM: Daisylike, single or double blooms usually 1 to 2 inches wide, but occasionally larger, in clusters.

SEASON OF BLOOM: Spring, or they may be forced at any time.

SOIL: Rich, lightweight, well-drained potting soil.

PH: 6.5 to 7.5.

FERTILIZER: Flower or high-phosphorus fertilizer.

WATER: Average to moist conditions.

EXPOSURE: Full sun or bright, dappled shade during cool weather; bring indoors during hot weather.

SPACING: One per 5- to 8-inch pot, or 1 foot in beds.

PROPAGATION: Seed or tip cuttings.

 ## Method

- **Start seeds indoors** at any time—in early summer for winter bloom or in fall for summer bloom. Plant seeds ⅛ inch deep in flats or small pots filled with moist potting soil. Water, cover with glass or plastic wrap, and keep at 70°F until seeds germinate. Grow seedlings in a sunny area or a few inches below a fluorescent light fixture, at 50° to 60°F for several weeks. Reduce temperature to 45° to 50°F for most of the growth period—four to six months—and then increase temperature to 50° to 60°F to set buds and finish plants. Whenever they are crowded, move them to larger pots. Seeds should not be started outdoors.

- **Take cuttings** several inches long from the strong shoots that appear after the flowering tops are removed. Dip the cut end in rooting hormone and plant it 1 inch deep in moist potting soil in a cool (55°F), humid, shady place indoors. Give plants more light after they root.

- **Thin or transplant** seedlings and cuttings to their permanent spacing indoors, one per 5- to 8-inch pot, when they are about 4 inches tall. Do not let the roots get crowded or growth and flowers will be impaired.

- **Set plants outdoors** in finely tilled, moist soil when weather is cool (though after any danger of frost is past) or warm (not hot), if you offer a mild climate. First harden them off outdoors for a day or two in shade.

- **Water** plants whenever the soil starts to dry out, but do not overwater or roots may rot.

- **Fertilize** periodically during growth.

- **Pests and diseases** can present a problem. Control aphids with nicotine sprays, and caterpillars, whiteflies, and other greenhouse pests with rotenone. Prevent viruses by using disease-free stock and soil.

- **Pinch off** the first flower buds if you want to promote bushy, wide, new growth and a larger crop of flower buds. This will delay flowering for about two weeks.

- **Remove** seedpods and discard plants when they become untidy. According to most sources, plants do not grow strongly from home-saved seeds.

Selected Cultivars

Originally bred in England, the florist types are crosses of various *Senecio* species and do best in cool, moist weather. Named cultivars include:

'Amigo' mixture, only 8 inches tall, but with flowers about 2 inches wide in a wide color range, including bicolors. Grow in 4-inch pots;

'Cindy,' with a domed shape and a full head of large flowers, early to bloom and attractive for a longer period than some types;

'Crimson and Gold,' a multiflora type 1 foot tall with large, cherry red flowers and golden central discs;

'Moll Strain Improved,' forming 18-inch plants flowering in a 2-foot spread with large flowers in bright shades. Grow in 8-inch pots; and

'Saucer Size Mixed,' with flowers up to 5 inches wide, on 16-inch plants. Strong plants grow in the full color range.

CLEOME

Botanical name: *Cleome* (Capparaceae)
Other common name: Spider plant

This native of Brazil and Argentina is a sweetly scented bee and butterfly plant that is attractive in a large border, as a cut flower, for a temporary shrublike background, and for accent planting. The extra-long stamens on this tall plant whose airy blooms open each afternoon until the stems are cut down by the gardener or by frost are what lend it its spidery look. If the main stem is removed, side shoots will appear and bloom. Rugged and heat tolerant, cleome grows quickly and easily from seed, blooming in as little as eight weeks. Its stems and palmlike leaves have sharp spines.

PLANT TYPE: Hardy to tender annual.
GROWING RANGE: All zones.
HARDINESS: Tolerates cool temperatures and light frost when young, thrives in heat.
PLANT HEIGHT: 3 to 4 feet, sometimes taller.
FLOWER COLOR: White, rose, lilac, magenta, purple.
FLOWER FORM: Elongated heads composed of flowers with 4 slim petals, each with long stamens. Each stem has whorls of unopened buds above the flowers that open each day and stringlike seedpods below.
SEASON OF BLOOM: Several months in summer in most regions; spring through fall in warm climates.
SOIL: Good to rich, moist.
PH: 6.5 to 7.5.
FERTILIZER: Well-rotted manure, all-purpose or high-phosphorus fertilizer, bonemeal.
WATER: Moist conditions.
EXPOSURE: Full sun in most areas, light shade in the South.
SPACING: 1 ½ to 2 feet.
PROPAGATION: Seed.

Method

- **Start seeds indoors** four weeks before last frost. Germination usually takes ten days. Grow in small pots or six-packs in moist potting soil, covering seed with barely ⅛ inch of soil. Water and use warm day/cool night temperatures (85°/60°F) until seeds germinate. Grow in a sunny area or a few inches below a fluorescent light fixture.

- **Prepare soil outdoors** in beds before planting by tilling in fertilizer, compost, bonemeal, and other soil improvers, as needed.

- **Sow seeds outdoors** where they will grow from two weeks before to two weeks after the last expected frost. In smoothly prepared and fertilized beds, plant seeds 4 or more inches apart and cover with ⅛ inch of soil. Do not let the seedbed dry out.

- **Thin or transplant** seedlings when they are about 4 inches tall. Shift indoor-grown seedlings to larger pots if they are crowded, or move them to outdoor beds. Thin and transplant outdoor-grown seedlings to their correct placement and spacing in the garden.

- **Set plants outdoors** after the danger of frost passes, after hardening them off in shade for a few days.

- **Water** often to prevent the soil from drying out.

- **Fertilize** lightly at planting time and steadily during growth. Boost blossoms by applying a low-nitrogen, high-phosphorus and -potassium fertilizer when plants are 5 to 6 inches tall.

- **Pests and diseases** seldom are problems.

- **Mulch** plants that grow in dry areas with several inches of bark chips or other mulch to keep soil cool and moist.

- **Pinch back** tips for bushiness, or leave plants unpinched for taller flower spikes.

- **Stake** tall bushy plants inside peony hoops if necessary, but usually it is not.

Selected Species and Cultivars

Cleome serrulata (Rocky Mountain bee plant). More delicate looking than *C. spinosa* hybrids, this pink or white variety is only 2 to 3 feet tall and tolerates colder weather—it is a hardy annual.

C. spinosa. This is the most popular garden cleome, a mainstay of gardens where summers are hot. Hybrid varieties include:

'Colour Fountain Mixed,' pink, rose, lilac, purple, or white flowers on bushy plants;

'Helen Campbell,' pure white, similar to 'Queen' series; and

'Queen' series (Rose, Ruby, White, Cherry, Violet, Purple, etc.), tall bushy plants with great vigor.

COLEUS

Botanical name: *Coleus* x *hybridus* (Labiatae)

Gaudy coleus, related to mint, is grown for its brightly colored and patterned leaves, not its inconspicuous or unsightly flowers. It is a tender perennial grown as an annual—often used in pots, window boxes, carpet beds, and semishaded borders in warm to hot conditions, and as a houseplant. Bedding schemes look more organized if plants of a single cultivar (just one leaf pattern) are chosen—a mixture of leaf patterns tends to be overwhelming. Look for bushy plants of an attractive color, remembering that colors may intensify when plants are set outdoors. Special drooping types have been bred for hanging containers.

PLANT TYPE: Tender perennial, usually grown as an annual.
GROWING RANGE: All zones as an annual; sometimes Zones 9 to 11 as a perennial.
HARDINESS: Killed by frost, thrives in heat.
PLANT HEIGHT: 6 inches to over 2 feet.
FLOWER COLOR: Blue. However, the plant is grown for its colorful patterned
    leaves—combinations of chartreuse, red, pink, purple, white, yellow, or green.
FLOWER FORM: Spires of tiny flowers above large rippled, toothed, or fringed leaves,
    in pairs.
SEASON OF BLOOM: Any time in warm weather.
SOIL: Average to rich, well drained.
PH: 6.5 to 7.5.
FERTILIZER: Well-rotted manure, all-purpose fertilizer.
WATER: Average conditions.
EXPOSURE: Light shade, denser shade in hot climates.
SPACING: 10 to 24 inches.
PROPAGATION: Seed or tip cuttings.

Method

- **Start seeds indoors** individually in small pots or an inch or two apart in flats filled with moist potting soil, about eight weeks before the last frost. Barely cover tiny seeds with soil, water, and keep at 75°F until they germinate, in about one week. Afterward temperatures may be reduced to 65° or 70°F if you wish. Grow seedlings in a bright but shaded area or a few inches below a fluorescent light fixture. When they have four to six leaves, step them up to larger pots if necessary.

- **Prepare soil outdoors** in beds before planting by tilling in fertilizer, compost, and other soil improvers, as needed.

- **Sow seeds outdoors** in partial shade one week after the last expected frost; though seedlings have more trouble surviving outdoors, you may wish to try this if you have extra seed. Plant in November or December in Zones 10 and 11. In smoothly prepared and fertilized beds, plant seeds 1 inch or more apart. Press them into the soil, barely covering them. Do not let the seedbed dry out.

- **Thin** seedlings when they are crowded. With care, thinnings may be transplanted.

- **Set plants outdoors** after the danger of frost has passed, after hardening them off in shade for a few days.

- **Water** seedlings often to prevent the soil from drying out. Mature plants will tolerate drier soil.

- **Take cuttings** 3 to 5 inches long during warm weather, before plants go to seed. Remove bottom leaves and root cuttings 2 inches deep in moist, sandy soil in a shaded position, or even in a glass of water on a windowsill.

- **Fertilize** lightly at planting time and periodically with all-purpose or houseplant fertilizer during active growth.

- **Pests and diseases** seldom are problems.

- **Mulch** plants in dry areas with several inches of bark chips or other mulch to keep soil moist.

- **Pinch back** tips for bushier plants and to remove flowers.

Selected Cultivars

The common coleus has many cultivars of varying leaf shapes, colors, sizes, and textures. When purchasing plants, look at large ones to check their true color and form. Seeds are sold for single color combinations, limited color or shape ranges, and in unsorted mixes. Self-sown seedlings may turn out to be quite attractive, too. Here are a few of the many cultivars available:

'Carefree,' a petite, fast-growing type 8 inches tall in a range of strongly contrasting colors with lobed leaves;

'Dragon,' 'Sunset,' and 'Volcano' hybrids. Many of these 9- to 12-inch plants will have gold-edged, deeply divided leaves with pink, chartreuse, and gold tones along with darker colors;

'Fairway' series, compact 8- to 10-inch plants for bedding. Small, slow-to-flower plants are available in separate colors—predominantly red, yellow, white, rose, or bronze, or the complete mixture; and

'Wizard' series, composed of large-leaved, well-branched 1-foot plants. 'Wizard Sunset' has rust-colored leaves with a thin, toothed, chartreuse margin.

COLUMBINE

Botanical name: *Aquilegia* (Ranunculaceae)

Columbine is a ferny-looking plant with bright, dancing, spurred flowers on wiry stems that makes a lovely cut flower. Hummingbirds gather nectar from the spurs—they are most attracted to red-flowered varieties, such as the native *Aquilegia canadensis*. New plants often grow from self-sown seeds—a help since their parents may be short lived. Use columbine in borders, rock gardens, and woodland gardens. It does well on slopes.

PLANT TYPE: Hardy perennial.
GROWING RANGE: Zones 4 to 9 (grow only as a biennial in Zones 9 and 10).
HARDINESS: Cold hardy but heat sensitive, growing best where summers are not too hot or wet.
PLANT HEIGHT: 1 to 3 feet.
FLOWER COLOR: White, yellow, pink, rose, red-orange, violet, or blue, with many bicolors.
FLOWER FORM: On each 2- to 3-inch-long nodding flower, 5 elegantly spurred petals are matched with 5 sepals, often in a contrasting color.
SEASON OF BLOOM: Late spring to midsummer.
SOIL: Well drained, rich in leaf mold.
PH: 6 to 7 (slightly acidic to neutral).
FERTILIZER: Well-rotted manure, compost, flower fertilizer.
WATER: Average conditions.
EXPOSURE: Light, dappled shade, with more shade farther south.
SPACING: 1 to 2½ feet.
PROPAGATION: Seed or division.

Method

- **Sow seeds indoors** individually in six-packs or 1 or 2 inches apart in flats filled with sterile seed starting medium any time from late winter to the end of spring, at temperatures near 60°F. Do not cover the tiny seeds, just pat them in place. Thin or transplant them to individual pots when they become crowded.

- **Prepare soil outdoors** in flower beds in spring or fall, incorporating peat moss and leaf mold.

- **Sow seeds outdoors** in summer in northern and central regions, as soon as they are ripe, in a prepared and fertilized shady bed. The seed germinates best when fresh. Plant them in late fall in Zones 9 and 10. Make rows about 1 inch deep and plant seeds an inch apart, without covering them. Do not let the seedbed dry out. You can also plant columbine in the cold frame at the end of summer (later in hot areas). Thin or transplant seedlings to 6 or more inches apart when they are 3 or 4 inches high. The next spring, thin or transplant them to permanent positions.

- **Set plants outdoors** in permanent places in spring or, farther north, early summer, after hardening them off for a few days in shade.

- **Divide** large clumps when new leaf growth begins in early spring without tearing individual taproots. Replant immediately and water. Divisions should bloom the same year.

- **Water** to keep the soil evenly moist.

- **Fertilize** lightly at planting time and keep plants steadily but not excessively fertilized. They do not like too much nitrogen.

- **Pests and diseases** are few. If leaf miners mar leaves with their winding trails, remove the affected portions.

- **Mulch** plants with several inches of composted leaves or small bark chips to help keep moisture in the soil.

- **Stake** tall plants with slim bamboo canes or inside peony hoops in windy areas.

- **Trim back** tops after they turn brown, for neatness.

- **Protect in winter** by mulching around plants.

Tips • A second crop of flowers may appear if spent flowers are removed immediately.
• To collect seed, let the pods ripen and start to split and curve. When seeds are black, they are ready. Strew them in prepared beds or on bare ground in shady woodland places. Species intermix readily, so seed will not stay true if more than one type is grown, but the offspring will be attractive anyway.

Selected Species and Cultivars

Aquilegia caerulea (Rocky Mountain columbine). One of our loveliest native plants, this has large blue and white flowers on springy stems about 2 feet tall.

A. canadensis (American columbine). This is a 2- to 3-foot-tall, vigorous wildflower with slim red-and-yellow blossoms, often grown in perennial borders and wild gardens.

A. chrysantha (Golden columbine). Growing up to 30 inches tall, this columbine grows very full and wide, with long-blooming yellow blossoms. The flowers of some cultivars are nearly white.

A. flabellata. A dwarf white or blue variety 9 inches tall with large flowers and pale, whitened leaves, this is good in rock gardens or borders.

A. x hybrida. Since columbines interbreed very freely, countless lovely cultivars have been developed, including:

'McKana Giants,' 2½ feet tall, with large, bright bicolored flowers;

'Music' hybrids, compact 15-inch plants with large flowers similar to those of 'McKana Giants';

'Nora Barlow,' 2 to 2½ feet tall, which tends to breed true, with double pink flowers; and

'Silver Queen,' a tall white columbine with a long-blooming season, 30 to 36 inches tall and very showy.

CORALBELLS

Botanical name: *Heuchera* (Saxifragaceae)

Slim, upright stems carrying plumes of bright flowers appear during the balmy days of late spring. This long-lived, sturdy, but shallow-rooted plant is a popular garden flower that is native to the Rocky Mountains. Its nearly evergreen, low basal rosettes have trim, rounded or kidney-shaped leaves. Though most are green with red veins, some types are reddish or purple. Use them in beds and rock gardens, where they attract hummingbirds, and as dainty cut flowers.

PLANT TYPE: Hardy perennial.
GROWING RANGE: Zones 3 to 9.
HARDINESS: Hardy in cold or hot weather.
PLANT HEIGHT: 12 to 30 inches.
FLOWER COLOR: Shades of red or pink, or greenish white.
FLOWER FORM: Plumes of tiny bell-shaped flowers on wiry stems.
SEASON OF BLOOM: Late spring into summer for many weeks.
SOIL: Average to rich, moist but well drained.
PH: 6 to 7.
FERTILIZER: Well-rotted manure and compost.
WATER: Average conditions.
EXPOSURE: Full sun or light dappled shade, partial shade in areas where highs are consistently in the 90's.
SPACING: 12 inches.
PROPAGATION: Seed, division, or leaf cuttings.

Method

· **Start seeds indoors** in spring after prechilling for four weeks in the refrigerator or outdoors in under 40°F temperature. Grow them in a bright place at 70°F, on top of moist potting soil 2 inches apart in flats or individually in six-pack pockets. Sprinkle a trace (less than 1/8 inch) of sand over them. Plants appear in three weeks.

· **Prepare soil outdoors** in beds by tilling in fertilizer, compost, leaf mold, and other soil amendments, as needed.

· **Sow seeds outdoors** in fall in a protected bed or cold frame for germination the following spring. Plant seeds an inch or two apart and barely cover them with 1/8 inch of sand.

· **Thin or transplant** seedlings when they are 2 or 3 inches tall, those grown outdoors to their permanent positions or to a nursery area when they become crowded. Those grown indoors can be shifted to individual 4-inch pots. When roots fill pots, transplant them outdoors to permanent positions.

· **Transplant** freshly dug, mature plants in spring or fall, during cool weather, if possible.

Those grown in pots may be moved in summer, too. Avoid setting crowns deeply, to avoid crown rot.

- **Divide** large clumps by separating roots every third year in early spring if they are crowded. Replant divisions immediately.

- **Take cuttings** in summer with a piece of main stem attached. Plant up to the leaf base in moist soil in shade. Move rooted plants to permanent places the next spring.

- **Water** frequently enough to keep the soil moderately moist in spring and somewhat drier in summer, but protect from drought.

- **Fertilize** lightly at planting time and again before plants show buds in spring. Mound an inch or two of compost or leaf mold over exposed roots each fall.

- **Pests and diseases** include mealybug (dislodge with streams of soapy water or treat with dormant oil), strawberry root weevil (soak roots with pyrethrum spray), and stem rot (remove and discard diseased portions and treat plants with fungicide).

- **Mulch** plants with 2 or 3 inches of composted leaves or small bark chips to help keep moisture in the soil.

- **Remove** flower stems after bloom is finished.

- **Protect in winter** with a 2-inch layer of mulch around each plant.

Selected Species and Cultivars

Heuchera americana (Alumroot, Rock geranium). This U.S. native with mottled red and green leaves and pale pink flowers is found in dry woods and rocky places. It grows up to 3 feet tall. A striking cultivar is 'Palace Purple,' with showy, lobed, dark red leaves and greenish white flowers on 2-foot stems.

H. x *brizoides* 'Pluie de Feu.' The cherry-red showy plumes of this hybrid are about 18 inches tall and unusually wide.

H. sanguinea. This species includes most of the garden types. One to 1½ feet tall, they produce many narrow plumes that flower freely all summer and are excellent for cutting and bedding. Some interesting varieties are:

'Bressingham Hybrids,' 1 to 1½ feet tall, usually propagated from seed in a mix that includes white, pink, and coral red;

'Firebird,' with deep scarlet flowers 16 inches tall;

'Green Ivory,' with white flowers on tall stems from 2 to nearly 3 feet tall; and

'June Bride,' 15 inches tall, creamy white.

COREOPSIS

Botanical name: *Coreopsis* (Compositae)
Other common name: Pot of gold

The name *coreopsis* covers a diverse group of golden, long-stemmed, daisylike flowers. Some are hardy annuals; some are hardy perennials. All are easily grown and attractive as bedding plants, meadow plants, and cut flowers. In the garden, mass them in large bands or groups.

PLANT TYPES: Hardy annual or perennial.

GROWING RANGE: All zones as an annual; Zones 3 to 10 as a perennial.

HARDINESS: Tolerant of heat and cold. Some perennials need chilling in winter.

PLANT HEIGHT: 2 to 4 feet.

FLOWER COLOR: Pale yellow, lemon yellow, gold, rust, bronze.

FLOWER FORM: Daisylike single or double blooms from one to several inches wide.

SEASON OF BLOOM: Summer in most areas, spring through fall in Zone 8 and southward.

SOIL: Any fair to good garden soil.

PH: 6.5 to 7.

FERTILIZER: Any flower or all-purpose fertilizer.

WATER: Keep soil somewhat moist, not too wet. Plants are moderately drought tolerant.

EXPOSURE: Full sun.

SPACING: 8 to 16 inches.

PROPAGATION: Annuals from seed, perennials from seed or by division.

Method

- **Start seed indoors.** In most regions, sow annuals six weeks before the last frost and perennials a few weeks earlier, at the same time, or in summer. In Zones 9 and 10, sow annuals and perennials in fall or winter. Fill flats or six-packs with moist sterile potting soil, and cover plant seeds an inch or two apart ⅛ inch deep. Water and keep at 60° to 75°F. Seeds germinate in about seven days. Grow in bright sunlight or a few inches below a fluorescent light fixture. Perennials often bloom the first year if started early.

- **Prepare soil outdoors** in beds by tilling in compost, fertilizer, and other soil amendments, if needed.

- **Sow seeds outdoors** after the danger of frost is past at least 3 inches apart and ⅛ inch deep. In Zones 9 and 10, sow annuals outdoors in late fall, during the winter, or very early in spring.

- **Thin or transplant** seedlings, whether grown indoors or out, when they are 4 inches tall, if they are crowded. Move them to larger pots or to their permanent position in the garden.

- **Set out plants** after the danger of frost passes, hardening off those grown indoors in the shade a few days. If annual plants are leggy, bury the stems deeper than they grew, up to the bottom two leaves. Plant perennials at the same depth at which they grew.

- **Divide** perennials in early spring or late fall.

- **Water** young or new plants more frequently at first. Mature plants should have drier conditions.

- **Fertilize** steadily but not heavily.

- **Pests and diseases** rarely are problems.

- **Mulch** plants with 2 or 3 inches of bark chips or shredded leaves in very dry areas to keep soil moist.

- **Stake** tall plants, especially in windy areas. Additional soil may be heaped on top of roots to help anchor plants.

- **Remove** flowers often to extend the bloom season, either by cutting fresh ones for bouquets or clipping off spent blooms. When annual plants become too branched and spent, remove and replace them. Deadhead and trim back perennials after bloom.

- **Protect in winter** by mulching around crowns of perennials.

Selected Species and Cultivars

Coreopsis lanceolata (Tickseed, Lance-leaved coreopsis). This type has golden composite flowers, single or double, about 2½ inches wide on tall straight stems. It is a hardy perennial for Zones 4 to 8 and some parts of 9. There are many dwarf, intermediate, and tall cultivars. 'Mayfield Giant' is one of the tallest, with 3-foot-tall stems. It is especially fine for cut flowers, but may need staking. 'Sunray' is an award-winning type well suited to bedding. It grows into bushy clumps 20 inches tall with bright yellow flowers. No staking is needed.

C. tinctoria (Calliopsis). Grow these flowers as hardy annuals, or, in mild-winter areas, as biennials. Dwarf types (under 15 inches) rarely need staking, but tall ones (up to 4 feet) need support. This species is easy to grow and floriferous. It makes a good cut flower, and is somewhat unusual and underrated. The colors range from bronzy reds through gold, with many patterns and markings. One of the most dramatic cultivars is 'Tiger Flower Improved,' only 8 inches tall, with large bicolored flowers of red and gold.

C. verticillata. This is a particularly easy and productive hardy perennial for Zones 3 to 10. It does very well in the humid East Coast. It offers golden, starry blooms on bushy, finely cut, ferny foliage in clumps. Straight stems appear at first, then branch out and bloom in early summer on plants up to 3 feet tall. This grows in sun or light shade, is tolerant of many soils, and is virtually pest-free. It is an excellent garden plant. Space large clumps 1½ feet apart. Mass in borders or naturalize in meadows. Recommended varieties are:

'Moonbeam,' a lovely pale yellow cultivar that grows 1½ feet tall and needs no staking. It is drought and mildew resistant. Like others of the species, it grows in Zones 3 to 10; and

'Zagreb,' a dwarf golden-yellow cultivar for the front of the border. It grows only 1 foot tall and is covered with hundreds of starry blossoms. Zones 3 to 10.

CORNFLOWER

Botanical name: *Centaurea* (Compositae)
Other common name: Knapweed

Centaurea is a genus that includes a range of favorite garden plants, some grown for their leaves and others for their flowers. Most typical and beloved is the cornflower, with its bright blue tufted round blossoms held on upright, nearly woody stems. The linear, willowlike leaves are whitened with small hairs that give them a silvery appearance. Dusty miller, closely related, has divided silver-gray leaves that are even more decorative. *Centaurea* species are used for bedding, containers, or cut flowers, fresh or dry.

PLANT TYPES: Hardy annual, biennial, or perennial.
GROWING RANGE: All zones as an annual, Zones 4 to 8 for most perennials.
HARDINESS: Most types tolerate frost but do not thrive in heat.
PLANT HEIGHT: 1 to 4 feet.
FLOWER COLOR: Blue, white, red, pink, yellow, purple, violet, burgundy.
FLOWER FORM: Round composite flowers, 1 to 2 inches wide.
SEASON OF BLOOM: Summer in northern and central areas, late winter through spring in Zones 9 to 11.
SOIL: Average to rich.
PH: 6 to 7.
FERTILIZER: Well-rotted manure, all-purpose fertilizer, or slow-release bedding plant fertilizer (14-14-14).
WATER: Average.
EXPOSURE: Full sun in most regions, partial shade in hot climates.
SPACING: 8 inches to 2 feet.
PROPAGATION: Annuals from seed, biennials and perennials from seed or by division.

Method

- **Start seeds indoors** eight to ten weeks before the last frost 1 inch apart in flats or individually in six-pack pockets filled with sterile seed starting medium. In Zones 9 to 11, start them in the fall. Cover seeds ⅛ inch deep, water them, and grow at 65° to 75°F. Seeds usually germinate in about a week. Grow seedlings in bright sunlight or a few inches below a fluorescent light.

- **Prepare soil outdoors** by tilling in fertilizer and soil amendments to a depth of 1 foot.

- **Sow seeds outdoors** 2 inches apart and cover them with ¼ inch of soil. Do not let the seedbed dry out. In northern and central regions, plant annual types in cool weather four to six weeks before the frost-free date. In areas with mild winters, plant annuals in the fall for bloom in spring. Gardeners in cold-winter areas can do the same if they bring plants through the winter in a well-insulated cold frame. Plant biennials and perennials any time from spring through fall, but not during the hottest weather.

- **Thin or transplant** all seedlings before they get crowded. Transplant indoor-grown seedlings to individual six-pack pockets or 4-inch pots when they are about 2 inches tall. Plants that are overwintered in pots do better in larger, 6-inch pots.

- **Set plants outdoors** in permanent places after hardening them off for several days in shade, in cool weather that will not dip below 25°F. Annual plants can tolerate light frost if they are used to cool temperatures, but do not need it to bloom.

- **Divide and reset** perennials in early spring when new growth begins, if they are overcrowded, usually every two to four years. Annual *Centaurea* varieties are not normally propagated vegetatively.

- **Water** frequently enough to keep the soil evenly moist.

- **Fertilize** at planting time and keep plants steadily fertilized.

- **Pests and diseases** rarely are problems.

- **Mulch** around growing plants with several inches of bark chips or shredded leaves to keep moisture in the soil.

- **Pinch off** the top inch of growth to promote bushiness when plants are about 8 inches tall. Cutting the flowers for indoor bouquets stimulates bushy new growth, too.

- **Stake** tall plants.

- **Protect in winter** by mulching around crowns of hardy plants and making sure they are in well-drained soil.

Selected Species and Cultivars

Centaurea cyanus (Cornflower, Bluebottle). This hardy annual is also well known as the bachelor's button. Cultivars include:
'Blue Boy,' 3-foot plants of rich medium blue (also 'Black Boy,' a blackish maroon, and 'Red Boy');
'Blue Diadem,' 2-foot-tall plants with large double flowers of intense deep blue;
'Frosty,' in mixed pastel colors frosted with white at the tips of petals. This type looks lovely when fresh but tends to look wilted very soon; and
'Polka Dot,' in mixed colors (red, white, blue, rose, wine, or lavender) on short bushy plants a little over a foot high.
C. dealbata (Persian cornflower). This valuable perennial for Zones 4 to 8 grows 2 feet high and nearly 3 feet wide when well established. Its rosy pink or lavender blossoms sometimes have pale centers. The cultivar 'John Coutts' (which is classified by some as *C. hypoleuca*), named for a former curator of Kew Gardens, is an excellent pink flower for perennial borders.
C. gymnocarpa (Dusty miller). Divided, feltlike white leaves make this 3-foot-tall tender perennial valuable in flower beds. It can be grown as an annual.
C. macrocephala (Globe centaurea, Lemon-tuft). Hardy in Zones 5 to 10, this perennial grows 3 or 4 feet tall and has golden, thistlelike 3-inch blossoms on stems 3 or 4 feet tall, with little foliage. The long-lasting blooms, good as cut flowers, are used fresh or dried.
C. montana (Mountain knapweed, Mountain bluet). With wide, feathery, pale blue florets about twice as wide as cornflowers, this 2-foot-tall flower with deep purple centers adorns a good-looking plant for dry, sunny areas in Zones 4 to 8.
C. moschata (Sweet sultan). This half-hardy annual from the Mediterranean needs warmer weather than *C. cyanus* and a longer growing period. Flowers are larger and silkier looking. The color range includes dark red, white, pink, lavender, purple, and yellow. 'The Bride,' 16 to 24 inches tall, is a pure white variety with fragrant flowers.

COSMOS

Botanical name: *Cosmos* (Compositae)

Cosmos is a popular tender annual with many bright, daisylike flowers on long stems. It is tall and bushy when well grown, with threadlike or ferny foliage. Some gardeners adore it, others dismiss it as too weedy. It can be grown throughout the United States in warm weather. Mass cosmos in large bands or groups in flower beds and borders, or grow in large tubs—space plants twice as close and add extra fertilizer. It may also be used in meadows, but needs annual replanting. Both foliage and flowers are excellent in fresh bouquets. Buy seed from good suppliers for strong, uniform plants that need less staking. Cosmos is well adapted to the hot summer climate found in most parts of the United States because it originated in the North American Southwest.

PLANT TYPE: Tender annual.
GROWING RANGE: All zones.
HARDINESS: Killed by frost but tolerant of high heat.
PLANT HEIGHT: 14 inches to 4 feet.
FLOWER COLOR: Yellow, orange, red, pink, white, deep rose, or violet. Some types have zones or streaks.
FLOWER FORM: Single or double disc and ray flowers.
SEASON OF BLOOM: Summer in most areas, spring through fall in Zones 8 to 11.
SOIL: Any good garden soil.
PH: 6.5 to 7.
FERTILIZER: Any all-purpose or flower fertilizer.
WATER: Moist but not saturated conditions.
EXPOSURE: Full sun in most areas, more shade in hot or dry climates.
SPACING: 8 inches to 2 feet.
PROPAGATION: Seed.

Method

- **Start seeds indoors** three to six weeks before the last frost an inch apart in flats, one per pocket in six-packs, or one per 4-inch pot filled with damp potting soil. The 4-inch pots are preferred if plants will be started early. Cover seeds with ¼ inch of soil. Water and keep in a warm (65° to 80°F), bright place. Seeds germinate in about five days. Grow seedlings in bright sunlight or a few inches below a fluorescent light fixture.

- **Prepare soil outdoors** in beds by tilling in compost, aged manure, fertilizer, or other soil amendments, as needed.

- **Sow seeds outdoors** after the danger of frost has passed in smoothly prepared and fertilized beds. Plant seeds at least 3 inches apart and cover with ¼ inch of soil. Do not let seedbeds dry out.

- **Thin or transplant.** When seedlings reach 4 inches tall, thin them to 3 inches apart, keeping the best ones. A week or so later, thin or transplant seedlings to permanent positions. From this point on they grow very fast.

- **Set out plants** after the last frost when weather is settled and warm, after hardening them off for several days in shade. Bury them an inch or two deeper than they grew, especially if they are leggy.

- **Water** frequently if needed.

- **Fertilize** plants steadily, either with a single application of slow-release fertilizer or occasional side-dressings of other fertilizer. Liquid feedings are helpful in hot weather.

- **Pests and diseases** rarely are problems. If slugs appear, remove mulch and dust the ground and plants with wood ashes or diatomaceous earth.

- **Mulch** with several inches of bark chips, shredded leaves, straw, or other material in dry areas to keep soil evenly moist.

- **Stake** tall types, especially those in partial shade or windy areas, before first buds open, by tying to 4-foot-tall bamboo canes with soft string. Additional soil may be heaped on top of roots when plants are large to help anchor them.

- **Remove** flowers often to extend the bloom season, either by cutting fresh ones for bouquets or clipping off spent blooms. When plants become too branched and spent, discard them.

Tip · It is practical to save homegrown seed for growing cosmos in quantity (especially for bouquets). Collect ripe seed from the strongest, best formed plants. Results are variable but attractive.

Selected Species and Cultivars

Cosmos bipinnatus. This tall bushy species offers pink, rose, lavender, or white flowers with golden discs. Some flowers are tufted or bicolored. Usually plants are 4 feet tall, or even taller in excellent conditions at the end of the season. Plants may need staking. It is not widely known that this species can be grown from stem cuttings in warm, moist weather as well as from seed. Named cultivars include:

'Candy Stripe,' with white petals splashed or striped with pink or crimson;

'Purity,' an all-white strain of the 'Sensation' type;

'Sea Shells,' in the range of colors above, with rolled, quilled petals. Some gardeners find that whites and pastels look better than deeper tones in this form; and

'Sensation,' the classic type, in all the colors above.

C. sulphureus. Flowers 1 or 2 inches wide may be yellow, orange, or rusty red. Leaves are broader and plants are smaller than *C. bipinnatus.* Named cultivars include:

'Bright Lights,' a mixture with yellow, gold, golden orange, or red-orange flowers on vigorous, easy-to-grow, 3- to 4-foot plants;

'Diablo,' with orange semidouble flowers on plants 18 to 30 inches tall;

'Sunny Gold,' with the same habit, but yellow flowers; and

'Sunny Red,' with bright, orange-red petals. The dwarf, bushy, 14-inch-tall plants are floriferous and heat tolerant.

CRINUM LILY

Botanical name: *Crinum* (Amaryllidaceae)
Other common names: Cape lily, Spider lily

Like most of their cousins in the amaryllis family, crinums cannot tolerate frozen soil. However, they thrive with little care in the delta soils of the lower South, where they are often included in perennial beds. Foliage appears in early spring, followed in early summer by huge flower clusters suitable for cutting.

PLANT TYPE: Tender bulb.
GROWING RANGE: Zones 8 to 11, and Zone 7 with winter protection.
HARDINESS: Low tolerance for hard freezes, can withstand heat.
PLANT HEIGHT: 2 to 4 feet.
FLOWER COLOR: Red, pink, white.
FLOWER FORM: 4-inch-wide lilylike blossoms, borne in clusters.
SEASON OF BLOOM: Summer.
SOIL: Moist, deep, well drained, with high organic content.
PH: 5.5 to 6.5.
FERTILIZER: Well-rotted manure added to the planting site.
WATER: Above average (weekly) in spring and early summer, below average other times.
EXPOSURE: Full sun, with brief midday shade.
SPACING: 1 to 2 feet.
PROPAGATION: Bulbs or division.

Method

- **Prepare soil outdoors** by digging a planting hole 2 feet deep. For three bulbs, make the hole 2 feet wide. Refill the hole with one part aged manure and two parts soil.

- **Plant bulbs outdoors** 6 inches deep. When planting in rows, allow 2 feet between bulbs. Two or three bulbs may be planted 1 foot apart where a specimen clump is desired. Dormant bulbs may be planted in fall or spring.

- **Mulch** with a 1-inch layer of leaves, grass clippings, or straw immediately after planting.

- **Water** after planting when bulbs are planted in spring. Water established plants every ten days during dry periods in spring and early summer.

- **Fertilizer** is seldom necessary if the planting site is prepared with manure.

- **Divide** crinums when flowers become sparse, indicating that the plants have become overcrowded. In Zones 9 to 11, division may be needed every five years; in cooler zones, less often. When digging, remember that the bulbs are quite deep. Crowded clumps may be divided any time the bulbs are dormant during late fall and winter. Incorporate a fresh supply of aged manure into the soil when resetting bulbs.

- **Pests and diseases** are seldom a problem.

· **Winter protection** is required in Zone 7. Cover the planting with a thick insulating mulch, such as 6 inches of chopped leaves. Remove the mulch after the danger of hard freezes has passed so the soil can warm up promptly in spring.

Tips · Crinums may be grown indoors in containers in colder climates and repotted only every four or five years. Move the containers outdoors in spring, and overwinter them in a dry place where the bulbs will not freeze.

Selected Species

Crinum x *powellii* (Powellii hybrids) are the hardiest, and perhaps showiest, of the crinums. They produce eight flowers on each flowering spike, flanked by twenty long straplike leaves.

Although not as hardy as the Powellii hybrids (hardy in Zones 9 to 11), *C. macowanii* grows to only 2 feet tall and has striped leaves, and *C. amabile* flowers late and has a rich, spicy fragrance.

CROCUS

Botanical name: *Crocus* (Iridaceae)

The vivid, early-blooming crocus resemble delicate tulips with no stems. Cup-shaped on cold, misty days, they widen to stars when it is warm and sunny. After blooms fade, the linear foliage remains for about two months. Native to the shores of the Mediterranean, the Near East, and southern Europe, crocus thrives in most of the United States. Grown from hardy corms (sometimes mislabeled bulbs), crocus are widely used in rock gardens, flower beds, and for naturalizing in lawns. Plant them in groups of seven or more of the same color.

PLANT TYPE: Hardy bulb.
GROWING RANGE: Zones 5 to 9, farther north with shelter.
HARDINESS: Most types will survive temperatures to −10°F.
   Tolerant of summer heat, crocus need chilling in winter to provoke blossoming.
PLANT HEIGHT: 4 to 9 inches.
FLOWER COLOR: Yellow, white, lavender, purple, violet-blue, or bronze petals with orange stigmata. Some flowers are striped or have contrasting colors on each side of petals.
FLOWER FORM: Cuplike, divided into 6 petals.
SEASON OF BLOOM: Most types bloom in early spring, before the narcissus, for several weeks. Several are autumn blooming.
SOIL: Any soil with good drainage.
PH: 6.5 to 7.5.
FERTILIZER: Bonemeal, slow-release fertilizer, or well-rotted manure.
WATER: Moderate moisture.

EXPOSURE: Sun or dappled shade under deciduous trees.

SPACING: 3 inches.

PROPAGATION: Most gardeners purchase full-size corms. Crocus may also be grown from seed or by division.

Method

- **Plant seeds indoors** ⅛ inch deep, ½ inch apart, in flats or small pots in spring. Grow in temperatures from 55° to 75°F. Crocus germinates in about a month but takes two or three years from seed to bloom.

- **Prepare soil outdoors** at planting time by tilling in bonemeal, compost, fertilizer, and builders' sand, if needed.

- **Plant seeds outdoors** when they ripen in late spring, ⅛ inch deep, 1 inch apart, in finely tilled soil. (This is easy, though rarely done.) Grow it near parent plants if possible. Home-saved seed may be scattered to naturalize where flowers are wanted. But be careful—the seedlings look like grass.

- **Thin or transplant** seedlings when they are 2 or more inches tall, whether they were grown indoors or out (unless they're being naturalized). Plant them in a nursery area, 2 or 3 inches apart, with the top of the root 1 inch deep. When corms develop the next year, plant them 3 inches deep in permanent places.

- **Plant corms** of spring-blooming crocus outdoors in the fall, 3 inches deep and 3 inches apart, where they will bloom. Fall-blooming species are planted in summer. Spring bloomers may be forced in pots set in cold frames in autumn and then brought indoors in January. Some gardeners find that yellow crocus forces less successfully than other colors.

- **Divide** clumps when foliage begins to yellow, every year or two, when plants are crowded. Tease tangled roots and corms apart, but do not cut through individual corms. Replant corms and cormels.

- **Water** during active growth in spring and after planting in summer or fall.

- **Fertilize** at planting time and just after blossoms fade, to nourish next year's bulbs.

- **Pests and diseases** are few. Rodents and deer eat crocus corms but will avoid them if they are interplanted with narcissus, which is toxic.

- **Remove** flower heads and stems after bloom is finished, unless seed is wanted. Let leaves disappear naturally or remove them when they yellow. Mark or remember the spot, for plants do not show again until the next year.

- **Protect in winter** by mulching with 4 inches of evergreen boughs, or 2 inches of pine bark chips, or shredded leaves. Remove mulch in stages in late winter when sprouts appear.

Tips · Forced or potted crocus can be saved for the garden. Let foliage ripen and plant the corms in the garden where they are wanted. Or you can dry the corms and save them for autumn planting.

· Crocus seed is easily collected and sown—tan seed heads are in the center of the foliage, partly underground. They begin to split when the seeds are ripe. Plant immediately.

Selected Species

Dutch crocus are hybrids of many species. These popular plants are later to bloom and somewhat larger than species crocus. Flowers are white, white veined with purple, purple, or violet, with orange stigmata.

Species crocus come in more colors and forms, and tend to bloom earlier, though this varies. Several species bloom in autumn. Many are bicolored or patterned. Species available to U.S. gardeners include:

Crocus angustifolius, synonym *C. susianus* (Cloth of gold). Deep golden yellow blossoms are touched with bronze. Plants bloom prodigiously.

C. kotschyanus, synonym *C. zonatus.* Rosy lavender blossoms appear in fall.

C. sativus (Saffron crocus). Discussed at greater length on pages 440–41.

C. sieberi 'Firefly.' Blossoms are nearly pink with orange stamens.

C. tomasinianus. Pale to darker lavender flowers, sometimes appear to be silvery on the outside of petals. This species is fast to increase.

CYCLAMEN

Botanical name: *Cyclamen* (Primulaceae)
Other common name: Persian violet

Cyclamen are grown for their sparkling flowers and round, leathery leaves, sometimes with a metallic sheen. Most types are from southern Europe or the Mediterranean and range from tender to hardy. The florist's strain of cyclamen is not cold hardy, but many species are. Hardy types are used in rock gardens and shady borders.

PLANT TYPE: Hardy or tender bulb.
GROWING RANGE: Zones 4 to 7 for most of the hardy types.
HARDINESS: Varies greatly with the species. Generally they do not tolerate hot, dry climates.
PLANT HEIGHT: 3 to over 16 inches.
FLOWER COLOR: Vibrant shades of red, rose, carmine, magenta, violet, pink, or white, sometimes bicolored.
FLOWER FORM: Large "shooting star"–shaped flowers are formed by 5-lobed petals, either smooth or frilled, swept back from a central ring. Each stalk bears one flower.

SEASON OF BLOOM: Spring or fall.
SOIL: Well-drained, gritty garden soil.
PH: 7 to 7.5.
FERTILIZER: Bonemeal, all-purpose fertilizer, and low-nitrogen, high-phosphorus and -potassium fertilizer.
WATER: Average to dry.
EXPOSURE: Partial shade.
SPACING: 3 to 8 inches.
PROPAGATION: Seed, corms, or division.

Method

- **Start seeds indoors** (for the houseplant varieties) at any time of year at 60°F. At temperatures above 65°F, seeds may fail to germinate and plants may fail to thrive. Germination can be improved by soaking overnight in hot water. Plant seeds ¼ inch deep, 1 inch apart, in flats or six-packs in sterile, sandy potting medium, and cover with foil. Once germinated, move to a cool, bright greenhouse or cold frame. Seedlings usually appear in thirty to sixty days.

- **Prepare soil outdoors** before planting by tilling in grit, sand, compost, bonemeal, fertilizer, and lime, if needed.

- **Sow seeds outdoors** (for the hardy types) during the fall or winter to break their dormancy with cold weather—or put them in the freezer for two months instead, and then plant them in late winter or early spring. Plant them ¼ inch deep in sandy soil or in flats (1 inch apart) or small pots in a cold frame. They germinate erratically in one to six months.

- **Thin or transplant** seedlings grown indoors when they are 2 inches high, by moving each one to a 4-inch pot filled with rich but free-draining soil. Shift them to 6-inch pots when they become crowded. Thin and transplant seedlings grown outdoors to permanent spacing if they are crowded.

- **Set store-bought hardy plants or corms outdoors** during cool weather in spring or fall.

- **Divide** established clumps in early spring by separating corms without cutting them. Division is rarely needed.

- **Water** only if soil is dry.

- **Fertilize** plants lightly but steadily throughout their growth. Boost blossoms by applying a low-nitrogen, high-phosphorus and -potassium fertilizer when plants start to form buds.

- **Pests and diseases** on outdoor plants are rare; indoors, mites and fungi can be problems. Treat mites by spraying plants with water and applying insecticidal soap. Use fungicide and improve air circulation if necessary.

- **Weed** and regularly keep competing flowers away from the hardy cyclamen beds, which may look bare for part of the year.

- **Protect in winter** by mulching hardy cyclamen with 2 or 3 inches of shredded leaves or fine bark chips. Uncover plants gradually as soil warms and new growth begins in spring.

Tips · Hardy cyclamen is slow to grow from seed. Growing the plants from their flat corms is difficult because it is hard to tell whether they are upside down or not, so it is safest to buy hardy types for the garden already growing in containers. They are available at nurseries in regions where they grow well, and from rock garden specialists.
· Hardy cyclamen grows easily in California, but is difficult to grow in eastern states.

Selected Species

Cyclamen cilicium. This autumn-flowering hardy cyclamen with twisted pink flowers and round leaves mottled with silver grows 3 inches tall.

C. coum. This very hardy cyclamen blooms in fall through early spring on 6-inch-tall plants. Leaves are silver-green, flowers are charming in shades of deep rose. This also can be grown in the cool parts of the West Coast.

C. hederifolium, synonym *C. neapolitanum* (Baby cyclamen). When mature, corky-textured black tubers are 6 inches in diameter on this 4-inch-tall, hardy garden variety. Gemlike rose or white flowers appear in late winter through very early spring, followed by round green leaves.

C. persicum. This is the well-known florist's cyclamen, which does best in temperatures around 60°F at all times—difficult to achieve outdoors. Some new F_1 hybrids come into bloom eight months after planting seed, but older types may require a year and a half. This species is found in all cyclamen colors and in varied sizes and shapes, from 6 to 12 inches tall, with flowers up to 4 inches long. Some strains resist heat or cold better than others. It blooms in winter and spring.

C. purpurascens, synonym *C. europaeum.* This very hardy 3-inch-tall species has fragrant red-violet flowers for many weeks, blooming from summer into fall, and evergreen silvery green leaves.

DAHLIA

Botanical name: *Dahlia* (Compositae)

Of Mexican origin, dahlias are fleshy, bright, flowery plants for bedding or cutting. Their shapes, sizes, and colors are immensely varied. Holland-grown tuberous roots of mature plants are available in season at garden centers, as are locally grown bedding plants, but dahlias are also easy to grow from seed. The short small-flowered varieties are often used as annuals. Tall large-flowered dahlias may be featured as specimens, or massed in large bands or groups. Dahlias of all types do well in large tubs (space plants twice as close and add extra fertilizer). Gaps may be filled with smaller plants such as alyssum or violas. Dwarf varieties are superb in window boxes, pots, and flower beds.

PLANT TYPE: Tender perennial.

GROWING RANGE: All zones. Winter hardy in Zones 9 to 11. Dig up roots in Zone 8 and north and store inside over the winter.

HARDINESS: Plants are killed if underground tuberous roots freeze.

PLANT HEIGHT: 8 inches to over 6 feet.

FLOWER COLOR: Yellow, orange, red, pink, white, deep rose, violet, or purple, including many bicolors.

FLOWER FORM: Single dahlias show their inherent disc and ray form. Doubles form round heads that may be quilled, pompon shaped, or peony flowered. Flower size ranges from about 2 to 10 inches wide.

SEASON OF BLOOM: Summer in most regions, most or all of the year in frost-free areas.

SOIL: Any good garden soil.

PH: 6 to 7.

FERTILIZER: Well-rotted manure, compost, flower fertilizer, all-purpose fertilizer.

WATER: Average soil moisture, high humidity.

EXPOSURE: Full sun in most areas. In hot, bright areas, dahlias prefer partial shade. Protect plants from harsh temperatures and winds.

SPACING: 6 inches to 3 feet.

PROPAGATION: Seed, tuberous roots, stem cuttings, or division.

Method

- **Start seeds indoors** eight weeks before the last frost 1 inch apart in flats or in six-packs filled with clean seed starting medium. Cover seeds 1/8 inch deep, water, and keep at 65° to 75°F. Seeds germinate in a week or two. Grow seedlings in bright sunlight or a few inches below a fluorescent light fixture. Harden off seedlings before planting them outdoors.

- **Start tuberous roots indoors** with crown up, showing slightly above the soil, several weeks before safe outdoor planting time. Start large varieties in deep (6 inches or more) pots or boxes and smaller types in 4-inch pots. Fill containers with a mixture of compost, peat, and sand, well moistened but not soggy. When sprouts appear, give them plenty of light.

- **Prepare soil outdoors** in beds by tilling in manure, fertilizer, compost, and other soil amendments, if needed.

- **Sow seeds outdoors** to raise quantities of bedding plants for the same or next year, after the danger of frost passes. In smoothly prepared and fertilized beds, plant seeds an inch or two apart and cover with 1/4 inch of soil. Do not let the seedbed dry out.

- **Thin and transplant** seedlings, whether growing indoors or out, when they are 4 inches high, if they are crowded. Indoors, seedlings grow best one to a 4-inch pot. Outdoors, sturdy seedlings should be thinned or transplanted to permanent positions.

- **Set plants or tuberous roots outdoors** in permanent places after the danger of frost passes, after mixing all-purpose or flower fertilizer into each planting hole. Firm plants into place and water well.

- **Stake** plants at planting time to prevent stabbing tuberous roots, or set in short sticks at planting time to mark locations for stakes to be added later. Tall cultivars become top-heavy and always need wind protection and staking before their first buds open. Tie each plant to a 4- to 6-foot-tall wooden stake, deeply set. Short cultivars grow without stakes or with shorter stakes.

- **Pinch back** tips before the first buds appear to promote bushiness.

- **Divide** large clumps of tuberous roots in half or thirds at planting time, if you wish. After eyes at the base of the old stem begin to swell, carefully slice down through the stem and between tuberous roots if possible. There should be at least one eye for each division. Treat cuts with fungicide before planting.

- **Root cuttings** under mist or in humid conditions. Take new sprouts or shoots when about 3 inches long. Cover all but the growing tip with moist rooting medium.

- **Water** to keep the soil evenly moist.

- **Fertilize** at planting time and keep plants steadily fertilized. As plants get large and weather gets hot, supplement dry feedings with liquid fertilizer.

- **Pests and diseases** rarely are problems. Protect plants from slugs by trapping or baiting them or dusting the ground with wood ashes or diatomaceous earth. Prevent cutworm damage by setting a cardboard collar around each plant.

- **Mulch** dahlias with 2 or 3 inches of composted leaves or small bark chips to keep the soil evenly moist.

- **Remove** spent blooms or cut fresh flowers for bouquets to extend the bloom season.

- **Disbud** by pinching off side buds from central bloom stalks if larger flowers are wanted.

- **Protect in winter** by storing dahlia tuberous roots indoors in Zone 8 and above. Dig up clumps of tubers after the first frost. Wash off soil and dry in the sun for a few days, without permitting them to freeze. Dust with fungicide and put each clump in a plastic bag with barely moistened peat moss, sand, or potting soil, carefully labeled. Punch ventilation holes and store bags in a cool, dark place for the winter. Do not permit to freeze. Check occasionally to be sure that roots are not rotting or becoming desiccated. If the tubers are totally desiccated, discard; if partially, moisten the peat moss a little or plant immediately. Large quantities of dahlias may be kept in root cellars or cool basements in boxes of moistened sand and peat.

    In Zones 9 to 11, protect tuberous roots from frost with 2 to 4 inches of mulch. Plants may remain in the ground all year. With deeper mulch and a sheltered exposure next to a building, dahlias may sometimes be overwintered in Zones 6 to 8. Remove mulch in gradual stages as new growth begins in spring.

Tips · Condition cut dahlia flowers for bouquets by soaking them up to their necks in cool water mixed with floral preservative for several hours or overnight.

· Smaller types of dahlias come into bloom earlier from seed than large ones. Tuberous roots of the best seedlings may be dug and saved for the next year.

Selected Cultivars

Dahlia hybrids. Dahlias are among the most varied of garden flowers, as a look at specialists' lists will show. Their parentage is mixed, but most likely includes *D. pinnata* and *D. coccinea.* Singles need less staking and have more flowers than doubles. Dahlias may be classified by flower size and form; according to *Hortus Third,* the twelve types recognized by the American Dahlia Society are:

Anemone dahlias, with central tubular petals in the disc area, and longer petals surrounding it;

Ball dahlias, with ray flowers only in a globose shape;

Colarette dahlias, often bicolored, with a central disc surrounded by short tufted petals and a row of ray flowers;

Formal decorative dahlias, with ray flowers only in many rows, and recurved outer petals;

Incurved cactus dahlias, with quill-like petals;

Informal decorative dahlias, with many rows of long rays, often twisted or curved;

Miscellaneous dahlias, a group for more unusual forms;

Peony dahlias, with two or more rows of nearly flat ray flowers;

Pompon dahlias, with globose shapes in petite sizes;

Semicactus dahlias, with partially quilled or rolled petals;

Single dahlias, with a central disc surrounded by less than two layers of ray flowers; and

Straight cactus dahlias, with quill-like petals.

The 'Coltness' cultivars are small singles and doubles that grow quickly from seed, and usually need no staking.

DAISY

Botanical name: *Bellis* (Compositae)

These tiny daisies, double or single, are used for edgings and among bulbs and later-blooming perennials. The dainty flowers have a long blooming period and will spread by self-sown seeds where conditions are right—cool and moist—but will not grow in hot, dry areas. Pretty as they are, they are considered weeds in northwestern states. In northeastern states, they are sometimes killed by extremes of temperatures. Most *Bellis* species grow as neat rosettes of leaves, though some have leafy stems. They need frequent thinning and dividing in areas where they do well.

PLANT TYPE: Hardy perennial, usually grown as a biennial.
GROWING RANGE: Zones 3 to 9.
HARDINESS: Not suited for hot weather.
PLANT HEIGHT: 3 to 8 inches.
FLOWER COLOR: Shades of white, lilac, rose, red, or wine with golden centers.
FLOWER FORM: Double or single disc and ray flowers ½ to 2 inches wide.
SEASON OF BLOOM: Late spring through early summer in northern and central states, earlier in southern and mild West Coast areas.
SOIL: Rich, moist.
PH: 6 to 7.
FERTILIZER: Well-rotted manure, compost, flower fertilizer.

WATER: Moist conditions.
EXPOSURE: Full sun or light shade, more shade in the South.
SPACING: 4 to 6 inches.
PROPAGATION: Seed or division.

Method

- **Start seeds indoors** in temperatures around 70°F, four to eight weeks before the last frost. In the South, start plants in the fall and treat them as biennials. Plant them ⅛ inch deep, ½ to 1 inch apart, in flats or six-packs where they germinate in ten to fifteen days and grow quickly. Harden off seedlings before planting them outdoors.

- **Prepare soil outdoors** very finely in flower beds, incorporating soil improvers and fertilizer.

- **Sow seeds outdoors** in cold frames two to six weeks before the last frost or a few weeks later in outdoor beds. Space them an inch or more apart, barely covering them. In Zone 9, plant in autumn for bloom in spring.

- **Thin or transplant** both indoor- and outdoor-grown seedlings to their permanent places when they become crowded, usually in the fall.

- **Set plants outdoors** in permanent places any time in spring or fall. Plants are often purchased in bloom in the spring.

- **Divide** clumps in early spring when new growth begins, if they are crowded. Replant divisions immediately.

- **Water** often enough to keep the soil moist.

- **Fertilize** at planting time and lightly throughout growth. Top-dress beds with an inch of compost or leaf mold each fall.

- **Pests and diseases** are few. If powdery mildew is a problem, use fungicide.

- **Mulch** is not needed in cool, damp spots. In warmer, drier areas, mulch with an inch or two of shredded leaves or bark chips.

- **Remove** flower stalks after bloom is finished unless you want to save the seeds.

- **Protect in winter** with an inch of light mulch, such as shredded leaves, taking care not to smother the tiny plants. Keep plants under a cold frame until spring in Zones 3 to 5.

Selected Species and Cultivars

Bellis perennis (English daisy). Wild types are tiny, single, and most often have golden discs surrounded by pink or white petals. Named cultivars include:
'Button' series, with neat 1-inch-wide double red or pink flowers;
'Kito,' with large flowers of semiquilled, cherry red petals;
'Meadow Daisy,' the wild English daisy, 2 to 4 inches tall with small white single flowers;

'Monstrosa,' with large flowers nearly 4 inches wide in red, pink, or white; and 'Prolifera,' branching but low plants with secondary flower heads.

B. rotundifolia. Similar to *B. perennis,* it has rounder leaves and likes sheltered moist places. *B. r. caerulescens* is a pretty lavender-blue type from North Africa.

DAYLILY

Botanical Name: *Hemerocallis* (Liliaceae)

Easy to grow and dependable, the daylily has been described as the perfect perennial flower. The individual blossoms last only a day, but a healthy clump may bear hundreds of them. Once planted, daylilies will multiply and bloom for years with minimal maintenance.

PLANT TYPE: Hardy perennial.
GROWING RANGE: Zones 3 to 9.
HARDINESS: Cold hardy and tolerant of heat and drought.
PLANT HEIGHT: 20 to 40 inches.
FLOWER COLOR: Orange, yellow, red, coral, white, pink.
FLOWER FORM: Lily-type blossoms up to 6 inches across.
SEASON OF BLOOM: Summer.
SOIL: Any good garden soil.
PH: 6 to 7.
FERTILIZER: Add compost or well-rotted manure to the planting site.
WATER: Below average; supplemental water is required only during severe midsummer droughts.
EXPOSURE: Full sun to partial shade.
SPACING: 2 feet apart.
PROPAGATION: Division.

Method

- **Prepare soil outdoors** by adding aged manure or compost to the soil to improve its drainage and ability to hold moisture. In alkaline soils, add peat moss to increase acidity.

- **Plant** by spreading the roots of the plants and covering them with soil. Daylilies can be planted at any time during the growing season, but spring and fall are preferred. In cool climates, plant them in spring.

- **Mulch** with 3 inches of leaves, pine straw, or grass clippings to control weeds and retain soil moisture. A thicker mulch may be used in arid climates.

- **Water** after planting to help settle the roots in the soil. Provide water every week to ten days during the summer droughts that coincide with the bloom time of your daylilies.

- **Propagate** plants by digging and dividing clumps, preferably during damp weather. Daylilies may be divided every five years or so, though division is seldom required to keep them healthy. Transplanted plants may not bloom well their first year. To divide, dig up a clump, shake off the soil, and gently pull the individual plants apart and replant them immediately. The best times to divide are in spring when new growth quickens, in the summer after the flowers fade, or in midfall.

- **Fertilize** lightly, if at all. When grown in good soil, daylilies should not require fertilizer.

- **Pests and diseases** of daylily are practically nonexistent.

Tip · Fading of daylily colors often can be corrected by moving the plants to where they will receive a little afternoon shade.

Selected Cultivars

Forty years ago there were hundreds of daylily cultivars, and today there are thousands. Many are specially adapted to certain climates. Before buying, ask your extension agent or a local nurseryman about cultivars that do especially well in your area.

Also consider bloom times when choosing cultivars. Daylilies are described as early, midseason (the largest group), and everbearing. Early and midseason cultivars bloom about three weeks apart, though there is considerable overlap.

Named hybrids are best for planting in flower beds and borders, but *Hemerocallis fulva,* the orange-flowered wild strain, remains the best choice for naturalizing in meadows or along roadsides.

DELPHINIUM

Botanical Name: *Delphinium* (Ranunculaceae)
Other common name: Larkspur

These gorgeous flowers do well in England's climate, but they are difficult to grow in many parts of the United States. Where cool nights and warm days promote their strong growth, delphiniums are perfect tall plants for the rear of the border. When the primary flowering stalk is cut for flower arrangements, a second flowering on shorter spikes usually follows.

PLANT TYPE: Hardy perennial.
GROWING RANGE: Zones 2 to 7.
HARDINESS: Very winter hardy, but cannot tolerate hot conditions.
PLANT HEIGHT: 2 to 6 feet.
FLOWER COLOR: White, lavender, pink, many shades of blue.
FLOWER FORM: 12- to 15-inch-tall spikes covered with 2-inch-wide single flowers.
SEASON OF BLOOM: Early summer.
SOIL: Fertile, well drained, rich in organic matter.
PH: 6.5 to 7.5.
FERTILIZER: Apply a balanced fertilizer in early spring and again when plants begin to flower.

WATER: Plants need water once a week during the growing season. They cannot tolerate drought.

EXPOSURE: Full sun with good air circulation. In marginal (hot) climates, plant in partial shade.

SPACING: 20 to 36 inches in rows, or a clump of three, spaced 15 inches apart.

PROPAGATION: Division or seed.

Method

- **Start seeds indoors** in early spring or late summer (for bloom the following year) by sowing them thinly on the surface of a premoistened flat. Keep in a cool (60°F) place until germination, in two to four weeks, in darkness. Move seedlings to a well-lit area after germination. Thin seedlings to 3 inches apart. Harden off outdoors for two weeks before transplanting.

- **Prepare soil outdoors** by tilling a 2-inch layer of compost or rotted manure into the planting site. Unless soil is alkaline, thoroughly mix in a heavy dusting of lime.

- **Sow seeds outdoors** in prepared beds in early spring or late summer.

- **Set plants outdoors** in early spring when new growth begins or early fall. Avoid transplanting delphiniums in very damp weather. Set the plants so that the roots are securely covered with soil, but make sure the crowns do not get buried. When transplanting in fall, surround young plants with a ½-inch collar of clean sand.

- **Thin** after plants are established in their permanent home if crowded conditions lead to problems with poor soil drainage or sluggish air circulation.

- **Water** by thoroughly wetting the root zones of the plants. Avoid dampening the leaves. Plants need water once a week throughout the growing season.

- **Fertilize** with a balanced fertilizer after rapid growth commences in spring, and again in early summer, when flowering is imminent. Choose a slow-release chemical fertilizer that includes minor plant nutrients, or a mixture of cottonseed meal, bonemeal, and alfalfa meal.

- **Divide** established plants every four years in early spring. When dividing plants, cut tangled roots cleanly with a sharp knife.

- **Pests and diseases** include snails, slugs, and several fungal diseases. Install sand collars around plants to discourage snails, trap slugs in beer traps or sprinkle the ground with wood ashes or diatomaceous earth, and attend to cultural details that affect soil drainage and air circulation to prevent problems with powdery mildew and crown rot. Delphiniums often fall victim to disease in warm, humid climates, so be especially vigilant of soil drainage to help prevent these problems.

- **Stake** plants when they are 10 to 12 inches high. Stakes should be as tall as the flowers are expected to grow. As the hollow flowering spike emerges, tie it to the stake in several places.

· **Protect in winter** by spreading a 3-inch layer of clean sand or sawdust, or a 6-inch pile of evergreen branches over the plants in late fall.

Tip · Although perennial, delphiniums often decline after their second year. Propagate them from plant divisions frequently to make sure you have healthy plants when you want them.

Selected Species and Cultivars

Delphinium belladona includes smaller varieties that produce numerous short flowering spikes 3 to 4 feet tall rather than one large one. They are easier to grow than the showier delphiniums. Varieties include 'Blue Bees' and 'Sapphire.'

D. elatum. Almost all cultivated delphiniums are hybrid forms of this species. 'Pacific Giants' grow over 4 feet tall and boast huge spikes of mostly double flowers. 'Blackmore & Langdon' is the show strain widely grown in England. Dwarf varieties include 'Blue Springs,' 'Pennant,' and 'Fantasia.'

DIANTHUS

Botanical name: *Dianthus* (Caryophyllaceae)
Other common name: Pinks

It is said that the name of the color pink comes from "pinks," a somewhat archaic common name for *Dianthus* species. The interrelated groups of dianthus are of many sizes and forms, but all have linear foliage with a bluish, powdery look and bright, flat-faced or ruffled flowers. Many have a sweetly spicy or clovelike aroma. The edges of the petals of these variably hardy plants range from smooth to deeply fringed—some look as if they were cut out with pinking shears. Blossoms grow singly or in clusters. The alpine types stay low and form attractive perennial evergreen tufts or mats (used in rock gardens or as ground covers), usually blooming just once per year. Larger-blooming dianthus types are often used as bedding plants, blooming continuously for months, but they tend to be killed in cold winters. Sweet Williams are cluster-flowered, spring-blooming biennials with a pleasant tendency to self-sow. The best-known *Dianthus* variety is the carnation, treated separately on pages 214–16, but there are countless others, originally from widespread regions of Europe, Asia, and Africa. The name *Dianthus* is from the Greek for "divine flower."

PLANT TYPES: Hardy annual, biennial, or perennial.
GROWING RANGE: All zones.
HARDINESS: Species vary, but there are types for all climates. Most do best in cool climates.
PLANT HEIGHT: 4 inches to over 2 feet.
FLOWER COLOR: White, red, pink, purple, yellow, or peach, often bicolored.
FLOWER FORM: Flat, ruffled, fringed, or lacy single or double flowers ½ to 2 inches wide. Single forms usually have 5 petals.

SEASON OF BLOOM: Varies with type: all year in Zones 10 and 11, spring and summer in most areas.

SOIL: Average to rich, well drained.

PH: 6 to 7.5.

FERTILIZER: Well-rotted manure, or flower or all-purpose fertilizer.

WATER: Average to moist conditions.

EXPOSURE: Full sun in most regions, full sun to light shade in hot or dry areas.

SPACING: 8 to 15 inches.

PROPAGATION: Seed, stem cuttings, or division.

Method

- **Start seeds indoors** in small pots or flats filled with moist potting soil, eight to twelve weeks before the last frost. Start perennials in spring or summer in northern and central areas or in fall or winter in Zones 9 to 11. Start biennials in late fall in Zones 9 to 11, early to late summer farther north. Plant seeds 1 inch apart and barely cover them with soil. Water and keep at 75°F until they germinate in about one week. Afterward reduce temperature to 60° to 70°F. Grow seedlings in a bright but shaded area or a few inches below a fluorescent light fixture. When they have four to six leaves, step them up to larger pots if necessary.

- **Prepare soil outdoors** before planting by digging in fertilizer, compost, and other soil improvers, as needed, making sure soil will drain well.

- **Sow seeds outdoors** at the time of the last expected frost or as soon as they ripen, usually about eight weeks after they bloom. Plant in November or December in Zones 10 and 11. In smoothly prepared and fertilized beds, plant seeds 2 inches or more apart. Press them into the soil, covering them 1/8 inch deep. Do not let the seedbed dry out.

- **Thin or transplant** seedlings grown outdoors when they are crowded to permanent positions. With extra care, thinnings may be transplanted.

- **Set plants outdoors** once the danger of frost is past, after hardening them off in shade for a few days.

- **Take tip or stem cuttings** 3 inches long of perennial species and root them in shaded, misted beds in a mixture of half peat moss and half sand, or your favorite rooting medium. Make the cuttings from plants in full growth and bloom in summer in Zone 7 and northward, or early to late fall after summer heat moderates in Zone 8 and southward. Do not let cuttings dry out. Roots appear in approximately four weeks.

- **Root layers** (especially of *D. plumarius,* but also of other species) by pulling an attached stem down to the ground, nicking it slightly about halfway from the tip, and covering the nicked portion with moist soil or rooting medium anchored with a rock. Do not let the main plant or the layered portion dry out. When the new roots are strong, about two months later, the layer can be cut from the mother plant and set into the garden.

- **Divide** perennial species in early spring when new growth begins.

- **Water** often enough to keep soil evenly moist.

- **Fertilize** lightly at planting time and periodically with all-purpose fertilizer during active growth. Annual dianthus requires more fertilizer than perennials because of its prolonged blooming period.

- **Pests** include cutworms and slugs. Treat plants with rotenone or pyrethrum. Diseases rarely are problems.

- **Mulch** plants in dry areas with several inches of small bark chips or other mulch to keep soil moist.

- **Pinch back** tips for bushier plants.

- **Deadhead** to remove spent flowers and stimulate new growth, unless seeds are wanted.

- **Protect in winter** by removing all blooms and lightly mulching after the ground freezes.

Selected Species and Cultivars

Dianthus alpinus 'Allwoodii.' Neat, petite, uniform 6- to 8-inch-tall, mat-forming perennial plants have lacy, flat, single blooms in white, deep rose, or lilac, often bicolored, in spring. The silvery cushion of foliage is evergreen in winter. Grows in Zones 3 to 9.

D. barbatus (Sweet William). Double or single, short or tall, these are cluster-flowered biennials for all zones that provide a bright burst of bloom in late spring, in shades of red, pink, or white. Some are eyed or bicolored. Height ranges from 6 to 18 inches.

D. deltoides (Maiden pinks). These are perennial, cushion-forming, evergreen pinks about 6 inches tall. Popular cultivars include the large-flowered 'Zing Rose,' sometimes grown as an annual, coming into bloom about eight weeks from seed and blooming all summer long, and 'Microchips,' which forms a carpet of tiny flowers in spring in shades of white, pink, rose, salmon, or crimson, often bicolored, either streaked or eyed. Perennials are most reliable in Zones 3 to 9.

D. gratianopolitanus, synonym *D. caesius* (Cheddar pinks). These fragrant perennial plants make low, wide, perennial mats (6 by 20 inches) or bright pink, 1-inch-wide flowers, perfect for banks, rock gardens, or edging. Blooms appear in late spring to midsummer. Grows in Zones 3 to 9.

Dianthus hybrids. Some of the many popular annual types include:

'Brilliancy,' with crimson blooms in spring and summer; only 6 inches tall but grows up to 15 inches wide, a perennial in Zones 3 to 9;

'Double Gaiety,' fringed double in color combinations of white, pink, rose, and red; 1 foot tall and showy as a border or pot plant;

'Snowfire,' 8-inch-tall plants bearing large, white, fringed, single flowers with bright red centers;

'Telstar,' bright and compact (8 inches tall), great for beds and edgings, available in a mixture of many pinks, reds, and whites in variegated patterns with a "pinked" edge, which is easy to grow from seed; and

'Telstar Picotee,' with bright red serrated flowers edged in white. Plants bloom all summer on 10-by-10-inch plants, tolerating heat well and covering faded blooms with eye-catching new blossoms.

D. knappii. Clusters of lemon-yellow scentless flowers on 18-inch-tall, branched, mound-shaped perennial plants bloom from late spring into summer. They are very hardy in cold, heat, and drought, and grow best in Zones 3 to 9.

D. plumarius (Cottage pinks). One-foot-tall branching perennial plants bear large flowers with delightful contrasting markings or zones. The frilly blooms with serrated edges may be double or single, in the purple, rose, pink, or white color range. Grows in Zones 3 to 9.

DICENTRA

Botanical Name: *Dicentra* (Fumariaceae)

Dramatic *Dicentra spectabilis* has graced American gardens since 1847, when these plants were first imported from Japan. Other dicentras are charming natives. Dicentra's elegant drooping flowers, lacy leaves, and autumnal yellow foliage make it an ideal specimen plant for shaded beds. Bleeding heart can be planted alongside spring-flowering bulbs or hardy ferns. The flowers are excellent for cutting.

PLANT TYPE: Hardy perennial.
GROWING RANGE: Zones 3 to 9.
HARDINESS: Very cold hardy and moderately heat tolerant.
PLANT HEIGHT: 2 to 3 feet.
FLOWER COLOR: Pink, white, red.
FLOWER FORM: 1-inch blossoms hang from arching 8-inch racemes.
SEASON OF BLOOM: Late spring to midsummer.
SOIL: Moist, fertile soil with high organic matter content.
PH: 5.5 to 7.
FERTILIZER: 1-inch layer of well-rotted manure or compost, applied in winter.
WATER: Average, with poor tolerance for drought.
EXPOSURE: Shade to partial sun.
SPACING: 2 feet apart.
PROPAGATION: Division or seed.

Method

- **Prepare soil outdoors** by tilling in organic matter (peat moss, compost, or leaf mold) to improve the soil's ability to hold moisture.

- **Sow seeds outdoors** in late fall in the prepared site 3 inches apart and barely covered by soil. Seeds sown in flats and then left in an unheated place for the winter germinate in spring, when it is time to move them to their permanent positions. Seedlings will be much smaller than purchased plants for a year or two.

- **Set plants outdoors** in early spring. Spread the roots carefully, and cover with soil until the crown is 1 inch below the surface.

- **Water** immediately after planting, and weekly throughout the first growing season. Water mature plants every ten days during dry periods in spring and summer.

- **Mulch** after planting with a thin, 1-inch layer of grass clippings or chopped leaves. Mulch again in late spring, adding a 3-inch layer of material in a circle around the plant.

- **Fertilize** by spreading a 1-inch layer of rotted manure over the dormant plant in winter. Organic fertilizers and mulches help keep soil the way dicentras like it—moist and friable.

- **Divide** mature plants to expand your supply by cutting a small rooted stem from the outside of the clump in midspring, when new growth appears. Transplant immediately and keep moist. Dicentras rarely need to be divided; do it only for propagation purposes.

- **Pests and diseases** rarely pose problems, though dicentras are subject to stem rot when grown in damp, poorly drained sites. Improve drainage with organic matter in soil; avoid overwatering.

- **Protect in winter** with a 3-inch layer of chopped leaves heaped on in the fall. In mixed beds, mark the dicentra's location in early winter so you won't disturb it while working with adjacent plants.

Tip · Dicentra makes a good flowering plant to place among hostas. Both plants prefer soil that remains constantly moist.

Selected Species

Dicentra spectabilis (Bleeding heart) is the popular 3-foot garden species with rose-red outer petals over white inner petals. A white-flowered variation, 'Alba,' is also available.

Dicentras also grow wild in some parts of the country, and wild species make good additions to woodland wildflower gardens. Western bleeding heart, *D. formosa,* and its eastern counterpart, *D. eximia* (fringed bleeding heart), can be grown from seed, and often self-sow after they are established. They grow best in shade, reaching 12 to 18 inches in height.

Another closely related plant, *D. cucullaria* (Dutchman's breeches), has white flowers shaped like inverted pantaloons and lacy foliage. It grows from underground clusters of small tubers in humus-rich soil in shade. This petite dicentra grows only 6 to 12 inches tall.

DUSTY MILLER

Botanical name: *Senecio cineraria* (Compositae)

Grown for foliage, not flowers, dusty miller has finely divided, lacy leaves of whitened gray. Each plant forms a neat mound that is useful for providing color contrasts in bedding, container, and edging designs. It is also nice in flower arrangements. Easy to grow, it tolerates practically any kind of weather—hot, cold, wet, or dry. Though it sometimes winters over in mild climates, young plants are better looking than older ones, which become ragged in time. Because dusty miller takes a long time from seed, most gardeners set out potted bedding plants. Low-growing, spreading types stay the neatest.

PLANT TYPE: Half-hardy perennial, grown as an annual.

GROWING RANGE: All zones.

HARDINESS: Withstands summer heat as well as temperatures down to freezing; prefers temperatures from 50° to 85°F.

PLANT HEIGHT: 8 to 12 inches.

FLOWER COLOR: Yellow.

FLOWER FORM: Inconspicuous daisylike flowers.

SEASON OF BLOOM: Foliage looks good in any season; blossoms appear in spring or summer of second year.

SOIL: Any well-drained soil.

PH: Near 7 (neutral).

FERTILIZER: Well-rotted manure or all-purpose fertilizer, applied lightly.

WATER: Moderate, not too wet.

EXPOSURE: Full sun.

SPACING: 8 to 12 inches apart.

PROPAGATION: Seed.

Method

- **Start seeds indoors** in late winter, no more than ⅛ inch deep in flats or six-packs in bright light in cool conditions about 50° to 60°F. Plants need light for germination. The potting mix should be part sand. Seeds germinate in about ten days. Shift to larger containers when seedlings become crowded.

- **Prepare soil outdoors** by digging the bed and turning in compost, fertilizer, sand (for drainage), and other soil amendments, as needed.

- **Sow seeds outdoors** in fall in mild climates for bedding plants the following spring. (In cold-winter areas, start seeds indoors or in a cold frame in early spring, because a long growing season is needed to produce bedding-size plants.) Make shallow furrows and plant seeds ⅛ inch deep and 2 inches apart.

- **Thin or transplant.** When indoor-grown seedlings are a few inches tall, transplant them to permanent places after the danger of frost passes. When seedlings grown outdoors become crowded, thin or transplant them to permanent positions.

- **Set out plants** in spring after the danger of frost passes.

- **Water** if soil becomes very dry. Plants are somewhat drought tolerant but look better if grown with ample moisture.

- **Fertilize** moderately during active growth with any all-purpose fertilizer.

- **Pests and diseases** rarely are problems.

- **Remove** flower heads if they appear, for neatness.

- **Mulch** beds with 1 or 2 inches of shredded leaves or bark chips.

Selected Cultivars

'Cirrhus,' with rounded, silvery leaves, not as finely divided as some types, is a vivid bedding plant, and rain resistant;

'New Look' offers a whiter leaf than most in oakleaf shape, on uniform plants 9 inches tall with a 12-inch spread;

'Silverdust' has finely divided, fernlike silver foliage on compact plants 9 to 12 inches tall; and

'Silver Queen,' only 8 inches tall, is a French strain with whitened leaves of oakleaf shape.

FLAX

Botanical name: *Linum* (Linaceae)
Other common name: Linum

Originally from North Africa, the many species of flax offer clouds of delicate single flowers on slender stems. Though poetic looking, flax is rugged and easy to grow; however, perennial types tend to be short-lived. The common blue flax used for linen cloth and linseed oil now grows wild in the United States, especially in the Northeast. In borders, rock gardens, or wildflower meadows, use flax in crowded masses because single plants look too wispy.

PLANT TYPES: Annual, biennial, or perennial of varied hardiness.
GROWING RANGE: All zones. In Zones 10 and 11, treat perennials like biennials for they may not be hardy in hot summers.
HARDINESS: Hardy to tender, varying with the species.
PLANT HEIGHT: 6 inches to 4 feet.
FLOWER COLOR: Pale or deep blue, white, yellow, deep rose.
FLOWER FORM: Single flowers about an inch wide with 5 oval petals.
SEASON OF BLOOM: Summer in most zones, all year in frost-free areas.
SOIL: Any good, well-drained garden soil.
PH: 6 to 7.
FERTILIZER: Well-rotted manure, all-purpose or high-phosphorus fertilizer.
WATER: Average to dry conditions.
EXPOSURE: Full sun.
SPACING: 3 to 12 inches.
PROPAGATION: Seed, stem cuttings, or division.

Method

- **Start seeds indoors** or in a cold frame six to eight weeks before the last frost. Grow in small pots or six-packs in sterile seed starting medium. Water and keep in a warm (65° to 75°F) place until seeds germinate, in about twenty-five days, then grow in cooler temperatures (50° to 60°F) in bright sunlight or a few inches below a fluorescent light fixture. Harden them off before planting them outdoors.

- **Prepare soil outdoors** before planting by tilling fertilizer, compost, and other soil improvers into the bed, as needed.

- **Sow seeds outdoors** where they will grow about four weeks before the last frost and repeat every few weeks for a continuing supply. A March planting will yield flowers in late May. In smoothly prepared and fertilized beds, plant seeds an inch or two apart and cover with ⅛ inch of soil. Do not let the seedbed dry out.

- **Thin or transplant** seedlings when they are 3 or 4 inches tall, if they are crowded. Move those grown indoors to larger pots or set them outdoors in permanent places. Thin or transplant those grown outdoors to their permanent positions. With care, thinnings may be transplanted while they are young, but will resist transplanting later in the season.

- **Set plants outdoors** about when tulips bloom in spring in northern and central areas. In Zones 9 and 10, with mild winters (a few light frosts), flax may be sown and set out at any time of year.

- **Divide** clumps of established nonwoody perennial plants in early spring when new growth begins, if they are very crowded. Replant divisions immediately. Do not divide woody or shrublike types such as *Linum arboreum.*

- **Take cuttings** of perennial types in summer and root them under warm, humid, shady conditions. Propagate woody or shrublike types this way rather than through division.

- **Water** often to prevent the soil from drying out until plants are 6 inches tall; after that, water often enough to keep plants from wilting.

- **Fertilize** lightly at planting time. Boost blossoms by applying a low-nitrogen, high-phosphorus and -potassium fertilizer when plants start to form buds.

- **Pests and diseases** rarely are problems.

- **Mulch** plants that grow in dry areas with several inches of bark chips or other mulch, but do not cover the crowns of the plants.

- **Pinch back** for bushiness if you prefer, but this adds to the need for staking by making plants top-heavy.

- **Stake** tall clumps inside peony hoops or with slender sticks.

- **Protect in winter** (perennials) by mulching about 2 inches deep and adding sand to soil for better drainage, for flax dislikes cold, wet soil. Remove mulch gradually in spring after the danger of hard frost passes.

Selected Species and Cultivars

Linum arboreum. This shrubby perennial for rock gardens grows a foot high with yellow flowers an inch wide. Originally from Crete, it is tender in cold areas. Grow in Zones 8 to 11.

L. flavum (Golden flax). A branched, somewhat woody perennial with many 1-inch-wide yellow flowers, this can be found in heights from 6 to 24 inches. It is hardy in Zones 7 to 11.

L. grandiflorum. This easy-to-grow, popular hardy annual garden plant grows 1 to 2 feet tall with 1-inch-wide flowers. Cultivars include 'Album,' with white flowers; 'Bright Eyes,' with bold, chocolate-centered white flowers; 'Caeruleum,' with blue-purple flowers; and 'Coccineum,' with bright scarlet flowers.

L. narbonense. Bright blue flowers appear in early summer on short-lived perennial plants 1 to 2 feet tall. For Zones 5 to 9.

L. perenne (Perennial flax). This European perennial for Zones 5 to 9 has medium blue ³⁄₄-inch-wide flowers on 10-inch-tall stems. The 'White Diamond' cultivar grows a foot tall with white petals and golden anthers.

L. usitatissimum (Common flax). This hardy annual is used to make linen and string. Its small plentiful flowers are blue or white on 2- to 4-foot-tall stems.

FORGET-ME-NOT

Botanical name: *Myosotis* (Boraginaceae)

With downy green leaves and sprays of tiny bright blue or pink flowers, this plant is a good choice for shady flower beds and moist places near water. It spreads rapidly by seed and with side shoots, and, because it is small and pretty, blends in well wherever it goes. It is effective when interplanted with bulbs, especially tulips, and in woodlands.

PLANT TYPES: Hardy biennial or perennial. In hot areas, grow perennials as biennials.
GROWING RANGE: Zones 5 to 11.
HARDINESS: Cold hardy in most regions if mulched, but harmed by prolonged heat above 95°F.
PLANT HEIGHT: 8 to 16 inches.
FLOWER COLOR: Usually blue, sometimes pink or white with yellow eyes. Blue and pink flowers may appear on the same plant.
FLOWER FORM: Loose terminal racemes several inches long formed of ¼-inch-wide, flat, lobed flowers and dotlike buds.
SEASON OF BLOOM: Late spring, summer, and fall.
SOIL: Rich, moist.
PH: 6 to 7.
FERTILIZER: Well-rotted manure, compost, flower fertilizer.
WATER: Average to wet conditions.
EXPOSURE: Partial shade, but adaptable to sun.
SPACING: 6 inches to 1 foot.
PROPAGATION: Seed, cuttings, or division. Plants self-sow.

Method

· **Start seeds indoors** in winter for flowers in summer, or in spring or summer for flowers the next year. Fill flats or six-packs with clean seed starting medium, an inch or so apart. Cover seeds ⅛ inch deep, water, and keep at about 65°F. Keep containers in a dimly lit or dark place until they germinate in about two weeks; then grow them in bright light.

· **Prepare soil outdoors** in beds before planting by tilling in soil amendments such as compost and fertilizer, as needed.

- **Sow seeds outdoors** after the danger of frost has passed, an inch or two apart under ⅛ inch of soil. Do not let the seedbed dry out.

- **Thin or transplant** indoor-grown seedlings to larger pots or garden beds when they are about 2 inches tall. Harden them off before planting them outdoors. Thin and transplant seedlings growing outdoors whenever they become crowded.

- **Set plants outdoors** in permanent places on an overcast day in spring or summer in northern and central areas, in fall or winter in Zones 9 to 11, or at any time in the mild Pacific Coast climate.

- **Divide** crowded plants when new growth begins in early spring to midspring.

- **Take cuttings** of side shoots and root them in moist soil in late spring or in summer under humid conditions for fast results. They will root in a glass of water, too.

- **Water** often to prevent soil from becoming dry.

- **Fertilize** lightly at planting time and in early and late summer.

- **Pests and diseases** are few; if powdery mildew whitens leaves, eliminate it with better air circulation and an application of fungicide.

- **Mulch** plants with an inch or two of shredded leaves or fine bark chips to keep moisture in the soil.

- **Pinch back** taller types for bushiness.

- **Remove** spent flowers to prolong flowering on new growth and for neatness.

- **Protect in winter** with 2 inches of mulch around plants. In early spring, make sure leaves are uncovered, though mulch may remain around them.

Selected Species and Cultivars

Myosotis alpina. These neat dwarf (7-inch) clumps or mats of ½-inch-wide blue flowers from the Pyrenees are perennial in cool climates. Grow them as fall-planted biennials where summers are very hot.

  M. sylvatica. This species includes garden forget-me-nots, sometimes classified as *M. alpestris.* These biennial flowers from 6 to 18 inches tall may be blue, pink, or white. 'Blue Ball' and 'White Ball' cultivars are short and compact, only 6 inches high and very tidy. 'Victoria Blue' is rich medium blue and 'Carmine King' is deep rose—both grow 8 inches tall. 'Blue Bird' grows from 1 to 2 feet tall and is effective for naturalizing in woodlands.

FOXGLOVE

Botanical name: *Digitalis* (Scrophulariaceae)
Other common name: Digitalis

Sometimes short-lived, foxglove is tall and stately with graceful spires of bell-shaped blossoms. Plants produce neat rosettes of leaves the first year and bloom the following year, self-sowing freely if you let the seed ripen on the plant and conditions are right. To collect seeds, let the pods ripen and turn brown. Crush them and save the seeds in a paper envelope or strew them where you want plants to grow. Foxgloves grow well in combination with ferns and look very nice on slopes. They are often used in borders, rock gardens, and woodland gardens. *However, a word of caution—foxglove, the source of the medicine digitalin, is a strongly poisonous herb, especially the purple-flowered* Digitalis purpurea. *All plant parts contain the toxin digitalis glycosides. If ingestion is suspected, contact a local poison control center. Severity of poisoning is dependent upon the amount ingested.*

PLANT TYPES: Hardy perennial or biennial.

GROWING RANGE: Zones 3 to 9 (grow as a biennial in Zone 9).

HARDINESS: Cold hardy but heat sensitive, growing best where summers are not too hot.

PLANT HEIGHT: 1 to 7 feet.

FLOWER COLOR: White, yellow, pink, rose, strawberry, apricot, or violet, with dark mottling inside the flowers.

FLOWER FORM: From large basal leaves, tall stems hold bell-like flowers an inch or two long and almost as wide. They open from bottom to top over several weeks. In some varieties the flowers hang down, but in others stand nearly straight out.

SEASON OF BLOOM: Late spring to midsummer.

SOIL: Humusy but well drained, rich in leaf mold.

PH: 6 to 7.

FERTILIZER: Well-rotted manure, compost, all-purpose fertilizer.

WATER: Average conditions.

EXPOSURE: Semishade, more shade needed farther south.

SPACING: 1 to 3 feet.

PROPAGATION: Seed or division.

Method

- **Start seeds indoors** in six-packs or flats filled with moist, sterile seed starting medium any time from late winter to the end of spring, in temperatures near 60°F. Do not cover the tiny seeds because they need light to germinate. Space them about an inch apart. Plants should appear in fourteen to twenty-one days. Harden them off before moving them outdoors.

- **Prepare soil outdoors** in beds, incorporating peat moss, compost, fertilizer, sand, and leaf mold, if needed.

- **Sow seeds outdoors** in a prepared and fertilized shady bed in spring after frost or summer in northern and central states, or in fall when the weather is cool in areas with little frost. Make rows about 1 inch deep and plant seeds sparsely, an inch apart, without covering them. Do not let the seedbed dry out. In the North, you may plant foxglove in a cold frame any time in early spring or at the end of summer, *not* during hot weather.

- **Thin or transplant** seedlings when they are 3 or 4 inches tall, or as soon as they are crowded. Shift indoor-grown seedlings to larger pots or set them outdoors in nursery beds. Thin or transplant outdoor-grown seedlings to 8 or more inches apart in nursery areas, or to permanent positions. The next spring, if necessary, thin or transplant them to their permanent positions when growth resumes in spring.

- **Set plants outdoors,** after hardening them off if they were grown indoors, in spring or early summer, when daytime temperatures are around 60° to 65°F.

- **Divide** large clumps with multiple basal rosettes when new leaf growth begins in early spring. Do not cut individual rosettes in half, just separate them. Replant divisions immediately and water them; they should bloom the same year.

- **Water** frequently enough to keep the soil evenly moist.

- **Fertilize** lightly at planting time and keep plants steadily but not excessively fertilized.

- **Pests and diseases** include mildew, leaf spot, and Japanese beetles. Treat mildew and leaf spot with fungicide. Control Japanese beetles with pheromone traps and pyrethrum.

- **Mulch** plants with 2 inches of composted leaves or small bark chips to help keep moisture in the soil.

- **Stake** tall plants before flowers open, especially in windy areas.

- **Remove** flowering stems after they bloom unless you want to harvest the seed. For neatness, trim back the tops after they turn brown in autumn.

- **Protect in winter** by placing 2 inches of mulch around each plant.

Selected Species and Cultivars

Digitalis grandiflora, synonym *D. ambigua.* This species is a 3-foot-tall perennial native to Europe and Asia which has yellow-brown bells in summer. A cultivar, 'Temple Bells,' is a dwarf type excellent for rock gardens, growing a little over a foot tall with neat yellow bells.

D. lutea. These 2-foot-tall perennial plants bear yellow or white flowers in late spring or early summer.

D. purpurea (Common foxglove). A biennial plant native to Great Britain, this 7-foot-tall wildflower is a phenomenal sight in the woodlands. Plant breeders have developed many varieties from it, but not all are as graceful as the native type, which has bells on only one side of the stalk. Some well-known types are 'Foxy,' which will bloom in only five months from seed; 'Alba,' a tall pure white form that really lights up the woods; and 'Excelsior,' a 5-foot hybrid with showy, outward-facing flowers of cream, pink, rose, or purple, handsomely marked.

FUCHSIA

Botanical Name: *Fuchsia magellanica* (Onagraceae)
Other common name: Lady's eardrops

If you live in a mild-winter area and have a rich spot of soil that receives dappled shade, you can grow fuchsias outdoors. Otherwise, these tropicals are best planted in dramatic hanging baskets that are kept outdoors in summer and overwintered indoors, while semi-dormant. The exotic flowers dangle from the stems like fine floral jewelry.

PLANT TYPE: Tender perennial.
GROWING RANGE: Zones 8 to 11 outdoors; all zones when grown in containers and overwintered indoors.
HARDINESS: Cannot tolerate hard freezes, tolerates heat to 90°F but not drought.
PLANT HEIGHT: Up to 6 feet in tropical areas. Basket-grown plants reach 3 feet in diameter.
FLOWER COLOR: Pink, red, purple, or white, including bicolored.
FLOWER FORM: Dangling double and single blossoms 2 inches long.
SEASON OF BLOOM: Summer to fall.
SOIL: Rich, humusy, with leaf mold or sphagnum moss added.
PH: 6 to 6.5.
FERTILIZER: Well-rotted manure or compost added to the planting soil. Apply liquid fertilizer to the plants every 2 to 3 weeks in summer.
WATER: Above average. Soil should never dry out completely.
EXPOSURE: Dappled shade.
SPACING: 3 feet (outdoors in beds).
PROPAGATION: Softwood stem cuttings.

Method

- **Prepare soil outdoors** by tilling in liberal amounts of peat or sphagnum moss, leaf mold, compost, and manure. The final mixture should be one-half organic matter and one-half sandy soil. In well-drained containers, use a planting mix of one part compost, one part peat moss, and one part sand.

- **Set out** purchased plants or rooted cuttings so that the tops of the roots are covered with 1 inch of soil. Container-grown fuchsias benefit from repotting every spring.

- **Water** thoroughly after planting, and once a week thereafter. In mild-winter climates, where fuchsias grow into small trees, watering can be less frequent, about once every two weeks. In summer, water plants grown in baskets or containers until thoroughly soaked. In winter, water lightly once a month—just enough to keep the plants alive.

- **Mulch** around fuchsias grown outdoors in beds with a 3-inch layer of chopped leaves.

- **Fertilize** with a liquid fertilizer every two weeks. Plants grown outdoors in a rich site may be fertilized by spreading a 2-inch layer of compost or rotted manure around the plants in late spring, followed by monthly applications of a liquid fertilizer until the plants drop their flowers.

- **Root cuttings,** about 5 inches long, in spring through early summer. Bury the bottom end of the cuttings in moist sand and keep them in a shady place. The cuttings will develop working roots within four weeks. Cuttings rooted in early spring often bloom by the end of summer. Sometimes cuttings will root in a glass of water on a windowsill.

- **Pests and diseases** are seldom a problem.

- **Winter protection** is a good idea where fuchsias are grown outdoors, even in mild-winter climates. Mound a few inches of compost over the base of the plants, or surround them with a 3-inch-thick mulch.

- **Prune back** fuchsias after they bloom to keep them from getting leggy. Also trim the plants lightly before bringing them indoors to winter over in low light in a cool place (about 50°F). First thing in spring, bring the plants into brighter light and provide water and fertilizer to stimulate new growth. When new buds emerge, prune the plants severely so that only two or three strong shoots remain growing from the base of the plants.

Tips · Where space and climate permit, fuchsias may be trained into espaliered trees.
· Two plants of compatible colors may be grown together in the same container.

GAILLARDIA

Botanical name: *Gaillardia* (Compositae)
Other common names: Blanket flower, Indian blanket

Like other plants with hairy leaves, gaillardia tolerates harsh conditions and resists pests, blooming continuously during hot weather. These brightly colored flowers native to the Southwest grow tall and daisylike in the wild. They can often be found growing in sand dunes near the seashore.

For the garden, gaillardia has been bred into different shapes and sizes. Flowers may be single or double, and plants may be tall or compact. Each plant has a basal clump of leaves from which stems of flowers grow in warm weather. Use gaillardia for bedding and borders, in containers, as fresh cut flowers, and naturalized in fields and sunny wild gardens.

PLANT TYPES: Hardy annual or perennial.
GROWING RANGE: Zones 4 to 11.
HARDINESS: Very hardy, tolerating cold, heat above 90°F, and changeable weather.
PLANT HEIGHT: 1 to 2½ feet.
FLOWER COLOR: Golden yellow, cream, orange, rusty red, wine, and related shades. Most have red petals tipped with gold around red or gold centers.
FLOWER FORM: Composite daisylike flowers, double or single. Petals have zigzagged edges.
SEASON OF BLOOM: Summer in most areas, but any time in warm weather; all year in Zones 10 and 11.
SOIL: Any well-drained soil, preferably sandy.
PH: 6.5 to 7.5.
FERTILIZER: Well-rotted manure, compost, all-purpose fertilizer.
WATER: Needs little water but tolerates damp soil at times.
EXPOSURE: Full sun.
SPACING: 1 to 2 feet.
PROPAGATION: Usually by division, occasionally from seed.

🌱 *Method*

- **Start seeds indoors** in bright light at about 70°F. Plant annuals in February or March and perennials in spring or summer in Zones 4 to 8 and in fall or spring in Zones 9 to 11. Fill six-packs, flats, or small pots with moist, clean seed starting medium that is one-third sand for good drainage. Plant seeds ⅛ inch deep and 1 or 2 inches apart. Germination occurs in fifteen to twenty days.

- **Prepare soil outdoors** before planting by tilling in fertilizer, compost, and sand for improved drainage, if needed.

- **Sow seeds outdoors** in a prepared bed in summer or when temperatures are about 75°F in Zones 4 to 8, or in fall or spring in Zones 9 to 11. Make rows about 2 inches deep and plant seeds at least 2 inches apart and only ⅛ inch deep. Do not let seedbeds dry out.

- **Thin or transplant** seedlings (indoor and outdoor grown) to at least 8 inches apart in their permanent beds or in nursery beds when they have more than four leaves.

- **Set plants outdoors** in permanent places after hardening them off in light shade.

- **Divide** crowded plants in spring when leaf growth begins.

- **Water** if soil becomes dry below the surface.

- **Fertilize** lightly at planting time or each year in early spring and again just before plants bloom.

- **Pests and diseases** are rarely a problem.

- **Mulch** plants with 2 or 3 inches of composted leaves or small bark chips only in very hot, dry areas.

- **Stake** tall types if necessary, but this is rare.

- **Deadhead** plants for neatness and to prevent reseeding (seedlings are not true to the cultivars). They will keep blooming even if you do not.

- **Protect in winter** by placing an inch or two of mulch around the crowns of perennial types. Remove it in early spring.

Tip · **Good drainage helps prevent winterkill.**

Selected Species and Cultivars

Gaillardia x *grandiflora*. This hybrid group of easy-to-grow perennials is perfect for flower borders and cutting. Varieties include:

'Burgundy,' with 4-inch-wide flowers of a rich wine-red on 30-inch-tall plants;

'Dazzler,' with large golden yellow flowers on 30-inch-tall plants;

'Goblin' and 'Goblin Yellow,' a compact type, 1 foot tall, covered with 3-inch-wide red-and-yellow or solid yellow flowers;

'Monarch Strain,' a vigorous type with strong 30-inch stems that do not sprawl. Single flowers bloom in a range of colors from burgundy to orange for months in hot weather;

'Portola Giants,' bearing large gold-tipped red flowers for months on strong stems in spite of heat and drought. Plants grow about 30 inches tall;

'Tokajer,' on 30-inch-tall plants, with rich yellow-orange petals surrounding a strawberrylike center. This one is distinctive as a cut flower or in the border; and

'Torchlight,' growing 30 inches tall, with 5-inch-wide yellow flowers bordered in red.

G. pulchella, synonym *G. picta.* This is a hardy annual species that resembles the perennials in appearance and size. Flowers may be single or double. 'Gaiety' is typical—attractive masses of brilliant double flowers appear throughout the summer, even in sandy soil. Start indoors in areas with short summers. The mixture includes many bicolors in wine, red, rose, yellow, orange, and maroon.

GERANIUM

Botanical name: *Geranium* (Geraniaceae)
Other common name: Cranesbill

True geraniums are hardy wildflowers native to Eurasia. Once established, they are very easy to grow and thrive with little care. Their excellent drought tolerance makes them good candidates for rock gardens and garden walls, as well as low-maintenance perennial beds and borders. These flowers are different from common garden geraniums, which are properly called pelargoniums (see pages 327–29).

PLANT TYPE: Hardy perennial.
GROWING RANGE: Zones 3 to 7.
HARDINESS: Good tolerance of cold and moderate heat.
PLANT HEIGHT: 8 to 24 inches.
FLOWER COLOR: Blue, purple, pink.
FLOWER FORM: Single 5-petaled flowers, 1 inch wide, borne in pairs.
SEASON OF BLOOM: May to August.
SOIL: Well-drained soil of average fertility.
PH: 6 to 7.
FERTILIZER: ½-inch layer of well-rotted manure, applied in spring.
WATER: Water every 10 to 14 days, more frequently during drought.
EXPOSURE: Full sun or partial shade.
SPACING: 12 inches.
PROPAGATION: Seed, division, or stem cuttings.

Method

- **Prepare soil outdoors** by adding sand to clay soils, and peat or sphagnum moss to extremely sandy sites. Small rocks may be left in the planting site to improve drainage.

- **Plant seeds outdoors** where you want them to grow four weeks before the last spring frost, ¼ inch deep and 2 inches apart. Seedlings may not appear for several weeks, for seed germination is slow.

- **Set out plants** purchased from a nursery any time in early spring. Handle the roots carefully for they are quite fragile.

- **Divide** if established plants every three to four years to keep them neat and free flowering by digging up plants, cutting off small clumps with a sharp knife, and replanting immediately. Although early fall is the best time to divide geraniums, you can also divide them in early spring. They also may be propagated by rooting cuttings taken in early summer. Cuttings should be about 4 inches long.

- **Water** all newly planted geraniums immediately after planting, and every week thereafter for a month. After they are established, geraniums are very drought tolerant and rarely require supplemental watering except in very dry climates.

- **Fertilize** lightly with a ½-inch layer of rotted manure in early spring. Too much fertilizer can lead to rank, invasive growth.

- **Pests and diseases** are rarely a problem with true geraniums, but watch out for four-lined plant bugs if leaves show sunken brown spots. Control light infestations with applications of soapy water or a rotenone insecticide to the leaves.

- **Protect in winter** with a 3- to 5-inch layer of chopped leaves or other organic material. Remove the mulch in early spring.

Selected Species

True geraniums include over two hundred species. Budding geranium collectors may begin with the following choices, which are widely available and easy to grow:

Geranium regelii (Lilac cranesbill) produces blue to lavender flowers in midsummer on 2-foot-tall, spreading plants.

G. sanguineum (Blood red cranesbill) grows only 8 inches tall, and produces dainty rose-pink flowers in late spring or early summer. The leaves turn deep red after the first fall frost.

GERBERA

Botanical name: *Gerbera jamesonii* (Compositae)
Other common names: African daisy, Transvaal daisy, Barberton daisy

Seen everywhere in Zones 9 to 11, gerbera looks like an elegant version of the common dandelion. Bright daisylike flowers in sunny shades of salmon, rose, cream, or gold bloom on slender stems above a neat rosette of downy leaves. These tender perennial plants are deeply rooted and withstand heat and pests. The flowers bloom for most of the year in warm climates, where they are used for bedding and cutting. They make good container or greenhouse plants where the climate is cooler—grow them indoors most of the year and set them out for summer bloom. In the appropriate climate, the plants live and thrive for many years. Individual blossoms last about two weeks in cut bouquets.

PLANT TYPE: Tender perennial.
GROWING RANGE: Zones 9 to 11, without protection.
HARDINESS: Withstands heat, killed by hard frost.
PLANT HEIGHT: 8 inches to over 2 feet.
FLOWER COLOR: White, cream, yellow, orange, peach, pink, red, or wine, with yellow discs.
FLOWER FORM: Daisylike single or double flowers from 3 to 10 inches wide on leafless stems over neat foliage rosettes.
SEASON OF BLOOM: All year in Zones 9 to 11 during warm weather, especially spring and fall; summer in other zones.
SOIL: Rich, well drained.
PH: 6.5 to 7.5.
FERTILIZER: Aged manure, all-purpose or high-phosphorus fertilizer.
WATER: Average conditions.
EXPOSURE: Full sun or bright, dappled shade.
SPACING: 1 to 2 feet.
PROPAGATION: Usually from seed, also by division.

Method

- **Start seeds indoors,** one seed per pot, in small pots or six-packs filled with moist potting soil, covering less than 1/8 inch deep. Water and keep at 70°F until seeds germinate, in about a week. In the North, start seeds in January with twelve hours of artificial light per day. Only very fresh seed will grow, and it needs light to germinate. Keep seedlings in a sunny area or a few inches below a fluorescent light fixture. When leaves are 2 inches long, move plants outdoors in warm climates or to larger pots if they are crowded. Harden off seedlings before moving them outdoors.

- **Prepare soil outdoors** in beds before planting by tilling in fertilizer, compost, and other soil improvers, as needed.

- **Sow seeds outdoors** in nursery beds in warm (around 70°F) spring weather or as soon as they ripen on plants. Plant them 1/8 inch deep and about 4 inches apart. Do not let them dry out.

- **Thin outdoor-grown seedlings** to their permanent spacing when they are a few inches wide.

- **Set plants outdoors** in spring, after the danger of frost has passed, for best blooms. Pot-grown plants may be set out at any time during warm weather. Do not bury crown when planting in the garden.

- **Divide** established plants in warm, moist weather only if they are overcrowded and have more than one crown. Dig deeply to avoid harming the central taproot of each plant, and replant immediately in well-prepared soil. Division is rarely needed.

- **Water** plants whenever the soil starts to dry out and when they wilt during hot weather.

- **Fertilize** lightly at planting time and each year in spring and fall. Boost blossom size by applying a low-nitrogen, high-phosphorus and -potassium fertilizer when the first buds show.

- **Pests** seldom are problems. Crowns may rot if planted too deep.

- **Mulch** plants in dry weather with 2 inches of pine needles or other lightweight mulch.

- **Remove** spent blossoms unless seed is wanted.

- **Protect in winter** by mulching around crowns with a lightweight mulch of 2 inches of pine straw. Pull back the mulch after the danger of frost ends so new leaves can come up.

Tip · In northern states (Zone 7 and north), grow gerbera as an annual or dig up plants each fall and grow them indoors in a well-lit area until you can put them outdoors in late spring.

Selected Cultivars

African daisy comes in many sizes and colors. F_1 hybrids come into bloom earlier than nonhybrids, but still take at least three and a half months from seed to bloom. Most gardeners purchase unnamed plants in bloom at garden centers. Cultivars available as seeds include:

'California,' with lovely single flowers on 2-foot-tall stems, excellent for cutting;

'Ebony Eyes,' with dark centers that set off large flowers on dwarf plants under a foot tall. 'T & M Blackheart' is similar but taller, 15 to 20 inches, with well-filled-out flowers with broad petals;

'Gigi,' with 4½-inch-wide flowers on long stems up to 2 feet tall, in pastel and bright shades;

'Happipot,' a dwarf type 12 inches tall with large flowers on strong stems, good in 4- to 6-inch pots of rich soil;

'Rainbow,' with dwarf, 8-inch-tall plants bearing 4- and 5-inch-wide blossoms in bright, strong colors; and

'T & M Sensation' hybrids, with huge flowers up to 10 inches across on 1½- to 2-foot-tall stems, in an array of shapes (including spider-flowered) and colors.

GLADIOLUS

Botanical name: *Gladiolus* (Iridaceae)

As cut flowers, gladioli have come in and out of fashion—many people still associate them with funerals. But with their dramatic spires, holding up to thirty large flowers in tropical colors, they never stay out of favor for long. Their swordlike leaves appear before the flowers do and persist after bloom. 'Glads' originated in Africa and southern Europe, and have been widely grown and hybridized. Variably tender, they grow from corms. The largest grade of corms produces flowers the fastest. The smaller cultivars look most graceful in the garden and tend to be hardier than the larger ones.

PLANT TYPE: Tender or hardy bulb.
GROWING RANGE: All zones when dug up and overwintered. Will overwinter in Zones 9 to 11 with no protection and as far north as Zone 6 with mulch and a sheltered site. A few strains are cold hardy.
HARDINESS: Usually killed by frost, tolerant of heat.
PLANT HEIGHT: 1 to over 5 feet.
FLOWER COLOR: Vibrant shades of red, rose, carmine, magenta, violet, pink, orange, yellow, green, or white, sometimes bicolored.
FLOWER FORM: With ruffled or smooth flaring petals, flowers are up to 4 inches across, lined up on one side of a tall spire.
SEASON OF BLOOM: Any time of year if temperatures are warm.
SOIL: Well-drained, average to rich garden soil.
PH: 5.8 to 7.
FERTILIZER: Bonemeal, all-purpose fertilizer, compost, and well-rotted manure.
WATER: Average.
EXPOSURE: Full sun.
SPACING: 3 to 8 inches apart.
PROPAGATION: Corms, division, cormels, or (rarely) seed.

Method

- **Start seeds indoors** in spring at 60° to 70°F, closely planted ⅛ inch deep in flats filled with sterile growing medium. Few home gardeners grow gladiolus this way because it will take plants several years to flower. Seedlings usually emerge in about two weeks.

- **Prepare soil outdoors** in beds by tilling in compost, bonemeal, and fertilizer, as needed. If you use manure, mix it into the soil half a year or a year before planting corms or it might damage them.

- **Sow seeds outdoors** during warm (over 70°F) weather in spring or early summer, in shallow rows. Space seeds 2 inches apart, barely covering them. They will grow leaves and a cormel by summer's end.

- **Transplant** seedlings grown indoors when they are about 2 inches high. After hardening them off, move them to nursery beds outdoors when the weather is warm and plant them an inch or two deeper than they grew indoors, several inches apart.

- **Plant corms outdoors** in spring after the danger of frost passes, 4 to 7 inches deep. In Zones 9 to 11, plant in late winter. Plant small corms more shallowly than large ones. Plant corms deeper in sandy soil than in clay or humusy soil. Make several successive plantings for months of bloom. Corms may be planted earlier indoors and transplanted outside when weather is warm. Indoors plant corms 6 inches deep (deeper if soil is sandy). The corms may be closely spaced, 1 or 2 inches apart since they will be transplanted outdoors. When pips break the soil, place them where they will get bright sunlight.

- **Divide** tender glads in fall in areas with cold winters when bringing the corms indoors. If they are crowded, dig and divide tender glads in Zones 9 to 11 in early spring before new growth begins; replant immediately. Hardy glads may be treated similarly.

- **Water** plants moderately, but do not let the soil dry out during the active growth period or it might stunt the plants. If corms spend their dormant period in the soil, keep somewhat dry to prevent rot.

- **Fertilize** plants lightly but steadily throughout their growth.

- **Pests and diseases** include slugs, sow bugs, several kinds of blight, and fusarium corm rot. Growing glads in a different spot each year will help you keep from passing diseases on to fresh corms. Propagate only disease-free plants. Do not use malathion on them because it harms the plants, but rotenone and pyrethrum are safe to use on insect pests. Wood ashes and diatomaceous earth strewn on the ground around the plants help prevent slugs and sow bugs.

- **Mulch** glads with 2 inches of small bark chips or other mulch to hold moisture in the soil.

- **Stake** plants growing in partly shaded or windy areas, or if plants show a need for support.

- **Pinch off** the top bud while it is small to encourage blossoms to open simultaneously instead of progressively from bottom to top, if you wish.

- **Remove** foliage after it matures and begins to yellow. Corms may be dug up and dried at this time, before the location of the plants is forgotten.

- **Protect in winter** by mulching glads where they are hardy. In other areas, dig up the plants after foliage begins to yellow or when frosty weather begins (including tiny first-year plants grown from seed). Cut off all but the bottom inch of foliage. Dry the plants in the sun for a few days to cure them; remove the leaves, roots, and the withered mother corm (each usually makes two large new corms that will flower the next year, plus cormels). Store the dry corms and cormels through the winter, labeled, in paper sacks containing a few mothballs, in a cool, dry place. Cormels can be saved and grown for several years until they are large enough to flower well.

Tips • Seeds ripen on the plants about a month after flowers are pollinated.
• Plunge the stems of cut gladioli into a deep bucket of tepid water as soon as they are cut and leave there for three hours to overnight to prolong their bouquet life. Cut them when the first blooms open—the rest will open indoors.

Selected Cultivars

There are over ten thousand recorded cultivars of gladiolus, of unclassifiably mixed genetic heritage. Most are killed by frost. Some well-known types for the garden include:

Butterfly hybrids, growing from fairly small corms, which bloom on plants from 1½ to 4 feet tall, with many ruffled flowers on each stem. These do not multiply as quickly as other types.

Large-flowered hybrids such as 'Dawn Glow,' a tall type with large rosy flowers touched with lavender. Similar are 'Easter Time,' pure white; 'First Kiss,' pale pink; 'Gold Coin,' golden yellow; 'Lavender Ruffles,' an intense rosy lavender; 'Intrepid,' a brilliant scarlet; and many others, growing 4 or more feet tall.

Nanus hybrids (winter-hardy gladiolus), for Zones 3 to 10, under mulch. These glads usually grow about 18 inches tall and have smaller flowers than standard types. They are gracefully shaped and often bicolored or vividly marked in tones of rose, peach, white, red, or orange. It is difficult to keep them alive over winter if the weather is cold and wet, or if soil is poorly drained. However, the corms may be dried and stored indoors like those of tender varieties.

GOATSBEARD

Botanical name: *Aruncus* (Rosaceae)
Other common name: Aruncus

Great white plumes of flowers adorn this imposing perennial native wildflower, which resembles astilbe. It is carefree and unusual, and makes a good background plant. A single plant may be used as an accent, or several clumps may be used together in large flower borders. The toothed, light green leaves turn bright yellow in autumn.

PLANT TYPE: Hardy perennial.
GROWING RANGE: Zones 4 to 9.
HARDINESS: Tolerates cold, does poorly above 90°F.
PLANT HEIGHT: 3 to 6 feet.
FLOWER COLOR: White.
FLOWER FORM: Showy upright plumes of tiny flowers.
SEASON OF BLOOM: Late summer.
SOIL: Humusy, rich.
PH: 6.5.
FERTILIZER: Well-rotted manure, compost, and flower or all-purpose fertilizer.
WATER: Wet or moist soil.
EXPOSURE: Part shade to full sun, more shade in the South.
SPACING: 2 to 4 feet.
PROPAGATION: Division or seed.

Method

· **Start seeds indoors** in spring, an inch apart in flats and two per six-pack pocket filled with sterile potting soil. Cover seeds with ⅛ inch of soil or finely milled vermiculite. Keep them at 40° to 60°F until they germinate, then grow at 60°F. They usually take thirty to sixty days to germinate. When plants are large enough to handle, shift them to one plant per six-pack.

- **Prepare soil outdoors** at planting time by tilling in compost, fertilizer, and other soil amendments, as needed.

- **Sow seeds outdoors** after the danger of frost passes. Summer is a good time in most areas, fall is better in Zone 9. In rows, plant seeds an inch apart and cover with ⅛ inch of soil. Keep them moist constantly until they germinate. Indoor sowing is more reliable.

- **Thin or transplant** seedlings when they are about 3 inches tall, if they are crowded. Outdoors, thin those growing in beds to nursery spacing at least 6 inches apart. Indoors, step up container-grown plantlets to 4-inch pots or, if the weather is right, move them outdoors after hardening them off. When they are 6 to 8 inches tall, move the young plants to permanent positions or larger pots.

- **Set out mature plants** in spring or early fall. Set out seedlings grown indoors after the danger of frost passes, after hardening them off in shade for several days.

- **Divide** plants in early spring when new growth begins, once every few years. Discard the center portion if it is past its prime; replant the new shoots from the outer ring in their permanent positions.

- **Water** if soil is dry. Keep small plants well watered.

- **Fertilize** lightly in spring and summer, preferably with aged manure and compost.

- **Pests and diseases** seldom are problems. Spray with rotenone or cut back plants if they are attacked by caterpillars. New shoots will grow.

- **Remove** stalks of flowers after blooming is finished, if seed and seed heads are not wanted.

- **Protect in winter** by mulching young or potted plants growing outdoors with 2 inches of finely shredded leaves or compost. Remove mulch from above crowns in spring when new growth begins.

Selected Species

Aruncus dioicus, synonym *A. sylvester.* This is the main garden type. It can grow 6 feet tall or more in good conditions. 'Kneiffii,' a dwarf cultivar that grows only 3 feet tall, is useful in smaller flower borders.

GOMPHRENA

Botanical name: *Gomphrena* (Amaranthaceae)

Gomphrena is a traditional flower in dried everlasting bouquets, but is also a strong grower for the sunny flower border, where it blooms constantly in spite of dry conditions. Dwarf types are often used for pots, edgings, and in rock gardens for summer color. North of Zone 7, these tender annuals flower sooner if started indoors and then moved outside after the last expected frost. The large fuzzy seeds are easy to handle. Preserve flowers by picking them with long stems and hanging them upside down in bunches in an airy place to dry. The stems will stiffen enough to use in arrangements without wires.

PLANT TYPE: Tender annual.
GROWING RANGE: All zones.
HARDINESS: Killed by frost, thrives in heat.
PLANT HEIGHT: 6 inches to 2 feet.
FLOWER COLOR: White, shrimp, orange, rose, magenta, purple.
FLOWER FORM: Cloverlike heads about an inch wide, several per stem.
SEASON OF BLOOM: Summer into fall in the North; any time of year where there is no freeze.
SOIL: Fair to rich, well drained.
PH: 6.5 to 7.5.
FERTILIZER: Well-rotted manure, all-purpose or high-phosphorus fertilizer.
WATER: Average to dry conditions.
EXPOSURE: Full sun.
SPACING: 10 to 16 inches.
PROPAGATION: Seed.

Method

- **Start seeds indoors** an inch or two apart in small pots or flats filled with moist potting soil, about eight weeks before the last frost. Cover seeds with ⅛ inch of soil, water, and keep at 75° to 80°F until seeds germinate, usually in less than two weeks. Afterward temperatures may be reduced to 65° to 70°F if you wish. Grow seedlings in a sunny area or a few inches below a fluorescent light fixture. When they have four to six leaves, step them up to larger pots if necessary.

- **Prepare soil outdoors** before planting by tilling in fertilizer, compost, and other soil improvers, as needed.

- **Sow seeds outdoors** where they will grow one week after the last expected frost. Plant seeds in November or December in Zones 10 and 11. In smoothly prepared and fertilized beds, plant seeds 3 or more inches apart and cover with ⅛ inch of soil. Do not let the seedbed dry out.

- **Thin** outdoor-grown seedlings to their permanent spacing when they are about 4 inches tall. With care, thinnings may be transplanted.

- **Set plants outdoors** after the danger of frost passes, first hardening them off in shade for a few days.

- **Water** seedlings often to prevent the soil from drying out. Later, mature plants tolerate fairly dry soil.

- **Fertilize** lightly at planting time. Boost blossoms by applying a low-nitrogen, high-phosphorus and -potassium fertilizer when plants are 5 or 6 inches tall.

- **Pests and diseases** seldom are problems.

- **Mulch** plants that grow in very hot, dry areas with several inches of bark chips or other mulch to keep soil cooler.

- **Pinch back** tips for bushiness if flowers are grown for ornamental appearance in gardens. For cut flowers, you may prefer longer stems.

- **Stake** tall plants if necessary with slim bamboo, wood, or wire stakes.

Selected Species and Cultivars

Gomphrena globosa (Globe amaranth). This is the type most often grown in gardens, and its cultivars may be dwarf, medium, or tall, ranging from 6 to 24 inches in height. There is a great deal of variation in flower size and quality, so shop around for what suits you best. In dried arrangements, the large pinks and oranges look especially showy; sometimes the whites look dusty. 'Dwarf Buddy' is short (6 to 8 inches tall) and mounded with bright purple flowers—it is a good choice for pots or bedding in hot, dry areas. It sometimes roots from cuttings. 'Strawberry Fields' is an unusually rich red.

 G. haageana. This type is similar, but actually is a tender perennial grown as an annual. 'Aurea' and 'Orange' are strains with 1-inch-wide fiery-colored flowers. This type is slower to grow.

GRAPE HYACINTH

Botanical name: *Muscari* (Liliaceae)

On slopes, for beds and borders, in rock gardens, and as an underplanting for deciduous shrubs and trees, grape hyacinths are an excellent, reliable, carefree flower. Very often they are interplanted with tulips for they bloom at the same time. Grape hyacinths continue to bloom attractively for more than a month, longer than most other spring bulbs. However, the grasslike leaves also last a long time after the plants finish blooming, before yellowing and disappearing in summer. They reappear in fall and stay green through winter except during exceptionally cold years. Interplant grape hyacinths with other plants to hide their foliage. They work particularly well with periwinkle vine, forming a hazy carpet of blue when both bloom simultaneously; this is especially effective on a slope. After blooms are finished, tuck grape hyacinth leaves under the vines to ripen and fade invisibly.

  PLANT TYPE: Hardy bulb.
  GROWING RANGE: Zones 5 to 8; Zone 4 with protection.
  HARDINESS: Withstands summer heat, requires cold winters.
  PLANT HEIGHT: 6 to 12 inches.
  FLOWER COLOR: Usually deep blue, also light blue, pink, or white, rarely greenish.
  FLOWER FORM: In most species, spikes bear small round flowers in clusters resembling an upside-down bunch of grapes. *Muscari comosum* has a feathery-looking flower instead.
  SEASON OF BLOOM: Several weeks in late spring, with tulips.
  SOIL: Any well-drained soil.
  PH: Near 7 (neutral).

FERTILIZER: Moderate. Well-rotted manure, bonemeal, and slow-release fertilizer, applied lightly.
WATER: Moderate, not too wet.
EXPOSURE: Full sun or partial shade.
SPACING: 3 inches apart, 3 inches deep.
PROPAGATION: Usually from bulbs, also from seed.

Method

- **Start seeds indoors** in late winter to early spring, ⅛ inch deep in flats or six-packs in bright light at about 60°F. The potting mix should be part sand. Seeds germinate irregularly, usually in about a month. It takes three to four years for seedlings to mature enough to bloom, so most gardeners plant bulbs.

- **Prepare soil outdoors** by digging the bed and turning in compost, fertilizer, sand (for drainage), and other soil amendments, as needed.

- **Sow seeds outdoors** in early summer or when they turn black and ripen, or in fall in cold frames, ⅛ inch deep, 1 inch apart, in finely tilled soil, in rows. Seeds can be scattered where you would like to naturalize the plants.

- **Thin or transplant** when indoor-grown seedlings are a few inches tall to their permanent places or to outdoor nursery beds, after the danger of frost passes. When seedlings grown outdoors become crowded, thin or transplant them to permanent positions.

- **Set out bulbs** in fall as soon as they are received; otherwise, they may dry out too much in storage.

- **Dig up and separate** crowded plants after they bloom, when foliage starts to yellow, without cutting into the bulbs, to start new colonies. Plantings may remain undivided for many years with little care if you prefer. After lifting a clump with a spade, tease the bulbs apart gently by hand and reset immediately.

- **Water** if soil is dry while plants have green foliage showing. Do not overwater or bulbs will rot.

- **Fertilize** during active growth in fall and spring with bonemeal and all-purpose bulb or flower fertilizer. In rich soils little or no fertilizer is needed.

- **Pests and diseases** rarely are problems.

- **Remove** flower heads and stems after bloom is finished, unless seed is wanted. Let leaves disappear by themselves, or remove them when they start to turn yellow.

- **Mulch** beds with 1 or 2 inches of shredded leaves or bark chips.

Selected Species and Cultivars

Muscari armeniacum. Clear blue grapelike flowers 6 to 10 inches tall are edged in white. Plants like sun. The cultivar 'Blue Spike' is sterile (will not form seeds), which makes its blossoms last longer than other cultivars.

M. botryoides. Six to 12 inches tall, this species has typical grape hyacinth form. Blue flowers appear from late March to May. 'Album' is a white form and 'Carneum' is pinkish; neither is as vigorous as the blue strain.

M. comosum (Plume hyacinth, Tassel hyacinth, Feather hyacinth). It is taller than *M. botryoides,* sometimes reaching 18 inches, and several weeks later to bloom.

M. racemosum (Musk hyacinth). Only about 9 inches tall, and not especially pretty, with insignificant brownish flowers, this is planted for its lovely scent. It blooms at the same time as *M. botryoides.*

HELENIUM

Botanical name: *Helenium* (Compositae)
Other common name: Swamp sunflower

One of the daisylike "weeds" from North America that had to travel to Europe to be appreciated, helenium has been cured by plant breeders of its bad habit of flopping over. New cultivars are flowery and sturdy if planted in full sun. Wild or cultivated types are well suited to wildflower gardens or the backs of borders, blooming late in the season, after phlox but before chrysanthemums. They last well as cut flowers and may be dried for everlasting bouquets. Leaves were once used to make snuff, hence the name *sneezeweed.*

PLANT TYPES: Hardy annual or perennial.
GROWING RANGE: All zones as an annual; Zones 4 to 9 as a perennial.
HARDINESS: Very hardy in cold and hot weather.
PLANT HEIGHT: 2 to 6 feet.
FLOWER COLOR: Shades of yellow, orange, rust, red.
FLOWER FORM: Moundlike discs surrounded by fringed petals the shape of a slice of pie, flowering one per stem or, more often, in clusters. Most types have 2-inch flowers.
SEASON OF BLOOM: Late summer.
SOIL: Rich, moist.
PH: 6 to 7.
FERTILIZER: Well-rotted manure, compost, flower fertilizer.
WATER: Moist or swampy conditions.
EXPOSURE: Full sun.
SPACING: 1 1/2 to 2 1/2 feet.
PROPAGATION: Seed or division.

Method

• **Start seeds indoors** four to six weeks before the last frost in bright light at about 70°F. Plant them 1/8 inch deep and an inch or two apart in flats or six-packs, where they germinate in about a week. When they are crowded, move them to larger pots or outdoors.

- **Prepare soil** finely in flower beds before planting, incorporating soil improvers and fertilizer, as needed.

- **Sow seeds outdoors** in cold frames two weeks before the last frost or a few weeks later in outdoor beds. Space them 2 or more inches apart, barely covering them. In Zone 9, plant in autumn.

- **Thin or transplant** outdoor-grown seedlings to their permanent places when they become crowded—usually by fall.

- **Set plants outdoors** in permanent places in spring, summer, or fall, after hardening off those grown indoors.

- **Divide** perennial clumps in early spring if they are crowded, usually every third year. Replant divisions immediately.

- **Water** often to keep the soil moist.

- **Fertilize** plants lightly when you set them out and throughout their growth. Top-dress beds with an inch or two of compost or leaf mold each fall.

- **Pests and diseases** are rarely a problem.

- **Mulch** is a help if growing plants in hot, dry areas, but is not needed in cool, damp spots. Use 2 or 3 inches of shredded leaves or bark chips.

- **Stake** 3-foot or taller plants before they bloom with 4-foot bamboo stakes about ¾ inch in diameter.

- **Protect in winter** with several inches of light mulch such as shredded leaves around crowns of plants.

Selected Species and Cultivars

Helenium amarum (Bitterweed). This wild annual is widespread in eastern and central parts of the United States. It is a bushy, 2-foot-tall plant with many yellow, daisylike flowers. Use it in wildflower meadows.

H. autumnale (Sneezeweed). This fibrous-rooted perennial is very hardy, growing from Canada to Florida. The well-branched, floriferous plants grow up to 5 feet tall. They make excellent cut flowers. Many cultivars have been bred, including:

'Brilliant,' with orange, gold, or red flowers on bushy 3-foot-tall plants that need no staking;

'Butterpat,' under 3 feet tall, bearing a profusion of solid yellow flowers;

'Mound' mixture, 4-foot-tall plants with 2-inch flowers, available in several autumnal colors, from seed;

'Redgold' hybrids, 2 to 4 feet tall, with flowers in autumn colors on bushy plants;

'Riverton Beauty,' with great quantities of golden flowers with brown eyes on 4- to 5-foot-tall plants. Stake plants before blossoms open; and

'Sunshine' hybrids, like 'Redgold' in size and color, from seed.

H. hoopesii. This perennial species, 2 to 3 feet tall, is similar to *H. autumnale* but has clusters of yellow flowers that bloom a few weeks earlier.

HELIANTHEMUM

Botanical name: *Helianthemum* (Cistaceae)
Other common names: Rock rose, Sun rose, Frostweed

Named for the sun, the roselike flowers of *Helianthemum* open freshly each day, with light-catching, transparent petals that give them a frosty look. These half-hardy perennial plants are low and shrubby with evergreen, silvery leaves. Well suited to the California climate, rock roses are used as ground cover, in rock gardens and flower borders, above retaining walls, and on sunny slopes. Plants are carefree in poor soil if the climate is right.

PLANT TYPE: Half-hardy perennial.
GROWING RANGE: Grows best in cool parts of Zones 6 to 9.
HARDINESS: Fairly hardy, but killed by cold below 10°F.
PLANT HEIGHT: 1 foot for most types, some are taller.
FLOWER COLOR: White, yellow, pink, rose, salmon, orange, rust, or cream, often bicolored.
FLOWER FORM: Single or double 1-inch blossoms with a conspicuous central cluster of shiny golden anthers.
SEASON OF BLOOM: Spring and early summer.
SOIL: Sandy or chalky well-drained soil.
PH: 7 to 7.5.
FERTILIZER: Compost, flower fertilizer, bonemeal.
WATER: Average to dry conditions.
EXPOSURE: Full sun.
SPACING: 1 to 2 feet.
PROPAGATION: Seed, division, or tip cuttings.

Method

- **Start seeds indoors** six weeks before the last frost in small pots or six-packs filled with moist, sandy potting soil. Barely cover seed with a layer of sand. Water and keep at 70°F until seeds germinate. Grow in a sunny area or a few inches below a fluorescent light fixture. When seedlings have four to six leaves, step them up to larger pots if necessary, or plant them outdoors, after hardening them off.

- **Prepare soil outdoors** in beds before planting by tilling in fertilizer, compost, bonemeal, lime, and other soil improvers, if needed.

- **Sow seeds outdoors** where they will grow after the danger of frost passes but before hot weather arrives. In smoothly prepared and fertilized beds, plant seeds 3 inches apart and cover with 1/8 inch of soil. Do not let the seedbed dry out.

- **Thin or transplant** outdoor-grown seedlings to their permanent spacing when they are about 4 inches tall. Extra seedlings may be transplanted with care, when plants are thinned.

- **Set plants outdoors** after the danger of frost has passed, after hardening them off in shade for a few days.

- **Divide** plants in early spring once every few years or trim them back if necessary.

- **Root cuttings** about 4 to 6 inches long in moist, sandy soil in semishade during the summer.

- **Water** only if soil is very dry. Plants tolerate dry summers well but are harmed by hot, humid conditions.

- **Fertilize** lightly at planting time and each year a few weeks before blossoms open.

- **Pests and diseases** seldom are problems.

- **Protect in winter** by mulching crowns with 2 or 3 inches of bark chips or shredded leaves. In Zones 3 to 6, grow in a cold frame during winter. Uncover new growth gradually in early spring.

Tips · **Plants live for only about four years, so root cuttings or divide plants to perpetuate them, or else you will lose them.**
 · **Where soil and conditions are not favorable, grow rock roses in pots of sweet, sandy soil. Bring them into a cold frame or cool greenhouse for the winter.**

Selected Species

Helianthemum nummularium. This is the predominant garden variety, with many hybrids, single or double flowered, in all the rock rose colors. Its profuse blossoms are usually 1 or 1½ inches wide.

H. oelandicum subspecies *alpestre.* This type makes a close carpet of twiggy growth bearing many small golden flowers.

HOLLYHOCK

Botanical name: *Alcea* (Malvaceae)
Other common name: Althea

Often pictured against a large barn, the common hollyhock, growing up to 10 feet tall, is one of many forms of *Alcea,* native to sunny places from the Mediterranean to the Orient. Its rosettes of roundish, cabbage-size hairy leaves are topped from summer through fall by elongated spires of hibiscuslike flowers in many sizes, shapes, and colors. Hollyhock is used as a background plant in borders, against walls and fences, and for cut flowers. The flowers open in progression from the bottom up, with a foot or two of the stem covered in bloom at any one time.

PLANT TYPES: Hardy annual, biennial, or short-lived perennial. Grown as a biennial in Zones 9 to 11.
GROWING RANGE: Zones 3 to 11.
HARDINESS: Hardy in cold to moderately hot weather, killed by high heat.
PLANT HEIGHT: 3 to 10 feet.

FLOWER COLOR: Shades of yellow, white, rose, red, cranberry, purple, or nearly black.

FLOWER FORM: Double or single hibiscuslike blooms are 3 to 5 inches wide. Old-fashioned types are single and cup-shaped, and newer types may be very double and fringed or ruffled.

SEASON OF BLOOM: Midsummer through fall.

SOIL: Average to rich, moist but well drained.

PH: 6 to 7.

FERTILIZER: Well-rotted manure, compost, flower or tomato fertilizer.

WATER: Moist conditions.

EXPOSURE: Full sun in most regions, bright partial shade in the South.

SPACING: 2 to 4 feet.

PROPAGATION: Seed or division.

 *Method*

- **Start seeds indoors** in February in Zones 3 to 8 for summer bloom the same year. Plant seeds of taller types from March through summer for bloom the following year. In Zones 9 to 11, start plants in the fall and treat them as biennials. Plant them ¼ inch deep, one per pot, in 4-inch pots where they germinate in about ten days and grow quickly.

- **Prepare soil outdoors** in beds in spring or fall, incorporating soil improvers and fertilizer, as needed.

- **Sow seeds outdoors** in beds in spring or summer after the danger of frost for flowers the next year has passed. In Zones 9 to 11, plant them in November. Space them 3 inches apart, ¼ inch deep.

- **Thin or transplant** outdoor-grown seedlings when they are several inches tall, to nursery spacing at least 1 foot apart, and then shift them to their permanent places in early spring the following year. Shift indoor-grown seedlings to larger pots or to positions outdoors.

- **Set plants outdoors** in permanent places any time in spring or fall, after hardening them off for several days in the shade if they were grown indoors.

- **Divide** roots of large clumps every other year in early spring if they are crowded. Replant divisions immediately. Side shoots can be separated and rooted.

- **Water** frequently enough to keep the soil moderately moist in spring, somewhat drier in summer.

- **Fertilize** at planting time and keep plants well supplied with fertilizer throughout their growth. Top-dress beds with compost or leaf mold each fall.

- **Pests and diseases** in some areas discourage people from growing hollyhocks. Problems can include Japanese beetles (use pheromone traps), slugs (dust ground and plants with diatomaceous earth), spider mites (spray off with insecticidal soap mixed in water), leaf miners (remove infected leaves), and several diseases: leaf spot, rust, anthracnose, and mildew. To combat, select disease-resistant varieties and treat them with fungicide. Discard diseased plants.

- **Mulch** plants with several inches of composted leaves or small bark chips to help keep moisture in the soil.

- **Stake** each plant, especially in spots that are windy or have less than full sun.

- **Remove** stalks after bloom is finished unless you want to save the seed.

- **Protect in winter** by mulching with 2 inches of shredded leaves or other fine mulch. Make sure soil has good drainage—add sand if needed.

Selected Species and Cultivars

Alcea rosea, formerly *Althaea rosea* (Garden hollyhock), can be tall, short, double, single, or fringed in unlimited variations. Shorter types are returning to favor because they look charming in borders and need less staking. They often bloom their first year. Popular varieties include:
  'Charter's Double,' with thickly massed blooms about 4 inches wide on 6-foot stems;
  'Majorette,' 2 to 3 feet tall, with fluffy pastel blooms;
  'Pinafore,' 3 to 3 ½ feet tall, with single or semidouble lacy or ruffled blooms on multiple stems from each plant; and
  'Powder Puffs,' with large, fully double flowers on spires reaching 8 feet in height.
  A. rugosa. This 5-foot-tall type is rust resistant and very hardy, with long-lasting spires of large, single, primrose-yellow blooms.

HOSTA

Botanical name: *Hosta* (Liliaceae)
Other common names: Funkia, Plantain lily

A broad-leaved member of the lily family, the hosta is a hardy plant that thrives in either wet or dry conditions once established. To most gardeners, its foliage is more important than its flowers—some gardeners cut down the flowers. Its conspicuous leaves may be solidly colored or streaked with contrasting zones of light to deep green, bluish green, chartreuse, gold, or white. Textures and sizes vary also. Some of the most dramatic types are puckered like seersucker, but most are smooth or ridged.

The large, wide, oval or pointed leaves grow directly from the crown of the plant, from which a flowering stem grows once each summer. Some types are fragrant and very attractive to bees. The glossy leaves disappear in winter, dying down to pips at ground level, but regrow late in spring, about when tulips bloom. Their dense covering of the ground prevents weeds. Small hostas are good for shaded rock gardens, and large-leaved ones—some over 3 feet tall and wide—are preferred for most ground covers or flower beds. Hostas are excellent woodland plants. Because they multiply rapidly, divide hostas every other year to keep their size at optimal level.

PLANT TYPE: Hardy perennial.
GROWING RANGE: Zones 3 to 9 (most types).
HARDINESS: Established plants withstand extremes of cold and heat.
PLANT HEIGHT: 6 inches to 4 feet (not including flowers).
FLOWER COLOR: White, lavender.
FLOWER FORM: 15 or so tubular flowers an inch or two long, aligned on a tall stem.
SEASON OF BLOOM: Briefly in summer.
SOIL: Loamy and moist.
PH: 6 to 7.
FERTILIZER: Well-rotted manure, all-purpose or flower fertilizer.
WATER: Keep plants moist.
EXPOSURE: Bright partial shade to deep shade, especially in hot climates.
SPACING: 10 inches to 3 feet, depending on plant size.
PROPAGATION: Usually by division, also from seed.

Method

- **Start seeds indoors** 2 inches apart, in flats or one per pot in small pots filled with damp, sterile potting soil, if you are patient enough to wait three years for blooms. Keep containers at 50°F for one to three months, until germination occurs. Grow seedlings under fluorescent or bright but indirect light. Strong sun will bleach or kill seedlings. Harden them off before setting them in place outdoors.

- **Prepare soil outdoors** in beds before planting by tilling in fertilizer, compost, and other soil improvers, as needed.

- **Sow seeds outdoors** after the danger of frost passes or as soon as they ripen, usually in late summer. In tilled, fertilized beds, plant seeds 2 inches apart and cover with ¼ inch of soil. Some may not germinate until the following year.

- **Thin** seedlings (indoor and outdoor grown) when they are 3 or 4 inches high, or whenever they become crowded, to permanent spacing.

- **Set plants outdoors** in spring or during cool weather. Dormant plants may be set out before the frost-free date, but plants with leaves should be set out after the danger of frost passes.

- **Divide** plants in early spring when new growth begins, if they are crowded. Work during damp or overcast weather. Use a strong, sharp knife to cut between pips, cutting straight down into the firm woody roots and soil. A large clump may be divided into quarters. Dig and replant divisions immediately.

- **Water** when soil becomes dry, more frequently in spring during active growth.

- **Fertilize** at planting time and periodically during growth.

- **Pests** are few, but slugs may be a problem. Slugs can be trapped under a board and killed each morning, or controlled with commercial baits. **Diseases** are uncommon. In some areas, leaves are affected by leaf miners or caterpillars. Treat with rotenone or pyrethrum.

- **Mulch** around crowns but under leaves in dry areas. In areas where there is little snow cover, plants should be mulched in winter with 2 or 3 inches of shredded leaves or other mulch.

Selected Species and Cultivars

Hosta fortunei. Cultivars include 'Albo-picta,' with 1-foot-long leaves that are yellow in spring but turn to light green as summer progresses; and 'Ribbed Beauty,' with 1-foot-long pointed leaves of medium green, deeply ridged. Flowers are lilac to violet, on stalks taller than the leaves.

H. gracillima 'Variegata.' This Japanese type stays neat and low, under 10 inches, with narrow leaves thinly edged in white, and lavender flowers in late summer.

H. lancifolia. Two-foot-tall plants with narrow green leaves have bell-like lavender flowers.

H. montana 'Aureomarginata.' With huge, heart-shaped green leaves irregularly margined with gold, this Japanese variety grows nearly 3 feet tall and over 3 feet wide. It is less hardy (but more spectacular) than most of the other hostas.

H. plantaginea. Huge, fragrant white flowers above rich green leaves make this type very special in deep shade. It will grow 3 feet tall and nearly 3 feet wide.

H. sieboldiana. These are tall hostas, 2 to 3 feet tall, with wide textured leaves and pale lavender or white flowers. Cultivars include:

'Brigham Blue,' with large, heart-shaped puckered leaves of rich blue;

'Elegans,' with whitened, bluish, textured leaves about a foot wide and 15 inches long, with white flowers in late summer; and

'Frances Williams,' also called 'Gold Edge,' a large-flowered plant with wide, puckered bluish-green leaves banded with yellow. A well-grown plant may be 3 feet tall by 4 feet wide.

H. venusta. Dwarf plants about 3 inches tall have narrow green leaves and 6-inch spires of lavender flowers.

HYACINTH

Botanical name: *Hyacinthus* (Liliaceae)

Fragrant, showy hyacinths bloom in midspring once a year. Each bulb sends up a stiff, cylindrical raceme of flowers of somewhat formal appearance, surrounded by canoe-shaped, straplike leaves an inch wide. Hyacinths are popular bedding plants in gardens in the United States and southern Canada, and are forced for early bloom indoors as well. They are grown in southern France for making perfume as well as for enjoyment in the garden.

In home gardens, these hardy flowers tend to bloom best the first year after bulbs are planted, and then get smaller each year, as the bulbs multiply. With plentiful water and fertilizer, plus frequent division, the plants may recover most of their size, but many gardeners prefer to buy fresh bulbs every few years.

Wood hyacinths are similar to Dutch hyacinths, but are taller, airier, and later to bloom. They belong to a different genus, *Endymion* (see pages 387–88), and multiply and naturalize more easily than Dutch hyacinths.

PLANT TYPE: Hardy bulb.

GROWING RANGE: Zones 4 to 8.

HARDINESS: Requires chilling in winter.

PLANT HEIGHT: 6 to 12 inches.

FLOWER COLOR: White, cream, orange-yellow, pink, red, violet, blue.

FLOWER FORM: Fat, cylindrical spires about 10 inches tall, composed of small lilylike blooms, double or single.

SEASON OF BLOOM: Spring, with the midseason tulips.

SOIL: Sandy loam, well drained.

PH: 6.5 to 7.5.

FERTILIZER: Well-rotted manure, all-purpose or high-phosphorus fertilizer, bonemeal.

WATER: Plentiful water during growth.

EXPOSURE: Full sun or light, dappled shade.

SPACING: 8 or 9 inches apart, 6 to 8 inches deep.

PROPAGATION: Bulbs, bulblets, or division.

Method

- **Prepare soil outdoors** in beds before planting by tilling in fertilizer, compost, and other soil improvers, as needed.

- **Plant bulbs outdoors** in midfall so roots have a chance to develop before the soil freezes. Use a bulb planter or excavate beds, being sure to place bulbs 6 inches deep and 8 or 9 inches apart.

- **Divide** established plants if crowded. Bulbs may be dug up and pulled apart when the foliage yellows after flowering, and replanted in renewed soil.

- **Water** plants whenever the soil starts to dry out in spring, decrease water after foliage has turned yellow.

- **Fertilize** at planting time with a scoop of bulb booster or bonemeal for each plant and lightly each year in early spring. Fertilize again just after plants flower.

- **Pests and diseases** seldom are problems.

- **Force bulbs indoors.** Prechilled bulbs will grow indoors in a glass of water on a windowsill, suspended so that the roots stay wet and bulbs stay dry (florists sell special pinch-necked hyacinth glasses). Change the water weekly. Or prechill the bulbs yourself in a refrigerator for one and a half to two months inside a paper or plastic bag.

  To grow hyacinths in soil, use a 5-inch pot for one bulb or an 8-inch pot for three. Fill the pots with sandy soil in fall and plant the bulbs, covering the tops with an inch of soil. Keep them in a cold frame or outdoors where temperatures will be 40° to 50°F for one and a half to two months. Then bring them into a cool (50°F) room or greenhouse for several weeks, and into a warmer room when foliage is 4 to 6 inches tall. Blooms will follow rapidly. After plants bloom, either discard them or let foliage ripen and plant them outdoors for bloom the following year.

- **Stake** double-flowered and large forms that are top-heavy with slim 15-inch-tall wooden or bamboo sticks.

- **Remove** spent blossoms immediately. Remove and discard foliage when it turns yellow, not earlier, so plants can build strength for the next year's flowers.

- **Protect in winter** by mulching with a few inches of evergreen branches or pine needles. Pull back the mulch after the danger of heavy frost so shoots can come up.

Tip · **If you are interested in propagating hyacinths from bulblets, increase production by scoring an X ½ inch deep across the bottom (flat end) of each bulb in the fall. Replant the bulblets that appear in spring. Of course this cuts down on flower quality of the mother bulb and it will take several years for the bulblet flowers to develop more size.**

Selected Species and Cultivars

Hyacinthus orientalis (Dutch hyacinth). The bulbs of garden hyacinths are graded by size—the larger the bulb, the larger the flower. Top size is 2½ inches or more in circumference, and these will grow strong, showy blossoms the first year. Popular cultivars include:
  'Blizzard,' pure white;
  'Blue Jacket,' deep blue;
  'City of Harlem,'' pale yellow;
  'Delft Blue,' true to name, good for forcing;
  'Gypsy Queen,' peachy orange;
  'Jan Bos,' deep rose-red, early blooming;
  'Orange Boven,' soft salmon;
  'Pink Pearl,' deep pink, good for forcing; and
  'Princess Margaret,' pale pink.
  H. orientalis var. *albulus* (Roman hyacinth). This is a variant of the species that is smaller and earlier, with airier racemes of flowers in white or blue shades.

IMPATIENS

Botanical name: *Impatiens* (Balsaminaceae)

Garden impatiens is probably the world's most popular flower. Of the several species available, one, *Impatiens wallerana,* is so popular that it has become synonymous with the genus, which also includes balsam *(I. balsamina),* touch-me-not *(I. noli-tangere),* jewelweed *(I. capensis),* and several others.

Impatiens deserves its popularity: The all-purpose everblooming plants are relatively carefree with no need for staking. Used for carpet bedding, edgings, planters, hanging baskets, window boxes, flower borders, and the greenhouse, impatiens can also be naturalized in woodland areas.

Impatiens, balsam, touch-me-not, and jewelweed differ in habit, leaf, and flower, but all have fat green seedpods that, when ripe, burst open at the slightest touch.

PLANT TYPES: Tender annual or perennial.
GROWING RANGE: All zones as an annual, Zones 9 to 11 as a perennial. However, perennials are grown as annuals in any zone.
HARDINESS: Easily killed by frost, tolerant of heat.
PLANT HEIGHT: 6 inches to over 4 feet.
FLOWER COLOR: White, peach, rose, red, fuchsia, lilac, or orange, sometimes bicolored with stripes or blotches.
FLOWER FORM: Single or double blossoms from 1 to 3 inches wide.
SEASON OF BLOOM: Continuous bloom any time of year that is frost-free.
SOIL: Average to rich, with peat added to retain moisture.
PH: 6.5 to 7.5.
FERTILIZER: Well-rotted manure, compost, flower or tomato fertilizer.
WATER: Moist conditions, with extra water in hot weather.
EXPOSURE: Bright partial shade, more shade in the South, heavy shade in areas where daily temperatures exceed 90°F.
SPACING: 6 inches to 1½ feet. Set low-growing types 8 inches apart to thickly carpet a bed.
PROPAGATION: Seed or tip cuttings.

Method

- **Start seeds indoors** eight to twelve weeks before the last frost in areas with cold winters, or any time of year in frost-free places. Sow small seeds sparingly in flats, six-packs, or small pots in moist potting medium, barely covering them with soil. Seeds germinate in seven to twenty days, and grow quickly in ideal temperatures between 65° and 75°F and bright light. Balsam grows in direct sunlight but impatiens (*I. wallerana*) does better in filtered light.

- **Prepare soil outdoors** at planting time, incorporating soil improvers such as peat moss, vermiculite, compost, and fertilizer, as needed.

- **Sow seeds outdoors** ⅛ inch deep and at least 3 inches apart in beds when soil is warm after the danger of heavy frost has passed.

- **Thin or transplant** outdoor-grown seedlings to their permanent places outdoors or indoor-grown seedlings to individual or larger containers when they are several inches tall.

- **Set plants outdoors** in permanent places after all danger of frost has passed. Plants are soft and delicate—harden them off carefully before planting them outside.

- **Take cuttings** of *I. wallerana* about 6 inches long and root them in a humid, shady place by covering their bottom half with moist soil or placing them in a glass of water on a windowsill. In as little as three weeks during warm weather, new plants are rooted well enough to plant outdoors.

- **Water** frequently enough to keep the soil moist. In hot areas, spray plants with water twice a day to cool them off in summer. Wilted plants revive in minutes.

- **Fertilize** at planting time and keep plants well supplied with fertilizer throughout their growth.

- **Pests and diseases** include slugs and damping off of seedlings. Repel or kill slugs with diatomaceous earth or wood ashes, slug and snail bait, or trap them in partly submerged pans of beer. Treat damping off with fungicide, and prevent it by planting seeds in sterile soil and supplying adequate light and ventilation.

- **Mulch** plants with several inches of composted leaves or small bark chips to help keep moisture in the soil.

- **Pinch back** the central tip once to stimulate growth of side branches.

Tip · The ripe seeds may be collected each summer, stored in a paper envelope indoors, and strewn in shady places the next year for naturalized plants when the weather is warm. In areas where winters are not too severe, plants will propagate themselves without assistance.

Selected Species and Cultivars

Impatiens balsamina (Balsam, Rose balsam). This annual plant tends to self sow and is often seen in gardens. It is easily and quickly grown in warm weather from fairly large seed. Few people grow it from cuttings, though it is possible. Two-inch camellialike flowers, often spotted, appear in the leaf axils on thick fleshy stems. Some forms of this plant are less than graceful because stems are thick and flowers grow close to the stems, below the leaves. In spite of this, they are attractive when planted in large colorful masses in sun or light shade. The best cultivars include 'Camellia Flowered,' about 2 feet tall with speckled or solid flowers of great size and doubleness; 'Carambole,' good for bedding, very bushy, spreading, and floriferous, growing about a foot high and wide; and 'Tom Thumb,' a dwarf type with many 3-inch double flowers that bloom on the tops of plants.

I. capensis (Jewelweed). A widespread annual wildflower in North America, jewelweed grows near streams and in damp ground, spreading by seeds that follow the multitudes of spotted orange tubular blossoms. Plants grow about 2 to 5 feet tall and are usually considered weeds, although they look very nice in wild areas. The juice in the watery stems is sometimes squeezed onto skin irritations from poison ivy, which grows in the same habitat, for a quick cure.

I. wallerana (Impatiens, Busy Lizzie, Sultana). The popular annual garden impatiens grows 1 to 3 feet tall with an unending parade of flat, bright blossoms an inch or two wide in unlimited cultivars of varying shapes and colors. Some are double and all have a sparkling quality when in bloom because of the light-reflecting texture of the blossoms.

Shapely and everblooming, it is ideal for all kinds of gardens and containers. Cuttings taken during warm weather root easily. This plant needs a great deal of moisture, especially during hot or sunny weather. Indoors, sweeping up after the plants can be a chore because they drop spent blossoms.

Typical cultivars include 'Blitz' hybrids, great for hanging baskets in nonstop bloom; 'Gem,' a spreading, low-growing type perfect for sunny areas; 'King Kong,' said to be the largest flowered of all; 'Rosette Hybrid,' with double flowers in mixed colors; 'Shady Lady,' with bushy everblooming plants 15 inches high, available in mixed or separate colors; 'Super Elfin,' petite plants with large flowers, in many colors; and 'Tempo Blush,' a large-flowered pastel type that is especially early to bloom.

There are also New Guinea hybrids, usually grown from cuttings, which have extra-large flowers in brilliant colors and striped or variegated leaves in shades of green, greenish gold, and reddish brown. Some of the flower/leaf color combinations are more appealing than others. They take full sun in the North, partial shade in the South, and lend a tropical look to gardens.

Seed-grown cultivars include 'Tango' hybrid, a more compact and earlier-blooming improvement over 'Sweet Sue.' 'Tango' has many bright orange blooms and rich green leaves, spreading to make an everblooming bushlike plant 18 inches wide.

IRIS

Botanical name: *Iris* (Iridaceae)

There are over two hundred species and innumerable cultivars of iris with great differences among them. They have rhizomatous, fibrous, or bulbous roots, swordlike or grasslike leaves, and large showy flowers. Some types, like Japanese and Louisiana iris, grow in standing water; others need well-drained soil or their roots will rot.

Most irises originated in temperate climates and are hardy and long-lived, even without care, but types vary in their ability to thrive in hot, cold, wet, and dry conditions. Iris leaves are attractive in the garden whether or not the plants are in bloom. Use iris as a ground cover (especially the dwarf types), in beds and borders, and for cut flowers.

In the United States, the bearded irises have been best known and most used, though other types are gaining popularity.

PLANT TYPE: Hardy or tender perennial.
GROWING RANGE: Species are available for all zones.
HARDINESS: Varies with the species, from very hardy to tender.
PLANT HEIGHT: 4 inches to over 4 feet, varying with the species.
FLOWER COLOR: All colors except true red, solid colored or in multicolor combinations.
FLOWER FORM: Orchidlike, composed of 6 segments.
SEASON OF BLOOM: Spring and summer in most areas, winter in Zones 10 and 11.
SOIL: Average to rich.
PH: 6.5 to 7.5.
FERTILIZER: Well-rotted manure, low-nitrogen, high-phosphorus fertilizer.
WATER: Varies with type, from dry to wet conditions.
EXPOSURE: Full sun or bright, dappled shade.
SPACING: 5 inches to 3 feet.
PROPAGATION: Division or seed.

🌸 *Method*

- **Start seeds indoors** in small pots or flats filled with moist potting soil, covering ⅛ inch deep. Plant hardy types after prechilling seeds six weeks in the refrigerator. Water and keep at 70°F until seeds germinate, which they will do sporadically from over a month to a year later. You can transplant each one to its own 4-inch pot when it is large enough to handle—at least an inch tall. Grow seedlings in bright light from 50° to 70°F. Most types need two or more years to reach flowering size.

- **Prepare soil outdoors** in beds before planting by tilling in fertilizer, compost, and other soil improvers, as needed.

- **Sow seeds outdoors** in nursery beds in summer or fall when seeds ripen, or in late fall or winter in a cold frame. Plant them ⅛ inch deep and about 4 inches apart. Do not let them dry out. Usually they will germinate in spring. If not, keep watching for the seedlings the following year.

- **Thin or transplant** seedlings grown outdoors to their permanent spacing when they are a few inches tall.

- **Set plants outdoors** in spring. Indoor-grown plants must be hardened off for several days in shade, after all danger of frost has passed. Plants grown outdoors in pots may be set out at any time, but field-grown plants are easiest to move in early spring or else in early summer, after blooming.

- **Set out** bulbous species, such as *Iris xiphium,* in fall, 3 or 4 inches deep, for bloom the next spring. For other species, refer to the previous step.

- **Divide** crowded plants in early spring if they are fibrous-rooted, but after they bloom if they grow on rhizomes or bulbous roots.

    Divide bearded (German) iris once every four or five years, in midsummer in most areas, but in early fall in hot regions. Trim foliage back to 5 inches tall a day or two before dividing clumps. Dig up clumps carefully to avoid damage to roots and branching, fleshy rhizomes. Discard any mushy or rotten parts of rhizomes, and pull apart or cut plants so that each division has one or two fans of leaves and a generous amount of root. Replant immediately 1 ½ feet apart in well-prepared soil so that part of the rhizome is partly above the soil. Newly divided plants will rebloom the following year or the year after.

- **Water** most irises when the soil gets dry, but check individual species' preferences.

- **Fertilize** at planting time and each year in spring and after bloom in summer.

- **Pests and diseases** are rarely troublesome except for the iris borer, a threat to bearded iris because it tunnels into rhizomes and spreads rot. Discourage borers by planting this kind of iris in full sun and keeping the soil relatively dry. Discard affected rhizomes and yellowed leaves. Treat plants with pyrethrum or all-purpose insecticide.

- **Mulch** nonbearded iris in dry weather with 2 inches of pine needles or other lightweight mulch.

- **Remove** spent blossoms unless seed is wanted.

- **Protect in winter** with a lightweight mulch such as pine needles. Pull back the mulch after all danger of frost ends if soil is too wet.

Selected Species and Cultivars:

Iris cristata (Dwarf iris). This quick-spreading plant grows only 6 inches high and makes a wonderful ground cover with a bonus of blue or white flowers 3 inches wide once a year in spring. It is a native of the semishaded parts of the East Coast, growing with ease in Zones 3 to 8 if it gets enough moisture. Cultivars include:
'Alba,' white with yellow markings;
'Shenandoah Sky,' a pale blue; and
'Summer Storm,' deep blue.
   I. germanica and related hybrids (Bearded iris, German iris). These colorful favorites are classified by size, from dwarf to tall. The central arching "claw," which consists of three central petals (the *standards*), rises erect from the blossom, surrounded by three wide petals arching downward the (the *falls*). Each fall has a central furry strip, the *beard*. Colors include white, yellow, peach, brown, blue, and purple, in many shades and color combinations. The broad, swordlike leaves are arranged in characteristic fans.
   Grow bearded iris in Zones 4 to 8 in full sun in well-drained soil with a neutral pH. Divide rhizomes after plants flower, in summer in most areas, but in fall in Zones 8 and 9. Remove old foliage in the fall to eliminate borer eggs.
   I. kaempferi, synonym *I. ensata* (Japanese iris). This fibrous-rooted species has immense, rather flat flowers up to 10 inches wide on branched stems up to 4 feet tall, above linear 3-foot-long leaves in thick, tidy clumps. Types with smaller, narrower petals hold up better in bad weather—wider petals get soggy. The colorful flowers, which bloom once a year in early summer, may be veined, marbled, or speckled in any of the usual iris colors, plus red shades. Japanese iris needs acid soil that is moist or boggy in full sun or light shade (more shade in the South) in Zones 4 to 9. It tolerates the heat and humidity of the eastern states. It is easy to propagate from seed or division, and effective in borders, water gardens, or naturalized in meadows. It is not susceptible to iris borers.
   I. pallida 'Dalmatica' (Sweet iris, Orris root). This is an old-fashioned purple bearded iris with gray-green leaves. Hardy in Zones 3 to 7, plants grow 3 feet tall and bloom in early summer. Divide clumps in summer once every four years, if necessary. Some forms have variegated leaves: 'Zebra,' with yellow- and green-striped foliage; and 'Albo-Variegata,' with white- and green-striped foliage. The powdered dry rhizome (called orris powder) gives an aroma of violets to potpourri and perfume. Provide full sun and well-drained soil with a neutral pH.
   I. pseudacorus (Yellow flag). This yellow iris resembles Japanese iris. Its linear leaves are an inch wide on plants 3 to 5 feet tall. Flowers are narrow and graceful on erect stems. Some types have variegated foliage. Sow seed in soil near 70°F and keep wet. Grow this iris in moist to wet soil in Zones 5 to 8. In hot or drought-prone areas, plant it in light shade; otherwise full sun is best.
   I. sibirica (Siberian iris). Similar to Japanese iris, this fibrous-rooted, 2- to 4-foot-tall plant has smaller, narrower flowers and leaves, and is only a little less showy. It is graceful and easy to grow, and blooms after bearded iris and before Japanese iris. It combines well with

shrubbery. The deeply rooted plants are often used on slopes. Seedpods remain on the stalks until winter and may be used in dried arrangements. Seeds are easily grown if they get a month or two of cold weather to break their dormancy. This iris may be divided, but lives many years with or without division. In its many colors and forms it thrives in Zones 3 to 9. Provide full sun and well-drained, neutral soil.

I. xiphioides (English iris). Originally from the Pyrennes, despite its name, this narrow-leaved iris grows from bulbs in Zones 5 to 8. Its large blooms with rounded falls appear a few weeks later than blooms of Dutch iris. Its cultural requirements are the same as for *I. xiphium.*

I. xiphium (Spanish iris). This plant and related species are the parents of the popular Dutch iris hybrids. Leaves are tall and narrow. Grown from bulbs, this is a popular florist's iris for bouquets in white, gold, bronze, blue, or purple. It grows well outdoors if planted in fall in Zones 6 to 8, 3 or 4 inches deep and 6 inches apart. It is also forced in greenhouses. In most areas, it needs full sun and neutral, well-drained soil, but requires partial shade in hot areas.

JACOB'S LADDER

Botanical name: *Polemonium* (Polemoniaceae)
Other common names: Greek valerian, Charity

These dainty native plants spread out in spring with crisp, fernlike foliage of paired leaflets and neat, long-lasting sprays of flowers, usually baby blue. There are shorter and taller types, most blooming in spring with bluebells and crocus, but lasting past the late tulips. Blooms also last fairly long in fresh bouquets. Handle the foliage carefully, for it is brittle and juicy. Plants are not invasive or creeping but will self-sow readily if they like their spot in the garden. Use tall types in the middle of the spring border, and short types in rock gardens or the front of the border. In the heat of late summer, foliage may droop or disappear, but a new leaf rosette will grow in the fall. Since the varied species are similar to each other, there is some confusion in their labeling when they are sold.

PLANT TYPE: Hardy perennial.
GROWING RANGE: Zones 3 to 8.
HARDINESS: Hardy in cold to hot weather.
PLANT HEIGHT: 1 to 3 feet.
FLOWER COLOR: Usually soft blue, sometimes deep blue, white, salmon, or yellow.
FLOWER FORM: ½- to 1-inch bell-like, 5-lobed flowers in sprays on long stems.
SEASON OF BLOOM: Early spring to midspring.
SOIL: Average to rich, humusy, moist.
PH: 6 to 7.
FERTILIZER: Compost, high-phosphorus fertilizer.
WATER: Moist but well-drained conditions.
EXPOSURE: Partial shade.
SPACING: 10 to 20 inches.
PROPAGATION: Seed or division.

Method

- **Start seeds indoors** in late winter to early spring, in small containers filled with moist potting soil, an inch apart and barely covered with soil. Germination usually takes place in two to three weeks at 60° to 70°F, especially if seed has been prechilled for several weeks in the refrigerator. Do not give seedlings direct sunlight, but provide bright light. Transplant seedlings to larger containers if they become crowded, or thin them to one per pot.

- **Prepare soil outdoors** before planting by tilling in fertilizer, compost, and other soil improvers, as needed.

- **Sow seeds outdoors** in nursery beds after frost in spring or in early summer as soon as they ripen on plants, which tend to self-sow. Self-sown plants are quite desirable. Plant the seeds ¼ inch deep and about 4 inches apart. Do not let them dry out. Some may not germinate until the following year. If you like, plant them in a cold frame in autumn. Thin and transplant seedlings to their permanent spacing when they are about 2 inches tall, if they are crowded.

- **Set plants outdoors** in spring after all danger of hard frost has passed, after hardening them off in the shade for several days.

- **Divide** established plants, if they are crowded, in early spring when growth begins, in late spring after they flower, or in the fall. Do not disturb them during very hot or very cold weather. Plants multiply rapidly.

- **Water** plants when the soil starts to dry out.

- **Fertilize** lightly at planting time and each year in spring.

- **Pests and diseases** seldom are problems, other than mildew on the leaves, which tends to disappear in summer anyway. Rodents or deer sometimes eat the foliage.

- **Mulch** plants in summer with 2 inches of peat moss, compost, small bark chips, or other mulch.

- **Remove** spent blossoms unless seed is wanted.

- **Protect in winter** by mulching around crowns with 2 inches of shredded leaves. Pull back the mulch after all danger of hard frost ends.

Selected Species and Cultivars

Polemonium caeruleum. In light to deep cobalt blue with orange stamens, this species flowers from late spring into summer. *P. c.* var. *lactaeum* is the white form.

P. carneum. These 2-foot-tall plants from California and Oregon have lovely large salmon-pink flowers. There is a white form, too.

P. foliosissimum. These late-blooming, 1½- to 2½-foot-tall natives of the Rocky Mountains typically have large, rich blue flowers. 'Sapphire' is a bright blue cultivar. Others may be white, cream, or violet.

P. mellitum. This type is a dwarf (under 1 foot) with fragrant white flowers, perfect for rock gardens.

P. reptans. Growing from 1 to 1 ½ feet tall, this is the earliest polemonium to flower. It usually has pale blue petals with white stamens, on foliage of a particularly bright spring green. It grows in wide, dense mats. 'Blue Pearl' is an admired variety about 1 foot tall, with a spread of 15 inches. 'Album' is a white cultivar.

LADY'S MANTLE

Botanical name: *Alchemilla* (Roseaceae)
Other common name: Alchemilla

Called lady's mantle because of the resemblance of its round, crimped leaves to a lady's cape, alchemilla is an easy-to-grow perennial that often self-sows. Its dainty sprays of yellowish-green straw-textured flowers are nice in bouquets, as are its silvery chartreuse leaves. Plant alchemilla in masses in borders or use it as a ground cover. Because it is invasive, keep the large variety out of rock gardens, or use it cautiously. Widely spaced plants spread and fill in quickly. Alchemilla once was commonly used medicinally. Its name reflects its former reputation as the alchemists' plant, used in the unsuccessful effort to transmute base metals into gold.

PLANT TYPE: Hardy perennial.
GROWING RANGE: Zones 3 to 8.
HARDINESS: Very cold hardy, but not suited for long, hot summers.
PLANT HEIGHT: 6 inches to 3 feet.
FLOWER COLOR: Lime green to greenish yellow.
FLOWER FORM: Loose sprays of small, starlike, straw-textured blossoms.
SEASON OF BLOOM: Late spring or early summer for about 3 weeks.
SOIL: Any good garden soil.
PH: 7.
FERTILIZER: Well-rotted manure, bonemeal, timed-release flower fertilizer.
WATER: Moist conditions.
EXPOSURE: Sun or light, dappled shade.
SPACING: 1 foot.
PROPAGATION: Usually by division, also from seed.

Method

- **Start seeds indoors** any time of year by planting ⅛ inch deep, 1 inch apart, in flats or six-packs in bright light at 60° to 70°F. Seedlings usually germinate within four weeks. When plants are a few inches tall, shift them to 4-inch pots for optimum root growth. In cold frames, sow six weeks before last frost or in autumn. Move plants outdoors any time in spring after hardening them off.

- **Prepare soil outdoors** by digging the bed and turning in compost, fertilizer, and other soil amendments, as needed. Add lime in acid soil areas.

- **Sow seeds outdoors** in late spring or summer, when seeds ripen, ⅛ inch deep and 2 inches apart, in finely tilled soil. Plants often self-sow.

- **Thin or transplant** during cool, moist weather. When outdoor-grown seedlings are 5 inches high, thin them to 6 inches apart, or, if you wish, to permanent positions. The next spring, move any still in the nursery bed to their permanent positions. Thin or transplant extras from overcrowded plantings each year.

- **Set plants outdoors** (whether purchased or homegrown) into permanent places in spring after the last frost. Mix fertilizer into planting holes, firm plants into place, and water.

- **Lift and divide** established plants in early spring. Replant divisions immediately.

- **Water** often enough to keep soil moist, more frequently while new plants are becoming established.

- **Fertilize** plants steadily during their active growth in spring and summer.

- **Pests and diseases** rarely are problems.

- **Mulch** plants in dry areas with an inch or two of shredded leaves or other fine mulch.

- **Trim** plants back if they look weedy.

Selected Species

Alchemilla alpina. This diminutive form grows only 6 to 8 inches tall. Plants flower in summer in greenish to golden shades. The fine-textured, lobed, palmate leaves touched with white are nice against walls and in rock gardens where there is room for plants to spread.

A. mollis. Usually 2 to 3 feet tall when in bloom, this type has large grayish leaves topped with foamy clusters of yellowish starlike blossoms. The straw-textured flowers may be dried for wreaths and bouquets—for this, pick them before they open fully.

LIATRIS

Botanical name: *Liatris spicata* (Compositae)
Other common names: Blazing star, Gayfeather

The mounded foliage of liatris is narrow and swordlike. Tall stems grow from the center of the clump of foliage and are topped with spikes of fuzzy flowers. Unlike most spiked flowers, the blooms of this hardy perennial open from top to bottom. Grow liatris in a mixed border or for cut or dried flowers.

PLANT TYPE: Hardy perennial.
GROWING RANGE: Zones 3 to 10.
HARDINESS: Tolerant of cold and heat; does not grow well in the desert or the hot, humid climates of the Southeast.
PLANT HEIGHT: 3 to 6 feet.
FLOWER COLOR: Reddish purple or white.
FLOWER FORM: Spikes 1 foot long of flowers each ½ inch across.

SEASON OF BLOOM: Midsummer to late summer.
SOIL: Sandy, well drained.
PH: 6 to 7.
FERTILIZER: Well-rotted manure, compost, or all-purpose fertilizer.
WATER: Average to moist conditions.
EXPOSURE: Full sun or light shade.
SPACING: 12 inches.
PROPAGATION: Seed or division.

Method

- **Start seeds indoors** in spring or summer up to three months before the first fall frost. Fresh seed needs to be prechilled for six weeks at about 40°F in the refrigerator. Sow in small pots or flats filled with sterile seed starting medium. Plant seeds ⅛ inch deep, water, and keep in a cool or warm place (55° to 75°F) until they germinate, in twenty to twenty-five days. Grow seedlings in bright sunlight or a few inches below a fluorescent light fixture.

- **Prepare soil outdoors** before planting by tilling in fertilizer and compost or other organic soil improvers, as needed.

- **Sow seeds outdoors** in smoothly prepared and fertilized beds in spring or summer up to three months before the first fall frost. Plant seeds 6 inches apart and ¼ inch deep. Do not let the seedbed dry out.

- **Thin** outdoor-grown seedlings to their permanent spacing when they are 4 to 6 inches high. If necessary, two months before the first fall frost, place plants in their permanent position.

- **Set indoor-grown plants outdoors** from spring after all danger of frost passes through summer up to two months before the first fall frost.

- **Divide** perennial plants in midspring when new growth begins if plants are too crowded.

- **Water** when the soil starts to dry out. Although liatris prefers average to moist conditions, it will tolerate drought.

- **Fertilize** annually in midspring.

- **Pests and diseases** are not a problem.

- **Mulch** around growing plants with 2 inches of bark chips or shredded leaves to keep moisture in the soil.

- **Protect in winter** in the colder limits of its hardiness with about 4 inches of evergreen boughs or 2 inches of shredded leaves. Remove mulch in gradual stages when new growth appears in spring.

Selected Cultivars

'Kobold' is a compact variety, growing 18 inches tall, with deep reddish purple flowers. 'White Kobold' is similar, but with white flowers.

LILY

Botanical name: *Lilium* (Liliaceae)

When you add lilies to the flower border, you add a long season of color and dazzling blooms. Depending on the species and cultivars, hardy lilies will bloom from late spring until early fall, adding a strong backbone to mixed borders. Flowers bloom singly or in clusters, and have six petallike parts and showy stamens. Plant lilies in mixed borders, in massed plantings or as accent plants. Shorter varieties can be grown in containers. Lilies make excellent cut flowers as well.

PLANT TYPE: Hardy bulb.
GROWING RANGE: Zones 4 to 10, depending on the species and cultivar.
HARDINESS: Resistant to cold, with some requiring cold winters; fairly resistant to heat if soil is kept cool.
PLANT HEIGHT: 2 to 9 feet.
FLOWER COLOR: Red, pink, orange, yellow, white, purple, or lavender, with some spotted or striped, or with contrasting throats.
FLOWER FORM: Funnel-, trumpet-, or bowl-shaped. Flowers face upward, outward, or downward, depending on species and cultivar; range from 2 to 10 inches across.
SEASON OF BLOOM: Late spring to early fall.
SOIL: Deep, rich, fertile, well drained.
PH: 6 to 7.
FERTILIZER: Well-rotted manure, compost, all-purpose fertilizer, or bonemeal.
WATER: Moist conditions.
EXPOSURE: Full sun, or light shade where summers are very hot.
SPACING: 6 to 8 inches.
PROPAGATION: Division, bulbils.

Method

- **Prepare soil** before planting by tilling in bonemeal and compost or other organic soil improvers, as needed.

- **Set bulbs outdoors** in early spring before the last chance of frost or, preferably, in fall. Lily bulbs are never dormant and should be planted right away. Madonna lilies must be planted early enough to start top growth if they are going to bloom the following year—fall is best. Plant them 8 inches deep, except for Madonna lilies, which are planted 1 inch deep, and turk's-cap lilies, which are planted 2 inches deep.

- **Divide** bulbs after they have bloomed and the foliage has turned brown if plants are too crowded or the flowers become smaller in size.

- **Propagation** through bulbils is possible. Bulbils that grow on the stems of lilies may be picked off and planted about 1 inch deep in moist soil. They will take about three or four years to grow to full-size bulbs and flower.

- **Water** frequently so the ground is never allowed to become dry.

- **Fertilize** with bonemeal and all-purpose fertilizer in spring when growth starts and again as blooms fade.

- **Pests and diseases** include viral diseases, for which there is no cure. Purchase disease-resistant varieties and discard any bulbs that become infected. Pests are normally no problem.

- **Mulch** around growing plants with 2 inches of bark chips or shredded leaves to keep moisture in the soil and to keep the soil cool.

- **Stake** tall plants with wooden or metal stakes that are placed far enough away from the base of the plant to not injure the bulbs.

- **Remove** flowers as soon as they fade and foliage after it has completely turned brown.

- **Protect in winter** with evergreen boughs, straw, or shredded leaves during the first winter after the bulbs are planted, and in following winters in the lower limits of their hardiness.

Tips · **For best effect, plant lilies in clumps of at least three bulbs of the same variety.**
· **Remove the stamens from lilies when bringing them indoors so their pollen does not stain the furniture, flowers, or your clothes.**

Selected Species

Lilies are classified into two groups, species and hybrids. Unless otherwise noted, all grow in Zones 4 to 10.

The most common species of lily grown are:

Lilium auratum (Gold-band lily). This species has fragrant, slightly drooping, bowl-shaped, 6- to 10-inch white flowers with crimson spots and a central gold stripe on each petal. Blooming late in summer, it is one of the last lilies to bloom in the garden. Plants grow 3 to 9 feet tall, in Zones 5 to 10.

L. lancifolium (Tiger lily). One of the most vigorous lilies, the tiger lily grows 4 to 6 feet tall and has very narrow leaves. The drooping flowers have recurved petals and are 5 inches across. They are orange spotted in purple and appear in midsummer. They grow in Zones 4 to 8.

L. longiflorum (White trumpet lily). This species for Zones 4 to 8 has fragrant, trumpet-shaped, pure white, 7-inch flowers that appear in midsummer and grows 2 to 3 feet tall. The variety *eximium* is the popular Easter lily and has slightly longer flowers.

L. Martagon (Turk's-cap lily). This plant for Zones 4 to 9 grows 4 to 6 feet tall and has drooping, reflexed, 2-inch flowers. Blooms range from white through pink and purple to almost black. It is one of the first lilies to bloom in late spring.

L. monadelphum (Caucasian lily). Fragrant, drooping, 5-inch golden-yellow flowers on 5-foot-tall stems adorn this species in late spring. Hardy in Zones 4 to 9.

L. regale (Regal lily). This plant for Zones 4 to 9 has funnel-shaped, fragrant, 6-inch flowers. They are white on the inside, with a yellow throat, and purplish-red on the outside. Bloom appears in midsummer on 2- to 5-foot-tall stems.

The best-known lily hybrids are:

American hybrids, which bloom in early summer to midsummer. These 4- to 8-foot-tall plants have nodding, spotted, 4- to 6-inch flowers of red, pink, orange, and yellow, with highly recurved petals. Grow in Zones 4 to 8.

Asiatic hybrids, which bloom in midsummer and include the well-known 'Mid-Century' hybrids. Flowers are 4 to 6 inches wide and come in many colors, including white, yellow, red, orange, pink, or lavender, in solids and in combinations. Some flowers are spotted. Plants grow 2 to 5 feet tall. Grow in Zones 4 to 7.

Aurelian hybrids, which bloom in midsummer in many colors, some with yellow throats or maroon stripes. Blooms are up to 8 inches wide. They grow 3 to 6 feet tall. Most varieties are fragrant. Grow in Zones 4 to 7.

Candidum hybrids (Madonna lilies). These have pure white, fragrant, trumpet-shaped flowers on 4-foot-tall stems. They bloom in early summer and do best in Zones 5 to 10. Foliage disappears after the flowers fade and reappears in fall.

Oriental hybrids, which have white, yellow, pink, or crimson 3- to 10-inch flowers that are spotted and fragrant. Some have backswept petals; others have bowl-shaped or flat flowers. They bloom in late summer and early fall. Stems are 2½ to 7 feet tall.

LILY OF THE VALLEY

Botanical name: *Convallaria majaus* (Liliaceae)

This popular shade-loving ground cover with long-lasting elliptic green leaves gives a fragrant bonus each spring: bell-like cut flowers. *Muguet* in French, lily of the valley is used in perfume. Plants are easy to grow and quick to spread, especially in woodland areas, because of rhizomatous roots. The dormant pips (sprouts) may be forced to bloom indoors in winter.

PLANT TYPE: Hardy perennial.
GROWING RANGE: Zones 3 to 9.
HARDINESS: Hardy in cold or hot weather.
PLANT HEIGHT: 6 to 12 inches.
FLOWER COLOR: Usually white, sometimes pink.
FLOWER FORM: Small bell-shaped, nodding blossoms aligned on slender stems 6 to 8 inches long (a double white is available).
SEASON OF BLOOM: Late spring.
SOIL: Average to rich, moist but well drained.
PH: 6 to 7.
FERTILIZER: Well-rotted manure and compost.
WATER: Average.
EXPOSURE: From light to deep shade, with more shade needed in the South.
SPACING: 6 inches.
PROPAGATION: Usually by division, also from seed.

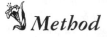 *Method*

- **Start plants indoors.** Lily of the valley is rarely grown from seed indoors, but plants from pips (sprouts) may be forced in a cool greenhouse or sunny window in temperatures from 60° to 65°F. Dig upright, dormant pips in winter (or order them by mail) and plant them about 3 inches deep in shallow bowls of soil or potting fiber. They will bloom two or three weeks later. After they finish blooming, and after all danger of frost passes, replant them outdoors.

- **Prepare soil outdoors** before planting in beds by tilling in fertilizer, compost, leaf mold, and other soil improvers, as needed.

- **Sow seeds outdoors** about ½ inch deep and 2 inches apart in beds in late summer when they ripen (the outer coat turns red). They probably will germinate the following spring but may take longer.

- **Thin or transplant** seedlings to their permanent places 6 or more inches apart the second year after they germinate.

- **Set pips or plants outdoors** in permanent places any time in spring or fall. Potted plants may be set out in summer, too.

- **Divide** large clumps by separating pips every other year in very early spring or late fall if they are crowded. Replant divisions immediately.

- **Water** frequently enough to keep the soil moderately moist in spring, somewhat drier in summer.

- **Fertilize** lightly at planting time and more heavily each fall, after foliage freezes. This can be done by top-dressing beds with compost or leaf mold each fall.

- **Pests and diseases** rarely are problems.

- **Mulch** plants with 2 inches of composted leaves or small bark chips to help keep moisture in the soil.

- **Remove** flower stems after bloom is finished, unless you want to save the seeds. Cut the leaves down in fall or winter after they turn brown, for neatness.

- **Protect in winter** with 2 inches of mulch around each plant.

Tip · The red berries containing the seeds are decorative, but are poisonous, so remove them if young children visit your garden.

Selected Cultivars

'Flora plena,' 8-inch-tall plants with double white flowers;
   'Fortin's Giant,' large and late blooming, with creamy white bells, 8 to 10 inches tall;
   'Giant Bells,' a good strain for forcing, with up to fifteen large white flowers on each 8- to 10-inch-tall spike;
   'Rosea,' with single pale pink flowers; and
   'Striata,' which has white flowers on green leaves narrowly striped with white.

LISIANTHUS

Botanical name: *Eustoma grandiflorum,* synonym *Lisianthus russelianus* (Gentianaceae)
Other common names: Prairie gentian, Seaside gentian

Returned to us after changes by Japanese and other breeders, our native prairie or seaside gentian has been glamorized into a large-flowered, showy plant for bedding and cutting. The silvery pale green foliage is attractive, too. Native to Texas, Colorado, and other western states, it grows 2 to 3 feet tall. The new strains still have the native plant's ability to thrive in hotter, drier places than most other garden flowers. They last three weeks indoors as graceful cut flowers.

PLANT TYPE: Hardy annual.
GROWING RANGE: All zones.
HARDINESS: Tolerates light frost and high heat.
PLANT HEIGHT: 1 to 4 feet.
FLOWER COLOR: Blue, violet, pink, white, purple.
FLOWER FORM: Several poppylike flowers up to 3 inches wide on 1- to 3-foot-tall wiry stems, single or double.
SEASON OF BLOOM: Summer in northern and central states, earlier farther south.
SOIL: Fair to rich, well drained.
PH: 6.5 to 7.5.
FERTILIZER: Low-nitrogen, high-phosphorus fertilizer.
WATER: Average to dry conditions.
EXPOSURE: Full sun in most areas, sun or partial shade in the South.
SPACING: 1 to 2 feet.
PROPAGATION: Seed.

Method

- **Start seeds indoors** in late fall to early spring at 70°F, pressing the fine seeds into the soil surface in flats or small pots filled with moist soil. Keep containers under a glass or plastic cover or in a polyethylene bag until seeds germinate, in three to six weeks, then uncover. Grow plantlets in a sunny area or a few inches below a fluorescent light fixture. When seedlings have several leaves, transplant individual seedlings to 3-inch pots. Seeds are not normally sown outdoors because seed is dustlike and plants take about five months from seed to bloom, sometimes longer. Some suppliers offer pelleted seed, which is easier to handle. Most gardeners buy plants because such a long developmental period is required from seed.

- **Prepare soil outdoors** before setting out plants by tilling in fertilizer, compost, and other soil improvers, as needed.

- **Set plants outdoors** when they have developed four to six true leaves after all danger of frost passes, after hardening them off in shade for a few days.

- **Water** young plants often to prevent the soil from drying out. Water plants during periods of drought or high heat. Later, mature plants thrive in dry soil.

- **Fertilize** lightly at planting time and periodically during active growth.
- **Pests and diseases** seldom are problems.
- **Mulch** plants to keep roots cool in very hot, dry areas. Use several inches of small bark chips or other mulch.
- **Deadhead** plants for a repeat show of bloom.
- **Stake** plants with slim bamboo sticks if necessary.

Selected Cultivars

'Colorado Bluebell,' an unusually tall, vigorous strain, up to 4 feet tall, with lavender-blue single flowers with deeper blue centers;

'Lion' hybrids, with double flowers, pink, blue-purple, or white. The 3 ½-inch flowers are larger than the single ones, but last just as long, and are excellent in flower arrangements;

'Prima Donna,' with double white, violet, or rose-pink flowers over 3 inches wide on wiry stems. Plants are 1 ½ feet tall; and the popular

'Yodel' hybrids, with 2 ½-inch poppylike single flowers of pink, deep rose, violet, blue-purple, or white, on plants 1 to 3 feet tall.

LUPINE

Botanical name: *Lupinus* (Leguminosae)
Other common name: Bluebonnet

Lupines are an excellent source of tall, richly colored spires of flowers. Though there are many species, the main type for gardens is the 'Russell' strain, which flowers in dense spires in early summer. Hybridized in 1911 by George Russell of York, England, a gardener and railroad guard, the Russell lupines have palmate, star-shaped leaves with long stems. They grow with ease in northwestern states and are also grown in northeastern and central states wherever summer heat is not too intense. Though perennial, plants tend to die out after a few years, but it is easy to grow new ones.

The Texas bluebonnet is another lupine, a wildflower for a hot, dry climate. Eastern and central states from Maine to Florida can enjoy wild blue lupines of several types in sunny fields. Because they are legumes, lupines create their own nitrogen when growing on poor soil. Lupines are used in flower beds, in wildflower gardens and meadows, and as cut flowers.

PLANT TYPES: Hardy perennial or annual.
GROWING RANGE: All zones for wild species; Zones 4 to 7 for garden perennials.
HARDINESS: Garden types tolerate temperatures below 0°F but are killed by high heat.
PLANT HEIGHT: 1 to over 3 feet, varying with the species.
FLOWER COLOR: Blue, pink, yellow, orange, white, or purple, often bicolored with white or yellow.
FLOWER FORM: Pealike flowers on dense, tall, showy racemes.

SEASON OF BLOOM: Early summer in northern states, earlier south of Zone 6.
SOIL: Good to rich, well drained.
PH: 6 to 6.5 (acidic) for 'Russell' lupine, 7 to 7.5 (sweeter soil) for Texas bluebonnets.
FERTILIZER: Low-nitrogen, high-phosphorus fertilizer.
WATER: Average to moist conditions.
EXPOSURE: Full sun or partial shade, more shade in the South.
SPACING: 1 to 2 feet.
PROPAGATION: Seed, cuttings, or division.

🌱 Method

- **Start seeds indoors** in spring (or, for perennials, summer at 70° to 80°F). Presoak seeds overnight before planting ¼ inch deep in flats or small pots filled with moist soil. Germination usually takes a week or two, but varies. Grow plantlets in a sunny area or a few inches below a fluorescent light fixture. When seedlings have several leaves, move them to larger pots if necessary.

- **Prepare soil outdoors** in beds before planting by tilling in fertilizer, compost, and other soil improvers, as needed.

- **Sow seeds outdoors** where they will grow at the time of the last expected frost, or later. In smoothly prepared and fertilized beds, plant seeds 4 or more inches apart and cover with ¼ inch of soil. Do not let the seedbed dry out.

- **Thin or transplant** seedlings grown outdoors to their permanent spacing when they are about 4 inches tall. Thinnings are not easy to transplant except when they are small—below 6 inches. Indoors, continue to move young plants to larger pots as they become crowded.

- **Set plants outdoors** after all danger of frost has passed, after hardening them off in shade for a few days. Move field-grown plants in spring when new growth begins. Set in outdoor-grown potted plants at any time.

- **Divide** crowded clumps when new growth begins in early spring.

- **Take cuttings** of side shoots growing next to the base of the main stem and root them in moist, shaded beds in late spring.

- **Water** young plants often to prevent the soil from drying out. Water plants often during periods of drought or high heat. Mature plants will thrive in drier soil. To prevent winter damage, keep lupine roots somewhat dry during winter.

- **Fertilize** lightly at planting time and periodically during active growth.

- **Pests and diseases** seldom are problems, except for slugs, which devour emerging seedlings and young plants.

- **Mulch** plants to keep roots cool in hot, dry areas. Use several inches of bark chips or other mulch.

- **Cut off** old flower stalks close to the ground to stimulate a repeat show of bloom.
- **Stake** tall plants with slim bamboo stakes, wires, or peony hoops.

Tip · Treat seed with legume inoculant (nitrogen-fixing bacteria) before planting, as you would treat edible pea seeds.

Selected Species and Cultivars

Lupinus luteus (Yellow lupine). This is a half-hardy annual lupine from the Mediterranean region. It is sometimes used as a green manure or cover crop to increase soil nitrogen, though its fragrant blooms are garden worthy, freely flowering on 2-foot-tall plants.

L. perennis (Sundial lupine, Wild lupine). This perennial lupine grows wild throughout eastern and prairie states from Maine to Florida. It has strong spikes of blue, pink, or white flowers on 2-foot-tall plants with palmate, compound leaves.

L. polyphyllus. Perhaps including the 'Russell' strain of cultivated hybrid lupines, this species is native to northwestern areas of the United States and adjacent parts of Canada. It has been introduced to the Northeast, where it does equally well. The 'Russell' lupines come in every color of the rainbow and reach up to 4 feet in height while in bloom. 'Gallery' is a dwarf version of 'Russell,' growing only 20 inches tall, with many flowering stems on each plant. Plants grow well in acid soil where summers are not too hot.

L. subcarnosus (Texas bluebonnet). Blooming in Texas grasslands in April and May, this 1-foot-tall plant has bright blue flowers with a white or yellowish spot that turns red with age. Similar but even showier is *L. texensis,* also called Texas bluebonnet, which reaches 2 feet in height in many western states where it grows wild. Both are annuals with biennial tendencies. Germination is unpredictable, with some seeds germinating in a few weeks and others taking a year or two to break dormancy.

LYTHRUM

Botanical name: *Lythrum* (Lythraceae)
Other common name: Loosestrife

This "weed" from Eurasia is beautiful but aggressive, and in some northeastern wetlands it crowds out other types of plants needed by wildlife. Since it has been outlawed in several states, check with your local agricultural extension agent before planting it. However, the popular named cultivars are better behaved, and some are sterile. Whatever its environmental impact, this hardy perennial makes an exceptionally attractive vista in meadows, especially where it grows with Queen Anne's lace and native sunflowers. As a tall, handsome border plant, it is very showy in stately, bushlike clumps—good near pools and brooks, too. Plants stay colorful for months, loved by bees and butterflies.

PLANT TYPE: Hardy perennial.
GROWING RANGE: Zones 3 to 9.
HARDINESS: Withstands temperature extremes.

PLANT HEIGHT: 2 to 5 feet.
FLOWER COLOR: Purple, red-purple, rosy red.
FLOWER FORM: Tiny, starlike, tubular blossoms are bunched on tall, pointed spires.
 The square mintlike stems bear linear leaves, narrowed at the base.
SEASON OF BLOOM: Several months in summer.
SOIL: Any moist or marshy soil.
PH: 6 to 7.
FERTILIZER: Well-rotted manure, all-purpose or high-phosphorus fertilizer.
WATER: Prefers moist conditions but tolerates drought.
EXPOSURE: Full sun or very light shade.
SPACING: 2 to 3 feet.
PROPAGATION: Seed, stem cuttings, or division.

 *Method*

- **Start seeds indoors** in late winter or early spring one or two per pot in small pots filled with moist potting soil, covering ⅛ inch deep. Water, cover, and keep at around 75°F until seeds germinate, in one or two weeks. Thin to one plant per pot. Grow seedlings in a sunny area or a few inches below a fluorescent light fixture, at 60° to 75°F. When they are crowded, move them to larger pots or outdoors.

- **Prepare soil outdoors** before planting by tilling in fertilizer, compost, peat moss, and other soil improvers, as needed.

- **Sow seeds outdoors** in nursery beds when they ripen in late summer, ⅛ inch deep and about 2 inches apart.

- **Thin** seedlings to 6 inches apart when they are 4 inches tall and again to permanent spacing when they become crowded.

- **Set plants outdoors** any time in spring or summer, after hardening off those grown indoors.

- **Divide** woody roots in early spring, once every three or four years, when new growth begins. Use a sharp spade to cut an old clump into two to four sections and dig them up. Replant them immediately at the same depth they grew or an inch deeper.

- **Take cuttings** that are 6 to 8 inches long after the flowering tip is removed, during summer while the plants are actively growing. Plant them 4 inches deep in peaty rooting medium in shade and keep cuttings moist at all times.

- **Water** plants whenever the soil starts to dry out, if possible.

- **Fertilize** at planting time and periodically during growth.

- **Pests and diseases** seldom are problems.

- **Mulch** plants in dry weather with 2 to 3 inches of bark chips, shredded leaves, or other mulch if you wish.

- **Deadhead** by removing spent flowers unless you want plants to spread from seed.

Selected Species and Cultivars

Lythrum salicaria (Purple loosestrife, Red Sally). Named varieties include:
   'Gypsy Blood,' with pinkish-purple flowers on 3- to 4-foot plants;
   'Morden's Gleam,' a red variety that may reach 4 feet, blooming from July to September. 'Firecandle' is similar; and
   'Morden's Pink,' with deep rosy pink flowers; has a relatively soft color. It is propagated by division or from cuttings. It will not spread into the wild.
   L. virgatum. With slender flower spires of purple or pink, this is a graceful border plant. Popular cultivars include:
   'Dropmore Purple,' 3 feet tall, rapidly spreading, a rich purple type that blooms profusely for the entire summer with an attractive upright habit; and
   'Rose Queen,' similar, bright rose-red, 2 feet tall.

MARIGOLD

Botanical name: *Tagetes* (Compositae)

Marigolds are among the easiest and most floriferous plants to grow. Plants are not too particular about soil pH. Though closely related to each other, the different types of marigolds may be tall, medium, or short, and are used in borders, beds, containers, and vegetable gardens, where they repel pests. The deep green foliage is fine and ferny, on sturdy plants. Flowers may be used in bouquets in spite of their sharp odor—some of the new types are said to be odorless.

PLANT TYPE: Tender annual.
GROWING RANGE: All zones.
HARDINESS: Thrives in heat, withstands cool weather above the freezing point.
PLANT HEIGHT: 6 inches to over 3 feet.
FLOWER COLOR: Yellow, orange, rust, or creamy white, sometimes bicolored.
FLOWER FORM: Daisy- or camellialike flower heads from ½ to several inches wide on bushy green foliage.
SEASON OF BLOOM: Late spring to frost.
SOIL: Good to rich.
PH: 6 to 8.
FERTILIZER: Well-rotted manure, all-purpose or high-phosphorus fertilizer.
WATER: Average to dry conditions.
EXPOSURE: Full sun in Zone 6 and north, sun or light shade south of Zone 6.
SPACING: 1 to 2½ feet.
PROPAGATION: Seed.

Method

· **Start seeds indoors** four to six weeks before the last expected frost. Germination usually takes five days. Grow one per container in small pots or six-packs in moist potting soil, covering seed with barely ⅛ inch of soil. Water and keep at 60° to 70°F until seeds germinate. Grow in a sunny area or a few inches below a fluorescent light fixture. When seedlings have four to six leaves, step them up to larger pots if necessary.

- **Prepare soil outdoors** before planting by tilling in fertilizer, compost, and other soil improvers, as needed.

- **Sow seeds outdoors** where they will grow at the time of the last expected frost, or later. Petite types will go from seed to bloom in less than two months. In smoothly prepared and fertilized beds, plant seeds 3 or more inches apart and barely cover with ⅛ inch of soil. Do not let the seedbed dry out.

- **Thin** outdoor-grown seedlings to their permanent spacing when they are about 4 inches tall. Thinnings are easy to transplant—plant them a little deeper than they grew.

- **Set plants outdoors** after all danger of frost has passed, after hardening them off in shade for a few days.

- **Water** seedlings often to prevent the soil from drying out. Mature plants will thrive in drier soil.

- **Fertilize** lightly at planting time. Boost blossoms by applying a low-nitrogen, high-phosphorus and -potassium fertilizer when plants are 5 or 6 inches tall.

- **Pests and diseases** seldom are problems. In fact, marigolds repel nematodes and other pests. The most serious problem is red spider mite during the heat of July and August. Spray plants with water or with water mixed with insecticidal soap.

- **Mulch** plants that grow in hot, dry areas with several inches of bark chips or other mulch.

- **Pinch back** tips once or twice for bushiness.

- **Deadhead** spent blossoms to stimulate more flowering.

- **Stake** tall plants with slim bamboo stakes, wires, or peony hoops.

Tip · **When planting, hold the slender seed by the "tail" (a tan tuft) and stick the "head" into the soil, slantwise, about ¼ inch deep, for faster germination. If the tufts have been milled off the seeds, plant them the usual way (level), and cover.**

Selected Species

Tagetes erecta (African marigold). Not really from Africa, but from Central America, this marigold has large flowers up to 5 inches wide on sturdy plants that are usually over 2 feet tall. They are used for borders and bedding, blooming for months in warm weather. Start plants indoors a few weeks earlier than smaller types. Camellia-shaped varieties are available and may be yellow, orange, or creamy white. Some of the marigolds with this appearance are "mules"—crossbreeds that are not able to form viable seeds. "Mule" marigolds keep blooming without needing deadheading.

T. filifolia (Irish lace). This type grows with fine lacy foliage on low shrubby plants used for edgings. Its numerous small flowers are considered less important than the leaves.

T. patula (French marigold). This low bushy marigold, 6 to 12 inches tall, has a broader color range and more variation in singleness and doubleness than the African types. Many are vividly colored with rust and red shades, or banded or splotched with contrasting reds and golds. The French marigolds are considered the most effective against pests.

T. tenuifolia, synonym *T. signata* (Signet marigold). One-inch, single or double marigolds in the full color range flower vigorously on plants about 6 inches tall. The foliage is threadlike and fine.

MONKSHOOD

Botanical name: *Aconitum* (Ranunculaceae)

Monkshood is a tall hardy perennial with flowers in a much appreciated shade of deep blue, along with several other colors. Spires of flowers top bushy foliage that is deeply veined and finely divided. Monkshood makes a good perennial border plant and looks best if grouped in threes, or, in larger gardens, in masses. *However, do not use the plant where small children play, for all parts of the plant are exceptionally poisonous, particularly the leaves and roots.*

PLANT TYPE: Hardy perennial.
GROWING RANGE: Zones 3 to 8.
HARDINESS: Cold hardy but heat sensitive.
PLANT HEIGHT: 2 to 6 feet.
FLOWER COLOR: Blue, mauve, yellow. Some blues are frosted with white.
FLOWER FORM: Tubular or hooded flowers on tall spires.
SEASON OF BLOOM: Summer.
SOIL: Average to good garden loam.
PH: 6.5 to 7.5.
FERTILIZER: Compost, well-rotted manure, bonemeal, high-phosphorus and -potassium fertilizer.
WATER: Average soil moisture, with extra water needed during hot spells.
EXPOSURE: Partial shade.
SPACING: 2 to 4 feet.
PROPAGATION: Seed or division.

Method

- **Start seeds indoors** after prechilling for six weeks. They germinate irregularly, usually taking from a week to a year at 55° to 60°F. Plant in six-packs or small pots in potting soil, two seeds per hole to guarantee against failure. Plant ¼ inch deep and keep containers in the light, watered, near 60°F, until seedlings grow several inches tall. Then shift to 8-inch pots and, after hardening them off, set them outdoors in shade.

- **Prepare soil outdoors** by digging the bed and turning in compost, fertilizer, and other needed soil amendments, as needed.

- **Sow seeds outdoors** in nursery rows in fall for germination in spring, or prechill and plant them outdoors in early spring. Plant seeds an inch apart and cover with ¼ inch of soil and an inch of dry grass clippings, marking the rows carefully.

- **Thin or transplant** outdoor-grown seedlings when they are 5 or 6 inches high. Thinnings may be transplanted if they are dug out carefully, then watered well for a week. Thin them to permanent spacing or temporary nursery spacing 10 inches apart. Transplant one-year-old seedlings to the flower border in spring when new growth begins.

- **Set plants outdoors** after all danger of heavy frost has passed, first hardening them off for several days in shade.

- **Divide** plants when new growth begins in spring, after the danger of heavy frost passes, once every three years if they are crowded.

- **Water** frequently if needed.

- **Fertilize** at planting time and side-dress with a light application of flower fertilizer in midsummer.

- **Pests and diseases** rarely are problems.

- **Mulch** lightly in dry areas.

- **Stake** plants just before flower stalks lengthen and bloom.

Selected Species and Cultivars

Aconitum x *bicolor.* Four feet tall, this type blooms from midsummer to late summer, forming spires of dark violet flowers with whitish tops. 'Bressingham Spire' is a bushy, 3-foot-tall type that needs no staking and makes a large patch of rich violet-blue spires in late summer.

A. carmichaelli, synonym *A. wilsonii.* Growing 3 to 6 feet tall, this type forms pyramids of 2-inch, hooded, amethyst-blue flowers in late summer.

A. napellus (Bear's-foot). Growing 3 to 4 feet tall, this type is relied on for deep blue flowers in summer. The cultivar 'Newry Blue' provides violet-blue, delphiniumlike spikes of flowers on 3-foot-tall plants, and is excellent in borders and for cutting.

A. volubile. This climbing, viny form with mauve hooded blooms in late summer may be trained against a wall on a trellis, or to climb through shrubs.

A. vulparia. These 2- to 6-foot-tall, summer-blooming plants with many stems of ¾-inch yellow flowers are dramatic in borders.

MORNING GLORY

Botanical name: *Ipomoea* (Convolvulaceae)

Morning glory is not aptly named, for its large circular flowers open either in morning or evening, depending on the variety. In any case, the blooms last just a few hours, but new buds open daily for months during warm weather.

Most morning glories are fast-growing, climbing tropical vines that can reach 10 feet in two months. With their heart-shaped leaves, twining stems, pointed buds, and tubular flowers, they were a popular subject in art deco ornamentation. Though they grow well in poor soil and drought, they grow even better in moist, rich soil if it is not too high in nitrogen. Do not plant morning glories too early indoors or they will outgrow their space and latch onto other plants. Outdoors, some reseed themselves as weeds. Nonetheless, they are appealing and useful on trellises or fences (adding height to the garden), as a screen for unsightly wire fences, trained on posts, or blooming in hanging baskets.

PLANT TYPES: Annual or tender perennial.

GROWING RANGE: All zones. Zones 9 to 11 as a perennial.

HARDINESS: Withstands heat, killed by frost.

PLANT HEIGHT: 1 to 20 feet.

FLOWER COLOR: White, blue, pink, red, brownish red, or violet, sometimes bicolored.

FLOWER FORM: Tubular, broadly flaring blossoms up to 6 inches wide.

SEASON OF BLOOM: All year during warm weather, especially summer.

SOIL: Rich, well drained.

PH: 6.5 to 7.5.

FERTILIZER: Well-rotted manure, high-phosphorus fertilizer.

WATER: Average conditions.

EXPOSURE: Full sun or bright, dappled shade.

SPACING: 5 inches to 1 1/2 feet.

PROPAGATION: Seed or stem or tip cuttings.

Method

- **Start seeds indoors** four to six weeks before the last expected frost in small pots or an inch apart in flats filled with moist potting soil, covering them with 1/2 inch of soil. The seeds have hard shells, so soften by presoaking overnight or nicking them, or by covering planted containers with glass or plastic to maintain high humidity, or all these measures. Water and keep seeds at 70° to 75°F until they germinate, in a week or two. Then remove the cover and keep seedlings in a sunny area or a few inches below a fluorescent light fixture at temperatures between 60° and 75°F. When plants start to become crowded or viny, move them to larger pots or outdoors.

- **Prepare soil outdoors** before planting by tilling in plentiful fertilizer, compost, and other soil improvers, as needed.

- **Sow seeds outdoors** near climbing supports in warm (around 70°F) spring weather, 1/2 inch deep and about 5 inches apart. Do not let them dry out.

- **Thin** seedlings grown outdoors to their permanent spacing when they are a few inches tall. It takes many plants to cover a fence or trellis because they do not branch especially well.

- **Set plants outdoors** in spring, after all danger of frost has passed after hardening off those grown indoors.

- **Take cuttings** 6 to 8 inches long of perennial types, such as moonflower, during warm weather. Plant them 4 inches deep in moist soil in shade. When well rooted, transplant to desired sites.

- **Water** plants whenever the soil starts to dry out and if they wilt during hot weather.

- **Fertilize** periodically during active growth.

- **Pests and diseases** seldom are problems.

- **Support** tall-growing vines with such structures as trellises, arbors, or wire fences. Plants will usually twine around them unassisted, but may need some training or extra strings to climb on.

- **Pinch** plants for bushiness if you wish, though this will delay blooming. If your summers are short, plant seeds more thickly instead.

- **Mulch** plants 2 or 3 inches deep in very dry weather—any mulch is fine.

- **Remove** spent blossoms to prolong bloom unless seed is wanted.

Tip · To plant a hanging basket, choose shorter types of morning glories and plant eight or nine seeds in the same basket, evenly spaced. Use liquid fertilizer often for best results. Pinch plants to keep them in shape.

Selected Species and Cultivars

Ipomoea alba, synonym *Calonyction aculeatum* (Moonflower). This tender perennial (usually grown as an annual) has round, fragrant white blooms up to 6 inches wide. Flowers open in the evening on tall sturdy vines and close the next day, but may be used for evening table arrangements. Try growing moonflowers near terraces enjoyed on summer evenings. If deeply mulched, plants may survive winter in Zones 7, 8, and 9.

I. x *hederaceae* (Minibar rose). These 4- to 5-foot-long annual vines produce red and white blooms with green and white foliage. 'Roman Candy' is one cultivar that makes a good hanging basket plant in hot areas.

I. x *nil.* Coming into bloom quickly from seed, this annual type is good for fences or trellises in northern areas. Blossoms are 4 or 5 inches wide and come in all the morning glory colors. 'Early Call' is especially fast from seed to bloom. 'Spice Island' is a dwarf type great for baskets.

I. purpurea. (Common morning glory). This is a popular annual and a sturdy climber.

I. quamoclit (Cypress vine, Cardinal climber, Star-glory). This is a tropical perennial vine that reaches 20 feet. Its multitudes of tiny red or, rarely, white stars are set off by dense but threadlike foliage that may be used as a ground cover. This type will bloom in the North if started indoors in February.

I. tricolor. The lovely annual strain 'Heavenly Blue' is the most popular of this species, and deservedly so. It grows a daily supply of huge, deep sky blue flowers on robust, 10-foot-long vines from seed in about two months. 'Summer Skies' is similar but paler blue, and 'Wedding Bells' is, too, in rosy lavender. All have a touch of white and gold at the throat.

NARCISSUS

Botanical name: *Narcissus* (Amaryllidaceae)
Other common names: Daffodil, Jonquil

In miniature or large sizes, cheerful narcissi mark the arrival of pleasant spring days. Those that are single and have long trumpets are usually called daffodils, and those with clusters of small flowers on each stalk are usually called narcissi, although there is little botanical difference between them. Easy to grow in temperate zones, narcissus varieties have few pests because of their toxicity. The long-lived plants are a better investment than tulips, which tend to die out or be eaten by deer, chipmunks, and squirrels. If you buy double-nosed bulbs, each will give you two flower stems the first year and more in the future. The individual flowers last several weeks if the weather stays cool, and of course there are early-, midseason-, and late-blooming types to stretch the season. Narcissi of all kinds are hardy bulbs and may be planted under deciduous trees, in fields, and in flower beds. Plant large narcissi toward the back of a mixed flower border, or else naturalize them among shrubs, in ground covers, or at the edges of the lawn where the lingering green foliage is less of a problem. Many garden designers feel that narcissi look best in large groups or drifts of the same type, not randomly mixed in color and form. Miniatures are best set in rock gardens or very close to paths and fronts of borders.

While most types need a climate with a cold winter, the paperwhites will thrive outdoors in Zones 9 and 10, or indoors for winter bloom in other zones. Other types may also be forced indoors. Outdoors, in the extreme climates of the far North and South (above Zone 4 and below Zone 8), the large yellow trumpet types usually do not grow well. Above Zone 4, try the small-cupped kinds.

After the flowers finish blooming, the foliage can be a problem, for it must be left in place for several months to develop the bulb for next year's flowers. You can hide the yellowing leaves by combining daffodils and narcissi with daylilies, violas, campanulas, lady fern, or gypsophila.

PLANT TYPE: Hardy or tender bulb.
GROWING RANGE: Zones 4 to 8 for most types, Zones 9 and 10 for paperwhites.
HARDINESS: Most types withstand heat but need cold winters.
PLANT HEIGHT: 6 to 20 inches.
FLOWER COLOR: Yellow, white, orange, or peach, sometimes bicolored.
FLOWER FORM: A central corona shaped like a large tube (the *trumpet*) or low cup (*eye*) is surrounded by a *perianth,* 6 pointed outer petals. Each flowering stem holds either a large single blossom or a cluster of 2 to 8 smaller ones, depending on the cultivar. Some have frilly double flowers or split coronas instead.
SEASON OF BLOOM: Spring for most types, winter for paperwhites, once a year.
SOIL: Good soil, well drained.
PH: 6 to 7.
FERTILIZER: Bonemeal, low-nitrogen, high-phosphorus fertilizer.
WATER: Average conditions.
EXPOSURE: Full sun or bright dappled shade.
SPACING: 4 to 12 inches.
PROPAGATION: Bulbs, seed, or division.

🌱 *Method*

- **Prepare soil outdoors** in beds before planting by tilling in fertilizer, compost, bone-meal, and other soil improvers, as needed.

- **Plant bulbs outdoors** in early fall, 6 to 8 inches deep and 6 to 12 inches apart for large types, shallower and closer together for small ones. A good rule of thumb is to plant them two to three times deeper than their length. In flower beds, plant them deeply to lessen the chance of their being cut accidentally by a spade or trowel. To naturalize bulbs in grassy or woodland areas, toss them onto the ground wherever plants are wanted and plant them where they fall, for a natural look. Use a bulb planter for this in order to do the least damage to the surrounding lawn or plants.

- **Sow seeds outdoors** 2 inches apart, ⅛ inch deep, in tilled soil, in nursery beds or where plants will be naturalized. Plant in late spring after seeds ripen. Fresh seeds are not hard to grow, but take four or more years to bloom. So that bulbs can develop, foliage should not be cut down until it yellows.

- **Thin** seedlings to their permanent spacing in their third year, in spring when their foliage starts to yellow.

- **Divide** bulbs if they are crowded and flower size starts to decrease, once every four or five years. When foliage begins to yellow, take out clumps with a spade, digging deeply

---

Tips · Never twist or bunch the leaves together with rubber bands, for it will prevent them from functioning. You can tuck the leaves under viny ground cover if plants are intermixed there.

· To force daffodils, dig or buy bulbs at the end of summer. Keep them in a warm, dry place until you are ready to begin—usually September. Plant several bulbs in a pot. Large bulbs should be planted with the noses showing, but small ones should be covered with an inch of soil. Water them, and place them in a cool (38° to 45°F) area or even the refrigerator to root. In ten weeks or so, after roots show at the bottom of the container, bring it into a cool, bright room so flowers will grow.

· To force paperwhites, plant them in pots of soil or simply set them in dishes of gravel or propped in glasses of water and grow them in a brightly sunlit room between 50° and 70°F.

· For longer-lasting cut flowers, cut daffodils at the "gooseneck" stage, when flowers have bent to an upside-down L shape and show color at the tip of the bud, but are not yet open. Condition them in warm water overnight, then arrange them.

· To increase numbers quickly, plant bulbs shallowly to stimulate them to split up. The next fall, plant the offsets at the proper depth so the bulbs will grow back to their full size. The offsets may take another full year or two to reach blooming size.

---

and carefully to prevent stabbing the bulbs. Gently pull clumps apart with your hands to minimize breakage. Discard any with signs of insect damage or disease. Replant immediately in desired places, or dry bulbs in an airy shed or attic and replant them in the fall.

· **Water** plants during their growing period if the soil starts to dry out and occasionally in summer, after plants become dormant, if soil is very dry. Resume watering in fall if needed, to stimulate growth of roots for the next year's flowers.

· **Fertilize** lightly at planting time and each year during active growth, to develop strong bulbs for the following year's flowers.

· **Pests and diseases** seldom are problems.

· **Deadhead** plants or cut flowers for bouquets to send energy back to the redeveloping bulb, unless seed is needed.

· **Protect in winter** by mulching with 6 inches of pine needles or 3 inches of shredded leaves in very cold northern areas. Remove the mulch in stages as winter ends, so shoots can come up freely.

Selected Cultivars

Narcissus species hybridize easily, so there are thousands of named cultivars available. Classic, easy-to-grow standbys include 'King Alfred' (yellow), 'Mount Hood' (white), 'Binkie' (yellow with a white trumpet), 'Actaea' (white with a red-gold pheasant's eye), and 'Geranium' (clustered small white flowers with orange centers). New types constantly appear—the trend recently is for pink or shrimp-colored kinds.

Because species are so intermixed, narcissi are classed as trumpet, large-cupped, small-cupped, double, triandrus (clustered, graceful), cyclamineus (small, reverse-flared), jonquilla (clustered with trumpets), tazetta (clustered, flat-cupped—this group includes the paperwhites), poeticus (pheasant's eye), species and wild types (including hoop-petticoat), and, where these classifications fail, other. Most types offered for sale belong to the first three groups.

NASTURTIUM

Botanical name: *Tropaeolum* (Tropaeolaceae)
Other common name: Indian cress

The charming nasturtium, native to South America, is one of the easiest flowers to grow because its seeds and seedlings are large and sturdy. Plants are used to add color quickly to mixed borders, in hanging baskets and containers, on trellises, as cut flowers, and in orchards, where they are said to repel woolly aphids on apple trees. Some types are bushy; others, viny. Nasturtiums look nice in pots, especially in combination with potted citrus trees. The flowers, stems, and leaves are edible—their spicy, mustardlike flavor adds piquancy to salads.

PLANT TYPES: Hardy annual or tender perennial usually grown as an annual.
GROWING RANGE: All zones during mild weather (50° to 80°F) as an annual, Zones 10 and 11 as a perennial.
HARDINESS: Killed by frost but withstands moderate heat. Plants do poorly when temperatures exceed 90°F, but recover in cooler weather.
PLANT HEIGHT: 1 to 6 or more feet.
FLOWER COLOR: Cream, yellow, orange, peach, rose, wine, or mahogany, sometimes veined or splotched.
FLOWER FORM: Spurred 2-inch flowers with 6 oval petals show through smooth round leaves.
SEASON OF BLOOM: Summer in northern and central areas; all year in mild, frost-free areas; fall, winter, and spring in hot parts of Zones 9 to 11.
SOIL: Good to rich, moist.
PH: 6.5 to 7.5.
FERTILIZER: Well-rotted manure, compost, high-phosphorus fertilizer.
WATER: Average to moist conditions.
EXPOSURE: Full sun in most areas, light shade in hot regions.
SPACING: 1 to 2 feet.
PROPAGATION: Seed or tip cuttings.

Method

- **Start seeds indoors** four to six weeks before the last frost, after soaking them overnight in water. Germination takes eight to twelve days. Grow in small pots in moist potting soil, covering seed with ½ inch of soil. Water and keep at 60° to 70°F until seeds germinate. Grow in a sunny area or a few inches below a fluorescent light fixture. When seedlings have four leaves, step them up to larger pots if roots are crowded. Harden them off before moving them outdoors.

- **Prepare soil outdoors** in beds before planting by tilling in fertilizer, compost, and other soil improvers, as needed.

- **Sow seeds outdoors** where they will grow from one week before to two weeks after the last expected frost. In smoothly prepared and fertilized beds, plant seeds 6 or more inches apart and cover with ½ inch of soil. Do not let the seedbed dry out. In Zones 10 and 11, sow in November.

- **Thin or transplant** seedlings growing outdoors to their permanent spacing when they have four to six leaves. With care, thinnings may be transplanted.

- **Set plants outdoors** after all danger of frost has passed, after hardening them off in shade for a few days. You can set out young plants with two to four leaves, or grow them indoors a few weeks longer.

- **Water** often to prevent the soil from drying out and in hot weather at midday to keep plants from wilting.

- **Fertilize** lightly at planting time. Boost blossoms by applying a low-nitrogen, high-phosphorus and -potassium fertilizer when plants are 5 or 6 inches tall. Too much nitrogen will result in more leaves and fewer flowers.

- **Root cuttings** 6 inches long in moist soil in shade, at temperatures from 60° to 85°F. Nasturtium cuttings also root in a glass of water.

- **Pests and diseases** seldom are problems. If black aphids appear, try a spray of soapy water. Discard leaves showing the winding trails of leaf miners.

- **Mulch** plants that grow in dry areas with several inches of bark chips or other mulch to keep soil cool and moist. This will prolong bloom in hot weather.

- **Pinch back** tips for bushiness, or leave plants unpinched for longer vines.

- **Make a hanging basket** of nasturtiums by filling the container to 1 inch from the rim with rich soil and a timed-release flower fertilizer (such as Osmocote pellets) according to product directions. The 'Whirlybird' and 'Gleam' hybrids are a good size for containers. Plant about fifteen presoaked seeds 2 inches apart and ½ inch deep, evenly spaced across the surface. Grow in bright light for twelve to sixteen hours per day (if possible) at about 65°F. Never let the soil dry out completely, but make sure drainage is satisfactory. In less than ten weeks, plants should be in full bloom.

Selected Species and Cultivars

Tropaeolum majus. Hardy annuals, these old-fashioned spurred flowers grow on semitrailing or viny plants. Cultivars include:

'Empress of India,' 2-foot-tall plants with rich scarlet flowers. Plants tend to cascade attractively and are good on terraces or for containers; and

'Fordhook Favorite,' a 6-foot climber with single flowers available in a good range of clear colors.

T. minus, synonym *T. nanus.* These bushy plants from 6 inches to 2 feet tall are hardy annuals with upright flowers, sometimes held above leaves, sometimes below. Cultivars include:

'Alaska,' a compact, 8-inch-tall plant with marbled leaves attractively touched with white, bearing citrus-colored flowers above them. Not vigorous in hot weather;

'Double Dwarf Jewel,' with dwarf plants a foot tall and large flowers in the full range of colors, held above the foliage;

'Peach Melba,' with cream-colored flowers vividly splotched with crimson, on plants 9 inches tall; and

'Whirlybird,' with colorful spurless blossoms covering compact plants, excellent for bedding and baskets, and available in mixed or single colors. This variety tolerates higher heat and humidity than some types.

T. peregrinum (Canary creeper, Canary bird vine). This is a vigorous climber 6 to 10 feet long with multitudes of small, feathery-looking golden blossoms. It is nice on fences or trellises if you tie it onto the supports. It is a hardy annual in cool or hot weather.

NICOTIANA

Botanical name: *Nicotiana* (Solanaceae)
Other common names: Tobacco flower, Flowering tobacco

Here is a great bedding plant for places with hot, humid summers. Nicotiana is bright and long blooming, with tubular flowers that flare into bright stars. Old-fashioned types close for part of the day and open toward evening with a strong, sweet smell. White varieties are especially attractive at night. New hybrids smell sweet and stay open all day and evening.

Dust sticks to nicotiana's fuzzy leaves and stems, so do not plant it near busy roads. It will self-sow if conditions are right, but most gardeners buy plants because the seeds are so small. Some types are perennial in warm climates, but in areas with cold winters are started in greenhouses to be used as summer annuals. At nurseries, look for healthy dark green leaves on budded plants with a few opened flowers. Mass nicotiana in borders—twelve or more plants together show well. In large tubs, space plants twice as close and add extra fertilizer. Nicotiana is a good greenhouse plant, too.

PLANT TYPES: Annual or tender perennial usually grown as an annual.
GROWING RANGE: All zones as an annual, Zones 10 and 11 as a perennial.
HARDINESS: Killed by hard frost, tolerant of high heat.
PLANT HEIGHT: 16 inches to over 4 feet.
FLOWER COLOR: Green, white, purple, red, cream, citron yellow, or deep rose—all in subdued, smoky tones.
FLOWER FORM: Tubular flowers 2 or more inches long, in clusters.
SEASON OF BLOOM: Summer in most regions, all year in frost-free areas.
SOIL: Any good garden soil enriched with organic matter.
PH: 6.5 to 7.
FERTILIZER: Well-rotted manure, flower fertilizer, compost.
WATER: Keep soil somewhat moist.
EXPOSURE: Full sun or light shade, more shade in the South.
SPACING: 1 foot or more.
PROPAGATION: Seed.

 *Method*

- **Start seeds indoors** ten weeks before the last frost. In Zones 9 to 11, also start seeds in September for winter bedding. Seeds germinate in ten to twenty days. Grow them an inch or two apart in flats, small pots, or six-packs in moist potting soil, keeping plants in a moderately warm (65° to 80°F) place. Grow in bright sunlight or a few inches below fluorescent lights. Try to give twelve or more hours of light per day.

- **Prepare soil outdoors** before planting by tilling in fertilizer, compost, and other soil improvers, as needed.

- **Sow seeds outdoors** a week or two before the frost-free date in smoothly prepared, fertilized beds. Make rows 2 inches deep. Mix seed with dry sand and plant sparsely, without covering them. Do not let the seedbed dry out.

- **Thin or transplant** seedlings when they are a few inches tall or whenever they become crowded. Indoor-grown seedlings may be shifted to individual 4-inch pots. Outdoors, thin plants to 4 or more inches apart. About two weeks later, thin or transplant them to permanent positions.

- **Set out plants** from indoors after the danger of frost passes, after hardening them off in shade for a few days. Mix fertilizer into each planting hole.

- **Water** frequently. Do not let seedbeds dry out. Keep plants from wilting.

- **Fertilize** plants steadily, supplementing with liquid fertilizer in hot weather.

- **Pinch back** tips to encourage bushiness.

- **Pests and diseases** rarely are problems.

- **Mulch** soil with several inches of bark chips or other mulch to keep it evenly moist.

- **Remove** spent blooms or cut flowers for bouquets to prolong blooming.

Selected Species and Cultivars

Nicotiana alata. Cultivars of this popular garden plant include:

'Domino,' in a bright color range on stocky, floriferous 14-inch-tall plants; stays open all day;

'Grandiflora,' strongly perfumed for the night garden, a white-flowered form about 3 feet tall that needs plenty of space and fertilizer. Flowers may close during the day;

'Nicki' hybrid, which blooms for months in a wide color range; an outstanding 16-inch-tall bedding plant with blossoms that stay open all day; and

'Sensation,' an evening-scented type in all colors that stays open all day, growing 2½ feet tall.

N. langsdorffii. This bushy, 3- to 5-foot-tall plant has abundant sprays of greenish bell-shaped flowers, unusual in the border. Use it as an accent plant.

N. sylvestris. Flaring, very long, tubular white blooms appear in masses on well-branched plants 3 to 4 feet tall. With large velvety leaves, this species is outstanding in borders where there is room. It is sweetly scented.

NIGELLA

Botanical name: *Nigella* (Ranunculaceae)

These poetic-looking members of the buttercup family deserve their common name, love-in-a-mist. Each delicate flower is surrounded by a cloud of light green, lacy, finely divided leaflike bracts, on branched plants with fine foliage. Later, each blossom becomes a balloon-like green seedpod, 2 inches long, striped with purple or bronze. The pods of these hardy annuals are used in dried flower arrangements, while the fresh blossoms are at home in flower beds as well as flower arrangements. The small black seeds are said to have been used as a substitute for pepper.

PLANT TYPE: Hardy annual.

GROWING RANGE: All zones.

HARDINESS: Killed by heavy frost, thrives in moderate to hot weather.

PLANT HEIGHT: 8 inches to over 2 feet.

FLOWER COLOR: Deep or pastel shades of blue, red, purple, or white, with dark or green stigmata.

FLOWER FORM: Flat single or double flowers 1 to 1½ inches wide with prominent stamens.

SEASON OF BLOOM: Any time in warm weather.

SOIL: Average to rich, well drained.

PH: 6.5 to 7.5.

FERTILIZER: Well-rotted manure, all-purpose fertilizer.

WATER: Average conditions.

EXPOSURE: Full sun to light shade, more shade in the South.

SPACING: 8 to 15 inches.

PROPAGATION: Seed.

Method

- **Start seeds indoors** individually in small pots or 2 inches apart in flats filled with moist potting soil, about eight weeks before the last frost. Barely cover the tiny seeds with soil, water, and keep at 75°F until they germinate, in about a week. Afterward temperatures may be reduced to 60° or 70°F if you wish. Grow seedlings in a bright but shaded area or a few inches below a fluorescent light fixture. When they have four to six leaves, step them up to larger pots if necessary.

- **Prepare soil outdoors** before planting by tilling in fertilizer, compost, and other soil improvers, as needed.

- **Sow seeds outdoors** at the time of the last expected frost or a week or two earlier. Plant in November or December in Zones 10 and 11. In smoothly prepared and fertilized beds, plant seeds 2 inches or more apart. Press them into the soil, covering them ⅛ inch deep. Do not let the seedbed dry out.

- **Thin seedlings** when they are crowded. With care, thinnings may be transplanted.

- **Set plants outdoors** after all danger of frost has passed, after hardening them off in shade for a few days.

- **Water** whenever soil becomes dry.

- **Fertilize** lightly at planting time and periodically during active growth with all-purpose fertilizer.

- **Pests and diseases** seldom are problems.

- **Mulch** plants in dry areas with several inches of small bark chips or other mulch to keep soil moist.

- **Pinch back** tips for bushier plants.

- **Deadhead** to remove spent flowers to prolong bloom, unless seeds or seedpods are wanted.

Selected Species and Cultivars

Nigella damascena (Love-in-a-mist). Each 1½-inch flower is surrounded by threadlike bracts. Seeds in current catalogs are sometimes sold by individual color, or under these names:

'Dwarf Moody Blue,' 6 to 8 inches tall, with changeable blue flowers on neat compact plants good for edgings and rock gardens. 'Blue Midget' is similar;

'Miss Jekyll,' with rich blue flowers among lacy leaves on strong, 18-inch-tall plants;

'Miss Jekyll Alba,' with white flowers;

'Persian Jewels,' with a full color range and large seedpods, growing on 15-inch-tall plants; and

'Red Jewel," with rose-red flowers on 15-inch-tall plants.

N. hispanica. Grown for its large, dark or medium blue single flowers with red stigmata.

N. sativa (Fennel flower). This 1-foot-tall, branching plant is grown for its blue flowers or as an herb—the small black seeds are used for seasoning. The arrow-shaped leaves are not divided or lacy like the other types.

ORNAMENTAL KALE

Botanical name: *Brassica oleracea* (Cruciferae)

This colorful cabbage cousin is most often used to enliven flower beds in fall, after most flowering annuals have declined. Very easy to grow, ornamental kale, a hardy biennial, has leaves that make great garnishes, though their flavor is not as sweet as nonornamental cultivars.

PLANT TYPE: Biennial, grown as an annual.
GROWING RANGE: Zones 2 to 8.
HARDINESS: Tolerates frost but not severe hard freezes.
PLANT HEIGHT: 8 to 15 inches.
FLOWER COLOR: Creamy white on green, rose-red on green.
FLOWER FORM: Grown exclusively for colorful curled foliage.
SEASON OF BLOOM: Inner leaves change from green to red or white when temperatures drop below 55°F.
SOIL: Any good garden soil of moderate fertility.
PH: 5.5 to 7.
FERTILIZER: Add a shovelful of well-rotted manure or compost to each planting hole. Provide a liquid fertilizer in early fall, when plants begin to grow vigorously.
WATER: Average. Water whenever soil becomes dry.
EXPOSURE: Full sun.
SPACING: 12 to 20 inches.
PROPAGATION: Seed.

Method

- **Start seeds indoors** in hot climates from midsummer to late summer. Plant seeds an inch or two apart in a flat and barely cover with soil. Keep moist. After germination, thin seedlings to 3 inches apart. Place in direct sunlight or under fluorescent lights. In cooler climates, it is better to start seeds outdoors.

- **Prepare soil outdoors** by cultivating the site until it is loose and friable. Add compost or well-rotted manure to the planting site, and mix in well.

- **Sow seeds outdoors** in the prepared site in late spring or in summer. Keep moist until seedlings emerge. In Zones 8 to 11, ornamental kale may also be sown in late winter for spring color. Seeds will take four to five months to grow to a mature plant.

- **Thin** seedlings to permanent spacing before they develop into round rosettes. Dwarf varieties may be grown closer together than nondwarfs. Space so the leaves will barely touch when the plants reach mature size.

- **Set plants outdoors** when they have four true leaves. Plant about ¼ inch deeper than they grew in the flat.

- **Water** after transplanting, and once a week during dry spells.

- **Mulch** with a 2-inch layer of chopped leaves, bark, or other mulch material.

- **Fertilize** planting holes with compost or manure, and follow up by drenching the roots with a liquid fertilizer like fish emulsion or manure tea when the plants form small rosettes, usually about a month after transplanting.

- **Pests** include aphids, which sometimes congregate on the leaves in late fall, and cabbage loopers. Spray with soapy water or an insecticidal soap to get them under control. **Diseases** are uncommon.

- **Winter protection** is beneficial in Zone 7, where the plants survive winter if surrounded with a thick, 6-inch-deep mulch.

Tips · Use the colorful leaves to garnish salads, dips, and other cold dishes.
· Plant ornamental kale in beds previously occupied by summer annuals. In areas where this plant is cold hardy, it can be planted in combination with pansies.

Selected Cultivars

New hybrids include 'Frizzy,' with deeply curled leaves, and 'Peacock,' with purplish-green outer leaves and large centers of finely divided white or red leaves. Both are available in individual colors or mixtures. Large open-pollinated varieties are widely available.

PANSY

Botanical name: *Viola* (Violaceae)

The blossoms and leaves of pansies and their close relatives, violas, are unharmed by light frost, making them ideal spring flowers where weather is unpredictable, and reliable winter bedding plants in Zones 9 to 11. In mild climates they are perennial, but they are treated as biennials or annuals in most parts of the United States, for temperatures in summer, winter, or both are too extreme. The pansy varieties listed in catalogs as winter-flowering tend to be the hardiest to cold.

Pansies and their kin have many affectionate names such as heartsease, ladies' delight, and stepmothers' flower. Plants are used in edgings, massed in beds, in window boxes and containers, and in rock gardens. The flowers are edible and may be used in salads or as a garnish. For the greatest economy, you can buy bundles of bare-rooted pansy plants (usually twenty-five or a hundred per pack) rather than potted ones. They will take a few weeks longer to establish themselves in the garden, but stretch the budget enough to let you get all the plants you want. Many nurseries sell these (if you ask), including some of the mail-order houses.

PLANT TYPES: Perennial or biennial, often treated as an annual.
GROWING RANGE: All zones.
HARDINESS: Variably hardy depending on species, but preferring cool weather (30° to 70°F) to hot. Plants are killed by prolonged heat over 90°F.
PLANT HEIGHT: 3 to 12 inches.
FLOWER COLOR: White, yellow, black, brown, lavender, purple, many shades of blue, or pink, often gaudily marked with blotches and "whiskers" in a way that suggests animal faces.
FLOWER FORM: Flat, sometimes round, 5-petaled flowers from 1 to 5 inches wide with a family resemblance to violets.
SEASON OF BLOOM: All year in cool temperatures, but in most areas, in spring 6 weeks before to 6 weeks after the last frost.
SOIL: Rich, moist.
PH: 6 to 7.
FERTILIZER: Well-rotted manure, compost, flower fertilizer.
WATER: Average to moist conditions.
EXPOSURE: Full sun or partial shade, more shade in the South.
SPACING: 6 inches to 1 foot.
PROPAGATION: Seed, tip cuttings, or division.

Method

· **Start seeds indoors** in temperatures from 55° to 70°F at any time of year. Fill flats or six-packs with dampened seed starting medium, space seeds an inch or two apart and ⅛ inch deep, water, and grow plantlets in bright light but not hot sun. With care, seed can be pregerminated before planting by wrapping it in a moist paper towel and keeping it inside a plastic bag at room temperature for about a week. Plant immediately (you may need to pick up seeds with tweezers).

· **Prepare soil outdoors** before planting by tilling in soil improvers and fertilizer.

· **Sow seeds outdoors** in late spring or summer in northern and central states, in fall in Zones 9 to 11, an inch or two apart under ⅛ inch of soil. Sow in a cold frame during cold weather. Do not let the seedbed dry out. Germination time can be variable and slow.

· **Thin or transplant** seedlings, indoors or out, to prevent crowding.

· **Set plants outdoors** in permanent places during cool weather in spring or fall when they are about 3 inches tall. Harden them off in shade for several days before planting them.

· **Divide** crowded plants if you are lucky enough to have them when new growth begins in early spring, harming main stems as little as possible. Plant them 2 inches deeper than they grew and keep them moist until they are well established.

· **Take cuttings** 6 inches long from leafy stems of violas and Johnny-jump-ups in spring, and root them in shade in moist soil. This is more difficult to do with pansies.

· **Water** often to prevent soil from becoming dry. Water often during hot weather to keep plants cool.

· **Fertilize** lightly at planting time and throughout the growing season.

· **Pests and diseases** occasionally are a problem. Repel or kill slugs with wood ashes, slug and snail bait, or diatomaceous earth, or trap them in partly submerged pans of beer. Treat leaf spot and crown rot with fungicide.

· **Remove** spent flowers and trim back main stems when they become leggy in hot weather.

· **Mulch** plants 2 or 3 inches deep with straw or leaf mulch to keep soil cool and damp in hot weather.

· **Protect in winter** with 2 inches of mulch such as fallen leaves around plants. Pull mulch back in spring.

Selected Species and Cultivars

Viola cornuta (Horned violet). From Spain and the Pyrenees, violas are increasingly popular for their ability to withstand more heat and cold than pansies. They come in all the pansy colors in sizes from 1 inch to nearly 3 inches across. Flowers are often solid colored, but also are blotched, shaded, or whiskered in pleasing ways. It is fun to see results from mixtures. Some named types that are easily grown from seed are:

'Bambini,' with pansylike faces 2 inches wide in a mixed rainbow of colors from cream to purple. Heights vary. Many are attractively whiskered; all are easy to grow and exceptionally weather tolerant. Since this type is open pollinated you get more seeds per pack. 'Monarch' is similar;

'Cuty,' with two purple petals above three white ones, the lowest one marked with a purple blotch. Flowers are about 2 inches wide on 6-inch-tall hardy plants;

'Princess Blue,' with 1-inch rich violet-blue flowers on compact 6-inch-tall plants. This type blooms in ten weeks from seed; and

'Yellow Charm,' with showy masses of 1½-inch flat, upturned blossoms on compact 6-inch-tall plants.

V. tricolor (Johnny-jump-up, Field pansy). Violetlike 1-inch flowers are vividly colored, with many of the most common ones a perky combination of gold and purple. This cheerful flower self-sows in gardens old and new. Some types are nearly or truly black—unexpectedly charming near the chartreuse flowers or leaves of other plants.

V. x *wittrockiana.* The indispensable garden pansy in its many sizes and forms is probably a hybrid of *V. tricolor, V. lutea,* and *V. altaica.* It is usually grown as a biennial—many gardeners purchase flowering plants from nurseries each spring. Named cultivars such as these have flowers from 2 to 5 inches across:

'Crystal Bowl,' violalike pansies 2½ inches wide in clear, unmarked color including blue, red, white, yellow, and rose;

'Floral Dance,' a hardy, winter-flowering mixture in red, purple, white, or yellow with black blotches;

'Majestic Giants,' with flashy 4-inch flowers with large blotches in a wide range of colors on heat-tolerant plants;

'Orange Prince,' with mahogany blotches on apricot faces;

'Rippling Waters,' with large royal purple flowers edged with a line of white; and

'Universal' series, an early-flowering multiflora strain with resistance to cold and heat, in many colors and patterns.

PELARGONIUM

Botanical Name: *Pelargonium* (Geraniaceae)
Common name: Garden geranium

The well-known garden geranium, most species of which are native to South Africa, is a favorite for window boxes and sunny beds since the bold flowers appear all summer with good care. These tender annuals often continue to flower when brought indoors for the winter. Scented geraniums are herbs grown for their fragrant leaves.

PLANT TYPE: Tender annual.
GROWING RANGE: All zones.
HARDINESS: Cannot tolerate frost.
PLANT HEIGHT: 8 to 30 inches.
FLOWER COLOR: Red, white, pink, salmon, or lavender, sometimes bicolored.
FLOWER FORM: Mostly double flowers in clusters.
SEASON OF BLOOM: Early summer to frost, all winter indoors.
SOIL: Any well-drained garden soil of average fertility.
PH: 6 to 7.
FERTILIZER: For pot-grown geraniums, a weak solution of liquid plant fertilizer. In outdoor beds, a fish emulsion.

WATER: Below average.
EXPOSURE: Full sun to partial shade.
SPACING: 12 inches for bedding plants, closer if used in containers.
PROPAGATION: Seed or stem cuttings.

Method

- **Start seeds indoors** six to eight weeks before the last spring frost. Plant them 1 or 2 inches apart, ⅛ inch deep in flats or small pots. Use a sterile potting mix and keep in a warm (70°F) place until the seeds germinate. Then, move to a sunny windowsill, or place the seedlings under fluorescent lights. Transplant seedlings to small individual pots when seedlings have two true leaves.

- **Take cuttings** 3 to 4 inches long from plants that have overwintered indoors in early spring. Plant the cuttings 1 inch deep in a sterile potting mix. Development of roots takes three to four weeks.

- **Prepare soil outdoors** by adding organic matter to clay soils, or peat moss to loose sand. Where verticillium wilt (see "pests and diseases") is common, grow pelargoniums in containers, using a sterile potting mixture.

- **Set out plants** after all danger of frost is past and the soil is warm, after hardening off those grown indoors. Potted geraniums, including the types with scented leaves, may be placed in beds and borders by burying the pots so that ½ inch of the container shows above the soil line.

- **Water** young plants immediately after planting, and keep moist (but not wet) for two to three weeks. Later, drier soil is tolerated. When growing in containers or hanging baskets, water before the soil becomes extremely dry, but avoid frequent heavy soakings.

- **Fertilize** with a weak liquid fertilizer solution immediately after planting, and about once a month during the summer. Increase the strength of the solution if new leaves become yellow. Fertilize pot-grown plants every two weeks, except for a two-month "rest period" in early winter.

- **Pests and diseases** include verticillium wilt, a soil-borne fungus that results in weak, yellowing leaves and overall lack of vigor. Where this disease is common, grow plants in containers. Bedding geraniums are sometimes bothered by leaf-eating caterpillars, which may be controlled with a *Bacillus thuringiensis* insecticide.

- **Winter protection** consists of potting up plants and bringing them indoors. When kept on a sunny windowsill, the plants often bloom during the winter. Or you can keep them in a cool, low-light environment (like the basement) and allow them to become semidormant. Prune back half of the tops and allow the roots to become rather dry, and water sparingly every few weeks. In early spring, bring the plants into good light, provide water and fertilizer, and use them as "donors" of rootable cuttings.

Tip · In hot climates, bring baskets of ivy-leaf geranium and other container-grown plants indoors where they can benefit from air-conditioning during hot, dry periods in the summer.

Selected Species and Cultivars

Pelargonium domesticum (Martha Washington geranium, Regal geranium) includes the fancy geraniums sold by florists. They are seldom planted outdoors, doing best in cool climates. They are propagated exclusively by stem cuttings.

P. hortorum hybrids include most cultivars used as bedding plants, including 'Bandit,' 'Orbit,' 'Elite,' 'Sprinter,' and 'Pinto.' These geraniums can be grown from seed or from stem cuttings. Colors include red, white, orchid, salmon, and pink.

P. peltatum (Ivy geranium) is ideal for hanging baskets. The leading variety, 'Summer Showers,' can be grown from seed, but propagation is faster when stem cuttings are rooted. Colors include red, pink, purple, and white.

Scented-leaf geraniums include several species, all of which are propagated by rooted cuttings. (See pages 446–48 for a more extensive discussion.)

PENSTEMON

Botanical name: *Penstemon* (Scrophulariaceae)
Other common name: Beard tongue

Native primarily to western states, *Penstemon* comprises hundreds of species of half-hardy annuals and perennials. Their preferred growing conditions vary greatly, with some types liking moisture and others drought. As a group, they have a reputation for being difficult to grow—the location must be just right, and because there are so many types, this is a challenge. They are especially difficult in the Northeast because just about all types are easily killed by wet winter soil. This can be guarded against by digging in several shovelfuls of sand for each plant. Some penstemons are low and matted, and others send up tall flowering stems from neat basal rosettes, much like foxgloves. The perennials become more floriferous with age, so, once established, they are very rewarding. Tall types are good as cut flowers and for bedding. The dwarf shrubby evergreen types are good for rock gardens and ground covers. Usually the low ones are happy in a well-drained, rocky soil, in a bright place but with protection from some of the full intensity of the sun.

PLANT TYPES: Half-hardy annual or perennial.
GROWING RANGE: All zones as an annual, Zones 3 to 9 as a perennial, varying with the species.
HARDINESS: Cold and heat tolerance varies greatly with the species.
PLANT HEIGHT: 2 inches to 6 feet, varying with the species.
FLOWER COLOR: Purple, scarlet, blue, rose, orange, pink, lavender, white.
FLOWER FORM: Spires or plumes of showy tubular flowers, usually hooded.

SEASON OF BLOOM: Summer into fall (earlier in the South).
SOIL: Average, very well drained. Slopes are ideal.
PH: Near 7 (neutral).
FERTILIZER: Well-rotted manure, all-purpose or high-phosphorus fertilizer.
WATER: Average to dry conditions.
EXPOSURE: Full sun to partial shade, depending on the species.
SPACING: 1 to 3 feet.
PROPAGATION: Usually from seed, also by tip and stem cuttings or division.

Method

- **Start seeds indoors,** one or two seeds per small pots filled with moist potting soil, covering ⅛ inch deep, usually in winter to early spring. Freeze seeds of perennials in an airtight container for four weeks before planting them. Water and keep at 55° to 65°F until seeds germinate, usually in eighteen to thirty-six days. Keep seedlings in a sunny area or a few inches below a fluorescent light fixture. When plants are 4 to 6 inches tall, harden them off and move outdoors or shift them to larger pots if they are crowded.

- **Prepare soil outdoors** before planting by tilling in fertilizer, compost, lime, sand, and other soil improvers, if needed.

- **Sow seeds outdoors** in nursery beds in fall or before the last frost in early spring, ⅛ inch deep and about 3 inches apart. Do not let seeds or seedlings dry out.

- **Thin or transplant seedlings** grown outdoors to their permanent spacing when they are about 4 inches tall. They are not difficult to transplant at this stage.

- **Set plants outdoors** in spring, after all danger of frost has passed. Harden them off in shade for several days before planting them in permanent places.

- **Take cuttings** 4 to 6 inches long in summer to propagate the best-formed perennial plants. Root them in shade in sand mixed with peat. Keep them in the cold frame through the winter and plant them outdoors in spring.

- **Divide** established perennial plants into two new clumps if they are overcrowded, in spring when new growth begins.

- **Water** newly established or young plants whenever the soil starts to dry out and when they wilt during hot weather. Mature plants need less water, although tall types tend to like water in the summer. Types with gray, hairy, or tiny leaves need little water. Keep all penstemons on the dry side in winter.

- **Fertilize** lightly at planting time and during active growth.

- **Pests and diseases** seldom are problems.

- **Mulch** tall plants in dry weather with 2 inches of bark chips or other mulch.

- **Shear off** spent blossoms for neatness and to keep plants vigorous.

- **Stake** with slim sticks if plants show need for support.

· **Protect in winter** by mulching around crowns with 3 inches of a lightweight, airy mulch, such as salt hay. Pull back the mulch after all danger of frost passes so new leaves can come up.

Selected Species

All those listed here are classed as perennials, though some (those that don't carry hardiness ranges), are grown as annuals because they are not reliably hardy.

Penstemon acaulis. Plants are only 2 inches tall with blue flowers and tiny green leaves. This type is good for rock gardens or rocky places.

P. albertinus. Plants stay low, usually 6 to 8 inches tall, with small leaves and light blue flowers.

P. alpinus. This strong perennial for Zones 5 to 9 with thick, glaucous leaves bears blue-purple flowers in summer on stems up to 3 feet tall.

P. angustifolius (Pagoda penstemon). This type has sky blue flowers on 1-foot-tall stems and tolerates widely varying conditions in Zones 3 to 9.

P. aridus. Drought tolerant, this species grows 4 to 6 inches tall with grayish-green leaves and bluish-purple flowers.

P. barbatus (Scarlet bugler). This popular 2- to 6-foot-tall perennial variety for Zones 5 to 9 stays low until it blooms on tall stems in summer. Flowers are white, pink, purple, or red, with many named cultivars on the market.

P. barrettiae. With 1-foot-long leathery leaves, this branched species bears large lilac-purple flowers. It is native to Oregon and prefers a mild climate, not too hot or cold.

P. caespitosus. Petite and thymelike, this mat-forming type has clusters of violet flowers. It does not tolerate high heat.

P. cardinalis (Cardinal penstemon). The many deep, rich, red, summer-blooming tubular flowers borne on 3-foot-tall stems make this a winning garden flower.

P. cardwelli. This type grows about 10 inches tall with dark toothed leaves and large purple flowers in summer. It grows in the cool, mild parts of the West Coast.

P. cyananthus (Wasatch penstemon). The 1-inch tubular flowers of rich blue bloom for months from spring to summer on 3-foot-tall stems in sun or partial shade.

P. digitalis (Foxglove beard tongue). This plant resembles its namesake with spires of bell-like white flowers up to 5 feet tall, and grows in Zones 4 to 9.

P. gentianoides. With 2½-foot-tall upright stems and lance-shaped leaves, this penstemon produces large tubular flowers of rose, red, lavender, or white in summer. It grows in Zones 7 to 9.

P. hallii. A petite form from Colorado, this grows 6 to 8 inches tall with narrow green leaves and violet flowers.

P. heterophyllus (Royal penstemon). The 2-foot-long gray-green foliage bears exquisite deep blue-purple flowers in summer. Perennial in Zones 5 to 9, it is evergreen in the southern part of its range.

P. hirsutus 'Pygmaeus.' Toothed gray-green foliage with hairy stems bears light blue flowers in summer. Plants are 3 feet tall and grow in Zones 3 to 7.

P. montanus. With gray leaves, this drought-tolerant type is 8 to 10 inches tall with large lilac flowers. It grows wild in Wyoming, Idaho, and Montana.

P. pinifolius. With needlelike leaves on 1-foot-tall plants, this species bears narrow scarlet flowers all summer and is hardy in Zones 4 to 8.

PEONY

Botanical name: *Paeonia* (Paeoniaceae)

Peonies are hardy, long-lived perennials from China that bloom once a year with magnificently showy blooms. They are a popular subject in ancient and modern Chinese, Korean, and Japanese art. In Western countries, they have been grown for several hundred years, at least. Undisturbed clumps known to date from eighty or a hundred years ago are not rare, and their fragrant flowers are as gorgeous as ever.

Choose early-, midseason-, and late-blooming varieties for six or more weeks of continuous bloom. The long-stemmed flowers are unsurpassed in bouquets. Use peonies in flower borders, as shrublike accent plants, and in the cutting garden.

Most peonies have foliage that dies back to "eyes," or underground buds, in the fall and reappears in spring as fleshy red shoots. These shoots must be protected from breakage and heavy frost. They get stronger as they turn green and leaf out. The large lobed leaves on the unbranched stems last many months and turn an attractive crimson in the autumn. There are also hardy shrubs, called tree peonies, which are related but have woody stems and branches. Tree peonies may be yellow or orange in addition to the usual peony colors.

PLANT TYPE: Hardy perennial.
GROWING RANGE: Zones 4 to 8.
HARDINESS: Withstands heat and cold, requires chilling in winter.
PLANT HEIGHT: 1 to over 3 feet.
FLOWER COLOR: White, cream, pink, rosy red, or magenta, sometimes bicolored.
FLOWER FORM: Rose- or camellialike single or double flowers from 3 to 6 inches wide
    on long stems with bushy green foliage.
SEASON OF BLOOM: Spring or early summer—May into June in most of the range.
SOIL: Preferably rich and loamy, but tolerant of all types.
PH: 6.5 to 7.5
FERTILIZER: Well-rotted manure, all-purpose or high-phosphorus fertilizer.
WATER: Average conditions.
EXPOSURE: Nearly full sun in Zone 6 and northward, bright, dappled shade in Zones
    7 and 8.
SPACING: 2 to 3 feet.
PROPAGATION: Usually by division, sometimes from seed.

🌱 *Method*

- **Start seeds indoors** after prechilling for four to eight weeks in the freezer to break dormancy. Plant four to six weeks before the last expected frost in small pots or six-packs filled with moist potting soil, covering 1/4 inch deep. Water and keep at 60° to 70°F until seeds germinate, which may take many weeks. (If they do not germinate the first year, move them outdoors to a shady location and keep them there for another year.) Grow indoor seedlings in a sunny area or a few inches below a fluorescent light fixture. When they are 4 inches tall, move them outdoors (either into gallon containers or beds), after the last frost and after hardening them off for several days. It may take five years for seed-grown plants to bloom.

- **Prepare soil outdoors** before planting by tilling in fertilizer, compost, and other soil improvers, as needed.

- **Sow seeds outdoors** in nursery beds in summer. Mark them well, for seedlings probably will not appear until the following year, or later. Plant them 3 inches apart, ¼ inch deep.

- **Thin or transplant seedlings** grown outdoors to their permanent spacing in their second or third year, in midspring.

- **Set plants outdoors** (from divisions or dormant roots) in early spring or in fall—fall is best in Zone 6 and above. Dormant roots are planted with the eyes facing upward, covered with 1 inch of soil in Zones 7 and 8 but with 2 inches in Zones 4 to 6. Plant divisions at the same depth at which they grew. Pot-grown plants may be set in place at any time of year, at the same depth at which they grew. It may take a year or two for new plants to become strongly established.

- **Divide** established plants if they are crowded on an overcast day when summer ends. Plants do not appreciate being disturbed, but it is possible to divide them safely. First, prepare planting holes about 2 feet deep and 2 feet wide, where divisions will grow. Enrich the soil for filling the holes with composted manure, compost, a handful of bonemeal for each plant, and peat moss. Put a layer of improved soil nearly a foot deep back into each hole. Divide plants with a straight-sided spade, cleanly and deeply slicing straight down through the center of the old clump, with at least three eyes on each side. Carefully lift the two divisions out, and cut off and discard any rotted or jagged edges. Replant the divisions so that the eyes are 2 inches below the top level of the soil—if you plant them too deep, they will not bloom the next year. Firm the soil around the plants and cover with 2 or 3 inches of mulch for the winter.

- **Water** plants whenever the soil starts to dry out.

- **Fertilize** lightly at planting time and each year in early spring. Boost blossoms by applying a low-nitrogen, high-phosphorus and -potassium fertilizer when plants have red shoots about 4 inches tall. Fertilize again lightly after plants flower.

- **Pests and diseases** seldom are problems. Destroy foliage in late fall to prevent its carrying the start of disease into the next year. If blight (sooty fungus on leaves and buds) is a problem, discard affected portions of the plant as well as the top inch of soil, replacing it with freshly limed topsoil.

- **Mulch** plants in dry weather with several inches of bark chips, salt hay, shredded leaves, or other mulch.

- **Do not pinch back** tips for bushiness or you will lose the flowers. Disbud (remove side buds near a central bud) for largest flowers if you wish, before buds are ½ inch wide.

- **Remove** spent blossoms unless seed is wanted.

- **Stake** plants by letting the shoots grow through peony hoops. In full sun, plants are less likely to need staking.

- **Protect in winter** with several inches of mulch. Pull back the mulch after the danger of heavy frost so shoots can come up.

Tip · Caution: Peony roots sold in soilless cardboard packages sometimes sprout and die in storage, so be sure to look for healthy sprouts or eyes before you buy them, and plant them right away.

Selected Species and Cultivars

Paeonia lactiflora (Chinese peony). This is the popular spring-blooming garden peony, found in many lovely cultivars. Local garden centers and mail-order perennial plant specialists will have these or others:

'Bowl of Beauty,' with huge single pink flowers and a large center of golden stamens, on large, 40-inch-tall plants;

'Edulis Superba,' with early-blooming, fragrant, wide pink blooms with paler pink central tufts;

'Festiva Maxima,' with huge double white blooms with crimson marks in the center—grown for over a hundred years, early blooming;

'Kansas,' with large double red flowers in midseason;

'Karl Rosenfield,' with large deep crimson blooms in midseason or a little later;

'Lady Alexandra Duff,' a semidouble with pale pink petals and prominent golden stamens, blooming early to midseason; and

'Sarah Bernhardt,' a classic flower with large peachy pink petals in midseason.

P. tenuifolia (Fernleaf peony). This plant is similar to the Chinese peony but has lacy, ferny, deeply divided foliage, usually with 3-inch single pink or red blossoms in lovely proportion to the plant. Usually 2 feet tall, it is small enough to use in rock gardens. There are larger doubles, too. This species grows from an underground creeping rhizome and should be marked carefully.

PETUNIA

Botanical name: *Petunia* x *hybrida* (Solanaceae)

As seen everywhere, petunias, originally from Argentina, are long-blooming, brilliantly colored, funnel-shaped flowers with many uses: bedding, hanging baskets, containers, and cutting. Some plants grow upright, others are trailing. Plants flower attractively for more months than most annuals. Leaves are fuzzy, sometimes slightly sticky—this helps repel pests. Petunias are a good winter bedding plant in Zones 9 and 10, for they withstand light frost; only a heavy frost kills them. They are good patio accents in containers—the deeper the pot, the better the plants will do. Eight-inch terra-cotta containers are recommended. Flowers will not form when nighttime temperatures remain over 85°F for an extended period. Most gardeners purchase greenhouse-grown plants in bloom because it takes about three months to grow petunias from seed. For best results, buy strong, young green plants that have been watered steadily and are not pot-bound. There should be many buds but few opened flowers. For outdoor bedding, single flowers are more weatherproof than heavy doubles. Trailing types are best for hanging baskets or tall containers.

PLANT TYPE: Tender annual.

GROWING RANGE: All zones.

HARDINESS: Hardy from about 30° to over 90°F.

PLANT HEIGHT: 1 to 2½ feet.

FLOWER COLOR: White, purple, red, pale yellow, lavender, deep rose, blue. Some are bicolors with contrasting dark veins, splotches, or stars of white.

FLOWER FORM: Tubular, flaring flowers 2 to 5 inches wide, often ruffled or double.

SEASON OF BLOOM: Summer in most regions, all year in frost-free but mild areas, winter and spring in hot parts of Zones 9 to 11.

SOIL: Any good garden soil high in organic matter.

PH: 6 to 7.

FERTILIZER: Timed-release and organic fertilizer, supplemented with liquid fertilizers in hot weather.

WATER: Keep soil somewhat moist at all times.

EXPOSURE: Full sun or light shade. More sun needed north of Zone 7.

SPACING: 1 foot, less in containers.

PROPAGATION: Usually from seed, also by tip cuttings.

Method

· **Start seeds indoors** ten to twelve weeks before the last frost. Plants sown about Christmastime will start to bloom around Eastertime. In Zones 9 to 11, also start seeds indoors in August or September for winter bedding plants. Grow in flats, small pots, or six-packs in damp potting soil. Keep them in a moderately warm (60° to 75°F) place in bright sunlight or a few inches below a fluorescent light fixture. Try to give twelve hours of light per day.

· **Prepare soil outdoors** in beds before planting by tilling in fertilizer, peat moss, compost, and other soil improvers, as needed.

· **Sow seeds outdoors** after the danger of frost has passed, if the climate is mild and the growing season is long; otherwise, you're better off starting seeds indoors. In smoothly prepared and fertilized beds, make rows about 2 inches deep. Mix seed with a few spoonfuls of dry sand and plant sparsely, without covering, and water.

· **Thin or transplant** seedlings whenever they are crowded. Indoors, step up tiny seedlings to individual six-pack pockets or small pots. When they become crowded again, step them up to larger pots or plant them outdoors. Outdoors, thin and transplant when seedlings are about 3 or 4 inches high, to 6 inches apart in nursery rows or to their places in the garden.

· **Set out plants** from indoors as soon as the danger of frost passes, when temperatures stabilize around 55°F. Harden off plants grown indoors before planting them.

· **Take cuttings** about 5 inches long and root them, covered 3 inches deep in moist soil, in a humid, shady area kept at 60° to 80°F for several weeks.

· **Water** frequently if needed; never let soil dry out completely. During unremitting hot weather above 90°F, refresh plants at midday with a spray of cool water.

- **Fertilize** lightly at planting time. Boost blossoms by applying a low-nitrogen, high-phosphorus fertilizer when plants start to form buds. As plants get large and weather gets hot, supplement their feeding with liquid fertilizer.

- **Mulch** plants with bark chips or other mulch several inches thick to keep soil moist and cool.

- **Pinch back** tips to encourage bushiness.

- **Pests and diseases** rarely are problems.

- **Deadhead** plants or pick flowers for bouquets to prolong blooming.

Selected Species and Cultivars

Garden petunias have been hybridized into innumerable forms, taking up several pages in popular seed catalogs. The three basic types are floribunda, grandiflora, and multiflora. In all types, the flowers are available in a wide range of colors and patterns.

Floribunda. Faster to come into bloom from seed than grandifloras or multifloras, this type offers plentiful single flowers in the usual array of colors and patterns on plants about 12 inches high. New strains such as 'Celebrity' have 3 1/2-inch-wide flowers and bloom in just forty-three days from seed.

Grandiflora types have the largest flowers. These are vigorous plants with single or double flowers 3 to 4 1/2 inches wide, on plants about 12 inches high. Some cultivars are upright, and others cascade. Most of these need ten to twelve weeks to develop from seed to bloom.

Multiflora types have many flowers of smaller size, 2 to 2 1/2 inches wide. There are singles and doubles in a wide range of colors. They make a long-lasting, everblooming, fairly weatherproof display on 1-foot-tall plants, which should be pinched back occasionally for bushiness. Blooms usually appear in eight to ten weeks from seed.

PHLOX

Botanical name: *Phlox* (Polemoniaceae)

The flowers of all the phlox have a strong family resemblance, but the plants vary from low creeping varieties to stiff tall ones. None need staking and all are easy to care for. The tall types have the drawback of being prone to mildew, although there are resistant cultivars. There are about fifty species, most native to North America but some to Asia. Phlox may be used in borders, as ground covers, for naturalizing, and as cut flowers.

PLANT TYPES: Hardy annual or perennial.
GROWING RANGE: All zones as an annual, Zones 4 to 9 as a perennial.
HARDINESS: Very hardy in cold and heat.
PLANT HEIGHT: 3 inches to 4 feet.
FLOWER COLOR: White, rose, salmon, lilac, magenta, purple, blue, or yellow, differing by species; some with deeper-colored eye.
FLOWER FORM: Compact, showy heads composed of tubular flowers opening out to flat circles about 1 inch wide.

SEASON OF BLOOM: Several months in spring and summer in the North, spring in hot southern areas, any time in mild climates.

SOIL: Any garden soil, but better growth in rich soil.

PH: 6 to 7.5, depending on variety.

FERTILIZER: Well-rotted manure, compost, flower or all-purpose fertilizer, bonemeal.

WATER: Average conditions.

EXPOSURE: Full sun in most areas, light shade in the South, but partial shade for *Phlox divaricata* and *P. stolonifera* in all zones.

SPACING: 6 inches to 2 feet; 6 to 12 inches for *P. drummondii.*

PROPAGATION: Seed or division.

Method

- **Start seeds indoors** six weeks before the last frost. Grow in individual small pots or six-packs in moist potting soil, covering seed with barely ⅛ inch of soil. Water and keep at 60° to 70°F until the seeds germinate, about ten days. Grow in a sunny area or a few inches below a fluorescent light fixture. When seedlings have four to six leaves, step them up to larger pots if necessary.

- **Prepare soil outdoors** before planting by tilling in fertilizer, compost, bonemeal, and other soil improvers, as needed.

- **Sow seeds outdoors** where they will grow after the danger of frost has passed. Sow seeds of Drummond phlox (annual) in fall or early spring in Zones 9 and 10. In smoothly prepared and fertilized beds, plant seeds 4 or more inches apart and cover with ⅛ inch of soil. Do not let the seedbed dry out.

- **Thin and transplant** seedlings growing outdoors to their permanent spacing when they are about 4 inches tall. With care, thinnings may be transplanted. Indoors, thin seedlings and move them to larger pots if they are crowded.

- **Set plants outdoors** after the danger of frost has passed, after hardening them off in shade for a few days.

- **Divide** established perennial plants once a year if they are crowded in early spring when new growth begins. Keep annuals and perennials well thinned.

- **Water** often to prevent the soil from drying out, wetting the ground directly to keep leaves dry and prevent mildew.

- **Fertilize** lightly at planting time. Boost blossoms by applying a low-nitrogen, high-phosphorus and -potassium fertilizer when plants are 5 or 6 inches tall.

- **Pests and diseases** seldom are problems, other than mildew in tall types which is controlled by thinning plants for good air circulation. Do not plant perennial phlox next to damp walls.

- **Mulch** plants that grow in dry areas with several inches of bark chips or other mulch to keep soil cool and moist.

- **Remove** spent flowers or cut fresh flowers for bouquets. *P. paniculata, P. carolina,* and *P. drummondii* will grow a second or third crop of flowers if the season is long enough.

- **Protect in winter** by mulching crowns and removing dead stems of tall types. Mat-forming phlox needs no protection.

Selected Species and Cultivars

Phlox carolina (Thick-leaf phlox). For Zones 3 to 9, these hardy, 3-foot-tall, clump-forming plants have sturdy stems and are especially resistant to mildew. This type flowers in midsummer, a few months earlier than *P. paniculata,* and has narrower clusters of flowers. They are graceful plants in the garden, blossoming in white, lilac, or shades of rose. The popularity of an excellent white cultivar, 'Miss Lingard,' has continued for over eighty years.

P. divaricata (Blue phlox, Woodland phlox, Wild sweet William). This spreading low perennial is best used as a ground cover, on slopes, in woodland gardens, and in the front of the border. It grows in light shade in Zones 3 to 9, and is well adapted to the filtered shade below leafy trees. It is an excellent plant for humid northern and central regions with a slightly acid soil. Its foliage makes a dense, stemmy mat. In spring, about tulip time, upright flowers bloom on top of slim stalks about 8 inches tall. It can be found in several shades of blue—one of the best is the intense true blue, 'Laphamii.' Whites are available, too, for instance, 'Fuller's White.' The native strain is pale blue.

P. drummondii (Drummond phlox). A native annual that grows as a biennial in southern and western states, this type often carpets fields for as far as the eye can see. It prefers a pH near 7, neutral, or even higher (more alkaline). It is always grown from seed. In northern and central states, this will bloom all summer. Domesticated cultivars come in all the phlox colors, including yellow. Some of the many good types are 'Twinkle,' with star-shaped blossoms; 'Dwarf Beauty,' on bushy 6-inch-tall plants; 'Cecily,' 8 inches tall and heat tolerant; and 'Tall Finest,' 14-inch-tall plants with large heads in brilliant colors. Some suppliers sell seeds separated by color, others do not.

P. paniculata, synonym *P. decussata,* hybrids (Summer phlox, Garden phlox). These are tall garden phlox of very robust constitution, hardy in Zones 3 to 9. They spread rapidly, so plant them 2 feet apart and thin them often. They bloom profusely late in summer.

Gardeners are often warned against allowing self-sown seedlings of this type of phlox to grow because they will tend to be "ugly magenta"—this is true for dark shades, but if you have only whites, you will get more whites and possibly some other shades from bee-carried pollen. After a few plant generations, offspring will tend to darken, but by then you will have added some nice perennial plants to your collection.

Some especially fine plants include cultivars of the Symons-Jeune strain developed in England for huge flower panicles on strong stems in clear colors. Resistant to mildew and other fungus diseases, the category includes 'Bright Eyes,' pale pink with crimson eyes; 'Blue Lagoon,' with immense lavender-blue heads of flowers on stems over 3 feet tall; 'Dramatic,' a clear, solid salmon-pink; and 'Everest,' snowy white with a rosy eye.

Other strains come in rose, lavender, fuchsia, salmon, and pure white.

P. stolonifera (Creeping phlox). In bloom and cultural requirements, this resembles *P. divaricata,* but has a more spreading, less dense pattern of growth. It increases rapidly, and because it is so lovely, this is rarely a problem. It combines well with spring bulbs and blooms with the daffodils, pansies, violas, and early tulips. 'Sherwood Purple' is very deeply colored; 'Blue Ridge' has large sky blue flowers; 'Pink Ridge' is similar in pale pink; and 'Osborne's White' is true white.

P. subulata (Moss pink, Moss phlox). This commonly used ground cover bursts into a carpet of bloom each spring in Zones 3 to 9 at about azalea time. The dense, leafy mats can flare into some fairly startling shades of cerise and fuchsia, so if you prefer pastels, select nursery plants while they are in bloom. This phlox is available in shades ranging from pure white to deepest red, including blues and violets. The cultivar 'Pink Surprise' often repeats its bloom in the fall—that is the surprise.

POPPY

Botanical name: *Papaver* (Papaveraceae)

Poppy flowers are cup-shaped and have a fine texture, almost like crinkled crepe paper. The flowering stems grow from a mound of divided foliage and provide gay color that moves with the breeze. Poppies are best grown in mixed borders, meadows, or rock gardens, and also make good cut flowers.

PLANT TYPES: Hardy annual or perennial.
GROWING RANGE: Zones 2 to 9.
HARDINESS: Resistant to cold, not tolerant of excessive heat.
PLANT HEIGHT: 5 inches to 4 feet.
FLOWER COLOR: White, yellow, pink, red, orange, salmon, purple.
FLOWER FORM: Single or double, cup-shaped, 2 to 4 inches across.
SEASON OF BLOOM: Spring or summer.
SOIL: Rich, with excellent drainage.
PH: 5.5 to 7.
FERTILIZER: Well-rotted manure, compost, or all-purpose fertilizer.
WATER: Dry conditions.
EXPOSURE: Full sun in most regions, partial shade in hot parts of Zones 8 and 9.
SPACING: 5 to 18 inches.
PROPAGATION: Seed or root cuttings.

Method

- **Start seeds indoors** in early spring (six to eight weeks before the last frost) for annual poppies and any time in spring through summer up to three months before the first fall frost for perennial poppies. Sow thinly in small pots filled with sterile seed starting medium. Press seeds into the soil but do not cover them with soil, and water. All except Oriental poppy seeds should be covered with black plastic until they germinate, as they need darkness. Keep in a cool (55°F) place until they germinate, ten to fifteen days. Grow seedlings in bright sunlight or a few inches below a fluorescent light fixture. Thin seedlings to a 3- or 4-inch pot when they become crowded.

- **Prepare soil outdoors** before planting by tilling in fertilizer and compost or other organic soil improvers, as needed.

- **Sow seeds outdoors** for both annuals and perennials in smoothly prepared and fertilized beds where plants are to grow in late fall or early spring. Plant seeds 6 inches apart and ⅛ inch deep. Seeds will germinate in spring. Water well after sowing, and do not let the seedbed dry out in spring until germination.

- **Thin** outdoor-grown seedlings to their permanent spacing when they are 3 to 4 inches high.

- **Set plants outdoors** in midspring. Transplant carefully as poppy seedlings do not like to have their roots disturbed.

- **Take cuttings** of perennial poppies in spring or summer after the plants have bloomed. Poppies can be divided, but root cuttings are more satisfactory because of their long roots.

- **Water** infrequently as poppies prefer dry soil.

- **Fertilize** lightly at planting time. Fertilize perennial poppies lightly in spring when growth starts.

- **Diseases** of the roots may develop if plants are overwatered. **Pests** are no serious problem.

- **Mulch** around growing plants with 2 inches of bark chips or shredded leaves to keep moisture in the soil and the soil cool.

- **Winter protect** perennial poppies in the colder limits of their hardiness with 3 to 5 inches of evergreen boughs or straw, or 2 inches of shredded leaves.

Tips • Annual poppies do not have a long blooming period, so sow seeds successively every two weeks for continual color.

• Oriental poppies lose their foliage in midsummer. They must be transplanted in early fall after the foliage starts to reappear. To fill in the blanks they leave when they go dormant in summer, plan on adding other annuals to where they grow.

• Keep faded flowers picked to prolong bloom.

• Plunge stems of poppies in hot water after cutting them to prolong their life as a cut flower.

Selected Species

Papavar alpinum (Alpine poppy). This perennial is hardy in Zones 5 to 9. It grows 5 to 10 inches high and has 1½-inch flowers of white, yellow, or pink that bloom in spring over blue-green leaves.

P. commutatum. This hardy annual grows 1½ feet tall and has 1½-inch flowers that are dark red with a black center, blooming in summer.

P. nudicaule (Iceland poppy). This perennial is hardy in Zones 2 to 9. It grows 12 to 24 inches high and has coarse, divided leaves at the base of the plant. The flowers are fragrant,

1 to 4 inches across, single or double, and white with yellow, red, orange, rose, or apricot markings. It blooms in spring. In Zones 8 to 11 it will die in summer heat.

P. orientale (Oriental poppy). This perennial is hardy in Zones 2 to 9. Leaves are coarse and deeply divided. Flowers are 3 inches across and bloom in early summer; they are white, orange, pink, red, or salmon with a black center. Plants grow to 4 feet high. The foliage disappears after the plant blooms and reappears in early fall.

P. rhoeas (Flanders poppy, Shirley poppy). A hardy annual that grows 2 to 3 feet tall, the Flanders poppy's flowers are 2 inches across and red, purple, white, pink, salmon, or orange, blooming in summer.

PORTULACA

Botanical name: *Portulaca* (Portulacaceae)

Two popular types of portulaca, moss rose and purslane, have succulent leaves and bright little flowers in neon colors. They open for a grand display for several hours each day, then usually close in midafternoon to late afternoon. Purslane has fat, oval leaves, and moss rose has fat, needle-shaped ones. The spreading matlike plants make good temporary ground covers or fillers for gaps in flower beds. They are also used in hanging baskets, rock gardens, and as edgings. They tolerate dry conditions and tend to self-sow.

PLANT TYPE: Tender annual.
GROWING RANGE: All zones.
HARDINESS: Killed by frost, thrives in heat.
PLANT HEIGHT: 6 to 8 inches.
FLOWER COLOR: White, yellow, orange, peach, pink, or red, sometimes striped.
FLOWER FORM: Small, roselike single or double flowers, usually about an inch wide.
SEASON OF BLOOM: Any time in warm weather.
SOIL: Any soil, well drained.
PH: 6.5 to 7.5.
FERTILIZER: Well-rotted manure, all-purpose fertilizer.
WATER: Average to dry conditions.
EXPOSURE: Full sun in most regions, sun or light shade in the South.
SPACING: 6 to 8 inches.
PROPAGATION: Seed, also tip cuttings for purslane.

Method

- **Start seeds indoors** in small pots or flats filled with moist potting soil, four to eight weeks before the last frost. Sowing thinly, barely cover tiny seeds with soil, water, and keep at 75°F until they germinate, in about a week. Grow seedlings in a bright but shaded area or a few inches below a fluorescent light fixture. When they have four to six leaves, step them up to larger pots if necessary.

- **Prepare soil outdoors** before planting by tilling it well and, if soil is exceptionally poor, adding fertilizer, compost, and other soil improvers, as needed.

- **Sow seeds outdoors** during warm weather. Plant seeds in November or December in Zones 10 and 11. In smoothly prepared nursery beds or where plants will grow, sow thinly. Press them into the soil, barely covering them. Do not let the seedbed dry out.

- **Thin** seedlings grown outdoors when they are crowded. With care, thinnings may be transplanted.

- **Set plants outdoors** after all danger of frost has passed, after hardening them off in shade for a few days.

- **Water** seedlings often to prevent the soil from drying out. Mature plants will tolerate drier soil.

- **Take cuttings** of purslane 4 inches long during warm weather. Remove bottom leaves and root cuttings 2 inches deep in shady, moist, sandy soil, or in a glass of water.

- **Fertilize** lightly at planting time. Fertilize periodically during active growth.

- **Pests and diseases** seldom are problems.

- **Mulch** plants in very dry areas with 2 inches of small bark chips or other mulch to keep soil moist.

Selected Species and Cultivars

Portulaca grandiflora (Moss rose, Rose moss). With needle-shaped leaves topped by fluffy translucent flowers, this is a favorite summer garden annual. Named cultivars include:
   'Cloudbeater,' an unusual double strain that is said not to close in the afternoon. The large blossoms in many colors are up to 1¾ inches wide. 'Afternoon Delight' is similar;
   'Magic Carpet,' a well-doubled, lively blend of pink, red, salmon, orange, white, and yellow, some striped, about 6 inches tall;
   'Sunny Boy,' 6-inch-tall plants with large bright flowers in rose, red, orange, salmon, white, and yellow; and
   'Swanlake,' a white-flowered strain of showy, large ruffled doubles with golden anthers.
   P. oleracea (Purslane, Pusley). This plant has bright single flowers all over mats of succulent, thick prostrate stems. Pieces of almost any size root easily as cuttings. The young, tender stems and fleshy leaves are edible—the wild form of this plant is used in soups or salads. This plant is excellent for hanging baskets because it tends to form a slightly dropping mound with flowers all over, and tolerates high heat and crowded conditions. It will bloom continually from spring until frost comes in autumn.

PRIMROSE

Botanical name: *Primula* (Primulaceae)
Other common name: Cowslip

The name *primrose* may come from the Latin *primus* (first), indicating its time of flowering. Hardy primroses are among the earliest plants to bloom in spring, along with the crocus and early tulips. There are about four hundred species and innumerable hybrids, tender or hardy, annual or perennial. They all show off pert, neat, clustered flowers in colors that may be pale, bright, or dark, sometimes in interesting multicolored combinations, rising from basal rosettes of thick, fuzzy, puckered, usually oval leaves. Although primroses grow in all colors, the color called primrose is the soft, bright yellow of the native wild English primrose, the cowslip.

Some species need a special environment such as an alpine area, a cool greenhouse, well-drained stony soil (called scree), or a bog, but many will grow in ordinary garden conditions in shade. Because of extensive interbreeding, it is difficult to classify and describe cultural needs. The genus is complex; many gardeners and horticulturists make a specialty of it.

There are primrose species for most gardens if the type of plant and the site are well matched. By and large, primroses grow well in shady places, humusy soil, cool temperatures, and at the edges of lakes and streams. They are used in natural and wild gardens as well as in rock gardens, greenhouse pots, and formal bedding plant designs.

PLANT TYPES: Perennial or annual.

GROWING RANGE: Zones 3 to 8.

HARDINESS: Varies from quite hardy to tender, but all types dislike prolonged heat above 90°F and handle cool weather down to 35°F well.

PLANT HEIGHT: 3 inches to 3 feet (often under 1 foot).

FLOWER COLOR: All colors, including black, but usually bright shades.

FLOWER FORM: Flat or ruffled flowers about an inch wide in small stemless clusters or in round or elongated racemes on leafless stems.

SEASON OF BLOOM: Winter (as pot plants), spring, or early summer; a few types rebloom in fall.

SOIL: Rich, humusy, and moist for most types.

PH: 6 to 8, depending on variety.

FERTILIZER: Well-rotted manure, compost, all-purpose or high-phosphorus fertilizer.

WATER: Moist conditions for most species.

EXPOSURE: Partial shade.

SPACING: 5 to 15 inches.

PROPAGATION: Seed or division.

Method

- **Start seeds indoors** in small pots or six-packs filled with moist potting soil high in peat moss or compost. Prechill seed of hardy types in the refrigerator for four weeks. Do not cover seed, just press it into the surface of the soil, spacing tiny seeds ½ inch or more apart if possible. Cover containers with transparent glass or plastic and keep them at 65° to 70°F until seeds germinate, usually in three to six weeks. Seeds that do not germinate the first year may germinate later if they are put into the freezer (still planted) for a month or two, then put back into a warm place or outside. Do not give seedlings direct sunlight, but provide bright light.

  Greenhouse types such as *Primula malacoides* are planted in January at 60°F for bloom the next winter. Seedlings are stepped up to progressively larger pots until September, and then grown on in pots they will bloom in.

- **Prepare soil outdoors** before planting by tilling in fertilizer, compost, and other soil improvers, as needed.

- **Sow seeds outdoors** in nursery beds in warm spring weather (around 70°F), or as soon as they ripen on plants—in late spring. Plant them less than ⅛ inch deep and about 2 inches apart. Do not let them dry out. Hardy types may not germinate until the following year. It is difficult to grow most types this way, but *P. japonica* will self-sow near streams in Zones 5 to 8.

- **Thin** seedlings (indoor and outdoor grown) to their permanent spacing when they are about an inch wide if they are crowded.

- **Set plants outdoors** in spring after all danger of hard frost has passed, after hardening them off in the shade for several days.

- **Divide** established plants after they flower if they are crowded in clumps with several long-rooted crowns (each crown is one plant). Dig deeply to avoid harming central taproots. Separate the plants gently with your hands and replant them in their new places immediately, supplying extra shade if sun is hot and bright. Keep soil damp. Some types multiply rapidly.

- **Water** plants when the soil starts to dry out.

- **Fertilize** lightly at planting time and each year in spring.

- **Pests and diseases** seldom are problems, but sometimes plants are affected by red spider mites (spray off with water), flea beetles, or aphids. Insecticidal soap or rotenone should take care of these two if they appear.

- **Mulch** plants in summer with 2 inches of peat moss, compost, small bark chips, or other mulch.

- **Remove** spent blossoms unless seed is wanted.

- **Protect in winter** by mulching around crowns with 2 inches of peat moss, compost, small bark chips, or other mulch. Pull back the mulch after the danger of hard frost ends.

Selected Species

Primula auricula (Auricula). This is a showy, hardy perennial type, 8 inches tall, with vivid coloring that may include contrasting zones or bands. It is often grown by collectors in cool greenhouses, and in Zones 5 to 8 in sheltered areas. Blooms appear in early spring.

P. denticulata (Himalayan primrose). This perennial has pink, lilac, or white flowers with yellow eyes in spring in round heads 2 inches across on 1-foot-tall stems. It needs moist or wet soil and grows in Zones 3 to 8.

P. japonica. This 2½-foot-tall perennial species naturalizes well near woodland streams in Zones 5 to 8. Its red, white, or pink flowers open in late spring on ball-shaped umbels that open in tiers. It needs moist to boggy acid soil—mulch plants with peat moss or pine needles. The ephemeral foliage disappears in late summer, fall, and winter. Prechill purchased seeds before planting, or allow plants to self-sow when seeds ripen in summer.

P. malacoides (Fairy primrose, Baby primrose, Annual primrose). This plant is often seen in pots blooming in spring. The pink, white, or violet blossoms seem frillier than most primroses and have attractive leaf rosettes. Plant this tender annual indoors in winter for blooms the next year.

P. x polyantha (Polyanthus). These popular polyanthus hybrid primroses are hardy plants for garden (Zones 3 to 8) or greenhouse. They bloom in early spring at the same time as daffodils, or earlier if grown indoors. They prefer humus-rich garden soil.

P. veris (English cowslip). Bright yellow in the wild, with hybrids in many other colors, the English cowslip grows about 8 inches tall and is hardy in cool, shady gardens in Zones 3 to 8. 'Grandiflora' is used in the names of various large-flowered cultivars.

P. vulgaris, synonym *P. acaulis* (English primrose). This popular primrose blooms very early in spring and is hardy if grown in cool, moist shade in Zones 3 to 8. Flowers are available in various bright colors, and foliage remains partly evergreen in winter.

RUDBECKIA

Botanical name: *Rudbeckia* (Compositae)
Other common name: Coneflower

In the hottest part of summer, rudbeckia shows stamina and bright beauty in fields everywhere. This easy-to-grow, daisylike native plant, the state flower of Maryland, has been bred into many fine cultivars, as well as some that are less pleasing than the wild plant. Seedling plants form neat rosettes of hairy green leaves the first year and then bloom later the same year or the following year, self-sowing freely. Rudbeckia is used in wildflower meadows, borders, and for cut flowers from Maine to Florida and Maryland to California. The flowers last a long time on the plant and in bouquets.

PLANT TYPE: Hardy perennial with biennial tendencies.
GROWING RANGE: Zones 3 to 10.
HARDINESS: Extremely hardy in both cold and hot weather.
PLANT HEIGHT: 2 to over 4 feet.
FLOWER COLOR: Deep golden ray flowers around a dark chocolate central disc. Petals of some cultivars are orange, pale yellow, bronze, or rust, sometimes bicolored.
FLOWER FORM: Long-petaled single or double disc and ray flowers up to 6 inches wide are borne on long, stiff, hairy stems. Petals appear somewhat pleated.
SEASON OF BLOOM: Summer, especially July in most areas, continuing through fall; all year in Zones 9 and 10.
SOIL: Well drained, average to rich.
PH: 6 to 7.
FERTILIZER: Well-rotted manure, compost, all-purpose fertilizer.
WATER: Average conditions.
EXPOSURE: Prefers full sun but tolerates light shade.
SPACING: 1 to 3 feet.
PROPAGATION: Seed or division.

Method

- **Start seeds indoors** in six-packs (two seeds per pocket) or sparsely in flats filled with moist, sterile seed starting medium at any time in temperatures near 70°F. Do not cover the small seeds, just pat them in place. Plants appear within fourteen days and need bright light. They will bloom the first year if planted early—about eight to twelve weeks before the last frost; if planted later in spring or in summer, they will bloom the next year.

- **Prepare soil outdoors,** incorporating soil amendments such as compost and fertilizer, if needed. Plants will grow in unimproved meadows, but will be more vigorous in good soil.

- **Sow seeds outdoors** in prepared and fertilized beds in summer in northern and central areas, in fall in Zones 9 and 10. Make rows 1 inch deep and plant seeds an inch apart without covering them. Do not let the seedbed dry out.

- **Sow seeds in a cold frame** when its interior temperatures range from about 65° to 85°F—fall or spring in most areas, winter in Zones 9 and 10.

- **Thin or transplant** seedlings when they are 3 inches tall, before they become crowded. Shift those grown indoors to individual pots 4 inches wide or larger, or to nursery beds outdoors. Thin or transplant those grown outdoors whenever they become crowded, but eventually to a foot or more apart. Gloriosa daisies are especially easy to transplant during cool weather in early spring.

- **Set indoor-grown plants outdoors** in permanent places after hardening them off in spring or, farther north, early summer, when daytime temperatures are around 65°F.

- **Divide** large clumps when new leaves grow in early spring by separating plants every other year or when crowded. Replant divisions immediately; they should bloom the same year.

- **Water** frequently enough to keep the soil moderately moist in spring, somewhat drier in summer. Moisten the ground, not the leaves, to help prevent mildew.

- **Fertilize** lightly at planting time and in midsummer.

- **Pests and diseases** rarely are problems. Sawfly and aphid may be treated with rotenone or insecticidal soap. Downy mildew can be prevented with better air circulation and fungicide.

- **Mulch** plants with 2 or 3 inches of composted leaves or small bark chips to help keep moisture in the soil.

- **Stake** tall plants in windy areas with 3-foot-tall bamboo or other stakes.

- **Remove** stems and spent flowers unless you want to save the seeds.

- **Protect in winter** with 3 inches of composted leaf mulch around each plant.

Tip · To collect seeds, let the heads ripen and turn grayish. Crush them and strew the seeds where you want them to grow or store them in paper envelopes. Seeds from wild plants are easy to grow in sunny gardens.

Selected Species and Cultivars

Rudbeckia fulgida. This is a widespread, small-flowered, wayside black-eyed Susan, as attractive in flower borders as it is in open fields. It is less subject to mildew than *R. hirta.* 'Goldsturm,' with 2-foot-tall plants featuring bright gold flowers with long, thin petals, is a popular cultivar. Flower heads are up to 5 inches wide and appear in handsome clusters on bushy plants.

   R. hirta (Black-eyed Susan). This widespread native has golden ray flowers around a velvety brown center. 'Gloriosa Daisy' is a domesticated tetraploid form that grows up to 3 feet tall with huge single flowers up to 7 inches wide. It is very easy to grow from seed. Flowers are often banded with autumnal colors from gold through reddish brown. *R. hirta tetra* 'Green Eyes' is an interesting variation with olive-green discs surrounded by pointed golden petals, growing nearly 3 feet tall when in bloom. 'Rustic Colors' is a mix with flowers ranging from orange, bronze, and brown, and includes bicolors, intershades, and solid colors. Plants are generally 18 to 24 inches tall.

   R. laciniata 'Gold Drop.' Charming double flowers with wiry stems a little over 2 feet tall, these are a paler yellow than most rudbeckias. They are reliably hardy in Zones 3 to 10.

   A hybrid rudbeckia worth mentioning is 'Nutmeg,' 2 to 2½ feet tall, a double form with well-proportioned 4-inch-wide flowers that keep the characteristic chocolate centers. Petals may be banded or solid in any of the autumnal hues of gold, brown, orange, and red.

SALPIGLOSSIS

Botanical name: *Salpiglossis sinuata* (Solanaceae)
Other common names: Painted tongue, Velvet flower

Brilliant veining on velvety, petunialike blossoms makes salpiglossis worth fussing with. It is one of those plants that do well if the weather is not too hot or too cold—easy to grow in Oregon, difficult in Virginia. Like violets, some salpiglossis plants have cleistogamous flowers—that is, some of the flowers never open because they pollinate themselves, especially in hot weather. This trait is being bred out, so newer cultivars are usually better. Salpiglossis is originally from Chile and may be grown in beds or in large tubs—space plants twice as close in containers and add extra fertilizer. It has a branched, upright habit. Dwarf hybrids are good pot or greenhouse plants. Salpiglossis is fascinating as a cut flower.

   PLANT TYPE: Tender annual.
   GROWING RANGE: All zones during moderate weather.
   HARDINESS: Prefers cool weather but is killed by frost as well as heat in the 90's (F).
   PLANT HEIGHT: 1 to 3 feet.

FLOWER COLOR: Yellow, orange, bronze, red, pink, white, pearl gray, deep rose, violet, purple, blue. Many bicolors, distinctively veined.

FLOWER FORM: Tubular, flaring, open-faced single blooms.

SEASON OF BLOOM: Summer in most areas, most or all year-round in cool but frost-free areas.

SOIL: Average to rich garden soil.

PH: 6.5 to 7.5.

FERTILIZER: Compost, well-rotted manure, flower or tomato fertilizer.

WATER: Keep soil moist at all times, but not saturated.

EXPOSURE: Full sun; in excessive heat areas, afternoon shade is beneficial.

SPACING: 1 foot (less in containers).

PROPAGATION: Seed.

Method

- **Start seeds indoors** eight to ten weeks before the last frost, sowing thinly in flats, six-packs, or small pots filled with damp potting soil. Barely cover seeds and grow them in a warm (60° to 70°F) place, in bright sunlight or a few inches below a fluorescent light fixture. Try to give plants twelve hours of light per day.

- **Prepare soil outdoors** in beds before planting by tilling in fertilizer, peat moss, compost, and other soil improvers, as needed.

- **Sow seeds outdoors** only if the climate is mild and the cool season is at least four months long. In smoothly prepared and fertilized beds, make seed rows about 2 inches deep. Plant seeds an inch apart, barely covered with ⅛ inch of soil. Do not let seedbed dry out.

- **Thin or transplant** seedlings when they are large enough to handle, 3 to 4 inches tall, if they are crowded. Indoors, move them to larger pots if they are crowded, one per 4-inch pot. Outdoors, when they are 4 inches high, thin them to 6 inches apart. A week or two later, thin or transplant them to their permanent garden positions. Choose an overcast or rainy day for transplanting field-grown plants.

- **Set plants outdoors** after hardening them off in shade for several days, after most danger of frost passes. Temperatures should be stabilized around 50°F. Mix fertilizer into each planting hole. Firm plants into place and water well.

- **Water** frequently if needed.

- **Fertilize** plants steadily, boosting blossoms when plants are 6 inches tall with additional low-nitrogen, high-phosphorus and -potassium fertilizer. As plants get large and weather gets hot, supplement their feedings with liquid fertilizer.

- **Pinch back** tips to encourage bushiness.

- **Pests and diseases** rarely are problems.

- **Mulch** plants with several inches of bark chips or other mulch to keep soil cool and moist.

- **Cut flowers** often for bouquets or deadhead spent blooms to extend the bloom season.
- **Stake** tall types with slim, 2-foot-tall bamboo sticks if necessary.

Selected Cultivars

'Bolero,' selected for its dramatic coloring, in mixed colors;

'Dwarf Friendship,' a 15-inch-tall mixture bred for increased heat tolerance and compact form;

'Gloomy Rival,' with pearl gray flowers veined with rich bronze, on 15-inch-tall plants. This somewhat startling color complements silver, white, and gray-leaved plants;

'Kew Blue,' with striking gold veins on velvety blue flowers, on dwarf plants 12 inches tall; and

'Splash,' a compact strain that is good for pots and has hybrid vigor that improves its outdoor performance.

SALVIA

Botanical name: *Salvia* (Labiatae)
Other common name: Sage

This large genus related to mint includes many species of half-hardy annuals and biennials, and some herbaceous perennials. Salvia is grown for showy spires of flowers. Best known is fiery red *Salvia splendens,* used for bedding even in hottest weather. *S. farinacea,* sometimes called mealycup sage, is increasingly popular for bedding and flower arrangements, fresh or dry. In flower beds, salvia looks best in large clumps. It also works well in tubs and large planters. Dwarf types are good in window boxes.

Most gardeners set out purchased bedding plants of annual salvia. Check plant name, color, and height before buying. Choose young plants that are not pot-bound; they will quickly outpace overstressed large ones.

 PLANT TYPES: Annual, biennial, or perennial.
 GROWING RANGE: All zones as an annual and biennial, usually Zones 5 to 9 as a
  hardy perennial. Tender perennials can be grown as annuals.
 HARDINESS: Variably hardy, depending on species.
 PLANT HEIGHT: 1 to 3 feet.
 FLOWER COLOR: Red, pink, purple, or white flushed with green, blue, or violet.
 FLOWER FORM: Tubular flowers in rings on long showy spires.
 SEASON OF BLOOM: Summer in most areas, year-round in frost-free areas.
 SOIL: Any good garden soil.
 PH: 6 to 7.5.
 FERTILIZER: Flower or all-purpose fertilizer, plus liquid fertilizer in hot weather.
 WATER: Keep soil somewhat moist.
 EXPOSURE: Full sun in most regions, partial shade in the South or where day tempera-
  tures are consistently over 90°F.
 SPACING: 8 inches to 3 feet.
 PROPAGATION: Annuals from seed, perennials from seed or by division, all types by
  stem cuttings.

🌾 *Method*

- **Start seeds indoors** eight weeks before last frost in flats or six-packs, thinly. In cold frames, sow six weeks before last frost. In frost-free areas, sow plants during the coolest part of the year. Cover with ⅛ inch of soil. Water and keep in a warm (65° to 75°F) place. Seeds germinate in about two weeks, sometimes less. Grow in bright sunlight or a few inches below a fluorescent light fixture.

- **Prepare soil** in flower bed by tilling in compost, fertilizer, and other soil amendments, if needed.

- **Sow seeds outdoors** after the danger of frost has passed. In tilled, fertilized beds, make seed drills (rows) about 2 inches deep. Plant seeds 2 inches apart and cover with ⅛ inch of soil. Keep evenly moist.

- **Thin or transplant** seedlings when they are about 4 inches high, if they are crowded. Indoor-grown plants should be stepped up to 4-inch pots for optimum root growth. Thin plants being grown outdoors to at least 4 inches apart. Within three weeks, thin or transplant them to their permanent positions in containers or the garden. Space most species about a foot apart—farther for large perennials. Salvia is easily transplanted, even when large.

- **Set indoor-grown plants outdoors** in their permanent places after the last frost, when weather is settled, after hardening them off in shade a few days. Mix fertilizer into the planting holes. If seedlings are leggy, bury roots and stems up to the first two leaves. Firm into place and water well.

- **Take cuttings** if desired, as salvia roots easily if cuttings are taken during warm weather. Root under high humidity in a damp potting medium such as a mixture of sand and peat. Perennial salvias with only one main stem should be propagated in this manner, not divided. If many rooted stems are clumped together, plants may be divided in early spring.

- **Water** more frequently at first, then just enough to keep soil slightly moist, not wet.

- **Fertilize** steadily with slow-release or occasional side-dressings of all-purpose, blossom booster, or tomato plant fertilizer.

- **Pests** include cutworms and slugs. Use cutworm collars (see Broccoli, page 464) when setting out plants, and dust with rotenone. Prevent slugs by dusting the ground and the plants with diatomaceous earth or lime and ashes, and trapping them in partly submerged pans of beer. **Diseases** are seldom a problem.

- **Pinch back** seedlings for bushiness.

- **Remove** flowers after bloom, unless seed is wanted.

- **Mulch** plants in dry areas with 2 or 3 inches of shredded leaves or other mulch.

- **Stake** tall plants if they are in especially windy areas.

Tip · Although fairly tender, seedlings of annual (as well as perennial) types tolerate some cold weather. In nearly frost-free areas, they often make it through the winter, especially in cold frames, and bloom earlier on stronger plants.

Selected Species and Cultivars

Salvia argentea (Silver sage). This is a biennial or short-lived perennial with an attractive rosette of leaves covered with tiny silver hairs. It has small pinkish flowers but is grown principally for its foliage. This variety reaches a height of 15 inches.

S. coccinea. (Texas sage). Grown as a half-hardy annual, this 3-foot-tall plant has long spires studded with rings of tubular red flowers. It is very attractive in mixed borders.

S. columbariae. This interesting half-hardy annual for sunny gardens is 1 to 2 feet tall, bearing spires of blue flowers within purple bracts.

S. farinacea (Mealycup sage). The graceful, linear spires of this tender perennial salvia are blue or silver, and smaller than those of *S. splendens.* In the 'Victoria' cultivar, flower heads are dense and intensely violet-blue. Flowers may be tied in bunches and hung upside down to dry for everlasting bouquets.

Other *S. farinacea* cultivars may be used similarly. Their color range is silvery white, shades of light blue, and dark blue. Though perennial, *S. farinacea* is tender and is usually grown as an annual north of Zone 8.

S. forskahlii. This 3-foot-tall perennial has lush foliage. Its flowers are long blue spires with white throats.

S. haematodes (Meadow clary). Also known as *S. pratensis,* this 3-foot-tall perennial grows tall sprays of lavender-blue claw-shaped flowers from a basal rosette. It blooms for several months in the summer.

S. patens (Gentian sage). This plant grows bright blue tubular flowers in spikes and is long blooming, on plants reaching from 1 to 3 ½ feet tall.

S. splendens (Scarlet sage). Usually bright red, this dependable annual blooms for several months, even longer in the South. Colors also available are white, pink, violet, and deep purple. Cultivars include:

'Carabiniere,' dwarf plants with scarlet flowers that grow to 10 inches tall. Is also available in white and purple;

'Fireworks,' which has unusual red and white striped bracts that are softer looking in the landscape than the usual types; it grows 12 to 14 inches tall;

'Pirate,' which produces extra-long, brilliant red flower spikes on 18-inch-tall plants; and

'Purple Blaze,' with deep purple flowers and dark green foliage on 16-inch-tall plants. It is great looking with yellow marigolds or pink or violet petunias.

S. x superba (Violet sage). This is a tall (up to 3 feet) perennial with violet-blue or purple flowers that does well in dry areas in sun or shade. It dislikes wet winters and needs well-drained soil. It does best in Zones 5 to 9. 'East Friesland,' purple, and 'Mainacht,' deep violet-blue, are good cultivars.

S. viridis, synonym *S. horminum* (Clary sage). The bracts of white, violet, or rose from this hardy annual are veined with green and may be dried for everlasting bouquets. 'Claryssa' is a compact, well-branched variety that grows 18 inches tall.

SANVITALIA

Botanical name: *Sanvitalia procumbens* (Compositae)

Here is a bright, useful little plant that can withstand summer heat. These low, wide, sun-loving plants with zillions of single or double bright golden to orange zinnialike flowers look great spilling down in a hanging basket or window box or covering the ground in mixed or unmixed flower beds. The deep green tidy leaves are oval or somewhat pointed and grow in pairs. One reason these plants are so easy to grow is their sturdy taproots. The flowers may be air-dried for everlasting bouquets and wreaths.

PLANT TYPE: Hardy annual.
GROWING RANGE: All zones.
HARDINESS: Thrives in heat, not in cold (below 45°F).
PLANT HEIGHT: 6 to 8 inches.
FLOWER COLOR: Yellow or orange with dark purplish centers.
FLOWER FORM: Masses of single or double daisylike flowers about ¾ inch wide.
SEASON OF BLOOM: All summer or during hot weather.
SOIL: Light, sandy, well drained.
PH: 6.5 to 7.5.
FERTILIZER: Well-rotted manure, all-purpose or high-phosphorus fertilizer.
WATER: Average to dry conditions.
EXPOSURE: Full sun.
SPACING: 10 to 12 inches.
PROPAGATION: Seed.

Method

- **Start seeds indoors** in individual small pots or thinly in flats filled with moist potting soil, about eight weeks before the last frost. Cover seeds with ⅛ inch of soil, water, and keep at 75° to 80°F until seeds germinate. Afterward temperatures may be reduced to 65° or 70°F if you wish. Grow seedlings in a sunny area or a few inches below a fluorescent light fixture.

- **Prepare soil outdoors** before planting by tilling in fertilizer, sand, compost, and other soil improvers, as needed.

- **Sow seeds outdoors** where they will grow one or two weeks before the last expected frost. Plant seeds from November through February in Zones 10 and 11. In smoothly prepared and fertilized beds, plant them 3 or more inches apart and cover with ⅛ inch of soil. Do not let the seedbed dry out.

- **Thin** seedlings grown outdoors to their permanent spacing when they are about 4 inches tall. With care, thinnings may be transplanted. Indoors, when they have four to six leaves, step them up to larger pots if necessary.

- **Set plants outdoors** after all danger of frost has passed, after hardening them off in shade for a few days.

- **Water** seedlings often to prevent the soil from drying out. Mature plants will tolerate fairly dry soil.

- **Fertilize** lightly at planting time. Boost blossoms by applying a low-nitrogen, high-phosphorus and -potassium fertilizer when plants are 4 inches tall.

- **Pests and diseases** seldom are problems.

- **Mulch** plants that grow in very hot, dry areas with several inches of bark chips or other mulch to keep soil cooler, keeping mulch around but not over the stems.

- **Pinch back** tips for bushiness and **deadhead** occasionally to encourage branching and flowering.

Selected Cultivars

'Gold Braid,' with double zinnialike ¾-inch flowers in a rich gold, forming mats 6 inches tall and up to 12 inches wide; and

'Mandarin Orange,' an award-winning cultivar with orange flowers up to 1 inch wide, looking like small orange sunflowers on vigorous, matlike, 6-by-12-inch plants.

SCABIOSA

Botanical name: *Scabiosa* (Dipsacaceae)
Other common name: Pincushion flower

Such a pretty flower deserves nicer names, and a place in the garden, too, where the mound-shaped plants are attractive in all stages of growth. This lacy-looking round flower, related to teasel, is good for bedding and cutting. Leaves are divided and linear. There are half-hardy annual as well as perennial types. As cut flowers, the blossoms last two weeks or more. Plant three or more plants together in the border for impact. Select the strain carefully—some plants, especially the annuals, need support, but this attribute has been eliminated in better types. Scabiosa is native to Mediterranean and nearby regions.

PLANT TYPES: Half-hardy annual or hardy perennial.
GROWING RANGE: All zones as an annual, Zones 3 to 8 as a perennial.
HARDINESS: Withstands cold and moderate heat.
PLANT HEIGHT: Variable, 1 to 3 feet.
FLOWER COLOR: White, cream, pink, lavender, blue, burgundy.
FLOWER FORM: Flattened round heads 2 to 3 inches wide, on long stems, are formed of florets opening in whorls.
SEASON OF BLOOM: Summer into fall.
SOIL: Rich, loamy, well drained.
PH: Near 7 (neutral).
FERTILIZER: Well-rotted manure, all-purpose or high-phosphorus fertilizer.
WATER: Average to moist conditions.
EXPOSURE: Full sun in most regions, bright partial shade in the South.
SPACING: 1 to 2 feet.
PROPAGATION: Annuals from seed, perennials from seed or by division.

Method

- **Start seeds indoors,** ⅛ inch deep, in small pots filled with moist potting soil. Water and keep at 65°F until seeds germinate, in one or two weeks. Keep seedlings in a sunny area or a few inches below a fluorescent light fixture. When plants are about 4 inches tall, move them outdoors or to larger pots if they are crowded.

- **Prepare soil outdoors** before planting by tilling in fertilizer, compost, lime if needed, and other soil improvers.

- **Sow seeds outdoors** in nursery beds in spring weather around 65°F, ¼ inch deep and about 4 inches apart. Plants do especially well if sown where they will grow. Do not let seeds or seedlings dry out.

- **Thin or transplant seedlings** grown outdoors to their permanent spacing when they are 4 inches tall. They are not difficult to transplant at this stage.

- **Set plants outdoors** in spring, after all danger of frost has passed, after hardening them off in shade for several days.

- **Divide** each established perennial plant into two new clumps if the old ones are over-crowded, in spring when new growth begins. Division is rarely needed.

- **Water** plants whenever the soil starts to dry out and when they wilt during hot weather.

- **Fertilize** lightly at planting time and during active growth.

- **Pests and diseases** seldom are problems. Slugs are troublesome in some areas. (See the table on pages 132–33 for ways to control slugs.)

- **Mulch** plants in dry weather with 2 inches of bark chips or other mulch.

- **Remove** spent blossoms and their stems for neatness and to encourage more flowering.

- **Protect in winter** by mulching around crowns with 4 inches of a lightweight, airy mulch such as salt hay. Pull back the mulch after the danger of frost ends so new leaves can come up.

Selected Species and Cultivars

Scabiosa atropurpurea (Sweet scabious, Mourning bride). These half-hardy annual plants are usually about 2 feet tall, but this varies. They may be set just 1 foot apart. Some types need staking with slim sticks. Cultivars include 'Blue Moon,' a tall blue good for cutting; 'Grandiflora,' a large-flowered type in the full color range; and 'Nana,' much shorter, in all colors, and well branched, good for bedding.

S. caucasica. These plants are bushy perennials 2 or more feet tall, with pale green foliage. The 2- to 3-inch-wide flowers continue to bloom for several months and last a long time in bouquets. Cultivars include:

'Alba,' with white flowers on 20-inch plants;

'Blue Perfection,' with light blue ruffled flowers, 2 feet tall;

'Fama,' 20 inches tall, with deep blue flowers, excellent when cut; and
'House's Mixture,' 30 inches tall, strong plants in a series of colors from pure white to
deep lilac blue.

SNAPDRAGON

Botanical name: *Antirrhinum* (Scrophulariaceae)

This sun-loving plant from the Mediterranean offers columns of flowers with a fanciful
resemblance to dragons' heads or butterflies. In low mat-forming types or tall linear ones,
snapdragons are among the most popular of garden flowers. Actually tender perennials,
they are most often grown as hardy annuals. Foliage may be green or bronze. They are
used for bedding, containers, cut flowers, and greenhouses.

PLANT TYPE: Tender perennial, usually grown as annual.

GROWING RANGE: All zones as an annual, Zones 8 to 11 as a short-lived perennial.

HARDINESS: Killed by hard freezes. Some strains are heat tolerant, others are not.

PLANT HEIGHT: 8 inches to over 4 feet.

FLOWER COLOR: Red, pink, peach, yellow, orange, rust, burgundy, violet, or white,
sometimes bicolored.

FLOWER FORM: Double-lipped, tubular flowers bloom in clustered short spires or on
fewer taller ones.

SEASON OF BLOOM: Summer in most areas, any time (but especially spring) in
frost-free areas.

SOIL: Average to rich, well drained.

PH: 6 to 8.

FERTILIZER: Well-rotted manure, boron (contained in Borax detergent), compost,
and slow-release bedding plant fertilizer (such as 6-6-6).

WATER: Average to plentiful.

EXPOSURE: Full sun in most areas, some light shade in areas where day temperatures
are consistently over 90°F.

SPACING: 1 to 2 feet.

PROPAGATION: Usually seed, also by division.

Method

· **Start seeds indoors** six weeks before the last frost, thinly, in flats or individually in
six-packs filled with clean seed starting medium. Cover seeds less than ⅛ inch deep,
water, and grow at 60° to 70°F. Seeds need light for germination, which takes eight to
twenty-one days. Grow seedlings in bright sunlight or a few inches below a fluorescent
light fixture.

· **Prepare soil outdoors** in beds at planting time. Till in compost, sand, fertilizer, and
other soil amendments, as needed. Snapdragons need more boron than most plants, so
add borax at a rate of 3 grams per square yard.

- **Sow seeds outdoors** in smoothly prepared and fertilized beds after the danger of frost has passed, making rows about 1 inch deep. Plant seeds 3 inches apart and barely cover with ⅛ inch of soil. Do not let the seedbed dry out.

- **Thin or transplant** indoor-grown seedlings to one per six-pack pocket or 4-inch pot when they are about 2 inches tall. Thin or transplant outdoor-grown seedlings to permanent places in beds before they get crowded.

- **Set out indoor-grown plants** after the danger of frost has passed, on an overcast day with temperatures around 60° to 70°F, after hardening them off in shade a few days, tilling in fertilizer and firming plants in place.

- **Divide** plants in early spring during cool, moist weather, if plants have survived winter. This is most likely to occur in Zones 8 to 11. Snapdragons are not normally propagated this way commercially because of the chance of transmitting disease, but it may be practical at home.

- **Water** often to keep the soil evenly moist.

- **Fertilize** at planting time and keep plants steadily but moderately fertilized with a bedding plant fertilizer such as 6-6-6.

- **Pests and diseases** include rust, mildew, and botrytis blight in some areas. Choose disease-resistant cultivars. Hose off aphids and mites with soapy water and treat with pyrethrum or rotenone. Where nematodes infest soil, grow snapdragons in sterilized potting soil in containers. Do not use malathion, for it harms the plants.

- **Mulch** plants with 2 or 3 inches of composted leaves or bark chips to keep moisture in the soil.

- **Stake** tall types with slim sticks.

- **Trim** plants for the effect you want. For large flowers on tall spires (for cut flowers), trim off side shoots and do not pinch plants back. For well-branched bedding plants, pinch them back once. In areas with short summers, do not pinch or trim plants—it delays flowering.

- **Remove** spent flowers or cut fresh flowers for bouquets to stimulate new growth, unless seed is wanted. Plants tend to self-sow.

- **Clear** stems and roots of snapdragons from beds at the end of the season to prevent diseases such as rust from overwintering in the garden.

Tip · In Zones 8 to 11, snapdragons may live through the winter as large leafy mats with no flowers. Do not get rid of them—when days get longer in spring, they will burst into bloom.

Selected Cultivars

Antirrhinum majus. The garden snapdragon has been developed by plant breeders into short (for bedding), medium (all-purpose), and tall (for cut flowers) cultivars in most colors as well as several different flower shapes—single or double (butterfly-flowered). Some of the many notable cultivars include:

'Cinderella,' a naturally branching type in all colors, 20 inches tall with erect spires of flowers on many side shoots;

'Double Madam Butterfly,' tall and frilly, 24 to 30 inches tall, with double, azalea-shaped blossoms in bright colors on strong stems;

'Little Darling,' a butterfly-flowered dwarf strain, early and floriferous, about a foot tall;

'Minaret,' 18 inches tall, early to flower, and quick to recover and reflower if spent blossoms are picked off;

'Purple King,' an 18-inch-tall type with classically shaped flowers in rich lilac touched with rose at the lips;

'Rocket' strain, a group of medium or tall snapdragons (up to 3 feet) bred for hot-weather tolerance;

'Royal Carpet,' 8 inches tall, with vigorous, rust-resistant flowers in low clumps a foot wide in many bright colors;

'Sonnet' series, wind tolerant, early-flowering, bushy plants 20 inches tall, available in white, yellow, pink, rose, orange-scarlet, crimson, bronze, or mixed colors; and

'White Wonder,' with large pure white flowers that grow 18 inches tall.

SNOWDROP

Botanical name: *Galanthus* (Amaryllidaceae)

Petite white snowdrops are among the earliest flowers to bloom as winter ends, while snow or frost is still on the ground. If the weather is not too hot, the flowers of these hardy bulbs last several weeks. They are very pretty in masses, and fortunately they thrive even when crowded in among later-blooming plants, as long as the straplike leaves are not shaded or cut for a month or more after blooming ends. Plant snowdrops near paths where they can be seen easily, and in parts of the garden or under trees where the bulbs will not be disturbed. Once planted, snowdrops spread or naturalize well if conditions are suitable. They resist forcing, but clumps in bloom may be dug up, planted in pots, and brought indoors for decoration. (Replant them outside after flowers fade, for they will bloom again the following year.) Snowdrops resemble later-blooming snowflakes *(Leucojum)* and are distantly related.

PLANT TYPE: Hardy bulb.
GROWING RANGE: Zones 4 to 8.
HARDINESS: Withstands heat and cold.
PLANT HEIGHT: 4 to 10 inches.
FLOWER COLOR: White touched with green.
FLOWER FORM: Bell-like, solitary pendant flowers about 1 inch wide with lilylike outer petals that open more on warm days.

SEASON OF BLOOM: Late winter, before crocus.
SOIL: Average, well drained.
PH: 6.5 to 7.5
FERTILIZER: Well-rotted manure, bonemeal, all-purpose fertilizer.
WATER: Average conditions.
EXPOSURE: Bright dappled shade.
SPACING: 2 inches apart and 3 inches deep.
PROPAGATION: Bulbs, division, or seed.

Method

- **Prepare soil** in outdoor beds before planting by tilling in fertilizer, compost, bonemeal, and other soil improvers, as needed.

- **Plant bulbs outdoors** in early fall, 3 inches deep and 2 inches apart, especially in spots near walkways where flowers can be seen easily.

- **Sow seeds outdoors** 2 inches apart, 1/8 inch deep, in nursery beds or naturalized under trees, in late spring after they ripen on plants. Fresh seeds are not hard to grow, though few gardeners bother because seedlings take two or three years to bloom.

- **Thin or transplant** seedlings to their permanent positions in their second or third year, in early spring while they are still green.

- **Divide** plants if they are crowded after flowers bloom, but while leaves are still green. Dig deeply to protect roots, and then gently pull clumps apart with your hands to minimize breakage. Replant immediately in desired places, 2 inches apart and 3 inches deep, in groups of ten or more. Plants do not seem to mind growing in crowded conditions.

- **Water** plants during their growing period whenever the soil starts to dry out.

- **Fertilize** lightly at planting time and each year after plants bloom, to develop strong bulbs for the following year's flowers.

- **Pests and diseases** seldom are problems.

- **Protect in winter** in very cold areas by mulching lightly with 3 inches of pine needles or 2 inches of shredded leaves. Remove the mulch in stages as winter comes to an end, so shoots can come up freely.

Selected Species and Cultivars

Galanthus x *grandiflorus.* This is a large-flowered type with leaves up to 10 inches long, with 1-inch pendant white flowers.

G. nivalis (Common snowdrop). This variety usually grows 4 or 5 inches tall with single white flowers, each with green dots on the central petals. Flowers are less than an inch long, but the plant is pretty in masses. This type is widely available as a bulb at garden centers in the fall. 'Viridapicis' is a large cultivar that has green tips on both inner and outer petals, and 'Flore Pleno' is a double form, with bunched inner petals tipped lime green.

SQUILL

Botanical name: *Scilla* (Liliaceae)

The squills are small bulbs that bring vivid colored patches of flowers, usually blue, to spring lawns and gardens. All species are ideal for naturalizing. One of their best uses is as a flowing mass in the lawn below a highly visible deciduous landscape tree—say in the center of the front yard. Multiplying by offsets and self-sowing freely once established, these spring blossoms appear early (just when we need them!) and then ripen and disappear before summer heat begins. Similar but larger are the wood hyacinths (see pages 387–88), *Endymion hispanicus,* sometimes called bell-flowered squills.

PLANT TYPE: Hardy bulb.
GROWING RANGE: Zones 5 to 8 for most types; Zone 4 with protection.
HARDINESS: Withstands summer heat; most types require cold winters.
PLANT HEIGHT: 6 inches (most types).
FLOWER COLOR: Bright to deep blue, white, purple, pink.
FLOWER FORM: Spikes usually bear 4 to 8 star-shaped flowers.
SEASON OF BLOOM: For most, several weeks in spring, with daffodils, but some
  bloom in fall.
SOIL: Any well-drained soil.
PH: Near 7 (neutral).
FERTILIZER: Moderate. Well-rotted manure, bonemeal, and slow-release fertilizer,
  applied lightly.
WATER: Moderate, not too wet.
EXPOSURE: Full sun or light shade.
SPACING: 3 inches apart, 3 inches deep, for most types.
PROPAGATION: Division, also from seed.

Method

- **Prepare soil outdoors** by digging the bed and tilling in compost, fertilizer, sand (for drainage), and other soil amendments, as needed.

- **Sow seeds outdoors** when they ripen (they turn black), usually in early summer, or in fall in cold frames, ⅛ inch deep, 1 inch apart, in finely tilled soil, in rows. Seeds can be scattered where you would like to naturalize the plants. An easy way to mark them is to plant them near their parents. It will take several years for them to mature and bloom.

- **Thin or transplant** seedlings to permanent positions when they become crowded.

- **Set out bulbs** in fall as soon as they are received; otherwise they may dry out too much in storage.

- **Dig and separate** crowded plants in spring after they bloom, when foliage starts to yellow, without cutting into the bulbs, to start new colonies. Plantings may safely remain undivided for several years. After lifting a clump with a spade, tease the bulbs apart gently by hand and reset immediately.

- **Water** if soil is dry while plants have green foliage showing. Do not overwater or bulbs will rot.

- **Fertilize** lightly during active growth in fall and spring with bonemeal and all-purpose bulb or flower fertilizer. In rich soils little or no fertilizer is needed.

- **Pests and diseases** rarely are problems.

- **Remove** flower heads and stems after bloom is finished, unless seed is wanted. Let leaves disappear by themselves, or remove them when they start to turn yellow.

- **Mulch** beds with 1 or 2 inches of shredded leaves or bark chips.

Selected Species

Scilla amoena (Star hyacinth). Bright blue star-shaped flowers ¾ inch wide appear on 6-inch stems in spring.

S. autumnalis (Autumn squill). Small purple flowers, up to twenty per stalk, bloom in fall on 6-inch stems.

S. bifolia (Twin leaf squill). Usually a soft gentian blue, these ½-inch-wide flowers grow on stems 6 inches tall in spring. A rare form is ivory-pink.

S. peruviana (Cuban lily). Though not really from Cuba, this showy scilla is a heat-loving type that differs from the better-known species. It likes a hot sunny site and grows outdoors only in Zones 8 and 9. Forty to sixty rich blue flowers ¾ inch wide make a large showy cluster on each sturdy 8-inch stem in spring. Plant bulbs in fall or winter, 5 inches deep, 6 to 8 inches apart.

S. siberica (Siberian squill). Deep blue, light blue, bright azure blue, or white, these early spring–blooming squills flower plentifully with up to six 6-inch flowering stems per mature bulb. Flowers are ½ inch wide.

STATICE

Botanical name: *Limonium* (Plumbaginaceae)
Other common name: Sea lavender

Statice has light, airy, sharply angled stems that are completely covered with delicate clusters of tiny papery flowers. The inner part of the flower is often white, and the outer part has a bright and long-lasting color, even when dried. The foliage is long and leathery, and is clumped at the base of the plant. The stems often have "wings." Statice is best known as a dried flower, but also makes an attractive plant for garden beds and borders. The perennial types take a few years to become established, but after that are a good addition to any sunny garden.

PLANT TYPES: Annual, biennial, or perennial.
GROWING RANGE: All zones as an annual or biennial; Zones 3 to 11 as a perennial.
HARDINESS: Tolerant of heat, cold tolerance depends on the species.
PLANT HEIGHT: 1 to 3 feet.

FLOWER COLOR: Yellow, lavender, pink, white, blue, red.
FLOWER FORM: Funnel-shaped, in long clusters, each flower ⅛ to ¼ inch across.
SEASON OF BLOOM: Summer.
SOIL: Sandy, light, well drained.
PH: 5.5 to 7.
FERTILIZER: Well-rotted manure, compost, or all-purpose fertilizer.
WATER: Average to dry conditions.
EXPOSURE: Full sun.
SPACING: 18 to 24 inches.
PROPAGATION: Seed or division.

Method

- **Start seeds indoors** eight to ten weeks before planting outside in individual small pots or thinly in flats filled with sterile seed starting medium. Plant seeds ⅛ inch deep, water, and keep in a warm (70° to 75°F) place until they germinate, in fifteen to twenty days. Grow seedlings in bright sunlight or a few inches below a fluorescent light fixture. Transplant seedlings to individual pots when they have two sets of true leaves.

- **Prepare soil outdoors** before planting by tilling in fertilizer and compost or other organic soil improvers, as needed.

- **Sow seeds outdoors** in smoothly prepared and fertilized beds. Annual seeds may be started outdoors after all danger of frost has passed, but this method will be successful only where summers are long. Where they are not, seeds must be started indoors. Perennial and biennial seeds are sown outdoors in late fall or early spring. Plant seeds 12 inches apart and ¼ inch deep. Do not let seedbed dry out.

Tips · Statice is very tolerant of salt spray and is therefore a good plant for a seashore garden.

· To dry statice, cut it when the flowers are fully open and hang it in bunches, upside down, in a cool, dry area.

- **Thin** outdoor-grown seedlings when they are 6 inches high to their permanent spacing.

- **Set plants outdoors** after all danger of frost has passed, after hardening off several days in shade. Set biennial or perennial plants outdoors in spring or summer up to two months before the first fall frost.

- **Divide** perennial plants in early spring when new growth begins if plants are too crowded.

- **Water** when the soil starts to dry out. Statice is very drought resistant and will withstand infrequent watering.

- **Fertilize** at planting time. Fertilize perennial and biennial statice in spring when growth begins. No other feeding is necessary.

- **Pests and diseases** include aphids, which can be controlled with insecticidal soap, and leaf spot, which can be controlled with a fungicide.

Selected Species

Limonium bonduellii (Algerian sea lavender). An annual or biennial that grows 2 to 3 feet tall, Algerian sea lavender has panicles of yellow flowers and lobed leaves.

L. latifolium (Wideleaf sea lavender). This perennial is hardy to Zone 3 and grows 2 to 3 feet tall. It has lavender, blue, white, or pink flowers on 2- to 3-foot-tall plants.

L. sinuatum (Notchleaf sea lavender). This species is an annual or biennial that has white, blue, lavender, or red flowers on 12- to 30-inch-tall plants.

STOCK

Botanical name: *Matthiola* (Cruciferae)

Beautiful as cut flowers or in flower borders, most stocks are easily grown hardy annuals. Flowers on tall spires may be single or double, and have a wonderful sweet scent. Seeds of singles and doubles are mixed in the same packet—some seedsmen offer tips for selecting seedlings that will prove to be the desirable doubles. Stocks grow best during cool, misty weather and are used in cool greenhouses as well as gardens.

PLANT TYPES: Hardy annual or biennial.
GROWING RANGE: All zones, winter only in hot climates.
HARDINESS: Cold hardy, but degree varies with type (biennials are hardiest); dislikes heat above 90°F.
PLANT HEIGHT: 1 to 2½ feet.
FLOWER COLOR: White, ivory, rose, lilac, magenta, peach.
FLOWER FORM: Single or double flowers about 2 inches wide on tall spires, sometimes branched.
SEASON OF BLOOM: Spring or summer in most areas, all year in cool but frost-free areas, late winter in hot parts of Zones 9 to 11.
SOIL: Any good well-drained garden soil.
PH: 6.5 to 7.5.
FERTILIZER: Well-rotted manure, bonemeal, all-purpose or low-nitrogen, high-phosphorus and -potassium fertilizer.
WATER: Average to moist conditions.
EXPOSURE: Full sun in most areas, light shade in hot parts of Zones 7 to 11.
SPACING: 4 to 12 inches.
PROPAGATION: Seed.

Method

- **Start seeds indoors** eight to ten weeks before last frost. Germination takes ten days. Grow in flats (sprinkle evenly) or six-packs in moist potting soil. Cover seed with no more than ⅛ inch of soil. Water and keep at 60°F until seeds germinate, usually in ten to fourteen days, then grow in a sunny area or a few inches below a fluorescent light fixture. When seedlings have six leaves, step them up to 4-inch pots.

· **Prepare soil outdoors** before planting by tilling in fertilizer, compost, bonemeal, and other soil improvers, as needed.

· **Sow seeds outdoors** where they will grow about four weeks before the last frost and repeat a few weeks later for a continuing supply of flowers. In smoothly prepared and fertilized beds, plant seeds an inch or two apart and cover with ⅛ inch of soil. Do not let the seedbed dry out.

· **Thin or transplant** seedlings (indoor or outdoor grown) when they are 4 inches high, to their permanent spacing and location, or to 8-inch pots. Handle them with care to avoid bruising stems.

· **Set plants outdoors,** after hardening off in the shade a few days, about when tulips bloom in spring in northern and central areas, after the danger of heavy frost passes. In Zones 9 to 11, with mild winters (a few light frosts), stock may be sown and set out at any time of year if heat will not exceed 90°F. Plants should be about 4 inches tall.

· **Water** often to prevent the soil from drying out.

· **Fertilize** lightly at planting time. Boost blossoms by applying a low-nitrogen, high-phosphorus and -potassium fertilizer when plants are 5 or 6 inches tall.

· **Pests and diseases** are few, but slugs sometimes are a problem. Kill or repel slugs with slug and snail bait and/or partly submerged pans of beer, or by sprinkling diatomaceous earth or wood ashes about the plants.

· **Mulch** plants that grow in dry areas with several inches of bark chips or other mulch, but do not cover the crowns of the plants.

· **Pinch back** tips for bushiness, or leave plants unpinched for taller cut flowers.

· **Stake** tall clumps inside peony hoops.

· **Protect in winter** with several inches of mulch; biennials may need cover, especially in windy areas. Remove mulch in gradual stages when new growth begins.

Selected Species and Cultivars

Matthiola incana (Stock, Gillyflower). This is the species of stock sold by florists and includes these popular cultivars:
  'Brompton,' hardy biennials, 18 inches tall and strong;
  'Large Flowering Ten Week,' half-hardy annuals, 12 or more inches tall;
  'Trysomic Giant Imperial,' hardy annuals up to 2½ feet tall that are taller and brighter than most types; and
  'Trysomic Seven Week,' quickly grown from seed into bushy flowering plants 12 to 15 inches tall. These are your best bet in hot summer areas—they finish blooming before the "dog days" arrive.

M. longipetala bicornis (Night-scented stock). Bears single pale violet flowers on plants 12 to 18 inches tall. Each night the flowers emit a pervasive sweet scent. Stems and flowers may wilt during the day, but will revive at night. Light shade is helpful for this hardy annual.

STRAWFLOWER

Botanical name: *Helichrysum* (Compositae)
Other common names: Immortelle, Everlasting

Here is a useful everlasting plant that southern gardeners can grow very easily. Strawflowers are native to Australia and tolerate all kinds of weather—if a lot of it is hot. There are annual and tender perennial species. In northern and central states, plants grow best if started indoors and then moved outside around the time of the last expected frost. Flowers are used in borders and in floral arrangements, fresh or dried.

PLANT TYPES: Annual or tender perennial.
GROWING RANGE: All zones for annuals, Zones 8 (with mulch) to 11 for perennials.
   Start plants indoors in Zone 5 and north.
HARDINESS: Very hardy, thrives in heat, survives light frost.
PLANT HEIGHT: 1 to 4 feet for most types.
FLOWER COLOR: White, yellow, pink, deep rose, orange, red, wine, magenta.
FLOWER FORM: Daisylike heads with central discs and strawlike pointed petals.
SEASON OF BLOOM: Late summer into fall in most regions, any time of year in
   frost-free areas.
SOIL: Good to rich, moist.
PH: 6.5 to 7.5.
FERTILIZER: Well-rotted manure, all-purpose or high-phosphorus fertilizer.
WATER: Average to dry conditions.
EXPOSURE: Full sun, sun or light shade in the South.
SPACING: 1 to 2 feet.
PROPAGATION: Seed.

❧ *Method*

- **Start seeds indoors** eight weeks before last frost. Grow in individual small pots or six-packs in moist potting soil, covering seed with barely ⅛ inch of soil. Water and keep at 60° to 70°F until seeds germinate, about ten days. Grow in a sunny area or a few inches below a fluorescent light fixture. When seedlings have four to six leaves, step them up to larger pots if necessary.

- **Prepare soil outdoors** before planting by tilling in fertilizer, compost, and other soil improvers, as needed.

- **Sow seeds outdoors** where they will grow from two weeks before to two weeks after the last expected frost. Plant seeds in November or December in Zones 10 and 11. In smoothly prepared and fertilized beds, plant seeds 3 or more inches apart and barely cover with ⅛ inch of soil. Do not let the seedbed dry out.

- **Thin** seedlings grown outdoors to their permanent spacing when they are about 4 inches tall. With care, thinnings may be transplanted. Indoors, when seedlings have four to six leaves, move them to larger pots if crowded.

- **Set plants outdoors** after all danger of frost has passed, after hardening them off in shade for a few days.

- **Water** seedlings often to prevent the soil from drying out. Mature plants will thrive in nearly dry soil.

- **Fertilize** lightly at planting time. Boost blossoms by applying a low-nitrogen, high-phosphorous and -potassium fertilizer when plants are 5 to 6 inches tall.

- **Pests and diseases** seldom are problems.

- **Mulch** plants that grow in very dry areas with several inches of bark chips or other mulch to keep soil cool and moist.

- **Pinch back** tips for bushiness.

- **Stake** tall plants with slim bamboo stakes, wires, or peony hoops.

- **Protect in winter** by mulching fall-planted annuals as well as perennials (as above) in Zones 8 to 9. In Zones 10 and 11, no mulch is needed except in dry areas.

Tip · Harvest flowers for drying before they open fully (before pollen shows). You can attach them to wires while they are still fresh. Discard the whole stem and stick a thin piece of florist's wire (or a dried plant stem) about 1/4 inch deep into the bottom of each fresh-picked flower head. Stand the flower-topped wires in jars and dry them in a cool, airy place, out of direct sunlight. The blossoms soon seal themselves onto the wires with no glue. Or hang flowers upside down in long-stemmed bunches to dry in the usual way.

Selected Species and Cultivars

Helichrysum belloides (Everlasting daisy). A trailing, low-growing, shrubby strawflower, this tiny, silvery white everlasting blossoms in summer. It is a tender perennial from New Zealand that needs protection from extremely hot or cold temperatures.

H. bracteatum (Strawflower). This popular annual is found in many dried flower arrangements. Seeds for tall or short, small- or large-flowered, mixed- or single-colored plants can be purchased. Though usually used for dried wreaths and bouquets, the flowers look fine in the border or freshly cut in live bouquets. Grow this as a fall-planted biennial in Zones 9 to 11, as an annual elsewhere. Popular cultivars are:

'Bright Bikini,' a floriferous dwarf type with flowers up to 2 inches wide, growing a little over a foot tall; and

'Monstrosum,' in all colors, usually 20 to 30 inches tall. This name is used for the largest flowered types.

SUNDROPS

Botanical name: *Oenothera* (Onagraceae)
Other common name: Evening primrose

These great-looking native prairie flowers grow in any sunny place with the minimum of care, spreading rapidly via stoloniferous roots. The sundrops open in the morning or afternoon, and the evening primroses open late, as their names suggest. All species of *Oenothera* are used in wildflower meadows, ornamental borders, and rock gardens. Lower-growing types stay neater than tall ones. All are easy to grow and have allelopathic roots: they kill weeds.

PLANT TYPE: Hardy perennial.
GROWING RANGE: Zones 3 to 10.
HARDINESS: Very hardy, tolerating cold, heat, and changeable weather.
PLANT HEIGHT: Under 1 to over 3 feet.
FLOWER COLOR: White, lemon yellow, soft rose.
FLOWER FORM: Clusters of flowers open in masses each day. Each 2- to 4-inch blossom
 has several slightly cupped, oval petals and prominent stamens.
SEASON OF BLOOM: Summer, for 4 or more weeks.
SOIL: Any well-drained soil, preferably somewhat sandy.
PH: 6.5 to 7 (slightly acidic to neutral).
FERTILIZER: Well-rotted manure, compost, all-purpose fertilizer.
WATER: Needs little water but tolerates damp soil at times.
EXPOSURE: Full sun in most areas, bright partial shade where temperatures are in the
 90's (F).
SPACING: 6 inches to 2 feet apart.
PROPAGATION: Usually by division, occasionally from seed.

Method

- **Start seeds indoors** in early spring and hope for germination in ten days or more. Pat the tiny seeds thinly onto the surface of six-packs or flats filled with moist, sterile seed starting medium that is one-third sand for good drainage. Sundrops and evening primroses are rarely grown from seed because they multiply so rapidly by division.

- **Prepare soil outdoors** in beds before planting by tilling in fertilizer, compost, and other soil improvers, as needed.

- **Sow seeds outdoors** in a prepared bed any time in spring or summer in northern and central areas, or in fall when the weather is cool in areas with little frost. Make rows about 1 inch deep and plant seeds sparsely, ½ inch apart, without covering them.

- **Thin or transplant** seedlings when they are about 3 inches tall. Shift indoor-grown seedlings to larger pots as they become crowded, or to nursery beds outdoors if weather permits. Plants started outdoors should be thinned to at least 4 inches apart.

- **Set plants outdoors** in their permanent positions after hardening them off several days in shade any time in spring or, farther north, early summer, when daytime temperatures are around 60°F. Set them a foot or two apart to let them spread and fill in, to prevent having to divide them for a few years, or plant them closer together for immediate effect.

- **Divide and thin** crowded clumps by separating and replanting the plantlets annually, early in spring when leaf growth begins (the new foliage of some types is red). They will bloom the same year.

- **Water** in spring while leaf growth is rapid if soil is on the dry side. In summer, water only if soil becomes dry an inch below the surface.

- **Fertilize** lightly at planting time or in early spring and again just before plants bloom.

- **Pests and diseases** rarely are problems. Trap Japanese beetles and treat whiteflies with insecticidal soap or pyrethrum.

- **Mulch** plants with an inch or two of composted or shredded leaves or small bark chips to help keep moisture in the soil.

- **Stake** tall types if necessary, but this is rarely the case.

- **Cut down** stems just after they flower, or after seed ripens if you want to grow it. Sometimes plants reflower in a few weeks.

- **Protect in winter** by placing mulch an inch or two thick around each low-growing plant (now in its rosette stage). Good drainage helps prevent winterkill.

Selected Species and Cultivars

Oenothera fruticosa (Sundrops). Sometimes confused with the similar *O. tetragona,* these sundrops are upright plants (1 to 3 feet) with quantities of 2-inch yellow flowers in clusters on stiff stems. Cultivars include 'Yellow River,' about 2 feet tall and very sturdy; and 'Fyrverkerii,' about a foot tall, floriferous, and neat—good for rock gardens.

O. hookeri (Hooker's evening primrose). The yellow blossoms of this western mountain wildflower open at dusk on 1 ½- to 8-foot-tall stems in moist areas. It adapts well to gardens.

O. missourensis (Ozark sundrops, Missouri sundrops). These sprawling plants are about a foot high with showy 4-inch yellow flowers opening in the evening. They prefer neutral or limy soil.

O. pilosella (Sundrops). This day-flowering erect plant is often grown in gardens. Its veined yellow flowers are about 2 inches wide, appearing in clusters on plants growing from 6 inches to 2 feet tall.

O. speciosa (White evening primrose). A lovely pink or white day-flowering, short-lived perennial with 3-inch blossoms, this is native from Kansas to Texas. It grows 1 to 2 feet tall on running rhizomatous roots.

SUNFLOWER

Botanical Name: *Helianthus* (Compositae)

Sunflowers, those tall golden-flowered plants usually grown for edible seed, are also available in a wide color range for the flower garden in smaller-flowered, branching varieties. They are easy to grow in sunny places. Used for cut flowers, temporary privacy screens, or bedding plants, sunflowers look best in bands or groups. Where there is room for them, small-flowered sunflowers such as 'Diadem' make outstanding background plants in mixed borders. Large-seeded types such as 'Russian Giant' are often grown in vegetable gardens. Though annual sunflowers are most familiar, perennials such as *Helianthus* x *multiflorus* and *H. tuberosus* are also useful in gardens. *H. tuberosus,* Jerusalem artichoke, grows from edible tubers.

PLANT TYPES: Annual or perennial.

GROWING RANGE: All zones.

HARDINESS: Tender or hardy in cold weather, varying with the species. All types tolerate high heat; most are killed by frost.

PLANT HEIGHT: 1½ to over 8 feet.

FLOWER COLOR: Gold, pale yellow, orange, red, rust, or white. Small-flowered types are sometimes banded or bicolored.

FLOWER FORM: Disc and ray flowers up to a foot wide grow on woody stalks. Central discs are smaller and ray flowers (the "petals" of sunflowers) longer on ornamental varieties.

SEASON OF BLOOM: Late summer in most zones, spring through late fall in Zones 8 to 10.

SOIL: Any garden soil.

PH: 6.5 to 7.

FERTILIZER: Any flower or all-purpose fertilizer. Well-rotted manure and compost help increase plant size.

WATER: Prefers moist soil but, when mature, tolerates drought.

EXPOSURE: 8 or more hours of sun per day.

SPACING: 1 to 2½ feet.

PROPAGATION: Annuals from seed, perennials from seed or by division.

Method

- **Start seeds indoors** three weeks before the last expected frost 2 inches apart in flats or six-packs, or earlier in individual 4- or 6-inch pots. Cover seeds with ½ inch of soil, water them, and keep them in a warm (65° to 75°F) place. Seeds germinate in about seven days and grow quickly. Grow in bright sunlight or a few inches below a fluorescent light.

- **Prepare soil outdoors** at the time of the last expected frost, tilling fertilizer and soil amendments into the bed. In Zones 7 to 11, several successive crops may be sown in spring and summer. Seeds may also be sown in winter in frost-free areas.

- **Sow seeds outdoors** after the danger of frost has passed. In tilled, fertilized beds, make rows about 2 inches deep. Plant seeds 4 inches apart and cover with ½ inch of soil. Plants may be sown where they will grow or in nursery beds for later transplanting.

- **Thin or transplant** seedlings when they are 4 inches tall. Shift indoor-grown plants to permanent positions in the garden or into larger pots—they may be grown in tubs. Thin and transplant outdoor-grown plants to desired spacing and placement.

- **Set plants outdoors** in their permanent places after the last expected frost, when the weather is settled. Mix fertilizer into the planting holes. Harden off indoor-grown plants in the shade several days. If seedlings are leggy, bury the stems (up to the first two leaves) as well as the roots. Firm into place and water well. Plant divisions or tubers of perennials in early spring.

Tips · Although fairly tender, annual sunflower seedlings tolerate some cold weather. In areas that are nearly frost-free, fall-planted sunflower seedlings sometimes make it through light frosts in the winter and then come into bloom much earlier on stronger plants in the spring.
  · In vegetable gardens, tall, large sunflowers may be interplanted with climbing beans or cucumbers.
  · Plants are rarely offered at garden centers because of their large size, but they are exceptionally easy to grow at home. Also, home-saved seed yields variable but good results.

- **Divide** perennial varieties in spring when new growth begins about once every three years, if needed.
- **Water** young plants frequently if soil is dry, but taper off as they get taller and sturdier. In hot areas, plants need more water.
- **Fertilize** plants steadily with the slow-release type or occasional side-dressings of all-purpose fertilizer.
- **Pests** include squirrels, birds, and other forms of wildlife. You can discourage pests attracted to the seeds by applying powdered cayenne pepper mixed with water and a spoonful of salad oil to the ripening flower heads. Mildew (treat with fungicide), caterpillars (try rotenone), and wind damage sometimes spoil the looks of the leafy part of the plant even though flowers remain attractive for cutting. Perennial types have fewer pest problems.
- **Mulch** several inches deep to keep the soil evenly moist with shredded leaves or other mulch.
- **Pinch off** the central growing tip when plants have about eight leaves if you want floriferous, branched plants. For single large seed heads, do not pinch.
- **Stake** bushy or tall plants, and heap a few inches of soil on top of the roots to help anchor plants.
- **Deadhead** plants frequently by removing spent blooms to extend the bloom season, unless seed is wanted. Cutting the fresh flowers for bouquets has the same effect. When annual plants become too branched and spent, discard them.
- **Harvest** seeds by cutting and drying mature flower heads when petals drop and seeds

are ripe—firm and well filled. If you like, leave stalks of annuals with ripe seed heads in place for the birds to feed on during the winter.

· **Protect in winter** by mulching perennials with several inches of shredded leaves or other mulch.

Selected Species and Cultivars

Helianthus annuus (Sunflower). Hybrids of this popular annual include:

'Autumn Beauty' or, similarly, 'Color Fashion,' growing about 5 feet tall with 6-inch banded or solid color flowers, in cream through mahogany including rosy shades;

'Piccolo,' growing 4 feet tall, with uniform, semidouble gold flowers, good for bedding and cutting;

'Russian Giant,' growing 8 feet tall or more, a large-centered, large-seeded variety primarily raised for the edible seed; and

'Sunspot,' with 10-inch blooms on dwarf plants 2 feet tall, which is a novelty for low beds.

H. debilis cucumerifolius (Cucumberleaf sunflower). This annual species makes a graceful border plant, growing 4 to 5 feet tall and, if pinched back, very wide and bushy. Long-petaled flowers are 5 or 6 inches in diameter. It deserves to be grown more often. Cultivars include:

'Diadem,' flowering in white to pale yellow with black centers and long, slender petals;

'Italian White,' nearly white with dark centers;

'Orion,' with twisted golden petals; and

'Stella,' with intensely golden, curled petals and purplish centers.

H. x *multiflorus* (Perennial sunflower, Prairie sunflower). Plants grow 3 to 8 feet tall, with plentiful flowers around 3 inches wide in clusters. The cultivar 'Maximilian,' for Zones 3 to 8, grows 6 to 8 feet tall and has golden blossoms with brown centers.

H. tuberosus (Jerusalem artichoke). See pages 489–91 for a more detailed description.

SWEET PEA

Botanical name: *Lathyrus* (Leguminosae)

Sweet peas, originally from Sicily, are known for their fragrant ruffled flowers of tremendous charm. They are emblematic of the Edwardian era in England, when "no dinner table, no wedding, no bouquet, and no buttonhole was complete without the sweet pea," according to Lys de Bray's *Manual of Old-Fashioned Flowers.*

In the garden, some types are low and spreading, while others are tall climbing vines that require support. Since they do poorly in hot weather, start them indoors in the Northeast and other areas where spring is short and summer is hot. They are used for cutting, bedding, edgings, and hanging baskets (dwarf types), in vertical gardens (climbing types), and in cool greenhouses.

PLANT TYPES: Hardy annual or perennial.
GROWING RANGE: All zones as an annual, Zones 3 to 9 as a perennial.
HARDINESS: Annuals are killed by heavy frost and prolonged heat in the 90's (F).
Perennials tolerate cold winters and hot summers.

PLANT HEIGHT: 6 inches to over 6 feet.

FLOWER COLOR: Shades of yellow, white, peach, rose, red, blue, purple, or nearly black.

FLOWER FORM: Pealike blooms an inch or more wide aligned on leafless stems several inches long

SEASON OF BLOOM: Any time of year in mild weather, especially late spring.

SOIL: Average to rich, moist but well drained.

PH: 7 to 7.5.

FERTILIZER: Well-rotted manure, compost, flower or tomato fertilizer.

WATER: Moist conditions, with extra water in hot weather.

EXPOSURE: Full sun in most areas, bright partial shade in Zones 7 to 11.

SPACING: 6 inches to 2 feet.

PROPAGATION: Seed or division.

Method

- **Start seeds indoors** in February for bloom in late spring. In parts of the South without heavy freezes, start plants in the fall and treat them as biennials. Plant them ½ inch deep in individual 4-inch pots where they germinate in ten to twenty days and grow quickly in ideal temperatures between 60° and 65°F. Provide bright sunlight or grow plants several inches below fluorescent lights.

- **Prepare soil outdoors** in beds at planting time, digging deeply to incorporate soil improvers such as compost and fertilizer.

- **Sow seeds outdoors** ½ inch deep and at least 3 inches apart in beds in spring or summer after the danger of heavy frost has passed, about four weeks before your frost-free date. In Zones 9 to 11, plant them in the fall.

- **Thin or transplant** seedlings to their permanent places at or near the frost-free date.

- **Set plants outdoors** in permanent places after the danger of heavy freezes passes, after hardening off in shade for several days.

- **Divide** roots of large clumps of perennial vines every other year in early spring if they are crowded, which is likely. Replant divisions immediately.

- **Water** frequently enough to keep the soil moist. Spray plants to cool them off in summer.

- **Fertilize** at planting time and keep plants well supplied with fertilizer throughout their growth. Top-dress beds of perennial types with compost or leaf mold each fall.

- **Pests and diseases** are few, but rabbits and deer eat the flowers and foliage if they can reach them. Use repellents or sprinkle cayenne pepper on plants to discourage them. Wire supports for the plants help repel deer, as the wire makes them unappetizing to chew.

- **Mulch** plants with several inches of composted leaves or small bark chips to help keep moisture in the soil.

- **Stake** vining plants on 6-foot-tall stakes or train them onto trellises or fences. Cultivars under 2 feet tall need no staking.

- **Pinch back** central tip once to stimulate growth of floriferous side branches.

- **Cut fresh** flowers often or deadhead plants to encourage repeated bloom.

- **Protect in winter** by mulching perennial plants with several inches of shredded leaves or other lightweight mulch.

Tips · Some growers report higher flower yields after treating seed with legume inoculant such as is used for edible peas. This helps the plants hold on to nitrogen, especially in soils where legumes have not been grown recently.

· Unwrinkled dark seed can be presoaked overnight to speed germination, but wrinkled or tan types should not be, because they are more likely to rot.

Selected Species and Cultivars

Lathyrus latifolius (Everlasting sweet pea). This hardy sweet pea resembling the annual types is a wildly vigorous and heat-resistant, summer-blooming climber with red, rose, or white blossoms. Although lovely, it can be invasive. It climbs over 8 feet high on trellises and fences or sprawls down slopes equally well. Keep this one trained and trimmed.

L. odoratus. This is the annual sweet pea grown on short spreading plants or tall vines (about 8 feet tall in good conditions). Both have stems carrying several large, pealike flowers. The many strains include heavily ruffled types in most of the colors of the rainbow, including true blue. Larger seed specialists such as Thompson & Morgan sell seed in separate colors. Popular cultivars include:

'Antique Fantasy,' a group of old-fashioned climbers, in many colors, smaller flowering than some new types, but appealing and sweet smelling.

'Bijou,' a type that needs no staking, growing 15 inches tall, in all colors, with flower stems about 6 inches long. This is early to bloom and continues for a long time because it is heat resistant;

'Cupid,' an unusual carpeting strain that grows just 4 to 6 inches high with masses of upright pink flowers, one or two per stem. Plants spread to 18 inches wide and are wonderful in hanging baskets and on well-drained slopes;

'Early Mammoth,' an American-bred climber with good heat resistance and large frilled flowers in the full range of colors;

'Floral Tribute,' a mixture of some of the best climbers, including many British and North American award winners, in all colors;

'Jet Set,' a compact, heat-tolerant 3-foot-tall type with strongly fragrant flowers in the whole range of colors;

'North Shore,' with rippled navy blue standards (lower portion of bloom) and richly purple wings (top portion of bloom) in large flowers of the Spencer type, an outstanding variety in flower arrangements or the garden;

'Snoopea,' an easy-to-grow carpeting type with no tendrils for climbing, in all colors. It grows a little over a foot high, and its well-filled flower stems are fine for cutting; and

'Spencer Varieties,' large-blooming climbers derived from frilled blooms that first appeared in Countess Spencer's garden in 1900. The many colors and forms are sold mixed or separately. If the weather is not too hot, these will bloom all summer.

TORENIA

Botanical name: *Torenia* (Scrophulariaceae)
Other common names: Wishbone flower, Florida pansy

These bushy, low-growing plants are constantly covered with small bright flowers during hot summer weather. Their tolerance for heat, rain, drought, and sandy soil have earned them the name *Florida pansy.* There are about forty species, but only a few are widely grown. *Torenia* species are from tropical and subtropical Asia and Africa, and are short-lived perennials, though they are most often grown as annuals. They are used as bedding plants in shade and in greenhouses, and in hanging baskets and other containers. Effective under deciduous trees, these easy-care plants bloom profusely in midsummer in the North.

PLANT TYPE: Tender perennial, usually grown as an annual.
GROWING RANGE: All zones.
HARDINESS: Withstands high heat where there is high humidity, but is killed by frost.
PLANT HEIGHT: Under 1 foot for most garden types.
FLOWER COLOR: Most often blue or violet, sometimes white or pink, touched with yellow or orange at the base.
FLOWER FORM: Multitudes of 1-inch, double-lipped tubular flowers that resemble snapdragons.
SEASON OF BLOOM: Any time of year during warm weather.
SOIL: Any soil.
PH: 6.5 to 7.5.
FERTILIZER: Well-rotted manure, all-purpose or high-phosphorus fertilizer.
WATER: Average to moist conditions.
EXPOSURE: Partial shade.
SPACING: 6 inches.
PROPAGATION: Seed or tip cuttings.

Method

- **Start seeds indoors** eight to twelve weeks before the last expected frost. Barely cover the thinly sown tiny seed (no more than 1/8 inch deep) in flats or small pots filled with moist potting soil. Water, cover with plastic (plants germinate in darkness), and keep at 70° to 80°F until seeds germinate, in one or two weeks. After seedlings appear, grow them in a sunny area or a few inches below a fluorescent light fixture, at 55° to 65°F—cool temperatures help keep them stocky, not leggy. When young plants are crowded, move them to individual pots.

- **Prepare soil outdoors** before planting by tilling in fertilizer, compost, and other soil improvers, as needed.

- **Sow seeds outdoors** in shaded nursery beds in late winter (Zones 10 and 11) or early spring. This is only practical where the growing season is very long, as in Zones 8 to 11. (Start seeds indoors or, in cooler areas, buy plants instead.) Plant seed thinly ⅛ inch deep. In warm climates, established plants, which are not long lived, often self-sow.

- **Thin** seedlings if they are crowded. Move them to their permanent spacing when they are 3 or more inches tall.

- **Set plants outdoors** when weather is warm, after the danger of frost has passed. Harden them off outdoors for a day or two in shade.

- **Water** seedlings whenever the soil starts to dry out. Mature plants tolerate dry conditions, but grow better with average to high moisture.

- **Take cuttings** 3 to 4 inches long during warm weather and plant them 1 or 2 inches deep in moist soil in shade. Do not let cuttings dry out, and they will root in two or three weeks.

- **Fertilize** lightly at planting time and periodically during growth.

- **Pests and diseases** seldom are problems.

- **Mulch** plants in dry weather with 2 inches of bark chips, shredded leaves, or other mulch if you wish.

- **Pinch back** tips for bushiness when plants are about 4 inches tall, or cut them back several inches if they become too leggy. The pieces pruned off may be rooted for new plants.

Selected Species and Varieties

Torenia fournieri (Blue wings). Blue, lavender, or white blooms have complex markings and a yellow blotch. These everblooming plants grow 8 to 12 inches tall. 'Alba' is a white cultivar, 'Compacta' is low and well branched, and 'Grandiflora' has especially large flowers.

T. 'Clown Mixed' is a popular F_2 hybrid of several species that blooms in ten weeks from seed, two to three weeks earlier than most types. It stays dwarf, about 8 inches tall, and comes in a wide color range that includes pink, red, white, violet, and many shades of blue, with a bright yellow mark on each underlip. Like other torenia, it is everblooming.

TRILLIUM

Botanical name: *Trillium* (Liliaceae)
Other common name: Wake robin

Trillium was aptly named for its three-part leaves and flowers. The foliage is usually deeply veined, pointed, and appears in whorls. Trillium is a hardy perennial used for shady edgings, borders, and woodland and wildflower gardens. Established clumps of *Trillium grandiflorum* make a handsome feature in a woodland garden. They combine well with ferns. Do not pick the flowers or the plant will be weakened.

PLANT TYPE: Hardy perennial (tuberous rhizome).
GROWING RANGE: Zones 3 to 8, varying with the species.
HARDINESS: Tolerant of cold, and must have cold winters; not tolerant of heat.
PLANT HEIGHT: 6 to 18 inches.
FLOWER COLOR: White, pink, brown, red, purple, green, yellow.
FLOWER FORM: 3-petaled, 2 inches across.
SEASON OF BLOOM: Early spring to midspring, once per year.
SOIL: Fertile, well drained, deep, and humus rich.
PH: 5.5 to 6.5.
FERTILIZER: Well-rotted manure, compost, all-purpose fertilizer.
WATER: Moist conditions.
EXPOSURE: Light to deep shade.
SPACING: 8 to 12 inches.
PROPAGATION: Seed or division.

Method

- **Start seeds indoors** in spring in individual small pots or thinly sown in flats filled with sterile seed starting medium. Before sowing, seeds must be refrigerated for three months, then held at 60° to 70°F for three months, then refrigerated again for three months. Plant seeds ¼ inch deep, water, and keep in a warm (60° to 70°F) place until they germinate. Germination may take several months; time varies. Grow seedlings in bright sunlight or a few inches below a fluorescent light fixture.

- **Prepare soil outdoors** before planting by tilling in fertilizer and compost or other organic soil improvers, as needed.

- **Sow seeds outdoors** in smoothly prepared and fertilized beds in late fall. Plant seeds 6 inches apart and ¼ inch deep. Do not let the seedbed dry out. Seeds will not germinate until the second spring.

- **Thin** outdoor-grown seedlings when they are 3 inches high to their permanent spacing. Plant the rhizome 2 to 6 inches deep—the larger it is, the deeper it should be planted.

- **Set plants outdoors** in late spring to summer, up to two months before the first fall frost.

- **Divide** perennial plants in early spring when new growth begins if plants are too crowded and the flower size seems diminished from the year before. However, division is rarely needed. Plants perform well in thick, well-established clumps.

- **Water** frequently to keep the soil constantly moist.

- **Fertilize** gently each year in early spring when growth starts.

- **Pests and diseases** are seldom a problem.

- **Mulch** around growing plants with 2 inches of bark chips or shredded leaves to keep moisture in the soil.

- **Protect in winter** with 4 inches of evergreen boughs or 2 inches of shredded leaves or bark chips in the colder limits of each species' hardiness range. Remove boughs before new growth begins in early spring. However, plants have no trouble emerging through shredded leaves of small bark chips—they need help with dense or rough cover.

Selected Species

Trillium erectum (Purple trillium, Stinking Benjamin). Attractive wine-red flowers 2½ inches wide have golden centers. They tend to nod rather than face outward. Leaves are about 7 inches tall. This is handsome but not as showy as *T. grandiflorum,* and is remarkable for its bad odor. It is native to the East Coast from southern Canada to Virginia and can be grown in Zones 4 to 8.

T. grandiflorum (Great white trillium). The showiest trillium, this garden-worthy type is 8 to 18 inches tall with white outward-facing flowers about 3 inches wide, which fade from white to pink and then purple before turning brown. Unusual forms of the species, varied in flower or leaf shape and color, are not uncommon. This species grows well in woodland shade in Zones 3 to 8, especially in East Coast states.

T. nivale (Snow trillium). The earliest trillium, this charming pygmy is 6 inches tall with white cup-shaped flowers, opening out to typical three-petal form. It is a rare native whose habitat extends from western Pennsylvania to Minnesota and Missouri and can be grown in Zones 6 to 8.

T. sessile (Toadshade, Red trillium). This is a stalkless trillium with a 1½-inch-wide flower that remains closed, otherwise resembling the purple trillium. It is not usually considered garden worthy but is of interest to collectors and rock gardeners growing in Zones 6 to 8. Its native habitat is from New York to Georgia.

T. undulatum (Painted trillium). Thin white petals have radiating red stripes and wavy edges. Flowers are about 2½ inches wide on plants 8 to 20 inches tall. Though beautiful, this trillium is difficult to grow unless you can provide it with a boggy, deeply acid soil, preferably under hemlock trees near ponds or streams in Zones 3 to 7. It is native to moist woods and swamps from Nova Scotia to mountainous parts of Georgia.

TULIP

Botanical name: *Tulipa* (Liliaceae)

Nothing says "spring" more than tulips. Native to Asia and particularly Turkey, these hardy bulbs have been made famous by the Dutch, who still produce most of the world's tulips. The smaller species tulips are best used in informal beds, borders, and rock gardens. The tall, larger, stately tulips are dramatic in formal, massed beds and in clumps in the flower garden or shrub border. Most tulips make excellent cut flowers as well.

PLANT TYPE: Hardy bulb.
GROWING RANGE: Zones 4 to 8.
HARDINESS: Tolerant of heat and cold; must have frost during the winter.
PLANT HEIGHT: 4 to 36 inches.
FLOWER COLOR: Red, pink, orange, gold, yellow, blue, lavender, purple, black, or white; many bicolors.
FLOWER FORM: Single, double, or lily-flowered.

SEASON OF BLOOM: Early to late spring.
SOIL: Rich, sandy, well drained.
PH: 6 to 7.
FERTILIZER: Well-rotted manure, compost, all-purpose fertilizer, or bonemeal.
WATER: Average conditions.
EXPOSURE: Full sun to partial shade; partial shade is preferred in hot areas.
SPACING: 6 to 8 inches.
PROPAGATION: Propagation of hybrid tulips is not recommended for the home gardener; it is best to purchase bulbs. Species tulips may be divided.

Method

- **Prepare soil outdoors** before planting by tilling in bonemeal and compost or other organic soil improvers, as needed.

- **Set bulbs outdoors** in midfall to late fall. Plant them at a depth of 4 to 6 inches.

- **Water** well after planting. Begin to water in spring when growth starts if spring rains do not provide 1 inch of water per week. Water is best applied to the ground so the flowers are not damaged.

- **Fertilize** in spring when shoots begin to emerge.

Tips · Tulips may be grown in Zones 9 and 10 if they are placed in a refrigerator for six to eight weeks during winter and planted outdoors in early spring.
· For best effect, always plant tulips in clumps. Use six bulbs of the smaller tulips and at least three bulbs of larger tulips per clump.
· Squirrels like to eat the flowers of some tulip bulbs. There is little that can be done to discourage them. Where squirrels are prevalent, choose low-growing varieties or lily-flowered tulips.
· Tulips may be forced to bloom indoors in the winter and early spring by potting the bulbs in fall, placing the pots in a refrigerator or outdoors if the temperature stays under 40°F for four to six weeks, and then bringing the pots indoors to grow and flower.

- **Pests and diseases** include a viral disease that causes the flowers to take on a greenish mottling. There is no cure, and bulbs severely infected should be dug up and discarded. Insect pests are not generally a problem. To protect from rodents digging up bulbs, plant bulbs inside a wire mesh cage, or secure a screen of wire mesh on top of the planting beds.

- **Mulch** around growing plants with 2 inches of bark chips or shredded leaves to keep moisture in the soil.

- **Remove** flowers as soon as they fade to prevent seed set and encourage bulb development.

- **Remove** foliage in the late spring after it has turned completely brown and pulls easily from the soil.

- **Divide** species tulips every two to three years when the flowers start to become smaller. When the flowers of hybrid tulips become small, it is best to discard and replace them.

- **Protect in winter** by mulching with 6 inches of evergreen boughs or 2 inches of shredded leaves in the fall. Remove evergreen boughs, if used, when leaf growth begins in early spring.

Selected Species and Varieties

Tulips are divided into two groups, species tulips and hybrid tulips. The most common species tulips are:

Tulipa acuminata (Turkish tulip). This species has 3- to 4-inch flowers with yellow or pink petals that are long and pointed, and somewhat twisted and spidery. It blooms in midspring to late spring on 12- to 18-inch stems.

T. clusiana (Candy-stick tulip). Fragrant, 2-inch flowers with pointed petals adorn this plant. Blooms are yellow or white, and striped on the outside in pinkish red. Flowers appear on 9- to 15-inch stems in midspring to late spring.

T. praestans. Growing 12 inches tall, the 2-inch flowers of this species are red and appear in bouquets of up to four. The most popular variety is 'Fusilier,' which has four to six flowers per stem. These tulips bloom in early spring.

Hybrid tulips include:

Cottage tulips, late-spring blooming tulips with single, egg-shaped, 4-inch flowers with pointed or rounded petals. Flower stems grow 36 inches long. They are available in most colors except purple and blue.

Darwin tulips, which come in every color and bloom in late spring. Single flowers are 3 to 4 inches long and are cup-shaped. Flowering stems are 30 inches tall.

Darwin hybrid tulips, which are descendants of Darwin tulips and bloom in midspring before the Darwins. They have oval- to egg-shaped flowers with a square base. They are one of the largest tulips, up to 4 inches long, and bloom on 30-inch-tall stems. Colors are mostly shades of red, orange, and yellow.

Double Early tulips, which have 4-inch double flowers that resemble a peony. They are very long lasting, and bloom on 6- to 12-inch-tall stems. Flowers are mostly red, yellow, orange, or white. Bloom time is early spring. These are sometimes sold as *peony-flowered tulips.*

Double Late tulips, which resemble the Double Early tulips but bloom in late spring. They are sometimes called *peony tulips.* Flowers are 6 inches across and bloom on 18- to 22-inch-tall stems.

Fosterana tulips, which have 4-inch single flowers that bloom in early spring on 8- to 12-inch stems. The most popular are the 'Emperor' varieties, with flowers of white, yellow, gold, orange, or red. Foliage is sometimes mottled or striped.

Greigii tulips, which grow 6 to 14 inches tall and have broad, wavy, mottled or striped foliage. Single flowers are 3 inches tall and slightly pointed. They bloom in midspring to late spring and are primarily red, yellow, or orange. 'Red Riding Hood' is a very common cultivar.

Kaufmanniana tulips, which are descendants of *T. kaufmanniana,* the water lily tulip. The hybrids grow 4 to 8 inches tall and have 3 ½-inch single flowers that open almost flat. These tulips are one of the first to bloom in early spring. They are also one of the longest-lasting tulips, living for many years.

Lily-flowered tulips, which have petals that are long, pointed, and curve outward like lily petals. Flowers are 2 to 4 inches long and bloom in late spring on 24-inch stems. Squirrels like them the least of the hybrid tulips.

Parrot tulips, which have large (6- to 7-inch) flowers with petals that are fringed, cut, or feathered, and often marked in green. Stems grow 24 inches tall; bloom is in late spring.

Single Early tulips, which are similar in appearance to Cottage or Darwin tulips, with egg-shaped 2- to 4-inch flowers, but bloom in early spring. Stems are shorter, 10 to 16 inches tall. Flowers are usually red, yellow, or white; some are fragrant.

Triumph tulips, which are crosses between Single Early tulips and later-flowering hybrids, and bloom in midspring between the two. Flowers are 2 to 4 inches high, single, egg-shaped, and bloom on 20-inch stems.

VERBENA

Botanical name: *Verbena* x *hybrida* (Verbenaceae)

Verbena has lobed or toothed, quilted or textured leaves and rounded clusters of small, tubular, fragrant, brightly colored flowers that often have a contrasting white eye. Verbena generally has a spreading habit, and is used for edging, borders, ground covers, rock gardens, slopes, in hanging baskets, and as cut flowers.

PLANT TYPE: Tender or hardy annual.
GROWING RANGE: All zones.
HARDINESS: Tolerant of heat, sensitive to frost.
PLANT HEIGHT: 8 to 12 inches.
FLOWER COLOR: Red, white, violet, purple, blue, cream, rose, pink.
FLOWER FORM: Clusters of small tubular flowers are 2 ½ to 4 inches across.
SEASON OF BLOOM: Summer.
SOIL: Rich, light, well drained.
PH: 6 to 7.
FERTILIZER: Well-rotted manure, compost, or all-purpose fertilizer.
WATER: Average to dry conditions.
EXPOSURE: Full sun in most regions, full sun to partial shade in hot regions.
SPACING: 12 to 15 inches.
PROPAGATION: Seed or stem cuttings.

Method

· **Start seeds indoors** ten to twelve weeks before the last spring frost in small pots or flats filled with sterile seed starting medium. Refrigerate seeds for seven days before sowing. Sow seeds heavily because the germination rate is usually low. Plant seeds thinly without covering them with soil, water, and keep in a warm (70° to 75°F) place until they germinate, in twenty to twenty-five days. Keep flats covered with black plastic during germination as they need darkness to germinate. Grow seedlings in bright sunlight or a few inches below a fluorescent light fixture. Transplant them to individual pots when they have two true leaves.

- **Prepare soil outdoors** before planting by tilling in fertilizer and compost or other organic soil improvers, as needed.

- **Do not sow** seeds outdoors.

- **Set plants outdoors** after all danger of frost has passed, after hardening off several days in shade.

- **Take cuttings** during summer or fall. Verbena can be grown indoors in winter in a cool (55°F) house or greenhouse.

- **Water** as soon as the soil starts to dry out.

- **Fertilize** at planting time and monthly during growth and flowering.

- **Pests and diseases** include damping off disease, which attacks seedlings; to combat, be careful not to overwater seedlings and drench seed flats with benomyl before sowing. Mature plants are susceptible to mildew, which can be controlled by not overwatering and not getting the foliage wet. Insect pests generally are not a problem.

- **Mulch** around growing plants with 2 inches of bark chips or shredded leaves to keep moisture in the soil.

Tip · Although verbena prefers a rich, fertile soil with average moisture, it will tolerate drought and poor soil. Verbena grows best where summers are hot.

Selected Cultivars

Several cultivars of verbena have been developed, all with a wide range of colors. 'Ideal Florist' is 12 inches tall and vigorous. 'Romance' is 8 inches high and grows into a dense carpet. 'Showtime' is 10 inches high and has a better rate of seed germination than many verbenas. The 'Sparkle' series includes the cultivars 'Amethyst,' 'Crystal,' 'Splendor,' 'Scarlet,' 'Blaze,' and 'Delight.' They all grow 8 inches tall. 'Springtime' blooms more quickly than other cultivars and also has a good rate of seed germination.

VINCA

Botanical name: *Catharanthus roseus* (Apocynaceae)
Other common name: Madagascar periwinkle

Vinca is one of the most heat-tolerant and carefree flowers for bedding in full sun. A tender, short-lived perennial, vinca is grown as an annual in states with cold winters. It has spread itself widely in vacant lots in Florida and other states with hot climates, where it is considered a weed. This just shows its value—it can grow without irrigation. The waxy coating on the small, glossy, oval leaves makes this rather pretty and delicate-looking plant suited for near-desert conditions, while offering a trim, leafy, everblooming appearance similar to water-loving impatiens. The plants have medicinal properties but are poisonous to cattle.

PLANT TYPE: Tender perennial, often grown as an annual.
GROWING RANGE: All zones as an annual, but better performance below Zone 4; Zones 9 to 11 as a perennial.
HARDINESS: Withstands high heat and light frost, killed by hard frost.
PLANT HEIGHT: 1 to over 3 feet.
FLOWER COLOR: White, pink, rosy red, magenta, or purple, sometimes with red eyes.
FLOWER FORM: Flat, starlike 1-inch blooms all over bushy plants.
SEASON OF BLOOM: Any time of year during hot weather.
SOIL: Any soil, well drained.
PH: 6.5 to 7.5.
FERTILIZER: Well-rotted manure, all-purpose or high-phosphorus fertilizer.
WATER: Average to dry conditions.
EXPOSURE: Full sun or bright, dappled shade.
SPACING: 1 to 2 feet.
PROPAGATION: Seed.

Method

- **Start seeds indoors** eight weeks before the last expected frost in individual small pots filled with moist potting soil, covering ¼ inch deep. Water, cover (plants germinate in darkness), and keep at 75° to 80°F until seeds germinate, in one or two weeks. Grow seedlings in a sunny area or a few inches below a fluorescent light fixture, at 60° to 75°F. When they are crowded, move them to larger pots or outdoors.

- **Prepare soil outdoors** before planting by tilling in fertilizer, compost, and other soil improvers, as needed.

- **Sow seeds outdoors** in nursery beds in spring in Zones 9 to 11. (Start seed indoors in most other areas.) Plant seeds ¼ inch deep and about 2 inches apart.

- **Thin or transplant** seedlings grown outdoors to their permanent spacing when they are 4 or more inches tall.

- **Set plants outdoors** when weather is warm, after all danger of frost has passed. Harden them off outdoors for a day or two in shade.

- **Water** seedlings whenever the soil starts to dry out. Mature plants tolerate dry conditions, but grow better with average moisture.

- **Fertilize** lightly at planting time and periodically during growth.

- **Pests and diseases** seldom are problems.

- **Mulch** plants in dry weather with 2 to 3 inches of bark chips, shredded leaves, or other mulch if you wish.

- **Pinch back** tips for bushiness when plants are about 5 inches tall.

Selected Cultivars

'Kermesiana,' with deep magenta-violet flowers on 18-inch-tall, sturdy, upright plants;

'Little' series, compact, branched, uniform vincas 10 inches tall including: 'Little Blanche,' pure white; 'Little Bright Eye,' white with red center; 'Little Delicata,' pink with rose center; and 'Little Pinkie,' rosy pink;

'Magic Carpet Mixed,' with whites and pinks, dwarf plants with a prostrate habit, good in beds, hanging baskets, and containers, 6 to 9 inches tall, spreading to 2 feet wide;

'Morning Mist,' bushy 1-foot-tall plants covered with white flowers, each with a rosy eye; and

'Snowflake,' 10 inches tall, a pure white with an excellent uniform dwarf habit.

VIOLET

Botanical name: *Viola* (Violaceae)

Sweet nodding flowers about an inch wide usually show above a rosette of heart-shaped leaves, but some types have other leaf shapes. Their rhizomatous roots are usually thick and fleshy. The plants are used in woodland gardens, as edgings, as a ground cover, in salads, in confections such as candied violets, in perfume, and as petite cut flowers. Most types are easily transplanted in early spring.

PLANT TYPE: Hardy perennial.
GROWING RANGE: Zones 4 to 8.
HARDINESS: Hardy in all temperatures, but flowers cease in hot weather.
PLANT HEIGHT: 3 to over 8 inches.
FLOWER COLOR: Lavender, purple, blue, white, yellow, or pink, varying with the species.
FLOWER FORM: ½-inch flowers usually borne on slender stalks, not on leaf stems.
SEASON OF BLOOM: Spring.
SOIL: Rich, moist.
PH: 6 to 7.
FERTILIZER: Well-rotted manure, compost, flower fertilizer.
WATER: Average to wet conditions.
EXPOSURE: Partial shade.
SPACING: 6 inches to 1 foot.
PROPAGATION: Seed or division. Plants self-sow.

Method

- **Start seeds indoors** in temperatures around 60°F at any time of year. Fill flats or six-packs with dampened seed starting medium, cover seeds ⅛ inch deep, water, and grow plantlets in bright light but not hot sun.

- **Prepare soil outdoors** before planting by tilling soil amendments such as leaf mold, compost, and fertilizer into beds.

- **Sow seeds outdoors** in late spring, summer, or fall, an inch or two apart under ⅛ inch of soil. Do not let the seedbed dry out. Germination time will vary—seeds planted in fall will germinate in spring and bloom the following year.

- **Thin or transplant** seedlings (grown indoors or out) to their places outdoors when they are about 2 inches tall, on an overcast day any time in spring. Harden off those grown indoors.

- **Divide and thin** crowded plants when new growth begins in early spring. The fleshy rhizomes and offsets are easily moved and will bloom later the same year.

- **Water** often in spring to prevent soil from becoming dry during the active growth period.

- **Fertilize** lightly at planting time and each year in early spring.

- **Pests and diseases** rarely are serious problems, but there are many possible afflictions. Hose off aphids with soapy water, discourage slugs and caterpillars by dusting the leaves and ground with diatomaceous earth or wood ashes, and treat violet sawfly with a soaking of pyrethrum in a liquid base. If leaf spot or root rot occur, treat plants with fungicide and remove damaged portions.

- **Mulch** plants with 2 inches of shredded leaves to keep moisture in the soil in hot weather.

- **Protect in winter** with 3 inches of mulch such as fallen leaves around plants. Pull mulch back in spring.

Selected Species and Cultivars

Viola blanda (Sweet white violet). This 6-inch species has 1-inch white flowers with navy blue stripes near the centers, above clumps of heart-shaped leaves. These pretty flowers grow wild by way of stoloniferous offshoots in many northern and central states.

V. labradorica (Labrador violet). This widespread U.S. native is now enjoyed in English gardens. It has 4- or 5-inch-tall mauve flowers.

V. odorata (Sweet violet). This is the European florist's violet (carried by 'Liza Doolittle in *My Fair Lady*). Plants bear masses of 1-inch flowers in late spring, above heart-shaped leaves. These popular plants spread quickly in cool damp shade, so they are widely naturalized in North America. Some named cultivars include:

'Red Giant,' with tall (8-inch) flowers of deep rose;

'Rosina,' colored deep rose, also fragrant;

'Royal Robe,' with deep purple flowers and a lovely fragrance; and

'White Czar,' white with yellow and blue streaks.

V. pedata (Bird's-foot violet). One of the loveliest of violets; its common name evolved because of the resemblance suggested by its divided leaves. Its root is a rhizome that grows vertically. It prefers a sandier, better drained but less rich soil and more sun than other violets. It grows 2 to 5 inches high with small two-toned flowers in shades of violet—the lower three petals are paler.

V. pubescens (Downy yellow violet). Golden flowers appear on the same fuzzy stalks as the heart-shaped, scalloped leaves. This tall (up to 16 inches) wild violet prefers shade and rich woodsy soil. It is widespread in northeastern and central states.

V. sororia (Woolly blue violet). The most widespread violet in the United States, this type is suitable in woodland or garden. It has a thick, fleshy rhizome and heart-shaped leaves several inches wide. The 1-inch flowers may be purple, blue, light blue, red, white, or grayish blue, the last called the Confederate violet.

VIRGINIA BLUEBELLS

Botanical name: *Mertensia* (Boraginaceae)
Other common name: Lungwort

Bluebells and their kin are ephemeral woodland plants. They disappear in summer, but only after blooming beautifully for several weeks in spring, so it is a good idea to interplant them with ferns or other groundcover plants. They are valued for their ability to flower in dense shade. With their rugged, woody taproots, they are among the most stable of perennials if their location suits them, though they look dainty and delicate. The type most used in wildflower and perennial gardens is the Virginia bluebell, native to woodland stream banks in the northeastern and central United States; related species are from western states, Europe, and Asia. Most types have oval, glaucous (whitened) leaves, but some have leaves that are linear, hairy, or spotted.

PLANT TYPE: Hardy perennial.
GROWING RANGE: Zones 3 to 8.
HARDINESS: Tolerates cold, harmed by prolonged high heat.
PLANT HEIGHT: 1 to 2½ feet (most species).
FLOWER COLOR: Usually bright medium blue, occasionally pink or white.
FLOWER FORM: Drooping clusters of showy tubular blossoms about an inch long.
SEASON OF BLOOM: Early spring to midspring for 6 weeks.
SOIL: Moist, humusy.
PH: 6 to 7.
FERTILIZER: Compost and high-phosphorus fertilizer.
WATER: Prefers moist conditions but tolerates drought in summer.
EXPOSURE: Light to deep shade.
SPACING: 1 to 2 feet.
PROPAGATION: Seed or division.

Method

- **Prepare soil outdoors** before planting by tilling in compost, peat moss, and other soil improvers, as needed.

- **Sow seeds outdoors** in shady nursery beds or where plants will grow, as soon as they ripen in late spring or early summer, planting them ⅛ inch deep and about 2 inches apart. They will germinate the following spring and bloom the year after that.

- **Thin or transplant** seedlings to permanent positions in late spring when they are a few inches tall. They are easy to transplant at this stage and will continue growing with no interruption.

- **Set store-bought plants outdoors** in spring, with the top of the thick root an inch below the surface of the soil.

- **Divide** woody roots in early spring as growth begins or in summer while plants are dormant, if you wish, although plants will grow well even when crowded. Use a sharp knife or spade to cut an old clump into large sections and dig them up. Replant them immediately at the same depth.

- **Water** plants during their active growth period in spring if the soil becomes dry.

- **Fertilize** lightly at planting time and during active growth.

- **Pests and diseases** seldom are problems.

- **Mulch** plants with 2 to 3 inches of small bark chips, shredded leaves, or other mulch, if soil tends to be dry.

- **Remove** spent flowers and stalks (for neatness) unless you want plants to spread from seed. Remove yellowed stems and foliage. Mark plants if necessary, for they are not visible in summer.

Selected Species

Mertensia alpina (Alpine bluebell). These 8-inch-tall plants with dark blue flowers are from the Rocky Mountains.

M. longiflora. Tuberous-rooted plants 1 foot tall have bright blue tubular flowers and are used in rock gardens.

M. virginica (Cowslip). This is the well-known Virginia bluebell, which grows 1 to 2½ feet tall. Plants remain in bloom for several weeks, at the same time of year as early season to midseason narcissi, with which they are often combined. Funnel-shaped flowers appear in showy, one-sided clusters, usually bright blue with buds and tubes touched with lilac. Some rare forms are white or pink. The stems of flower clusters elongate rapidly during the period of bloom.

WALLFLOWER

Botanical name: *Cheiranthus cheiri* (Cruciferae)

Narrow, bright green leaves are set off by clusters of fragrant 1-inch flowers on bushy plants. Wallflower is planted in beds, borders, and rock gardens, and for cut flowers. Wallflower grows as a perennial only in cool, humid areas, such as the Pacific Northwest. It is not propagated vegetatively.

PLANT TYPE: Perennial, often grown as an annual or biennial.

GROWING RANGE: All zones as an annual; Zones 7 to 10 where summers are not hot as a perennial.

HARDINESS: Sensitive to heat, slightly sensitive to frost.
PLANT HEIGHT: 12 to 30 inches.
FLOWER COLOR: Yellow, mahogany, red, orange.
FLOWER FORM: Erect, showy clusters.
SEASON OF BLOOM: Spring and early summer.
SOIL: Average, well drained.
PH: 6 to 7.5.
FERTILIZER: Well-rotted manure, compost, or all-purpose fertilizer.
WATER: Moist conditions.
EXPOSURE: Full sun or light shade.
SPACING: 12 to 15 inches.
PROPAGATION: Seed.

Method

- **Start seeds indoors** in midwinter six to eight weeks before outdoor planting time. Sow in small pots or flats filled with sterile seed starting medium. Plant seeds ¼ inch deep, water, and keep in a cool (60°F) place until they germinate, in five to seven days. Grow seedlings in bright sunlight or a few inches below a fluorescent light fixture. Transplant them to individual pots when they have developed two sets of true leaves.

- **Prepare soil outdoors** before planting by digging in fertilizer and compost or other organic soil improvers.

- **Sow seeds outdoors** in smoothly prepared and fertilized beds in late summer where winter temperatures do not drop below 20°F. Plant seeds 12 inches apart and ¼ inch deep. Do not let the seedbed dry out. Move plants into their permanent place two months before the first fall frost. Where winter temperatures drop below 20°F, sow seeds outdoors in early spring as soon as the soil can be worked, or in a cold frame in late summer.

- **Thin** outdoor-grown seedlings to their permanent spacing when they are 6 inches high.

- **Set plants outdoors** in early spring as soon as the soil can be worked, after they have been hardened off in shade for several days.

- **Water** frequently so the soil never dries out.

- **Fertilize** at planting time. Where perennial, fertilize each spring as growth begins.

- **Pests and diseases** include aphids, which are easily controlled with insecticidal soap. The major disease is club root. Avoid it by not planting wallflower in the same place two years in a row and by raising the pH from 7.2 to 7.5.

- **Mulch** around growing plants with 2 inches of bark chips or shredded leaves to keep moisture in the soil and the soil cool.

- **Protect in winter** with evergreen boughs or oak leaves where grown as a perennial.

Tips · Combine wallflower with forget-me-nots for an attractive color contrast, as is done traditionally in English cottage gardens.

· Where summers are hot, grow wallflower as a spring-blooming annual and replace it with a heat-tolerant annual in the late spring or early summer.

WOOD HYACINTH

Botanical name: *Endymion* (Liliaceae)
Other common names: Bell-flowered squill, Bluebells

Wood hyacinths are easy to grow. Taller than squills (see pages 359–60), which they resemble, and later to bloom, they are ideal plants for naturalizing among ferns and Virginia bluebells in woodland gardens. As cut flowers, they are fragrant and attractive. The long-lived bulbs multiply rapidly and tend to set themselves into the soil very deeply as clumps mature. Since their straplike foliage persists for a long time in summer and can be a nuisance, do not use wood hyacinths in the front of the border.

PLANT TYPE: Hardy bulb.
GROWING RANGE: Zones 4 to 9.
HARDINESS: Withstands summer heat, requires cool or cold winters.
PLANT HEIGHT: 10 to 18 inches.
FLOWER COLOR: Blue, purple, rose, pale pink, greenish white.
FLOWER FORM: Tall spires usually bear 8 or more pendant, bell-shaped flowers less
     than 1 inch long.
SEASON OF BLOOM: Late spring, with Darwin (late) tulips.
SOIL: Well drained, humusy.
PH: 6.5 to 7.5.
FERTILIZER: Moderate. Well-rotted manure, bonemeal, compost, and/or slow-re-
     lease fertilizer, applied lightly.
WATER: Moderate, not too wet.
EXPOSURE: Partial shade.
SPACING: 6 to 8 inches apart, 4 to 6 inches deep.
PROPAGATION: Division, also from seed.

Method

· **Prepare soil outdoors** by digging the bed and turning in compost, fertilizer, sand (for drainage), and other soil amendments, as needed.

· **Sow seeds outdoors** in summer when they turn black and ripen, or in fall in cold frames, ⅛ inch deep, 1 inch apart, in finely tilled soil, in rows. Seeds can be scattered where you would like to naturalize the plants. An easy way to mark them is to plant them near their parents. It will take at least four years for them to mature and bloom.

- **Thin or transplant** seedlings to permanent positions when they become crowded. Plants may be transplanted while leaves are green.

- **Set out bulbs** in fall as soon as they are received; otherwise they may dry out too much in storage.

- **Dig up and separate** crowded plants after they bloom, when foliage starts to yellow. If you prefer, move them in early spring when foliage appears or else while they are in full flower, digging carefully. This will affect flowering the year it is done, but plants will recover the next year. Transplanting flowering plants allows you to rearrange the colors. In any case, try not to cut into the soft bulbs. Plantings may remain safely undivided for many years. After lifting a clump with a spade, tease the bulbs apart gently by hand and reset them immediately.

- **Water** if soil is dry while plants have green foliage showing.

- **Fertilize** lightly during active growth in fall and spring with bonemeal and all-purpose bulb or flower fertilizer. Leaf mold and compost are beneficial. In rich soils, little or no fertilizer is needed.

- **Pests and diseases** rarely are problems.

- **Remove** flower heads and stems after bloom is finished, unless seed is wanted. Let leaves disappear by themselves, or remove them when they start to turn yellow.

- **Mulch** beds with 2 inches of shredded leaves or bark chips.

Selected Species

Endymion hispanicus (Spanish bluebell, Spanish squill). This is the common garden wood hyacinth, and it is a dependable and attractive plant in shady gardens. Strong cultivars (usually scentless) with up to thirty flowers per stalk 15 inches tall include 'Excelsior,' blue; 'Rosabella,' pink; and 'Alba Maxima,' white.

    E. non-scriptus (English bluebell). The English bluebell is a graceful woodland plant with four to sixteen violet-blue flowers per arching 15-inch stalk. Flowers have cream-colored anthers. Culture and time of bloom are similar to Spanish bluebell, but this species is sweetly scented. However, it is slightly less hardy, doing best in Zones 5 to 8.

YARROW

Botanical name: *Achillea* (Compositae)
Other common names: Achillea, Milfoil

Yarrow is hardy and easy to grow. Its flat, wide, pastel flower heads filled with tiny composite blossoms are often used in fresh and dried flower arrangements. It is grown in mixed borders, with three to five clumps to a group, or in cutting gardens in rows. It may be naturalized in sunny meadows. Most species originated in central Europe, but are naturalized widely in the United States.

PLANT TYPE: Hardy perennial.
GROWING RANGE: Zones 2 to 9.
HARDINESS: Unusually tolerant of both low and high temperatures.
PLANT HEIGHT: 9 inches to 5 feet, usually 2 feet.
FLOWER COLOR: White, mustard, yellow, pink, or rose shades.
FLOWER FORM: ¼- to 1-inch composite flowers, sometimes in platelike clusters to 6 inches across.
SEASON OF BLOOM: Summer in most regions, spring through summer in areas with mild winters.
SOIL: Well-drained, average to good garden loam.
PH: 6 to 7.5.
FERTILIZER: All-purpose or flower fertilizer.
WATER: Average to dry. Water young plants frequently.
EXPOSURE: Full sun to partial shade.
SPACING: 6 to 12 inches.
PROPAGATION: Seed or division.

Method

- **Start seeds indoors** eight to ten weeks before the last frost. Seeds germinate irregularly, taking from thirty to a hundred days. Grow seeds thinly in flats or six-packs filled with moist, sterile potting soil. Cover seed no more than ⅛ inch deep, water, and grow at 60° to 70°F in a sunny area or a few inches below a fluorescent light fixture. If seedlings are crowded, step them up to larger pots.

- **Prepare soil outdoors** by digging the bed and turning in compost, fertilizer, and other soil amendments, as needed.

- **Sow seeds outdoors** where they will grow after the danger of frost passes. In a smoothly prepared and fertilized bed, make rows about 2 inches deep. Plant seeds an inch apart and cover with ⅛ inch of soil. Do not let seedbed dry out.

- **Thin or transplant** seedlings to nursery spacing, 6 or more inches apart, when they are 4 inches tall. Move plants to their permanent places the following spring.

- **Set plants outdoors** when they are about 4 inches tall, after the danger of heavy frost passes. Harden them off in shade for several days.

- **Divide** plants, if necessary, in early spring after the danger of heavy frost passes, when new growth begins.

- **Water** frequently if needed until plants are 6 inches tall. By then roots are deeper and plants can resist drought. Water whenever plants seem wilted or listless.

- **Fertilize** at planting time and in midsummer.

- **Pests and diseases** rarely are problems.

- **Mulch** lightly around plants in dry areas.

- **Harvest** flowers for drying when they begin to open. Hang them upside down in small bunches in a dark, airy place for about two weeks.

- **Deadhead** plants unless seed is wanted.

Selected Species and Cultivars

Achillea ageratum (Sweet Nancy, Sweet yarrow). Growing 8 inches high and 1 foot wide, this species makes a beautiful silvery rosette of foliage with white flowers in summer.

   A. clavennae. This type is only 8 inches tall, with silver-gray foliage and white flowers 1 inch wide.

   A. filipendulina (Fernleaf yarrow). See pages 458–59 for a more detailed discussion.

   A. millefolium (Common yarrow). See pages 458–59 for a more detailed discussion.

   A. ptarmica (Sneezewort). With ¾-inch, white button flowers in loose heads good for cutting or drying, this is an excellent border plant. Named cultivars include:

   'Ballerina,' with many sprays of white flowers on sturdy, 2-foot-tall stems; and

   'The Pearl,' a late-summer bloomer, 4 feet tall, spreading vigorously and hardy in Zones 3 to 9.

   A. tomentosa (Woolly yarrow). This species has mustard-yellow flowers in flat-topped clusters. It grows in low, ferny green mats 9 inches tall and a foot wide.

YUCCA

Botanical name: *Yucca* (Agavaceae)
Other common names: Adam's needle, Joshua tree

There are many types of yucca, a large, moundlike, spiky, hard-leaved plant associated with semitropic or desert areas. These herbaceous or woody perennials grow in colonies. *Yucca filamentosa,* used throughout most of the United States, has a prolonged rosette stage, followed by a 5-foot-tall flowering stem that bursts open into a tower of white, bell-shaped flowers in summer. Some cultivars have variegated leaves. Several other species are also common in hot, southern areas. All types are most useful as specimen plants or as substitutes for shrubs, and are evergreen through winter.

   PLANT TYPE: Hardy perennial.
   GROWING RANGE: Zones 4 to 10, varying with the species.
   HARDINESS: All types withstand high heat and cold.
   PLANT HEIGHT: 5 or more feet when in flower.
   FLOWER COLOR: Greenish to ivory-white or lavender.
   FLOWER FORM: Bell-like flowers an inch or more wide, in huge spires.
   SEASON OF BLOOM: Summer in most regions, any time of year in hot climates.
   SOIL: Any well-drained soil, preferably sandy.
   PH: 6.5 to 7.5.
   FERTILIZER: Well-rotted manure, all-purpose or high-phosphorus fertilizer.
   WATER: Average to dry conditions.
   EXPOSURE: Full sun or bright dappled shade.

SPACING: 3 or more feet.
PROPAGATION: Division or seed.

Method

- **Start seeds indoors** ¼ inch deep at any time in individual small pots filled with moist potting soil. Water, cover, and keep at about 80°F until seeds germinate. Grow seedlings in a sunny area or a few inches below a fluorescent light fixture, at 60° to 85°F. When they are crowded, move them to larger pots or outdoors.

- **Prepare soil outdoors** before planting by tilling in fertilizer, sand, compost, and other soil improvers, as needed.

- **Sow seeds outdoors** in nursery beds during warm weather, about ½ inch deep and 4 inches apart.

- **Thin** seedlings grown outdoors to their permanent spacing when they are 4 or more inches tall.

- **Set plants outdoors** when weather is warm, after the danger of frost has passed. Harden them off outdoors for a day in shade.

- **Divide** plants, if necessary, by cutting off and replanting offshoots during cool weather—spring in cooler northern regions. Wear gloves and use a sharp knife! Do not cut individual plant rosettes in half, but respace those that are crowded. Some plants die after they flower, so it is important to cultivate offshoots.

- **Water** young plants whenever the soil becomes dry. Mature plants thrive in dry conditions.

- **Fertilize** lightly at planting time and periodically during growth.

- **Pests and diseases** seldom are problems.

- **Mulch** plants with 2 to 3 inches of bark chips, shredded leaves, or other mulch if you wish. Do not bury the crown.

- **Remove** stalks of seedpods unless seed is wanted.

Selected Species

Yucca baccata (Spanish bayonet). Forming short-stemmed clumps of tough, swordlike, 2-foot-long leaves with 2-foot-tall clusters of red-brown and white flowers in summer, this species grows in New Mexico and other southwestern states. Sow seeds in spring.

Y. elata (Soap tree yucca). A very showy type that is the state flower of New Mexico. Its lilylike white flowers appear on tree-trunklike stems up to 20 feet tall.

Y. filamentosa. Hardy in Zones 4 to 10, the 2-foot-tall, spiky evergreen mounds of green or bluish green leaves produce plumes of bell-like flowers on 5-foot-tall stems. 'Gold Sword' is a fine cultivar that features green leaves with an inner stripe of bright yellow.

Y. glauca (Narrow-leaved yucca). This variety grows in Zones 3 to 9, from South Dakota to New Mexico. Its stiff, narrow, pointed leaves make a moundlike base for slender, 4-foot-tall flower spikes of white or rose. Plant seeds in fall.

ZINNIA

Botanical name: *Zinnia* (Compositae)

Zinnia flowers range from tiny buttonlike heads to large double flowers up to 7 inches across. Although they are always at the end of the list, they are one of the easiest garden annuals to grow. This tender annual comes in a wide variety of heights, and is used as edging, in borders, massed plantings, and containers, and for cut flowers. Zinnias are not propagated vegetatively.

PLANT TYPE: Tender annual.
GROWING RANGE: All zones.
HARDINESS: Resistant to heat, sensitive to frost.
PLANT HEIGHT: 6 inches to 4 feet.
FLOWER COLOR: Pink, rose, red, cherry, lavender, purple, orange, salmon, cream, gold, yellow, white, light green.
FLOWER FORM: Single, double, round, ball-shaped, or quilled, 1 to 7 inches across.
SEASON OF BLOOM: Early summer until frost.
SOIL: Rich, fertile, well drained.
PH: 5.5 to 7.
FERTILIZER: Well-rotted manure, compost, or all-purpose fertilizer.
WATER: Average to moist conditions; keep foliage dry to reduce chance of disease.
EXPOSURE: Full sun.
SPACING: 4 to 24 inches, depending on variety and mature size.
PROPAGATION: Seed.

Method

- **Start seeds indoors** four weeks before the last spring frost in individual small pots or 2 inches apart in flats filled with sterile seed starting medium. Plant seeds ¼ inch deep, water, and keep in a warm (70° to 75°F) place until they germinate, in five to seven days. Grow seedlings in bright sunlight or a few inches below a fluorescent light fixture. When seedlings develop two pairs of true leaves, transplant them to small pots or cell-packs.

- **Prepare soil outdoors** before planting by tilling in fertilizer and compost or other organic soil improvers, as needed.

- **Sow seeds outdoors** in smoothly prepared and fertilized beds after all danger of frost has passed. Plant seeds a distance apart equal to half their permanent spacing and ¼ inch deep. For example, sow seeds 9 inches apart if the final spacing is to be 18 inches. Do not let the seedbed dry out.

- **Thin** outdoor-grown seedlings when they have four to six leaves to their permanent spacing. Zinnias should be spaced a distance apart equal to half their mature height. For example, plants that grow 36 inches tall should be spaced 18 inches apart.

- **Set plants outdoors** after all danger of frost has passed, after hardening them off in shade for several days.

- **Water** as soon as the soil starts to dry out. Water in the morning and try not to get the foliage wet to reduce mildew disease.

- **Fertilize** at planting time and again monthly during growth and flowering.

- **Pests and diseases** include mildew, which is a serious problem, especially when days are hot and nights are cool. Do not crowd plants to improve air circulation and reduce the chance of disease. When necessary, spray with a fungicide. Mites might pose a problem in summer heat. If so, spray plants with water or a solution of water and insecticidal soap.

- **Mulch** around growing plants with 2 inches of bark chips or shredded leaves to keep moisture in the soil.

- **Pinch back** after plants have developed four to six leaves to encourage bushiness.

- **Stake** tall plants with wooden or metal stakes.

Tips · Keep faded flowers removed to encourage bushy growth and repeat flowering.
· Zinnias are an excellent choice for hot-weather gardens as long as they receive sufficient water.

Selected Species and Cultivars

Zinnia elegans. Garden zinnias come in many varieties, heights, and flower forms. All of the following come in a wide range of colors. 'Border Beauty' has 3½-inch, dahlialike flowers on 2-foot-tall plants. 'Cut & Come Again' has 2½-inch flowers on 36-inch-tall stems and is a good cut flower. 'Peter Pan' has slightly curled, double flowers up to 5 inches across on 12-inch-tall plants. 'Pulcino' has 2½-inch flowers on 10- to 15-inch plants and is more resistant to disease than most zinnias. 'Rose Pinwheel' has 3-inch pink flowers and is very mildew resistant. 'Ruffles' has 2½-inch, ball-shaped, ruffled flowers on 24- to 30-inch plants. 'Small World' has beehive-shaped, 2½-inch flowers on 10- to 12-inch plants. 'Thumbelina' grows 8 inches tall and has 1½-inch semidouble or double flowers.
There are several species related to garden zinnias:
Z. angustifolia, formerly *Z. linearis.* This plant has single, golden orange flowers with yellow stripes. Plants grow 8 to 12 inches tall and have very narrow leaves.
Z. haageana (Mexican zinnia). Growing 12 to 18 inches high, this plant has 1½- to 2-inch single or double flowers in tones of red, mahogany, yellow, or orange. Some blooms are solid-colored; others are two-toned. 'Old Mexico' has double, 2½-inch flowers of mahogany highlighted in gold on 18-inch-tall plants. 'Persian Carpet' has 2-inch, double, two-toned flowers of gold, maroon, purple, chocolate, pink, or cream on 15-inch plants.

HERBS

ANGELICA

Botanical name: *Angelica archangelica* (Umbelliferae)

The leaves of angelica, the "herb of angels," are used fresh or dried as seasonings, particularly in drinks, and the stems are often candied or cooked as a vegetable. This aromatic herb has large, 2- to 3-foot long, three-part leaves. Legend holds that it was a gift from the angels to protect humankind from the plague, hence its name.

PLANT TYPE: Biennial.
GROWING RANGE: Zones 4 to 11.
HARDINESS: Resistant to cold, fairly tolerant of very hot weather.
PLANT HEIGHT: 5 feet.
FLOWER COLOR: Greenish white.
FLOWER FORM: Flat to rounded large clusters.
SEASON OF BLOOM: Early summer.
SOIL: Rich, cool, moist but well drained.
PH: 5 to 7.
FERTILIZER: Vegetable or all-purpose fertilizer.
WATER: Keep moist but do not overwater.
EXPOSURE: Full sun or light shade.
SPACING: 3 feet.
PROPAGATION: Seed or division.

 *Method*

- **Start seeds indoors** in early spring after storing them in moist sphagnum moss in the refrigerator for six to eight weeks, sowing them in flats placed in full sun or under fluorescent lights. You should be aware that seeds remain viable for only a short time, so it is far better to sow directly in the fall or let them self-sow.

- **Prepare soil outdoors** in either spring or fall before planting, adding organic matter, such as peat moss, leaf mold, or compost, to enrich it.

- **Sow seeds outdoors** ¼ to ½ inch deep, 12 inches apart, in late fall for germination the following spring. Plant seeds immediately as they are not long lived.

- **Set plants outdoors** in midspring as soon as the soil has warmed up and the plants have not yet established a taproot.

- **Thin** seedlings when they are 1 foot high to stand 3 feet apart.

- **Divide,** if necessary, in the early spring by separating the self-sown seedlings from the parent plant to give each more room to grow.

- **Water** regularly to keep the soil evenly moist.

- **Fertilize** in early spring as plant growth starts.

- **Pests and diseases** include aphids or leaf spot. Control aphids by spraying leaves with water or chemical insecticide approved for use on vegetables. Leaf spot can be treated by spraying plant with diluted insecticidal soap or a fungicide.

- **Mulch** the soil after the seedlings are 1 foot high and during hot, dry spells to keep the soil cool and moist.

- **Pinch** the plants when they are 1 foot high to keep them compact.

- **Harvest leaves** in the fall of the first year, being careful not to damage the stem, or in the spring of the second year before the plant flowers. For candied stems, cut the stalks in the second year just before the flowers open. Seeds are also edible and are used mostly as a flavoring for liqueurs and gin.

- **Dry leaves** in a cool, dry, dark, airy place.

- **Store** leaves, roots, and seeds in a tightly sealed container.

ANISE

Botanical name: *Pimpinella anisum* (Umbelliferae)

This dainty, spreading herb has small, lacy leaves, and forms small, grayish brown licorice-flavored seeds after flowering. Mentioned in the Bible, anise was brought to Europe from Egypt during the Roman Empire. Traditionally, anise has been used as a flavoring in breads, cookies, cakes, candy, and Italian sausage. The seeds may also be used in drinks, soups, and salads or chewed after dinner as an aid to digestion.

PLANT TYPE: Annual.
GROWING RANGE: Zones 1 to 11.
HARDINESS: Tolerates light frost and heat extremes.

PLANT HEIGHT: 18 to 24 inches.
FLOWER COLOR: White.
FLOWER FORM: Flat clusters.
SEASON OF BLOOM: Early summer.
SOIL: Well drained, light, sandy, rich in nutrients.
PH: 6 to 7.
FERTILIZER: Vegetable or all-purpose fertilizer.
WATER: Prefers average to slightly moist conditions, but will not tolerate swampy or constantly moist low areas.
EXPOSURE: Full sun.
SPACING: 6 to 9 inches.
PROPAGATION: Seed.

 Method

- **Sow seeds indoors** in late winter. Anise does not transplant well, and seeds should be started in individual pots. Do not try to save seeds from year to year as they are very short lived.

- **Prepare soil outdoors** in spring before planting, adding organic matter, such as peat moss, leaf mold, or compost, to enrich it.

- **Sow seeds outdoors** ⅛ inch deep and 6 inches apart in a sunny area, as soon as the soil can be worked in spring.

- **Thin** seedlings when they are 3 inches high to stand 6 to 9 inches apart.

- **Set plants outdoors** in early spring as soon as the soil can be worked.

- **Water** when the ground starts to become dry; do not overwater.

- **Fertilize** soil before planting; no other feeding will be necessary.

- **Insects** do not cause a problem

- **Diseases** can be treated by spraying leaves with a fungicide approved for use on vegetables. Anise may be susceptible to rust or leaf spot. **Insects** do not cause a problem.

- **Stake** plants if they become leggy, or mound soil around the base of the plants to support weak stems.

- **Harvest leaves** at any time all summer and use them fresh or dried. Dry them on a screen in a cool, dry, dark, airy place.

- **Harvest seeds** when the flowers mature, approximately two to three weeks after flowering, by cutting off the flowering stem. Seeds should be grayish brown. Handle flower heads carefully to keep seeds from falling off. Tie the stems in a bunch and hang them in a cool, dark place inside a paper bag; the seeds will drop off into the bag. Be sure they are dry before storing them.

- **Store** leaves and seeds in airtight containers.

BASIL

Botanical name: *Ocimum* (Labiatae)

Basil is a favorite seasoning for Italian sauces and soups. Its oval, pungent leaves are the main ingredient of pesto. There are varieties with either green or purple leaves that make this plant equally useful as an herb or as a garden ornamental. In India, basil is considered sacred by many and its possession is thought to make passage to heaven easier. Its affinity to tomatoes and pasta is surely nothing short of heavenly.

PLANT TYPE: Annual.
GROWING RANGE: Zones 1 to 11.
HARDINESS: Resistant to heat; not frost hardy, it is one of the first plants to be damaged by frost.
PLANT HEIGHT: 15 to 24 inches.
FLOWER COLOR: White to purplish.
FLOWER FORM: Terminal spikes.
SEASON OF BLOOM: Early summer until frost.
SOIL: Light, medium rich, well drained.
PH: 5 to 8.
FERTILIZER: Vegetable or all-purpose fertilizer.
WATER: Prefers even moisture but not wet conditions.
EXPOSURE: Full sun.
SPACING: 10 to 12 inches.
PROPAGATION: Seed.

Method

- **Sow seeds indoors** six to eight weeks before last frost, in flats placed in full sun or under fluorescent lights.

- **Prepare soil outdoors** in spring before planting, adding small amounts of organic matter, such as peat moss, leaf mold, or compost, to slightly enrich it.

- **Sow seeds outdoors** ¼ to ½ inch deep and 6 inches apart, in a sunny area after all danger of frost has passed.

- **Thin** seedlings when they are 4 inches high to permanent spacing.

- **Set plants outdoors** after all danger of frost has passed.

- **Water** when the soil starts to dry out. Water the ground, not the foliage, to prevent leaf spotting.

- **Fertilize** soil before planting. No further feeding will be necessary.

- **Diseases** are not generally a problem. Soil may become infested with nematodes. To combat an infestation, cultivate soil frequently in order to expose larvae to sunshine. Also, you can add compost, rotate crops, or try a nematicide.

- **Pinch** growing tips when plants are 4 to 6 inches high to encourage bushiness.

- **Mulch** the soil with a sheet of black plastic when temperatures are consistently in the 70°F range to keep the roots warm at night and evenly moist during dry weather. Be sure to cover plants with row covers or inverted bushel baskets if there is even a hint of frost expected.

- **Harvest leaves** at any time for fresh use. Leaves used for drying should be harvested before the flowers open. Continued removal of flower stalks will increase the harvesting time by several weeks. Handle harvested leaves with care as bruising them will cause the leaves to turn black and lose much of their flavor.

- **Dry leaves** on a screen in a warm, dry, dark, airy place.

- **Freeze leaves,** as an alternative to drying, by packing them tightly in plastic bags.

- **Store** dried leaves in an airtight container, or fresh leaves in olive oil or vinegar.

Selected Species and Varieties

Ocimum basilicum (Sweet basil) is the most common type of garden basil. It generally has bright green foliage, but the opal varieties *O. b. purpurascens* ('Dark Opal' and 'Purple Ruffles') have purple foliage. 'Minimum' and 'Spicy Globe' are dwarf varieties 8 to 12 inches tall with tiny leaves, excellent choices for growing in pots or indoors.

O. kilimandscharicum (Camphor basil) grows more than 3 feet tall and has a camphor scent. It is far better for repelling moths than for culinary use.

BEE BALM

Botanical name: *Monarda* (Labiatae)
Other common name: Bergamot

Bee balm is a tall, stately, hairy perennial with a minty fragrance. It is a favorite with bees and hummingbirds and very attractive in the flower garden. The leaves are used in making teas (bee balm gives Earl Grey tea its characteristic flavor) and can be added to salads and jellies. The plant is well rooted in American history; it was one of the "Liberty Teas" used by those protesting the tea taxes in the Colonies. Its less common name, Oswego tea, refers to the Indians who showed colonists how to use it.

PLANT TYPE: Perennial.
GROWING RANGE: Zones 4 to 11.
HARDINESS: Resistant to extreme cold and heat.
PLANT HEIGHT: 2 to 4 feet.
FLOWER COLOR: Red, pink, purple, salmon, white.
FLOWER FORM: Slender, tubular flowers in pompon clusters.
SEASON OF BLOOM: Summer.
SOIL: Light, sandy, well drained. Will be less invasive in dry, infertile, poor soil.

PH: 6 to 8.
FERTILIZER: Flower or all-purpose fertilizer.
WATER: Grows in moist or dry soil; is not as aggressive in dry soil.
EXPOSURE: Full sun to light shade.
SPACING: 12 inches.
PROPAGATION: Seed or division.

Method

· **Start seeds indoors** in early spring, in flats placed in full sun or under fluorescent lights. The growing medium must maintain a temperature of 55°F.

· **Prepare soil outdoors** before planting, incorporating a small amount of organic matter, such as peat moss, leaf mold, or compost.

· **Sow seeds outdoors** ¼ to ½ inch deep and 6 inches apart in early spring, as soon as the soil can be worked.

· **Thin seedlings** when they are 6 inches high to permanent spacing.

· **Set plants outdoors** in midspring to late spring, after the danger of frost has passed.

· **Divide** plants in early spring as soon as early growth starts or early fall. Bee balm grows rapidly and yearly division may be necessary. It tends to die out in the center of established clumps, so new growth from the edges may need to be transplanted back into the center.

· **Water** when the soil starts to dry out.

· **Fertilize** very lightly in early spring.

· **Pests and diseases** are not a problem.

· **Harvest leaves** before the flowers bloom and dry by hanging in an airy place. Use them fresh or dried for teas.

Tip · Bee balm can be highly invasive, especially if planted in moist, rich soil. Keep it under control by installing metal underground barriers of the type used to separate the lawn from flower beds.

Selected Species

Monarda didyma is the best known of the bee balms. The species is bright red, and varieties have been developed in dark red, pink, salmon, purple, and white. It grows to 2½ feet tall and prefers a slightly acid soil.

M. fistulosa (Wild bergamot) is slightly shorter (1½ to 2 feet) and has lavender flowers. It prefers an alkaline soil.

BORAGE

Botanical name: *Borago officinalis* (Boraginaceae)

Since Roman times borage has symbolized courage; it was added to the farewell cup of departing Crusaders, and its blue flowers are still floated in drinks and punch bowls. The flowers may be candied and used as garnish on cakes, ice cream, and other desserts. Both leaves and flowers have a cucumberlike flavor. This decorative plant has coarse, hairy leaves and its flowers are a favorite of bees.

PLANT TYPE: Hardy annual.
GROWING RANGE: Zones 1 to 11.
HARDINESS: Resistant to both heat and cold.
PLANT HEIGHT: 2 to 3 feet.
FLOWER COLOR: Blue, purple.
FLOWER FORM: Star-shaped, in drooping clusters.
SEASON OF BLOOM: Early summer until frost.
SOIL: Average to poor, dry soil.
PH: 5 to 8.
FERTILIZER: Vegetable or all-purpose fertilizer.
WATER: Average to slightly dry conditions.
EXPOSURE: Full sun or light shade.
SPACING: 12 inches.
PROPAGATION: Seed.

Method

- **Starting seeds indoors** is not recommended.

- **Prepare soil outdoors** in fall or spring before planting, adding little or no organic matter.

- **Sow seeds outdoors** ½ inch deep and 6 inches apart in fall or very early spring, as soon as soil can be worked. Be sure seeds are kept covered as darkness is needed for germination, which will occur in one to two weeks.

- **Thin** seedlings when they are 6 inches tall to permanent spacing.

- **Water** when the ground starts to become dry.

- **Fertilize** lightly before planting; no further feeding will be needed.

- **Pests and diseases** include beetles and leaf spot. Beetles can be picked off by hand and drowned in a cup of water, if only a few. Or spray with a chemical insecticide approved for use on vegetables. Treat leaf spot by spraying with diluted insecticidal soap.

- **Pinch** plants when they are 6 inches tall to encourage bushiness. If plants become leggy or sprawling in midsummer, they may be pruned back by half; they will produce a new crop of tender leaves.

- **Harvest leaves** when young, before they develop hairs, at any time during the growing season, to add a cucumberlike flavor to salads. *Use them sparingly, as they contain potentially toxic substances if ingested in large quantities. A leaf or two is fine; just don't make a whole salad out of them.*

- **Harvest flowers** as they first open.

CALENDULA

Botanical name: *Calendula officinalis* (Compositae)
Other common name: Pot marigold

Pot marigold, not to be confused with *Tagetes,* the marigolds common as bedding plants, have a proud history in both medicine and literature. Shakespeare referred to them in more than one play, noting in *A Winter's Tale* their habit of closing at sundown. Their flower petals are used for garnishes in soups and on hors d'oeuvres, in rice as a substitute for saffron, and in herbal teas. They impart almost no flavor or scent, but are colorful additions to both food and potpourri. Plant these in your flower beds where their colorful orange and yellow blossoms will continue all summer long.

PLANT TYPE: Hardy annual.
GROWING RANGE: Zones 1 to 10.
HARDINESS: Fairly resistant to cold, does not tolerate heat.
PLANT HEIGHT: 6 to 24 inches.
FLOWER COLOR: Yellow, gold, apricot, orange, cream.
FLOWER FORM: Daisylike, double, with crisp petals. Flowers close at night and on cloudy days.
SEASON OF BLOOM: Spring and fall where climates are hot, summer in cool areas.
SOIL: Rich, well drained.
PH: 5 to 8.
FERTILIZER: Vegetable or all-purpose fertilizer.
WATER: Prefers moist conditions, but with good drainage.
EXPOSURE: Full sun, light shade.
SPACING: 12 to 15 inches.
PROPAGATION: Seed.

Method

- **Start seeds indoors** six to eight weeks before transplanting outdoors, in flats placed in full sun or under fluorescent lights. Cover seeds completely, as they need darkness to germinate.

- **Prepare soil outdoors** before planting, adding generous amounts of organic matter, such as peat moss, leaf mold, or compost, to enrich it.

- **Sow seeds outdoors** ¼ to ½ inch deep and 6 inches apart in early spring, as soon as the soil can be worked. In mild areas, they can be sown in late summer for fall and winter blooming.

- **Thin** seedlings 4 inches high to permanent spacing.

- **Set plants outdoors** in midspring after all danger of frost has passed or early fall.

- **Water** regularly to keep the soil evenly moist.

- **Fertilize** soil prior to planting and again when buds start to form.

- **Pests** are snails and slugs. Either trap them with slug or snail bait or in partially submerged pans of beer. You may also dust the ground with wood ashes or diatomaceous earth.

- **Mulch** in early spring to keep the roots moist and cool.

- **Harvest flowers** as soon as they are fully open. Petals may be used fresh or dried. Be sure to deadhead flowers as they fade to ensure continuous bloom.

- **Dry flowers** on a screen in a warm, airy, dry place. The petals may be removed from the flower head either before or after drying.

- **Store** dried petals in an airtight container.

CARAWAY

Botanical name: *Carum carvi* (Umbelliferae)

Reputed to keep lovers faithful and constant, caraway is grown for its thin, crescent-shaped seeds. These are sprinkled over breads, cakes, cookies, and other desserts, and used in applesauce, sautéed cabbage, and cheese. The somewhat rangy plants are covered with finely cut, dark green leaves that are almost evergreen. The tender leaves are used in salads. The taproot, which looks like a white carrot, is edible and very nutritious. The plant was known in the ancient world for its medicinal value, especially for stomach disorders.

PLANT TYPE: Biennial.
GROWING RANGE: Zones 3 to 11.
HARDINESS: Resistant to both heat and cold.
PLANT HEIGHT: 2 to 2½ feet.
FLOWER COLOR: White.
FLOWER FORM: Flat clusters.
SEASON OF BLOOM: Summer.
SOIL: Average, fertile, well drained.
PH: 6 to 7.5.
FERTILIZER: Vegetable or all-purpose fertilizer (5-10-5).
WATER: Prefers evenly moist conditions.
EXPOSURE: Full sun.
SPACING: 6 to 8 inches.
PROPAGATION: Seed.

![leaf] *Method*

- **Sowing seeds indoors** is not recommended.

- **Prepare soil outdoors** in early fall or spring before planting, adding organic matter, such as peat moss, leaf mold, or compost, to enrich it.

- **Sow seeds outdoors** ⅛ inch deep and 6 inches apart in early fall, to have flowers and seeds by the following summer. Seeds sown in early spring will not produce flowers or seeds until the second summer. Seeds will germinate in one to two weeks.

- **Thin** seedlings when they are 4 inches high to permanent spacing.

- **Water** when the soil first becomes dry, without letting it become deeply dry. Watering should be stopped when flowers begin to form in order to encourage seeds to mature more quickly.

- **Fertilize** lightly when growth starts in spring.

- **Pests and diseases** are aphids, caterpillars, and aster yellows, a virus that causes flowers to lose their color and become malformed. Treat aphids by spraying leaves with water and caterpillars with Bt, an organic insecticide.

- **Harvest leaves** when young and tender and use fresh.

- **Harvest roots** as soon as flowering is finished. Roots may be harvested before flowering, but at the expense of the seed crop.

- **Harvest seeds** after flowering in midsummer by cutting off the flowering stems. Seeds should be brown when harvested.

- **Dry seeds** by hanging stems upside down in a paper bag in a dark, dry, cool place. The seeds will fall into the bag. Seeds may need to be sifted through a ¼-inch mesh screen to remove the chaff. Alternately, drop the seeds in a thin stream into a bowl on a breezy day and the chaff will blow away.

- **Store** seeds in an airtight container.

CATNIP

Botanical name: *Nepeta cataria* (Labiatae)

"If you set it, the cat will get it, but if you sow it, the cat won't know it" advises an old jingle. It's true: Catnip planted from seed has a far better chance of making it to harvest than "set" or transplanted catnip. This is because the fuzzy, gray-green foliage that has been bruised or rubbed against during planting releases an oil that attracts cats. Not only does it attract felines of nearly all varieties, it also causes them to roll in it and behave in altogether outlandish ways! Dried leaves are made into toys for cats, which have the same effect. Catnip tea has a pleasant flavor and is said to be comforting to those suffering from head colds.

Catmint (alternatively cataloged as *Nepeta mussinii* and *N. faassenii*) is a more tidy garden perennial than catnip, and although attractive to cats, it doesn't make them behave in such an undignified way.

PLANT TYPE: Perennial.
GROWING RANGE: Zones 3 to 11.
HARDINESS: Resistant to both cold and heat.
PLANT HEIGHT: 2 to 4 feet.
FLOWER COLOR: White with light purple spots.
FLOWER FORM: Terminal spikes.
SEASON OF BLOOM: Early summer to midsummer.
SOIL: Any soil, either poor and dry or rich and moist, but produces more foliage with the latter.
PH: 5 to 7.5.
FERTILIZER: Vegetable or all-purpose fertilizer.
WATER: Tolerates wet or dry conditions.
EXPOSURE: Full sun or partial shade.
SPACING: 18 to 24 inches.
PROPAGATION: Seed or division.

Method

- **Start seeds indoors** in early spring through early summer, in flats placed in full sun or under fluorescent lights.

- **Prepare soil outdoors** before planting, incorporating moderate amounts of organic matter, such as peat moss, leaf mold, or compost, if soil is very poor or sandy; this will help it hold water.

- **Sow seeds outdoors** ¼ inch deep and 9 inches apart in late spring or summer, up to two months before the first fall frost.

- **Set plants outdoors** after the last spring frost. They may be added to the garden up until six weeks before the first fall frost.

- **Thin** seedlings when they are 6 to 8 inches tall to permanent spacing.

- **Divide** plants every three to four years in midspring or early fall.

- **Water** when the soil starts to dry out. Catnip will tolerate considerable drought.

- **Fertilize** in early spring as growth starts. Use very little fertilizer as the growth of catmint is quite rampant.

- **Pests and diseases** rarely are a problem.

- **Prune back catnip** almost to the ground every spring to improve its appearance.

- **Winter protect** stalks left on the plant with evergreen boughs or other mulch. Remove after the ground thaws.

- **Harvest leaves** before the flowers bloom.

- **Dry leaves** on a screen in a cool, dry, airy place. Chopping the leaves or rubbing them with your fingers will release more flavor and scent.

- **Store** catnip in an airtight container.

Tips · Catnip can become weedy from rapidly growing underground stems. Keep it under control by installing metal underground barriers of the type used to separate the lawn from flower beds.
  · Young seedlings should be protected from cats.

CHAMOMILE

Botanical name: *Chamaemelum nobile,* sometimes known by its previous classification, *Anthemis nobilis* (Compositae)

The confusion over two distinctly different chamomiles is widespread and historic. Although German chamomile *(Matricaria recutita)* is a different genus and species, the two share so many characteristics that the confusion is inevitable. Perennial chamomile *(Chamaemelum nobile)* is a creeping plant with gray-green lacy foliage that is finely cut and fragrant, smelling somewhat like apples. Tiny, strongly scented flowers bloom at the ends of the stems and are used for tea or as a hair rinse. In the British Isles, where the climate is very humid and of more even temperatures, chamomile is grown as a dense lawn. German chamomile grows taller, with somewhat straggly stems, and its flowers have hollow centers. The two chamomiles have identical uses, and except for being an annual, German chamomile has the same growth and soil requirements.

PLANT TYPE: Perennial.
GROWING RANGE: Zones 4 to 10.
HARDINESS: Resistant to cold, not as tolerant of heat.
PLANT HEIGHT: 3 to 8 inches.
FLOWER COLOR: White, with a yellow center.
FLOWER FORM: Daisylike, with a solid center.
SEASON OF BLOOM: Late summer to frost.
SOIL: Sandy, well drained, not too rich.
PH: 6 to 7.
FERTILIZER: Vegetable or all-purpose fertilizer.
WATER: Average; will tolerate drought or moist conditions.
EXPOSURE: Full sun or light shade.
SPACING: 3 to 4 inches.
PROPAGATION: Seed or root cuttings.

Method

- **Sow seeds indoors** in early spring, in flats placed in full sun or under fluorescent lights.

- **Prepare soil outdoors** in spring or summer before planting. Use small amounts of organic matter, such as peat moss, leaf mold, or compost. Rich soil produces lush foliage for ground cover but fewer flowers.

- **Sow seeds outdoors** ¼ to ½ inch deep and 2 inches apart, any time in spring or summer. For a good ground cover, planting from seed is most often disappointing, especially in the North American climate.

- **Thin** seedlings when they are 2 inches tall to permanent spacing.

- **Set plants** into the garden after all danger of frost has passed.

- **Root 3- to 5-inch cuttings** of chamomile indoors in early spring or outdoors in pots in midsummer, using a medium of peat moss and perlite.

- **Water** before the ground becomes dry until plants are well established.

- **Fertilize** each spring when growth starts.

- **Pests and diseases** are not a problem.

- **Mow** chamomile in early spring before growth starts for better ground cover.

- **Harvest flowers** when the plants are in full bloom but before seeds start to form by cutting them off with a small piece of stem.

- **Dry flowers** on a screen in a warm place or loosely in a paper bag.

- **Store** flowers in an airtight container.

CHERVIL

Botanical name: *Anthriscus cerefolium* (Umbelliferae)

Found most abundantly in the French kitchen and garden, chervil is an ingredient of the fines herbes blend, but is rarely used alone. A dainty plant, it has finely cut, richly aromatic light green leaves and is a self-sower. These have a slight anise flavor and are often used in place of parsley in soups, stews, sauces, and salads, although they lack parsley's ability to balance garlic.

PLANT TYPE: Hardy annual.
GROWING RANGE: Zones 1 to 7 as a summer crop; in more southern zones as a spring, fall, or winter crop.
HARDINESS: Grows well only where nights are below 55°F; very frost resistant.
PLANT HEIGHT: 18 to 24 inches.
FLOWER COLOR: White.
FLOWER FORM: Flat clusters.
SEASON OF BLOOM: Midspring.
SOIL: Sandy, rich, well drained.
PH: 7 to 8.
FERTILIZER: Vegetable or all-purpose fertilizer.
WATER: Keep evenly moist.

EXPOSURE: Partial to full shade.
SPACING: 6 to 8 inches.
PROPAGATION: Seed.

Method

- **Start seeds indoors** in late winter. Chervil resents transplanting and should be sown into individual pots placed in full sun or under fluorescent lights. If you transplant from flats and disturb the roots, it encourages premature bloom and results in a shorter leaf harvest.

- **Prepare soil outdoors** in late fall or early spring, adding organic matter, such as peat moss, leaf mold, or compost, to enrich it.

- **Sow seeds outdoors** ¼ inch deep and 3 inches apart in early spring, as soon as the soil can be worked.

- **Thin** outdoor-grown seedlings when they are 3 inches high to permanent spacing.

- **Set seedlings outdoors** in early spring as soon as the soil can be worked.

- **Water** frequently so the ground is always evenly moist.

- **Fertilize** at planting time; no further feeding should be necessary.

- **Insects and diseases** are not generally a problem.

- **Mulch** the soil 4 inches deep in early spring to keep roots cool in hot climates.

- **Harvest leaves** at any time for immediate use and just before the flowers open for drying or freezing.

- **Dry leaves** on a screen in a cool, dry, airy place; freeze by packing tightly in a plastic bag.

- **Store** dried leaves in an airtight container.

CHIVE

Botanical name: *Allium schoenoprasum* (Amaryllidaceae)

Attractive enough for the perennial flower border, chives are bulbous perennial plants with tidy, dense clumps of slender, hollow leaves that possess a delicate onion flavor. The leaves are frequently mixed with sour cream for baked potatoes, chopped into cold and hot soups, and used with eggs and fresh tomatoes. You can use them in any recipe where you would use raw onions. The pink blossoms are highly flavored as well and make attractive additions to salads and omelets. Bottled in white distilled vinegar, the blossoms will color the vinegar to a rosé wine hue and imbue it with an onion flavor perfect in salads.

Allium tuberosum, or garlic chive, sometimes called Chinese chive, has much the same growing habits and requirements, but has flat leaves, white flowers, and a distinctly garlic flavor.

PLANT TYPE: Perennial.
GROWING RANGE: Zones 3 to 11.
HARDINESS: Resistant to both cold and heat.
PLANT HEIGHT: 8 to 12 inches.
FLOWER COLOR: Pale to pinkish purple.
FLOWER FORM: Globe-shaped clusters.
SEASON OF BLOOM: Midspring to early summer.
SOIL: Rich, moist, well drained.
PH: 6 to 8.
FERTILIZER: Vegetable or all-purpose fertilizer.
WATER: Keep soil evenly moist.
EXPOSURE: Full sun to light shade.
SPACING: 6 to 8 inches.
PROPAGATION: Seed or division.

Method

- **Start seeds indoors** from late winter until early summer, in flats placed in full sun or under fluorescent lights.

- **Prepare soil outdoors** before planting, adding generous amounts of organic matter, such as peat moss, leaf mold, or compost, to enrich it.

- **Sow seeds outdoors** ¼ inch deep and 3 inches apart from early spring, as soon as the soil can be worked, until the last spring frost date.

- **Set seedlings outdoors** from early spring, as soon as the soil can be worked, through midsummer.

- **Thin** seedlings when they are 3 inches high to permanent spacing.

- **Divide** plants in early spring or early fall every three to four years.

- **Water** frequently to keep soil evenly moist.

- **Fertilize** in early spring when growth starts.

- **Pests and diseases** are not a problem.

- **Winter protection** is not necessary. Plants may be dug up before frost and grown indoors on a sunny windowsill over winter, but first must be placed in a paper bag in the freezer for four weeks to simulate winter dormancy.

- **Harvest leaves** at any time for immediate use. Chives do not dry well, but may be frozen by packing tightly into plastic bags.

- **Store** leaves in the refrigerator or freezer.

Tip · **Keep well weeded as weeds are difficult to remove once they become entangled with chives' roots.**

CORIANDER

Botanical name: *Coriandrum sativum* (Umbelliferae)

Coriander is a large coarse plant that has finely divided, soft green leaves that are used in salads, soups, Central and South American dishes. Its lemon-flavored white seeds resemble peppercorns and are used in Indian curries, Oriental stir-fry dishes, and Scandinavian bread. Coriander flowers are very attractive to bees.

PLANT TYPE: Hardy annual.
GROWING RANGE: Zones 1 to 10.
HARDINESS: Resistant to cold, moderately resistant to heat.
PLANT HEIGHT: 12 to 30 inches.
FLOWER COLOR: White or pale pink.
FLOWER FORM: Flat cluster.
SEASON OF BLOOM: Late summer.
SOIL: Average, well drained.
PH: 6 to 8.
FERTILIZER: Vegetable or all-purpose fertilizer.
WATER: Keep soil evenly moist.
EXPOSURE: Full sun.
SPACING: 8 to 10 inches.
PROPAGATION: Seed.

Method

- **Starting seeds indoors** is not recommended.

- **Prepare soil outdoors** in late fall or early spring, adding a moderate amount of organic matter, such as peat moss, leaf mold, or compost.

- **Sow seeds outdoors** ¼ to ½ inch deep and 4 inches apart, in early spring as soon as the soil can be worked.

- **Thin seedlings** when they are 3 inches high to permanent spacing.

- **Water** frequently so the ground is always evenly moist.

- **Fertilize** at planting time. No further feeding is necessary.

- **Pests** are nematodes, which can be repelled by planting marigolds nearby or by cultivating the soil frequently to expose the larvae to sunshine. **Diseases** include anthracnose, identified by black spots on leaves. To control, spray with a chemical fungicide approved for use on vegetables.

- **Harvest leaves** for use fresh or dry before the flowers bloom.

- **Dry leaves** on a screen in a dark, cool, airy place.

- **Harvest seeds** in late summer when they start to brown. Cut the stem off at ground level in the early morning and place it upside down in a paper bag in a dry, airy spot till the seeds drop into the bag.

· **Store** leaves and seeds in airtight containers.

CUMIN

Botanical name: *Cuminum cyminum* (Umbelliferae)

An ancient plant of biblical note, cumin is popular in such diverse culinary cultures as Mexico, North Africa, India, and Portugal. Cumin is a spreading plant with threadlike leaves that is grown for its pungent seeds. The seeds are used whole or ground in chili and curry dishes, cheeses, and sausage.

PLANT TYPE: Tender annual.
GROWING RANGE: Zones 5 to 11.
HARDINESS: Resistant to heat, not tolerant of cold. Needs a long growing season.
PLANT HEIGHT: 6 inches.
FLOWER COLOR: White, rose.
FLOWER FORM: Small flat clusters.
SEASON OF BLOOM: Summer.
SOIL: Average, well drained.
PH: 6 to 7.5.
FERTILIZER: Vegetable or all-purpose fertilizer.
WATER: Prefers average moisture conditions, neither too wet nor too dry.
EXPOSURE: Full sun.
SPACING: 6 inches.
PROPAGATION: Seed.

Method

· **Start seeds indoors** six to eight weeks before the last spring frost, in flats placed in full sun or under fluorescent lights. Seeds must be started indoors in areas with less than three months of summer temperatures above 65°F.

· **Prepare soil outdoors** before planting, adding average amounts of organic matter, such as peat moss, leaf mold, or compost.

· **Sow seeds outdoors** ¼ inch deep and 6 inches apart, after all danger of frost has passed.

· **Do not thin** plants since a thick growth will help support the fragile stems when the weight of the ripening seeds bends them over to the ground.

· **Set seedlings outdoors** after all danger of frost has passed.

· **Water** when the soil starts to dry out.

· **Fertilize** at planting time; no further feeding will be necessary.

· **Pests and diseases** include aphids and leaf spot. Treat aphids by spraying leaves with water or chemical insecticide, leaf spot with diluted insecticidal soap.

- **Harvest seeds** when they begin to dry by cutting the stems and hanging them upside down in a paper bag in a cool, dry place. The seeds will fall into the paper bag as they ripen.

- **Store** seeds in an airtight container.

DILL

Botanical name: *Anethum graveolens* (Umbelliferae)

Dill, which was once believed to "hinder witches from their will," takes its name from the Saxon word "to lull," referring to its supposed effectiveness in lulling cranky babies to sleep. Easy to grow and a self-sower, dill plants have finely divided, light green foliage and airy flower clusters. The leaves are used either fresh or dry to season eggs, vegetables, fish, and sauces. The seeds are used for flavoring and pickling.

PLANT TYPE: Hardy annual.
GROWING RANGE: Zones 3 to 11.
HARDINESS: Tolerates both cold and heat.
PLANT HEIGHT: 2 to 3 feet.
FLOWER COLOR: Yellow.
FLOWER FORM: Flat clusters.
SEASON OF BLOOM: Midsummer.
SOIL: Slightly acid, moderately rich, well drained.
PH: 5.5 to 6.5.
FERTILIZER: Vegetable or all-purpose fertilizer.
WATER: Prefers moist conditions.
EXPOSURE: Full sun.
SPACING: 4 to 8 inches.
PROPAGATION: Seed.

Method

- **Start seeds indoors** in late winter. Sow into individual pots placed in full sun or under fluorescent lights, as dill does not like to be transplanted. Do not cover the seeds—they need light to germinate.

- **Prepare soil outdoors** in early spring as soon as the soil can be worked, adding moderate amounts of organic matter, such as peat moss, leaf mold, or compost.

- **Sow seeds outdoors** ¼ inch deep in early spring, as soon as the soil can be worked, by scattering seeds over a 2-foot-wide area. Rake lightly and keep the area well watered with a fine spray until plants are established.

- **Do not thin** seedlings unless they are tightly crowded, since a group of stems helps to support the heavy seed heads that must otherwise be staked.

- **Set plants outdoors** in middle to late spring, when the soil is warm during the day, but before really hot weather develops.

- **Water** as soon as the soil starts to dry out until plants are established. Then water during dry spells of a week or more.

- **Fertilize** the soil at planting time. No further feeding should be necessary.

- **Pests and diseases** include aphids, caterpillars, and leaf spot. Eliminate aphids by spraying the leaves with water or an insecticide approved for use on vegetables. Leaf spot can be treated by spraying infected areas with insecticidal soap. An effective deterrent to caterpillars is Bt, an organic insecticide.

- **Harvest leaves** any time before flowering for fresh use or drying. If you are growing dill for the leaves and not the seeds, do not allow flowers to form to extend the harvest period.

- **Dry leaves** by wrapping them in a paper towel, sealing it in a paper bag, and placing it in a frost-free refrigerator until crisp and dry. Dried any other way, they will lose both flavor and color.

- **Harvest seeds** when they start to turn brown. Cut the stems and place them upside down in a paper bag to collect the seeds as they ripen. The seeds need very warm surroundings (90°F) in order to dry properly; an attic may be the best place to hang them.

- **Store** leaves and seeds in an airtight container.

Tip · Dill self-sows easily and can become weedy unless flower heads are removed before they set seed. It should not be allowed to self-sow near fennel, since the two will cross-pollinate with unpredictable results.

ELECAMPANE

Botanical name: *Inula helenium* (Compositae)

Elecampane is a tall robust plant perfect for a large garden or the back of a perennial border. The leaves at the base of the plant can grow up to 2 feet long, and decrease in size toward the growing tips. The flower is bright yellow, with showy clusters. Only the root of this herb is used, either candied as a cough drop to relieve congestion or added as a flavoring for drinks, although its flavor is sharp and a little bitter. It earned its place in the herb garden of old as an ingredient in veterinary medicine for bronchial disorders, for which purpose early colonists brought it from its native Europe.

PLANT TYPE: Perennial.
GROWING RANGE: Zones 3 to 8; grows wild throughout eastern and midwestern North America.
HARDINESS: Resistant to both cold and heat.
PLANT HEIGHT: 6 to 8 feet.
FLOWER COLOR: Golden yellow.
FLOWER FORM: Daisylike.

SEASON OF BLOOM: Late spring to late summer.
SOIL: Rich and moist, but will tolerate poor soil.
PH: 4.5 to 6.
FERTILIZER: Vegetable or all-purpose fertilizer.
WATER: Prefers moist conditions.
EXPOSURE: Full sun or partial shade.
SPACING: 18 to 36 inches.
PROPAGATION: Division or seed.

Method

- **Start seeds indoors** in early spring six to eight weeks before the last frost, in flats placed in full sun or under fluorescent lights.

- **Prepare soil outdoors** before planting, incorporating generous amounts of organic matter, such as peat moss, leaf mold, or compost, for maximum growth.

- **Sow seeds outdoors** 8 to 12 inches apart after the last spring frost or in the fall.

- **Set plants outdoors** after the last spring frost.

- **Thin seedlings** when they are 8 inches high to permanent spacing.

- **Divide** roots in the fall when harvesting, if necessary. Be sure that each root division contains at least one "eye."

- **Water** as soon as the soil starts to dry out, keeping it evenly moist.

- **Fertilize** the soil prior to planting. In the spring, when growth starts, apply fertilizer again.

- **Pests and disease** are not problems.

- **Winter protection** is not necessary. Cut the stalks to the ground in the fall to prevent the plants from being uprooted by the winter wind.

- **Harvest roots** in the fall of their second year. After digging up the root, slice it into small pieces to dry on a screen or lay in a single layer on brown paper.

- **Store** pieces of roots in an airtight container.

FENNEL

Botanical name: *Foeniculum vulgare* (Umbelliferae)

Fennel gave the name *marathon* to the long-distance run, since the Battle of Marathon was named for the fields of fennel in which it was fought. Fennel has threadlike, bright yellow-green leaves similar in appearance to those of dill, but distinctly anise flavored. Fresh leaves are used in soups, salads, and fish dishes, but do not retain their flavor when dried. Seeds are used in bread and cookies, and as a seasoning in sausage. Try placing fennel stalks on the fire when grilling fish for a delicate smoked flavor.

Fennel is a difficult neighbor in the garden; its growth is deterred by coriander or wormwood if planted close by, and it, in turn, can interfere with the growth of bush beans, caraway, tomatoes, and kohlrabi. Also, be aware that fennel will cross-pollinate with dill if it is planted close by.

PLANT TYPE: Perennial, though best grown as a tender annual.
GROWING RANGE: Zones 1 to 11 as an annual.
HARDINESS: Resistant to heat, slightly frost tolerant.
PLANT HEIGHT: 4 to 5 feet.
FLOWER COLOR: Yellow.
FLOWER FORM: Large flat clusters.
SEASON OF BLOOM: Summer.
SOIL: Moderately fertile, alkaline, well drained.
PH: 6 to 8.
FERTILIZER: Vegetable or all-purpose fertilizer.
WATER: Tolerates all moisture ranges except soggy soil.
EXPOSURE: Full sun.
SPACING: 8 to 12 inches.
PROPAGATION: Seed.

Method

- **Start seeds indoors** six to eight weeks before the last frost. Cover the seeds completely as they require darkness to germinate. It is best sown into individual pots placed in full sun or under fluorescent lights as it is difficult to transplant.

- **Prepare soil outdoors** before planting, incorporating generous amounts of organic matter, such as peat moss, leaf mold, or compost.

- **Sow seeds outdoors** ⅛ inch deep and 4 inches apart, in spring after all danger of frost has passed.

- **Thin** seedlings when 6 inches high to permanent spacing.

- **Set plants outdoors** after all danger of frost has passed.

- **Water** when the soil becomes dry.

- **Fertilize** at planting time.

- **Pests and diseases** include nematodes and root rot. To prevent nematodes, plant marigolds nearby. Avoid root rot by not overwatering and making sure soil has proper drainage.

- **Harvest leaves** for fresh use before the flowers open. If you do not want to harvest seeds, prevent flowers from forming by pinching out the flower stems; this will increase the harvesting period for the leaves.

- **Harvest seeds** as they begin to turn brown. Since they do not always ripen evenly, hold each flower head over a paper bag and knock ripe seeds off gently. Repeat every few days. If you cannot do this, wait until the ripest seeds begin to fall, then cut the flower heads and hang them upside down in paper bags till seeds fall off.

· **Store** seeds in an airtight container.

Selected Variety

Foeniculum vulgare nigra is a beautiful border plant with feathery rust- to bronze-colored foliage. Grow them 3 to 4 feet apart and remove flower heads to promote lush foliage.

FENUGREEK

Botanical name: *Trigonella foenum-graecum* (Leguminosae)

Fenugreek was used in ancient Egypt as a component of kuphi, an incense and embalming oil. It is commercially used in Europe as a flavoring for imitation maple syrup and extract. The seeds have a spicy odor when crushed and are used in curries, chutneys, and halvah, a Middle Eastern candy. The seedpods resemble string beans, are 6 inches long, and grow upright. The growing plant has a strong, sweet clover scent, pleasant to brush against in the garden but repellent to some insects. Its seeds are often sprouted like bean sprouts, and used to flavor sandwiches and salads.

PLANT TYPE: Hardy annual.
GROWING RANGE: Zones 1 to 10.
HARDINESS: Resistant to cold, moderately resistant to heat.
PLANT HEIGHT: 2 feet.
FLOWER COLOR: White to pale yellow.
FLOWER FORM: Pealike.
SEASON OF BLOOM: Summer
SOIL: Rich, well drained.
PH: 6 to 7.
FERTILIZER: Not recommended.
WATER: Average to dry conditions.
EXPOSURE: Full sun.
SPACING: 6 inches.
PROPAGATION: Seed.

Method

· **Starting seeds indoors** is not recommended.

· **Prepare soil outdoors** before planting, incorporating moderate amounts of organic matter, such as peat moss, leaf mold, or compost, to enrich it.

· **Sow seeds outdoors** 1/4 inch deep and 3 inches apart in early spring, as soon as the soil can be worked.

· **Thin** seedlings when they are 3 inches high to permanent spacing.

- **Water** as soon as the soil starts to dry out.

- **Pests and diseases** include beetles and root rot. If beetles are few, just pick them off and drown them. If not, spray with an insecticide approved for use on vegetables. Root rot can be avoided by not overwatering and making sure soil has good drainage.

- **Mulch** the soil in early spring to keep the roots cool.

- **Harvest seedpods** when the seeds are firm and the pods start to open by uprooting the entire plant and hanging it upside down in a paper bag until the seeds are hard and the pods crisp.

- **Store** dried seeds in an airtight container after removing them from the pods.

GINSENG

Botanical name: *Panax quinquefolius* (Araliaceae)

The Chinese have held ginseng in esteem and reverence for its medicinal, restorative, and aphrodisiac qualities for centuries. A woodland plant with whorls of five-part leaves, it is a wild native in eastern North America, but has been overharvested to the point of near-extinction. After the plant flowers, small clusters of red berries appear. The deeply branched roots, used to make teas, have a strong, bitter flavor. Growing ginseng is a challenge even to the experienced gardener.

PLANT TYPE: Perennial.
GROWING RANGE: Zones 3 to 8.
HARDINESS: Resistant to cold; will tolerate some heat, but will not thrive in tropical regions.
PLANT HEIGHT: 15 to 18 inches.
FLOWER COLOR: Greenish white.
FLOWER FORM: Small cluster.
SEASON OF BLOOM: Early summer
SOIL: Light, rich, well drained.
PH: 6 to 7.
FERTILIZER: Bonemeal. Do not use soluble fertilizers.
WATER: Moist conditions.
EXPOSURE: Full shade, preferably that of deciduous trees, which will maintain the cool, moist atmosphere needed for growth.
SPACING: 15 inches.
PROPAGATION: Seed or root cuttings.

Method

- **Starting seeds indoors** is not recommended.

- **Prepare soil outdoors** before planting, adding generous amounts of woodland organic matter such as leaf mold.

- **Sow seeds outdoors** ½ inch deep and 3 inches apart in the fall. Seeds may germinate the following spring, but don't be surprised if they take two years to germinate. Seeds should be rinsed in a 10 percent bleach solution before planting to hasten germination.

- **Thin** seedlings when they are 3 inches high to permanent spacing.

- **Take cuttings** in spring and plant them 1 inch deep.

- **Water** as soon as the soil starts to dry out, and keep it evenly moist but not soggy.

- **Fertilize** in the spring when growth starts.

- **Pests and diseases** include leaf blight, root rot, wilt, and rodents. Leaf blight can be treated with a chemical fungicide; prevent root rot by not overwatering. To avoid attracting rodents, clear away dead leaves and pull mulch back away from plants. Wilt is not something you can control; just pull up affected plants.

- **Winter protect** with a heavy mulch of straw or leaves. Remove early in the spring.

- **Harvest roots** in the fall of the fifth or sixth year after planting from seed, and the fourth or fifth year after growing from roots. Carefully dig up the roots and wash them with water.

- **Dry roots** on racks or screens in a warm, airy spot. It may take four weeks to dry them.

- **Store** roots in an airtight container.

HOREHOUND

Botanical name: *Marrubium vulgare* (Labiatae)

One of the bitter herbs of the Passover seder, horehound has been gathered and grown for centuries as a medicine to relieve coughs and sore throats. Horehound drops are still a popular cough drop. This spreading plant has deeply veined, wrinkled, woolly, aromatic leaves covering square stems that are covered in gray down. The bitter leaves and flowers are used in making tea, which some people drink to relieve coughs. Its name is derived from its historic use as a remedy for dog bites. It is a favorite of bees.

PLANT TYPE: Perennial.
GROWING RANGE: Zones 3 to 11.
HARDINESS: Resistant to both cold and heat.
PLANT HEIGHT: 18 to 24 inches.
FLOWER COLOR: White.
FLOWER FORM: Tubular, in whorls.
SEASON OF BLOOM: All summer.
SOIL: Average, sandy, well drained; tolerates poor soil.
PH: 4.5 to 8.
FERTILIZER: Vegetable or all-purpose fertilizer.
WATER: Dry to average conditions.
EXPOSURE: Full sun.

SPACING: 8 to 10 inches.
PROPAGATION: Seed, stem cuttings, or division.

 *Method*

- **Starting seeds indoors** is not recommended as horehound is very difficult to transplant.

- **Prepare soil outdoors** before planting, adding moderate amounts of organic matter, such as peat moss, leaf mold, or compost.

- **Sow seeds outdoors** ½ inch deep and 6 inches apart from early spring, as soon as the soil can be worked, till about two months before the first fall frost. Horehound may take two years to bloom when grown from seed.

- **Thin** seedlings when 4 inches high to permanent spacing so that the somewhat spindly stems can provide support for each other.

- **Divide** plants in midspring or early fall when plants become crowded. (Horehound may become weedy and rangy, and should be divided and reset every few years to keep beds attractive.)

- **Root cuttings** 4 to 6 inches long in spring or summer in a mixture of peat moss and perlite or sharp sand. Cuttings are the preferred method of propagation because, as previously noted, horehound is difficult to transplant.

- **Water** when the soil starts to dry out. Horehound tolerates drought very well.

- **Fertilize** very lightly at planting time and again in early spring when growth starts.

- **Diseases** are nematodes or leaf spot. Control nematodes by planting marigolds nearby or by adding compost (it contains organisms that attack nematodes). Leaf spot can be controlled by spraying with diluted insecticidal soap.

- **Harvest leaves and flowers** when the plant is in full bloom.

- **Dry leaves and flowers** on a screen in a dry, airy spot. The flowers dry easily but are difficult to handle because they are very sticky with tiny hairs.

- **Store** dried leaves and flowers in an airtight container.

HYSSOP

Botanical name: *Hyssopus officinalis* (Labiatae)

There is considerable disagreement over whether the hyssop we know today is the same as the one so frequently mentioned in the Bible as a cleanser and purifier. It is the same herb used for strewing on floors to walk on in England, and it was sprinkled on the altar during the consecration of Westminster Abbey in the eleventh century. This shrubby semi-evergreen perennial has aromatic dark green leaves and square stems. The leaves and flowers have a musky smell that reminds one of a skunk standing in the hot summer sun. Its principal modern use is as one of the herbs in monastic liqueurs such as Chartreuse and as a border or hedge plant for formal herb beds and knot gardens. It can be clipped to a neat, compact shape, perfect for this use. Hyssop tea is used occasionally to relieve sore throats and coughs.

PLANT TYPE: Perennial.
GROWING RANGE: Zones 3 to 7.
HARDINESS: Resistant to both heat and cold.
PLANT HEIGHT: 18 to 24 inches.
FLOWER COLOR: Blue-violet, sometimes white or pink.
FLOWER FORM: Spikes.
SEASON OF BLOOM: Early summer.
SOIL: Dry to average, well drained, alkaline.
PH: 7 to 8.
FERTILIZER: Fish emulsion, especially after harvest.
WATER: Tolerates dry to average conditions.
EXPOSURE: Full sun or light shade.
SPACING: 18 inches.
PROPAGATION: Seed, division, or stem cuttings.

Method

- **Start seeds indoors** in early spring, in flats placed in full sun or under fluorescent lights.

- **Prepare soil outdoors** before planting, adding a small amount of organic matter, such as peat moss, leaf mold, or compost. If soil is too rich, the leaves and flowers will lose their fragrance.

- **Sow seeds outdoors** ¼ inch deep and 9 inches apart in early spring, as soon as the soil is workable, or in the fall.

- **Thin** seedlings when they are 4 inches high to stand 18 inches apart, or 12 inches apart for use as a hedge or in a knot garden.

- **Set plants outdoors** in spring or summer up to two months before the first fall frost.

- **Divide** plants in midspring or early fall if they grow sparse after a few years.

- **Root cuttings** 4 to 6 inches long taken from growing tips during the summer after removing any flowers or flower buds.

- **Water** when the soil becomes dry. Hyssop tolerates drought very well.

- **Fertilize** lightly at planting time, again in spring when growth starts, and after leaves are harvested.

- **Diseases** are not a problem, but scales and nematodes may be bothersome. Repel nematodes by planting marigolds nearby, adding compost (it contains organisms that will kill nematodes), or cultivating frequently to expose larvae to sunshine. Scales can be picked off, if only a few, otherwise use an insecticide approved for vegetables.

- **Winter protection** is not necessary. Cut plants almost to the ground in early spring or late fall.

- **Harvest leaves and flowers** when the plant begins to bloom.

- **Dry leaves and flowers** on a screen in a dry, airy place.

- **Store** leaves and flowers in an airtight container.

LAVENDER

Botanical name: *Lavandula* (Labiatae)

Well loved by the ancient Greeks and Romans for its fragrant and cleansing properties, lavender fell into disuse during the Middle Ages. In Tudor England it blossomed once again into the popularity it still enjoys. Its distinctive fragrance and attractive growing habits make it a favorite in the garden. Lavender is a mounded, aromatic perennial with gray-green needlelike foliage and spikes of purple flowers that are used in sachets, potpourris, bath salts, soap, cosmetics, and tea. Its spikes are used to make fragrant fans, and its crisp, clean fragrance was used by some to invigorate and prevent fainting. Its compact shape works well in a hedge or knot garden, where its gray foliage contrasts nicely with boxwood, germander, and hyssop.

PLANT TYPE: Perennial.
GROWING RANGE: Zones 5 to 11.
HARDINESS: Resistant to both heat and cold.
PLANT HEIGHT: 18 to 24 inches.
FLOWER COLOR: Blue-violet.
FLOWER FORM: Spikes.
SEASON OF BLOOM: Early summer.
SOIL: Light, sandy, well drained, alkaline. Rich soil produces less fragrant lavender.
PH: 6 to 8.5.
FERTILIZER: Vegetable or all-purpose fertilizer.
WATER: Average to dry conditions. Soil should be dry during freezing weather to prevent killing the plant's crown and tearing the roots during alternate freezing and thawing.
EXPOSURE: Full sun.
SPACING: 12 inches.
PROPAGATION: Seed, division, or stem cuttings.

🌿 *Method*

- **Start seeds indoors** in early spring after four to six weeks of refrigeration, in flats placed in full sun or under fluorescent lights.

- **Prepare soil outdoors** before planting, adding small amounts of organic matter, such as leaf mold or compost, to slightly enrich it. Peat moss is too acidic for lavender.

- **Sow seeds outdoors** ½ inch deep and 6 inches apart in late fall. Seeds will germinate the following spring.

- **Set plants outdoors** in late spring or summer up to two months before the first fall frost.

- **Thin** seedlings when they are 4 inches high to permanent spacing. Nip off all the flower buds the first year for healthier, stronger plants.

- **Divide** plants in early spring only when plants are large.

- **Root cuttings** 4 to 6 inches long in spring or summer in a medium of peat moss and perlite. Since seed germination is slow, division and cuttings are the preferred methods of propagation.

- **Water** only when the soil becomes dry—do not overwater!

- **Fertilize** very lightly at planting time and again each year in early spring as soon as growth starts.

- **Pests and diseases** include caterpillars, leaf spot, and root rot, but healthy plants are usually resistant to these problems. If you have an infestation, caterpillars can be controlled by applications of soapy water sprays to the leaves (the spray tears through their webs). Leaf spot can be eliminated by spraying the leaves with water or an insecticide. Root rot can be treated by improving air circulation between plants and drainage.

- **Prune back** the plant to a compact shape after it flowers to keep it well shaped and to prevent degeneration. Even so, it may need frequent division and resetting. Never cut it back to the ground as it needs the leaves for continued growth.

- **Winter protect** with evergreen boughs or loose straw as a windscreen, but do not mulch. Remove boughs after ground thaws.

- **Harvest flowers** as they begin to open.

- **Dry flowers** in a dark, airy place on a screen or by hanging them upside down.

- **Store** dried flowers in an airtight container. The freezer is a good place for long-term storage, since dried flowers are subject to infestation.

Selected Species

Be aware that the nomenclature in common names for lavender is not consistent, and even the Latin names are subject to some disagreement among botanists. The oil of *Lavandula angustifolia* subsp. *angustifolia* (English lavender), which is one of the highest quality, is the most fragrant, making it best for commercial uses. It has narrow leaves and blue-green foliage, and is the hardiest for American gardens. 'Munstead Dwarf' and 'Hidcote' are compact, low cultivars. *L. angustifolia* is usually taller, produces a greater quantity of both flowers and oil, but is less fragrant. *L. dentata* (Fringed lavender) has dark green, fernlike foliage and the same climate requirements as *L. stoechas*. *L. stoechas* (French or Spanish lavender) is not quite as sweet as English lavender, has a more herblike fragrance, and is the classic lavender of the Greeks and Romans. Darker blue in bloom, it is not hardy for northern climates and will winter over only in Zone 7 and farther south. It can be grown indoors in pots, but needs five to six hours of direct sun daily.

LAVENDER COTTON

Botanical name: *Santolina chamaecyparissus* (Compositae)
Other common name: Santolina

No relation to lavender, lavender cotton is characterized by a scent that neither humans nor insects like. This makes it an excellent choice for moth-repelling potpourris, where its scent blends well into the more attractive smells of other herbs. Lavender cotton produces shrubby mounds of aromatic, woolly, fernlike, silver-gray foliage. It is excellent in borders and is popular in knot gardens. The flowers are often clipped off the plants when they are used as borders or in knot gardens to keep the shape more uniform and compact.

PLANT TYPE: Perennial; can be grown as an annual north of Zone 6.
GROWING RANGE: Zones 6 to 11 as a perennial, Zones 3 to 5 as an annual.
HARDINESS: Resistant to heat, moderately resistant to cold. It is salt tolerant and therefore a good seashore plant.
PLANT HEIGHT: 18 to 24 inches.
FLOWER COLOR: Golden yellow.
FLOWER FORM: Buttonlike.
SEASON OF BLOOM: Summer.
SOIL: Average, well drained. Grows very well in poor or sandy soil.
PH: 6 to 8.
FERTILIZER: Vegetable or all-purpose fertilizer.
WATER: Prefers dry conditions.
EXPOSURE: Full sun.
SPACING: 18 to 20 inches.
PROPAGATION: Seed, stem cuttings, layering, or division.

Method

· **Start seeds indoors** in early spring to early summer, in flats placed in full sun or under fluorescent lights. Plants started early will flower the first year.

· **Prepare soil outdoors** before planting, adding a small amount of organic matter, such as peat moss, leaf mold, or compost.

· **Sow seeds outdoors** ¼ inch deep and 9 inches apart in spring, as soon as the soil can be worked, or summer up to two months before the first fall frost.

· **Thin** seedlings when they are 5 inches high to permanent spacing.

· **Set plants outdoors** in spring when the ground can be worked or summer up to two months before the first fall frost.

· **Divide** plants in early spring before new growth begins.

· **Root cuttings** in summer in a medium of peat moss and perlite. These are slow to reach full size and should be grown indoors until the following spring. **Layer stems** as soon as they are long enough by laying long side stems along the ground and anchoring them with a rock. Cut the new plants off after roots have formed where the stem touches the ground.

- **Water** when the soil has dried out. Do not overwater.
- **Fertilize** very lightly at planting time and again each spring when growth starts.
- **Pests and diseases** are generally not a problem.
- **Prune back** the plants to 4 to 6 inches high each spring to encourage new growth.
- **Winter protect** with a light mulch of a few evergreen boughs or salt hay.
- **Harvest leaves and flowers** when the plant starts to bloom.
- **Dry leaves and flowers** on a screen in a warm, dry, airy spot.
- **Store** leaves and flowers in an airtight container.

Selected Species

Santolina virens is a similar plant in every respect except for the color of its foliage, which is bright green. It makes a good contrast in a border or a knot garden.

LEMON BALM

Botanical name: *Melissa officinalis* (Labiatae)

The regular consumption of lemon balm tea was credited for the longevity of many of the citizens of early England, but most people drink it for its refreshing flavor. Lemon balm oil is used in furniture polish; you can achieve the same results as polish by rubbing the fresh leaves on wooden surfaces. Lemon balm has crisp, lemon-scented, deeply ridged leaves that are used in teas, jellies, fruit salads, and cold drinks. The leaves have more flavor when used fresh in teas, although they can be dried. Bees like lemon balm; in fact, it is often rubbed inside hives to attract new bees and keep the more restless inhabitants at home.

PLANT TYPE: Perennial.
GROWING RANGE: Zones 4 to 10.
HARDINESS: Resistant to cold, moderately resistant to heat.
PLANT HEIGHT: 2 feet.
FLOWER COLOR: White.
FLOWER FORM: Whorls.
SEASON OF BLOOM: Summer.
SOIL: Poor to moderately fertile, light, sandy, well drained.
PH: 5 to 8.
FERTILIZER: Vegetable or all-purpose fertilizer.
WATER: Prefers moist conditions but tolerates drought.
EXPOSURE: Light shade.

SPACING: 18 inches.

PROPAGATION: Seed, division, or stem cuttings.

 *Method*

- **Start seeds indoors** in flats placed in full sun or under fluorescent lights in early spring, at least ten weeks before the last frost, since they germinate slowly and plants need a long time to become established. Do not cover the seeds; they need light to germinate.

- **Prepare soil outdoors** before planting, adding a small amount of organic matter, such as peat moss, leaf mold, or compost.

- **Sow seeds outdoors** in warm zones in early spring as soon as the soil can be worked, or in the fall in colder regions. Seeds should be pressed into the soil about 4 inches apart but not covered.

- **Set plants outdoors** midspring through summer up to two months before the first fall frost.

- **Thin** plants when they are 6 inches high to permanent spacing.

- **Divide** plants in spring when growth starts or in the fall, allowing three to four weeks for plants to become established before hard frost. Be sure there are several growth buds on each division. **Root cuttings** 4 to 6 inches long in summer in a medium of peat moss and perlite.

- **Water** as soon as the soil starts to dry out, keeping it evenly moist. Lemon balm will tolerate drought after it is established.

- **Fertilize** very lightly at planting time and again in early spring when plants start to grow.

- **Diseases** include botrytis and leaf spot. To control botrytis, spray with a fungicide. Leaf spot can be controlled by spraying the leaves with water or an insecticide approved for use on vegetables. **Pests** are not a problem.

- **Winter protect** with a light covering of leaves, evergreen boughs, or straw. Remove when ground thaws in spring.

- **Harvest leaves** before the plant comes into bloom by cutting off stems at their base.

- **Dry leaves** by hanging small, loosely tied bunches of stems upside down in a dark, dry, airy space. Be careful not to bruise the leaves during harvesting or drying. To retain color, dry at 90° to 110°F.

- **Store** leaves in an airtight container.

Tip • Shear back after flowering to keep the plants compact. Lemon balm spreads in a good growing environment and can be contained by an underground barrier or by removing the seedlings that come up from lemon balm's self-seeding.

Lemon Verbena

Botanical name: *Aloysia triphylla* (Verbenaceae); also known by its former designations, *Lippia citriodora, Aloysia citriodora,* and *Verbena triphylla*

Lemon verbena is the only herb that retains its true lemon scent after drying, often remaining fragrant for many years. It is an open-growing shrub with lance-shaped leaves that are used fresh in teas, and dried in potpourri and sachets.

PLANT TYPE: Deciduous or semi-evergreen shrub.
GROWING RANGE: Zones 9 to 11; may be grown in other areas if roots are dug in fall and stored indoors over the winter.
HARDINESS: Resistant to heat, not tolerant of cold.
PLANT HEIGHT: 4 to 10 feet in its native South and Central America; smaller in northern zones.
FLOWER COLOR: White to pale lavender.
FLOWER FORM: Spikes; very insignificant.
SEASON OF BLOOM: Late summer.
SOIL: Rich, sandy, well drained.
PH: 5.5 to 6.5.
FERTILIZER: Vegetable or all-purpose fertilizer.
WATER: Prefers constant moisture.
EXPOSURE: Full sun.
SPACING: 2 to 3 feet.
PROPAGATION: Stem cuttings.

Method

- Lemon verbena cannot be grown from **seeds.**

- **Prepare soil outdoors** before planting, adding a generous amount of organic matter, such as leaf mold or compost, to enrich it.

- **Plant dormant roots outdoors** 1 inch deep in spring, after all danger of frost has passed.

- **Root cuttings** 4 to 6 inches long in midsummer to late summer in a medium of peat moss and perlite.

- **Water** before the soil starts to dry out to ensure constant moisture.

- **Fertilize** at planting time. Where hardy, lemon balm should be fed each spring when growth starts.

- **Pests** include the red spider, which can be controlled by spraying the undersides of the leaves frequently with plain water. **Diseases** are not a problem.

- **Winter protect** in areas with winter frosts by digging up the roots after the first frost and storing them in moist sand or peat moss in a cool, dark, frost-free area. Check the roots regularly to make sure they are not drying out. Replant them in spring after all danger of frost has passed, at the same depth at which they were dug up.

· **Harvest leaves** throughout the summer.

· **Dry leaves** on a screen in a cool, dark, airy spot.

· **Store** leaves in an airtight container.

Tip · Lemon verbena can be grown outdoors in containers and overwintered indoors, although the chances of survival are about fifty-fifty. Keep the plant even if the leaves fall off and it appears dead. Continue to water; it may regrow.

LOVAGE

Botanical name: *Levisticum officinale* (Umbelliferae)

Lovage is a tropical-looking plant that resembles celery. It has celery-flavored leaves and seeds, and hollow stems that are used as a substitute for celery in soups. The leaves are used fresh or dried in salads, stews, and soups. Crushed seeds may be used as celery powder; whole seeds are used in baking.

PLANT TYPE: Perennial.
GROWING RANGE: Zones 3 to 8.
HARDINESS: Tolerant of cold and moderately tolerant of heat. Lovage must have freezing temperatures during the winter.
PLANT HEIGHT: 2 to 3 feet when not in bloom, 6 feet in bloom.
FLOWER COLOR: Greenish yellow.
FLOWER FORM: Flat clusters.
SEASON OF BLOOM: Summer.
SOIL: Rich, well drained.
PH: 5.5 to 7.5.
FERTILIZER: Vegetable or all-purpose fertilizer.
WATER: Prefers moist conditions.
EXPOSURE: Full sun to partial shade.
SPACING: 12 to 15 inches.
PROPAGATION: Seed or division.

 *Method*

· **Start seeds indoors** in early spring in individual pots placed in full sun or under fluorescent lights, as lovage does not like to be transplanted.

· **Prepare soil outdoors** before planting, adding generous amounts of organic matter, such as peat moss, leaf mold, or compost, to enrich it.

- **Sow seeds outdoors** in fall, ½ inch deep and 12 inches apart, for germination the following spring, or, in warmer climates (Zone 6 and south), sow in early spring as soon as the soil can be worked. Fresh seeds have the best chance of germination.

- **Set plants outdoors** in spring when night temperatures can be expected to remain above 40°F.

- **Thin** plants when they are 2 inches high to permanent spacing.

- **Divide** plants in early spring or late fall when necessary.

- **Water** before the soil starts to dry out to ensure evenly moist conditions.

- **Fertilize** yearly when growth starts. Feed again during the summer if foliage starts to turn yellow.

- **Pests and diseases** are not a problem.

- **Harvest leaves** for fresh use when they are young by cutting the outside leaf stalks. Harvest for dried leaves by cutting the stem before the flowers bloom. This will, of course, be at the expense of a seed crop.

- **Dry leaves** on screens in a warm, dry area or in a warm oven (no more than 200°F) until crisp.

- **Harvest seeds** as soon as they start to turn tan in color. Place the seed heads upside down in a paper bag, letting the seeds drop as they ripen.

- **Store** leaves and seeds in an airtight container.

MARJORAM

Botanical name: *Origanum majorana* (Labiatae); also known by its former designation, *Majorana hortensis*
Other common name: Sweet marjoram

No other herb has caused so much confusion among botanists as the marjorams and oreganos. Sweet marjoram, the most popular of those grown in the United States, is the only one on which there is agreement regarding the botanical name. Sweet marjoram has oval, slightly velvety, 1-inch-long, aromatic leaves. It is used in tomato dishes, and to flavor meats, vegetables, and salads.

PLANT TYPE: Tender perennial, usually grown as an annual.
GROWING RANGE: Zones 1 to 8 as an annual, Zones 9 to 11 as a perennial.
HARDINESS: Resistant to heat, tolerates light frosts.
PLANT HEIGHT: 8 to 10 inches.
FLOWER COLOR: Pinkish white.
FLOWER FORM: Inconspicuous knotlike clusters that resemble seeds.
SEASON OF BLOOM: Midsummer.
SOIL: Light, slightly rich, sandy, well drained.

PH: 7 to 8.
FERTILIZER: Vegetable or all-purpose fertilizer.
WATER: Prefers average to slightly moist conditions.
EXPOSURE: Full sun.
SPACING: 6 to 8 inches.
PROPAGATION: Seed.

 ## *Method*

- **Start seeds indoors** in late winter, in flats placed in full sun or under fluorescent lights.

- **Prepare soil outdoors** before planting, adding moderate amounts of organic matter, such as leaf mold or compost.

- **Sow seeds outdoors** ¼ to ½ inch deep and 3 inches apart in early spring, as soon as the soil can be worked. Seeds are so tiny that indoor sowing is usually more successful, since it is easier to care for the plants in a controlled environment.

- **Thin** when seedlings are 4 inches high to permanent spacing.

- **Set plants outdoors** in early spring to midspring as soon as the soil can be worked.

- **Water** as soon as the soil starts to dry out and keep evenly moist.

- **Fertilize** lightly at planting time; no other feeding will be necessary.

- **Pests and diseases** are usually not a problem.

- **Remove flower buds** to extend the harvest period of the leaves.

- **Harvest leaves** at any time until the plant blooms for fresh or dry use.

- **Dry leaves** on a screen in a warm, dry, airy place.

- **Store** dried leaves in an airtight container.

MINT

Botanical name: *Mentha* (Labiatae)

Mint is among the most commonly grown herbs, popular both to the gardener and the cook. Native to the Near East, mint is mentioned in the Bible and in Greek mythology. For such an old herb, there are unusually few legends or superstitions connected with it. Mints include a large number of aromatic herbs that spread quickly by underground runners and are difficult to keep confined in beds. Leaves of mint are used in teas, cold drinks, salads, and vegetables. In the Near East, mint is added to salads and is commonly served with peas and lamb. The leaves can also be used as a garnish or in potpourri.

PLANT TYPE: Perennial.
GROWING RANGE: Zones 3 to 11.

HARDINESS: Resistant to both cold and heat.
PLANT HEIGHT: 1 to 3 feet.
FLOWER COLOR: Lavender, purple, pink, white.
FLOWER FORM: Spikes.
SEASON OF BLOOM: Midsummer through fall.
SOIL: Rich, light, well drained.
PH: 6.5 to 8.
FERTILIZER: Vegetable or all-purpose fertilizer.
WATER: Prefers moist conditions.
EXPOSURE: Full sun or light shade.
SPACING: 12 to 24 inches, since runners will quickly fill in spaces.
PROPAGATION: Seed, division, or stem cuttings. Since mints do not grow true from seeds, it is best to begin with divisions or cuttings of a variety whose flavor is pleasant to you.

Method

- **Start seeds indoors** in early spring through midsummer, up to three months before the first fall frost, in flats placed in full sun or under fluorescent lights.

- **Prepare soil outdoors** before planting, adding generous amounts of organic matter, such as peat moss, leaf mold, or compost, to enrich it.

- **Sow seeds outdoors** ¼ to ½ inch deep and 6 inches apart from early spring, as soon as the soil is workable, through midsummer.

- **Thin** plants when they are 4 inches high to permanent spacing.

- **Set plants outdoors** from midspring to late summer, up to two months before the first fall frost.

- **Divide** plants when growth starts in early spring. **Root cuttings** in summer from new growth. Root division is so easy and reliable that stem cuttings are rarely used.

- **Water** when the soil starts to dry out, keeping it evenly moist.

- **Fertilize** lightly at planting time and again every summer after leaves are harvested.

- **Pests and diseases** include nematodes, aphids, mealybugs, mites, leaf spot, and mildew, but mint is so prolific that these rarely interfere with the harvest.

- **Harvest leaves** for fresh use at any time. Harvest leaves for dried use just before the plant flowers by cutting off the flowering stem.

- **Dry leaves** by tying stems together and hanging them upside down in a dry, cool, airy spot.

- **Store** dried leaves in an airtight container. To preserve the flavor, keep leaves attached to the stems until use.

Tip • Mint can become very invasive; control it by yearly thinning or by an underground barrier. A barrier is about the only way to control spearmint. Also, pinching off growing stems regularly gives a supply of fresh mint as well as prevents the plants from becoming leggy.

Selected Species

Mentha aquatica var. *crispa* (Curled mint) grows 3 feet tall and has purple flowers. Leaves are crisped or crinkled, with a spearmint flavor. *M.* x *piperita* (Peppermint) grows 2 to 3 feet tall and has purple flowers and smooth leaves. This is the best mint for drying. Its shallow root structure sends aboveground runners instead of the deep and hard-to-control runners of spearmint. *M.* x *piperita* var. *citrata* (Orange mint) grows 2 to 3 feet tall and has purple flowers and leaves that carry the odor of orange rind. It is preferred for potpourri use, producing an almost colognelike scent.

M. spicata (Spearmint) grows 1 to 2 feet high and has lavender flowers and wrinkled leaves. Often called garden mint, it is the type most commonly grown.

M. suaveolens, sometimes called *M. rotundifolia* (Apple mint), grows 4 feet tall and has white or pink flowers. 'Variegata,' pineapple mint, is lower growing. Pineapple and apple mint must be used fresh as they lose their flavor when dried.

OREGANO

Botanical name: *Origanum* (Labiatae)

The name *oregano* is used to describe a wide variety of plants of the genus *Origanum,* and there is very little agreement among botanists or herbalists as to nomenclature. For the gardener, however, the main importance is not the name, but the flavor. Good oregano should have a distinctive, almost sharp flavor. Since oregano planted from seed ranges wildly in its pungency—at one extreme it may even be tasteless—it is best to purchase oregano as a plant. You can tell its flavor by rubbing a leaf and looking for a strong, pleasant fragrance. One fact to keep in mind when shopping for plants is that the flavorful oreganos usually have white blossoms. Species you may see are *O. heracleoticum, O. vulgare, O. onites,* and *O. virens,* all of culinary quality. *O. dictamnus* (Ditany of Crete) is an ornamental herb with round gray leaves.

Dried oregano bought at the market is usually a mixture of many different varieties blended together for their flavor, rather than being from one particular plant. Oregano is best known in Italian dishes and is often combined with basil. It also blends well in many egg dishes.

PLANT TYPE: Tender perennial, grown as an annual in the United States.
GROWING RANGE: Zones 1 to 11 as an annual.
HARDINESS: Resistant to heat, variable resistance to cold.
PLANT HEIGHT: 1½ to 3 feet.
FLOWER COLOR: Purple, pink, white.

FLOWER FORM: Clusters.
SEASON OF BLOOM: Midsummer to fall.
SOIL: Light, poor, well drained.
PH: 6.5 to 8.
FERTILIZER: Vegetable or all-purpose fertilizer.
WATER: Prefers dry conditions.
EXPOSURE: Full sun.
SPACING: 12 inches.
PROPAGATION: Stem cuttings, division, or seeds; however, seeds often produce tasteless plants.

Method

- **Start seeds indoors** in late winter, in flats placed in full sun or under fluorescent lights. Seeds are slow to germinate, sometimes taking several weeks.

- **Prepare soil outdoors** before planting, adding little or no organic matter.

- **Sowing seeds outdoors** is not recommended.

- **Set plants outdoors** in spring after all danger of frost has passed.

- **Divide** plants in early spring when growth starts if necessary. **Root cuttings** 4 to 6 inches long in summer from new growth in a sterile medium.

- **Water** sparingly when the ground dries out.

- **Fertilize** at planting time; no other feeding will be necessary.

- **Pests and diseases** are not a problem.

- **Harvest leaves** when the plants start to bloom by cutting off the stems to half their length.

- **Dry leaves** by hanging the stems upside down in a dry, cool, airy spot.

- **Store** dried leaves in an airtight container.

ORRIS

Botanical name: *Iris germanica* var. *florentina* (Iridaceae)

The growing plant is usually called iris and the dried root orris. The dried root is either powdered or broken into chips for use as a fragrance fixative in potpourri and in many cosmetics. Broken orris root works better and lasts longer than the powdered form, and is also less likely to irritate eyes and nasal tissue (those with cosmetic allergies should not handle orris root); unfortunately, it is very difficult to break up the dried root into the chips. Orris, being an iris, has the flat, strap-shaped leaves of the genus.

PLANT TYPE: Perennial.
GROWING RANGE: Zones 4 to 10.

HARDINESS: Resistant to both heat and cold.
PLANT HEIGHT: 2 feet.
FLOWER COLOR: White, veined with blue and crested in yellow.
FLOWER FORM: Irislike.
SEASON OF BLOOM: Early summer.
SOIL: Rich, well drained.
PH: 7 to 8.
FERTILIZER: Vegetable or all-purpose fertilizer.
WATER: Prefers dry to average conditions.
EXPOSURE: Full sun.
SPACING: 12 inches.
PROPAGATION: Division.

 ## Method

- **Starting from seeds** is not recommended.

- **Prepare soil outdoors** before planting, adding organic matter, such as peat moss, leaf mold, or compost, to enrich it.

- **Set rhizomes outdoors** in midspring or early fall. They should be placed at or just below the soil surface, with the top of the rhizome exposed.

- **Divide** plants in summer or fall every two to three years.

- **Water** when the soil starts to dry out. Do not overwater.

- **Fertilize** in spring when growth starts.

- **Pests and diseases** are the same as for other irises (see page 293). It also may be bothered by root rot or borers. Root rot can be controlled by proper drainage, and borers can be eliminated by the application of a chemical pesticide.

- **Harvest roots** after the flowers fade or in early fall.

- **Dry roots** in the sun for at least a week after peeling them.

- **Store** roots in a dry place for at least a year before grinding or chipping. After cutting them into pieces, store in airtight containers.

Tip · Remove flowers as soon as they fade so the plant will concentrate its energies on root development.

PARSLEY

Botanical name: *Petroselinum crispum* (Umbelliferae)

Parsley seeds are so slow to germinate that it was once thought that they went to the devil and back nine times first. Its lore is filled with sinister associations, but its closest association in the kitchen is with garlic. Use parsley in partnership with garlic to cut garlic's aftertaste. Parsley is used fresh or dry in almost any meat, fish, egg, or vegetable dish, and sprigs of parsley are often used as garnishes. The leaves are curled, crinkled, or finely cut, depending on the variety, and are best cut with scissors. Parsley is best grown as an annual, as foliage becomes bitter and tough the second year.

PLANT TYPE: Biennial, usually grown as an annual.
GROWING RANGE: Zones 1 to 10 as an annual, Zones 3 to 10 as a biennial.
HARDINESS: Resistant to cold, not tolerant of high heat.
PLANT HEIGHT: 6 to 12 inches in foliage, 3 feet in flower.
FLOWER COLOR: Yellowish green; no flowers if grown as an annual.
FLOWER FORM: Flat clusters.
SEASON OF BLOOM: Late spring of the second year of growth.
SOIL: Rich, deep, well drained.
PH: 6 to 8.
FERTILIZER: Vegetable or all-purpose fertilizer.
WATER: Prefers moist conditions.
EXPOSURE: Full sun or light shade.
SPACING: 6 to 8 inches.
PROPAGATION: Seed.

Method

· **Start seeds indoors,** after soaking them in water for twenty-four hours, in individual pots placed in full sun or under fluorescent lights, as parsley does not like to be transplanted. Completely cover the seed as darkness is needed for germination. Seeds are very slow to germinate, taking several weeks.

· **Prepare soil outdoors** before planting, adding generous amounts of organic matter, such as peat moss, leaf mold, or compost, to enrich it.

· **Sow seeds outdoors** ¼ inch deep and 3 inches apart two to four weeks before the last frost, after soaking them in water for twenty-four hours or freezing them in ice cubes. In warm areas (south of Zone 5), sow seeds in fall for harvest the following spring.

· **Set plants outdoors** two to four weeks before the last frost.

· **Thin** when plants are 3 inches high to permanent spacing.

· **Water** before the soil becomes dry.

· **Fertilize** when the plants are 4 inches tall and again one month later.

· **Pests and diseases** are caterpillars, root rot, and leaf spot. To eliminate caterpillars, spray with Bt, an organic insecticide. Root rot can be controlled by proper drainage. Plants afflicted with leaf spot should be sprayed with a diluted insecticidal soap.

· **Harvest leaves** at any time for fresh or dried use. If grown as a biennial, harvest leaves before the plant flowers.

- **Dry leaves** on a screen in a warm, dry, airy place, or, to retain color, wrap them in a paper towel and place them in a frost-free refrigerator until they are crisp.

- **Store** dried leaves in an airtight container.

Tip · Parsley may be dug up in the fall and grown indoors on a sunny windowsill, but you must dig very deeply to get the large taproot, and you will need a deep pot. For potting, it is best to use smaller plants that have been started later in the season (midsummer) since they will be at their peak during winter and will not have developed a taproot that is too large for transplanting.

PENNYROYAL

Botanical name: *Mentha pulegium* (Pennyroyal); *Hedeoma pulegioides* (American pennyroyal) (Labiatae)

Once used medicinally and as a tea, pennyroyal has been shown by modern research to be an abortive, so it is now grown primarily for its pungent, citronella-scented leaves. These are used as a repellent to fleas, moths, and mosquitoes, and in potpourri. Perennial pennyroyal is a spreading plant with dark green leaves; the annual is lighter green and upright. Though of different genuses, the two are in the same plant family and are identical in use and fragrance, as well as growth needs.

PLANT TYPES: Perennial (pennyroyal) and annual (American pennyroyal).
GROWING RANGE: Zones 3 to 10.
HARDINESS: Tolerant of cold, not tolerant of excessive heat.
PLANT HEIGHT: 6 inches, perennial; 12 inches, annual.
FLOWER COLOR: Lavender-blue.
FLOWER FORM: Spikes.
SEASON OF BLOOM: Summer.
SOIL: Rich, sandy, well drained.
PH: 5.5 to 8.
FERTILIZER: Vegetable or all-purpose fertilizer.
WATER: Prefers moist conditions.
EXPOSURE: Full sun or light shade.
SPACING: 1 to 2 feet.
PROPAGATION: Seed, division, or stem cuttings.

 *Method*

- **Start seeds indoors** in early spring to midsummer up to three months before the first fall frost, in flats placed in full sun or under fluorescent lights. Since the perennial is slow to germinate and develop, divide it or buy plants rather than grow it from seed.

- **Prepare soil outdoors** before planting, adding generous amounts of organic matter, such as peat moss, leaf mold, or compost, to enrich it.

- **Sow seeds outdoors** ¼ to ½ inch deep and 6 inches apart in midspring (after heavy frosts) to midsummer, up to three months before the first fall frost.

- **Set plants outdoors** in midspring to midsummer, up to two months before the first fall frost.

- **Divide** root runners in spring or early fall when necessary. **Root cuttings** 4 to 6 inches long of new growth in summer.

- **Thin** when plants are 6 inches high to stand 12 inches apart. If plants become crowded, rethin to stand 2 feet apart.

- **Water** before the soil dries out.

- **Fertilize** at planting time and again each summer after harvesting.

- **Pests** are not a problem; **diseases** include leaf spot and mildew. Leaf spot can be treated by spraying with a diluted insecticidal soap or fungicide. Mildew can be prevented by not crowding plants and allowing for good air circulation, and can also be treated by spraying with a fungicide that has been approved for use on vegetables.

- **Winter protect** perennial pennyroyal with a light layer of leaves, evergreen boughs, or straw in the northern limits of its hardiness. Remove when ground thaws in spring.

- **Harvest leaves** before the plants bloom by cutting off the flowering stem.

- **Dry leaves** by hanging the stems upside down in a dry, cool, airy place.

- **Store** dried leaves in an airtight container.

PERILLA

Botanical name: *Perilla frutescens* (Labiatae)
Other common name: Beefsteak plant

The crisp, deeply cut, green or reddish-purple foliage of perilla has a metallic, bronzy sheen. Although it flowers, it is primarily grown for its foliage; 'Atropurpurea' has very dark purple leaves, and 'Crispa' has ruffled, crinkled leaves. Both mild-flavored leaves can be used fresh in salads and with fruit, as can their flowers in fish dishes or soup. Perilla is a favorite in Japanese cooking, where its leaves make a striking addition to quickly sautéed dishes of mixed meat and vegetables.

PLANT TYPE: Tender annual.
GROWING RANGE: Zones 1 to 11.
HARDINESS: Resistant to heat, not tolerant of cold.
PLANT HEIGHT: 18 to 36 inches.
FLOWER COLOR: Lavender, pink, white.

FLOWER FORM: Spikes.
SEASON OF BLOOM: Early fall.
SOIL: Average to rich, well drained.
PH: 5.5 to 6.5.
FERTILIZER: Vegetable or all-purpose fertilizer.
WATER: Prefers dry conditions.
EXPOSURE: Full sun or light shade.
SPACING: 12 to 15 inches.
PROPAGATION: Seed.

🌿 *Method*

- **Start seeds indoors** four to six weeks before the last spring frost, in individual pots placed in full sun or under fluorescent lights. The beefsteak plant does not like transplanting. Do not cover the seeds as light is needed for germination.

- **Prepare soil outdoors** before planting, adding moderate amounts of organic matter, such as peat moss, leaf mold, or compost.

- **Sow seeds outdoors** in spring after all danger of frost has passed, 6 inches apart and barely pressing seeds into the soil surface.

- **Thin** plants when they are 6 inches high to permanent spacing.

- **Set plants outdoors** after all danger of frost has passed.

- **Water** when the soil has dried out.

- **Fertilize** at planting time; no other fertilizing is necessary.

- **Pests and diseases** are not a problem.

- **Pinch back** growing tips when plants are 6 inches high to encourage bushiness.

- **Harvest leaves and flowers** at any time and use both fresh.

ROSEMARY

Botanical name: *Rosmarinus officinalis* (Labiatae)

A native of the Mediterranean, rosemary has long been associated with remembrance. This is perhaps due to the length of time the dried leaves retain their scent, also making it a good choice for potpourri, where it combines well with roses. Rosemary is also associated with constancy, its sprigs used in bridal crowns and bouquets. Its name is believed to arise from the legend that Mary spread her wet laundry to dry on its branches. Rosemary has aromatic stems and aromatic, gray-green needlelike leaves that are used in all types of meat and poultry dishes, most especially with lamb. A rosemary infusion is said to be a good hair rinse for brunettes.

PLANT TYPE: Tender perennial that must be brought indoors in winter except south of Zone 6. It is sometimes treated as an annual, but its slow growth produces few leaves.

GROWING RANGE: Zones 6 to 11 as a perennial, all zones as an annual.

HARDINESS: Resistant to heat, not tolerant of cold.

PLANT HEIGHT: 3 feet; up to 5 feet where it can develop as a shrub.

FLOWER COLOR: Pale blue.

FLOWER FORM: Whorls on short spikes.

SEASON OF BLOOM: Winter and early spring where hardy or where brought indoors for the winter.

SOIL: Light, well drained.

PH: 5 to 8.

FERTILIZER: Vegetable or all-purpose fertilizer.

WATER: Prefers well-drained conditions, but soil must not dry out, especially in pots.

EXPOSURE: Full sun or partial shade.

SPACING: 12 to 18 inches.

PROPAGATION: Seed, stem cuttings, division, or layering.

Method

- **Start seeds indoors** in late winter in a cool room, in flats placed in full sun or under fluorescent lights. Seeds develop into plants so slowly that most gardeners begin with purchased plants or propagate it from cuttings.

- **Prepare soil outdoors** before planting, adding small amounts of organic matter, such as peat moss, leaf mold, or compost.

- **Sow seeds outdoors** ¼ to ½ inch deep and 6 inches apart in early spring, as soon as the soil can be worked.

- **Set plants outdoors** in midspring two to four weeks before the last frost.

- **Thin** when seedlings are 6 inches high to permanent spacing.

- **Divide** plants when growth starts in spring, if necessary. **Root cuttings** 4 to 6 inches long in midsummer in a sterile medium. Rosemary is slow to root and may take several weeks. **Layer** plants at any time during the growing season by weighting an outside branch to the ground to form roots.

- **Water** before the soil has dried out; take note, however, that rosemary cannot survive wet roots. Do not overwater! Rosemary benefits from having its foliage misted daily when hot.

- **Fertilize** at planting time; where hardy, fertilize when growth starts in winter or early spring.

- **Pests** are not a problem. Rosemary may be susceptible to root rot, which can be prevented by having proper drainage and taking care not to overwater.

· **Prune back** where hardy, as needed, to control size and use the harvested leaves.

· **Winter protect** with a single layer of evergreen boughs, leaves, or straw. Remove when ground thaws in spring. Where winters are severe, it must be brought indoors, where it profits from daily misting.

· **Harvest leaves** before the plant flowers for fresh or dry use.

· **Dry leaves** on a screen in a cool, dry, airy place.

· **Store** dried leaves in an airtight container.

Tip · Growing zones are somewhat misleading for rosemary because its success depends as much on humidity as temperature. Therefore, you might have more trouble growing the herb in a warmer but drier climate than you would in a colder but more humid climate.

Selected Species

Rosmarinus prostratus is a trailing, lateral-growing variety that cascades nicely from walls and does well in pots. It is more sensitive to cold and its flowers are bluer than those of the upright variety.

RUE

Botanical name: *Ruta graveolens* (Rutaceae)

Rue, the herb of grace, was used by the ancient Greeks and in the Middle Ages to ward off witches, and some suggest that its smell would ward off anything! Since the fresh leaves and oil may cause an allergic rash, many gardeners prefer to handle it with gloves. Rue is a shrubby, evergreen perennial that has deeply cut, lacy, fernlike blue-green foliage. *Although old recipes including rue are sometimes seen, it should not be ingested, because of a possible allergic reaction.* It should be grown strictly as an ornamental. Legend has it that stolen rue thrives better than plants acquired through more legitimate means.

PLANT TYPE: Perennial.
GROWING RANGE: Zones 4 to 11.
HARDINESS: Resistant to both heat and cold.
PLANT HEIGHT: 1½ to 3 feet.
FLOWER COLOR: Yellow.
FLOWER FORM: Clusters of buttonlike flowers.
SEASON OF BLOOM: Early summer to midsummer.
SOIL: Poor, well drained.
PH: 5.5 to 8.
FERTILIZER: Vegetable or all-purpose fertilizer used only in exceptionally poor soil.
WATER: Prefers moist conditions.

EXPOSURE: Full sun.
SPACING: 6 to 12 inches.
PROPAGATION: Seed, stem cuttings, or division.

Method

· **Start seeds indoors** in late winter, in flats placed in full sun or under fluorescent lights.

· **Prepare soil outdoors** before planting, adding no organic matter.

· **Sow seeds outdoors** ½ inch deep and 3 inches apart in spring, as soon as the soil can be worked.

· **Set plants outdoors** in spring as soon as the soil can be worked.

· **Thin** seedlings when plants are 6 inches high to permanent spacing.

· **Divide** plants in spring when new growth begins or **root cuttings** in summer; however, cuttings are rarely successful.

· **Water** deeply and heavily before the soil dries out.

· **Fertilize** very lightly in early spring.

· **Pests and diseases** are not a problem.

· **Prune back** lightly in early spring to encourage compact growth.

· **Harvest leaves** before the plant flowers.

· **Dry leaves** on a screen in a cool, dry, airy place. Handle the leaves carefully until dry, since the oils cause allergic reactions in many people.

· **Store** dried leaves in an airtight container.

SAFFLOWER

Botanical name: *Carthamus tinctorius* (Compositae)
Other common name: False saffron

Safflower has large, toothed, thistlelike leaves studded with short, prickly orange hairs. The flower petals are dried to produce a powder often used as a substitute for saffron in coloring and flavoring rice. Its oil, taken from the seeds, is important in cooking, since it is polyunsaturated. The powder can also be used as a dye for silk and it is the principal ingredient of rouge. The dried flowers are attractive in bouquets and add color to potpourri.

PLANT TYPE: Tender annual.
GROWING RANGE: Zones 1 to 11.
HARDINESS: Resistant to heat, does not tolerate cold.
PLANT HEIGHT: 3 feet.
FLOWER COLOR: Deep yellow to orange.
FLOWER FORM: Thistlelike.

SEASON OF BLOOM: Summer.
SOIL: Average, well drained.
PH: 6 to 7.
FERTILIZER: Vegetable or all-purpose fertilizer.
WATER: Prefers dry conditions.
EXPOSURE: Full sun.
SPACING: 12 inches.
PROPAGATION: Seed.

Method

- **Start seeds indoors** eight weeks before the last spring frost, in individual pots placed in full sun or under fluorescent lights, as safflower is very difficult to transplant.

- **Prepare soil outdoors** before planting, adding small amounts of organic matter, such as peat moss, leaf mold, or compost.

- **Sow seeds outdoors** ¼ to ½ inch deep and 6 inches apart, after all danger of frost has passed.

- **Thin** seedlings when they are 6 inches high to permanent spacing.

- **Set plants outdoors** after all danger of frost has passed.

- **Water** when the soil is dry; do not overwater.

- **Fertilize** at planting time; no further feeding will be necessary.

- **Pests** are not a problem; **diseases** include anthracnose, root rot, and mildew. Anthracnose, a fungal disease that grows in warm, wet spring weather, can be controlled by removing and destroying infected plant parts. For root rot, try to improve soil drainage and cut back on watering. Mildew can be prevented by not crowding plants to allow for good air circulation and can be treated by spraying with a fungicide that has been approved for use on vegetables.

- **Harvest flowers** when they are fully open but before they begin to fade.

- **Dry flowers** on a screen in a warm, dry, airy place.

- **Store** dried petals in an airtight container.

SAFFRON

Botanical name: *Crocus sativus* (Iridaceae)

Unlike our popular spring-blooming crocus, the saffron crocus blooms in the fall. It was well known in the ancient world, originating in Persia and moving both east and west. The three stigmata (central orange or red section) of the saffron flower are mostly used to color and flavor bread and rice dishes. It takes hundreds of flowers to produce enough saffron to fill one tiny packet and sixty thousand stigmata to make one pound. The foliage is grasslike and lasts throughout the winter.

PLANT TYPE: Hardy bulb (corm).
GROWING RANGE: Zones 6 to 11.
HARDINESS: Tolerant of heat, slightly tolerant of cold.
PLANT HEIGHT: 3 to 6 inches.
FLOWER COLOR: White, lavender.
FLOWER FORM: Cup-shaped, crocuslike.
SEASON OF BLOOM: Early fall.
SOIL: Rich, well drained.
PH: 5.5 to 7.
FERTILIZER: Vegetable or all-purpose fertilizer.
WATER: Prefers moist conditions during the growing period.
EXPOSURE: Full sun or light shade.
SPACING: 3 inches.
PROPAGATION: Division.

Method

- **Starting from seeds** is not recommended.

- **Prepare soil outdoors** before planting, adding generous amounts of organic matter, such as peat moss, leaf mold, or compost, to enrich it.

- **Plant corms outdoors** in early fall, 3 to 4 inches deep.

- **Divide corms** in fall after the flowers have faded, or in early spring after the foliage fades when new plants are wanted.

- **Water** deeply when the plant is in its growing stage.

- **Fertilize** in early spring as foliage starts to brown or in late summer when growth restarts.

- **Insects and diseases** are not a problem; rodents may eat the corms.

- **Winter protect** with a light layer of straw, leaves, or evergreen boughs. Remove in spring when the ground thaws.

- **Harvest flowers** in the early morning as soon as they bloom; remove the orange or red stigmata from the center of the flower.

- **Dry stigmata** by spreading on a screen, in a warm, dry, airy place.

- **Store** the dried stigmata in an airtight container.

SAGE

Botanical name: *Salvia officinalis* (Labiatae)

Sage is a shrubby perennial with oblong, woolly leaves and hairy stems. A native of the Mediterranean, it was first valued as a medicinal herb and spread with the Roman legions. In the Orient it was more highly valued than tea because it was believed to prolong life.

It is most widely used as the seasoning in poultry stuffing and sausage, as well as in other meat or cheese dishes and teas. In Italian cooking it is used with veal.

PLANT TYPE: Perennial.
GROWING RANGE: Zones 3 to 11.
HARDINESS: Resistant to both cold and heat.
PLANT HEIGHT: 2 to 2½ feet.
FLOWER COLOR: Blue-violet, pink, white.
FLOWER FORM: Spikes.
SEASON OF BLOOM: Late spring or early summer.
SOIL: Light, sandy, well drained.
PH: 5 to 8; 6 to 6.5 is best.
FERTILIZER: Vegetable or all-purpose fertilizer.
WATER: Prefers average to moist conditions.
EXPOSURE: Full sun, light shade.
SPACING: 12 to 18 inches.
PROPAGATION: Seed, stem cuttings, division, or layering.

Method

- **Start seeds indoors** in late winter, in flats placed in full sun or under fluorescent lights. Seeds are slow to start, and propagation is usually done by division.

- **Prepare soil outdoors** before planting, adding small amounts of organic matter, such as peat moss, leaf mold, or compost.

- **Sow seeds outdoors** ½ inch deep and 6 inches apart in early spring, as soon as the soil can be worked.

- **Set plants outdoors** in early spring to midspring, as soon as the soil can be worked.

- **Thin** seedlings when they are 6 inches high to permanent spacing.

- **Divide** plants in spring when growth starts. **Root cuttings** 4 to 6 inches long in spring from new growth. These should root in two weeks. **Layer** plants in early fall by weighting down an outer branch with a rock until roots form, and transplant the following spring.

- **Water** when the soil starts to dry out. Be sure soil is dry over the winter.

- **Fertilize** at planting time and again when growth starts in spring.

- **Pests and diseases** include aphids, mites, caterpillars, mildew, and leaf spot. Aphids can be eliminated by spraying the leaves with water or an insecticide approved for use on vegetables. Special pesticides will also get rid of mites. To eliminate caterpillars, spray with Bt, an organic insecticide. Mildew can be prevented by allowing for good air circulation and, like leaf spot, can be treated with a fungicide that has been approved for use on vegetables.

- **Prune back** plants lightly in early spring to encourage bushiness.

- **Harvest leaves** before the plant blooms and again in late summer. Harvest only the upper third of the plant, leaving plenty of leaves. If you harvest too far down, the plant will have trouble surviving the winter.
- **Dry leaves** on a screen in a warm, airy, dry place.
- **Store** dried leaves in an airtight container.

Selected Cultivars

'Purpurascens' has dark purple leaves, and although not as hardy (Zone 6 and south), it makes an attractive bedding plant; and 'Tricolor' has foliage of green, pink, and purple.

SALAD BURNET

Botanical name: *Poterium sanguisorba* (Rosaceae)

The distinct cucumber flavor of burnet's leaves has earned it a place in the salad garden. It is especially favored by those who have problems digesting raw cucumbers. This pretty herb has finely cut leaves bunched at the base of the plant and sends up gracefully arching stems covered with small toothed leaflets. The leaves have no flavor when dry, but keep both their color and flavor when stored fresh in vinegar. What's more, the vinegar takes on a delightful cucumber taste.

PLANT TYPE: Perennial.
GROWING RANGE: Zones 3 to 11.
HARDINESS: Resistant to both cold and heat; will stay green and flavorful under winter's snow.
PLANT HEIGHT: 18 to 24 inches in bloom, 6 inches in leaf only.
FLOWER COLOR: White, rose-pink.
FLOWER FORM: Dense tufts.
SEASON OF BLOOM: Early summer to midsummer.
SOIL: Average, sandy, alkaline, well drained. Will tolerate poor soil.
PH: 7 to 8.
FERTILIZER: Vegetable or all-purpose fertilizer, but use sparingly.
WATER: Prefers dry conditions.
EXPOSURE: Full sun; light shade in hot climates.
SPACING: 12 to 15 inches.
PROPAGATION: Seed or division.

Method

- **Start seeds indoors** from early spring through early summer, in flats placed in full sun or under fluorescent lights.
- **Prepare soil outdoors** before planting. Remove stones or debris but do not add fertilizer or organic matter. Add gypsum or coarse sand to improve drainage if soil is heavy.

- **Sow seeds outdoors** ¼ to ½ inch deep and 6 inches apart from midspring, before the last frost, up until two months before the first fall frost.
- **Set plants outdoors** from midspring until six weeks before the first fall frost.
- **Thin** seedlings when they are 4 inches high to permanent spacing.
- **Divide** plants in early spring to midspring, after new growth begins, or in early fall. Burnet has a long taproot and may be difficult to divide.
- **Water** infrequently, only when the soil dries out.
- **Fertilize** very little or not at all.
- **Insects** are generally not a problem. **Diseases** include leaf spot and mildew. Leaf spot can be eliminated by spraying the leaves with water or a chemical insecticide that has been approved for use on vegetables. Prevent mildew by not crowding plants—allow for good air circulation. Treat mildew by spraying plants with a fungicide that has been approved for use on vegetables.
- **Harvest leaves** at any time for fresh use. Burnet is not generally dried.
- **Preserve** fresh leaves in vinegar that you can then use as a salad dressing.

Tip · Burnet easily reseeds and can become weedy unless flowers are removed as they start to fade.

SAVORY, SUMMER

Botanical name: *Satureja hortensis* (Labiatae)

The Romans used this wild native of their region to make a sauce for meat, much as we make mint sauce for lamb. Summer savory is a bushy annual with linear gray-green leaves that have a peppery flavor and are used fresh or dried to flavor beans and other vegetables. It is especially good at cutting the cooking odors of cabbage, turnips, and other strong vegetables when a few leaves are added to the cooking water. It has a more delicate flavor than winter savory and is an excellent substitute for sage in poultry dressings.

PLANT TYPE: Hardy annual.
GROWING RANGE: Zones 1 to 11.
HARDINESS: Tolerant of heat, not tolerant of cold.
PLANT HEIGHT: 12 to 18 inches.
FLOWER COLOR: White to pale lavender.
FLOWER FORM: Loose spikes.
SEASON OF BLOOM: Summer.
SOIL: Light, sandy, well drained.
PH: 6.5 to 7.5.
FERTILIZER: Vegetable or all-purpose fertilizer.
WATER: Prefers average to moist conditions and should not be allowed to dry out.

EXPOSURE: Full sun.
SPACING: 4 to 6 inches.
PROPAGATION: Seed.

Method

- **Start seeds indoors** in early spring in individual pots placed in full sun or under fluorescent lights, as savory does not like to be transplanted. Do not cover, as they need light to germinate.

- **Prepare soil outdoors** before planting, adding moderate amounts of organic matter, such as peat moss, leaf mold, or compost, to enrich it.

- **Sow seeds outdoors** in early spring as soon as the soil can be worked by scattering. Press the seeds into the soil but do not cover them. Successive plantings ensure a continuous harvest.

- **Thin** seedlings when they are 4 inches high to permanent spacing. Since they are spindly, summer savory stems planted close together will support each other.

- **Set plants outdoors** in spring four weeks before the last frost.

- **Water** as soon as the soil starts to dry out.

- **Fertilize** at planting time; no other feeding is needed.

- **Pests and diseases** are not a problem.

- **Remove flower buds** to extend the harvest season of the leaves.

- **Harvest leaves** before the flowers bloom, cutting the entire stem.

- **Dry leaves** in a warm, airy, dry place by hanging the stems upside down in loose bunches.

- **Store** leaves in an airtight container.

SAVORY, WINTER

Botanical name: *Satureja montana* (Labiatae)

Winter savory is a stiff, spreading plant with thick, linear, gray-green leaves that are used fresh or dried to flavor beans and other vegetables. It has a stronger, more peppery flavor than summer savory, and less of it is needed.

PLANT TYPE: Perennial.
GROWING RANGE: Zones 5 to 11.
HARDINESS: Resistant to both heat and cold.
PLANT HEIGHT: 6 to 12 inches.
FLOWER COLOR: Pink, white.
FLOWER FORM: Loose spikes.
SEASON OF BLOOM: Summer.

SOIL: Sandy, light, slightly rich, well drained.
PH: 6.5 to 7.5.
FERTILIZER: Vegetable or all-purpose fertilizer.
WATER: Prefers average to moist conditions.
EXPOSURE: Full sun.
SPACING: 12 to 15 inches.
PROPAGATION: Seed, division, stem cuttings, or layering.

Method

- **Start seeds indoors** in early spring in individual pots placed in full sun or under fluorescent lights, as winter savory does not like to be transplanted. Do not cover seeds; they need light to germinate.

- **Prepare soil outdoors** before planting, adding small amounts of organic matter, such as peat moss, leaf mold, or compost.

- **Sow seeds outdoors** 6 inches apart in early spring, as soon as the soil can be worked. Press the seeds into the soil but do not cover them.

- **Set plants outdoors** in spring four weeks before the last spring frost.

- **Thin** seedlings when they are 3 inches high to permanent spacing.

- **Divide** plants every few years in spring when growth starts. **Root cuttings** 4 to 6 inches long in summer. **Layer** plants during the summer and transplant the new plants the following spring.

- **Water** as soon as the soil starts to dry out.

- **Fertilize** at planting time and again each spring when growth starts.

- **Pests and diseases** are not a problem.

- **Pinch back branch tips** to encourage bushiness. Prune back hard in late fall or early spring.

- **Winter protect** in cold climates with a light covering of evergreen boughs or straw. Remove when ground thaws in spring.

- **Harvest leaves** before the flowers open.

- **Dry leaves** on a screen in a cool, dry, airy place.

- **Store** dried leaves in an airtight container.

SCENTED GERANIUM

Botanical name: *Pelargonium* (Geraniaceae)

Native to South Africa, scented geraniums are among the most varied fragrant-leaved plants in the world, with scents ranging from rose to nutmeg, from lime to peppermint.

The scent is released in the hot sun and by rubbing the leaves. Some foliage is large and woolly; other is finely cut. The plants have small flowers, but they are secondary to the foliage. Fresh leaves are used in baked goods, cold drinks, jellies, and with fruit; dried leaves are used in teas and potpourris.

PLANT TYPE: Tender perennial, usually grown as an annual.
GROWING RANGE: Zones 1 to 11 as an annual; Zones 9 to 11 as a perennial.
HARDINESS: Resistant to heat, not tolerant of cold.
PLANT HEIGHT: 1 to 4 feet.
FLOWER COLOR: White, pink, rose, purple.
FLOWER FORM: Loose clusters.
SEASON OF BLOOM: Summer.
SOIL: Rich, light, well drained.
PH: 5.5 to 6.5.
FERTILIZER: Houseplant fertilizer used at half strength.
WATER: Prefers dry to average conditions.
EXPOSURE: Full sun.
SPACING: 1 to 2 feet.
PROPAGATION: Seed; stem cuttings are more reliable.

Method

- **Start seeds indoors** twelve weeks before the last frost, in flats placed in full sun or under fluorescent lights.

- **Prepare soil outdoors** before planting, adding generous amounts of organic matter, such as peat moss, leaf mold, or compost, to enrich it.

- **Set plants outdoors** after all danger of frost has passed.

- **Root cuttings** 4 to 6 inches long from new growth in summer.

- **Water** when the soil starts to dry out. The plant prefers to be dry, but not too dry, because then leaves will drop.

- **Fertilize** twice monthly when the plants are in flower; monthly the rest of the growing season.

- **Pests and diseases** include botrytis, edema, and mites. Botrytis can be controlled with a fungicide. To prevent edema, check soil for proper drainage. To eliminate mites, use a pesticide approved for vegetables.

- **Pinch back** growing tips to encourage bushiness; otherwise, plants will get leggy.

- **Harvest leaves** at any time.

- **Dry leaves** on a screen in a dark, cool, airy place.

- **Store** leaves in an airtight container.

Tip · **Plants or rooted cuttings may be taken indoors over the winter.**

Selected Species

Pelargonium crispum (Finger bowl geranium) is 3 feet high, small leaved, and has pink flowers. Leaves are lemon scented.

P. x *fragrans* (Fragrant geranium) is a trailing plant 1 foot high with white flowers and nutmeg-scented leaves.

P. graveolens (Rose geranium) is 3 feet high and has rose-colored flowers. Foliage is scented like a rose.

P. x *limoneum* (Lemon geranium) is 2 feet high, has purple and lavender flowers and lemon-scented leaves.

P. odoratissimum (Nutmeg geranium) is 1½ feet high, trailing, and has white flowers. Contrary to its common name, its foliage is apple scented.

P. quercifolium (Oakleaf geranium) grows 4 feet high and has an almond fragrance. Flowers are rosy purple.

P. tomentosum (Peppermint geranium, Woolly geranium) is 3 feet high and has white flowers splotched in red. Foliage is strongly mint scented and velvety to the touch.

SESAME

Botanical name: *Sesamum indicum* (Pedaliaceae); also known by its former designation, *S. orientale*
Other common name: Benne seed

A native of tropical Asia and Africa, sesame was an important food source in the Orient. Egyptians and Persians ground its seeds for flour, and ground sesame seeds are still used in Near Eastern cooking. The term *open sesame* in the *Arabian Nights* probably was inspired by the way ripened pods burst open suddenly to expel seeds. Sesame plants are covered with attractive, long, pointed leaves that are dark green and slightly hairy. The seeds have a nutty flavor and are used in baking cakes, cookies, and bread, and in candy. They are the main ingredient of benne wafers, a Charleston favorite.

PLANT TYPE: Tender annual.
GROWING RANGE: Zones 7 to 11.
HARDINESS: Resistant to heat, not resistant to cold. Needs a long, hot growing season of at least 120 days.
PLANT HEIGHT: 2 to 3 feet.
FLOWER COLOR: Pale rose, white.
FLOWER FORM: Bell-shaped, in spikes.
SEASON OF BLOOM: Summer.
SOIL: Average, well drained.
PH: 6 to 7.
FERTILIZER: Vegetable or all-purpose fertilizer.
WATER: Prefers average conditions.
EXPOSURE: Full sun.
SPACING: 6 inches.
PROPAGATION: Seed.

🍃 *Method*

- **Start seeds indoors** six to eight weeks before the last spring frost in individual pots placed in full sun or under fluorescent lights, as sesame does not like to be transplanted. Seeds must be started indoors in places that don't have three to four months of 75°F temperature in summer.

- **Prepare soil outdoors** before planting, adding moderate amounts of organic matter, such as peat moss, leaf mold, or compost.

- **Sow seeds outdoors** ¼ inch deep and 4 inches apart after all danger of frost has passed and night temperatures remain above 60°F.

- **Thin** seedlings when they are 6 inches high to permanent spacing. Sesame plants grown thickly will be bushier.

- **Set plants outdoors** after all danger of frost has passed.

- **Water** when the ground starts to dry out.

- **Fertilize** at planting time; no further feeding will be necessary.

- **Pests and diseases** are not a problem.

- **Harvest seeds** before the most mature pods begin to open by cutting off the flowering stem at ground level and hanging it upside down in a paper bag. The seeds will fall into the bag as they ripen.

- **Store** dried seeds in an airtight container.

SWEET WOODRUFF

Botanical name: *Galium odoratum* (Rubiaceae); also known by its previous designation, *Asperula odorata*

Long admired in its native Europe as a medicinal herb and the flavoring for May wine, sweet woodruff grows wild in the deep woods. In England it was traditionally used in flower arrangements in churches along with roses and lavender on St. Barnabas Day. Sweet woodruff is an attractive, spreading plant whose leaves are also used dried in mattresses, pillows, and sachets to prevent musty smells in closed places. The leaves are odorless when fresh but smell like freshly mown hay when dried.

PLANT TYPE: Perennial.
GROWING RANGE: Zones 4 to 11.
HARDINESS: Tolerant to heat and cold.
PLANT HEIGHT: 6 to 8 inches.
FLOWER COLOR: White.
FLOWER FORM: Star-shaped, in loose clusters.
SEASON OF BLOOM: Late spring.
SOIL: Rich, well drained.

PH: 4.5 to 5.5
FERTILIZER: Not recommended.
WATER: Prefers moist conditions.
EXPOSURE: Partial to full shade.
SPACING: 6 to 12 inches.
PROPAGATION: Division or root cuttings.

 *Method*

- **Starting from seeds** is not recommended as they germinate erratically or not at all.

- **Prepare soil outdoors** before planting, adding generous amounts of organic matter, such as peat moss or leaf mold, to enrich it.

- **Set plants outdoors** any time in midspring.

- **Root cuttings** 4 to 6 inches long from new growth in late spring and summer. Woodruff is not easy to root as a cutting and may take several weeks.

- **Divide** plants in early spring to midspring, when growth starts, if necessary.

- **Water** frequently and deeply to keep soil moist.

- **Pests and diseases** are not a problem.

- **Prune back** the plant slightly in early summer after flowering to encourage bushiness.

- **Harvest leaves** before the plants flower.

- **Dry leaves** on a screen in a cool, dry, airy place.

- **Store** dried leaves in an airtight container.

TANSY

Botanical name: *Tanacetum vulgare* (Compositae); also known by its former designation, *Chrysanthemum vulgare*

A dramatic addition to the perennial garden, tansy has attractive, fernlike 3- to 5-inch-long leaves and bright yellow flowers that dry beautifully for arrangements. It is often planted around foundations as it wards off ants. Dried leaves and flowers are used in sachets, potpourri, and dried flower arrangements, and to repel moths. One of the herbs of the Passover seder, it has a bitter flavor and was used widely at one time in Lenten recipes. It is now known, however, to contain a poisonous drug and should not be used in food or drink.

PLANT TYPE: Perennial.
GROWING RANGE: Zones 3 to 11.
HARDINESS: Resistant to both cold and heat.
PLANT HEIGHT: 4 feet.
FLOWER COLOR: Yellow.
FLOWER FORM: Buttonlike, in clusters.

SEASON OF BLOOM: Late summer.
SOIL: Rich, well drained.
PH: 5 to 7.
FERTILIZER: Vegetable or all-purpose fertilizer.
WATER: Prefers moist conditions.
EXPOSURE: Full sun.
SPACING: 12 to 18 inches.
PROPAGATION: Seed or division.

Method

· **Start seeds indoors** in midspring, in flats placed in full sun or under fluorescent lights.

· **Prepare soil outdoors** before planting, adding generous amounts of organic matter, such as peat moss, leaf mold, or compost.

· **Sow seeds outdoors** ½ inch deep and 6 inches apart in early spring, as soon as the soil can be worked.

· **Set plants outdoors** after all danger of frost has passed.

· **Thin** seedlings when they are 6 inches high to permanent spacing.

· **Divide** plants in spring when new growth appears or in fall when necessary. Any piece of root that has a bud eye will grow into a plant.

· **Water** deeply and frequently to keep the soil moist.

· **Fertilize** in spring each year as growth starts.

· **Pests and diseases** are not a problem.

· **Harvest flowers and leaves** just before the plant is in full bloom.

· **Dry leaves and flowers** by hanging the stems upside down in a dark, dry, airy place. Flowers retain their shape and color well if they are picked before they are in full bloom.

· **Store** dried leaves and flowers in an airtight container.

Tip · Tansy creeps rapidly by underground rhizomes and will need to be thinned regularly or contained by underground barriers to keep it within bounds.

TARRAGON

Botanical name: *Artemisia dracunculus* var. *sativa* (Compositae)
Other common name French tarragon

Tarragon is a true aristocrat of the culinary herb garden, since it has survived as an herb strictly on its culinary merits. Unlike almost any other herb, tarragon has little medicinal history or lore or mythology attached to it. There are two varieties of tarragon, French tarragon and Russian, or Siberian, tarragon, but only French tarragon is used in cooking. It is a woody perennial and has linear dark green leaves. French tarragon may be dried, but has much better flavor when used fresh. It sets no seed, so it must be started from plant divisions. If you are buying tarragon plants, be sure to taste a leaf. Unless you notice a distinct licorice flavor, you are not getting the culinary type. Tarragon is used on fish, with chicken, and as an ingredient in béarnaise sauce.

Russian tarragon, *A. dracunculus,* is the invasive flavorless weed that grows tall and rangy and will take over any area where it is planted. Whenever you find tarragon seeds, be aware that it is the seed of this species.

PLANT TYPE: Perennial.
GROWING RANGE: Zones 5 to 8.
HARDINESS: Resistant to both heat and cold; must have cold winters.
PLANT HEIGHT: 3 feet.
FLOWER COLOR: Hardly any flowers; an occasional yellow bloom.
FLOWER FORM: Loose, tiny clusters.
SEASON OF BLOOM: Early summer to midsummer.
SOIL: Rich, well drained.
PH: 6.2 to 7.8.
FERTILIZER: Fish emulsion.
WATER: Prefers average conditions.
EXPOSURE: Full sun or light shade.
SPACING: 1 to 2 feet.
PROPAGATION: Division.

Method

- **Prepare soil outdoors** before planting, adding generous amounts of organic matter, such as peat moss, leaf mold, or compost, to enrich it.

- **Set plants outdoors** in midspring, two to four weeks before the last spring frost.

- **Divide** plants in early spring; 1-inch sections of roots will grow into new plants. Mature plants need to be divided every three or four years to keep them vital.

- **Water** when the soil starts to dry out. Roots must be dry during the winter or the plants will die.

- **Fertilize** in early spring when growth starts and again in early summer.

- **Pests and diseases** are not a problem.

- **Winter protect** with a light covering of straw or evergreen boughs after the ground freezes in the fall. Remove before the ground is completely thawed in spring.

- **Harvest leaves** at any time for fresh use and in the early fall for drying. Handle them carefully during harvest and drying as bruising will cause them to lose much of their essential oil.

- **Dry leaves** on a screen or in paper bags in a warm, dry, airy place.

- **Store** leaves in an airtight container.

THYME

Botanical name: *Thymus* (Labiatae)

An ancient herb, thyme has a two-thousand-year history and over a hundred varieties. Its history is associated with bees, which are attracted to its bloom, and a distinctive honey is produced by bees that feed on its nectar. Thyme was believed to be one of the manger herbs and is used in crèches at Christmastime. Its antiseptic oil is still used in herbal medicines and antiseptic salves. Thyme is a woody, spreading perennial with small, aromatic gray-green leaves that are sometimes evergreen. It is perhaps the most universal culinary herb, used in poultry stuffing, soup, egg dishes, and with meat and vegetables. Lemon thyme makes a fine garnish for fish or poultry dishes.

PLANT TYPE: Perennial.
GROWING RANGE: Zones 5 to 11.
HARDINESS: Resistant to both cold and heat.
PLANT HEIGHT: 6 to 12 inches.
FLOWER COLOR: Lavender-blue.
FLOWER FORM: Clusters.
SEASON OF BLOOM: Spring and early summer.
SOIL: Light, sandy, well drained.
PH: 5.5 to 7.
FERTILIZER: Cottonseed or bonemeal.
WATER: Prefers dry conditions.
EXPOSURE: Full sun.
SPACING: 10 inches.
PROPAGATION: Seed, stem cuttings, division, or layering.

Method

- **Start seeds indoors** in late winter through late spring in a cool room, in flats placed in full sun or under fluorescent lights.

- **Prepare soil outdoors** before planting, adding moderate amounts of organic matter, such as peat moss, leaf mold, or compost.

- **Sow seeds outdoors** ¼ to ½ inch deep and 3 inches apart in early spring, as soon as the soil can be worked.

- **Thin** seedlings when they are 3 inches tall to permanent spacing.

- **Set plants outdoors** in early spring when the ground is workable through early summer.

- **Divide** plants in spring when growth starts, if necessary. **Root cuttings** 4 to 6 inches long from tip growth during the summer. **Layer** stems in the summer by weighting down outer stems until they form roots where they touch the ground. Transplant the new plants in the fall or the following spring.

- **Water** sparingly when the soil starts to dry out.

- **Fertilize** in spring when growth starts, with a tablespoon of cottonseed or bonemeal scratched in around the base of each plant.

- **Pests and diseases** that can bother thyme include mealybugs, botrytis, and root rot. Mealybugs can be controlled with an application of insecticidal soap. Botrytis should be treated with fungicide, and root rot can be avoided by having proper drainage and not overwatering.

- **Prune back** heavily in summer to encourage bushiness.

- **Winter protect** with a light mulch of evergreen boughs or straw, which should be removed before the ground is completely thawed in spring.

- **Harvest leaves** any time for fresh use or just before the plant blooms for drying.

- **Dry leaves** on a screen in a warm, dry, airy place.

- **Store** dried leaves in an airtight container.

Selected Species

Thymus x *citriodorus* (Lemon thyme) closely resembles *T. vulgaris,* but has slightly rounder leaves, semitrailing growth, and a delicious lemon flavor.

T. herba-barona is a small-leaved, caraway-flavored thyme that is excellent rubbed on lamb before roasting or grilling.

T. serpyllum (Wild thyme) is a creeping variety used as an ornamental between rocks and paving stones.

T. vulgaris 'Variegatus' is a white-edged thyme and *T.v.* 'Aureus' is golden edged. Both are used more as ornamentals and are beautiful additions to any garden.

VALERIAN

Botanical name: *Valeriana officinalis* (Valerianaceae)
Other common name: Garden heliotrope

Once highly valued medicinally, valerian is now grown in the perennial border mostly for its fragrant flowers. Its feathery leaves make a lovely background and it attracts earthworms to the garden. Unfortunately, the delightful fragrance is lost in drying. The long slim roots, which have an unpleasant odor until they are dried, are used medicinally and as a fixative in potpourri. The fresh root is attractive to rats and legend holds that it was carried by the Pied Piper of Hamlin.

PLANT TYPE: Perennial.
GROWING RANGE: Zones 3 to 11.

HARDINESS: Resistant to both heat and cold.
PLANT HEIGHT: 3 to 5 feet.
FLOWER COLOR: White, pink, lavender, blue.
FLOWER FORM: Flat to round clusters.
SEASON OF BLOOM: Late spring to late summer.
SOIL: Nutrient-rich, with plenty of moisture-retentive humus.
PH: 6 to 7.
FERTILIZER: Vegetable or all-purpose fertilizer.
WATER: Prefers moist conditions.
EXPOSURE: Full sun or partial shade.
SPACING: 12 inches.
PROPAGATION: Seed or division.

Method

- **Start seeds indoors** in late winter or early spring, in flats placed in full sun or under fluorescent lights. Seeds are not long lived and should not be stored from year to year. Do not cover seeds as they need light to germinate. They are difficult to germinate and it is better to start from plants that have self-sown.

- **Prepare soil outdoors** before planting, adding generous amounts of organic matter, such as leaf mold or compost, to enrich it.

- **Sow seeds outdoors** in early spring as soon as the soil can be worked, 6 inches apart and just pressed into the soil.

- **Thin** seedlings when they are 6 inches high to permanent spacing.

- **Set plants outdoors** in midspring four weeks before the last spring frost.

- **Divide** plants in spring when new growth starts or in fall at least once every three years.

- **Water** deeply and frequently to keep soil constantly moist.

- **Fertilize** in spring when growth starts.

- **Pests and diseases** are not a problem.

- **Harvest roots** in the fall of the second year before the first frost. Wash all soil from the roots and split any that are thicker than ¾ inch.

- **Dry roots** until crisp at a high temperature (above 120°F).

- **Store** roots in an airtight container.

Tips · **Though hard to germinate if seed isn't fresh, plants readily self-sow and can become weedy.**
· **Plants may need to be staked. Since they are tall, they make a good planting against a fence or wall behind other shorter perennials.**

WINTERGREEN

Botanical name: *Gaultheria procumbens* (Ericaceae)
Other common names: Checkerberry, Teaberry, Mountain tea

A favorite North American woodland plant, hikers often chew on the leaves of wintergreen for its refreshing minty flavor. Wintergreen is an evergreen shrub spreading to 12 inches across; it is more suitable for a woodland garden than for the herb garden full of sun-loving plants. Its leaves are used to flavor candy and beverages, especially teas.

PLANT TYPE: Evergreen shrub.
GROWING RANGE: Zones 3 to 11.
HARDINESS: Resistant to cold and heat.
PLANT HEIGHT: 3 inches.
FLOWER COLOR: White.
FLOWER FORM: Bell-shaped, drooping.
SEASON OF BLOOM: Spring.
SOIL: Rich, well drained, woodland.
PH: 4.5 to 6.
FERTILIZER: All-purpose fertilizer.
WATER: Prefers moist conditions.
EXPOSURE: Partial to full shade.
SPACING: 12 inches.
PROPAGATION: Layering.

Method

- **Starting from seeds** is difficult and not recommended.

- **Prepare soil outdoors** before planting, adding generous amounts of organic matter, such as peat moss or leaf mold.

- **Set plants outdoors** from midspring through early fall. (Since it is very difficult to establish plants taken from the woods, it is best to buy nursery-grown plants that are accustomed to garden conditions.)

- **Layer** outer branches by securing them to the ground in summer and transplanting in early fall when roots have formed.

- **Water** frequently to keep the soil constantly moist.

- **Fertilize** in spring when growth starts.

- **Mulch** with 2 to 4 inches of pine needles in midspring.

- **Pests and diseases** are not a problem.

- **Prune back** the plant to control its growth and to shape it in spring.

- **Harvest leaves** at any time for fresh or dry use.

- **Dry leaves** on a screen in a cool, dry, airy place.

- **Store** dried leaves in an airtight container.

WORMWOOD

Botanical name: *Artemisia absinthium* (Compositae)

Medicinally valued since antiquity, wormwood is wreathed in superstition and legend and is a mainstay of the British cottage garden. Coarse, white, hairy, deeply divided leaves clothe this spreading plant. The bitter-tasting leaves were the main ingredient in the now-outlawed drink absinthe, outlawed because *wormwood contains a volatile poison that should not be ingested.* It should also be noted that wormwood can inhibit the growth of neighboring plants. Dried leaves are one of the most effective herbs for repelling moths in stored clothing.

PLANT TYPE: Perennial.
GROWING RANGE: Zones 2 to 11.
HARDINESS: Tolerant of both heat and cold.
PLANT HEIGHT: 3 feet.
FLOWER COLOR: Yellow.
FLOWER FORM: Inconspicuous.
SEASON OF BLOOM: Late summer.
SOIL: Well drained, rich or poor, but does better in good soil.
PH: 6.5 to 8.
FERTILIZER: Bonemeal.
WATER: Tolerates wet or dry conditions.
EXPOSURE: Full sun.
SPACING: 18 inches.
PROPAGATION: Seed, stem cuttings, or division.

Method

- **Start seeds indoors** in flats in late winter, not covering the seeds, which are very fine and need light to germinate. The flats should be placed in full sun or under fluorescent lights.

- **Prepare soil outdoors** before planting by adding small to generous amounts of organic matter, such as peat moss (used sparingly), leaf mold, or compost.

- **Sowing seeds outdoors** is difficult and not recommended.

- **Set plants outdoors** in midspring, four weeks before the last spring frost.

- **Divide** plants in spring or fall. **Root cuttings** 4 to 6 inches long taken from new growth during the summer.

- **Water** when the soil becomes dry; wormwood will tolerate moist soils as well.

- **Fertilize** in spring each year when growth starts.

- **Pests and diseases** include aphids, beetles, mealybugs, mites, and mildew. To control aphids, spray leaves with water. Beetles may be picked off and drowned. Mealybugs can be eliminated with an application of insecticidal soap. Various pesticides get rid of mites, and mildew can be prevented by good air circulation and treated by spraying with a fungicide that has been approved for use on vegetables.

- **Harvest leaves** by cutting entire stems to the ground when the plants start to bloom. Remove woody stems and dry only the upper green portion.

- **Dry leaves** by hanging the stems upside down in a dry, cool, airy spot.

- **Store** dried leaves in an airtight container.

YARROW

Botanical name: *Achillea millefolium* (Compositae)

Yarrow's botanical name comes from its association with Achilles, who was taught its healing properties by the centaur. It was carried as a first aid for wounds into the Elizabethan era. Yarrow plants, while often spreading rapidly, are an attractive addition to the flower garden; the foliage is finely cut and fernlike, and the flowers are showy and long blooming. Today yarrow flowers are used in dried flower arrangements, and both flowers and leaves as an ingredient in herbal bath products because of their powerful astringent qualities.

PLANT TYPE: Perennial.
GROWING RANGE: Zones 3 to 8.
HARDINESS: Resistant to heat and cold; likes cold winter temperatures.
PLANT HEIGHT: 3 feet.
FLOWER COLOR: Pink, magenta, white.
FLOWER FORM: Flat cluster.
SEASON OF BLOOM: Early summer and again in early fall.
SOIL: Poor, well drained.
PH: 4.5 to 7.
FERTILIZER: Bonemeal.
WATER: Prefers dry conditions.
EXPOSURE: Full sun.
SPACING: 8 to 12 inches.
PROPAGATION: Seed or division.

 *Method*

- **Start seeds indoors** in early spring to midsummer, up to three months before the first fall frost, in flats placed in full sun or under fluorescent lights. Do not cover the fine seeds as they need light to germinate. Plants started from seed take two years to become established.

- **Prepare soil outdoors** before planting, adding no organic matter unless the soil is almost pure sand; then add small amounts of peat moss, leaf mold, or compost.

- **Sow seeds outdoors** in midspring to midsummer, up to three months before the first fall frost, 6 inches apart and pressing the seed into the soil.

- **Thin** seedlings when they are 4 inches high to permanent spacing.

- **Set plants outdoors** in midspring to late summer, up to two months before the first fall frost.

- **Divide** plants in early spring or early fall. Frequent division is necessary because of the rampant growth of this perennial.

- **Water** sparingly when the ground becomes dry.

- **Fertilize** lightly in spring when growth starts.

- **Pests and diseases** are not a problem.

- **Harvest leaves and flowers** just before the plants are in full bloom by cutting the flowering stems off at the base.

- **Dry leaves and flowers** by hanging the stems upside down in a dark, dry, warm place.

- **Store** dried leaves and flowers in an airtight container.

Tip · The native white variety of yarrow spreads quickly and will need frequent thinning to keep it under control.

Selected Species

Achillea filipendulina (Fernleaf yarrow). Growing 5 feet tall, it has bold mustard-yellow flowers on long stems in 5-inch-wide, flat-topped clusters. 'Cloth of Gold' is an excellent cultivar and a good border plant.

VEGETABLES

ARUGULA

Botanical name: *Eruca sativa* (Cruciferae)
Other common names: Rocket, Rucola, Roquette

A native of the Mediterranean, where it grows wild, arugula was used by the ancient Romans. It was once popular in the New World, but since Colonial times was nearly forgotten until its recent "discovery" by American cooks. This relative of mustard is easy to grow as an early green and provides a distinctive flavor in salads. Its pungent flavor is the most delicate when the leaves are small and tender. Although arugula most common use is in a mixed green salad, its flavor makes a dramatic counterpoint to a grilled steak served on a bed of it. Try adding a few leaves to gazpacho.

PLANT TYPE: Annual.
GROWING RANGE: Zones 2 to 11.
HARDINESS: Withstands frost; quickly bolts to seed in hot weather.
SOIL: Any cool soil.
PH: 6 to 7.
FERTILIZER: None required.
WATER: Needs moist soil for quick growth.
EXPOSURE: Full sun.
SPACING: 6 to 10 inches, in rows 18 inches apart; or use a 10-by-10 grid.

 *Method*

· **Prepare soil outdoors** as soon as it can be worked in the spring. In most regions, a fall crop can be planted in late summer as well, about six weeks before the arrival of cold weather.

- **Sow seeds** ½ inch deep in permanent spacing, making successive plantings every three weeks. Will germinate in one to two weeks.

- **Water** often to keep soil moist and encourage rapid growth.

- **Remove** flower stalks as soon as buds form in the center of the plant. This will prolong harvest.

- **Pests** are not a problem.

- **Harvest** leaves at any time, preferably before flower stalks form. To keep crisp in the refrigerator, wash, shake off excess water, and wrap loosely in paper towels before placing in a plastic bag. Punch several small perforations in the bag to permit some air exchange.

ARTICHOKE, GLOBE

Botanical name: *Cynara scolymus* (Compositae)

Although it is raised commercially only in a limited area of coastal California where winters are mild and the climate is humid, the careful gardener in other parts of the country can also raise this vegetable successfully. The thistlelike plants grow to 6 feet tall, so they are not for the tiny kitchen garden plot. Although it produces globes the first year in very warm, moist, long-season climates, in many areas it will not flower until the second year. The delicious globes we eat are actually the flower bud. Best at its tightly closed stage, only about the size of a lime or lemon, the artichokes we see in the grocery store are usually much larger and have begun to open, at which time they offer more food per plant, but must have the choke removed, along with some of the outer leaves.

PLANT TYPE: Perennial.
GROWING RANGE: Zones 6 to 11, occasionally farther north.
HARDINESS: Will withstand frost.
SOIL: Very rich, moist but well drained with plenty of humus. Should do well in raised beds to which heavy amounts of well-rotted compost have been added.
PH: 7.5 to 8.5.
FERTILIZER: 5-10-5, manure.
WATER: Requires moist soil.
EXPOSURE: Full sun.
SPACING: 18 inches, in rows 24 to 30 inches apart.
PROPAGATION: Side shoots may be separated and planted 18 inches apart.

Method

- **Start seeds indoors** in late winter in cold climates, in 3-inch peat pots.

- **Prepare soil outdoors,** working in plenty of compost or well-rotted manure, at least a shovelful per plant.

- **Sow seeds outdoors** ¼ inch deep in permanent spacing in rows, just before last frost is expected.

- **Set plants outdoors** after the danger of frost is past, about a week after tomatoes are set out.

- **Thin** seedlings to permanent spacing when they are well established.

- **Water** frequently to keep soil evenly moist.

- **Fertilize** once, about halfway through the summer and again the following spring, using only ¼ cup scratched into the soil around each plant.

- **Fungus disease** can be a problem, so be sure that drainage is good and plants are never allowed to stand in water that has gathered around the base of the stem.

- **Winter protect** in northern climates by cutting back plants to 18 inches tall and heaping straw around the crown. Cover them with a tall bushel basket and heap manure around and over them to help protect the plants from extreme low temperatures. Remove when danger of frost is low. With this protection, winter temperatures as low as 5° to 10°F can be tolerated.

- **Harvest** for the finest product when the buds are small and tightly closed. At this stage the artichoke can be eaten whole. Or, for a larger crop, harvest when they are large and partly open, as they are sold in the supermarket. They may be stored in the refrigerator for two weeks or the hearts may be blanched and frozen.

Tip · **Larger artichokes have formed the fuzzy "choke," or center, which must be removed. Enjoy tiny artichokes whole, as the Italians do, by parboiling slightly and deep-frying in a coating of seasoned crumbs. Prepare larger ones by boiling or by scooping out choke and center leaves and filling with breadcrumbs, herbs, and garlic, then steaming.**

ASPARAGUS

Botanical name: *Asparagus officinalis* (Liliaceae)

It takes three or four years to get a bed started, but once established this perennial will thrive for generations. It is one of the first vegetables to produce in the spring, a welcome sight to any gardener. Most home growers start asparagus from one- or two-year-old plants (called *crowns*) in the spring, set out as soon as the soil can be worked. Although it can be grown from seed, that adds another year before production, making it four or five years before harvest.

Asparagus produces a bonus for the flower arranger as well: Its feathery, fernlike foliage cut just before frost in early fall is a favorite in fresh bouquets, especially with roses or carnations. Since it is a permanent bed that can't be plowed, most gardeners grow it as a border plant just inside the garden fence or edge.

In Europe, asparagus is blanched by covering it with soil as it grows to keep the entire stalk white, but Americans have always preferred the enhanced color, flavor, and nutrition of green asparagus.

PLANT TYPE: Perennial.
GROWING RANGE: Zones 3 to 8.
HARDINESS: Withstands subzero winters, but does not do as well in the warm Gulf Coast winters.
SOIL: Sandy loam, moderately rich, well drained.
PH: 6 to 8.
FERTILIZER: 5-5-10, or a special asparagus formula of 17-16-28.
WATER: First-year beds need moist soil, others only moderate moisture.
EXPOSURE: Full sun.
SPACING: 18 to 24 inches, in rows 4 feet apart.

Method

- **Start seed indoors** in midwinter, first soaking them overnight in tepid water to hasten germination, then planting in flats 1 inch apart and ½ inch deep.

- **Plant outdoors** in nursery beds (a well-protected growing area) after danger of frost is past, spacing 5 inches apart. Thinning will not be necessary. They can be transplanted into the permanent garden site early the following spring after a year's growth in a more protected environment. You can start the plants by seeding directly into the permanent garden bed, but as the plants are small and slow to grow, extra care will be needed in weeding.

- **Prepare soil** deeply before setting out one-year-old plants or roots in the early spring by digging a trench 2 feet wide and 9 inches deep and mixing in well-rotted manure.

- **Plant roots,** covering with 2 inches of firmly packed soil. Water to keep the soil moist until the delicate new growth appears above the soil. Add new soil throughout the summer as the new stems grow, until the soil level is even with the rest of the garden.

- **Fertilize** two or three months after planting roots, using 1 pound to every 20 feet and scattering it in a 1-foot band on each side of the plants. Early each following spring, repeat, using 1 pound to each 50 feet.

- **Water** only during prolonged dry spells. Southwestern gardeners should avoid watering asparagus in the winter since it needs a period of dormancy.

- **Harvest** when the stalks are about 9 inches tall and the top buds still are firm and tight. A light harvest, perhaps of one week, could begin the second season after the roots are set into the garden. Bend stalks sideways until they break; do not use an asparagus knife, which cuts belowground parts of the plant and roots and can injure other stems that have not yet emerged. Pick even the very thin stems at this height, since allowing them to grow taller will weaken the plant. Use asparagus within a few days, storing in the refrigerator in plastic bags to maintain high humidity. It can be blanched and frozen, but the product is not nearly as good in either taste or texture as fresh.

Selected Cultivars

'Mary Washington' is an old favorite that produces well in most climates. 'Lucullus' is a new hybrid with slightly earlier and exceptionally heavy production and good flavor. 'Roberts' and 'Brock Imperial' also yield heavy crops of good flavor. In the Midwest, 'Mary Washington Improved' and 'Viking KB3' achieve good results. Both are widely adopted. For best long-term success, check with the county agricultural extension office for the best varieties used in your area.

BROCCOLI

Botanical name: *Brassica oleracea italica* (Cruciferae)

A cool-weather vegetable, broccoli is a friend to the northern gardener. In warmer climates, it is planted as a spring and fall crop. Easy to grow, it is rich in vitamin B_2 and iron, but very low in calories. It is eaten both raw and cooked, and it freezes well. Romanesco broccoli have pale green heads made up of clusters of pointed spears instead of rounded clusters. They are not as easy to grow and require very fertile soil, but they have a fine flavor. Save the stems and leaves of broccoli and simmer in chicken broth for a delicious cream soup.

PLANT TYPE: Annual.
GROWING RANGE: Zones 2 to 11.
HARDINESS: Withstands fall frosts; blossoms quickly in extreme heat.
SOIL: Fertile and humus-rich.
PH: 6 to 7.
FERTILIZER: 5-10-5.
WATER: Average.
EXPOSURE: Full sun.
SPACING: 18 inches, in rows 3 feet apart.

 *Method*

- **Start seed indoors** one or two months before the last spring frost is expected. Newly emerged plants quickly become leggy if indoor temperatures exceed 70°F and if full sun is not provided.

- **Prepare soil outdoors** early in the spring, about two weeks before planting, digging in ½ pound of fertilizer for each 30 row feet.

- **Sow seeds outdoors** in groups of three or four, ½ inch deep, each group 18 inches apart.

- **Set plants outdoors** when frost is no longer expected. Cutworms can be a problem at this stage, so it is wise to put paper "collars" around the stems, pushed about 1 inch into the soil.

- **Thin** to the best seedling in each group when plants are 2 to 3 inches tall. Protect the seedling or the cluster with a paper collar as you would a transplant.

- **Water** enough to keep soil moist and to prevent wilt. In dry seasons, broccoli will need extra water to develop large heads.

- **Fertilize** when plants are 6 and 12 inches tall, and just as buds begin to form. Scatter fertilizer alongside plants at a rate of 1 pound for 30 row feet. It is better to fertilize broccoli lightly and frequently since it needs a steady growth.

- **Pests and diseases** can be discouraged by planting seedlings and starting seeds in a sterile medium (many gardeners skimp on this, though it is an important precaution for all plants) and by rotating broccoli each year to an area where no member of the cabbage family has grown in the past three years. Cabbage worms may get into the buds, but usually don't do much harm. Dislodge them by soaking heads of broccoli in salt water for about 30 minutes before cooking. Rotenone will protect plants from these as well as from flea beetles. Since pesticide controls vary from state to state, it is best to contact your county agricultural extension office for the most current guidelines for your gardening area.

- **Harvest** the early heads promptly as soon as they form, while they are still tight. Cut the main stem just below the point where it begins to branch. Use a sharp knife and cut at a slight angle so water will not remain and form a puddle on the cut stem. This causes the stem to rot and prevents the formation of new side shoots. These side shoots, which will develop on most varieties, will provide a second crop of perfect smaller heads, extending broccoli's season throughout the summer by providing a second harvest.

Selected Cultivars

'Emperor' and 'Green Valiant' are particularly good for a second crop of side shoots, 'Emperor' producing heads a week earlier. 'Green Comet' is the earliest, with large heads, but fewer side shoots. 'Minaret' is the easiest to grow of the Romanesco cultivars. 'Purple' broccoli produces smaller shoots, much like the second crop of others, which turn bright green when cooked. 'Cruiser' does well in hot, dry weather, also producing a second harvest. 'Premium Crop' is one of the best standard cultivars.

BROCCOLI RAAB

Botanical name: *Brassica rapa* (Cruciferae)
Other common names: Broccolini di rapa, Rapini

This hardy biennial is really the tender shoots of turnips wintered over, one of the first green vegetables to appear in the spring. During the first year it develops a root and lush leaves. Although any turnip can be grown this way, it is better to use one bred especially for its greens. Although it is still not a commonly grown vegetable, raab is well known to those of Italian heritage. The turnip was an important food among country Italians as far back as the Roman Empire, and Pliny records that turnip greens were well liked among the upper classes. Cook and serve these shoots as you would asparagus, lightly simmered and served with butter and lemon juice or a sauce. Or blanch quickly and toss lightly in hot olive oil and garlic.

PLANT TYPE: Biennial.
GROWING RANGE: Zones 2 to 11.
HARDINESS: Very hardy; roots winter well under mulch.
SOIL: Moderately well drained; will survive poor soil.
PH: 6.5 to 7.5.
FERTILIZER: 10-10-10.
WATER: Moisture is required during summer heat when seeds are germinating and plants are sprouting.
EXPOSURE: Full to partial sun.
SPACING: 2 inches, in rows 20 inches apart.

 Method

- **Prepare soil outdoors** in late summer in a section of your garden that will not be plowed before the plant can produce its leafy harvest the following spring. Dig soil deeply, working in well-rotted manure or other fertilizer.

- **Sow seeds** in late summer, 1/2 inch deep.

- **Thinning** is not necessary since there will be some loss over the winter.

- **Water** well to be sure germinating seeds do not dry out in summer heat.

- **Fertilize** only if soil is very low in nitrogen. You might try a modest application of 10-10-10.

- **Pests and diseases** are rare since late planting protects the plant from most of the pests that afflict the Brassica genus.

- **Mulch** 6 to 8 inches in severe climates and leave plants in the ground through the winter. Remove mulch early in the spring.

- **Harvest** in the spring of the second year, before blossoms appear, when the plants are about 6 to 8 inches in height. A second, smaller crop will follow the first, then the roots can be dug and discarded. The space can then be used to grow another vegetable for summer or fall harvest. Store raab in the refrigerator, but plan to use it within a week.

BRUSSELS SPROUTS

Botanical name: *Brassica oleracea gemmifera* (Cruciferae)

The British have long been fans of the Brussels sprout, and even today they account for half its consumption worldwide. Although they do best in cool weather, Brussels sprouts have a very long growing season, so they usually are started indoors in all but southern climates. Rich in vitamin C, they also freeze well. They grow on fairly tall plants (1 1/2 to 2 1/2 feet), as lateral buds clustered around the central stalk of the plant (whereas the head on a cabbage plant is a terminal bud, the sprouts on Brussels sprouts plants are lateral buds). Brussels sprouts have a stronger flavor than others in the cabbage family and should be cooked only to the tender-crisp stage. Rinse quickly in cold water to set the color without cooling the vegetable.

PLANT TYPE: Annual.
GROWING RANGE: Zones 3 to 9, except in the Midwest.
HARDINESS: Withstands moderate freezes (20° to 25°F), but intense, dry summer heat causes sprouts to open and fluff out, especially those on lower portions of stem.
SOIL: Fertile and humus-rich.
PH: 6 to 7.5 (alkaline).
FERTILIZER: 5-10-10 or 10-10-10.
WATER: Average moisture.
EXPOSURE: Full sun.
SPACING: 18 inches, in rows 3 feet apart.

Method

- **Start seeds indoors,** sowing thinly in flats six to eight weeks before the last expected frost.

- **Set out plants** after the danger of frost is past.

- **Prepare soil outdoors** for direct seeding about four weeks before the last expected frost, digging in fertilizer.

- **Sow** seeds directly in the garden only in climates where you can expect 110 consecutive days of temperatures between 40° and 70°F. Plant about two weeks before the last expected frost, three or four to a group, each group 18 inches apart.

- **Thin** all but the strongest plant in each group when they are 1 inch tall. Protect from cutworms with paper collars (see Broccoli, page 464).

- **Water** as needed to prevent soil from drying out. Be especially careful during dry weather, since Brussels sprouts need evenly moist soil.

- **Fertilize** at heights of 6 and 12 inches and just as sprouts begin to form.

- **Pests and diseases** are much the same as those affecting broccoli and can be treated the same way (see page 465).

- **Pick off** lower leaves of the plant as they begin to yellow so that Brussels sprouts will form faster. In early fall, remove the topmost foliage and growing crown from each plant several days before harvest to encourage the sprouts to mature more rapidly.

- **Harvest** when the sprouts become large and crowded on the stem, waiting, if you can, until after the first frost. Cold weather improves their flavor, and since the plants are very hardy and prefer cold weather, they will continue to grow after this. When the time comes to harvest the last sprouts, don't leave the tiny ones that have failed to mature. These are tedious to pick, but are delicious and tender. Where winters are mild, the plants may continue to grow and multiple harvests can be made, each one taking sprouts progressively higher on the stem.

Selected Varieties

'Jade Cross' is the most commonly grown in all regions, but 'Oliver' is a new extra-early cultivar that matures ten days sooner. 'Teal' is a favorite in England and is gaining favor in the United States since its recent availability here. Newly developed is 'Rubine,' a red late-season cultivar with the same flavor as green sprouts. 'Dolmic' is an earlier cultivar introduced by Cook's Garden.

CABBAGE

Botanical name: *Brassica oleracea capitata* (Cruciferae)

One of the few green vegetables that keep well in the winter, cabbage has been a mainstay of peasant populations for centuries. The globular, conical or flattened (drumhead) heads contain tightly packed leaves, which are, in the case of the Savoy types, deeply crinkled. Leaves of Savoy types are not as stiff and are wrinkled even in the center of the head. This makes them less likely to split during heavy rains, as smooth cabbages are likely to do. Cabbage varies in color as well. There are the purple-headed varieties (known as red cabbage) and those of a slightly bluish-green color (known as green cabbage). There is very little difference in flavor between them. There are also "ornamental" cabbages in purple and pink, but these are leafy, not tightly headed, and grown more as a novelty than a food crop (although they are edible and make an attractive garnish). Consult the entry on pages 323–24 if you are interested in growing them.

Cabbage is shredded raw for salads, stir-fried with caraway seeds, and served in wedges as part of a traditional boiled dinner. Blanched leaves are rolled around rice and meat fillings for stuffed cabbage, a Middle European favorite. In France, entire heads of Savoy cabbage are stuffed with a veal mixture. The leaves of the Savoy are more pliable, making it possible to open the head slightly.

PLANT TYPE: Annual.
GROWING RANGE: Zones 2 to 11.
HARDINESS: Withstands frost.
SOIL: Fertile, humus-rich, and moist.
PH: 6 to 7.5.
FERTILIZER: 10-10-10.
WATER: Requires even moisture; sudden, heavy watering late in summer causes heads to split, but dry soil stops its growth.
EXPOSURE: Full sun.
SPACING: Early varieties, 12 inches; late, 18 inches; in rows 30 inches apart.

 *Method*

- **Start seeds of early varieties indoors** six to eight weeks before the last frost is expected.

- **Prepare soil outdoors** about two weeks before the last expected frost, working in compost if the soil is poor or sandy.

- **Set out plants** after last frost. Protect with paper collars (see Broccoli, page 464).

- **Sow seeds** of late varieties directly in the garden, about a week before last expected frost, 1 inch deep. In regions where freezing temperatures are rare, sow seeds directly in the garden in late summer.

- **Thin** seedlings to permanent spacing when plants touch. Use collars, as with broccoli, to control cutworm.

- **Water** as needed to prevent soil from drying out. Be especially careful during dry weather since cabbage needs evenly moist soil.

- **Fertilize** at three-week intervals, scattering along each side of the row, using 1 pound for each 20 row feet.

- **Pests** include cabbage worms and several fungal and viral diseases. Rotenone and crop rotation (see explanation in Broccoli entry) can help combat these. Since pesticide controls vary from state to state, it is best to contact your county agricultural extension office for the most current guidelines in your area. Cabbage profits from companion planting with the herb hyssop, which repels the cabbage worm.

- **Harvest** by cutting off the stalk close to the ground when cabbages have reached full size. Although cabbage needs ample water to develop, a long wet spell late in the season can cause heads to split, particularly in early-maturing varieties. Harvest immediately if this should happen, since they will rot quickly if left in the garden.

Selected Cultivars

Smooth green types include 'Stonehead' and 'Jersey Wakefield' for early cabbage, 'Grand Slam' and 'Grand Prize' for midseason, and 'Wisconsin' and 'Superior Danish' for late crops. 'Solid Blue' is a midseason cultivar with an especially sweet flavor and heads weighing as much as 4 pounds. 'Ruby Ball' is an excellent early red that resists splitting well, as does 'Ruby Perfection,' a midseason cultivar. Savoys such as 'Chieftain Savoy' are almost totally immune to splitting and are more disease resistant as well. If you are interested in storing cabbage beyond the harvest season, be sure to check your garden seed catalog carefully to choose varieties that store well.

CARROT

Botanical name: *Daucus carota* (Umbelliferae)

The carrot is the domesticated cousin of the wildflower Queen Anne's lace and would be a biennial if left unharvested, blooming in the second year with a lacy white flower. Requiring relatively little attention in the garden, carrot varieties are available for most soil types, but prefer a loose, deep soil for smooth, straight root formation. More than one crop is possible in mild areas, and succession planting can provide a steady crop all summer long. Carrots are rich in vitamin A and calcium.

PLANT TYPE: Biennial, grown as an annual.
GROWING RANGE: Zones 2 to 9.
HARDINESS: Withstands frost and heat.
SOIL: Any type, but performs better in light loam than in clay.

PH: 5.5 to 6.5.
FERTILIZER: 5-10-10.
WATER: Requires moist soil.
EXPOSURE: Full sun.
SPACING: 2 to 3 inches, in rows 16 inches apart. Can be planted no-rowed (in beds).
 Spacing can be closer if soil is very loose.

 *Method*

- **Prepare soil outdoors** deeply, as early in the spring as it can be worked, a week before planting seeds, adding humus if soil is too heavy or too sandy. Be sure to remove all stones. Work soil to a depth of 12 inches for long varieties such as 'Imperator,' but at least 8 inches. For an added boost to poor or clay soil, add a mixture of cottonseed meal, bonemeal, and wood ashes in a 1-1-4 ratio, worked in at a rate of 1 quart per 20 row feet.

- **Sow seeds** in wide rows, about ½ inch apart, ½ inch deep. Rake soil very lightly every few days and after rain until seedlings appear, to prevent its crusting over and presenting a barrier to fragile new shoots. Or you may want to cover the rows with an organic mulch after planting and carefully remove it upon plant emergence. The mulch should help prevent crusting. Continue planting at three-week intervals for a succession of tender carrots. Since carrots are slow to germinate and seeds are tiny to handle, some gardeners prefer to space seeds along rows of dampened paper towels, roll loosely, and store in the refrigerator for about six days until they sprout. Then they lay the towel and seeds along with the prepared soil, and cover with ½ inch of peat moss. This makes better use of seeds, makes later thinning unnecessary, and gives plants a good head start. You should never transplant carrots, as the roots will probably fork.

- **Thin** after tiny carrots have begun to form so they stand 3 inches apart. Use these small carrot thinnings raw in salads.

- **Water** during early stages to a depth of 2 inches or more, never allowing the soil to dry out. Consistently moist soil, even later in their growth period, gives carrots better shape and tenderness.

- **Fertilize** when greens are about 4 inches tall and again at 8 inches, spreading a 6-inch band on either side of the foliage at a rate of 1 pound per 30 row feet.

- **Hoe** surrounding soil to cover crowns as they push out of the ground to prevent tops of carrots from turning green.

- **Pests and diseases** are not a severe problem with carrots, but can include root maggots. If this has been a problem, soak soil with diazinon at planting time. Since pesticide controls vary from state to state, it is best to contact your county agricultural extension office for the most current guidelines for your gardening area. Occasionally a blight will cause leaves to turn black or shrivel; treat with appropriate fungicide from your local garden center. Crop rotation every three years will help control damage—carrots thrive where members of the cabbage family have recently grown. Sage is a good companion plant for carrots and helps repel the carrot fly.

• **Harvest** carrots at any time after they develop a good bright orange color and reach sufficient size to meet your need. If left in the ground too long, they may crack or become woody. Carrots intended for winter storage should be dug up before the ground freezes and stored without tops in barely moist sand or in moist peat moss, just above freezing temperature.

Selected Cultivars

Any carrot with 'Nantes' in its name will be cylindrical, blunt-tipped, and tender, with 'Early' and 'Express Nantes' being among the earliest by as much as two weeks. 'Paris Market' produces sooner, but with a compact, round carrot. 'Imperator' is a particularly long carrot. 'Danvers' and 'Chantenay' are broad and stocky; 'Chantenay' has a blunt tip and stores well. 'Suko' is a good choice for difficult soils. 'Chantenay,' 'Caramba,' and especially 'Amstel' are shorter and produce well in heavier soils, even in clay. 'Napoli,' a new variety from Johnny's Seeds, matures much earlier than even the other 'Nantes' types. Baby (miniature) carrots have become popular among gardeners in recent years and an increasing number of varieties are available, such as 'Baby Orange,' 'Minicor,' 'Baby Finger Nantes,' and 'Baby Sweet Hybrid.'

CAULIFLOWER

Botanical name: *Brassica oleracea* (Cruciferae)

A member of the cabbage family, cauliflower is a little more difficult to grow successfully, but not nearly as difficult as its reputation. It requires cool temperatures, even moisture, fertile soil, and harvesting at just the right time. The only secret to growing good cauliflower is consistency. By protecting young plants from frost, watering often, and fertilizing regularly throughout the growing season, the plants will reward the gardener with a vegetable far superior to what has been shipped and stored and then presented for sale in grocery stores. Although cauliflower heads normally may reach a diameter of 6 to 7 inches or more, the extra-small heads of minicauliflower are produced by reducing the spacing among the plants. Minicauliflower produce more in a small space and give neat, small clusters ready for eating raw or steaming. Since cauliflower does not keep well, plan to refrigerate it immediately after harvest and use within a few weeks.

PLANT TYPE: Annual.
GROWING RANGE: Zones 3 to 8.
HARDINESS: Withstands frost if tops have been blanched (see method, page 472).
   Will not tolerate heat above 75°F.
SOIL: Light and sandy, but fertile.
PH: 6 to 7.5.
FERTILIZER: 10-10-10 with added lime.
WATER: Requires even moisture during entire growth period.
EXPOSURE: Full sun.
SPACING: 18 to 24 inches; as close as 6 inches to produce minicauliflower.

 *Method*

- **Start seeds indoors** four to six weeks before the last expected frost, in flats or individual peat pots. Fall crops started outdoors in late summer and harvested as the first frosts/ freezes occur can be excellent.

- **Set seedlings outside** when they are about five weeks old, protecting from cutworms with paper collars (see Broccoli, page 464). Plants kept inside too long before setting out suffer from checked growth and do not perform well. They may produce small, cracked, discolored heads.

- **Prepare soil outdoors** for direct seeding of minicauliflower in midspring. In warm climates, cauliflower is usually started indoors so it can head before really hot weather.

- **Sow seeds outdoors** in groups of two or three, about 7 inches apart, ½ inch deep, in rows 24 inches apart.

- **Thin out** to the strongest plant in each group when about 2 inches tall. Seedlings may have to be protected from cutworms at this stage by the use of paper collars.

- **Water** if necessary to keep the ground evenly moist. It is important to remember that cauliflower cannot withstand periods of inactivity in their growing season. Continued, even growth as a result of adequate water and fertilizer is important.

- **Fertilize** every three or four weeks, using 1 pound for every 20 feet. Scatter as a 2-foot-wide band (1 foot on each side of the row), work in lightly, and water thoroughly.

- **Pests and diseases** are the same as those that trouble cabbage and broccoli and are treated the same.

- **Blanch** white varieties to keep heads white and of good texture by tying up the green leaves to cover the heads as the white begins to form. Purple varieties and minicauliflower do not need to be blanched.

- **Harvest** while buds (called *curd*) are still tight and have not begun to open even the slightest bit. Cut just below the head. Harvest minicauliflower when they are from 1 ½ to 3 ½ inches in diameter.

Selected Varieties

'Early Snowball,' 'Snowball 123,' and 'Snow Crown' are suitable for summer crops, since they withstand heat better than most, but are also good choices for colder regions because of their short growing season. 'Imperial 10-6' is also extra-early. 'Montano,' 'Andes,' and 'Elgon' are self-blanching, with leaves that wrap around the head as they grow. 'Alert' is a good choice for northern and high-altitude growing, maturing earlier and producing good leaves to tie up for blanching and frost protection. 'Snow King' is recommended in the southern states. 'White Bishop' is a new variety with self-blanching, well-textured heads that mature fifty days after transplant. 'Purple Head' and 'Violet Queen' are both purple, turning green when they are cooked. Minicauliflower are currently marketed in only two types, labeled simply as early- or late-maturing minicauliflower. Almost any variety can be forced to produce as a minicauliflower if spaced closely, although the exact spacing will differ from variety to variety.

CELERIAC

Botanical name: *Apium graveolens rapaceum* (Umbelliferae)
Other common name: Knob celery

Celeriac is a firm, crisp root vegetable with a smooth, fiberless texture and a nutty celery flavor. Its origins are as a wild celery, first used as a flavoring. The strong wild flavor was moderated by selective breeding in the seventeenth century when it became a popular garden vegetable in the Mediterranean countries and England. Its essentially inedible leaves and stalks have retained the strong, bitter flavor and toughness of its wild ancestors. A middle European favorite, celeriac is not common in American gardens, but stores well for winter use and is grown much like celery, to which it is closely related. Braising and blanching until just tender-crisp are favorite cooking methods. In Europe it is often boiled and added to potatoes before mashing. Raw, it can be grated for salads. It is hard to peel the whole root, so slice it first, then peel each slice.

PLANT TYPE: Annual.
GROWING RANGE: Zones 3 to 8.
HARDINESS: Withstands frost; heat is not a problem.
SOIL: Very rich and moisture retaining, but well drained; does well in sandy soils
    fortified with large amounts of humus or well-decomposed compost.
PH: 6 to 7.
FERTILIZER: 10-10-10.
WATER: Requires regular watering.
EXPOSURE: Full sun with light protection during extreme heat.
SPACING: 6 inches, in rows 2 feet apart.

Method

- **Start seeds indoors** in more northern climates twelve weeks before the last frost is expected in the spring in seeding trays. Germination can be hastened by scattering seeds in a dampened paper towel and keeping it moist and warm (70°F) for a few days until they sprout. If you have not presprouted, mix seeds with cornmeal for easier planting. When seedlings have two true leaves, transplant into flats, about 2½ inches apart. Keep seedlings well watered and close to 75°F during the day and 65° to 70°F at night.

- **Set seedlings** in the garden after the weather has settled in the spring. Like celery, celeriac seedlings are likely to bolt if exposed to low temperatures, in the 30's and 40's, for more than a week or two.

- **Prepare soil outdoors** well in advance of planting, with a 3- to 4-inch layer of compost and a pound of fertilizer for every 10 feet, both worked well into the soil to a depth of 8 to 12 inches.

- **Sow seeds outdoors** 2 to 3 inches apart and ½ inch deep in late winter in mild climates.

- **Water** regularly to keep soil evenly moist. If roots dry out they will become tough.

- **Fertilize** every two weeks with a weak solution of 10-10-10 liquid fertilizer poured around the base of the plant at a rate of 1 pint per plant.

- **Pests and diseases** including carrot fly can be controlled by keeping weeds away from plants and by interplanting with chives.

- **Remove** some of the lateral roots near the surface when the root has begun to bulge, and mound some soil around the swollen root.

- **Harvest** by digging up when roots are 2 to 3 inches in diameter (pull mounded soil away from one or two plants to check size). Although they will grow larger in areas with long growing seasons, they are best harvested no larger than 3 or 4 inches in diameter, before they become pithy in the center.

Selected Varieties

'Large Smooth Prague' is the most commonly grown and available in the United States, but 'Jose' is a noteworthy new variety with larger roots not subject to becoming hollow and pithy. 'Alabaster' also gives good results and can be allowed to grow larger than the suggested 3 inches in diameter at harvest.

CELERY

Botanical name: *Apium graveolens* (Umbelliferae)

Celery requires a long but cool growing season, two conditions that are largely incompatible throughout much of North America, except in certain coastal areas. But the home grower can still grow celery by using extra-early hybrids, planting indoors for an early start, and offering the plant some protection from the worst heat of summer. Celery is rich in minerals and vitamins, and even if the crop does not produce tender stems, at the very least you will have an abundant supply of tasty, nutritious leaves for flavoring soups, salads, and other dishes. The leaves are easy to dry between layers of paper towel in the microwave oven.

PLANT TYPE: Annual.
GROWING RANGE: Zones 3 to 8.
HARDINESS: Withstands fall frosts; will bolt in hot weather.
SOIL: Very rich and able to hold moisture well, but well drained.
PH: 6 to 7.
FERTILIZER: 10-10-10.
WATER: Requires even moisture throughout season.
EXPOSURE: Full sun, with light protection for shade during extreme heat of summer.
SPACING: 8 to 12 inches.

 *Method*

- **Start seeds indoors** twelve weeks before the last frost is expected in the spring, about ¼ inch apart and ¼ inch deep. When seedlings have two true leaves, transplant to individual pots or thin in flats to about 2½ inches apart. Keep seedlings well watered and close to 75°F during the day and 65° to 70°F at night to assure steady growth.

- **Set seedlings outdoors** in well-dug, well-fertilized soil after weather is settled and warm in the late spring. Young plants bolt to seed easily if exposed to temperatures below 55°F for a week or more, so do not harden off plants first by reducing temperature. Instead, expose them to outdoor conditions during the day and reduce water for a week. Severe stress should be avoided, however.

- **Water** regularly to keep soil evenly moist throughout all stages of growth.

- **Fertilize** every two to three weeks with a weak solution of 10-10-10 fertilizer poured around the base of plants at a rate of 1 pint per plant of half-strength solution.

- **Pests and diseases** are mostly in the form of blights that can be prevented by controlling aphids, which carry them. A good strong stream of water direct from the garden hose weekly will help control them, as will interplanting with garlic or chives. Black heart, a disease that sometimes affects celery, is easily prevented by increasing the calcium in the soil with ground eggshells or bonemeal.

- **Blanching** is suggested for the "golden" varieties to keep the stalks white and more tender, but keep in mind that you do this at the expense of valuable nutrients that are present in the greener stalks. If you wish to blanch, hoe soil up around the stems in the fall, but not all the way to the leaves. Let alone for about two weeks. Do not blanch in the summer.

- **Harvest** at any stage of growth by cutting entire plant close to the ground. Leaves may be harvested for flavoring at any time without harming the plant, as long as not too many are removed from any single plant. Store celery immediately in a place with high humidity and near-freezing temperature, if possible.

Selected Varieties

'Waltham Improved' and 'Ventura' are early varieties. 'Golden Self-Blanching' is not as early, but is very tender, has a nutty flavor, and a waxy, greenish-yellow color. 'Utah 52-70R' and 'Improved 52-70R' are proven dark green types. 'Florida 683' is a medium green well adapted to the Southeast. Other, newer varieties are 'Deacon,' 'Starlet,' and 'Green Giant.' The latter two have good disease resistance; all are of medium to dark green color.

CHINESE CABBAGE

Botanical name: *Brassica rapa* (Cruciferae)

Chinese cabbage is the most commonly grown of the many vegetables that have come into the modern kitchen from the Orient. There are two principal types, *Brassica pekinensis* (wong bok), which grows in a tight cluster of wide-ribbed leaves forming an elongated head; and *B. chinensis* (bok choy or pak choi), which grows in a loose cluster more like Swiss chard or celery with white stems and dark green leaves. In recent years many variations on these two types have been introduced. Their culture and use in the kitchen are much the same.

PLANT TYPE: Annual.
GROWING RANGE: Zones 3 to 11.
HARDINESS: Withstands some frost; runs to seed quickly in hot weather.
SOIL: Ordinary, but with compost to help retain moisture.
PH: 6 to 7.7.
FERTILIZER: 10-10-10.
WATER: Needs steady moisture.
EXPOSURE: Full sun.
SPACING: 6 to 8 inches until they almost touch, then 12 to 18 inches, in rows 18 to
    24 inches apart.

 *Method*

- **Prepare soil outdoors** by digging a heavy layer of compost or well-rotted cow manure into a 12-inch-wide strip, then adding fertilizer at a rate of 1 pound per 10 feet.

- **Sow seeds** about three months before the first expected frost. (It is important to follow package directions for each individual variety, since planting times vary between spring and summer. Planting a variety at the wrong time will result in bolting—developing into a seed head.) Plant in groups of four, ½ inch deep and 4 inches apart.

- **Thin** all but the best plant in each group when seedlings are 1 inch tall, then pull alternate plants when they are 8 inches tall and again when they become crowded. The thinned plants at each stage are perfect for use in the kitchen.

- **Fertilize** every three to four weeks at a rate of 1 pound for every 30 row feet.

- **Pests and diseases** are rare, except for cabbage worms, which can be discouraged by dusting plants with *Bacillus thuringiensis* (Bt), an insect-killing microbe, or by planting garlic or chives nearby. Since pesticide controls vary from state to state, it is best to contact your county agricultural extension office for the most current guidelines for your gardening area.

- **Harvest** whenever heads are the desired size by cutting plant at the base or, if only a little is needed, by cutting outer leaves close to the ground.

Selected Varieties

The most popular variety of *Brassica pekinensis* is 'Michihili,' but 'Two Seasons,' 'Tip Top,' 'China Doll,' and 'Jade Pagoda' are newer varieties that are said to be slow to bolt if planted in the spring.

Bok choy (pak choi) types include 'Prize Choy' and 'Lei-Choi,' as well as 'Mei Quing Choi,' also called 'Baby Pac Choi,' a small, compact, and bolt-resistant cultivar that is very tender and flavorful. 'Tsai Shim' is a bok choi from China that is highly resistant to heat, but is deliberately allowed to bolt for its tender stalks.

COLLARD

Botanical name: *Brassica oleracea* var. *acephala* (Cruciferae)

The collard, a nonheading form of cabbage, has been grown in the New World since the 1600s. Collards have changed very little since their wild ancestors were used by the ancient Greeks and Romans. Well loved throughout the southern United States, the collard is sadly neglected elsewhere. Collards are rich in minerals and vitamins, containing many times the vitamin A of cabbage, vitamin C equal to the same weight in oranges, and calcium equal to that in milk. They withstand enormous temperature ranges and produce an abundance of greens from very few plants. In mild climates, such as in the South, collards can be grown and harvested throughout the year.

In cooking collards, be sure to reach a high temperature very quickly to seal in their sweet flavor. Slow initial cooking will make them bitter. Chunks of ham are often added to collards as they cook.

PLANT TYPE: Annual.
GROWING RANGE: Zones 2 to 7.
HARDINESS: To 15°F; flavor is actually improved by frost; heat resistant.
SOIL: Sandy loam, but will tolerate most conditions.
PH: 6 to 7.5.
FERTILIZER: 10-10-10.
WATER: Requires regular watering.
EXPOSURE: Full sun, but will tolerate some shade.
SPACING: From 6 inches to 3 feet, depending on growing stage; in rows 24 inches apart.

✤ *Method*

- **Prepare soil outdoors** as soon as it can be worked in the spring, or in the late summer for a winter crop, adding aged manure to enrich it.

- **Sow seeds** about 3 inches apart, ½ inch deep, very early in the spring or sixty days before the first expected frost.

- **Thin** seedlings to 6 inches apart when they are 5 inches tall and continue to thin plants as they become crowded, to permanent spacing.

- **Fertilize** every four weeks by scattering a 10-inch band of fertilizer along each side of the plants at a rate of 1 pound for each 20 row feet.

- **Pests and diseases** are few except for flea beetles and cabbage worms, which are discouraged by interplantings of garlic or chives. *Bacillus thuringiensis* (Bt) can be used for the worms, but if frost is near, they will not trouble you for very long. Since pesticide controls vary from state to state, it is best to contact your county agricultural extension office for the most current guidelines for your gardening area.

· **Harvest** at any time, even into snowy weather, when their flavor is even better. Gather the lower leaves without disturbing the center crown growth, and you will have a continuing crop.

Selected Varieties

'Hi-crop' and 'Georgia' are both good, and 'Champion' is more compact than the others. 'Vates' is an old popular standard.

CORN

Botanical name: *Zea mays* (Gramineae)

Possibly the most popular of all fresh grown vegetables, corn is a native of the New World, grown by Native Americans in both North and South America. Only those who have tasted corn fresh from the field know its true flavor, since it deteriorates rapidly from the moment it is picked. Although it takes up a lot of room in proportion to its yield, corn is not difficult to grow and is among the most rewarding crops for the home gardener. Plant in blocks rather than in long single rows of each variety, as this will assist in pollination. Unless they tassel at different times, popping and ornamental corn should not be planted in the same garden with sweet corn as they cross-pollinate. Although corn is best enjoyed fresh from the cob, it also freezes well if blanched carefully, retaining a good fresh flavor. Dried corn can be ground into meal and used in making corn bread, tortillas, polenta, and as a hot cereal. Sweet corn is not well adapted to these uses, however, and older varieties with less sugar content or blue corn should be used.

> PLANT TYPE: Annual.
> GROWING RANGE: Zones 3 to 11.
> HARDINESS: Not frost hardy, thrives in hot weather; cool weather near harvest assists in quality retention.
> SOIL: Moderate to rich.
> PH: 6 to 7.
> FERTILIZER: 10-10-10.
> WATER: Requires even moisture.
> EXPOSURE: Full sun.
> SPACING: 12 inches on the square, if moisture and fertilizer are abundant; otherwise 12 inches, in rows 2 to 2½ feet apart.

 *Method*

· **Prepare soil outdoors** about a week before the last spring frost is expected, working in compost or other organic material if the soil is sand or clay.

· **Sow seeds** 1 to 1½ inches deep in frost-free regions any time after the average nightly temperatures can be expected to remain above 40°F. Corn can be planted when one or two light frosts are yet expected. If frosted and killed back after emergence it generally recovers nicely, as the growing point remains below ground for the first several weeks.

Corn will not germinate in cold, wet soil, so if a week of wet weather follows planting, it would be wise to check on the seed and perhaps plant a second crop as soon as the soil dries. Plant all varieties at the same time, choosing an early, midseason, and late variety to assure continued supply. If you stick to a single variety, sow successive plantings when the last planting is at about the two-leaf stage.

- **Thin** when plants are about 5 inches tall or before small suckers form. This will often not be necessary, since corn is the proof of the old saying "one for the crow, one to die, and one to grow." At that ratio, you will be left with a perfect spacing of about 12 inches! If this natural thinning is uneven, leaving clumps and bare spots, you can move plants. Do this carefully and very quickly, using an unbroken chunk of soil. You must do this before plants are 5 inches tall. However, the transplanted plants generally will be set back, as the roots are frail and widespread and will be disturbed somewhat.

- **Water** corn whenever it shows signs of wilting, especially during the time when tassels (clusters of corn silk) appear.

- **Fertilize** close to plants using 1 pound for each 20 row feet, when plants are 4 to 8 inches tall.

- **Pests and diseases,** while not plentiful, are very destructive. The corn borer can be a major problem. Insect-damaged tips can be cut off before cooking or look for broken tassels and treat crop with cabaryl, repeating at five-day intervals for three more applications. Since pesticide controls vary from state to state, it is best to contact your county agricultural extension office for the most current guidelines for your gardening area. Unless the garden is fenced, animals are likely to cause more damage than borers, since raccoons, skunks, and porcupines are especially fond of corn. Unfortunately, they like it just before we do, and many a gardener has found his field in shambles only days before his first harvest. A radio or a dog in the cornfield may help keep these night marauders away during the critical period.

- **Harvest** corn as each ear is ready with even rows of fully packed kernels, checking by carefully stripping down husks from the top until the kernels are visible. Corn should be harvested and either eaten fresh or frozen directly after picking, since its "shelf life" is short. Optimum maturity generally is reached at about nineteen to twenty-one days after silking, but it depends on the temperatures over that three-week period.

Selected Varieties

One of the most significant improvements in corn is the recent development of the supersweet or high-sugar hybrids. They have achieved a high-sugar content that holds at maturity instead of converting to starches as quickly as in the standard sweet corns. There are two main types on the market: the shrunkens *(sh2)* and the sugary enhancers *(se)*. The shrunkens are reduced in quality if pollinated by either the *se* or by standard sweet corns. Look for varieties with 'E.H.' as part of the name. Among these are 'Earliglow E.H.,' 'Kandy Korn E.H.,' and 'Pearls and Gold E.H.' An old-fashioned open-pollinated favorite is 'Golden Bantam,' introduced in 1902 and still going strong, a firm-textured large-kernel yellow corn that should be picked and used promptly. 'Jubilee' and 'Florida Staysweet' *(sh2)* now are probably the most widely grown and available sweet corn cultivars. 'Silver Queen' is a late white corn that should not be planted until after the soil is quite warm. Extra Sweet varieties (*sh2* type) are very sweet, have an improved shelf life, but are highly susceptible to cross-pollination. Seeds are smaller, so you get a lot more seed per pound. 'Early Xtra Sweet' and 'Sweetie' are midseason corns, 'Illini Extra Sweet' and 'Florida Staysweet' late, and 'Northern Extra Sweet' an early variety.

Bicolor (white-yellow) varieties also have become popular in recent years. These also are available in normal or *se* or *sh2* types. Some possibilities are 'Sweet Sal' and 'Sweet Sue,' which are normal sweet corns, 'Ivory 'N' Gold,' an *sh2* type, and 'Calico Belle,' an *se* type.

Popcorn has a long growing season, since it dries on the stalk. If dried completely it can stand below zero freezing. However, it usually is picked before it is completely dry and allowed to finish drying indoors. The earliest popcorn is 'Tom Thumb,' which has been refined from an early heirloom corn. 'Matinee' has excellent popping qualities, as does 'Purdue.' 'Strawberry Popcorn' combines popping corn with an ornamental, a dark red, round-eared type that can be used for harvest decoration, then popped. 'Symphonie' is a miniature ornamental, 'Indian Fingers' has a small 4-inch-long ear, and 'Ornamental Squaw' produces a wide variety of colors in each ear, as does 'Fiesta.' These last two are full size.

CORN SALAD

Botanical name: *Valerianella locusta* var. *olitoria* (Valerianaceae)
Other common names: Mache, Lamb's lettuce

The puzzling name of corn salad comes, like the plant itself, from Europe, where it was a troublesome weed in grain fields. All grains are called *Korn* in Europe (what we call "corn" is *Mais*) and this edible green that grew among the "corn" became known as corn salad. It has become naturalized in some parts of the United States as well, having escaped from gardens. This is a good salad green for hot areas of the Midwest and South where lettuce does not do well. Although known for generations, it has never been as popular in America as in Europe, especially in France. Its delicate leaves are unlike any other salad green, neither crisp nor chewy. Whole rosettes look best and are less likely to be lost among the other ingredients in a salad. Mache has one-third more iron than spinach, and it may be cooked quickly and served in the same way. It is grown as a spring crop in the North and a winter crop in the South.

PLANT TYPE: Annual.
GROWING RANGE: Zones 3 to 11.
HARDINESS: Will withstand some frost; more heat resistant than most greens.
SOIL: All soil types.
PH: 5.5 to 6.5.
FERTILIZER: 10-10-10.
WATER: Does best in moist soil, but will withstand some drought.
EXPOSURE: Full sun.
SPACING: 4 inches, in rows 1 to 1½ feet apart, or 5 to 6 inches on the square.

Method

- **Prepare soil outdoors** as soon as ground can be worked in the spring and, except in the far North, again in August for a fall crop.

- **Sow seeds** thickly in furrows ½ inch deep. Germination is often poor.

- **Thin** seedlings when they are about 3 inches tall to permanent spacing, using the thinnings in salads.

- **Water** whenever soil is dry to a depth of 1 inch.

- **Harvest** whole plants fifty to sixty days after planting, or use individual leaves throughout the growing season. Flavor deteriorates when plants become overmature, but unlike most greens, it doesn't become bitter after it has run to seed.

Selected Varieties

'Elan' is a small, smooth-leaved, upright plant that does well even in cold, wet conditions. 'Coquille' is the prettiest of the maches, with cupped leaves like the scallop for which it is named. 'D'étempes' has larger flat leaves and overwinters well in the South. 'Piedmont' is the largest, with long leaves and better heat resistance.

CUCUMBER

Botanical name: *Cucumis sativus* (Cucurbitaceae)

Almost as popular in their pickled form as they are fresh from the garden, cucumbers can also be braised or used in soups. Although varieties developed for pickling make good salads, slicing varieties do not pickle as well because the seeds mature faster and the fruit quickly grows too large for whole dills. Long Japanese varieties and European and American greenhouse varieties are excellent for slicing, and since most of these varieties are seedless they make good sliced and chunk pickles as well. Most cucumber vines take up a lot of room, although there are also bush varieties. The normal vining types are more prolific, however, and can be trained to grow on fences or trellises to save space.

PLANT TYPE: Annual.
GROWING RANGE: Zones 3 to 11.
HARDINESS: Will not withstand even a light frost; thrives in hot weather.
SOIL: Rich and limy is preferred, but it will tolerate ordinary soil.
PH: 5.5 to 7.
FERTILIZER: 5-10-5.
WATER: Requires even moisture to prevent bitter flavor.
EXPOSURE: Full sun.
SPACING: Trailing vines in hills of several plants each, 3 to 4 feet; climbing vines, 1 foot apart; bush, 2 feet apart.

 *Method*

- **Start seeds indoors** in peat pots three weeks before last frost date. Plant three seeds in each pot, trimming out the weaker ones when they are 2 inches tall.

- **Prepare soil outdoors** after weather is settled and soil is warm in the spring, incorporating plenty of organic material to hold moisture.

- **Set out** 4-inch-tall plants after the last frost, four to a hill or singly at 1-foot intervals along a fence for climbing and tying. A continuous supply of water can be assured in dry climates by punching holes in the bottom of an empty milk carton and burying it in the hill before planting, its neck 2 inches above the surface. Plant the seedlings around it. By filling the jug with water during dry weather, the water seeps in a steady stream into the roots where it is needed. Place the nozzle of the watering hose directly into the neck of the jug or fill the jug from carried jugs. Fill a number of times to achieve a thorough watering.

- **Sow seeds outdoors** ½ to ¾ inch deep, five or six to a hill a week after the last frost, when the soil has warmed to at least 70°F.

Tip · Bush cucumbers can be grown in containers for patio gardens as long as the pot is at least 12 inches wide and 12 inches deep. They perform best in full sun, unless conditions are very hot, in which case they can have some shade during the hottest part of the day. Be sure to keep them well watered and fertilized. They probably will require daily watering in midsummer when plants are full size.

- **Thin** to the four best plants in each hill when the plants are 3 inches tall.

- **Water,** especially when the plants are small, to prevent the roots from drying out. Cucumbers that are grown in alternately wet and dry soil will be bitter. Slow seepage irrigation hoses are best for cucumbers since it is important to water roots deeply.

- **Fertilize** by scattering about ¼ cup of fertilizer around each hill every two weeks. Take care to avoid direct contact between the fertilizer and the plant stem or foliage.

- **Pests and diseases** include the striped cucumber beetle, which not only chews the leaves and weakens the plant, but also carries bacterial wilt. These can be avoided by covering the seedlings with translucent caps available in gardening stores. They prevent the beetles from laying their eggs around the roots of the plant. If beetles appear later, spray with a solution of 8 tablespoons of Sabadilla (the pulverized seeds of a plant native to the Caribbean) in a gallon of water. Placement of bright yellow trap materials a short distance away from the cucumber plants also will help attract the beetles away.

- **Harvest** cucumbers when they are 6 to 8 inches long for slicing varieties, 3 to 4 inches for whole dills, and 2 inches for gherkins. Never harvest cucumbers when the vines are wet, as diseases will spread rapidly. Check pickling cucumbers daily, since they grow too fat very quickly. Gherkin-size pickles require picking off the tiny vegetables just as the blossom is falling off, so you will need to inspect plants carefully each day. Cukes for use as dills should be nicely shaped, but not have begun to bulge. Keep all cucumbers refrigerated after harvest. The pickling process should be begun immediately after cucumbers are picked, to assure crisp pickles.

Selected Varieties

Good slicing cucumbers are 'Early Triumph,' 'Supersett,' 'Marketmore,' and 'Sweet Success.' 'White Wonder' is an heirloom variety still popular and prolific, but not suggested for gardens where disease has been a problem. 'Tasty Green Burpless' and 'Sweet Slice' are both burpless varieties. 'Patio Pik,' 'Salad Bush,' and 'Bush Champion' are very prolific bush cucumbers; 'Chinese Long' and 'Kyoto' are long Oriental varieties.

Great progress has been made in recent years in developing many disease-resistant varieties. Among these, 'Marketmore 76,' 'Marketmore 80,' 'Comet A,' 'Sprint,' 'Pacer,' and 'Slicemaster' have become popular among the slicers.

EGGPLANT

Botanical name: *Solanum melongena* (Solanaceae)

Eggplant is a major crop in the Mediterranean (especially Italy and Greece) and the Orient, but has never been a common home garden crop in this country. Although eggplants require a long season and warm weather, they can be grown quite easily as far north as Zone 5 and, with a little extra care, even farther north. Perhaps grocery store eggplants, which are so large that they have often become seedy and bitter, are to blame for the general inattention from which this vegetable suffers.

Oriental eggplant varieties generally have longer and thinner fruit and a milder flavor. Some varieties grow 7 to 12 inches long, but are shaped more like thin cucumbers. The yield on these is higher, with as many as forty-five fruits per vine.

PLANT TYPE: Annual.
GROWING RANGE: Zones 4 to 11.
HARDINESS: Will not withstand frost, grows best in warm weather; tends to be chill damaged at low temperatures, especially in the seedling and transplant stages and at bloom.
SOIL: Moist, sandy, warm.
PH: 5.5 to 6.5.
FERTILIZER: 5-10-5.
WATER: Performs best with evenly moist soil.
EXPOSURE: Full sun.
SPACING: 2 to 2½ feet, in rows 2 to 3 feet apart.

 *Method*

· **Start seeds indoors** eight to ten weeks before the last expected frost, keeping soil between 80° and 90°F until leaves appear, 70°F thereafter. Placing seed trays in a sunny window will keep temperatures high. Transplant to individual peat pots when they are 2 to 3 inches tall.

- **Prepare soil outdoors** at least a week before transplanting, working in fertilizer at a rate of ¼ pound per 20 row feet.

- **Set plants** in garden when all danger of frost is past and when night temperatures below 45° to 50°F are uncommon. In northern regions, eggplant will do best if planted with a black plastic mulch. To do this, lay a strip of mulching plastic over the prepared soil and anchor the edges by burying them. Cut holes along the center about 2 feet apart by making crossed slits in the plastic and plant the eggplants in these holes. This keeps the ground warm around the roots, absorbs warmth during the day, and helps preserve moisture in the soil.

- **Water** whenever there has been less than an inch of rain within a week, soaking the ground thoroughly.

- **Fertilize** every three weeks with about ¼ cup of diluted liquid fertilizer per plant. Be sure the soil is thoroughly wet, and has been for twenty-four hours, before fertilizing.

- **Pests and diseases** include flea beetles, which can be controlled with pyrethrum when plants are first brought outdoors. Check the undersides of leaves frequently and remove any clusters of orange beetle eggs.

- **Harvest** regularly when eggplants are about 6 inches long, to encourage continued production. The harvest can continue past frost if the plants are covered with cloths at night when temperatures are expected to be low and uncovered after the day has warmed a little. Eggplants should be used within a few days and kept refrigerated.

Selected Varieties

'Black Beauty,' 'Dusky,' 'Classic,' 'Black Magic,' and 'Black Prince' are standard cultivars; 'Orient Express' and 'Ichiban' are the more slender and tender-skinned Oriental eggplants; 'Easter Egg' is small and white, with much the same flavor as the others. The new 'Small Ruffled Red,' also known as 'Italian Pink Bicolor,' is delicious both in its young green stage and at maturity when it turns red. 'Baby Bell' is the earliest, maturing at fifty-five days as a miniature plant, well suited for small containers, and producing six eggplants each only 2 inches long.

EGYPTIAN ONION

Botanical name: *Allium cepa* var. *viviparum* (Amaryllidaceae)
Other common names: Garden rocambole, Top onion, Circle onion

Unlike other onions, this one grows its bulb not at the base of the plant, but in clusters atop the long, hollow, flowering stem. An ungainly plant, it is rarely placed in an ornamental garden. Allow it plenty of room in a permanent bed, where its clusters of bulbs can drop when they grow heavy and regenerate the plant by sprouting where they hit the soil. This tendency results in a ring of small plants surrounding the parent and gives rise to the name *circle onion.* Use in place of shallots in cooking or where a small amount of onion is required.

Egyptian onions make excellent pickling onions. Clusters of them are a favorite among dried flower arrangers for their deep, almost purple color.

PLANT TYPE: Perennial.
GROWING RANGE: Zones 4 to 11.
HARDINESS: Overwinters even in the northern tier of states; tolerant also to heat and drought.
SOIL: Any soil with good drainage.
PH: 5.8 to 6.5.
FERTILIZER: None required but will respond to a balanced vegetable garden fertilizer.
WATER: Will withstand drought.
EXPOSURE: Full sun to light shade.
SPACING: 15 to 20 inches.

 *Method*

- **Prepare soil outdoors** in midsummer in the North, or late summer in the South, in a part of the garden where you can leave them in the bed from year to year.

- **Set bulbs** ½ inch deep. They will sprout simply sitting on the moist soil, but planting helps protect them from birds.

- **Watering** is useful though unnecessary; if absent, the bulbils stay dormant until rain.

- **Weed** often to give new plants plenty of sunlight and space.

- **Mulch** in the summer to help keep bed weed-free, but pull mulch back before bulbs fall if you wish them to form a circle of new plants.

- **Harvest** all but those clusters of bulbs that you intend for propagation. Hang clusters in a cool, airy place, where they keep very well.

ENDIVE

Botanical name: *Cichorium endiva* (Compositae)
Other common name: Escarole

Similar to lettuce, endive is an easy-to-grow salad green with a somewhat sharper, almost bitter flavor. It is used in Europe in "hot salads" that call for sautéing the leaves briefly before adding to potatoes and other ingredients. Because the leaves are sturdier than other lettuce, endive gives substance to a salad, either hot or cold. It can be added to stir-fry dishes toward the end of cooking and makes a delicious cream soup.

PLANT TYPE: Annual.
GROWING RANGE: Zones 3 to 10.
HARDINESS: Withstands frost; bolts to seed in very hot weather.
SOIL: Ordinary.
PH: 5.8 to 7.
FERTILIZER: 10-10-10.

WATER: Requires evenly moist soil.
EXPOSURE: Full sun.
SPACING: 8 to 12 inches on the square; 8 inches, in rows 2 feet apart.

 ## *Method*

- **Prepare soil outdoors** early in spring or, for a fall crop, about three months before first expected frost. In regions where winter temperatures don't dip below 25°F, prepare soil in fall for winter and spring harvest.

- **Sow seeds** directly in the garden ¼ inch deep, in groups of four, 8 to 12 inches apart on the square, or in rows, 1 to 1½ feet apart.

- **Thin** when plants are 2 inches tall, leaving the strongest in each group, or a row of plants spaced 8 inches apart.

- **Water** whenever soil becomes dry to a depth of 1 inch.

- **Fertilize** every three to four weeks, scattering fertilizer alongside plants at a rate of 1 pound per 30 row feet.

- **Blanch** endive about three days before harvest, if light-colored hearts are desired, by placing a plastic container (the 1-pound deli or cottage cheese ones work well) over the top of the plant. It should not cover the entire plant, but simply gather the top leaves together. This is much easier than the old method of tying each plant at the top.

- **Harvest** at any time after blanching by cutting the entire plant. Do not leave in the garden more than three weeks after blanching. Store in the refrigerator and use within two weeks.

Selected Varieties

'Salad King' and 'Green Curled Ruffee' have finely curled leaves, and 'Full Heart' is upright with broad leaves. 'Nuvol' is similar but self-blanching. 'Nina' is a new variety, smaller and earlier than the others, and 'Frisan' is the most tolerant of late-fall weather. 'Florida Deep Heart' is one of the most popular southern cultivars.

FINOCCHIO

Botanical name: *Foeniculum vulgare* var. *azoricum* (Umbelliferae)
Other common name: Florence fennel

A Mediterranean favorite for centuries, finocchio has been used as food, flavoring, tea, and medicine. The ancient Greeks employed it as a reducing aid, and Romans thought it would improve their eyesight. It has been held to have many medicinal qualities since then, especially as a cough suppressant. Because finocchio tends to bolt quickly, it is best to start the plant in autumn in warmer climates so it can produce in the early spring. The edible part is the bulbous base of the thick leaf stalk, which forms a round, layered, bulblike ball. Its anise flavor and crisp texture are a pleasant addition to salads, or it may be served as a cooked vegetable, after braising or stir frying. Or steam it lightly, sprinkle with grated cheese, and run quickly under the broiler. Use its feathery foliage as you would use the herb fennel.

PLANT TYPE: Annual.
GROWING RANGE: Zones 5 to 10.
HARDINESS: Will not withstand frost; bolts quickly in hot weather.
SOIL: Rich, cool, moist.
PH: 6 to 8.
FERTILIZER: 5-10-5.
WATER: Needs even moisture.
EXPOSURE: Full sun.
SPACING: 6 to 8 inches, in rows 24 inches apart.

Method

· **Prepare soil outdoors** at least eighty days before fall frost is expected, working in compost and fertilizer.

· **Sow seeds** thinly, about ½ inch deep.

· **Thin** seedlings when they are 2 inches tall to permanent spacing.

· **Water** frequently to prevent bolting, never allowing soil to become dry more than an inch deep.

· **Fertilize** when plants are 5 to 7 inches tall at a rate of 3 ounces per 10 row feet, scratching fertilizer into soil near the base of the plants.

· **Cut off** flower heads before they bloom to encourage a thicker base.

· **Blanch** when base is the size of an egg by mounding soil about halfway up. If you do not blanch the bulb, it will be tough and fibrous.

· **Harvest** by cutting plant at ground level slightly below the bulb in late fall when bulb is about 3 inches in diameter. Delay harvest until about three weeks after blanching. If bulbs are allowed to get too much larger they will be tough and stringy. Store in the refrigerator and use within two to three weeks.

Selected Cultivar

'Mammoth' is the best cultivar available for home gardens.

GARLIC

Botanical name: *Allium sativum* (Amaryllidaceae)

A native of the Himalayas, garlic's popularity quickly spread throughout the ancient world. It is said to be a mild antibiotic, renowned as a staple in the diet of the builders of the pyramids and as a deterrent to vampires. Its lore is almost endless and its use almost universal; in Castroville, California, there is even an annual garlic festival.

Each underground bulb is made up of separate cloves, and the entire bulb is encased in a papery covering. Only *Allium sativum* is a true garlic, but elephant garlic *(A. scorodoprasum)* has the same growing habits and requirements and a distinct but milder flavor. Its size (weighing in sometimes to as much as half a pound a head) and more gentle nature make it suitable for serving as you would onion, sliced raw in salad or cooked whole with pot or oven roasts. *A. sativum* is available in white and yellow varieties, the white having a more subtle and delicate flavor. Use any kind with parsley to counteract the latter's strong aftertaste without affecting its flavor.

PLANT TYPE: Annual.
GROWING RANGE: Zones 3 to 11.
HARDINESS: Very hardy.
SOIL: Fertile, well-drained loam or light sand.
PH: 5.5 to 8.
FERTILIZER: 5-10-5.
WATER: Needs even moisture.
EXPOSURE: Full sun.
SPACING: 4 to 6 inches, 12 for elephant garlic, in rows 12 to 18 inches apart.

Method

- **Prepare soil outdoors** by cultivating deeply early in the spring. In the Deep South, garlic may be planted in the fall for a plentiful early crop in the spring.

- **Set** individual cloves 2 to 4 inches apart, root end (blunt end) down, and cover with 2 to 3 inches of soil.

- **Water** when soil is very dry, except after tops have begun to wither. After this, the soil should be allowed to dry out if the weather permits.

- **Fertilize** when leaves are 5 to 6 inches tall, scratching in a light application around the base of the plant.

- **Cut off** flower stalks of elephant garlic that may appear in the summer. If tops of either type have not withered and fallen over by midsummer, bend them over so the cloves will develop.

- **Harvest** when tops are yellow and shriveled, lifting bulbs carefully and curing by laying them out for a few days in a dry, airy place before storing. Garlic is often stored by braiding the tops together after they dry. This braid may be hung in the kitchen within handy reach of the cook.

GARDEN CRESS

Botanical name: *Lepidium sativum* (Cruciferae)
Other common names: Curled cress, Pepper grass

Originally a wild herb of western Asia, cress varies in appearance from species to species, giving rise to a confusing variety of common names. Like all the wildlings, it requires little attention in the garden. Garden cress is even richer in vitamin A than watercress, to which it is only distantly related botanically, and contains ample vitamin C, iron, and calcium as well. Be sure to save the dried stems of its seedpods for use in everlasting arrangements.

PLANT TYPE: Annual.
GROWING RANGE: Zones 3 to 11.
HARDINESS: Very frost resistant; heat tolerant.
SOIL: Ordinary, but cool and well drained.
PH: 6 to 7.
FERTILIZER: 5-10-5.
WATER: Will thrive in low-moisture locations.
EXPOSURE: Partial shade or full sun.
SPACING: 3 inches.

Method

· **Prepare soil outdoors** early in the spring, incorporating a little fertilizer (¼ pound for 10 row feet) only if the soil is very poor.

· **Sow seeds** thinly before the danger of frost has passed and cover very lightly or simply rake seeds lightly into the soil.

· **Thin** seedlings when they are 2 or 3 inches tall to permanent spacing, saving the thinnings for use in salads.

· **Water** only in severe drought, since cress thrives in dry soil.

· **Pests and diseases** are not a problem with these sharp-flavored "weeds."

· **Harvest** the entire plant any time after it reaches 6 inches in height, or individual leaves at any time before flowers drop. Tiny new sprouts can be harvested for a peppery garnish for salads or sandwiches. Store in a sealed container in the refrigerator.

Selected Varieties

Broadleaf cress is the best for salads, with its crisp, peppery flavor. 'Curley Cress' is tightly curled and ruffled, perfect for a garnish, and has a good sharp flavor.

JERUSALEM ARTICHOKE

Botanical name: *Helianthus tuberosus* (Compositae)
Other common names: Girasole, Sunchoke

A member of the sunflower family, but not a close relation of the globe artichoke, and certainly differing in flavor, this North American native grows wild from Nova Scotia to Mexico. Champlain sent some home, where they became a popular vegetable in France and Italy. These perennials grow to be 6 to 12 feet tall, with yellow daisylike blossoms. The edible underground tubers develop quickly, looking like long lumpy potatoes. Immediately after harvest they are completely starchless. Starches begin to form during long storage, during which time the tuber begins to shrivel. They have one-tenth the calories of the potato, and are best steamed or simmered and served with butter or sliced raw in salads. The Jerusalem artichoke can be used as a screen in the garden, but it tends to spread rapidly, so many prefer to plant it away from the rest of the garden in a bed of its own. Included in a garden corner, it may be restrained in a tight bordered bed or in vertical, sunken, 10- to 12-inch concrete drain tile.

PLANT TYPE: Perennial.
GROWING RANGE: Zones 3 to 10, but they perform best in cooler zones.
HARDINESS: Hardy.
SOIL: Loose, sandy.
PH: 5.5 to 6.5.
FERTILIZER: None required.
WATER: Requires only moderate moisture; drought resistant.
EXPOSURE: Full sun.
SPACING: 18 to 24 inches, but can be grown more densely in small beds.
PROPAGATION: From tubers dug and reset in the spring.

Method

- **Prepare soil outdoors** deeply in a corner beyond the reach of the plow and where the tall plants won't shade others in the garden.

- **Plant** the tubers as they are sent by seed houses or cut in chunks, each with one or more eyes, as you would potatoes. The eyes look like potato eyes, and each one will send off a new shoot when planted. Plant 3 to 4 inches deep, with eyes pointing up. They will spread to form beds, so trying to plant them in rows is pointless. A corner is a better place. When the plants reach 4 to 5 inches in height, the stalks of the bed or clump might be tied as a group, or fenced, to prevent them from falling over onto other plants in the garden.

- **Water** in dry climates.

- **Mulch** with wood chips *only* in very dry, hot climates, about 2 inches deep.

- **Pests and diseases** rarely trouble these, but mice will nibble on the tubers. Fortunately, the tubers are plentiful enough in a bed so there is no serious loss of the crop.

- **Weed** when plants are small, but as soon as they are established they will out-tough any weed.

- **Harvest** the tubers after the first frost, when the flowers die, digging carefully to avoid damaging the tender tubers. These grow off lateral roots about a foot from the stem of the plant. In milder climates, Jerusalem artichokes can be left in the ground and dug up as needed. In severe climates, dig only as many for storage as can be used in two or three weeks, using fresh from the ground until then. Longer storage will require a container of damp sand or peat moss and temperatures ideally in the 30's or low 40's.

Selected Cultivars

Several cultivars are available, although they may not always be easy to find. These are 'Mammoth French White,' 'Oregon White,' and 'M-6.'

KALE

Botanical name: *Brassica oleracea* var. *acephala* (Cruciferae)

Similar to the collard but having a shorter stem, kale was grown by the ancient Greeks and Romans, and is still a favorite in Europe, especially in Portugal, where it is grown under the wine grapes that provide it with shade in the heat of the summer. It is the basis there for the nutritious and flavorful Caldo Verde soup. It is rich in vitamins A and C, as well as in minerals, and is low in calories. Flowering kale has a longer growing season, but is otherwise grown just like the conventional varieties. In addition to its use in soups, kale makes a good cooked green, since it stays firm when heated. Both kale and collard are among the most nutritious of vegetables.

PLANT TYPE: Annual.
GROWING RANGE: Zones 1 to 11.
HARDINESS: Very hardy; will withstand temperatures into the teens.
SOIL: Tolerates any soil, but prefers sandy with humus.
PH: 5.5 to 6.7.
FERTILIZER: 10-10-10 or well-rotted manure.
WATER: Tolerates dry soil.
EXPOSURE: Full sun or partial shade, especially in hot climates.
SPACING: 8 to 12 inches on the square or in rows 1½ to 2 feet apart.

Method

· **Prepare soil outdoors** as soon as it can be worked in the spring, or forty-five to sixty days before early fall frosts. In the South, a fall sowing produces a winter and spring crop.

· **Sow seeds** ½ inch deep and 18 inches apart.

· **Thin seedlings** to 8 to 12 inches apart when plants begin to touch.

· **Fertilize** only if soil is quite poor, by side-dressing with ¼ pound to every 10 row feet early in the spring.

· **Pests and diseases** rarely trouble kale, even where it is grown extensively.

· **Harvest** after the first frost, which brings out the flavor. Pick outer leaves and leave the crown to grow.

Selected Varieties

'Winterbor' is a very hardy, high-yield, very curly type of kale. 'Konsera' is less curly, very tall, and does better in milder climates. 'Dwarf Blue Curled' (also known as 'Blue Curled Vates') has long been a popular standard.

KOHLRABI

Botanical name: *Brassica oleracea caulorapa* (Cruciferae)

Kohlrabi is like no other vegetable in its appearance. About the size of a golf ball at its prime, it is covered with little stems radiating from it, each with a leaf attached. Another little tuft of leaves is at the top. The entire vegetable sits on a stiff stem about an inch above the ground. Botanically it is very much similar to a potato tuber; both arise from thickened stems.

The flavor of kohlrabi has been described as similar to that of a turnip, but it is the texture, not the taste, that is turniplike. It is mild and pleasant, almost nutlike; German cooks serve it with a cream sauce or scoop out a bit of the center and stuff it with veal. It is an excellent source of calcium, iron, and several vitamins.

PLANT TYPE: Annual.
GROWING RANGE: Zones 3 to 11.
HARDINESS: Will tolerate some freezing; heat resistant.
SOIL: Moist and light.
PH: 5.5 to 6.7.
FERTILIZER: 10-10-10.
WATER: Needs evenly moist soil.
EXPOSURE: Full sun; can tolerate some shade.
SPACING: 4 to 6 inches, in rows 12 inches apart.

Method

- **Prepare soil outdoors** in the spring as soon as the ground can be worked. Since the roots of kohlrabi are shallow, the soil does not have to be dug to great depth.

- **Sow seeds** ½ inch deep, in groups of four, spaced 6 inches apart. Continue to plant at two-week intervals for a continuous crop. In areas where temperatures rarely go below freezing, seeds can be sown in the fall for a winter and spring crop.

- **Thin** to the strongest in each group when the seedlings are 2 inches tall. No further thinning is needed, since plants should be harvested before they outgrow that spacing.

- **Water** to keep soil constantly moist to avoid woodiness. Stress will cause them to be tougher and more fibrous.

- **Fertilize** around plants every three weeks at a rate of 1 pound per 30 row feet.

- **Keep well weeded,** pulling any weeds before they form deep roots that would disturb the shallow roots of the kohlrabi when pulled. For the same reason, do not hoe or cultivate close to plants.

- **Harvest** when kohlrabi is the size of a golf ball, never larger than a small apple. Cut the stem just above the ground to avoid disturbing its neighbors by uprooting. Keep refrigerated for up to four weeks.

Selected Varieties

'Early White Vienna' and 'Early Purple Vienna' are the best known, but 'Kolpak' is earlier than either and does not get woody or fibrous. 'Purple Danube' is of equal quality and almost as early. 'Grand Duke' is a Japanese-developed hybrid variety that won the All-American award for its uniform shape and longer shelf life.

LEEK

Botanical name: *Allium porrum* (Amaryllidaceae)

Although little grown in the New World until recently, the leek has a history of several thousand years in Europe. It was sacred to the ancient Egyptians and has been a national emblem in Wales since A.D. 640 when the Welsh army wore leeks in their hats to distinguish themselves from the opposing Saxons. Leek soup is a national dish among the Welsh.

Low in calories, high in vitamins, a good companion plant for carrots and all members of the cabbage family, leek is also easy to grow. Those grown by home gardeners are less likely to be full of sand than commercial leeks. It is served braised and is most commonly known as an ingredient in leek and potato soup. Cock-a-leeky is a popular chicken and leek dish in the British Isles.

PLANT TYPE: Annual.
GROWING RANGE: Zones 3 to 11.
HARDINESS: Very hardy to heat and cold.
SOIL: Ordinary.
PH: 5.8 to 6.7.
FERTILIZER: 5-10-5.
WATER: Needs evenly moist soil.
EXPOSURE: Full to moderate sun.
SPACING: 4 to 6 inches, in rows 18 inches apart.

Method

- **Start seeds indoors** in flats two months before the last expected frost and keep seedlings well fertilized.

- **Prepare soil outdoors** early in the spring by digging a 6- to 8-inch-deep trench along the garden row.

- **Set out seedlings** when they are between 10 and 15 inches tall, in the trench, but do not fill it in. Add only about an inch of soil, and water. As the plants grow, add more soil to the trench, covering the white stems just to the level of the green leaves. Do not cover the tops. The soil blanches and tenderizes the white stems. An ideal stem for harvest will be cylindrical and 1 to 1½ inches in diameter.

- **Sow seeds outdoors** ½ inch apart and ½ inch deep in the bottom of the trench and add soil, as described above, as the seedlings grow.

- **Thin** seedlings to permanent spacing as they grow larger, using the thinnings in soups.

- **Fertilize** every four weeks by scattering a narrow line along each side of the trench, at a rate of 1 pound for 30 row feet.

- **Water** whenever the ground is dry to a depth of 1 inch.

- **Harvest** leeks as soon as they are large enough to use (at least ½ inch in diameter) by pulling up the entire plant. Leeks can be harvested until the ground around them freezes solid. **Mulch** in regions of mild winters, and harvest all winter. They store well in the refrigerator, lasting several weeks.

Selected Varieties

'Large American Flag' (also called 'Broad London') and the giant leek, 'Molos,' are good for mild climates. 'Nebraska,' 'Varna,' and 'King Richard' are recommended for northern growing. 'Electra' has also found a place in the market, though some people aren't keen on the taste.

LETTUCE

Botanical name: *Lactuca sativa* (Compositae)

There are so many different lettuces that it is difficult for the gardener (or the cook) to know just where to begin. Head lettuces are widely used, but difficult to grow except near the Great Lakes and in parts of California, or in special cold-frame and greenhouse environments. Looseleaf types form a crown of loose, tender leaves, and butterhead lettuce is somewhere between the two with a lightly compressed head. All are used raw in salads. The best salads may combine several different lettuces for variety; the home gardener may want to use a seasonal mixture that some seed houses (such as Cook's Garden) offer, in order to have a variety throughout the growing season. Looseleaf and cos (romaine) varieties are the best choice where summers are hot; butterhead and crisphead (iceberg) varieties are more adapted to cooler weather.

PLANT TYPE: Annual.
GROWING RANGE: Zones 3 to 11.
HARDINESS: Withstands frost; bolts easily in hot weather.
SOIL: Ordinary, well drained.
PH: 6 to 7.
FERTILIZER: 10-10-10.
WATER: Requires even moisture.
EXPOSURE: Full sun except in extreme summer heat.
SPACING: Depends on the type: crisphead lettuce, 10 to 12 inches; butterhead and romaine, 8 inches; leaf types, 4 to 6 inches; all in rows 18 inches apart.

 *Method*

- **Start seeds indoors** about a month before the last frost is expected in the spring.

- **Prepare soil outdoors** as soon as the ground can be worked in the spring, digging in a little fertilizer.

- **Set out seedlings** when they are 3 inches or taller and nights are not likely to be colder than the mid-20's.

- **Sow seeds outdoors** ¼ inch deep, directly into the garden at intervals of two weeks for continuous salads throughout the summer. In areas where daytime temperatures are expected to remain consistently above 80°F, discontinue planting about two months before hot weather. Begin sowing fall crops as soon as temperatures begin to drop below 80°F.

- **Thin** seedlings carefully when outer leaves of neighboring plants begin to touch, using the thinnings in salads.

- **Water** to keep the soil moist, but avoid top watering that keeps the foliage wet. Lettuce is better watered from beneath with a drip irrigation hose.

- **Fertilize** every three weeks by scattering it alongside plants at a rate of 1 pound for 30 row feet.

- **Pests and diseases** are few, but lettuce mosaic can sometimes be a problem. Check seed packet to see if they have been tested for this virus. If slugs are found on the lettuce (check in the morning or on a cloudy day), sprinkle them with salt or set out shallow pans of beer in the early evening to trap them.

- **Harvest** leaf lettuces at any time, including at the thinning stage for use in salads. Head varieties can be harvested when heads are firm and of desired size, or they can be harvested at the preheading stage and used as you would leaf lettuce.

Selected Varieties

'Black-Seeded Simpson,' 'Summer Bibb,' and 'Salad Bowl' are favorite green leaf lettuces, along with 'Oak Leaf,' with narrow and very tender leaves. One of the most upright and vigorous is 'Grand Rapids.' Red-leaved varieties include 'Red Salad Bowl,' 'Lollo Rossa,' 'Flame,' 'Red Sails,' the newer 'Cocard' (shaped like 'Oak Leaf'), and 'Garnet.'

'Buttercrunch,' 'Salad Bibb,' 'Tania,' and 'Nancy' are popular butterhead types, along with 'Pirat' and 'Red Boston,' both red butterheads. Romaine varieties include 'Cosmo,' 'Winter Density,' 'Green Towers,' and 'Parris Island,' the most versatile of these. 'Crispino' is an iceberg (crisphead) lettuce that performs well even outside those areas where it is usually grown. Another excellent crisphead variety is 'Ithaca.' 'Tom Thumb' is a miniature lettuce that does well in container gardens.

OKRA

Botanical name: *Abelmoschus esculentus* (Malvaceae)

A native of North Africa, okra has found its way into many other cuisines. Primarily associated with Creole cooking, it was brought here by the French. Its pods are a necessary ingredient of gumbo, where the gelatinous material inside the pods provides the thickening. Small pods are also pickled. Its growth is sprawling, like that of tomatoes, and it can be grown almost anywhere tomatoes grow. If you have a surplus, dried okra pods are a favorite among dried flower arrangers.

PLANT TYPE: Annual.
GROWING RANGE: Zones 5 to 11.
HARDINESS: Will not withstand frost.
SOIL: Ordinary.
PH: 6 to 8.
FERTILIZER: 5-10-5.
WATER: Can tolerate some drought.
EXPOSURE: Full sun.
SPACING: 12 to 18 inches, in rows 3 feet apart.

Method

- **Start seeds indoors** about a month before night temperatures can be expected to remain above 50°F. Soaking seeds overnight helps speed germination. Sow in peat pots, thinning to one strong plant in each pot. Keep the soil warm (80°F) as the seedlings develop.

- **Prepare soil outdoors** by loosening with a spade or fork as you would for any vegetable.

- **Set out seedlings** after the last frost and when nights have warmed. A mulch of black plastic sheet (see Eggplant, page 484, for method) will help keep soil warm.

- **Sow seeds outdoors** in frost-free regions when night temperatures can be expected to remain above 50°F. Plant in groups of three, ½ inch deep and 12 to 18 inches apart, in rows 3 feet apart.

- **Thin** to best plant in each group when seedlings are 2 inches tall. No further thinning should be needed.

- **Fertilize** when plants are 12 inches tall and again as they begin to bloom, scattering a band of fertilizer along each side of the row at a rate of 1 pound for 30 feet.

- **Water** during dry spells of a week or more. Avoid overwatering.

- **Pests and diseases** are more likely to trouble okra in the South, where it has been grown for many years. Crop rotation can help keep wilt and southern blight under control, as does keeping the area well weeded.

- **Harvest** okra by picking pods when they are between 2 and 4 inches long, wearing gloves, for it can irritate the skin. Once it begins, okra produces very quickly and until frost, so you will need to harvest daily. If left unpicked, the plant will stop producing. Store in the refrigerator or pickle in vinegar.

Selected Varieties

'Tenderpod' is compact and without the sprawling nature of some okras. 'Clemson Spineless 80' produces longer pods on a fairly compact bush. 'Blondy,' an All-American winner, is a newer early dwarf variety developed in the South, but it should be tried also in the North. 'Burgundy' has deep red pods that are tender and plentiful as well as striking in the garden. 'Annie Oakley,' producing a good yield in cooler weather, may be the best for northern gardens.

ONION

Botanical names: *Allium cepa* and *A. fistulosum* (Amaryllidaceae)

There are many types of onion, but the two most common garden crops are the bulb, or ordinary, onion *(Allium cepa)* and the bunching onion *(A. fistulosum)*. Their culture is much the same. *A. fistulosum* varieties never produce bulbs, whereas *A. cepa* always produces bulbs, provided that the variety you grow is adapted to the day length of the growing season in your region. "Green onions," often referred to as "scallions," may be harvested in either species while the tops are still green. Bulb onions have red, yellow, brown, or white skins. Neither type is difficult for the home gardener, and both are frequently grown from small bulbs, known as sets, or from small nursery plants, but also can be direct seeded in the garden.

Well known in ancient times, onions were a staple in the diet of the builders of the pyramids, and were eaten by ancient Greeks and Romans, supposedly to give them strength before battles. It is one of the most versatile of the culinary vegetables, finding its way into a wide variety of dishes from nearly all of the world's cuisines. It can be boiled, roasted, fried, or served raw in salads and sandwiches. It is a basic ingredient for sauces, soups, stews, and combination dishes from nearly all cultures.

PLANT TYPE: Annual.
GROWING RANGE: Zones 2 to 11.
HARDINESS: Withstands frost and heat.
SOIL: Ordinary to rich.
PH: 5.5 to 7.
FERTILIZER: 5-10-5.
WATER: Requires evenly moist soil.
EXPOSURE: Full sun.
SPACING: 4 inches, more for extra-large varieties but down to 1 inch if harvested as scallions, in rows 18 inches apart.

Method

· **Prepare soil outdoors** by digging to a depth of 8 inches and working in fertilizer if soil is poor.

· **Plant sets or young plants** in the spring as soon as the soil can be worked. Since onions may take five or more months to reach full bulb maturity from seed and the seedlings are so tiny to handle, home gardeners (and commercial growers as well) usually begin with purchased plants or sets. Plant sets 2 inches deep and 2 to 4 inches apart, depending on the anticipated size of the mature onion. Started plants should be planted ¾ to 1¼ inches deep.

- **Thin** as necessary if onions seem crowded, using the small onions.

- **Water** as needed to keep soil moist, since dry conditions produce fiery flavor and smaller bulbs.

- **Fertilize** when onions are 6 and 12 inches tall, scattering a 3-inch band along each side of the row at a rate of ¼ pound to 10 row feet.

- **Pests and diseases** are not a problem except for onion root fly (maggot), which you can't do much about.

- **Watch** for a normal dropping of the tops when bulb growth stops. Do not water plants after this signal. Leaves begin to yellow and bulb scales develop their characteristic color. Plants can now be undercut at about 2 inches below the bulb to hasten maturity. To do this, push in a spade at an angle to cut the roots. Do not break down green tops as diseases may enter bulb, but let bulb ripen naturally.

- **Harvest** when tops are brown, pulling up bulbs and cutting off tops an inch from the onion. Spread bulbs out to dry in an airy place for at least a week. Store in a cool, dark place. Bunching onions are harvested green as needed, starting as soon as they are thick enough for use.

Selected Varieties

'Stuttgart' is a medium-size yellow onion, normally grown from sets; it is very firm and a good choice for winter storage. 'Early Yellow Globe,' 'Downing Yellow Globe,' and 'Sweet Sandwich' are also firm, yellow onions that keep well, good for northern regions. White varieties include 'Crystal White'; 'Redman' and 'Red Burgundy' are red southern varieties. 'Grano' and 'Creole' types are also adapted to the South. Three famous mild, nonstoring salad onions that are specifically adapted to the regions they take their names from are Walla Walla (Washington), Vidalia (Georgia), and Maui (Hawaii). Care should be taken if one tries to grow these in other regions as day length and other conditions may not be satisfactory.

Good bunching onions are 'Evergreen Hardy White,' 'White Lisbon' (the earliest), and 'Ishikura,' an outstanding thick-stalked choice.

PARSNIP

Botanical name: *Pastinaca sativa* (Umbelliferae)

The delicate-flavored roots of the parsnip are one of the earliest vegetables enjoyed in the spring, since they may be harvested either in the fall or the following spring. The plant is a relative of parsley, carrot, and celery and among the easiest vegetables to grow. Parsnips keep very well in a cool, moist environment. Serve them boiled and buttered or mash them like potatoes. They are good in soups and stews and make an excellent cream soup. A dash of nutmeg brings out their fine flavor.

PLANT TYPE: Bienniel.
GROWING RANGE: Zones 3 to 9.
HARDINESS: Very hardy.
SOIL: Light loam.
PH: 5.5 to 7.
FERTILIZER: 5-10-5.
WATER: Requires even moisture until plants are well established.
EXPOSURE: Full sun.
SPACING: 2 to 3 inches, in rows 18 to 24 inches apart.

Method

- **Prepare soil outdoors** as soon as ground can be worked in the spring, digging deeply and removing all stones to a depth of 18 inches. In regions where temperatures rarely fall far below freezing, plant parsnips in late summer or fall. Do not incorporate manure unless it is very well rotted as it may cause the roots to fork.

- **Sow seeds** thickly, since germination is often poor. Be sure to use fresh seeds each year as they do not keep well. Plant seeds ½ inch deep and cover with fine soil, tamped gently. Never transplant parsnips, as the roots will fork and essentially be unusable.

- **Thin** seedlings to permanent spacing when plants are 2 inches tall.

- **Water** well until plants are well established. Before plants have appeared, rake *lightly* if soil forms a hard crust as the surface dries after watering or rain, or the crust will prevent new sprouts from breaking through. As a safer alternative, cover the row with ¼ inch of grass mulch after planting to reduce soil crusting.

- **Fertilize** once a month; 1 ounce for every 10 feet is about average.

- **Pests and diseases** are not a major problem. Root canker can best be prevented by choosing a canker-resistant variety, such as 'Andover.' If carrot flies have been a problem with your carrots, protect young parsnip plants with a floating row cover until they are a few weeks old.

- **Harvest** by digging out of the ground as soon as the ground thaws the following spring, before the new green shoots appear.

Selected Varieties

'Harris Model' is the standard, with long cylindrical roots and a raised crown. 'White Gem' is a smooth, white-skinned parsnip with some canker resistance. 'Andover' is a new variety specially developed for canker resistance. 'Cobham Improved Marrow' from England has a high sugar content. 'Guernsey' matures early, at ninety-five days, and is especially flavorful for spring harvest. 'All American' is an earlier variety of the old standby 'Hollow Crown,' but its wider crowns need to be kept covered with soil to prevent rot, so many gardeners prefer to stay with the older variety.

PEAS

Botanical name: *Pisum sativum* (Leguminosae)

Although we associate peas with the British (we still call the shelling varieties—*Pisum sativum*—English peas to distinguish them from Oriental edible pod types—*P. Sativum* var. *macrocarpon*), dried peas were found in the tombs of ancient Egyptians. But it was the British fondness for them, and the fact that they did well in the often cool climate there, that led British horticulturists to perfect the modern table peas.

Because of the short shelf life of fresh peas, they, like corn, are among the most rewarding vegetables for the home gardener. The difference between freshly picked peas and those that have survived shipping and standing on the grocery counter is dramatic. Edible pod varieties do not freeze as well as the English ones, but keep quite well if refrigerated immediately after harvest. Peas do best in cool weather and are among the earliest crops of the season. In the Deep South, gardeners hope for peas by Easter; in New England, gardeners vie to have them by Independence Day, where they are a traditional dish.

PLANT TYPE: Annual.
GROWING RANGE: Zones 3 to 10.
HARDINESS: Withstands frost; dies in hot weather.
SOIL: Ordinary and light.
PH: 6 to 7.5.
FERTILIZER: 5-10-10, but very little is needed.
WATER: Requires even soil moisture.
EXPOSURE: Full sun.
SPACING: 2 inches apart in double rows.

Method

- **Prepare soil outdoors** as early as possible in the spring, placing a chicken wire or other support for the vines along the center of the row before planting.

- **Sow seeds,** having soaked them overnight in cold water, about 1 inch apart and 1 inch deep on either side of the fence. Be sure to plant early since pea vines will stop producing and die when hot weather comes.

- **Thin** seedlings, if the cutworms have not done it for you, to permanent spacing when plants are 3 or 4 inches tall.

- **Water** if the soil dries out more than 1 inch deep, since peas have very shallow roots.

- **Pests and diseases** are not common because of the fast growth of peas during cool weather. Varieties resistant to wilt disease are available. If blight strikes your pea patch, showing up in the form of gray spots on the pods and thin areas on the stems, remove and burn all affected plants to prevent its spread.

- **Harvest** English peas while the pods are crisp and green and the seeds have begun to swell inside. Check by opening a few pods to be sure they are ready. Peas should be round, not crowded into flattened shapes inside. Edible pod varieties are harvested just as the seeds begin to form tiny lumps. Don't let these develop into round peas before picking, or the pods will be tough and flavorless. Peas will continue to bloom and develop pods until hot weather.

Selected Varieties

'Lincoln' is an old English pea favorite for its resistance to summer heat and its fine freezing qualities, as is 'Wando.' 'Progress #9' is a good choice, producing peas a week earlier than most. 'Dark Skin Perfection,' one of the later, more vigorous bush types, is most broadly adapted and reliable in yield. 'Little Marvel' has a longer vine life than others, and 'Thomas Laxton' holds its quality for a longer shelf life after picking. Newer varieties, such as 'Knight,' 'Green Arrow,' and 'Frosty,' have excellent quality and better disease resistance.

'Dwarf Gray Sugar,' an Oriental bush type and a favorite, produces an abundance of small edible pods. 'Mammoth Melting,' a pole type, is the crisp giant used by Chinese restaurants for its better keeping qualities. 'Oregon Sugar Pod II' produces medium broad pods and has become the most popular. 'Sugar Snap,' 'Sugar Ann,' and 'Sugar Daddy' are new thick pod-wall varieties that are supposed to combine the qualities of edible pod and shelling peas, but they fall short of the qualities of either. Those who wish to dry peas for soup should grow 'Alaska,' which will ripen in August and have plenty of time to dry on the vine.

Gardeners who wish to reduce the extra and abundant foliage common in peas may wish to grow the so-called semileafless bush varieties, such as 'Novella,' which have abundant tendrils and hence are easy to trellis.

PEPPERS

Botanical name: *Capsicum* (Solanaceae)

Popular vegetables both raw and cooked, peppers are a favorite of home gardeners, even in the North, where their popularity is increasing rapidly. Although they require warm weather and warm soil, peppers do well in colder climates if planted under a mulch of black plastic that keeps the roots warm and absorbs the sun's warmth during the day. The use of a layer of clear plastic over the black plastic will create a greenhouse effect, capturing and holding more heat.

Hot peppers are a staple of pungent cuisine as found in many cultures, including Mexican, Italian, Indian, West African, Hungarian, and South and Central American. The "fire" comes from capsaicin, concentrated especially in the seeds and in the tissue that holds the seeds. All peppers are particularly rich in vitamin C and have significant vitamin A as well. These nutrients increase as the peppers ripen.

Although it is commonly believed that hot peppers need a hot climate, both the sweet and the hot types thrive under the same conditions, preferring warm temperate weather instead of extremes of either hot or cold. In choosing varieties, remember that the days to maturity listed on the seed packets refer to days from transplanting into the garden, not days from planting the seeds indoors.

PLANT TYPE: Annual.
GROWING RANGE: Zones 4 to 11.
HARDINESS: Will not withstand frost, thrives in hot weather; fruit set may decrease with temperatures for a few days below 50° to 55°F.

SOIL: Rich for sweet varieties, ordinary for hot. If too rich, may reduce fruit set in
  either.
PH: 5.5 to 7.
FERTILIZER: 5-10-5, with added bonemeal or crushed eggshells for calcium.
WATER: Requires evenly moist soil.
EXPOSURE: Full sun.
SPACING: 12 to 18 inches, in rows 2 to 2½ feet apart.

Method

- **Start seeds indoors** six to eight weeks before nighttime lows can be expected to exceed 55°F. Transplant seedlings to individual pots and keep at temperatures between 70° and 80°F.

- **Set out plants,** using black plastic mulch (see Eggplant, page 484, for method), after the temperature can be depended upon to remain above 55°F at night. Peppers will not grow in cold soil, and cold nights cause them to drop blossoms without setting fruit. Peppers should be spaced so that the leaves of mature plants just touch neighboring plants. Plants of the jalapeño are bushier than other types, so be sure to leave at least 2 feet between them.

- **Fertilize** sweet peppers when plants are set into the garden and again, lightly, when they are 12 inches tall. Do not fertilize hot peppers the second time. Use a liquid fertilizer diluted to half strength for plants under black plastic and feed only after soil has been well soaked for twenty-four hours. If plants are making fast growth and are green and lush, delay the addition of fertilizer.

- **Cover** plants with fabric or inverted bushel baskets in the evening when frost is expected. Peppers are highly sensitive to frost, but can continue to produce despite cold nights in the fall if fruit was set earlier and plants are protected before the air becomes too chill. The warmth stored in the ground during the day has a radiation effect and the covers prevent frost from killing the sensitive leaves. Be sure to remove covers soon after the sun hits the garden in the morning.

- **Pests and diseases** are not a serious problem, especially for hot peppers, but cutworms may threaten young seedlings unless they are protected by paper collars (see Broccoli, page 464) when set into the garden. Tarnished plant bugs (that's their name!), aphids, and flea beetles can be controlled with pyrethrum. Blossom end rot is a sign that you may not be watering thoroughly and that you need more calcium in the soil. Combat by scratching in bonemeal or powdered eggshells at a rate of 1 pound for each 20 row feet.

- **Harvest** peppers at any stage of their development. For larger varieties it may be necessary to harvest a few peppers early to thin an especially prolific plant of fruit that is too heavy for it.

Selected Varieties

'Ace' is a good choice for northern gardens, since it is highly resistant to the blossom drop suffered by most during periods of low temperatures. 'Lipstick' is another early sweet pepper with cold-resistant qualities. Both turn red if left on the plant to ripen. 'Calwonder' and 'Early Calwonder' have been popular in the South, but are broadly adapted. 'Bell Tower' is a larger pepper with a longer season. 'Gold Star,' 'Golden Summer,' and 'Oro-belle' are yellow varieties (like red peppers, these start out green) that mature midseason.

Mini-red and Mini-yellow are perfect miniatures of sweet peppers, only 1 to 2 inches long at maturity. 'Italian Sweet' is a flavorful long pepper that is good for frying. 'Karlo' is a semihot, thick-fleshed bell pepper, and 'Sweet Banana' is a Hungarian-style frying pepper. 'Mexi Bell,' shaped like a bell pepper, has a moderately hot chili flavor. Purple peppers have joined the colorful array recently; 'Purple Bell' is a good choice.

'Super Chili' is very hot and can be used fresh or dried. Jalapeño is a small hot pepper with a distinctive flavor, which does very well in northern gardens. Habanero is even hotter.

POTATO

Botanical name: *Solanum tuberosum* (Solanaceae)

A staple crop in northern and central Europe, potatoes originated in South America, where they are still widely cultivated in an astonishing number of varieties. The Incas stored them dried in enormous caves in the Andes for use in times of famine. They are easy to grow, but not commonly cultivated by the home gardener. Baby new potatoes are among the culinary treats that come only to those with a garden (or a neighbor's garden), since they do not keep well and commercial growers are unlikely to sacrifice later, larger crops to dig them. Potatoes are grown from seed potatoes, which are tubers saved from the previous year's crop. Most gardeners purchase these from commercial growers who produce certi-fied disease-free stock, and who have the facilities to keep them at just the right temperature and to treat them to prevent fungus diseases. But if you have some sprouted potatoes of your own, it is fun to plant them as well. Avoid using as seed any potatoes purchased in the market as they may have been treated with a sprout inhibitor and may not germinate.

PLANT TYPE: Annual.
GROWING RANGE: Zones 3 to 11.
HARDINESS: Plants will not withstand frost, but unharvested potatoes will be un-harmed as long as the soil around them does not freeze.
SOIL: Light, sandy.
PH: 4.8 to 5.5; higher pH levels are okay, but the tubers will be more likely to develop "scab" disease.
FERTILIZER: 15-15-15.
WATER: Requires only moderate moisture, since roots are deep, but should be well watered and unstressed for best yield, tuber smoothness, and yield.
EXPOSURE: Full sun.
SPACING: 12 to 15 inches, in rows 2 to 2½ feet apart.

Method

- **Prepare seed potatoes** for planting, say a typical 2-by-4-inch tuber, by cutting it in half first the long way and then each half across into two. Each seed piece should contain from one to three eyes. Spread out in a single layer in a well-ventilated place to dry for about three days. Tubers of about 1 ½ to 2 by 1 ½ to 2 inches need not be cut and, planted whole, may be the most desirable seed, giving more stems per hill.

- **Prepare soil outdoors** in the spring as soon as it can be worked, digging deeply and incorporating fertilizer into soil at a rate of 1 pound per 50 feet. Prepare a furrow about 3 inches deep.

- **Plant seed potatoes** in the furrow, covering with 3 inches of soil. Germination does not occur below 48°F. Frost after emergence is not very serious as new shoots will quickly replace them.

- **Hill** potatoes when they are 8 to 10 inches tall by hoeing soil up around the stems to about 4 inches high. Be careful not to break plants. Potatoes form very close to the surface and are easily damaged by hoeing. Hilling will keep the root system cooler—hot soils may result in reduced tuber set.

- **Pests and diseases** include the Colorado potato beetle, which can be controlled with rotenone and by crop rotation. Do not plant potatoes where they or tomatoes or peppers have been the previous year. Nematodes are not usually a problem, but if they are, plant a few French marigolds among the potatoes.

- **Harvest** whenever the tubers are large enough to use. You can harvest a few at a time from each of several plants, leaving the rest to grow, any time after the blossoms appear. The main crop for winter storage should be dug in dry weather, about three weeks after the plants have died. Dig carefully with a potato fork, taking care not to bruise or split the tubers. Dry large unblemished potatoes for a few hours before storing, and use any damaged or very small ones promptly. Potato tubers must be stored in the dark at cool temperatures.

Selected Varieties

Early potatoes include 'Irish Cobbler' and 'Early Gem.' 'Norgold M' is a good choice for southern gardens or those with drought problems. 'Kennebec' and 'Russet Burbank,' a baking potato, are good midseason varieties. Red potatoes include 'Red Pontiac,' 'Red Norland,' 'Reddale,' and 'Sangre,' the latter two early. 'Viennese Fingerling' has small tapered tubers with light yellow flesh and a delicious nutlike flavor. 'Peruvian Purple Fingerling' keeps all winter. 'Butte' is a baking variety, late maturing and 20 percent higher in protein. For best and most reliable yields across a wide range of environments, 'Kennebec' and 'Red Pontiac' are favorites.

PUMPKIN

Botanical name: *Cucurbita pepo* (Cucurbitaceae)

The pumpkin is a relative of winter squash, summer squash, and common bird's-nest gourds, and occasionally they will be cross-pollinated in the garden, producing bizarre hybrids. Like squashes, pumpkins are easy to grow. Even those with small gardens can plant pumpkins with the newer bush varieties. These produce small sweet pumpkins well suited to use in pies. Pumpkin pies are the traditional Thanksgiving dessert, but this vegetable may be used in breads and muffins, as thickening for minestrone, as the base of a cream soup, or in pickles and marmalades. In South America they are candied in strips and chunks, and also may be hollowed out to use as a "serving pot" for savory beef stews. Many gardeners grow them along the edge of the garden and let the long vines trail outside to expand garden space. For information on growing giant pumpkins, see Tips on page 506.

PLANT TYPE: Annual.
GROWING RANGE: Zones 4 to 11.
HARDINESS: Although plants are killed by light fall frosts, the ripe fruit will not be damaged until the temperature drops a few more degrees.
SOIL: Medium to rich.
PH: 5.5 to 7.5.
FERTILIZER: Well-rotted cow manure, fish emulsion, 10-10-10.
WATER: Very large pumpkins require considerable moisture; others need extra water only during prolonged dry spells.
EXPOSURE: Full sun to light shade.
SPACING: vines, 8 feet; bush, 4 feet.

Method

- **Start seeds indoors** only if your season is very short. Pumpkins do not transplant well, so large peat pots that can later be put right in the ground are best.

- **Prepare soil outdoors** after it has warmed to 60°F by digging holes ("hills" is the gardener's term for these areas where several plants will grow together), 8 feet apart and 1 foot deep. Work in well-rotted manure. If soil is sandy or clay, work in a bushel of compost as well. Pack the soil so that if it rains after planting it will not settle into a dish that is too slow to dry. The hill should be just that—a slightly raised mound that heats and drains well.

- **Set plants outdoors** after night temperatures can be expected to remain above 55°F, although pumpkins and squashes are not as cold sensitive as muskmelons and watermelons. Protect transplants for a few days with light covers, such as plant caps or gallon plastic milk jugs with the bottoms removed.

- **Plant seeds outdoors** 1 inch deep, four seeds to each hill. If your growing season is short, soak seeds overnight before planting to speed germination.

- **Thin** all but the two strongest plants from each hill when seedlings are about 4 inches tall. Unless you are pruning the plant to produce one giant pumpkin, a vine will produce three to six pumpkins, a bush two to three.

- **Water** heavily, especially for large display pumpkins. Any variety will need extra water during dry spells.

- **Fertilize** a wide area around the base of the plant every two weeks with fish emulsion and also with 10-10-10 for larger pumpkins.

- **Pests and diseases** include the striped cucumber beetle, which feeds on young plants and carries wilt disease. These can be controlled by using floating row covers while plants are young and by locating and crushing eggs that are laid in clusters on the undersides of the leaves. Watch for brown shriveled leaves and yellow spots, which may be a sign of mildew. Remove these leaves immediately to keep the mildew from spreading. To prevent vine borers, use rotenone around the base of the plants when they are young.

- **Harvest** when leaves begin to die and pumpkins are bright orange. Cut, leaving 3 inches of stem. Set pumpkins in the sun for a week after cutting to season, covering them at night to protect from frost. Then store them in a cool (50° to 60°F), dry place.

Tips · If you want to win prizes for your giant pumpkins, first choose a variety that has been bred for size. Select a site with plenty of room, full sun, and well-drained soil. Space hills 25 feet apart and dig holes 2 feet deep and 3 feet in diameter. Fill with well-rotted cow manure and cover with 4 to 5 inches of good topsoil mixed with ¼ pound of 10-10-10 fertilizer. When the soil reaches 70°F, set out the plants. Prune away early fruit and those that are within 10 feet of the base of the plant. In mid-July choose the best pumpkin on each vine—about 15 feet from the roots—and prune away all others. Water profusely near the base of the vine and fertilize with fish emulsion, especially near the "knees," the knobby area where vines set down additional roots. During the entire growing season, water vines heavily, as much as several gallons a day. If your pumpkin breaks the 500-pound record, contact the Guinness Book of World Records at 2 Park Avenue, New York, New York 10016. Good luck!

· Pumpkin and squash seeds can be saved for a healthy snack. Wash them well and spread on a cookie sheet in a single layer. Allow to dry several days, then toast in a 300°F oven until they are lightly browned. Store sealed in a jar.

Selected Varieties

'Big Max,' actually a winter squash, is one of the largest field "pumpkins," often 22 inches in diameter. 'Jack-o'-Lantern' is another ornamental type, although not as large. 'Jack Be Little' is a delightful miniature pumpkin, only 3 inches in diameter, good for pies or table decorations. 'Cinderella' is a compact bush variety, good for pies and for smaller gardens. 'Small Sugar' and 'New England Pie' are two famous, excellent vining pie pumpkins. 'Spirit' has become a popular Halloween pumpkin because of its "tall" shape when set on end, and hence its attractiveness for carving. 'Atlantic Giant' has been specially bred for its enormous size. 'Godiva' and 'Trick or Treat' have "naked" seeds, with no hull to remove, and are useful to those who grow pumpkins for their nutrient-rich seeds as well as their tasty flesh. Rinse these seeds well and dry on a tray or screen. They may be eaten raw or toasted.

RADICCHIO

Botanical name: *Cichorium intybus* (Compositae)

This variety of chicory is known for its deep red color and slightly bitter flavor, both of which become more pronounced with cold weather. In its native northern Italy, all heading types of chicory are called by this name, but in the United States only the red ones are called radicchio. Usually found in Italian salads, it can also be brushed with oil and cooked lightly over the grill. Fresh, it adds color and zest to salads and does not wilt quickly. Sometimes it can be wintered over for a second crop in the spring. Not entirely predictable as a garden crop, it is best to try several varieties and see which does best in your garden.

PLANT TYPE: Annual, though may winter over and produce seed in the second season.
GROWING RANGE: Zones 3 to 11.
HARDINESS: Very hardy; some varieties bolt in hot weather.
SOIL: Light and fertile.
PH: 5.5 to 7.5.
FERTILIZER: None required if soil humus content is high.
WATER: Moderate.
EXPOSURE: Full sun.
SPACING: 8 inches, in rows 18 inches apart.

Method

· **Prepare soil outdoors** in the fall in areas where winter temperatures stay above 10°F. In colder areas, prepare soil in May or early June.

· **Sow seeds** thinly in rows.

· **Thin** seedlings when they are about 3 inches tall to permanent spacing. The thinnings are very good in salads.

· **Water** when there is severe drought, but radicchio will withstand dry soil.

· **Blanch heads** by tying them together or placing a clay flowerpot over each head about two weeks before harvest. This makes the leaves a paler green and more tender.

· **Harvest** when heads are the size of tennis balls by pulling up the whole head. Leave the root attached for better storage.

Selected Varieties

'Giulio' is a bolt-resistant early-spring variety, as is 'Silla.' 'Red Verona' is the best known and most widely available, producing bright red heads. 'Red Treviso' is shaped more like romaine and is less winter hardy. 'Castelfranco' is a hard-to-find variety, beautifully marbled in red and white, with a loose head and good resistance to bolting.

RADISH

Botanical name: *Raphanus sativus* (Cruciferae)

Although round red salad radishes are the type most commonly grown in North America, there are others. Icicle radishes are long and white, usually quite hot, and are often grated as a condiment with Oriental food. Round radishes come in white as well, and there are black varieties, either round or long, that keep very well in the winter. Some Chinese types have green or red interiors and green exteriors. Radishes are among the first vegetables harvested in the spring, a great encouragement to the gardener. Succession planting assures a continuous crop until very hot weather, and there is time for a fall crop in most areas. For a mild flavor, be sure the watering is even and the growth fast.

PLANT TYPE: Annual.
GROWING RANGE: Zones 2 to 10.
HARDINESS: Withstands both spring and fall frosts, but not intense heat.
SOIL: Sandy loam.
PH: 6 to 7.
FERTILIZER: 10-10-10 or well-rotted cow manure.
WATER: Requires even moisture.
EXPOSURE: Full sun.
SPACING: Small varieties, 1 inch apart; larger varieties, 2 inches.

 *Method*

- **Prepare soil outdoors** two weeks ahead of planting, digging in 1 pound of fertilizer for each 10 row feet.

- **Sow seeds** ½ inch deep in early spring, as soon as the soil can be worked, scattering them thinly, and continue planting each week. After you have begun to harvest radishes, simply drop a seed into the hole left by each one picked and cover it up. This assures a continuous supply. You can do this until really hot weather, when they will bolt to seed.

- **Thin** when they are 2 inches tall: an inch apart for small varieties and 2 inches for larger ones. If you have planted in wide rows, you can wait until the tiny radishes have formed and thin by harvesting these for use in salads.

- **Water** enough to keep the soil evenly moist, since radishes become woody and peppery if the soil dries out.

- **Fertilize** well before planting, but any applied during the growing season will not have much effect on these fast-growing vegetables.

- **Pests and diseases** are rare in radishes, but root maggots and flea beetles may be a problem. If damage occurs, soak the ground around the plants with diazinon. This will not help the plants already in progress, but will prevent damage in subsequent plantings.

- **Harvest** when radishes reach the optimum size described for each variety. Some radishes push themselves out of the ground slightly when they are ready, a handy sign for the unsure gardener! Be sure to harvest them regularly, before they begin to form seed stalks.

Selected Varieties

Red varieties include 'Cherry Belle,' 'Scarlet Knight,' 'Marabelle,' 'Red Prince,' 'Scarlet Globe,' and 'French Breakfast,' as well as 'Prinz Rotin,' which has a longer harvesting period and doesn't split during heavy rains. White radishes include 'White Globe,' 'White Icicle,' and 'April Cross' for spring planting and 'Summer Cross,' 'China White,' 'Okura Cross,' and 'Miyashige' for fall. 'Round Spanish Black' is a fall radish that keeps well, but needs peeling. 'Munchen Bier' is a unique variety grown for its tasty seedpods, which can be eaten raw or steamed. This must, of course, be left to go to seed in the garden; the pods are picked green.

RHUBARB

Botanical name: *Rheum rhaponticum* (Polygonaceae)
Other common name: Pie plant

An old favorite once found in every kitchen garden, rhubarb is again enjoying popularity as a home garden crop. Marco Polo is credited with bringing it from China, where its history dates from the third millennium B.C. Its popularity in the United States dates from the early 1800s, and large clumps of it still mark the sites of long-gone New England farms.

It is a flowering, cool-season perennial, grown for its thick leaf stems, which are ready to harvest the second year after roots are planted. *The roots and leaves are poisonous and should not be eaten.* Rhubarb is propagated by divisions of the root crowns; instead of by seed (which rarely breeds true), plants are started from roots that can be purchased from seed and garden supply houses. It thrives in cold climates where the ground freezes in the winter. Although botanically not a fruit, it is used for jams, pies, and as a condiment sauce, often combined with berries.

PLANT TYPE: Perennial.
GROWING RANGE: Zones 3 to 8.
HARDINESS: Very hardy; plants withstand summer heat as long as winters are cold.
SOIL: Light, ordinary to rich, slightly acid.
PH: 5.5 to 7.
FERTILIZER: Well-rotted cow manure, 5-10-5.
WATER: Moderate.
EXPOSURE: Full sun to light shade.
SPACING: 3 feet, in rows 4 feet apart.

Method

- **Prepare soil outdoors** early in the spring by digging a hole for each plant 2 feet deep and working well-rotted cow manure into the soil.

- **Set root crown** 2 to 3 inches below the surface and cover.

- **Fertilize** lightly in midsummer if soil is very poor.

- **Divide** when first leaf buds just appear aboveground. Ideally, divisions should be at least 4 to 6 inches across.

- **Remove** the tall flower stalks that form early each summer, since these weaken the roots for next year's crop.

- **Pests and diseases** are not a problem.

- **Harvest** the large outer stalks the third year and after, by grasping firmly close to the base and pulling sharply to the side to break the stalk in its socket. Do not cut the stems since this leaves stubs that will rot and damage the roots. Don't remove more than 1/3 to 1/2 of the stalks from a crown in any one year of harvest. A strong crown should yield 2 to 3 pounds of stalks. Store, refrigerated, for up to two weeks.

Selected Varieties

'Victoria' and 'Linnaeus' are old varieties, still dependable. 'Valentine' and 'Cherry' are especially good for areas with milder winters. Also very dependable are 'MacDonald Crimson,' 'Canada Red,' and 'Strawberry.'

SALSIFY

Botanical name: *Tragopogon porrifolius* (Compositae)
Other common names: Oyster plant, Vegetable oyster

This old-fashioned favorite of wild Mediterranean origin was once a standby of the kitchen garden. It has fallen out of style, but is still carried by European seed houses. Cultivated in Europe as early as the sixteenth century, it was one of the first plants brought by settlers to the New World from England, where it was grown as both a vegetable and an ornamental.

Although it takes four months to mature to usable size, it is hardy enough to be planted early and harvested late in the season. Use salsify soon after harvest, since it loses flavor in long storage. Steam the root until tender, peel—as you would beets—by rubbing off the skin, slice, and serve with butter. Or mash, mix with egg, and roll in breadcrumbs to fry for a dish very similar in taste to oysters (which gives rise to its old-fashioned name, vegetable oyster).

PLANT TYPE: Annual.
GROWING RANGE: Zones 3 to 11.
HARDINESS: Will withstand spring and fall frosts; heat resistant.
SOIL: Rich, loose loam.
PH: 7 to 8.
FERTILIZER: 5-5-10 or seaweed mixed with wood ashes.
WATER: Moderate.
EXPOSURE: Full sun.
SPACING: 4 to 6 inches, in rows 15 inches apart.

Method

- **Prepare soil outdoors** deeply and thoroughly to loosen and lighten it and to remove all stones to a depth of 12 inches, incorporating fertilizer at a rate of ¼ pound per 10 row feet. Do this in June in the South or about a month before the last frost is expected in the North.

- **Sow seeds** thinly, 1 inch deep.

- **Thin** seedlings when they are well established, 4 to 5 inches high, to permanent spacing.

- **Water** thoroughly until plants are well established, then whenever the top inch of soil is dry.

- **Weed** carefully and frequently to give tiny slow-growing shoots plenty of room and sunlight. They are easily mistaken for grass as they sprout.

- **Fertilize** halfway through the summer—but do not use manure.

- **Pests and diseases** are not a problem.

- **Harvest** as needed after several frosts, leaving the remaining crop in the ground until just before the ground is expected to become too frozen to dig. In mild climates, cut off tops and mulch deeply in order to harvest all winter. Store in sand in a cold cellar.

Selected Variety

'Mammoth Sandwich Island' is an old standard.

SCORZONERA

Botanical name: *Scorzonera hispanica* (Compositae)
Other common name: Black salsify

Like the similar but unrelated salsify, black salsify is of Mediterranean origin and is treated like salsify in the garden. Black salsify became a major vegetable during the Middle Ages and was used as a remedy for snakebite. It lost its popularity during Victorian times when overfastidious cooks insisted on peeling off its black skin before cooking. This robbed it not only of its food value, but of its flavor as well. It is a valuable food for diabetics, since it contains no sugar-forming starches. Its oyster flavor is even stronger than that of salsify, and it is prepared in the same ways.

PLANT TYPE: Annual.
GROWING RANGE: Zones 3 to 11.
HARDINESS: Withstands spring and fall frosts.
SOIL: Rich, loose loam.
PH: 7 to 8.
FERTILIZER: 5-5-10 or seaweed mixed with wood ashes.
WATER: Moderate.

EXPOSURE: Full sun.
SPACING: 4 to 6 inches, in rows 15 inches apart.

Method

- **Prepare soil outdoors** deeply and thoroughly to loosen and lighten it, removing all stones to a depth of 12 inches, incorporating ¼ pound of fertilizer per 10 row feet. Do this in June in the South or about a month before the last frost is expected in the North.

- **Sow seeds** thinly, 1 inch deep.

- **Thin** seedlings when they are 4 inches tall to permanent spacing.

- **Water** thoroughly and often until plants are established.

- **Weed** very carefully since new shoots look just like grass.

- **Fertilize** halfway through the summer, using ½ pound to 20 row feet. Do not use manure since it is too high in nitrogen for salsify.

- **Pests and diseases** are not a problem.

- **Harvest** as needed after several frosts, leaving the remaining crop in the ground until just before the ground is expected to become too frozen to dig. In mild climates, cut off the tops and **mulch** with about a foot of hay that can be pulled back to harvest roots all winter. In climates where they must be dug up, store in sand in the cold cellar.

Selected Varieties

'Geante Noire de Russie' is an extra-long French variety, with a slim, cylindrical root. 'Flandria,' developed in the Netherlands, produces earlier and has a fine flavor. 'Duplex,' a cultivar with very long, black, cylindrical roots, also should be tried.

SHALLOT

Botanical name: *Allium ascalonicum* (Amaryllidaceae)

A hardy bulb of the onion family, shallot grows much like garlic in bulbs made up of several individual flat-sided bulblets. It is the most delicately flavored of all the onion family and is a great favorite of French chefs. It is used for its very subtle onion flavor in béarnaise sauce, and it can be substituted for onion whenever small amounts are required for flavoring.

PLANT TYPE: Annual.
GROWING RANGE: Zones 3 to 11.
HARDINESS: Very hardy to heat and cold.
SOIL: Rich, but will tolerate moderate.
PH: 5.5 to 7.
FERTILIZER: 5-10-5.

WATER: Requires moderate but even moisture.
EXPOSURE: Full sun.
SPACING: 6 inches, in rows 16 inches apart.

Method

- **Prepare soil outdoors** very early in the spring, as you would for onions.

- **Set individual bulblets** at a depth equal to their length, blunt end down and about 6 inches apart.

- **Water** during prolonged dry spells, if soil becomes dry to a depth of 1 inch. Discontinue watering when tops become yellow and begin to wither in the fall.

- **Fertilize** by side-dressing at a rate of ¼ pound per 12 row feet when plants are 5 to 6 inches tall.

- **Pests and diseases** are not a problem and shallots are often interplanted with other crops to protect them from damage by insects.

- **Weed** by hand since cultivation with a tool could harm the delicate bulblets and roots, which grow close to the surface. Flower stalks rarely form, but should be removed if they do.

- **Harvest** as soon as the leaves have withered in the fall and cure by spreading out in a single layer in a warm, airy place for two weeks. Store loosely in a dry, airy place at a cool temperature, 50° to 60°F. Young leaves may also be harvested sparingly to use as you would chives, but too much harvesting will reduce the yield of bulbs.

Tip · Shallots are often braided like garlic and hung in the kitchen for easy access.

SHELL BEAN

Botanical name: *Phaseolus vulgaris* (Leguminosae)

As the name implies, these beans must be shelled before use. Along with the old-fashioned horticultural beans, this group includes butter beans and limas. All have a slightly mealy texture and a nutlike flavor. They come in both bush and pole varieties. The latter sometimes are planted in "hills" with a 6-foot pole in the center for them to twine around.

Although they are easy to grow, flavorful and highly nutritious, they are not as commonly grown as snap beans and are rarely found in grocery stores. They are richer in protein than snap beans and may be cooked as a hot vegetable dish or chilled for use in salads. They are a favorite addition to soups as well.

PLANT TYPE: Annual.
GROWING RANGE: Zones 3 to 11.

HARDINESS: Plants will not withstand frost, but the beans themselves are inside shells and are not damaged by light frosts.
SOIL: Ordinary, well drained.
PH: 6 to 7.5.
FERTILIZER: 5-10-5.
WATER: Performs best with even moisture.
EXPOSURE: Full sun.
SPACING: Bush, 12 inches, in rows 2 to 4 feet apart; pole, in hills 24 inches apart.

Method

- **Prepare soil outdoors** after ground has warmed to 60° to 65°F or more, putting in poles if planting those varieties. To set poles firmly, dig a hole at least 18 inches deep, set pole in hole, and refill with soil, tamping it firmly with your feet.

- **Sow seeds** 1 inch deep where they are to grow. Beans do not transplant well and can be transplanted readily only when in the "crook" stage shortly after emergence. Space seeds about 4 inches apart. For pole beans, plant in groups of six, leaving about 2 feet between "hills" and sprinkling the soil with a granular legume inoculant at a rate of ¼ pound for every ten hills. This provides the rhizobia bacteria, which fix nitrogen in the soil, with a necessary nutrient for beans. However, if you have grown beans for a couple of years in your garden, the inoculant should no longer be necessary as it should by then be a part of the normal soil microbe makeup.

- **Thin** pole varieties to the three or four strongest plants in each hill (or group of seeds), thin bush beans to 12 inches when plants are about 4 inches tall.

- **Fertilize** when plants are about 6 inches tall, taking care not to get fertilizer on stems or leaves. Sprinkle fertilizer lightly and scratch into the soil. Do not work too deeply, since beans have feeder roots fairly close to the surface.

- **Pests and diseases** include those that attack other bean varieties (Mexican bean beetle, powdery mildew), but horticultural beans seem to withstand these better. Crops should be rotated at least every three years, especially if diseases have been a problem. Dead plants and leaves should be thoroughly removed in the fall to control overwintering of pests.

- **Harvest** when beans have grown plump inside the pods, before the pods become dry and brittle. If you wish to save any of these as dried beans, leave them on the vine until pods are brittle and beans hard. Then pull up entire plants and hang upside down in bundles, roots still attached. Shell when they are thoroughly dry and store in jars.

Selected Varieties

'Vermont Cranberry' and 'Wren's Egg,' sometimes known as 'Speckled Cranberry,' are old favorites, both pole beans. There is also a bush variety of 'Wren's Egg.' Another popular bush type is 'French Horticultural.' Lima beans come in both pole and bush types, with 'King of the Garden' and 'Carolina' probably the most popular for pole growing and 'Fordhook 242,' 'Henderson,' 'Early Thorogreen,' and 'Kingston' the best baby limas.

'Henderson,' an old cultivar, has been very reliable and prolific, with a long season of productivity. 'Florida Speckled Butterbean' (pole) does well in the South, as do 'King of the Garden' and 'Dixie Butterpea.' 'Geneva' is a new baby bush lima that will germinate in cool soil, a boon to northern gardeners.

SKIRRET

Botanical name: *Sium sisarum* (Umbelliferae)

A hardy perennial of the carrot family and grown as an annual, skirret produces clusters of roots. It is well liked in China and Japan, where it originated, and is still grown in England. Like salsify, skirret was among the first vegetables brought by early settlers, but it is now considered an old-fashioned oddity here, despite its delicious flavor, and roots for starting it are hard to find. Scrub and slice the roots, which are mild flavored, before boiling and serving with butter. They can also be shredded raw and tossed with oil and vinegar for a salad as you would raw turnip.

> PLANT TYPE: Hardy perennial, grown as an annual.
> GROWING RANGE: Zones 4 to 11.
> HARDINESS: Will withstand frost and heat.
> SOIL: Sandy loam.
> PH: 6 to 8.
> FERTILIZER: 5-5-10.
> WATER: Moderate.
> EXPOSURE: Full sun.
> SPACING: 9 to 12 inches, in rows 18 inches apart.

Method

- **Prepare soil outdoors** very early in the spring, or in the South, prepare soil in the fall for a spring crop. Unless soil is very poor, there is no need to add fertilizer.

- **Set roots,** each piece containing an eye, about 9 inches apart. Cover with 2 inches of soil. If roots are not available, sow seeds thinly, 1 inch deep.

- **Thin** seedlings once established to permanent spacing.

- **Water** often until seeds germinate or roots sprout. After that, water when the ground is dry to a depth of 1 inch.

- **Fertilize** in midseason by side-dressing with well-rotted manure.

- **Cut back** flower heads before plants go to seed.

- **Pests and diseases** are not a problem.

- **Harvest** after the first frosts have improved the flavor. Leave roots in the ground and harvest as needed until a hard freeze is expected. In mild climates, plants can be deeply mulched and roots left all winter to be dug up as needed.

SNAP BEAN

Botanical name: *Phaseolus vulgaris* (Leguminosae)
Other common names: Green bean, Wax bean

Nutritionally, beans are one of the most valuable crops for the home gardener. A good protein source (especially when combined with grains in a meal to provide a "complete protein"), they are easy to grow and harvest, and yield heavily for the space they occupy. They freeze well for winter use. The larger and more mature the seeds in the pods at harvest, the higher the protein content. For that reason, shell beans, dry beans, and limas regularly are higher in protein than are snap beans.

If picked when they are very slender and about 4 inches long, they can be blanched quickly and plunged into cold water to set their color and used in salads. Seeds of over-grown snap beans of any variety can be removed from the pod and used as shell beans.

Many growers feel that the pole varieties have a better flavor. This may be due to the greater number of leaves that provide greater photosynthesis, increasing sugar and other flavor components. Northern gardeners find, however, that bush varieties survive the first light frosts better. Pole beans produce more in a small space.

PLANT TYPE: Annual.
GROWING RANGE: Zones 3 to 11.
HARDINESS: Highly susceptible to frost; heat resistant.
SOIL: Well drained, ordinary.
PH: 6 to 7.5.
FERTILIZER: 5-10-5.
WATER: Performs best with even moisture.
EXPOSURE: Full sun.
SPACING: Trellised pole varieties, 6 to 8 inches, in rows 3 to 4 feet apart; bush, 12 inches, in rows 1 1/2 to 2 1/2 feet apart.

Method

- **Prepare soil outdoors** after ground has warmed, since beans will not germinate quickly in cool soil below 65° to 70°F and the germination process stops below 50° to 55°F. If you are using them, put poles in before planting the beans (see Shell Beans on page 514 for advice on how).

- **Sow seeds** of bush varieties 1 inch deep and about 4 inches apart and pole beans in hills of four to six around poles set 2 feet apart. For increased yield, sprinkle a granular legume inoculant into the furrow at a rate of 1/2 pound for 50 row feet. This provides the rhizobia bacteria, which fix nitrogen in the soil, with a necessary nutrient for beans. However, if you have grown beans for a couple of years in your garden, the inoculant should no longer be necessary as it should by then be a part of the normal soil microbe makeup.

- **Thin** pole beans to the best three or four in each hill, bush varieties to permanent spacing.

- **Water** before seeds have sprouted only if the soil is warm, since bean seeds rot in cool, wet soil. Drip irrigation is better than overhead watering, since water penetrates closer to the roots without soaking the large spreading leaves. Overhead watering before seedling emergence also commonly crusts many types of soil, making emergence difficult. Once beans are established, they will not need extra watering, except in very dry seasons, but this will depend somewhat on how closely the plants are spaced.

- **Fertilize** when plants are about 6 inches tall with 1 pound for every 20 row feet. Keep fertilizer away from the stems and leaves and at least 3 inches from the base of the plant, to avoid burning tender stems.

- **Pests and diseases** can be a serious problem with beans, especially with plants grown in soil where beans have been grown in previous years. Rotate beans at least every three years. Mexican bean beetles can be controlled with pyrethrum. Beans quickly develop wide leaves that shade the ground and discourage the growth of weeds. If possible, avoid overhead watering and never harvest or work with the plants when the foliage is wet, since this spreads disease. In the fall after harvest, remove bean plants from the garden.

- **Harvest** beans when the pods are long and glossy, before the seeds have begun to swell into lumps.

Selected Varieties

Bush green beans include 'Tendercrop,' 'Blue Lake Bush 274,' 'Tendergreen,' and the slightly smaller 'Provider,' which is popular in the North for its shorter season. 'Mini Green,' a new variety from Park Seeds, produces tiny, slender "gourmet" beans only fifty-two days from planting. 'Romano' is a broad, flat Italian bean. 'Jumbo' is an extra-wide pod Italian type. Newer purple varieties include 'Royalty' and 'Royal Purple Burgundy.' These beans turn green when cooked and retain a deeper green color when frozen. 'Purple Teepee,' new in 1989 from Thompson and Morgan, is a dwarf bush bean whose pods grow above the foliage. This makes harvest easier and the plants more prolific in wet seasons. Wax cultivars include 'Pencil Pod Wax,' 'Golden Rod,' and 'Early Wax,' which freezes especially well. 'Rocdor' has an excellent flavor. Green pole types include 'Kentucky Wonder,' one of the best known. 'Kentucky North' and 'Northeaster' produce nearly a week earlier than most. 'Jeminez,' introduced in 1989 by Johnny's Seeds, is a highly flavorful pole bean with a reddish tint and an extended vine life. For a real heirloom pole bean, try 'Case Knife,' one of the earliest recorded beans in American history.

SORREL

Botanical names: *Rumex scutatus* (French sorrel); *R. acetosa* (Garden sorrel) (Polygonaceae)

This hardy perennial green adds life to salads and soups, and is the main ingredient of a favorite tart sauce for fish. Popular in France and elsewhere in Europe, it is also an ingredient in the traditional pease porridge. Wild varieties growing throughout the United States and Canada have leaves of the same shape, but are smaller. The leaves of French sorrel are larger than those of garden sorrel. Once planted, it requires very little care. Sorrel's uncontrollable spreading habits make it advisable to find a spot outside the regular garden, where it can become a weed. Sorrel is rich in vitamins A and C. A few sorrel leaves may be added to other cooked greens, such as spinach, to give them a little extra tang.

PLANT TYPE: Hardy perennial.
GROWING RANGE: Zones 3 to 11.
HARDINESS: Very hardy; heat resistant.
SOIL: Any soil will do, but thrives best in rich, moist conditions.
PH: 5.5 to 7.5.
FERTILIZER: 10-10-10 or fish emulsion.
WATER: Moderate.
EXPOSURE: Full sun or partial shade.
SPACING: 6 to 8 inches.

 *Method*

- **Prepare soil outdoors** early in the spring, in a location where the bed can remain year after year.

- **Sow seeds** ¼ inch deep, about 2 inches apart.

- **Thin** seedlings when they are 2 or 3 inches tall to permanent spacing. Use thinnings in salads.

- **Water** when soil becomes dry to a depth of 1 inch.

- **Fertilize** midseason with a side-dressing of fish emulsion for heavier leaf growth.

- **Pinch off** the flower stalks as they form to prevent even faster spreading and to preserve the flavor of the leaves.

- **Pests and diseases** are not a problem with these highly flavored leaves.

- **Harvest** at any time before the flowers form, picking outer leaves and allowing the centers to remain and grow. Pick just before use since sorrel wilts quickly.

Tip · Sorrel plants will last for many years, each increasing to a clump by multiplying underground. If their spread becomes a problem, either weed out the unwanted new plants or surround the patch with a band of garden lime to help discourage its spread.

SPINACH

Botanical name: *Spinacia oleracea*

Spinach was among the vegetables introduced to Europe by the Moors. Very rich in vitamin A, it thrives in northern gardens where it can get the required six-week cool growing season. It is quick to bolt to seed, especially in the long day length of June, July, and August in the North. Spinach is popular in Mediterranean dishes, often combined with white cheeses, and is delicious as a salad green or lightly steamed as a side dish.

Although not of the same botanical family, New Zealand spinach *(Tetragonia tetragon-oides)* is popular with gardeners and has much the same growth requirements, and its food value is excellent. It has the advantage of continuous production even during hot weather and does not require as much water as spinach.

PLANT TYPE: Annual.
GROWING RANGE: Zones 2 to 9.
HARDINESS: Frost resistant, but heat sensitive. New Zealand spinach is sensitive to frost.
SOIL: Rich loam.
PH: 6 to 7.5.
FERTILIZER: 10-10-10.
WATER: Requires even moisture.
EXPOSURE: Full sun.
SPACING: 6 inches, in rows 12 to 18 inches apart.

Method

· **Prepare soil outdoors** as soon as the ground can be worked in the spring, working in fertilizer at a rate of ¼ pound to each 10 row feet.

· **Sow seeds** ½ inch deep and 1 inch apart after soaking overnight in cold water, as early in the spring as possible. For New Zealand spinach, wait until a week before the last frost is expected.

· **Thin** seedlings when they are about 4 inches tall to stand 3 inches apart. When plants begin to touch, thin alternate plants (all these thinnings are good in salads).

· **Water** after disturbing the soil by thinning or weeding, and every three to four days during dry weather.

· **Fertilize** after first thinning with 3 ounces per 10 row feet.

· **Pests and diseases** are unlikely to be a problem.

· **Harvest** about six weeks after planting, when the leaves are full and large. Cut off the entire plant at ground level. New Zealand spinach can be harvested by picking individual leaves and young shoots, since the plants will continue to produce all summer without bolting.

Selected Varieties

Savoy types of common spinach have crinkled leaves (which catch sand as soil is splashed up during rains) and include 'Indian Summer,' 'Melody,' 'Dixie Market,' 'Winter Blooms-dale,' and 'Tyee.' The latter is slower to bolt and grows more upright, making it less sandy. 'Viking' is a good smooth-leaved spinach. There is only one variety of New Zealand spinach and it is sold as a kind rather than as a variety. While frost sensitive, New Zealand spinach does not bolt and is highly recommended for summer crops and continuous harvest. Its upright growth and smooth leaves keep it free of sand.

SUMMER SQUASH

Botanical name: *Cucurbita pepo* (Cucurbitaceae)

Summer squash is light fleshed, with thin, edible skin, and is picked young for fine, delicate flavor. It is a bush plant, often with large showy foliage under which the squash is shaded and hidden from the gardener's view (often until overgrown!). Squash blossoms are delicious fried in a light batter or stuffed. While few gardeners would want to pick the productive female blossoms and compromise their crop, the male blossoms are easy to distinguish. They have long thin stems with no sign of the thickening of beginning fruit at their base. All squashes are usually planted in hills, or groups, although it is not necessary to use this style of planting.

PLANT TYPE: Annual.
GROWING RANGE: Zones 4 to 11.
HARDINESS: Will not withstand frost; heat resistant.
SOIL: Light, ordinary, must be well drained.
PH: 6 to 7.5.
FERTILIZER: 5-10-5.
WATER: Requires moderate moisture.
EXPOSURE: Full sun.
SPACING: In hills (groups) 4 feet apart.

Method

- **Start seeds indoors** in very cold climates for an early start four weeks before the last frost is expected. Use peat pots to avoid disturbing roots during transplanting. Keep soil warm; squash will not germinate at temperatures below 60°F, and will germinate quickly only when the soil temperature exceeds 70°F.

- **Prepare soil outdoors** deeply, digging a hole 18 inches deep and filling it with well-rotted cow manure mixed with garden soil.

- **Set plants** in the garden as soon as all danger of frost is past, planting in hills, or groups, spaced 4 feet apart, four or five to a hill with 4 to 5 inches between plants.

- **Sow seeds outdoors** 1 inch deep and 4 to 5 inches apart, six or seven to a hill, after night temperatures no longer fall below 50°F.

- **Thin** to the three strongest plants when they are 3 inches tall.

- **Fertilize** when plants begin to vine, scattering ¼ cup around each hill.

- **Water** during dry periods of over one week.

- **Pests and diseases** can be a problem, especially cucumber beetles, squash bugs, and vine borers, most of which can be controlled with pyrethrum. Keep area free of weeds and check undersides of leaves for eggs.

- **Harvest** summer squashes when they are small (zucchini is at its best when only slightly larger than a cigar) by twisting the stems off the plant. Look hard for the fruit, since overgrown ones will prevent the plant from setting new ones. Since the fruit grow very rapidly, plan to harvest every two to three days.

Selected Varieties

There are many excellent varieties of summer squash and only a few can be mentioned here. 'Yellow Crookneck,' 'Zucchini,' 'Sunburst,' and 'Pattypan' offer a variety of shapes and flavors in summer squash. 'Sakiz Zucchini' from Turkey is only 5 inches long at maturity and has a creamy white color. 'Butter Blossom' is specially bred for its abundance of large, highly flavored male blossoms for cooking.

SWEET POTATO

Botanical name: *Ipomoea batatas* (Convolvulaceae)

Strictly a warm climate crop, requiring a 150-day frost-free season, sweet potatoes are popular with both southern cooks and gardeners, where they have been a major crop since Colonial times. However, they are also popular among gardeners in the middle and border states. A native of Peru, the sweet potato has found its way throughout the world to become an important crop in places as widely separated as Japan and Africa. Sweet potatoes produce long, spreading vines and are started from sprouts or slips produced on the farm or purchased from commercial propagators. "Sprouts" are the new shoots pulled from the whole or sectioned thickened (edible) roots placed in nursery beds, while slips are the cut tips (usually 10 to 14 inches) from growing plants. Either can be set directly into the garden.

Both white and orange varieties of sweet potatoes are rich in carotene, and the orange ones are also rich in vitamin A, particularly if harvested late. They have about half the vitamin C of an orange, as well as calcium and iron. They may be baked, steamed, or fried in batter.

PLANT TYPE: Annual.
GROWING RANGE: Zones 4 to 11.
HARDINESS: Will not withstand frost; chill injury can occur at temperatures below 40° to 45°F.
SOIL: Any open, well-drained soil; likes sandy soil in northern climates.
PH: 5.2 to 6.7.
FERTILIZER: 5-10-10.
WATER: Requires very little.
EXPOSURE: Full sun.
SPACING: 12 to 15 inches, in rows 4 to 5 feet apart.

Method

- **Prepare soil outdoors** in the early spring, after night temperatures are not likely to drop below 60°F, by digging 5 to 8 inches deep and mixing in fertilizer at a rate of ¼ pound for each 10 feet. Make a mounded ridge along the row, about 6 inches high.

- **Set slips or sprouts** into the ridge so that 4 inches of each is buried and one or two leaves remain above the soil.

- **Fertilize** only during soil preparation.

- **Pests and diseases** are plentiful in the South, where sweet potatoes have grown for years. Crop rotation every four years, care in purchasing disease-free sprouts, and careful handling of sprouts and plants to avoid stress and injuries all help. Avoid overwatering, which encourages rot.

- **Harvest** by digging late in the fall in regions where frost does not kill the vines or after they have been killed in other regions. Where frost is slow to come, harvest before soil temperatures persist below 55°F. Allow potatoes to dry and cure for a few days in a warm, well-aerated place, handling them very gently, before storage. Success in storage can be increased by curing them for a week in a warm, shaded, open place. Store, spread out on layers of newspaper, in a dry area no colder than 50°F.

Selected Varieties

'Orange Jersey' and 'Nugget' have dry flesh; 'Georgia Jet,' 'Puerto Rico,' and 'Centennial' have moist flesh. The moist type is often called yam, although it is no relation to the several *Dioscorea* species that are the true yams of the tropics. 'Nancy Hall' is a favorite pale-colored, fine-textured sweet potato "yam" in the South; it is resistant to rot.

SWISS CHARD

Botanical name: *Beta vulgaris* var. *cicla* (Chenopodiaceae)

This relative of the beet is grown for its leaves and tender, mild-flavored white or burgundy-red stalks. These are usually separated from the rich green leafy portion that is cooked as a green. Unlike most greens, this one produces a steady crop over a long growing season. Chard is one of the easiest and most reliable green vegetables for the home gardener, performing well in a wide variety of soils and climates. If spared from fall plowing and left in the ground over the winter in mild climates, it will usually produce a very early crop the next spring, a welcome sight indeed to the gardener still busy protecting tender seedlings of other vegetables in his or her greenhouse!

PLANT TYPE: Annual.
GROWING RANGE: Zones 2 to 11.
HARDINESS: Withstands frost.
SOIL: Nearly any type is suitable.
PH: 6 to 7.5.
FERTILIZER: 5-10-5.
WATER: Moderate.
EXPOSURE: Full sun.
SPACING: 8 inches, in rows 2 feet or wider apart.

Method

- **Prepare soil outdoors** 8 to 12 inches deep as early in the spring as it can be worked, incorporating compost or other organic material to aid in moisture retention.

- **Sow seeds** ½ inch deep and about 4 inches apart as soon as ground can be worked in the spring.

- **Thin** seedlings when they are about 8 inches tall to permanent spacing, steaming the entire plants of the thinnings for a delicious spring green.

- **Fertilize** every four weeks by scattering fertilizer around the plants at a rate of ¼ pound for each 10 row feet.

- **Pests and diseases** are, happily, rare.

- **Harvest** by cutting off individual outer leaves near the ground with a sharp knife. The plant will continue to produce more.

Tip · Swiss chard grows well in containers for a patio garden, especially if a minivariety is selected. Sow directly into a pot or planter at least 12 inches wide and 12 to 18 inches deep. Water regularly, especially when the seedlings are small. Container plants perform well even if they are partially shaded during part of the day.

Selected Varieties

'Fordhook Giant' is the most popular variety of this old-fashioned vegetable, with deep green crinkly leaves and tasty white stems. Other white stem types are 'Lucullus' and 'Large White Rib.' 'Nihon' is a Japanese cultivar with thick stalks. 'Rhubarb Chard' has such attractive red-veined leaves that many prefer to plant it in their flower garden as a stunning background for shorter annuals. 'Italian Green' and 'Italian Red Chard,' available from Shepherds Seeds, is a miniature variety perfect for container gardens.

TOMATILLO

Botanical name: *Physalis ixocarpa* (Solanaceae)

A standby of Mexican cuisine, the tomatillo is easily grown as far north as New England. Like the ground cherry, a relative, the small fruit is encased in papery husks that are easily removed for cooking. It is the primary ingredient of salsa verde, and although it looks and even tastes a bit like a green tomato, the two are not interchangeable in cooking. The plant yields profusely, even in the North, doing well even in those seasons when tomatoes are disappointing in yield. To prepare for sauce, husk, wash, and simmer in very little water until just softened. Then liquefy in a blender. This may be frozen until needed. Freshly harvested tomatillos keep well for over a month if refrigerated promptly and kept in their husks.

PLANT TYPE: Annual.
GROWING RANGE: Zones 4 to 11.
HARDINESS: Plants will not withstand frost, but fruit on the vine will survive.
SOIL: Ordinary.
PH: 6 to 8.
FERTILIZER: 5-10-5.
WATER: Resists drought well.
EXPOSURE: Full sun.
SPACING: 12 to 18 inches, in rows 2 to 3 feet apart.

Method

- **Start seeds indoors** six weeks before the last expected spring frost.

- **Prepare soil outdoors** for direct seeding in mild climates when the danger of frost is past.

- **Sow seeds** thinly, about ½ inch deep, since germination rate is high.

- **Set plants outdoors** when all danger of frost is past. Shade plants from midday sun for a few days if the weather is hot, and keep well watered.

- **Thin** seedlings when plants stand 6 to 8 inches high.

- **Water** when soil is dry to a depth of 1 inch.

- **Fertilize** by side-dressing, only if soil is very poor, halfway through summer. Use ¼ cup per foot, at least 2 feet away from the base of the plant.

- **Pests and diseases** are rare, but newly set plants should be protected from cutworm attack with paper collars (see Broccoli, page 464).

- **Weed** early in the season, but the tomatillo's rapid growth and sprawling habits soon discourage the growth of surrounding weeds.

- **Harvest** when fruit fills husk but is still green. Leave in husks until ready to use. Leave a few mature fruit in the garden and plow them under. These will provide ample volunteer plants early the next spring, which may be transplanted into rows. They will be hardier and produce earlier than indoor-started plants.

TOMATO

Botanical name: *Lycopersicon lycopersicum* (Solanaceae)

Tomatoes, the most popular crop for home gardeners in all climates, have—possibly more than any other vegetable—fallen victim to mass marketing. Those varieties that can be kept the longest and that survive shipping best have won out over the juicy, tender varieties with more flavor. The home gardener has the luxury of choosing the most flavorful variety suitable for his own climate without regard to shipping problems. Tomatoes can be grouped into several categories such as the common slicers, the Italian or plum type, and the cherry types, but their horticultural requirements are the same.

PLANT TYPE: Annual.
GROWING RANGE: Zones 3 to 11.
HARDINESS: Will not withstand frost; requires warmth.
SOIL: Rich, with plenty of humus.
PH: 5.5 to 7.5.
FERTILIZER: 5-10-5.
WATER: Requires even watering while fruit is forming.
EXPOSURE: Full sun.
SPACING: Averages 24 inches apart, in rows 3 feet apart, but depends on vine size
of the variety chosen.

Method

- **Start seeds indoors** five to seven weeks before night temperatures stay above 60°F. Plant ⅛ to ¼ inch deep in flats, then transplant to individual pots when plants are 2 inches tall.

- **Prepare soil outdoors** deeply as soon as the ground can be worked in the spring. Scatter fertilizer at a rate of ½ pound to each 8 row feet and work it into the soil thoroughly.

- **Sow seeds** ½ inch deep directly into the garden as soon as night temperatures stay above 60°F. Plant in groups of three or four, spacing the groups about 2 feet apart.

- **Set** plants in the garden after all danger of frost is past. Protect newly set plants from cutworms by surrounding the stems with heavy paper collars (see Broccoli, page 464) until they have toughened.

- **Thin** all but the strongest one in each group when the plants are 2 or 3 inches tall.

- **Water** whenever soil is dry to the depth of an inch, especially while fruit is forming.

- **Fertilize** monthly by scratching in a cup of fertilizer around the base of the plants in a 2-foot diameter. Then water thoroughly to carry the fertilizer to the root system.

- **Pests and diseases** used to be more of a problem before the development of the now-abundant resistant varieties. There are many tomato diseases. Two of the most serious have been the fusarium and verticillium wilts. Some of the older varieties do not have resistance to these, and there is no other way to combat wilt. However, it may still be worth growing some of the old varieties just for their fine flavor, even at the risk of losing the plants. Blossom end rot, a serious fruit disease, can be controlled by covering the ground at the base of the plants with grass clippings or straw coupled with periodic long, slow, thorough watering. Also, you must avoid overfertilizing with nitrogen, especially the ammonia form.

- **Stake** or contain indeterminate varieties in wire tomato cages. These varieties continue to send up new shoots and set new fruit until the plant is killed by frost, hence their sprawling habit. After staking, pinch out new shoots when they are about 2 inches long to concentrate the plant's efforts on ripening the fruit that have already formed. Leave one or two shoots at or near the top of the plant.

- **Harvest** as tomatoes ripen. The harvest can be extended significantly by covering plants at night with old sheets, blankets, curtains, etc., when frost is expected and uncovering them again in the morning. A period of warm weather often follows the first series of killing frosts and the vines will have several weeks more harvest.

Tip · Most tomato varieties featured in seed catalogs have been bred not for commercial use but for direct fresh use. Choose varieties that can mature in your climate. Look also for the VF designation, indicating a high level of resistance to the wilts. Some varieties are now sold under a VFNT designation or possess two or three of these letters, which denote resistance to verticillium (wilt), fusarium (wilt), nematodes, and tomato mosaic virus.

Selected Varieties

Although early tomatoes tend to have less flavor, 'Sprint' is a sixty-day variety with excellent flavor. It is disease resistant and continues to bear for a long harvest, so northern gardeners should do well with it. 'Earlirouge' was developed in Canada for northern gardeners and is also a good choice.

Those of you who have not yet tried 'Celebrity,' an All-America Award Winner for 1984, should sample this very disease-resistant variety. Numerous older flavorful varieties bred for American home gardens are also available and many are favorites in one region or another. Although citing a few unintentionally ignores many good varieties, one must mention such varieties as 'Big Boy,' 'Fantastic,' 'Duke,' 'Sweet 100,' 'Springset,' and 'Spring Giant.'

'Heinz' is a good plum tomato that ripens early and has the thick flesh and rich flavor needed for canning and cooking, and 'Bellstar' is another slightly later Italian type. 'Washington Cherry' is a good cherry tomato, as is 'Camp Joy,' which has an even better flavor. Both continue to produce over a long season.

TURNIP AND RUTABAGA

Botanical names: *Brassica rapa* (turnip); *B. napobrassica* (rutabaga) (Cruciferae)

Although much maligned, the turnip is a staple food of much of central Europe. Turnips and rutabagas (called Swede turnip in Canada) do best in cool weather, producing well nearly anywhere north of the Mason-Dixon Line. Their culture is almost identical, but rutabagas keep well over the winter, whereas turnips do not. Rutabagas are larger at maturity and have yellow flesh; turnips are small and white. Either is good cooked or raw. Turnip greens are good cooked, but rutabaga greens are not. White turnips may be grated raw and tossed with dill, white vinegar, and oil for a delicious salad. A little nutmeg enhances the flavor of cooked rutabaga.

PLANT TYPE: Annual.
GROWING RANGE: Zones 3 to 11.
HARDINESS: Withstands frost and heat.
SOIL: Ordinary.

PH: 5.5 to 7.

FERTILIZER: 5-10-5.

WATER: Requires even moisture.

EXPOSURE: Full sun.

SPACING: Turnip 2 to 4 inches apart, in rows 1 to 2 feet apart; rutabaga 6 to 8 inches
apart, in rows 2 to 2½ feet apart.

Method

- **Prepare soil outdoors** deeply as soon as ground can be worked in the spring. Select a site free of stones and other coarse debris.

- **Sow seeds** ½ inch deep in groups of three or four, spaced as noted above. Continue planting at two-week intervals in the North until three months before night temperatures can be expected to go below 20°F on a regular basis. In the South, start successive plantings in late summer for winter and early-spring harvest. The rutabaga probably will need more time to mature.

- **Thin** to the best plant in each group as soon as seedlings are 2 inches tall.

- **Water** after dry spells of a week.

- **Fertilize** when plants are 4 inches tall, scattering a 6-inch band at one side of the plant at the rate of ¼ pound to 10 row feet.

- **Pests and diseases** are few, but root maggots may be a problem. Covering the seedlings with floating row covers may help to prevent these, as will soaking the ground with diazinon solution before planting. Soft brown spots inside rutabagas indicate a deficiency of boron in the soil, which may be corrected with an application of agricultural borax.

- **Harvest** turnips when they are 2 inches in diameter, rutabagas at 4 to 5 inches. Grasp the tops as near to the base as possible and pull sharply to free root from soil. Turnips keep for a few weeks in the refrigerator, but rutabagas will keep for five or six months if stored at near-freezing temperatures and high humidity.

Selected Varieties

'American Yellow,' 'American Purple Top,' 'Laurentian,' and 'Pike' are good rutabagas. 'Purple-Top White Globe' is a popular turnip, as is 'Tokyo Cross,' a very early variety that matures in only thirty-five days, and 'Just Right,' a white hybrid cultivar. 'Gilfeather' is an extra-sweet, egg-shaped turnip that is especially good eaten raw.

WATERCRESS

Botanical name: *Nasturtium officinale* (Cruciferae)

A native of Europe and western Asia, watercress's Latin name *officinale* derives from its use as a cure for every ailment from baldness to scurvy. It was effective, at least for the latter, since it is very rich in vitamin C, as well as in vitamin A and calcium. Once established, watercress is a perennial. The best place to grow this plant is in the margin of a slow-moving brook, but adventurous gardeners without a handy stream will want to try making their own watercress bed.

PLANT TYPE: Perennial.
GROWING RANGE: Zones 3 to 11.
HARDINESS: Will withstand frost.
SOIL: Rich and exceedingly wet.
PH: 6 to 8.
FERTILIZER: 5-10-5 in liquid form, or fish emulsion.
WATER: They grow in water.
EXPOSURE: Shade or partial shade.
SPACING: 6 inches.

 *Method*

· **Prepare soil** for a watercress bed by making a 6-inch-deep basin, flat on the bottom, and lining it with sheet plastic. Punch a few holes in the lowest points to allow for some drainage, since you don't want the water to become stagnant. Fill with peat moss and potting soil mixed with wood ashes and soak it thoroughly.

· **Sow seeds** by scattering and covering with a fine layer of soil in a prepared bed or by scattering them along the edge of a slow-moving stream after the rush of spring runoff.

· **Thin** to about 6 inches if plants appear crowded.

· **Water** prepared bed frequently to maintain water level as plants grow.

· **Fertilize** bed-grown plants with fish emulsion several times during the season.

· **Harvest** every fifteen to twenty days to keep leaves tender and mild flavored.

WINTER SQUASH

Botanical names: *Cucurbita maxima, C. moschata,* and *C. pepo* (Cucurbitaceae)

Although the culinary characteristics of summer and winter squashes are quite different, the gardener treats them much the same. Winter squashes have a more dense orange flesh and hard skins (called *rinds*), which are not eaten. These characteristics make them ideal for winter storage. Most are vining plants, but there are bush varieties of winter squash as well. The vines tend to be quite long and sprawling, so it is a good idea to plant these toward the edge of a garden where they can sprawl. They are planted in hills, or groups.

PLANT TYPE: Annual.
GROWING RANGE: Zones 4 to 11.
HARDINESS: Will not withstand frost; heat resistant.
SOIL: Light, ordinary, well drained.
PH: 6 to 7.5.
FERTILIZER: 5-10-5.
WATER: Requires even moisture.

EXPOSURE: Full sun; will tolerate some shade.
SPACING: Bush, 4 by 4 feet; vine, 8 by 8 feet.

Method

- **Start seeds indoors** in very cold climates for an early start, four weeks before last frost is expected. Use peat pots to avoid disturbing roots during transplanting. Keep soil warm; squash will not germinate at temperatures below 60° to 70°F.

- **Prepare soil outdoors** deeply, digging a hole 18 inches deep and filling it with well-rotted cow manure mixed with garden soil.

- **Set** plants in the garden as soon as the danger of frost is past, planting in hills, or groups, of four or five.

- **Sow seeds outdoors** 1 inch deep, six or seven to a hill, after night temperatures no longer fall below 50°F.

- **Thin** to the three strongest plants when seedlings are 3 inches tall.

- **Fertilize** when plants begin to vine, scattering ¼ cup around each hill.

- **Water** when soil becomes dry to 1 inch.

- **Pests and diseases** can be a problem, especially cucumber beetles, squash bugs, and vine borers, most of which can be controlled with pyrethrum. Keep area free of weeds and check undersides of leaves for eggs. To prevent blossom end rot, increase the calcium in the soil with bonemeal or crushed eggshells, scratching them into the soil near the base of the plants at a rate of ½ cup per hill. When watering, keep the water near the base of the plants. Let the water run slowly for thorough irrigation.

- **Harvest** before heavy frost, cutting stems about an inch from the squash. Leave squash in the field for at least a week to cure, covering at night to protect from frost, or remove them to a warm, airy space. If the squash are frost-bitten, they will not store well. Wash cured squash in a weak bleach solution before storing to prevent rot. Stored in a cool (60° to 65°F), dry atmosphere, squash will keep for several months.

Selected Varieties

'Waltham' and 'Ponca' are good choices for butternut squash, with firm texture and good flavor. They are also known for their small seed cavities and thick necks. 'Zenith' is a new extra-early butternut, ready two weeks before any others and yielding heavy crops. 'Acorn,' 'Blue Hubbard' (often weighing 15 to 20 pounds), and 'Buttercup' are all good baking squashes. These three are available in different strains that may differ greatly in quality—know your source as a seed buyer. 'Red Kuri,' also called 'Orange Hokkaido,' has a rich color and especially smooth texture. 'Mountaineer' is a small Blue Hubbard developed in Montana for high altitude and short season gardens. 'Chestnut' is a sweet, dry-fleshed squash and 'Golden Nugget' is a bush variety good for small gardens, where the vining varieties above would take up too much room. Many novelty squashes differing in shape and/or color and texture from the old standards have become available in recent years. 'Sweet Dumpling,' 'Delicata,' and 'Vegetable Spaghetti' are examples.

FRUITS

BLACKBERRY

Botanical Name: *Rubus* (Rosaceae)

Eating fresh blackberries is such a treat that they might never make it into the kitchen and into great-tasting jams, jellies, pies, and wine! They also freeze easily, making it easy to serve them all year long. Blackberries have three basic growth forms: plants with erect canes that look more like red raspberries, semi-erect canes that grow like bushes and are similar in form to black raspberries, and trailing canes that grow like vines. A few varieties lack thorny canes, but most are thorny. The canes grow from the base of the plant, or from root suckers in the case of erect types, in one year, produce fruit the next summer, and then die in the fall.

PLANT TYPE: Perennial.
GROWING RANGE: Zones 4 to 10 for erect-growing blackberries and Zones 5 and 6 (though, depending on the variety, range may extend up to Zone 10) for semitrailing or trailing vines.
HARDINESS: Erect varieties and adequately protected trailing varieties are hardy to −30°F; unprotected trailing varieties are hardy only to −10°F.
CHILL REQUIREMENT: 100 to 600 hours at 45°F or below to break dormancy, depending on variety.
SOIL: Well-drained loam.
PH: 5.8 to 6.6 (slightly acid).
FERTILIZER: Well-rotted cow or steer manure or 10-10-10 fertilizer.
WATER: Requires moderate amount of water. Avoid standing water.
EXPOSURE: Full sun.
SPACING: 4 to 5 feet, in rows 8 to 9 feet apart for erect forms; 6 to 10 feet, in rows 8 to 9 feet apart for trailing and semitrailing forms that have longer canes.
TIME TILL BEARING: 2 years till first crop but 3 or more for full production.

YIELD: Over 25 pounds per plant to less than 8 pounds, depending on variety and spacing.

PROPAGATION: Tip layering

🍓 *Method*

- **Prepare soil** by digging or tilling to a depth of 1 foot. If organic matter is needed, mix your soil with liberal amounts of compost for planting preparation. Add equal parts of compost or sand to clay soils in the planting area (1 foot deep and 2 feet wide the length of your row) to lighten and increase the drainage. Add compost at the same rate to light sandy soils to increase its water-holding capacity. Prepare holes about 8 inches deep and 8 to 12 inches wide for each plant.

- **Plant** in early spring by spreading the roots in the hole and then covering with dirt. Bury the stem to the same depth it was in the nursery, generally indicated by a brown line on the stem. Water each plant to settle the soil around the roots.

- **Mulch,** if desired, using light compost, rotted sawdust, or peat moss 3 inches thick around the plants and on walkways next to plants. Renew this layer every spring.

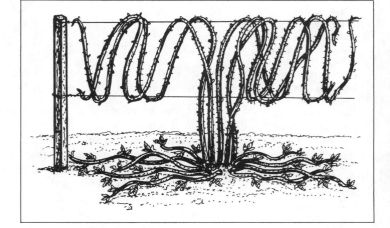

- **Trellis** your trailing and semitrailing varieties whose canes are longer than 4 feet to support the vines and increase yields. In mild-winter areas where temperatures seldom dip below 10°F, trellis the canes in August after planting. In areas with colder winters, the canes should be trellised in the early spring after being mulched during the winter. Use a wire trellis supported by sturdy 4- by 4-inch or larger end wooden posts set so that 4½ to 6 feet shows aboveground. Place lighter posts 20 feet apart in the row. Attach two wires, one to the top of each post and the other 18 inches below the top wire. Spiral the canes over the top wire, under the bottom wire, and so forth until the cane has been supported totally—these canes can be over 20 feet in length. Train half the plant in each direction. Spread the canes so that they don't shade each other. Each spring new canes will sprout from the base of the plant and grow along the ground; trellis these in August after pruning out the harvested trellised canes or do it in the spring. Trellis erect blackberries to a hedgerow. A two-wire trellis, one on each side of the row, at the height of 3 to 5 feet, will prevent canes from bending into the aisles.

- **Water** using drip or sprinkle irrigation when the top inch of soil is dry. Berries will require less water on a regular basis if mulched and watered by a drip irrigation system.

- **Fertilize** in the early spring by spreading ⅓ to ½ pound of well-rotted steer or cow

Early in the spring, blackberry canes that bore fruit the year before are spiraled on trellis wires, while canes that will bear fruit this coming season are on the ground. To train, cut last year's canes at the base of the plant and remove them from the wires. Carefully spiral the canes that were on the ground around the trellis wires and space them in such a way that they do not shade one another.

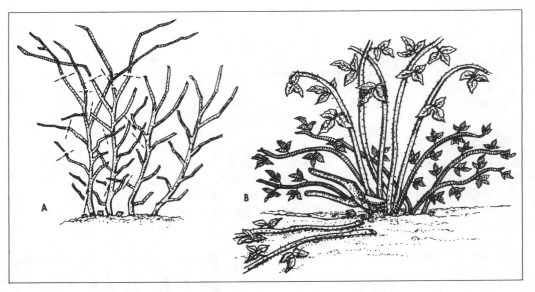

A. Erect blackberries are pruned differently during each of the first two growing seasons. The positions of the cuts are indicated by the dotted lines. During the middle of the first growing season, prune back first-year canes to 3 feet, as shown at the top of the plants. Early in the following spring, before leafing out, cut back the longer laterals to 12 to 18 inches long. Thin hedge-grown plants to one large cane for each 5 inches of row, cutting the canes at the base of the plant.

B. Prune trailing blackberries in August by cutting out the thinnest canes and leaving six to twelve of the thickest, healthiest canes for each plant.

manure or 10-10-10 per 20 row feet on the soil between the canes. Blackberries that are grown in too much nitrogen will be slow to ripen.

- **Prune** old fruiting canes of all types as soon as you've harvested their fruit by cutting them off at the base.

  In erect blackberries, prune the canes in their first growing season to 3 feet, encouraging the production of side branches that will bear fruit the following season. In the spring of the second growing season, when the canes are still dormant, prune these laterals back to 12 to 18 inches (this increases the size of the berries). If you have the plants growing in a hedgerow, thin canes to one large cane per every 5 inches in the row.

  For trailing varieties, cut out the thin canes, leaving the healthiest six to twelve canes in August as you trellis. For harsh winter areas, thin canes in the spring as you trellis. If the berries are small in the trailing varieties, cut back the side branches to 15 inches in the spring before summer fruit-bearing.

- **Pest and disease** prevention starts with planting certified disease-free plants away from any wild blackberries or raspberries and planting them in soil that has not grown potato family members (tomatoes, peppers, potatoes, and eggplants) or strawberries during the last two years to prevent verticillium wilt infection.

  Orange rust is a common fungal disease of blackberries and is easily identified by the bright yellow pustules covering the undersides of leaves. There is no cure, and infected plants should be removed promptly. Remove any wild blackberries nearby that may be a source of infection.

- **Propagate** blackberries in the spring after new growth begins by bending first-year canes to the soil and burying the tip about 4 inches deep. At the end of the summer, by which time the tip will have sprouted roots, cut the cane 1 to 1½ feet from the ground, dig up the sprouted tip, and transplant to a new location.

- **Harvest** when berries are ripe; most blackberries are fully black when ripe and need a little pull to be removed. Taste the berries to determine what berry color is best for maximum sweetness.

- **Winter protection.** Trailing varieties can be coaxed through harsh winters by covering the canes with a 1-foot layer of mulch as soon as the leaves drop off the canes in the fall. Remove the mulch in early spring. There is no successful way to winter-protect upright blackberries as the canes are too stiff to lay on the ground. Select hardy varieties for best winter survival and plant in an area that is protected from winter wind.

Selected Varieties

(*Rubus* species and hybrids)

Erect:

'Thornfree Blackberry' is a thornless cultivar well adapted to the South. 'Cheyenne' is an early-producing erect type. Berries are very large, firm, and attractive, with excellent flavor. Bushes are vigorous and thorny. 'Chester Thornless,' a thornless semi-erect cultivar, is more adapted to the North and can withstand winter temperatures in Zone 5. Fruit are produced later than most varieties. Berries are medium-size, with good flavor. 'Hull Thornless' is a semi-erect, midseason to late-season cultivar. Berries are large, firm with good flavor. 'Darrow Blackberry' is an old-favorite erect blackberry developed in Geneva, New York. This is adapted to survive in Zones 4 to 6.

Trailing:

'Waldo,' a thornless variety well adapted to the West Coast, is truly thornless and won't have thorns on root suckers either. It produces about midseason, and berries are medium-size, glossy, black, and firm. The flavor is mild, but good. Canes are low in vigor so plant 4 feet apart in the row. 'Loganberry' is a hybrid between the raspberry and blackberry, but the berry separates at the base, as do most blackberries. The berry color is a dark red rather than the deep purple of most other blackberries. There is a thornless loganberry as well as the thorny original. Although these plants do not produce large yields, the berries are large and less sweet than most blackberries. They are especially good in pies. 'Boysenberry' is a hybrid between a loganberry and a trailing blackberry. The fruit is deep purple and can be up to 2 inches long. Berries are soft, but have a very distinctive flavor. Canes are thorny. 'Marionberries,' a well-adapted western trailing blackberry, abundantly produces medium to large berries with better flavor than most trailing varieties. Canes are thorny. 'Tayberries,' a trailing loganberry-raspberry hybrid, has very large red or reddish-black berries that have slightly less acid than the loganberry. Canes are thorny.

Check your local nurseries for varieties adapted to your region and ripening times.

BLUEBERRY

Botanical name: *Vaccinium* (Ericaceae)

Fresh, ripe blueberries have a wonderful sweet-tart flavor and can be used in jellies, pies, pancakes, and many other delicious baked goods. These berries are also easy to freeze. Blueberries come in two commercially available forms, highbush *(Vaccinium corymbosum)* and rabbit-eye *(V. ashei).* The highbush varieties (2 to 6 feet tall) can be grown over most of the United States except the Deep South, but the rabbit-eye varieties (6 to 12 feet tall) must be grown in the Deep South. Use highbush blueberries in your landscaping plans to provide vivid red or yellow leaf color in the fall.

PLANT TYPE: Perennial.

GROWING RANGE: Zones 4 to 8 for highbush blueberry and Zones 7 to 10 for rabbit-eye varieties needing warmer winters.

HARDINESS: Cold hardy to as low as −35°F for some highbush varieties, and as low as −16°F for certain rabbit-eye varieties.

CHILL REQUIREMENT: 800 to 1400 hours at −45°F for hardier highbush varieties; 260 to 600 hours for rabbit-eye blueberries.

SOIL: Light, well-drained, easily penetrated soil such as a peat, sandy, or loam soil that is high in organic material.

PH: Acid. 4.5 to 5 for highbush blueberries, 4.5 to 5.5 for rabbit-eye blueberries. Yellow leaves on new growth are often a sign that the pH level is too high.

FERTILIZER: For highbush blueberries, none the first year of planting. In the following years, ammonium sulfate or rotted manure. To both fertilize and make the soil more acid in one step, use a commercial acid fertilizer such as Miracid as recommended on the box. Do not feed rabbit-eye blueberries unless the leaves turn yellow.

WATER: Moist soil conditions, but no standing water or flooding.

EXPOSURE: Full sun.

SPACING: 4 to 6 feet, in rows 10 feet apart for highbush varieties. Allow a 5-foot-square area for rabbit-eye blueberries or, if planting them in rows, allow 10 to 12 feet between rows and 5 to 6 feet between the bushes.

TIME TILL BEARING: 4 to 6 years for highbush varieties. Rabbit-eye take 3 or 4 years to reach full production.

YIELD: The yield of highbush varieties varies from 4 to 8 pints per plant to 25 pints for a plant grown under ideal conditions. Rabbit-eye blueberries are larger plants and produce up to 30 pints per plant.

PROPAGATION: Stem cuttings.

🍓 *Method*

· **Prepare soil** in the early spring by digging an 8-inch-deep, 2-foot-square hole. Add sulfur at the rate of 1 pound per 100 square feet to reduce the pH of the soil, if necessary, from 5.5 to 4.5 in a light sandy soil, even more sulfur for heavier loam soil. Another way to lower the pH is to mix equal parts of acid peat moss with your soil before planting and then add an extra 3 to 6 inches of peat moss around the base of the plant in the spring of each year to help keep the soil acid. Fertilizing with ammonium sulfate fertilizer will also gradually lower the pH, if the acid peat moss is not sufficient.

· **Plant** by using this mixture to fill in the hole so that the roots are only about 1 inch below the soil level. Spread the roots out and cover with the rest of the soil. Water the plant and gently press the soil around it.

· **Mulch** after the first year with a 3- to 6-inch layer of peat moss, pine straw, sawdust, or any other loose acid organic material.

- **Water** plants frequently so that the soil around their roots is constantly wet but not standing in water. Blueberries do well with drip irrigation, but also can be sprinkle irrigated if the soil moisture is maintained.

- **Fertilize** highbush blueberries in the early spring of the second year before the plants leaf out, with ¼ pound of ammonium sulfate per plant or a 1-inch layer of well-rotted manure around the dripline of the plant (the dripline is the circumference of the plant, as described by the place on the ground where water drips off the outermost leaves). Add peat moss mulch in place of fertilizer to rabbit-eye blueberries in the early spring.

- **Prune** any broken or dead canes from newly planted highbush blueberries. Other than this, blueberries require no pruning until their third year in your garden. Fruit is produced on the past season's growth. After the third year, prune out older canes that are highly branched (twiggy) as they will only produce small berries. Remove these canes either at the base of the plant or, if there is little new growth on the plant, cut the cane back to an unbranched part. Prune to leave thicker or stouter branches, as they will produce larger berries than thin branches.

  Prune rabbit-eye blueberry bushes to 4 to 6 inches at planting. Remove any weak shoots and flower buds at this time. For the first two to six years, cut out the twiggy or weak lower growth and any dead or damaged shoots in the dormant season. After this, prune to open up the bushes to sunlight by removing older canes from the interior of the bush and trim the remaining canes to picking height.

- **Winter protection** can be achieved by piling snow around the base of highbush plants in areas with below zero temperatures.

Tips · If possible, buy two-year-old plants in pots. Otherwise, order two-year-old plants from the nursery—they will most likely come bare-rooted.

· For the best-tasting pies and jams as well as improved pollination and larger berry size, order several blueberry varieties.

· Never leave bare-rooted plants immersed in water longer than twenty-four hours or you will drown them.

· For easy maintenance of acid soil, grow plants next to other acid-loving plants such as azaleas and rhododendrons.

- **Pests and diseases** are not often a problem with these berries. Mummy berry is a fungal disease indigenous to the Pacific Northwest and can be recognized by a hardening of the berry that drops to the ground and in the spring reinfects new blossoms. Control this disease by cleaning up all fallen berries and using fungicides in the early spring.

  Birds may be the worst pest as they can literally strip your bushes of all ripe fruit. The easiest prevention is to cover the bushes with nets after the berries begin to turn color.

- **Propagation.** By misted stem cuttings.

- **Harvest.** Blueberries ripen over a period of a month to six weeks. Plan to pick at least twice a week during the harvest time. Don't use a dark blue color to judge ripeness, as the berries turn color before ripening. Just pick them by lightly touching the berry—if there is any resistance, then they aren't ripe. For the best keeping quality, pick the berries directly into the container used to store them in the refrigerator or freezer.

Selected Varieties

Highbush *(Vaccinium corymbosum)*
'Bluecrop' is a medium-large, light blue, firm blueberry that ripens midseason. The flavor is best when the berry is picked fully ripe. 'Blueray,' bearing very large light blue berries on productive bushes, ripens early-midseason and has an excellent flavor. 'Herbert' is a very large medium blue, moderately firm blueberry that grows on vigorous plants. It ripens late-midseason and also has good flavor. 'Berkeley,' bearing very large light blue berries with a mild flavor, ripens in midseason. 'Northsky' is a dwarf, 18-inch-high blueberry that produces only 1 to 2 pounds of fruit a year. It is one of the most cold-hardy varieties and can withstand temperatures to −40°F. The fruit are medium-size, light blue with good flavor. 'Northblue,' a 2-foot-tall blueberry, is also very winter hardy and survives temperatures to −22°F. This bush produces up to 7 pounds of large dark blue, firm blueberries per bush. Its fruit has a "wild" taste. 'Northland' is a cold-hardy 4-foot-tall bush that produces very sweet, medium-size berries.

Rabbit-eye *(V. ashei)*
'Tifblue' has sweet, medium-large berries on very productive bushes. 'Woodward' features aromatic, delicious berries on productive bushes. Use this variety to pollinate 'Tifblue.' Check local nurseries for varieties adapted to your region and ripening times.

CRANBERRY

Botanical name: *Vaccinium macrocarpon* (Ericaceae)

The tangy red berries we associate with turkey dinners are the smallest and strangest members of the blueberry family. Over thousands of years they evolved to fit into a special ecological niche—the acid bogs of northern maritime climates. The trailing woody stems of cranberries entwine to form a mat of foliage, and berries are produced on upright shoots that emerge in spring. Since cranberries lack the root hairs typical of plants that grow in soil, they grow best when planted in places that can be flooded periodically, or places that flood naturally in fall and stay covered with water all winter. Fresh cranberries are very high in vitamin C and can be used in cakes and muffins, as well as in cranberry relish.

PLANT TYPE: Perennial.

GROWING RANGE: Zones 2 to 6.

HARDINESS: With wind protection, cranberries are cold tolerant, to −20°F, but not very heat tolerant. Fruit quality suffers and pest problems increase when cranberries are subjected to summer temperatures above 85°F.

CHILL REQUIREMENT: High; about 2500 hours below 45°F.

SOIL: Peat bog or leafy swamp bottom, covered by 3 inches of sand.

PH: 4 to 5 (acidic). If the pH is too high (not acid enough), plants will not grow, and weeds may become a serious problem.

FERTILIZER: Nitrogen fertilizer, but none is required after first year. Too much fertilizer can result in berries of poor quality.

WATER: Requires frequent, heavy watering.

EXPOSURE: Full sun.

SPACING: Set pairs of vine cuttings 10 inches apart. Within three years they will run together and form a tangle of woody stems.

TIME TILL BEARING: 3 years, with full production after 6 years. Cranberries are self-propagating and can be expected to produce for 50 years or more.

YIELD: About 6 quarts from a mature 4-by-12-foot bed annually.

PROPAGATION: Tip cuttings.

🍓 Method

· **Prepare soil** by eliminating weeds in the planting site. The "soil" should be a layer of peat, sphagnum moss, or leaf mold at least 1 foot deep, topped by 3 inches of sand. Dig a trench around the planting so you will be able to flood and drain it quickly. Soil from the trench can be used to build a dike around the planting. The dike, which holds water in while providing wind protection, should be at least 8 inches high, with a "drain" at the low end, such as sturdy boards held in place with large stones. Small beds can be enclosed with wide boards instead of earthen dikes.

· **Plant** in early spring, just after the last frost, by pressing stem cuttings into the sand so that the bottom ends are planted in peat and 1 inch of the tips is exposed.

· **Water** immediately after planting until the bed holds 2 inches of water. If the water is still standing two days later it may be drained off, but the sand should remain moist at all times. In warm weather, water twice a week, but avoid flooding the bed.

· **Fertilize** lightly with a nitrogen fertilizer in June or July of the first year to encourage strong, fast growth. After the bed is established and growing well, supplemental fertilizer is rarely needed.

· **Pests and diseases** include several insects and a few fungal and viral diseases, all of which can be controlled by flooding the planting for one day after fruit set has occurred, or up to three weeks after harvest.

· **Pruning** is not necessary with cranberries, but diseased plants should be removed when they are noticed.

· **Winter protection,** necessary in the Northeast, consists of flooding the planting as soon as the ground begins to freeze. In spring and fall, blankets or thin sheets of canvas may be spread over the bed to protect tender new growth, flowers, or underripe berries from sudden frosts.

· **Harvest** in the fall, when the outsides of the berries turn red, but before they lose their crisp texture and show red color inside the berries.

· **Propagation.** Take 3- to 4-inch cuttings from established plants in early spring. Plant them immediately in a prepared site.

Tips • Since special facilities are needed to keep cranberry plants healthy, they are seldom sold by major nurseries. In places where cranberries are grown commercially, fresh cuttings can often be obtained at local garden supply stores or from owners of cranberry bogs.

• Freeze cranberries, storing them in small batches for later use. Fresh, unblemished cranberries can be stored in the refrigerator for several weeks.

Selected Varieties

Selection is usually limited to four or five cultivars, and only one variety should be planted in a site. Listed by the regions in which they are best adapted, the most widely grown varieties are as follows:

New England: 'Early Black,' which features a deep red color and ripens early. 'Howes,' a later-maturing plant, stores well. 'Beckwith' has large berries and a good flavor.

Upper Midwest: 'Searles Jumbo' is a very productive midseason producer with large berries. 'McFarlin' is late producing with frost-resistant dark red berries of oblong, irregular shape.

Pacific Northwest: 'Crowley,' a very early-producing variety, is an improved 'McFarlin.' 'Stevens' is an early producer and features glossy dark red berries. 'Searles' is the same as 'Searles Jumbo.'

CURRANT

Botanical name: *Ribes* (Saxifragaceae)

Currants are quite popular in Europe and the USSR, but they have had several problems establishing themselves in North America. In the 1920s it was determined that the currants introduced from Europe played a role in the spread of a devastating forest disease called white pine blister rust. Many states passed laws prohibiting the culture of currants, but scientists have since found that only black currants are deserving of blame for the spread of the disease. Plant breeders in Ottawa, Ontario, have introduced several black currant varieties that are rust resistant, but shipment to some areas is still restricted. As garden plants, currants grow into lovely fruit-bearing hedges. The tart berries are very high in vitamin C, and make excellent jam and juice. Unpicked currants are enjoyed by many birds and small animals.

PLANT TYPE: Perennial.

GROWING RANGE: Zones 3 to 5.

HARDINESS: Very cold tolerant, and will tolerate temperatures above 90°F if roots are protected by a cooling mulch.

CHILL REQUIREMENT: 3 months of winter dormancy.

SOIL: Moist, fertile soil with plenty of organic matter added.

PH: 5.5 to 6.5 (slightly acid to neutral).

FERTILIZER: Currants' shallow roots make best use of organic soil amendments, such as stable litter, compost, and bonemeal.

WATER: Cannot tolerate dry soil. Water weekly during droughts.

EXPOSURE: Almost-full sun or partial shade. When grown in part shade, good air circulation is crucial to prevent mildew.

SPACING: 4 feet apart for red and white currants, and 5 feet for black currants. The rows should be at least 8 feet apart.

TIME TILL BEARING: 2 years, with full yield when plants are 5 to 7 years old.

YIELD: Up to 4 quarts per mature bush annually.

PROPAGATION: Stem cuttings.

🍓 *Method*

- **Prepare soil** by digging in plenty of organic matter such as compost, rotted manure, or peat moss.

- **Plant** stock promptly. Currants may be planted very early in the spring, but early-fall planting is preferred since the plants break dormancy very early, often in late winter. Press soil firmly around the roots until the plants are a little deeper than they grew at the nursery (which is generally indicated by a brown line on the stem).

- **Water** immediately after planting, and as needed to maintain even soil moisture throughout the first growing season. Supplemental water is needed only during periods of extremely dry weather.

- **Mulch** with a 3-inch layer of sawdust, weathered hay, leaves, or another organic mulch, and keep the mulch pulled back 2 inches from the canes.

- **Fertilize** each spring by raking back the mulch and blanketing the area beneath the bushes with a 1-inch layer of compost or manure, and sprinkle on ½ cup of bonemeal per bush. Then replace the mulch.

- **Prune** in late winter to early spring while the plants are dormant. Cut off branches that lie close to the ground, and all canes that are weak or broken, by cutting them off at ground level. Next, remove canes that are more than three years old, for they will bear inferior fruit and may harbor pests. Old, removable canes will look brittle, and may show splits and discolored patches on the bark. Keep a total of ten to twelve canes per mature bush.

- **Pests and diseases** can be serious problems if plants do not receive proper care. They include currant borers (a small yellowish larva), aphids, and four-lined plant bugs. If necessary, cut out limbs that become infested with the currant borer in midsummer and burn them. Infected shoots may leaf out late and die. Currant aphids and the four-lined plant bug can often be controlled with soap sprays applied every two weeks from midspring onward. If the insects are persistent, use rotenone (a low-toxicity pesticide) to get them under control.

  Remove mildewed branches to limit the spread of the disease, and prune to keep the growth habit of the bushes open so air can move freely through the leaves.

  Currants that are not resistant to white pine blister rust act as hosts for the disease, though they seldom become seriously damaged by it.

- **Winter protection** is unnecessary, especially if the plants are mulched year-round. Mice may attempt to nest in the mulch in winter, so keep the material pulled away from the canes.

- **Harvest** in summer, when the fruits are well colored and begin to soften a bit, for they do not become sweet until they are fully ripe. Pick when the berries are dry by gently stripping the fruit from individual clusters.

- **Propagation:** Nurseries propagate currants by rooting 8-inch-long cuttings taken in late winter and rooted in sand. If only a few plants are desired, layer stems by bending the tips to the ground, cover with 2 inches of soil, and hold in place with a board or stone until new roots develop.

Tips · **Order one-year-old plants.**
· If you live in the northern Appalachians, check with your extension service before ordering plants to make sure there are no legal restrictions on their culture.
· Currants will last in your refrigerator for about three weeks. They do not have enough moisture in them to freeze well. Currant juice can be mixed with light juices, like apple, or can be used to darken the color of wine.

Selected Varieties

Red currants *(Ribes sativum):* 'Red Lake' and 'Wilder' have large, red, tart fruit and are vigorous, productive, highly resistant to white pine blister rust, and moderately resistant to mildew. 'Cascade' has large red fruit that ripens earlier than 'Red Lake.' 'Stephens' has very large fruit of excellent quality, and plants are very hardy.

White currants *(R. sativum)* are a color variation of the red species, and include the 'White Dutch' and 'White Imperial' varieties.

Black currants *(R. nigrum):* 'Consort,' 'Crusader,' and 'Coronet' are the most rust-resistant black currant cultivars.

Plant more than one variety to help stretch the harvest season, for all currants do not bear at exactly the same time.

ELDERBERRY

Botanical name: *Sambucus canadensis* (Caprifoliaceae)

Elderberries were one of the first native American fruits tasted by early settlers, who quickly learned how to make them into wine, jam, and vitamin-rich health tonics. Today many gardeners enjoy not only elderberry wines and jellies, but also elderberry flowers, which are often dipped in batter and fried. The shrubby, thornless stalks leaf out in spring. Showy white flowers appear in early summer, followed by umbrella-shaped clusters of dark purple berries. The fast-growing bushes may reach 6 feet in height by midsummer. Elderberries multiply by means of seeds and creeping underground stems, and are ideal for woodland border areas where their vigorous growth will not crowd other cultivated plants.

PLANT TYPE: Perennial.
GROWING RANGE: Zones 2 to 8. Elderberries are not adapted to elevations above
8000 feet.

HARDINESS: Elderberries are extremely tolerant of both heat and cold, from $-20°$ to 105°F.

CHILL REQUIREMENT: None.

SOIL: Elderberries adapt to a wide range of soils, but prefer a well-drained clay loam.

PH: 5.5 to 7 (slightly acid to neutral).

FERTILIZER: Rotted compost or manure, or 6-12-12—but only if plants lack vigor. Not generally required for small-fruited varieties.

WATER: Tolerates drought well, but supplemental water can help improve fruit size during an unusually dry summer.

EXPOSURE: Full sun or partial shade.

SPACING: 3 to 6 feet. Within 2 years plants will spread into a bushy hedge.

TIME TILL BEARING: Elderberries bear annually after their first year.

YIELD: 15 pounds of cleaned berries per mature bush annually.

PROPAGATION: Seed or division.

🍓 *Method*

- **Prepare soil** by digging out large rocks and clumps of weeds. Dig planting holes large enough to accommodate the roots when spread out. Break up compacted soil as you dig.

- **Plant** elderberries in early spring, just before the last frost, deep enough so that the roots stretch from 3 to 6 inches below the soil's surface.

- **Water** after planting, and thereafter as needed, until plants are growing vigorously. It is seldom necessary to water mature plants.

- **Mulch** around young elderberries with a 3-inch-deep layer of leaves or sawdust to control weeds and retain soil moisture.

- **Fertilize** in winter when plants are dormant with a 1-inch layer of rotted compost or manure to ensure vigor, especially when growing large-fruited varieties. Or apply 6-12-12 at a rate of ½ pound per year of age of the plant (limit of 6 pounds per plant) in early spring.

- **Prune** out old canes in late winter to early spring to improve the appearance of the bushes and to control the size of the planting. Reduce vigorous plants to five or six 1-year-old canes and one or two 2-year-old canes. Remove any unwanted suckers that formed between plants.

- **Pests and diseases** are few. Birds like to eat the fruits. Viral diseases have been identified in isolated areas, but rarely cause problems in home gardens.

- **Winter protection** is seldom necessary. In very cold climates, mulch with a 4-inch layer of leaves or sawdust to protect the shallow roots from freeze damage.

- **Harvest** in midsummer when berries are dark purple and fall easily from the stem when pulled. Cut off the whole fruit cluster and then remove the fruit.

- **Propagation.** Suckers may be carefully dug up and replanted in midspring if more plants are needed.

Tips · Elderberries are low in sugar and high in nutritional value. Use them in jellies, wines, and syrups; they will last in your refrigerator for about one week. Do not freeze.
· Two plants are necessary for cross-pollination. Nurseries sell one-year-old rooted plants.
· Berry clusters may be gathered, dried, and fed to winter birds.

Selected Varieties

'Johns' is extremely hardy, very vigorous, and ripens very early. 'Adams,' created in New York, produces large berries and ripens about two weeks after 'Johns.' 'York,' a descendant from the 'Adams' line, is considered the most productive elderberry because its bushes and berries are larger than those of other varieties.

FIG

Botanical name: *Ficus carica* (Moraceae)

One of the most ancient of all cultivated fruits, the fig has been regarded as a symbol of fertility in cultures from China to India to Greece. Gardeners in the warmer regions of North America know the fig as a dependable, low-maintenance fruit with a life span as long as that of its human keepers. Along the Gulf Coast and in southern California, figs grow into small trees. But in cooler climates where they are marginally hardy, figs produce best when several shoots are allowed to rise from the ground and flourish, more like bushes than trees. Never expect to see flowers on a fig, though, for the fig fruits themselves are fleshy flowers, turned inside out.

PLANT TYPE: Perennial.
GROWING RANGE: Zones 5 to 10. Winter insulation is necessary in cold-winter areas.
HARDINESS: The roots of figs can survive when the air temperature drops to 10°F, but top growth is killed back to the ground by hard freezes. New shoots that grow from the roots in spring will usually bear fruit, but not until late summer.
CHILL REQUIREMENT: Low, under 800 hours below 45°F in winter.
SOIL: Reasonably fertile, well-drained soil. Clay is preferred over sand, especially in hot, dry climates where sand quickly heats up, dries out, and may host root-knot nematodes.
PH: 5.5 to 6.5 (slightly acid to neutral).
FERTILIZER: Well-rotted manure. Mature trees may be fertilized with 10-10-10.
WATER: Fig trees have large drought-resistant root systems, but shrub-size plants rely more on shallow roots. In dry weather, soak them thoroughly every two weeks.
EXPOSURE: Full sun.
SPACING: 15 feet in semitropical areas where figs grow into small trees. 6 feet for garden-size bushes.
TIME TILL BEARING: 2 years.
YIELD: 1 bushel per small bush to 3 bushels per tree annually.
PROPAGATION: Stem cuttings.

🍓 *Method*

- **Prepare soil** two weeks before planting by excavating a planting hole about 2 feet deep and 18 inches wide. Refill with one part stable manure to two parts soil. In soils that tend to be very acidic (with a pH less than 4.5), thoroughly mix in ½ cup of lime.

- **Set** fig plants in the prepared holes in early spring, just after the last frost, making sure roots are in firm contact with surrounding soil. In semitropical areas where the figs will grow into trees, plant them at the same depth that they grew at the nursery (indicated by the brown line on the stem). In colder climates, where a bush habit is desired, set the plants 2 inches deeper to stimulate production of multiple shoots.

- **Prune back** the tops of the plants immediately after planting. In semitropical areas, cut the top back to 18 inches the first year, and prune away low-growing suckers in subsequent springs. In warm climates, mature plants may be pruned by occasional thinning of large branches and light pruning of younger branches to balance the shape of the tree. Where cold injury is common and a more compact growth habit is desired, prune back the top of the plant to 6 inches after planting and leave all suckers intact.

- **Water** immediately after planting by flooding the root area. Water established plants every two weeks during droughts.

- **Mulch** in a wide circle around each plant with 3 inches of straw, hay, chopped leaves, or other organic mulch to control weeds and help retain soil moisture.

- **Fertilize** each year, beginning the second spring the plants are in the ground. In spring, rake back the mulch and apply either a 2-inch layer of stable manure beneath each bush or 1 cup of 10-10-10 fertilizer. Then replace the mulch. When figs are grown as small bushes in good soil, a thick, year-round mulch can eliminate the need for supplemental fertilization.

- **Pests and diseases** are only occasional problems in small home gardens. As soon as the figs begin to ripen, you may find yourself competing with large noisy beetles. They probably are June bugs, which are harmless to humans but love to eat figs. To beat them at their game, collect ripe fruits very early in the morning, before the dew is dry and the beetles start flying.

  Figs are moderately susceptible to soil-borne root-knot nematodes, which occur in warm climates. To strengthen their resistance, add plenty of decomposed organic matter to the planting site.

- **Winter protection** for the roots can be provided by a 3-inch-thick layer of mulch. There are several ways to protect the wood from winter injury. In semitropical areas, wrap or paint the trunks with white latex paint to protect them from sunscald. In warm temperate climates where old wood is sometimes winter-killed, you may bind the branches together loosely with twine to make a compact bundle. Then enclose the bush with a wire mesh cage that is roomy enough to allow for packing loosely with leaves, which you can drop in from the top of the cage. Wrap the outside of the filled cage with plastic, leaving the top uncovered.

  In cold climates, some gardeners bury their fig bushes in the fall—the only known method (besides greenhouse container culture) that makes fig growing possible in Zone

6. First, bind the bush loosely with string, followed by a layer of newspapers or burlap, until it resembles a mummy. Then bend it over and bury it in a shallow grave, with just enough roots severed on three sides to make it possible to lay the bush in the excavated trench. Cover the bush with old blankets or other porous material, followed by an inch or two of soil. The bush then can be raised upright a few weeks before the last spring frost, and mulched heavily to promote growth of new roots.

- **Harvest** figs from midsummer to fall when they begin to droop and change from green to a rosy brown color. Always allow figs to ripen fully before picking, for they do not become sweet until they are fully ripe.

- **Propagation.** Take 6-inch cuttings from one-year-old stems in late winter. Plant in a 1-to-1 mixture of sand and peat moss, and keep moist. New roots should be evident after six weeks.

Tips · Nurseries sell one- and two-year-old plants. Keep roots constantly moist until plants are set out.
· Figs are highly perishable, so keep them in the refrigerator, or promptly dry them in a food dehydrator, or preserve them in a heavy syrup.

Selected Varieties

'Brown Turkey' and 'Texas Everbearing' are the hardiest varieties for home gardeners. 'Texas Everbearing' produces fruit over a long period rather than all at once and is well adapted in places with short growing seasons. Fruit is medium to large with purplish skin. 'Brown Turkey' is sometimes sold as 'Black Spanish.' It has soft reddish-brown fruit best eaten fresh.

Although less hardy, 'Celeste' is extremely sweet, and 'Mission' is well adapted in the South and West. 'Mission' bears large flavorful fruit with purplish-black skin.

GOOSEBERRY

Botanical name: *Ribes grossularia* (Saxifragaceae)

Easy to grow and cold hardy, gooseberries are an excellent bush fruit for cold-climate fruit gardens and make delicious preserves. They will also grow in the South provided they are shaded from the summer sun. Gooseberries are seldom seen in markets because they do not become sweet until they are fully ripe, and ripe fruits cannot tolerate the rigors of shipping. The thorny bushes grow wild in many parts of the country, but cultivated varieties are preferred since they are more productive and resistant to most diseases. Cultivation of gooseberries is restricted in some Appalachian states because of the susceptibility of some varieties to white pine blister rust, a major fungal disease of white pine trees.

PLANT TYPE: Perennial.
GROWING RANGE: Zones 2 to 8.
HARDINESS: Very cold tolerant but easily stressed in hot weather above 90°F.

CHILL REQUIREMENT: Low, though plants may remain dormant in cold climates for as long as 6 months.

SOIL: Fertile soil with moderate to high organic matter content.

PH: 5.5 to 6.5 (slightly acid to neutral).

FERTILIZER: Compost or well-rotted manure. After flowering and fruiting begins, 10-10-10.

WATER: Average requirements if mulches are used. In warm climates, supplemental water is often needed in midsummer.

EXPOSURE: Full sun in the North, dappled sun in the South.

SPACING: 5 feet, in rows 8 feet apart.

TIME TILL BEARING: 2 years, with maximum productivity after 5 to 10 years.

YIELD: Up to 10 quarts per mature bush annually.

PROPAGATION: Layering or stem cuttings.

🍓 Method

- **Prepare soil** by clearing out weeds, and dig in humus-building organic matter such as rotted manure, compost, peat moss, or leaf mold. In heavy clay soil, incorporate sand to improve drainage.

- **Plant** gooseberries in early spring or in fall at the time of the last predicted frost. Set the plants in the prepared soil slightly deeper than they grew at the nursery (generally indicated by a brown line on the stem).

- **Mulch** with 3 to 5 inches of sawdust, leaves, hay, or other organic mulch to control weeds and maintain soil moisture close to the surface, where many of the roots are found. Year-round mulching also improves the condition of the soil and provides a constant supply of new organic matter.

- **Water** weekly during dry spells, especially in hot weather.

- **Fertilize** in winter with an organic soil amendment such as a 1-inch layer of compost or manure, tucked beneath the mulch. Bearing plants also benefit from a booster feeding in early summer. Spread 6 ounces of 10-10-10 in a 1-foot circle around each mature plant. Use of a nutrient-rich mulch like alfalfa hay or stable litter can eliminate the need for frequent fertilization.

- **Prune out** canes more than three years old by cutting them off at ground level in late winter. Mature bushes may have only three such elderly canes, which look gray and weathered compared to younger wood. A mature bush should have nine to twelve canes, including equal numbers of one-, two-, and three-year-old canes. Branches may be pruned as needed to help air circulate freely through the bushes, and to make the fruits easier to pick.

- **Diseases** include white pine blister rust, which may cause premature leaf drop, but otherwise does not severely damage the plants. Cane blight, which may cause canes to wilt and die suddenly, can be controlled by pruning out old canes. Powdery mildew causes leaves and berries to become covered with a white powder (fungus). Promote good air circulation and plant mildew-resistant varieties to reduce risk of infection. Avoid anthracnose (another fungal disease) by growing resistant varieties.

- **Winter protection** of 2 inches of packed mulch is sufficient. Avoid mulching with fresh hay in winter, as it attracts mice that may chew on the dormant canes. Where mice are a problem, keep all mulch pulled 2 inches away from the canes as a safety precaution.

- **Harvest** in summer when fruits become sweet, somewhat soft, and fall from the stem when touched. Some varieties become pink when fully ripe. When picking gooseberries, wear heavy gloves and use both hands—one to loosen the fruits from the stem and one to catch them. Or knock the ripe fruits to the ground and pick them up.

- **Propagation.** To propagate by layering, bend a cane to the ground and mound 2 inches of soil over the stem near the tip. Hold in place with a board or stone until new roots develop.

  Cuttings are more difficult but can be done by taking 6-inch stem cuttings in the summer and planting 2 inches deep in sandy potting medium. Cover the cutting and container with a plastic bag to maintain moisture and humidity until growth appears and roots develop. When the cutting shows strong new growth, plant outdoors in permanent location.

Tips · Healthy one-year-old plants are preferred for planting.
· Use thorny gooseberries as a living fence. Since sugar content and other flavor characteristics vary with variety, plant several varieties (two plants each) and propagate new plants from the one you like best.
· If you live in the Appalachians, check with your extension service before ordering plants to make sure there are no legal restrictions on their culture.
· You can freeze gooseberries but they tend to become mushy when defrosted. They will last in your refrigerator about ten days.

Selected Varieties

A 1930s vintage variety called 'Pixwell' is easy to pick since the fruits hang below the thorns. Its fruit is pink in color and resistant to mildew. 'Welcome' resists anthracnose. 'Oregon Champion' has whitish-green, tart fruit with tender skin; plants are resistant to mildew, a problem in the Northwest. 'Poorman' has sweet, red, well-flavored fruit when fully ripe. These plants are vigorous with few short thorns.

GRAPE

Botanical name: *Vitis* (Vitaceae)

The different species and hybrids of grapes differ widely in their taste and often have a special use. For instance, American grapes are eaten fresh, or as a jelly, and drunk as juice. Thompson seedless can be dried as raisins and are delicious when eaten fresh. Most wine grapes aren't sweet enough to be eaten fresh and are used strictly for wine-making. The hybrids between American and wine grapes, most often called French-American hybrids, have been bred to withstand colder winter temperatures than wine grapes and are used mainly in wine-making, but some varieties are used for fresh eating or to dry as raisins. The muscadines are grown mainly in the southeastern portion of the United States and can be used for fresh eating, and jelly- and wine-making.

PLANT TYPE: Perennial.

GROWING RANGE: Zones 5 to 8 for most American grapes. Zone 8 for wine grapes and Thompson seedless that need warm winter temperatures. The muscadines are adapted to Zones 7 to 9. French-American hybrids can be grown in Zones 3 to 8.

HARDINESS: American varieties are adapted to cooler summers and can withstand cold winters with winter mulching. European varieties require mild winter temperatures and a frost-free growing season of at least 170 days to more than 180 days to mature a crop. French-American hybrids are very winter hardy and can withstand cooler summers than European varieties. The muscadines need mild winters and thrive in hot, humid weather.

CHILL REQUIREMENT: As few as 100 hours of 45°F or below, but grapes will begin growth much sooner when longer chilling is given.

SOIL: Well-drained, deep topsoil.

PH: Between 6.5 and 8 (neutral to slightly alkaline).

FERTILIZER: Fertilize only if soil is nutrient deficient, with nitrogen-containing fertilizer.

WATER: Moderately moist but well-drained soil.

EXPOSURE: Full sun and a site that is free from early frosts. A south-facing slope will maintain warmth better than a level site and may promote earlier grape maturity in the fall. Another northern technique is to grow grapes in stony or rocky soil. The rocks heat up during the day and keep the soil warm for the grapes at night. Growing the vines on a trellis next to your house will help shelter and warm them in the winter.

SPACING: 8 to 10 feet apart for vigorous varieties or American and French-American types planted in deep soil, but only 6 to 7 feet in shallow soils or for European types. Muscadines need 20 feet or more for their vigorous growth. Rows should be 9 feet apart.

TIME TILL BEARING: 3 to 4 years for production of a harvestable crop.

YIELD: From 8 to 70 pounds per vine, depending on the variety.

PROPAGATION: Stem, leaf, or root cuttings.

🍓 Method

- **Trellis** before planting the vines. Grapes need a sturdy support to maximize exposure of fruit clusters and leaves to sunshine and support the heavy fruit crop. Trellising can be accomplished by installing a simple wood trellis against your house, a wood frame over a walkway, a linear wooden fence, or posts with wires stretched between them. For better yield, use a Geneva Double Curtain (GDC) system, only for vigorous varieties. For this system, use heavy, 4-inch-wide, 8-foot-tall redwood or other rot-resistant wooden posts. Bury them 2 feet deep and 24 feet apart. Attach a 48-inch-long crossbeam to the top, reinforced with two support pieces joined to the end of the crossbeam and then angled (about 35°) down to the wooden post. Two heavy-gauge metal wires, called

The Geneva Double Curtain (GDC) training method for grapes features three trellis wires. The top two wires (cordon wires) provide support for the canes and fruit while the bottom wire (trunk support wire) supports the two trunks of the plant. Every other plant is trained to the same cordon wire to maximize the sunlight to each plant. During the growing season each plant produces a "curtain" of leaves and fruit hanging down from the cordon wire, hence the name *double curtain.*

cordon wires, are strung from each end of the crossbeam. A trunk support wire is also strung from wooden post to wooden post, at a height of 48 inches. The grapes are spaced 6 to 8 feet (use the wider spacings for the more vigorous varieties) from the end post and then 6 to 8 feet between the next two vines, using a total of four vines in the 6-foot spacing, or three vines, using 8-foot spacing, for every 24 feet of trellis. Place wooden posts only 20 feet apart for muscadines and plant one vine per 20 feet of trellis.

For European varieties, a vertical hedgerow or two-cane Kniffin system is preferred. Use heavy, 4- to 6-inch-wide end posts set 2 to 3 feet deep with 6 feet of post above-ground. Set line posts 18 to 21 feet apart (line posts can be smaller in diameter than the end posts). Attach four wires (12-gauge or heavier), equally spaced, to the posts. Attach the top wire at 5½ feet from the ground and the bottom wire at 2½ to 3 feet. Set out three vines, equally spaced, between each two line posts. The trunk is trained to the lowest wire with one cane, or *cordon,* in each direction along the wire. The shoots are trained vertically and are woven among the three top wires (see figure on pages 96–97).

- **Prepare soil** in the early spring by digging deeply (as deep as your topsoil is or 2 to 3 feet if your topsoil is very deep) to loosen the soil. Work in sand for heavy clay soils. Dig a hole approximately 1-by-1 by-1-foot deep or large enough to accommodate the roots.

- **Plant** in early spring after the last expected 15°F frost. Plant varieties on their own roots by burying the roots slightly deeper in the ground than the dark soil line on the stem. With grafted vines, make sure that the graft or knob in the stem is above the soil level to prevent sucker formation. Firm the soil around the plants and water.

- **Water** by drip or sprinkle irrigation. During hot, dry spells grapes may need to be watered once or twice a week. Plants that aren't receiving adequate amounts of water

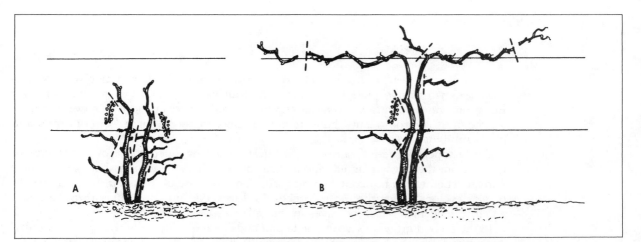

A. For GDC training, during the early spring of the second growing season prune off all canes except the top or strongest cane on each trunk. (Cutting locations are indicated by dotted lines in this illustration.) Tie the trunk canes loosely to the trunk support wires. If long enough, loop each cane around the upper cordon wire and tie each end of the cane to the wire. If too short, do this later in the growing season after the cane becomes long enough. Remove the flower clusters as soon as they appear. Throughout the summer, remove lower buds on the trunk as they emerge.

B. For GDC training, during the early spring of the third growing season prune each cordon arm to 3 to 4 feet, and remove any extra canes or branches from the cordons or from the trunks. During the season allow the buds on the cordon branches to form canes, which will bear your first crop.

have yellow-green shoot tips early in the spring; later in the spring, the internodes (spaces along the stem, between the leaves) at the tip of the plant shorten and the tendrils on the tip dry up.

- **Fertilize** in the early spring only if your vines are slow growing or have small or yellow leaves, with a nitrogen-containing fertilizer (10 ounces of 10-20-20 per plant) or rotted cow or steer manure. But beware—too much nitrogen will delay fruit maturation, decrease winter hardiness, and the vine may be killed by mild winter temperatures. Grapes deficient in potassium will have reddish or burnt-looking leaves and pale-colored fruit that may ripen unevenly. If this is a problem, apply a fertilizer high in potassium.

- **Train vines** during the first summer after planting. For the GDC trellis system, as soon as the buds begin to grow, cut back all canes except the two longest ones with the thickest diameters. This double trunk system has the advantage that if harsh winter conditions or disease affect your vines, one of the trunks will probably survive and the vine won't be totally lost. After the buds have grown out to about an inch, rub off all the buds except the top two to four. As these buds grow out, they should be loosely tied to the trunk support wires so that they will have full sunlight. Remove any flower clusters as soon as they appear.

  In the second year, select the best single cane on each trunk to continue a double trunk system to the upper wire and prune off other canes. Tie the two trunk canes close together to the lower 48-inch trunk support wire. Loop the canes in the opposite direction from one another two or three times around the upper cordon wire and tie each end of a cane to the wire. Each trunk on the upper wire will become a cordon arm. The next plant should have its trunks placed on the other cordon wire so that the plants of the row alternate from one cordon wire to the other. Remove the lower buds on the trunk as they emerge and any flower clusters for the most vigorous growth.

  In spring of the third year, trim each cordon arm to 3 to 4 feet. Buds will sprout from the cordons, forming canes. These canes will bear fruit this year.

In the fourth year, the canes should be pruned to five buds per cane for Concord varieties, two to five buds for French-American varieties, and two to four buds for European wine and muscadine varieties. On each plant leave no more than twenty (thirty for the most vigorous plants) buds, removing canes that were shaded or not exposed to much sunlight.

For European varieties trained to a vertical hedgerow, select the strongest shoot that grows from the newly planted vine and cut off all others. Train this shoot to a vertical wire attached to the horizontal cordon wires and the base of the plant so that a straight trunk develops. Once the shoot reaches the lower cordon wire, cut it through a bud when it is dormant (lost its leaves in the fall) and tie it to the wire.

In the second growing season, the lateral buds on the trunk will grow. Select two that grow just below the lowest wire, and wrap one on each side of the trunk along the wire (see figure on pages 96–97). Remove any flower clusters that form and all shoots other than the two selected. In the second winter, prune back the two canes to seven or eight buds each. Fruit will be produced from these buds, and it is important that young vines not be allowed to overproduce. In the third growing season, train shoots up among the top three wires.

In the fourth season, when the vine is still dormant, new fruiting wood must be selected; almost 90 percent of the vine should be removed in the pruning process. Select two new fruiting canes, those that grew last season, and cut each back to about fifteen to twenty-five buds; keep fewer buds on plants low in vigor. Wrap these canes around the lower wire. Leave a one- to two-bud renewal spur near each side of the trunk. Remove all other canes (see figure on pages 96–97).

- **Prune** vines grown in the GDC trellis system after five or more years in the early spring before growth begins. Along each cane that branched off the cordon, there will be numerous branches. Cut back the first branch closest to the cane's attachment to the

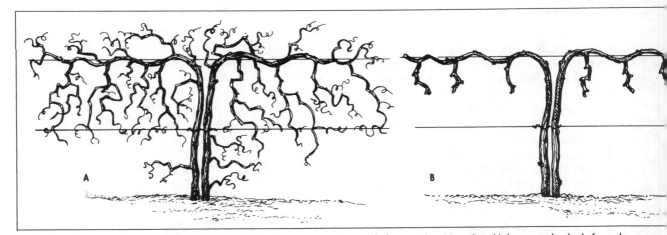

A. This GDC-trained grapevine is early in the spring of its fourth growing season, before pruning. Note that third-year cordon buds formed canes.

B. This pruned GDC vine is early in the spring of its fourth growing season, and all the canes from the trunk and top of the vine have been removed. Vigorous, downward-directed canes are chosen as fruit-bearing canes, which are pruned back to a certain number of buds (depending on variety), leaving between twenty and thirty buds per plant.

This mature grapevine is trained in a vertical hedgerow (two-cane Kniffin system), in which the cordon arms (the stout branches along the lowest wire of the trellis) produce fruit-bearing upright canes that are woven through three upper wires.

cordon to two buds to form a renewal spur. Cut the next branch to form the fruiting cane for this year. As in the fourth year, cut the branch back to the appropriate number of buds. Remove all other canes of the branch system. As the vines get older and more vigorous, leave forty buds per plant (seventy for the most vigorous varieties). In cold-climate areas where late-spring freezes often kill new growth, leave the fruit cane unpruned until the tenth to twelfth buds on the cane begin to swell. During the fifth growing season (and all subsequent years), the renewal spur will produce two canes. In the sixth spring (and all subsequent years), cut out the weaker cane. The remaining cane will be that year's fruit cane and should be pruned to two to five buds, depending on variety. Cut the last year's (year five) fruit cane back to the branch closest to its base. Prune this branch to one or two buds to form the renewal spur for next year.

In the vertical hedgerow system, prune mature plants in spring before growth begins by selecting one of the shoots produced by each renewal spur for the fruiting cane; cut this back to ten to twenty-five buds, depending on variety. Cut the other shoot on the renewal spur back to two buds to form next year's renwal spur. If either shoot is weak, select another cane arising near the trunk. Remove all other parts of the "branch" system.

- **Pests and disease** protection involves use of preventive sprays and the immediate removal of diseased or dying foliage, branches, or fruit.

  For leaf diseases, train shoots so that they are spread out, promoting air circulation. In severe infestations, use fungicides, such as a bordeaux spray. Proper canopy management (spreading the shoots) also decreases the incidence of fruit rots.

  Leafhoppers, 1/8-inch-long insects that hop when the vines are moved, can cause disease to spread, as well as damage vines. Spray vines with a pyrethrum compound or other insecticide.

  Cover the vines with netting if birds are eating your crop.

- **Harvest** grapes in late fall when they are sweet to taste and fully colored. To cut the stem of the grape cluster, use scissors or a sharp knife.

- **Winter protection.** Commercial growers invest in electric windmills and smudge pots to keep their plants safe from frost, but the only way a concerned home gardener can protect vines is to carefully lay the vines on the ground after they lose their leaves and cover them with a 1-foot layer of leaves or other light airy mulch. This can be done with the vertical hedgerow or the cane Kniffin system by mounding the leaves up and over

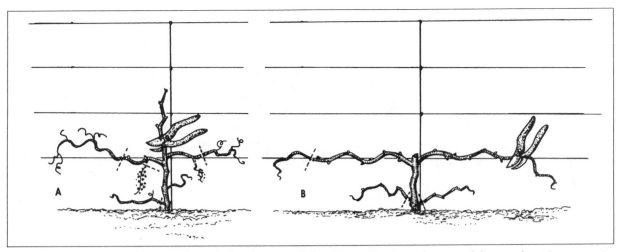

A. The vertical hedgerow system occurs during the first dormant period and the early spring and summer of the second growing season. As soon as the vine loses its leaves in the fall, cut it through a bud just above the lower wire (indicated by the pruning shears in the illustration). This vertical branch will thicken over the years and will be known as the trunk. In the second spring, select two buds that sprout just below the lower trellis wire. When long enough, wrap each around opposite sides of the lower trellis wire. Remove all other branches and flower clusters that form during the growing season. The cuts should be done at the dotted lines.

B. During the second winter, prune the canes on the lower trellis wire back to seven or eight buds so that the vine won't produce too much fruit. The cuts are indicated by the pruning shears and the dotted lines. Remove all other branches from the trunk.

the plant to just over the lower (2 ½ feet) cordons. The canes are then carefully removed from the trellis and covered with a foot of leaves. There's no winter protection for the GDC system, which is the reason for using two canes.

· **Mulch.** For best weed control, mulch a 3-foot-wide strip through the length of the row, so that the base of each vine is surrounded by mulch. Use compost or other material and spread 6 inches deep.

· **Propagation.** Take cuttings in the spring after new growth begins and plant 2 inches deep in sandy potting medium. Cover the cutting and the container with a plastic bag to maintain moisture and humidity until growth appears and roots develop. When the cutting shows strong new growth, plant outdoors in a permanent location.

Tips · European grapes are generally sold on grafted rootstocks that protect them from disease, except in Oregon and Washington. Most nurseries ship one-year-old, bare-rooted vines.

· Muscadine grapes need pollinators so you must buy at least one variety that can act as a pollinator for every two vines of another variety.

Selected Varieties

American *(Vitis labrusca)*
'Candace,' an early-season, red seedless grape that is hardy and good for eating fresh, wine-making, and drying for raisins.

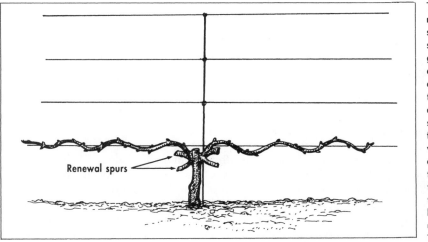

This vertical hedge-row-trained vine is shown early in the spring of the third growing season after pruning. Two canes close to the trunk have been chosen to fruit this summer, detached from the upper wires, wrapped around the lower trellis wire and then cut back to ten to twenty-five buds, depending upon the variety. The short spurlike branches in the lower area are the two bud renewal spurs that could be used the next year if the upper canes are damaged. The canes that bore last year are cut back to the new fruiting canes.

Renewal spurs

'Catawba,' a late-season red grape for fresh eating; its juice is used in making champagne and other wines. Grow only on the warmest sites.

'Concord,' a late-season, deep purple, rich-tasting berry that is widely used for jelly and juice. The fruit has the typical *labrusca* "foxy" flavor.

'Delaware,' an early-season to midseason red grape for wine-making. Fruit is small.

'New York Muscat,' an early to midseason reddish black grape that has a muscat, or spicy, flavor. Plants are moderately hardy.

'Niagara,' a late-season, large, white, sweet-flavored grape. Fruit can be eaten fresh or used for juice or wine. Plants are hardy in Zones 5 to 7.

European *(V. vinifera)*

'Flame Seedless,' an early, medium-size, round, red seedless grape. The flesh is firm and crisp and has an excellent flavor for a dessert grape.

'Thompson Seedless,' a late-season, white seedless grape that is great to eat fresh and can be dried to make raisins. Grow only in the warmest sites or else fruit will not mature.

French-American hybrids

'Himrod,' an early white seedless grape for eating fresh and for raisins. Plants are moderately hardy.

'Interlaken,' a hybrid formed from crossing 'Ontario' and 'Thompson Seedless,' hardy in Zone 6. These small, sweet, white seedless grapes can be eaten fresh or dried to make raisins.

'Kay Gray,' a very hardy hybrid grape that survives in Zone 3 and is used to make a white wine.

'St. Pepin,' hardy in Zone 4. The juice of this grape is used to make a spicy, German-type wine.

Muscadine *(V. rotundifolia)*

'Cowart,' a deep blue-black muscadine grape. 'Cowart' and 'Scuppernong' can be used to pollinate one another.

'Scuppernong,' a bronze-green muscadine grape.

JUNEBERRY

Botanical name: Various species of the genus *Amelanchier,* most often *A. oblongifolia* and *A. alnifolia* (Rosaceae)
Other common names: Serviceberry, Shadbush, Saskatoon

An important food to the American Indians, this low-maintenance, blueberrylike fruit has many names since it grows wild in so many places. Over twenty-five species are native to North America, and at least two wild species can be found in each of the United States. Besides bearing tasty berries, Juneberries are beautiful in early spring, when their dainty white flowers cluster along bare branches. Some large treelike species, such as *Amelanchier laevis,* or the Sarvis tree, are grown exclusively as ornamentals, but the best fruit production comes from species that can be managed as bushy hedges. Juneberries are interchangeable with blueberries in recipes. Cooking enhances their flavor.

PLANT TYPE: Perennial.
GROWING RANGE: All zones.
HARDINESS: Very cold and heat tolerant, from about −20° to 105°F.
CHILL REQUIREMENT: Varies with species. Three months of near-freezing weather are required for good seed germination.
SOIL: Tolerates a wide range of soils, but prefers the light, loamy soils typical of wooded riverbanks.
PH: Widely adaptable; 4 to 7.5.
FERTILIZER: None generally required, especially if the plants are mulched.
WATER: Supplemental water is seldom needed except in years when spring is very dry. Under these conditions, soak the plants once a week to ensure good fruit size.
EXPOSURE: Full sun to partial shade. A little shelter from large trees helps to mimic Juneberries' natural woodland habitats.
SPACING: 5 feet for nursery-grown plants. Eventually the plants will grow together to form a hedge about 5 feet tall and 5 feet wide.
TIME TILL BEARING: 2 years from the planting of 1-year-old plants, or 4 years from seed.
YIELD: 1 gallon per mature bush annually.
PROPAGATION: Seed, stem cuttings, or division.

🍓 *Method*

· **Prepare soil** by digging out large rocks and tree roots. Add peat moss to sandy soil to improve its ability to hold moisture. Dig planting holes wide enough to accommodate the roots when spread out.

· **Plant** Juneberries deep enough so all roots can be covered with 2 inches of soil. Refill the planting hole, making sure all roots are in firm contact with surrounding soil. One-year-old nursery-grown plants should be set out in early spring. Small plants dug from the wild transplant best in early fall or late winter.

· **Water** after planting, and then soak the root area weekly until new growth appears.

- **Mulch** around little bushes to control weeds. A 3-inch layer of leaves, replenished each fall, is ideal.

- **Fertilize** in late fall to early spring only if plants lack vigor or appear seriously stressed, and keep applications light, using organic soil amendments like compost or manure.

- **Prune** around the outside of the bushes if the plants spread too much. Typically, numerous stems arise from the plants' roots; they do not require thinning or pruning.

- **Pests and diseases** rarely bother Juneberries.

- **Winter protection** is not required. However, when mulches are used to control weeds and condition the soil, pull them away from the base of the plants in winter to keep mice from nesting there.

- **Harvest** when berries are dark purple to black.

- **Propagation.** To grow from seed, plant the seed ½ inch deep in a nursery bed in fall. Keep moist. Seed will not break dormancy until it has been chilled and moist for at least three months. **Rooting cuttings** (done in the summer) is difficult, but experienced propagators may get good results. To take new plants from an established clump, use a sharp spade to sever the roots below two or three adjoining stems. Dig the root ball without breaking it up. Replant immediately, water well, and mulch with a 2-inch-deep layer of leaves.

Tip · Plant Juneberries along fencerows or in front of an evergreen background where the contrast will highlight the pretty spring flowers.

Selected Varieties

Juneberries are normally not sold by variety name, though several improved selections exist. Superior self-pollinating cultivars include 'Smoky,' an unusually sweet and well-flavored berry; 'Pembina,' which matches good flavor with long fruiting clusters; and 'Success,' which has been in cultivation for a hundred years—a testament to its popularity. Where variety names are absent but plants are listed as saskatoon, shad, or shadblow, they are hardy species appropriate for cold climates.

MELON

Botanical name: *Cucumis melo* (Cucurbitaceae)

On a hot day, eating one of many varieties of sweet melons is really refreshing. While most store-bought melons fall into the cantaloupe, honeydew, or crenshaw flavor group, home gardeners can grow varieties that taste like pears, pineapples, and fruit punch, as well as the more traditionally flavored varieties. Varieties also include a multitude of flesh colors— orange, yellow, green, and almost white. Although many melon varieties require a long growing season, with season extension techniques and the new fast-maturing varieties, even short-season gardeners can grow these sweet fruits.

PLANT TYPE: Annual.

GROWING RANGE: 65° to 75°F daytime temperatures are best. If your area has cool summers, plant the fastest-maturing varieties and use season-extending devices such as black or clear plastic mulch, row covers, or Wall-O-Water to achieve suitable growing temperatures.

HARDINESS: Killed by frost.

SOIL: Rich, well-drained, sandy loam soil. Do not plant in soil that has grown watermelon, cucumbers, or other melons in the last 2 years.

PH: Around 7 (neutral).

FERTILIZER: 10-10-10 or fish emulsion.

WATER: Requires constant moisture.

EXPOSURE: Full sun.

SPACING: Grow in hills of 2 or 3 plants, spacing the individual plants in the hill 4 to 6 inches apart (in the form of a triangle). Space the hills 2 to 3 feet apart, with rows 3 to 6 feet apart, depending upon the variety.

TIME TILL BEARING: From 80 to 100 frost-free days for the fastest-maturing varieties grown in cool summers to over 100 days for later-maturing varieties.

YIELD: 2 to 8 melons, weighing from as little as a pound to over 14 pounds, depending on the variety.

PROPAGATION: Seed.

🍓 *Method*

- **Prepare soil** by adding compost or well-rotted cow or steer manure at the rate of ½ pound per square foot in the spring. Add fresh manure six weeks before planting; rotted manure or compost can be added just before planting. To warm up the soil and discourage weeds, cover the soil with fibrous landscape cloth two weeks prior to planting. Right before planting or transplanting, cut a large X in the cloth, then cut around it in a circle so that there is a hole 1 foot in diameter in the cloth. Dig three shallow holes for seeds in a triangular pattern.

- **Plant** seeds (two to a hole) either directly in warm soil one week before the last date of frost or start plants indoors in sterilized potting soil or in a frost-free cold frame or other season-extending device three to four weeks before the last date of the frost. It takes about one week to germinate seeds in 68°F soil; below 60°F the seeds often do not germinate. For indoor seeding, plant in plastic pots that are at least 4 inches deep and 2 inches wide, placing two seeds ½ inch deep in the soil. Thin to one plant per pot as soon as leaves have expanded by cutting the extra plant off at the base with scissors. Place them in a very sunny window or take them outside during warm (above 65°F) days. If you choose to grow them in a cold frame, open the frame to direct sun daily. Many gardeners use Wall-O-Water to grow melons by planting week-old seedlings underneath these water-filled tepees. Open up the top during the day and close it during the night. Wall-O-Water will protect the plant from temperatures down to −10°F.

- **Transplant** seedlings, started indoors or in cold frames, into the garden after the last spring frost. For fastest growth, cover the plants with row covers until they begin to blossom.

- **Weed** in areas not covered by the landscape cloth every two to three weeks after germination or transplanting, or until the plant starts to vine if no landscape cloth has been used.

- **Water** to keep the soil constantly moist without forming puddles, until after the plants have set fruit. Then water as soon as the top inch of soil is dry. If you have fungus or wilt diseases, keep your soil drier, watering only after the top 2 inches are dry. If you are using a plastic mulch system, a drip or trickle irrigation system works best for keeping the soil moist under the mulch.

- **Fertilize** during the growing season with 10-10-10 fertilizer or fish emulsion if the leaves turn yellow.

- **Pest and disease control** starts with rotating melon, watermelon, and cucumber crops, allowing at least two years before planting melons in these soils.
  To combat powdery mildew, which causes grayish-white areas on the older leaves, plant resistant varieties or apply sulfur dust according to the directions on the package.
  Control aphids or cucumber beetles by using insecticides approved for vegetables or, if you don't have many, squash cucumber beetles by hand. Ladybugs will help keep down the aphid population. Aphids and cucumber beetles often spread fungal or viral diseases.

- **Harvesting** melons—knowing when they're ripe—can be tricky. Most cantaloupe or muskmelon varieties turn from gray-green to buff yellow when ripe; they smell aromatic, and often the stem slips off easily. Honeydew melons are more difficult to judge. Indications of ripeness are that the hard, smooth white rind begins to take on a slight yellow coloration, and the blossom end is slightly soft and has a honeydew smell. French Charentais melons are harvested when the small leaf next to the stem end of the fruit turns pale; an orange skin color indicates that the melon is overripe. Crenshaw melons turn a yellow color and the flesh next to the blossom end yields with firm pressure.

Tip · Honeydew, crenshaw, and casaba will last about two weeks after harvesting, but should not be refrigerated as their flesh is damaged by cold air. Cantaloupe, muskmelon, and French Charentais can be refrigerated and will last about five to fourteen days after harvesting.

Selected Varieties

Cantaloupe or muskmelon

'Earligold' is early ripening (seventy-three days from transplanting) and tolerates cooler weather than many other varieties. The melon averages about 4 pounds and has thick, juicy orange flesh. 'Sweet Granite' takes only seventy days from transplanting to mature sweet 2½- to 3½-pound melons. 'Rocky Sweet' has sweet, thick, lime-green flesh in 3- to 4-pound melons. 'Burpee's Ambrosia Hybrid' has sweet 4½- to 5-pound melons with very thick salmon-colored flesh and a small seed cavity. 'Sweet 'n Early Hybrid' takes only seventy-five days from transplanting to ripe melons. These vines bear six to eight melons per plant and continue producing fruit over a longer season than many other varieties.

'Sweet Dream Hybrid,' another sweet and juicy, green-flesh cantaloupe, takes only seventy-nine days from transplanting to mature melons. 'Honeybush' grows in bush form and the vine takes up only 5 to 7 feet in diameter to produce 2½- to 3-pound thick-fleshed melons. 'Muskateer' is a small bush-forming vine, 2 to 3 feet across, producing sweet-tasting melons. 'Alaska Hybrid' is an early-maturing cantaloupe that produces 4- to 4½-pound melons.

Honeydew
'Honeydew Drip Hybrid' is a melon with cream-colored flesh and a very sweet taste. 'Ogen Hybrid' has the taste of Anjou pears! 'Pineapple Hybrid' bears 5-pound melons whose flesh has the flavor of pineapple, and 'Fruit Punch Hybrid' features the flavor of fruit punch. 'Early Dew Hybrid' is an early-maturing honeydew for short-season climates. The melons weigh 2½ to 3 pounds. 'Limelight Hybrid' features 7- to 7½-pound sweet melons that are ripe when the melon stem slips off, making it much easier to judge picking. 'Venus Hybrid' is an early hybrid that ripens eighty-eight days from transplanting. These also are ripe when the stem slips.

French Charentais
'Flyer' is a very early-maturing (sixty-eight days from transplanting) Charentais. These small 2-pound melons have thick, sweet, deep orange flesh. 'Savor' is also early (seventy-eight days from transplanting) and very sweet and aromatic. 'Cantaloupe Chaca Hybrid' is a larger 3- to 3½-pound Charentais type of sweet melon.

Crenshaw
'Burpee Early Hybrid Crenshaw' is early for a crenshaw, taking ninety days to mature from transplanting. Large, up to 14 pounds, these melons have thick, tasty salmon-pink flesh. 'Honeyshaw Hybrid' is another ninety-day variety that has juicy, thick-fleshed melons averaging 8 pounds.

RASPBERRY

Botanical Name: *Rubus* (Rosaceae)

Easy to grow, raspberries are great to eat fresh or to make jellies, jams, or syrup. The purple and black raspberries have a rich taste similar to that of concord grapes or blackberries, and the red and yellow berries are lighter flavored. Hedgerow-grown (when canes are trained to form a solid 1½- to 2-foot-wide row) berries can be used as fences or edible edgings along the garden or property. Fall-bearing or everbearing raspberries can bear two crops in one year, once in June or July, and then again in late August through September. Plants grow with stiff erect canes unlike trailing types of blackberry.

> PLANT TYPE: Perennial.
> GROWING RANGE: Zones 3 to 8 for red and yellow raspberries, the hardiest forms (though special red varieties will grow in the low-chill areas of Zone 10); Zones 4 to 8 for purple raspberry, slightly less hardy; and Zones 5 to 8 for black raspberry, which requires milder winters.
> HARDINESS: Hardy red raspberry varieties can withstand −31° to −40°F; hardy purple raspberries survive in −20° to −30°F; black raspberries need winter temperatures warmer than −20°F.

CHILL REQUIREMENT: From 800 to 1800 hours at or below 45°F are needed to break dormancy, depending on the raspberry variety.

SOIL: A well-drained loam soil high in organic material.

PH: 5.5 to 6.8

FERTILIZER: Well-rotted steer or cow manure or 10-10-10.

WATER: Requires moderate amounts of water. Avoid standing water.

EXPOSURE: Full sun.

SPACING: 3 feet, with rows 7 to 9 feet apart for black and purple raspberries, which are grown in hills. Red and yellow raspberries, most commonly grown in hedgerows, should be planted 2 feet apart, in rows 7 to 9 feet apart. These plants will spread by suckers so that a 1½-foot-wide hedgerow is formed.

TIME TILL BEARING: Canes bear in their second growing season (the second summer), except for fall-bearing red raspberries, which will bear at the end of their first growing season or in the fall. Most varieties come into full production in the third year after planting.

YIELD: Small crops can be expected in the autumn from fall-bearing red raspberries and during the summer of the second year for all other raspberries. In mature plantings, red and yellow raspberries produce 3 to 6 gallons of berries per 25 foot row; black raspberries produce only ½ gallon per hill. Without disease problems, most plants should be productive for 9 to 12 years.

PROPAGATION: Red and yellow raspberries are grown from suckers arising from the base of the plant; purple and black raspberries are tip-layered.

🍓 Method

· **Prepare soil** by adding liberal amounts of compost and then loosening and mixing it to a depth of 1 foot either by digging or rototilling. Add equal parts of compost or sand to clay soils to lighten and increase drainage. Dig a small hole, 8 inches deep and 8 to 12 inches wide, for each plant.

· **Set** bare-rooted plants in prepared hole in early spring after the last frost or as dormant plants in fall. Spread the roots and cover with dirt. Bury the stem to the same depth as it was in the nursery, generally indicated by a brown line on the stem.

· **Trellis** or stake raspberries to support the canes and keep the fruit from touching the ground. For those grown in a hedgerow, use a wire trellis with sturdy 4- by-4-inch or larger wooden end posts. About 4½ to 5 feet of post should show aboveground. Set lighter posts every 15 to 20 feet in the row. Make two crossbars as wide as your row (1½ feet) and attach one to the top and another at 1 foot on each post so that they cross the row. Fasten heavy wires (12-gauge or heavier) to the edge of one crossbar and string the wire to the next crossbar along the same side and height and fasten the wire tightly. Repeat this for all the crossbars. In the early spring, before the canes leaf out, fasten the canes that grew the last summer to the wires, making it easy to pick the fruit. The canes that will grow this summer will grow up in the middle of the row and will not bear fruit until the next summer.

When growing a few red raspberry plants, drive a wood stake next to the plant and tie the canes with a string or light wire to prevent them from falling to the ground.

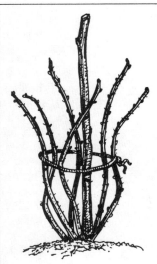

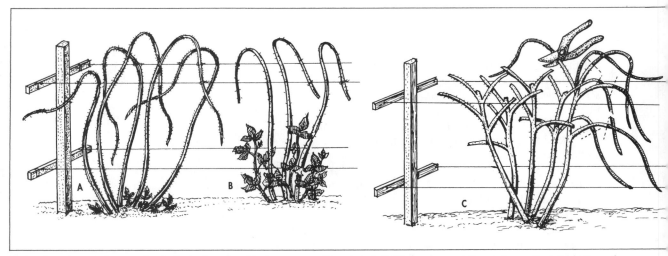

A. A red raspberry before pruning in the early spring. The long canes will produce fruit this summer, and the small growth at the bottom of the plant will produce canes that won't fruit until the following summer.

B. You may thin raspberry canes in the early spring by removing small-diameter or weak canes at the base of the plant. By cutting back the tops of the canes, you can increase the size of the berries. Tie canes to either side of the top wires so that about half of them are tied to each wire. Berries on fruit-bearing canes will be borne to the outside of the trellis, and the canes that fruit next year will grow upward in the middle of the row.

C. Prune black or purple raspberries in the early spring by cutting back lateral branches. The dotted lines show where branches should be cut. The canes that fruited last year, as well as the weak (small-diameter) canes for this year, have already been removed from this plant.

If you are growing only a few plants in hills, drive a stake beside each hill, attaching a wire or string to encircle and support the canes.

· **Water** using drip or sprinkle irrigation when the top ½ to 1 inch of soil is dry. If plants are mulched or the soil is high in organic matter, water when the top 2 inches of soil are dry.

· **Fertilize** in the early spring before the canes leaf out. Spread 1 to 2 pounds of well-rotted manure or 10-10-10 fertilizer per 20 row feet on the soil between the canes. If a hardy variety continues to grow very late into the fall and is easily winter-killed, too much nitrogen has been applied.

· **Prune** fruit canes as soon as they have been harvested in the summer by cutting them off at the base; these canes will die after they have fruited anyway. In the spring after the first growing summer, cutting the cane of red or yellow raspberries to 4 to 5 ½ feet when still dormant will increase the size of each individual berry, but also reduce the overall yield of the plant. For larger berries of red and yellow varieties, cut the canes to 4 feet in the spring before they start to leaf out; otherwise, don't cut them. With fall-bearing red raspberries, clip off only the top of the cane that bore fruit in the fall if you want to harvest berries from the lower part of the cane during the next summer. Thin the remaining canes to ten to twelve per hill or four to five of the strongest per foot of hedgerow. You can grow fall-bearing raspberries for only a fall crop by cutting off all canes at ground level in the early spring before growth starts. The new suckers that develop should be thinned and kept to a 1 ½-foot-wide row. No summer crop is produced by this method, but it has advantages in areas with cold winter temperatures, in that it eliminates the possibility of cane damage. For black and purple raspberries, prune 2 inches off the tops of the first-year canes as soon as they are 2 feet long for black raspberries and 2½ feet for purple raspberries. This will encourage many lateral branches that will bear fruit the next summer. The next spring when canes are still dormant, cut these lateral branches back to 8 to 10 inches for black raspberries and 12 to 14 inches for purple raspberries. These lateral branches bear the fruit. Remove the dead canes that fruited last season. Thin the remaining canes to about five of the strongest per hill.

Tips · Catalogs offer two forms of red raspberries—everbearing (fall bearing) and regular. The everbearing varieties bear at the tips of the first year canes, late in the summer or early fall and in the next summer on the lower part of the cane. In areas with short seasons (90 to 120 frost-free days), these varieties often don't ripen before the first fall frost. Purchase one plant per 2 row feet for red or yellow raspberries and as many plants as you need for purple and black raspberries.

· Crumbly berries can be caused by many things. The individual bumps on the berries (called *drupelets*) have tiny hairs that hold them together. If there aren't enough drupelets, the berry crumples. Poor pollination, resulting from rainy and cloudy weather or few bees during bloom, often causes crumbly berries. But this problem could also be due to insufficient water, soil deficiencies in phosphorus, nitrogen, or iron, or exposure to 2, 4-D, a common weed killer. If your berries do not have any of these problems, then the crumbly berries are caused by a virus and the plants should be discarded.

· **Pests and diseases** include many virus diseases that can cause the berries to crumble and not hold their shape. Buy certified virus-free stock, and remove any plants whose leaves curl or are spotted or streaked with yellow. Unfortunately, there is no cure for virus disease, and plants with this problem should be dug up and discarded in the garbage or burned. Plant any new raspberry beds as far from the old infected beds as possible for at least four years.

Raspberry cane borers cause the tips of raspberry canes to wilt suddenly. When this occurs, cut the cane below the slight swelling that indicates where the borer is in the cane. Raspberry crown borer also causes the canes to wilt or break off at the base because the grub feeds on the crown or the roots. Prompt removal of the old fruit canes will help control this pest, as well as using an approved insecticide for at least two years in the early spring before growth begins. You should also plant your raspberries away from wild raspberries that may carry the crown borer and remove old fruit canes (which are a haven for the insect) promptly after harvest.

Keep deer from eating the canes by hanging bars of soap from the trellis or sprinkling dried blood meal around the outside edge of the hedgerow.

· **Harvest** the fruit when they are fully colored and detach easily from the plant—if you have to pull the fruit, it isn't ripe. Place the fruit directly in small containers to avoid crushing it and refrigerate quickly.

- **Mulch** with a 4- to 6-inch layer of compost, rotted sawdust, peat moss, or other light material around the base of the plants and in walkways. Renew each spring.

- **Winter protection.** In areas where winter temperatures drop below −40°F, red raspberry canes should be covered with 1-foot layer of mulch as soon as the leaves drop off the canes in the fall. Remove the mulch in the early spring. There is no way to winter protect black raspberries as the canes are too stiff to lay on the ground. Select hardy varieties for best winter survival and plant in an area that is protected from winter wind.

- **Propagate** red and purple raspberries by digging up young suckers in early summer and transplanting them to a new area. Black raspberries can be propagated by bending first-year canes to the soil and burying the tip about 4 inches deep. At the end of the summer, when the tip will have sprouted roots, cut the cane 1 to 1½ feet from the ground, dig up the sprouted tip, and transplant to a new location.

Selected Species and Varieties

Red Raspberry and Yellow Raspberry *(Rubus idaeus* x *R. strigosus)*
'Canby' is a large and flavorful berry borne on nearly thornless, hardy canes. A popular variety for northern or cold-winter areas, but very susceptible to root rot.

'Dormanred' is a red raspberry adapted for the South, with a low chill requirement and a high tolerance for hot summer temperatures.

'Fallgold,' an everbearing plant with sweet, large, golden-yellow berries. Ripens ten days before 'Heritage.' Plants are very hardy.

'Heritage' is a fall-bearing or everbearing red raspberry. First-year canes bear in September and then again the next summer.

'Summer' bears medium-size, firm, sweet fruit with an intense flavor. Canes are hardier than 'Willamette' or 'Meeker' and plants are tolerant of heavy soils. Popular home-garden variety in the west.

'Willamette' bears large dark red fruit. It is a favorite in mild-winter areas as it cannot withstand below 0°F temperatures. It does not produce well in heavy soils.

Purple Raspberry *(R. occidentalis* x *R. idaeus* x *R. strigosus)*
'Brandywine' is a large purple berry that is tart when compared to 'Royalty.' These plants form large canes (up to 10 feet) and should be grown in a hill system as no root suckers are formed.

'Royalty' is a summer-bearing, very large, sweet, purple berry. Suckers are produced from the roots like red raspberries.

Black, or Blackcap, Raspberry *(R. occidentalis)*
'Bristol' is a large, juicy, rich-tasting berry. The canes are so strong that they don't need staking.

'Jewel' bears large, black, great-tasting berries. The plant is hardy and not susceptible to any serious disease.

'Munger' bears medium-size, black, rich-tasting fruit. Plant does not require staking. Most popular variety in temperate regions of the West.

Check with local nurseries for varieties adapted to your region and for ripening times.

STRAWBERRY

Botanical name: *Fragaria* x *ananassa* (Rosaceae)

Strawberries have three different fruiting forms: those that bear once a season, those that bear twice a season, and those that fruit periodically throughout the growing season. June-bearers are often used by homeowners who want to freeze or make jam in large quantities because they yield one large crop during the early summer. They stop producing flowers after this one crop and start to produce runners (a cordlike appendage that sprouts a new plant at the end) because of the long summer day lengths. Everbearing strawberries generally produce one crop in the summer and another in the fall. These also make great-tasting pies, jams, and freeze well, but they don't produce as many berries at a time as June-bearers. While northern gardeners enjoy harvesting strawberries in the summer and early fall, gardeners with less than fifteen hours of daylight in the summer are often disappointed with everbearers because they do not receive enough day length to encourage blossoming.

Recently, day-neutral varieties have been developed that are unaffected by the day length. These produce fruit relatively continually throughout the growing season. The fruit of these types may be small and have less flavor than June-bearers.

Everbearers and day-neutrals are great for gardeners whose first crops often are destroyed by late frosts or wet May or June harvest weather as they will produce flowers and fruit in long summer day lengths; even if the first crop is destroyed by weather, the later crop will be fine.

PLANT TYPE: Perennial.

GROWING RANGE: Can be grown everywhere in the United States as long as the proper varieties for the area are chosen. Call your cooperative extension agent for advice on varieties for your area.

HARDINESS: Both cold hardy (to 0°F) and heat tolerant. However, the blossoms of most strawberry varieties are killed by freezing temperatures.

CHILL REQUIREMENT: Only 100 to 300 hours below 45°F are needed to break dormancy in most strawberry varieties.

SOIL: A well-drained loam high in organic matter.

PH: Slightly acid; 6 to 7 is best.

FERTILIZER: Rotted steer manure, poultry manure, or 10-20-20. For one-year-old and older plantings, 10-10-10 fertilizer, well-rotted manure, or compost.

WATER: Keep the soil moist. Avoid standing water.

EXPOSURE: Full sun and protection from late-spring frosts.

SPACING: Strawberries can be grown in several different ways. The most common is a matted row system where individual plants are spaced 12 inches apart for everbearers and day-neutral varieties that produce few runners, to 18 inches apart for June-bearers that produce many runners. During the next 2 to 5 years the runners are allowed to fill in the spaces to form a matted row 1½ feet wide. Allow paths of 1½ feet between rows. The disadvantage of this method is that the plants often become overcrowded, causing a decrease in yield and an increase in disease. To decrease crowding, remove older plants in the fall so that there is a density of no more than 5 plants for every square foot of row.

Another way is to grow your plants in a hill system. This system is ideal for everbearers and day-neutrals that produce few runners. In 3-foot-wide beds, 3 rows are planted, 1 foot apart, and the plants in the rows are staggered so that there are at least 12 inches between all plants for everbearers and day-neutral varieties and 18 inches between June-bearers. All runners should be removed in the hill system.

To grow strawberries in pots, use a light potting soil. Keep the soil moist and fertilize once a month. The pot should be placed in full sun, but be careful not to place it where it gets too hot.

TIME TILL BEARING: Everbearers and day-neutral varieties should have just the first set of blossoms removed after planting and the next blossoms will set fruit ready for harvest in July or August after the spring planting. June-bearers should have their blossoms removed in the year of planting and so do not bear until the following summer.

If you are growing strawberries as an annual or 2-year crop, do not remove the first blossoms, but rather let the plants bear fruit.

YIELD: With good growing conditions, 25 plants can yield 15 to 30 quarts of berries. Disease and overcrowding cause a decrease in yield, making it advantageous to replace most plantings every 3 to 4 years.

PROPAGATION: Runners.

🍓 *Method*

- **Prepare soil** by tilling or digging in 5 pounds of steer manure or 1 ½ pounds of poultry manure per 10 square feet, or 1 pound of 10-20-20 per 100 square feet. If you are using fresh manure, till it in the fall before planting, or to plant immediately, use nonburning, rotted, or composted manure. Work the soil to the depth of 1 foot. Dig a 6- to 8-inch-wide and 8-inch-deep hole. Form soil into an upside-down cone shape in the middle of the hole.

- **Plant** in the fall, early spring, or in the late winter in the South or in parts of California. Call your cooperative extension agent for the proper planting time in your area. Place the plant on top of the cone and fan out the roots along the sides of the cone. Bury the plant until all the roots are covered. It is very important that the roots are not exposed to air and that the top of the crown that produces leaves is not buried. Press the soil down around the plant and water.

- **Weed** plants every two weeks or use a 2- to 4-inch mulch of grass clippings, straw, or other loose organic mulch, or apply landscape cloth or plastic mulch to control weeds. If you cultivate with a hoe, go no deeper than ½ inch as strawberry roots are very shallow.

- **Water** by drip or trickle irrigation when the top inch of soil is dry. For sprinkle irrigation, use a landscape cloth or organic mulch layer to provide easy water penetration and help keep the soil moist.

- **Fertilize** when plants are slow growing or have yellow leaves. Side-dress with 1 pound of 10-10-10 fertilizer per 25 row feet. For one-year-old and older plantings, fertilize with rotted manure, compost, or 10-10-10 fertilizer in the late summer. If your plants are mulched, pull back the mulch layer and place organic fertilizers such as compost or rotted manure next to the plants and reapply the mulch.

- **Mulch** after the soil warms up in the spring. Apply a 1- to 2-inch layer of grass clippings, pine needles, bark mulch, or other shredded organic material around the plant and up to 3 inches on the paths. Make sure that you do not cover the growing point or crown with mulch.

- **Pest and disease** prevention begins with planting certified, virus-free, or disease-free, stock in soil that hasn't grown strawberries, raspberries, or tomato family plants such as tomato, pepper, potato, and eggplant for at least ten years.

  Strawberries suffer from a multitude of diseases, some of which kill the plant and others that just reduce the yield. Often the best protection is careful inspection of the plants and immediately destroying those that have yellowed, twisted, wrinkled, or flattened leaves or those that are obviously not growing properly. Controlling sucking insects such as aphids also will help prevent the spread of disease. In moist, humid conditions, the berries are often afflicted with fruit rots and other leaf and berry diseases. To control this problem, it is absolutely necessary to pick and remove the rotted berries from the plant or the fruit rot will spread throughout the bed. To help the plants dry out, grow the strawberries in narrow 1- to 1½-foot-wide rows with the plants spaced at least 6 inches from each other so that the leaves do not form a moisture-holding canopy. Grow resistant varieties, if available, and varieties that bear their strawberries above the leaves or in an upright fashion rather than lying on the ground.

  If you have problems with slugs, fruit rots, or leaf diseases, do not use an organic mulch, such as grass clippings or bark mulch, because it encourages these problems. Instead, use landscape cloth that will prevent weed growth, help maintain soil moisture, and yet keep the berries and plants dry.

  For insects such as aphids, either use biocontrols like ladybugs or spray with an insecticide approved for use on food crops. Handpick or use a strong hand-held vacuum cleaner to remove lygus bugs, a small greenish-yellow to brown-with-yellow bug that sucks on the buds and fruit. Strawberry crown borers are ⅕-inch-long brown beetles that feed on the stems and leaves of strawberries. Their grubs cause the most damage because they bore into the crowns and roots of the plant. For the best control, start a new bed with fresh, disease-free plants at least 300 yards away from the old infected bed. Strawberry root weevils are black to gray beetles that feed on leaves, causing a notched appearance. The larvae, or grubs, of this beetle feed on roots, killing the plant. Check with your local county agent for methods of control.

  Birds love strawberries as much as, if not more than, humans. To protect your plants, cover them with bird netting. For easier net removal, place stakes or other light framing around the berries before covering with the net. This method also works to prevent deer from eating the leaves.

- **Harvest** strawberries when they are totally red by pulling gently on the stem where it should separate from the top of the berry or, if you want the stem, pinch the stem off.

- **Winter protect** in areas of temperatures below 0°F, with little or no snow cover, by mulching the plants with a 2- to 4-inch layer of straw once growth has stopped in the fall. Promptly remove the mulch in the spring as soon as expected lows are above 20°F. Mulching for winter protection is not recommended in western North America, as the amount of rainfall in winter promotes plant rot.

Tips · Plants that are shipped from nurseries are shipped bare-root. Store these in moist towels in the refrigerator if you can't plant them immediately. Healthy plants will have many root hairs appearing as tiny white hairlike projections on the roots. Plants grown in flats or pots will transplant well and are often available at local nurseries.

· The first blossom to open in the strawberry cluster always produces the largest berry. This is why it is important to cover or protect your flowering strawberries from frost, as blossoms with black centers will not produce fruit. Spotty frosts often cause disfigured berries where only part of the berry is large and fleshy, the rest being small, hard, and firm. In areas where there are frequent spring frosts during the time that strawberries are blooming, or wet spring weather during ripening that causes berry rot, plant ever-bearing or day-neutral varieties so that you can be assured of a crop later when there is no frost or drier ripening times.

Selected Varieties

June-bearers
'Benton' bears large bright red fruit that ripens later than that of other varieties. The plant is somewhat disease resistant and tolerates wetter soils than average.

'Brighton' is a large productive strawberry that bears sweet berries.

'Hecker' is very high in vitamin C.

'Hood' bears large, bright red, firm fruit with great flavor. Ripens early. Plants are susceptible to virus.

'Honeoye' is a great-tasting strawberry that is winter hardy and resistant to berry rot.

'Stark Crimson King Strawberry' is a very large, late June-bearer with a great sweet taste. These are also hardy and do well in areas that have early-spring frosts as they bloom later than most June-bearers.

'Totem' ripens midseason, bearing large attractive, dark red fruit with good flavor.

Day-neutrals
'Tristar' is a productive strawberry that is hardy and disease resistant. Sweet medium-size fruit.

'Selva' bears large firm fruit. The flavor may be disappointing in some areas.

Everbearers
'Fort Laramie' is a very hardy everbearer that can take northern winter temperatures without winter mulching. The blossoms can even stand light frosts.

'Ogallala' is an old-time favorite that is hardy and disease resistant.

'Ozark Beauty,' another hardy everbearer, bears sweet scarlet-red berries.

'Quinalt' is a great-tasting everbearer that isn't quite as productive as the newer day-neutral varieties.

Check with local nurseries for varieties adapted to your region and for ripening times.

WATERMELON

Botanical name: *Citrullus lanatus* (Cucurbitaceae)

Watermelons now come in so many different varieties—red and yellow flesh, seed and seedless, large and small fruit size, vine and bush forms, early and late maturing—that it is easy for the gardener to pick just the right variety for his or her needs. For small gardens, use bush varieties that require only 3 square feet to grow. Many varieties have smaller-size melons that are easier to store in the refrigerator or can be eaten in one meal. Seedless varieties need to be grown with another seeded variety (called the *pollinator variety*) to produce melons, and seed companies enclose the pollinator seed with the seedless variety, as well as any special instructions. In short- or cool-season areas, use only the fastest-maturing varieties to grow sweet melons.

PLANT TYPE: Annual.

GROWING RANGE: 70° to 85°F daytime temperatures are best. If your area doesn't have warm summers, you might want to use black plastic, row covers, Wall-O-Water, or other season-extending devices to warm up the temperature.

HARDINESS: Freezing temperatures kill watermelons.

SOIL: Rich, organic soil. Do not plant in soil that has grown watermelons, cucumbers, or other melons in the last 2 years.

PH: approximately 7 (neutral).

FERTILIZER: 10-10-10 fertilizer or fish emulsion.

WATER: Needs constant moisture.

EXPOSURE: Full sun.

SPACING: Watermelons are generally grown in hills of 2 to 3 plants. Space individual plants in the hill 4 to 6 inches apart in the shape of a triangle. Space the hills 3 to 4 square feet apart for small bush-type watermelons; the smaller (5- to 8-pound) vine melons need 3 feet between hills with rows spaced at 5 to 8 feet, and large (over 15-pound) vine melons need at least an area 10 feet in diameter around each hill.

TIME TILL BEARING: 100 frost-free days for the fastest-maturing forms of watermelon in cool short-season areas to over 120 days for the slower-ripening varieties.

YIELD: 1 or 2 melons from 15 to over 100 pounds for large vine plants. Smaller bush plants can produce up to 10 melons, weighing 3 to 4 pounds each, though the average is more often 1 or 2 melons, weighing from 3 to 15 pounds.

PROPAGATION: Self-sows by seed, except for hybrid varieties.

🍓 *Method*

· **Start seed indoors** or in a frost-free cold frame or other season-extending device three to four weeks before the last date of frost. Plant in plastic pots that are at least 4 inches deep and 2 inches wide, two seeds per pot. Use a rich, loose potting soil, and plant the seeds ½ inch deep. Germination should occur in three to five days at temperatures between 75° and 95°F. Thin to one plant per pot by cutting the extra plant off at its base with a pair of scissors. Place the plants in a very sunny window or take them outside during warm (above 65°F) days. If you choose to grow them in a cold frame, open the frame to direct sun. Many gardeners use Wall-O-Water to grow watermelons by planting week-old seedlings underneath these water-filled tepees. Open up the top during the day and close it during the night. Wall-O-Water will protect the plant from temperatures down to −10°F.

- **Prepare soil outdoors** by adding compost or well-rotted cow or steer manure at the rate of ½ pound per square foot in the spring. If you use fresh manure, plan to add it at least six weeks before planting. Compost can be added just before planting. To warm up the soil and discourage weeds, cover the soil with fibrous landscape cloth two weeks prior to planting. Right before planting or transplanting, cut a large X in the cloth, then cut around it in a circle so that there is a hole, 1 foot in diameter. Dig a hole 4 inches in diameter, 4 to 6 inches deep for each plant.

- **Sow seeds outdoors** 2 to a hole in warm soil one week before the last date of frost.

- **Transplant** seedlings, started indoors or in cold frames, into the garden after the last spring frost. Cover the plants with row covers until they begin to blossom for fastest growth.

- **Weed** in areas not covered by the landscape cloth every two to three weeks after germination or transplanting, or until the plant starts to vine if no landscape cloth has been used.

- **Water** to keep the soil constantly moist without forming puddles, until after the plants have set fruit, then water as soon as the top inch of soil is dry. If you are using a plastic mulch, use a drip or trickle irrigation system for best results.

- **Fertilize** with 10-10-10 fertilizer or fish emulsion if the leaves turn yellow.

- **Pest and disease control** starts with rotating watermelon, cucumber, and melon crops, allowing two years to pass before planting in the same soil.
  For diseases such as fusarium and verticillium wilt, plant resistant varieties. Since these diseases are often spread by aphids or cucumber beetles, either control these with an insecticide or use ladybugs for the aphids and squash cucumber beetles when you see them.

- **Harvest** watermelon when the nearest tendril (curl) to the fruit stem is brown or dead and the portion of the fruit where it rests on the ground has turned from white to yellow. Another way to determine ripeness is to tap the melon and listen for a "punk" rather than "pink" or "pank" sound.

Tips · Refrigerated at between 40° and 50°F, watermelons will keep for two weeks, after harvesting.
· **To get very large watermelons, grow large varieties in rich, very moist soil. Remove all but one melon per plant.**

Selected Varieties

Bush varieties

'Burpee's Sugar Bush' should be planted on a 3-by-3-foot spacing. It yields two to four melons weighing 6 to 8 pounds each. 'Sweet Treats' vines grow 4½ to 5 feet long and generally bear two 9- to 14-pound melons. 'Bush Sugar Baby' features short 3- to 3½-foot vines that yield two 8- to 12-pound round or oval-shaped melons. 'Bush Charleston Gray' has vines only 3 to 5 feet long, yet can produce 17-pound watermelons! This is an extra-sweet melon with a fine deep red color to the flesh. 'Bush Jubilee' produces 12- to 14-pound fruit on 3- to 5-foot vines. 'Garden Baby' is a fast-ripening hybrid that takes only seventy days from transplanting to mature melons and is great for short-growing-season areas. The juicy, sweet fruit averages 7 pounds. 'Watermelon Yellow Doll' is another fast-growing hybrid (sixty-five days from transplanting) whose melons have sweet yellow flesh weighing 5 to 8 pounds.

Vine varieties

'Honey Cream Watermelon' is another fast-growing watermelon (sixty-five days from transplanting) that has a yellow-orange flesh. The melons weigh 3 to 4 pounds, and each plant can bear up to ten melons each. 'You Sweet Thing' is a round, juicy, sweet melon weighing up to 13 pounds. 'Black Diamond' is a variety that under the best conditions can produce huge, 125-pound melons! 'Charleston Gray' is an old-time favorite variety that produces 28- to 35-pound melons.

Seedless varieties

'Redball Seedless' hybrid is a 10- to 12-pound melon with firm, bright red flesh that's great to eat. It has a few small but soft seeds that are edible. 'Seedless Tri-X-313' is a very sweet seedless watermelon weighing 10 to 15 pounds.

ROSES

ROSE

Botanical name: *Rosa* species (Rosaceae). Over 300 species have been identified worldwide.

People have admired and collected roses for more than ten thousand years, and the result is an amazing selection of types and varieties. Today roses range from sprawling miniatures that can be grown in hanging baskets to huge climbers and ramblers. Much has changed in rose culture since 1980, when breeders began releasing new cultivars that show superior resistance to many of the diseases that have plagued rose growers for decades. At the same time, interest in old roses of unknown pedigree is increasing. These changes have made it much easier for gardeners to find the right rose for any landscape situation.

All roses are perennials that can be expected to grow and flower for many years. They reach their maximum size two to three years after planting. Cold hardiness varies tremendously among roses, from 20° to −20°F. If you live in a cold climate, investigate roses that grow well in your area before choosing varieties for your yard. Ungrafted roses that grow on their own roots are usually the best bets. If the canes of these roses are winter-killed, new plants just like the old ones will grow back from the roots. Hybrid tea roses usually are grafted, and they are the least cold hardy of popular garden roses.

SITE SELECTION

The availability of suitable planting sites will determine the size of your rose collection. All roses require at least six hours of sun each day. Morning sun is especially beneficial since it dries dew promptly, and thus lessens the risk of mildew. Ideally, air should circulate freely around roses at all times. However, gardeners in cold climates may find that roses grow best in the shelter of a south-facing wall. In warm, humid climates, situate roses where air movement is not blocked by shrubs or buildings.

When locating roses along walkways or sidewalks, set the bed back far enough so that the thorny canes will not invade walking space. Where space is limited, you might try planting different types of roses together, arranged to create visual depth and lasting color. For example, a climbing rose might be planted behind hybrid teas or floribundas, with a miniature or low-growing shrub rose in the foreground.

PLANTING ROSES

Prepare the soil by removing all grass, weeds, and tree roots. Loosen the soil to a depth of 18 inches. Work in a liberal amount of organic matter, such as peat moss, rotted compost or manure, or rotted sawdust. In thin sand or heavy clay, organic matter should constitute one-fourth of the final mixture of soil and soil amendments. Sharp sand also may be added to clay soil to improve drainage. Along with these soil amendments, work in a light dusting of lime if the soil is acidic. The ideal pH for roses ranges between 5.5 and 6. Bonemeal (4 pounds per 100 square feet) may be added to boost soil fertility, but avoid using chemical fertilizers until the plants are well established as they could "burn" the young plants. Allow two weeks or more between bed preparation and the day you plant your roses.

If your soil is infected with nematodes, apply an approved nematicide after the site is prepared. Or solarize the plot by covering it with clear plastic for several weeks. Chitinous materials such as pulverized crab shells can help slow the proliferation of new nematodes.

Plant dormant bare-root roses in early spring, a few weeks before the last spring frost. Container-grown plants may be set out later in the spring if necessary. In Zones 8 to 10, roses also may be planted in fall. Before planting, make sure the roots of your roses never dry out. If you cannot plant them within three days, set them in a shallow hole and heap damp soil or sawdust over the roots.

For each plant, dig a hole large enough to accommodate the roots when they are spread out. Place a small mound of soil in the bottom of the hole, and then gently place the plant over it. Backfill one-third of the excavated soil into the hole, and firm in around the roots with your hands.

Water well, and check for proper planting depth after the soil settles. In cold climates, the bud union (a thick section of stem just above the roots) should be just below the soil surface. In warm climates, it should be just above the soil line. Gently adjust the depth before adding the remainder of the soil. After the planting holes are refilled, water again.

In cool climates, protect the tender buds near the base of newly planted roses by covering the base with an 8-inch-high cone of loose soil. After the danger of frost has passed, remove the hilled soil, being careful not to bruise the new shoots.

Most nursery-grown roses are pruned before they are shipped. Unpruned plants should be pruned back to 6 to 8 inches above the ground. Cut back to ½ inch above an outward-facing bud.

Water newly planted roses twice a week during dry weather. After they begin growing vigorously, roses need about 1 inch of water per week, provided the soil has been prepared properly. When watering roses, avoid wetting the leaves.

Mulch roses in early summer, after the soil has warmed. Choose a clean, attractive mulch material such as pine needles or bark nuggets. A 2-inch layer of mulch usually gives sufficient weed control while helping to retain soil moisture.

MODERN GARDEN ROSES

TYPE	ZONES	GROWTH HABIT	FLOWERS	USES
Climbers	5 to 11	Cane length varies with variety, from 6 to 30 feet, and may be upright or spreading. Long canes must be secured to a wall, fence, or trellis. Space at least 6 feet apart.	Blossoms of either floribunda or hybrid tea type in clusters or on single stems, depending on variety. Some imported species and older varieties have single flowers.	Plants may be trained onto pillars on upright trellises near entries, or trained to cover arches or fences. When growing on walls, sunlight and fresh air must be in good supply.
English roses	4 to 11	Large bushes form a mound of flowers and foliage on softly arching canes. Three to 4 feet tall and 4 to 5 feet wide. Plant 5 feet apart.	Ruffled, heavily scented cupped blossoms in salmon, white, and all shades of pink. Stems may droop from weight of open blossoms.	Specimen shrubs. Plant near outdoor living areas so the scent can be enjoyed.
Floribunda	4 to 11	Stiff, somewhat twiggy canes develop into bushes 2 to 4 feet tall. Plant 3 feet apart.	Clusters of ruffled or tea-type blossoms in broad color range. Fragrance varies. Repeat-flowering strongest in newer varieties.	Groups of three or more plants in all one color create a dazzling display. Good specimen shrubs or border plants.
Grandiflora	4 to 9	Large robust bushes similar to hybrid teas, only larger and capable of producing more flowers. Height ranges from 4 to 8 feet. Plant 4 feet apart.	Flower form varies with variety. Most typical are slightly ruffled hybrid tea types, borne in loose, long-stemmed clusters.	Commonly planted as specimen shrubs in mixed beds, or used at the rear of a collection of smaller hybrid teas.

Fertilization requirements vary with the type of roses grown and the texture of your soil. Roses grown in sandy, porous soils may need frequent light applications of fertilizer. General fertilization requirements for the most popular garden roses are summarized in the table above.

Organic fertilizers, such as compost and manure, provide nutrients and improve soil texture, and they should be part of your spring fertilization program. For booster feedings

FERTILIZER	PRUNING	CULTIVARS
Fertilize in spring by spreading a 3-inch layer of well-rotted manure or compost over the root zone of the plant. Apply a light dusting of bonemeal in early summer.	Remove dead wood in winter and deadhead in summer. Additional pruning may be needed to keep plants shapely. Secure new canes to trellis in fall.	'Blaze' (red), 'Golden Showers' (yellow), 'Joseph's Coat' (orange-yellow), others.
Fertilize in early spring with a 2-inch layer of well-rotted manure or compost. Top-dress lightly with bonemeal or a balanced chemical fertilizer when flowering begins.	Leave new plants unpruned for 2 years. At maturity, remove dead or diseased wood in late winter, then prune lightly to shape the plants. Deadheading enhances repeat flowering.	'Gertrude Jekyll' (pink), 'Othello' (deep pink), 'Fair Bianca' (white), others.
Fertilize in early spring with a 2-inch layer of well-rotted manure or compost. Top-dress lightly with bonemeal or a balanced chemical fertilizer when flowering begins.	Prune lightly to remove damaged canes and shape bushes. Deadheading helps prolong flowering period.	'Cherish' (pink), 'Iceberg' (white), 'Showbiz' (red), many others.
Fertilize in early spring with a 2-inch layer of well-rotted manure or compost. Fertilize lightly with a balanced fertilizer when flowering begins and again in midsummer. In Zones 8 and 9, fertilize again in early fall.	Prune back by one-third to one-half in late winter. In summer remove dead flowers and canes that crowd the plants' centers.	'Queen Elizabeth' (pink), 'Gold Medal' (yellow), 'White Lightnin'' (white), 'Viva' (red), others.

Continued

during the summer, choose a chemical fertilizer blended especially for roses, or a blended organic fertilizer such as a mixture of bonemeal, feather meal, and blood meal.

Winter protection also varies with the type of roses grown. In Zones 4 to 7, all roses except hardy shrub species need good protection around the base of the plants so that if the high canes are winter-killed, a few buds, close to the ground, will survive. After the first hard freeze, bring soil from another part of your yard and hill it over the base of each

MODERN GARDEN ROSES *(Continued)*

TYPE	ZONES	GROWTH HABIT	FLOWERS	USES
Hybrid shrub roses	3 to 11	Varies with variety. Most grow to less than 4 feet tall and 4 to 6 feet wide. Plant 6 feet apart.	Single, double, or ruffled blossoms, depending on variety. Colors include red, white, and pink. Light fragrance.	Flowering hedges, ground covers on gentle slopes, or in massed beds where low maintenance is desired.
Hybrid tea	4 to 9	Stiff canes form angular bushes. Large glossy leaves are somewhat sparse. Height ranges from 3 to 5 feet. Space at least 3 feet apart.	Classic vase-shaped buds open into elegant, long-lasting blossoms. Extensive color range; fragrance good.	Use large vigorous varieties as specimen shrubs. To simplify maintenance, plant collections of several varieties together in a custom-prepared bed.
Miniatures	5 to 11	Stiff, twiggy bushes similar to hybrid teas, only miniature. Height varies with variety from 12 to 24 inches. Plant 2 feet apart.	Tiny blossoms of hybrid tea type, but less than 1 inch wide. Broad color range with good fragrance.	Plant in containers, small patio beds, or in front of hybrid teas.
Tree roses	5 to 9	The upright trunk is topped by grafts of hybrid tea or floribunda roses. Staking usually needed. 3 feet tall. Space 4 feet apart.	Blossoms in the form and color of variety used for grafts.	Specimens near entries or walkways, or accent plants at the ends of rose beds.

plant to a depth of 8 inches. In Zones 4 and 5, reinforce this protection by erecting a 12-inch-high collar (made of chicken wire, cardboard, old baskets, etc.) around each plant. Fill it with shredded leaves, corncobs, or crumpled newspapers.

In Zones 8 to 11, a 3-inch mulch of leaves or pine needles gives sufficient winter protection. Pull the mulch away from the base of the plants to help prevent problems with canker and other diseases.

Tree roses need special winter protection since their least hardy parts are 2 to 3 feet above the ground. After the plants have become dormant, but before the first 20°F night, prune the tips at the tops to 6 inches. Wrap both the head and the trunk loosely but securely with burlap strips or special wrapping materials (sold at garden supply stores). Remove the wrapping when new growth commences in spring.

FERTILIZER	PRUNING	CULTIVARS
Top-dress in early spring with a 2-inch layer of well-rotted manure or compost.	Prune in winter to remove dead and damaged wood. In spring, prune back tips to shape the plants. Deadheading is beneficial but not necessary.	'Bonica' (pink), 'La Savillana' (red), 'Amorette' (white), others.
Fertilize in early spring with a 2-inch layer of well-rotted manure or compost. Fertilize lightly with a balanced fertilizer when flowering begins and again in midsummer. In Zones 8 and 9, fertilize again in early fall.	Frequent pruning and deadheading are needed to enhance plant vigor. Improve light penetration by pruning to an inverted cone shape, with an open center.	'Peace' (creamy yellow), 'Mister Lincoln' (red), 'Tropicana' (orange-red), 'Pascali' (white), 'Double Delight' (red-and-white bicolor), hundreds more.
Fertilize in spring with a slow-release organic fertilizer. Feed container-grown plants with a balanced liquid fertilizer monthly during the summer.	Give good winter protection and prune off dead tips in spring. Plants are sparse by nature, so prune lightly. Deadhead to enhance repeat flowering.	'Cupcake' (pink), 'Party Girl' (light apricot), 'Winsome' (deep lavender), others.
Fertilize in early spring with a 2-inch layer of well-rotted manure or compost. Fertilize lightly with a balanced fertilizer when flowering begins and again in midsummer. In Zones 8 and 9, fertilize again in early fall.	Prune tips back to 6 inches in late fall, and thin to 6 evenly spaced branches. In summer, remove old blossoms and prune as needed to maintain balanced shape.	Most hybrid teas and floribundas may be used. Grafting is best done at the nursery.

Pest control of shrub roses is limited to spraying with insecticidal soap if aphids or other leaf-eating pests appear. Most shrub roses, and some new floribundas and hybrid teas, have good resistance to common fungal diseases. However, the most famous hybrid teas require regular spraying with a fungicide to prevent black spot and mildew. Spray requirements vary according to climate. Check with your county extension agent for the recommended spray schedule for your area.

Roses may be bothered by a number of insect pests, including Japanese beetles, thrips, leaf rollers, or spider mites. In small plantings, many of these pests can be controlled by handpicking or spraying with an insecticidal soap. If problems are severe and a chemical insecticide is necessary, apply it late in the day to lower the risk of burning tender leaves.

Pruning of roses is not nearly as complicated as most gardeners think, unless you are growing large perfect blossoms for exhibition. The table on pages 572–75 describes the pruning needs of various types of roses. Always use sharp, clean shears, and cut diagonally across the stem. Whenever possible, preserve outward-facing buds to help maintain an open center in the plant, facilitating good penetration of fresh air and sunshine. In summer, remove dead flowers promptly to preserve plant vigor. When deadheading roses, remove as few leaves as possible.

Propagation of roses, though restricted on patented varieties, **can be** an interesting project. The most practical method for home gardeners is to root cuttings taken in early summer. Begin with 4- to 6-inch sections of mature wood. Remove all but one set of leaves. Fill containers or a small nursery bed with a half-and-half mixture of peat moss and sand. Place the cuttings in the mixture 2 inches deep, and keep constantly moist and out of full sun. Cuttings that "take" should begin to produce new growth within four weeks. Transplant the rooted cuttings to larger containers or a permanent bed at least six weeks before the first fall frost.

Roses grown in containers have the same needs as those grown in a garden. Drainage in the container must be excellent, and frequent weak applications of a liquid fertilizer are needed to keep the plants in bloom. In cold climates, the roots and base of container-grown plants require winter protection. If you have a spot of ground available, sink the pots into snug holes and protect them with a mound of soil topped by a loose mulch. Container-grown roses that must spend the winter on a patio should be grouped together and wrapped in several layers of cloth. Some low-maintenance landscape roses are small enough to grow in containers and require no winter protection.

SELECTING ROSES

The subject of rose classification is complex. Traditional botanical groupings (species and varieties) are of some help in understanding the various types of roses, but roses are further divided into "classes," such as the well-known hybrid teas and floribundas. To add to the confusion, many of the newest hybrids are crosses between classes, or crosses between wild species and elite, refined varieties. To clarify rose classification, the predominant types will be discussed in building block order, beginning with the oldest types still in cultivation and ending with the most up-to-date hybrids.

Old Roses

Many old roses still carry their species names, as well as a variety name. They are best known as the parents to modern hybrids, but collectors often seek out representatives of the original strains. Most old roses bloom only once a summer.

Rosa centifolia translates as hundred petals, and is commonly called the cabbage rose since the petals spiral and overlap like a cabbage. Blossoms are mostly pink, or white blushed with pink. The 3- to 6-foot plants are very cold hardy.

R. chinensis, or China rose, occurs primarily in pink, with less vigorous forms in red. The elegant flower form of this strain has been incorporated into many modern roses, most notably the hybrid teas. Plants grow to 5 feet, are hardy to 20°F, and disease resistance is low.

R. damascena, or damask rose, has been grown since the tenth century B.C. for a fragrance that made it worthy of the cult of Aphrodite. Flowers usually are double and borne in clusters, in pink, white, or red. Varieties vary in size and vigor. The best-known named variety, 'Mme. Hardy' (white), probably includes *R. gallica* and *R. centifolia* in its pedigree.

R. gallica, called Gallicas or French roses, are red, vigorous, and very fragrant. Flowers are semidouble with a cluster of yellow stamens in the center. Plant size varies from 2 to 6 feet. Winter hardiness is good.

R. moschata, or musk rose, is almost obsolete in its pure form, as it was backcrossed early on with *R. multiflora* and various French roses. Flowers may be single or double, depending on variety, and occur in shades of pink, yellow, and red. Fragrance is generally good. Most hybrid musks are climbers with good disease resistance. They may produce two or three "trusses" or waves of blossoms during the summer.

Shrub Roses include the bushy wild species of North America, along with those from other parts of the world. Although less refined in appearance and flower than most cultivated roses, they are unsurpassed in terms of cold hardiness and disease resistance. The best known of the shrub roses is *R. rugosa,* or rugosa hedge rose. Flower form may be single or double, fragrant or not, depending on variety. Rugosas may bloom once a year or in light flushes. Used as landscape shrubs, rugosas stretch the ornamental season by developing colorful edible hips in fall.

Polyanthas were created in the late nineteenth century by crossing *R. multiflora,* from Japan, with *R. chinensis.* Flowers appear in tight clusters over a long blooming period. Most polyanthas grow to less than 3 feet high and are very winter hardy. They are usually used in mass plantings. Polyanthas are prominent parents of modern floribundas. Time-tested varieties include 'Cecile Brunner' (pink), 'Margot Koster' (salmon), and 'The Fairy' (pink).

Ramblers, or climbing polyanthas, were very popular in the 1940s. They are covered with flowering clusters once a summer on new canes. The color range is broad and cold hardiness is excellent. Ramblers have fallen from favor among gardeners because of their space requirements and chronic problems with mildew.

Hybrid Perpetuals were created in the early 1800s by crossing China roses with hardy shrub roses such as damasks. Hybrid perpetuals bloom repeatedly in warm climates, but may bloom only once where summers are short. Most selections are fragrant. Today hybrid perpetuals are found only in the gardens of collectors, having been almost completely supplanted by their offspring, the hybrid teas.

Modern Roses

Floribundas are an extremely large group of bushy roses that bear clusters of flowers on rather short stems. The flowering habit comes from polyanthas and hybrid perpetuals; the elegant flower form can be traced to teas. Color range is extensive, but fragrance often is missing. In home landscapes, floribundas are usually used in mass plantings of all one color. Some of the most recent crosses with hybrid teas have stems long enough for cutting. Generally, floribundas are hardier and more stress and disease resistant than hybrid teas.

Hybrid Teas began as crosses between hybrid perpetuals and Chinese teas *(R. chinensis)*. The beauty and fragrance of their blossoms and extensive range of colors and bicolors have made them the dominant roses grown today. Pruning, fertilization, and spraying are usually required as the plants bloom heavily and repeatedly, and have low resistance to black spot and other diseases.

Grandifloras are a class of roses created by crossing hybrid teas and floribundas. Color range is extensive and the large vigorous plants are more stress resistant than hybrid teas. Blossoms of the classic hybrid tea type are produced in loose, long-stemmed clusters, and fragrance varies with variety.

Climbers include sprawling hybrids that bloom on old wood and new wood. Many began as mutations, or "sports," of hybrid teas. They grow best in mild climates where the mature canes are not subject to winter injury. Modern varieties bloom all summer and most are at least slightly fragrant.

English Roses began entering American gardens in the 1980s. They are carefully blended mixtures of many of the finest characteristics of old roses: the perfume of damasks, disease resistance of shrub roses, and propensity for repeat flowering of perpetuals. The flower form is cupped and ruffled. Availability of colors is expanding, but pink remains dominant.

Hybrid Shrub Roses are another recent development. Using rugosa and other shrub species, rose breeders have created a new class of disease-resistant, free-flowering shrub roses and ground covers. Because of their hardiness and ease of culture, this new group is often called "landscape roses." When planted in a favorable site, they require minimal pruning, fertilizing, and spraying.

Miniatures are usually dwarf forms of *R. chinensis*. They have tiny flowers, leaves, and canes, and are excellent for containers and small patio gardens. Color range is broad, and plant forms include upright or sprawling bushes, climbers, and miniature trees. Miniature roses have the same pest problems as hybrid teas, but require less pruning.

Tree Roses are really two roses in one: a rootstock and trunk of a vigorous shrub rose, with a named variety of hybrid tea or floribunda grafted onto the tops. They create a unique landscape effect, especially around entrances. Cold injury of the grafted tops is often a problem, and the number of shoots at the top should remain constant from year to year to keep the head from becoming too heavy.

SHRUBS

Shrubs provide a gradation of height between trees and buildings and flowers, ground covers, and lawns, allowing your eye to move easily about the landscape. Foundation plantings, those grown in front of a building, are often made up of various shrubs either by themselves or in combination with other plants. Second, shrubs can often take the place of trees, since some grow as tall as 20 feet or more. Third, they are frequently used as hedges, for privacy, aesthetics, or as a windbreak. And fourth, shrubs can be used as ground covers to help stabilize a slope or reduce maintenance of portions of your property.

All of these reasons are secondary to those attributes that shrubs themselves possess: beauty of leaf or flower, fragrance, edible fruit, and, in the case of evergreens and even some deciduous shrubs, winter interest. In addition, many flowering shrubs grow rapidly, some maturing in five years, and seem to do well for a long time with little maintenance.

Shrubs are often confused with trees because some can grow to heights of 20 to 30 feet. Both shrubs and trees are woody plants (their stems and branches survive from year to year in areas where they are resistant to winter cold), but shrubs have multiple trunks or stems and a tree usually has only one. Some species of common trees like Norway maple contain varieties that are shrubs. Shrubs have spreading, round, or weeping habits.

SELECTING SHRUBS

The variety of shapes and sizes of shrubs, the colors of their fruits and blossoms, and their individual textures provide you with material to fit your every need, whether you wish to enclose your garden with a hedge, create a background for your annuals and perennials, or just add color and fragrance to your landscape.

Deciduous versus Evergreen

Many gardeners choose evergreen shrubs, which hold their foliage even when dormant in winter.

The term *evergreen* can be misleading, since not all plants in this category are green. Some are yellow, blue, bronze, or deep purple, depending on the variety, the plant's age, and the season.

Evergreen shrubs are the basis for most landscapes. They are usually the first plants put in around a new house by the builder or new homeowner, and they are the most often misplaced. They provide a constant green backdrop for your house and garden and blend the seasonal changes of deciduous shrubs, annuals, and perennials into a harmonious whole.

Some, like the privet and boxwood, are often used as hedges in formal gardens. In addition, they are most effective as screens to provide privacy or pruned into fanciful shapes of animals as topiary.

There are two kinds of evergreen shrubs—needle-leaved evergreens, or conifers, with narrow needlelike foliage; and broad-leaved evergreens, with flat, broadened foliage.

Conifers, such as junipers and spruce, are characterized by waxlike leaves that are shaped like needles or scales. Some junipers are extremely hardy and will tolerate drought, poor soils, and low winter temperatures. Spruce are quite variable in requirements, depending on the species.

The foliage of most broad-leaved evergreens resembles that of deciduous shrubs. They are flowering plants, and many have beautiful blossoms and showy fruit. Unlike conifers, which have a fine-textured appearance, broad-leaved varieties offer an assortment of textures for your garden.

Deciduous plants, on the other hand, lose their leaves in autumn. Some flowers appear early, like the flowering quince and forsythia, shrubs that in the Deep South bloom as early as January and in Maine as late as April or early May, if at all, as the flower buds of most varieties of quince and forsythia are often killed by late frosts in the northernmost part of their range.

Some shrubs, such as *Ilex* or *Taxus,* have male and female plants that require cross-pollination to produce their ornamental fruit. If you want the shrubs to fruit, make sure to plant both kinds of plants close enough so they can cross-pollinate.

Few plants are as versatile as flowering shrubs. They may be appreciated for their colorful and often fragrant blossoms, but they can also fulfill utilitarian needs, such as screening an unsightly shed or concealing unattractive features of your house or yard. Sometimes they are used to keep people or animals from going where you don't want them to go. And many varieties, such as azaleas and hydrangeas, can thrive in containers to decorate a patio or deck if their tender roots are protected from winter freezing.

There are thousands of flowering shrubs to choose from. Rhododendrons, for example, have more than nine hundred species and over ten thousand named varieties, including those commonly known as azaleas. These feature a wide array of colored blossoms and a few kinds are hardy to very low winter temperatures.

Some flowering shrubs known for their fragrant blossoms include mock orange and lilac, which will not only fill your garden but the whole neighborhood as well with sweet-smelling scents. These, as well as forsythia and flowering quince, are relatively easy to grow and maintain.

Autumn brings another outburst of color as the green foliage of many deciduous shrubs turns the colors of the rainbow, from golden yellow and bronze to rich orange and scarlet. Even the leaves of some evergreens take on darkened hues of red and purple for the cold winter months. The Japanese snowball *(V. plicatum)* and American cranberrybush *(V. opulus),* both in the *Viburnum* genus, are good examples.

Before you purchase any shrubs, make a list of those that offer the best in each season in your zone. You will find some of the most popular shrubs and their characteristics in the table on pages 584–89. This way you can plan for the best features of each variety.

Growth Pattern

Besides color, fragrance, and fruit, another factor that must be weighed in the selection of shrubs is their pattern of growth. Some, such as the arborvitae, grow upright like small trees; others, like the spreading junipers, grow sideways and sprawl close to the ground. Most shrubs, however, grow in a rounded pattern—as much up as out—and achieve a balanced look, even without pruning. Others, like the forsythia, have extra-long branches that grow up and then bend over in a weeping fashion.

Most shrubs grow quickly. Allow your shrubs room to grow by choosing shrubs whose mature size and pattern of growth will be in keeping with the site. Don't put in foundation plantings that will block windows or doorways. For instance, a planting of prostrate junipers is more appropriate in front of a large bay window than a planting of upright yews. In just a few years, the yews will outgrow their space and block your view from indoors unless they are pruned back mercilessly and often. Also, set shrubs far enough away from a building so that even when grown they will be a foot away from the walls. This space permits the painting and maintenance of the building and prevents the development of mildew from the lack of air circulation.

In addition to the expected height and width of a shrub, you'll want to know the growth rate—whether it is rapid, reaching a maximum height in five years; moderate, taking six to ten years; or slow, taking up to twenty years to make its mark on your garden.

Choosing a Healthy Shrub

A strong healthy shrub has a number of canes or stems that branch out from the central stem close to the ground. Look for dense, bushy plants with many stems coming off the main branches, and with leaves that are free of blemishes. The more buds the stems have, the better.

If you select shrubs that are balled in burlap, make sure that the burlap is as tight as a drumhead. If it is loose, the roots can tear away from the soil. The ball should be the same soil the shrub was growing in when transplanted.

If you have selected container-grown shrubs, make sure that the soil is firmly packed, indicating that the shrub has been growing in the container for a year or more. Too often shrubs are simply dug up and put in containers; if this is the case, their roots will show on the surface of the soil.

Unhealthy shrubs often will have many dead twigs, brown leaves, and bark that is shriveled. Beware of plants with yellow-green foliage when it should be green. This indicates that it is growing in the wrong soil or is suffering damage to its roots.

When to Buy Shrubs

You should purchase shrubs immediately before you plant them, especially those sold with their roots balled in burlap. Those grown and sold in containers can wait a bit longer to be planted, but often dark-colored containers will heat up if left in the sun and the shrub's roots will be damaged.

If you are purchasing flowering shrubs, buy them when they are in flower to make sure you are getting what you want. Don't choose the smallest or the largest in the group, but rather medium-size ones that have a good balance between top and root growth.

Evergreens are almost never sold with bare roots except as very small seedlings. Deciduous shrubs can be sold with bare roots if the shrub is in its dormant period, since there are no leaves to make demands on the roots for moisture. The main advantage in buying bare-rooted shrubs is their lower cost when purchased through mail-order houses. These plants are usually smaller than those available at local nurseries.

Whether you purchase your shrubs from a nursery or by mail, make sure you use the Latin botanical name, since many plants have similar common names or may be called by different names in different parts of the country.

GROWING CONDITIONS

Many of the hardier shrubs will grow in a variety of soil conditions, but nearly all shrubs grow best in well-drained soils. The easiest way to provide good drainage is to add organic material, such as peat moss, leaf mold, compost, or decayed sawdust, to the soil before planting. Once shrubs are in the ground, it is difficult to add organic materials without injuring the roots.

Most shrubs, especially evergreens, prefer a mildly acidic soil between 6 and 7 on the pH scale. Some of the most popular flowering shrubs, like azaleas, prefer acid-loving soils with a pH reading of 4.5 or so.

The most popular shrubs grow well in Zones 5 through 8. Some, like junipers, have a much broader range and will do well in Zones 3 to 8 or 10. Depending on where you plant the shrubs in your garden, you can often grow borderline varieties if you provide shelter from walls or make use of the microclimates existing in your garden.

Most varieties will grow well in either full sun or partial shade. However, the farther south your garden, the more likely full sun will be too hot for them. And the farther north your garden, the more likely your shrubs will do better in a sunnier exposure.

PLANTING

As explained in Chapter 4, planting small shrubs is relatively easy. However, larger shrubs might best be planted by professionals. You will find general planting instructions on pages 92–93 of that chapter.

In most areas, early spring is a good time to plant many shrubs. The plants are dormant, or nearly so, and moderate air temperatures cause a limited amount of stress on the plants. In the South, evergreens are best planted in the fall, when temperatures are moderate and the soil is relatively warm, encouraging root growth.

Flowering shrubs are best planted in the early spring, when their root systems will have as much time as possible to take hold before hot weather. If they are planted in the fall, it must be about the time of leaf drop and then they should be mulched up to 3 inches deep to protect the roots from freezing and encourage the soil to retain its heat for root growth.

The most common error in planting shrubs is placing them too close together. Space your shrubs according to their mature height and spread. Those used for privacy hedges should be placed twice as close as those used in borders. A good rule for spacing hedge plants is to space them at a distance equal to one-fourth their mature height. Showy varieties, such as yews and rhododendrons, look quite attractive standing alone as specimens.

While it is often easier to purchase new shrubs, you can propagate them yourself if you are willing to devote time to the project. A simple way to gain new plants is by regular layering (see pages 122–23), the reproduction method used for most broad-leaved evergreens. Another method is air layering (see pages 121–22), which is good for those shrubs that do not have long flexible branches near the ground.

Some flowering shrubs can be propagated by using one of several types of stem cuttings or pieces of stem with a piece of the root attached. Shrubs such as border forsythia will root easily from cuttings; others are more difficult.

The least practical method of propagation for many shrubs is by seed. Some shrub seeds remain dormant for up to two years in the ground and need warm weather followed by moist and cool conditions for germinating.

MAINTENANCE

Maintaining your new shrubs is just as important as the care you take in planting them.

Mulching is one of the best things you can do for your new shrubs. It helps keep soil cool and encourages delicate feeder roots that cannot tolerate hot soil to explore the soil's surface. Pine needles, sawdust, tree bark, and compost are some of the most common mulches, but any material that does not compress and exclude air is a possibility. Do not use sawdust or chips from treated wood as they can contain harmful chemicals.

If you plant any shrubs that are especially susceptible to drying winter wind or frost, you might want to construct a wrap of burlap that encircles it or even covers it completely. Where snow is heavy, construct a frame to support the cover. You should also cover the area beneath the spread of branches with a 3- to 4-inch layer of mulch to protect the roots.

Some evergreens don't require a lot of fertilizer but benefit from yearly application when young. Deciduous shrubs benefit from frequent light fertilization and moisture when a new set of leaves is grown in the spring.

Pruning (discussed in Chapter 5) is the one aspect of shrub maintenance that causes the most concern. The frequency and amount of pruning can affect the appearance and flowering of your shrubs. The best time of year varies with the species and the climate.

Some flowering shrubs should be pruned annually, some occasionally, and some hardly ever. A slow-growing plant, like an azalea, can go without pruning indefinitely. If you have to prune any shrub more than once a year, it is the wrong shrub for the location.

Most evergreens, such as yews, arborvitae, and juniper, thrive on pruning, which produces denser foliage and controls the size. Privet and boxwood are often shaped into formal hedges with constant pruning, but most evergreens require only annual pruning to maintain their shape. Dead, damaged, or diseased branches should be removed from all shrubs.

You can also train fast-growing evergreen shrubs, such as Japanese yew, into fanciful sculptured forms called topiary. By choosing a shrub that is close to the form you wish to create and then embedding a wire frame into the shrub, you can train the branches into the shape easily as it grows.

RECOMMENDED SHRUBS

COMMON NAME (BOTANICAL NAME)	ZONES	TYPE	GROWTH HABITS/ HEIGHT	FLOWERS OR FRUIT	SEASON OF BLOOM OR FRUITING	COLORS	EXPOSURE
ARBORVITAE (Thuja occidentalis)	3–7	E	40–60'				FS is best
Oriental arborvitae (T. orientalis)	5–8	E	15–25'				
Giant arborvitae (T. plicata)	5–9	E	to 50'				
KNAP HILL HYBRID (Rhododendron)	5–9	D	R/4–5'	Flowers	Late spring	WYRPi	S/PS
Sweet azalea (R. arborescens)	8–9	D	4–6'	Flowers	Mid-summer	W	S/PS
Royal azalea (R. schlippenbachii)	5–8	D	6–8'	Flowers	Mid-spring	Pi	S/PS
Mollis hybrid (R. kosteranum)	5–8	D	4–5'	Flowers	Late spring	WYOPi	S/PS
Ghent azalea (R. gandavense)	6–9	D	4–6'	Flowers	Late spring	WYORPi	S/PS
JAPANESE BARBERRY (Berberis thunbergii)	6–9	D	R/5–6'	Flowers and red berries	Spring	Y	S/PS
Wintergreen barberry (B. julianae)	6–9	E	to 8'	Flowers and blue-black berries	Spring	Y	S/PS
Mentor barberry (B. x mentorensis)	6–8	E	6–8'	Flowers and red berries	Spring	Y	S/PS
BOXWOOD (Buxus sempervirens)	6–9	E	R/6–20'				S/Sh
Littleleaf boxwood (B. microphylla)	5–8	E	3–7'				S/Sh
WINTERCREEPER (Euonymus fortunei)	5–8	E	S/3–6'	Orange berries	Fall		S/PS
Evergreen euonymus (E. japonica)	7–9	E	S/8–15'	Orange berries	Fall		S/PS
Spreading euonymus (E. kiautschovica)	6–9	E	S/to 9'	Red berries	Fall		S/PS
Winged euonymus (E. alata 'Compacta')	4–8	D	R/6–10'	Orange berries	Fall		S
NARROWLEAF FIRE-THORN (Pyracantha angustifolia)	6–9	D	to 12'	Orange-red berries	Fall		FS
Scarlet firethorn (P. coccinea)	6–9	E/D	6–12'	Orange berries	Fall		FS
Tiny Tim firethorn (P. 'Tiny Tim')	7–9	E	to 13'	Red berries	Fall		FS

KEY TO ABBREVIATIONS

Growth Habits	Colors		Exposure	Growth Rate	Type
R = round	B = blue	P = purple	FS = full sun	M = moderate	D = deciduous
S = sprawling	Bl = black	R = red	PS = part shade	R = rapid	E = evergreen
U = upright	O = orange	W = white	S = sun	S = slow	
	Pi = pink	Y = yellow	Sh = shade		

GROWTH RATE, REQUIREMENTS, AND CHARACTERISTICS	PROPAGATION	PRUNING	FALL FOLIAGE/FRUIT
R; moist soil, humid air; aromatic foliage; good for hedging	Seed; hardwood cutting, Nov–March Seed; softwood cutting, late spring Seed; hardwood cutting, Oct.–Jan.	Little needed; before growth in spring	
M; cool, moist, acid soil; cold to very hardy; fall foliage with leaf drop in fall; single to clustered flowers	Seed; softwood cutting (can be difficult); root cutting (all seasons); layering	Deadhead; can cut back after bloom; little or no pruning required	
M; can be good for hedging; light, acid, sandy/clay loam; can tolerate heat and drought	Seed; softwood cutting, June–Oct. Seed; hardwood cutting, winter Semihardwood cutting, Aug.	Little needed	Fruit: Oct. Leaves: yellow-orange-red
S; grows in climates without extremes; mulch—has shallow root system	Seed; cuttings, July–Nov.; root divisions	Prune and shear for hedge or topiary	
M; leathery leaves; good for hedges; resists frost, smog, dog urine; any soil but wet	Seed; cuttings any time	Little needed	Fruit: Oct.–Nov.
S; rodent prone			
R; well-drained, nonacid soil; good for hedging, espaliers; resists pollution but not disease—choose disease-resistant varieties	Seed; cuttings any time	Shorten "wild" shoots during summer	Fruit: fall

Continued

RECOMMENDED SHRUBS *(Continued)*

COMMON NAME (BOTANICAL NAME)	ZONES	TYPE	GROWTH HABITS/ HEIGHT	FLOWERS OR FRUIT	SEASON OF BLOOM OR FRUITING	COLORS	EXPOSURE
COMMON FLOWERING QUINCE (Chaenomeles speciosa)	5–9	D	R/6–10'	Flowers and fruit	Spring	WPiR	FS
FORSYTHIA (Forsythia x intermidia)	5–9	D	R/to 9'	Flowers	Early spring	Y	S/PS
Weeping forsythia (F. suspensa)	5–9	D	7–10'	Flowers	Early spring	Y	S/PS
ENGLISH HOLLY (Ilex aquifolium)	6–9	E	4–40'	Yellowish orange-red berries	Fall		PS/Sh
Wilson holly (I. x altaclarensis)	6–9	E	6–20'	Red berries	Fall		PS/Sh
Chinese holly (I. cornuta)	7–9	E	2–10'	Large red berries	Fall		PS/Sh
Japanese holly (I. crenata)	6–8	E	2–15'	Small blue berries	Fall		PS/Sh
HOLLY OSMANTHUS (Osmanthus heterophyllus)	7–9	E	U/8–15'	Flowers	Summer	W	PS/Sh
BIGLEAF HYDRANGEA (Hydrangea macrophylla)	6–9	D	6–10'	Flowers	Mid- to late summer	BRP	FS
Peegee hydrangea (H. paniculata)	4–8	D	to 20'	Flowers	Late summer	W	FS
Hills-of-snow (H. arborescens)	4–9	D	3–5'	Flowers	Early summer	W	FS
CHINESE JUNIPER (Juniperus chinensis)	4–10	E	S/2–75'	Blue berries	Fall		FS
Shore juniper (J. conferta)	6–10	E	to 2'				FS
Savin juniper (J. sabina)	3–10	E	to 4'				FS
ENGLISH LAUREL (Prunus laurocerasus)	7–9	E	R/to 5–20'	Flowers	Spring	W	S/PS
Carolina cherry laurel (P. caroliniana)	7–9	E	U/20–30'	Flowers	Early spring	W	S/PS
LILAC (Syringa vulgaris)	4–8	D	U/to 15'	Flowers	Spring	WYRBP	S preferred
Chinese lilac (S. x chinensis)	3–7	D	U/8–15'	Flowers	Spring	P	S preferred

KEY TO ABBREVIATIONS

Growth Habits	Colors		Exposure	Growth Rate	Type
R = round	B = blue	P = purple	FS = full sun	M = moderate	D = deciduous
S = sprawling	Bl = black	R = red	PS = part shade	R = rapid	E = evergreen
U = upright	O = orange	W = white	S = sun	S = slow	
	Pi = pink	Y = yellow	Sh = shade		

GROWTH RATE, REQUIREMENTS, AND CHARACTERISTICS	PROPAGATION	PRUNING	FALL FOLIAGE/FRUIT
M; tolerates wide range in temperature and soil; good for hedging, espaliers, flower arrangements	Seed; cuttings, June–Aug.	Maintenance prune after bloom	Fruit: yellow-green with reddish blush, Oct.
R; shallow roots; good for hedging, cutting, forced blooms in winter	Seed; cuttings any time	Maintenance prune after bloom	Leaves: green to yellow-green
S; most soils; male/female plants; good for hedging; tolerates salt air and pollution	Seed (difficult); terminal cuttings of firm wood, June–Feb.	Little needed	Fruit
Good for screen; urban tolerant	Cuttings late summer	Little needed	
R; rich, well-drained acid or alkaline, moist soil; sheltered position best	Seed; cuttings any time seed; softwood cuttings, June–July Division of suckering roots	Maintenance prune after bloom Cut previous year's shoots back by 1/3 Cut slightly above the ground in spring	
S; well-drained soil, acid or alkaline; best dry, sandy soil	Seed; for greenhouse, take hardwood cuttings in winter; for cold frame, late-summer or early-fall cuttings	Little needed; some can be pruned and sheared for hedges	
R; well-drained, moist soil; aromatic leaves; good for hedging	Seed; cuttings any time Seed; softwood, semihardwood cuttings, June–Sept.	Little needed; can be pruned and sheared for hedges (in summer)	
M; neutral to alkaline moist, fertile soil	Seed; cuttings any time; division of suckers; layering root cuttings Seed; softwood, hardwood cuttings	Remove suckers; can be pruned severely to rejuvenate	

Continued

RECOMMENDED SHRUBS *(Continued)*

COMMON NAME (BOTANICAL NAME)	ZONES	TYPE	GROWTH HABITS/ HEIGHT	FLOWERS OR FRUIT	SEASON OF BLOOM OR FRUITING	COLORS	EXPOSURE
SWEET MOCK ORANGE *(Philadelphus coronarius)*	5–8	D	10–12'	Flowers	Early summer	W	PS/Sh
Virginalis mock orange *(P. x virginalis)*	4–8	D	to 6–8'	Flowers	Mid-summer	W	FS
NANDINA *(Nandina domestica)*	6–9	E	U/6–10'	Flowers and red berries	Mid-summer	W	S/PS
OLEANDER *(Nerium oleander)*	8–11	E	R/to 8–20'	Flower	Spring/summer	WYPR	S/PS
JAPANESE PRIVET *(Ligustrum japonicum)*	7–11	E	to 10'	Flowers and black berries	Mid-summer	W	S/PS
Glossy privet *(L. lucidum)*	8–11	E	to 20–40'	Flowers and blue-black berries	Late summer	W	S/PS
Amur privet *(L. amurense)*	4–7	D	U/12–15'	Flowers and black berries	Early summer	W	S/PS
CAROLINA RHODODENDRON *(Rhododendron carolinianum)*	6–9	E	6–8'	Flowers	Early summer	Pi	S/PS
PJM rhododendron *(R. 'PJM')*	5–8	E	5–8'	Flowers	Spring	P	S/PS
Catawba rhododendron *(R. catawbiense)*	5–9	E	R/6–12'	Flowers	Spring	WPiPR	S/PS
JAPANESE SNOWBALL *(Viburnum plicatum)*	5–8	D	8–12'	Flowers and red berries	Late spring	W	S/PS
Cranberry bush *(V. opulus)*	3–8	D	8–15'	Flowers and red berries	Late spring	W	S/PS
BUMALD SPIREA *(Spiraea bumalda)*	4–8	D	R/2–3'	Flowers	Early summer	Pi	S
Vanhoutte spirea *(S. x vanhouttei)*	5–8	D	R/6–9'	Flowers	Late spring	W	S
NORWAY SPRUCE *(Picea abies)*	2–8	E	U/to 75'	Cones			FS
Alberta spruce *(P. glauca 'Conica')*	2–5	E	to 7'	Cones			FS
ENGLISH YEW *(Taxus baccata)*	6–8	E	U, R, or S to 65'	Red berries	Fall		S/PS
Japanese yew *(T. cuspidata)*	5–7	E	to 50'	Red berries	Fall		S/PS

KEY TO ABBREVIATIONS

Growth Habits	Colors		Exposure	Growth Rate	Type
R = round	B = blue	P = purple	FS = full sun	M = moderate	D = deciduous
S = sprawling	Bl = black	R = red	PS = part shade	R = rapid	E = evergreen
U = upright	O = orange	W = white	S = sun	S = slow	
	Pi = pink	Y = yellow	Sh = shade		

GROWTH RATE, REQUIREMENTS, AND CHARACTERISTICS	PROPAGATION	PRUNING	FALL FOLIAGE/FRUIT
M; well-drained loamy soil; tolerates salt air	Seed; softwood cuttings, June–July	Flowers on 2- to 3-year-old wood; remove a few older shoots each year after flowers	
R	Seed; semihardwood or hardwood cuttings in fall	Little needed	Fruit: fall into winter
M; any soil; good for hedging; resists drought, wind, heat, pollution; fragrant flower; poisonous	Seed; cuttings any time	Can be pruned and sheared as hedge or topiary	Fruit
R; tolerates poor soil, drought, neglect Good for hedging; tolerates salt air	Fruit: fall into winter	Fruit: fall into winter	Fruit: fall into winter
S; acid soil; good drainage; woodsy plant; use extra mulch; protect from wind	Seed; semihardwood cuttings Aug.–Nov.; layering, late summer	Deadhead; prune after bloom	
M; moist soil; tolerates salt air and pollution	Seed; cuttings throughout growing season; layering	Little needed	Fruit: fall into winter Leaves: reddish purple
M–R; any drained soil good for hedging; widely adapted	Seed; cuttings any time in leaf	Blooms on 1-year-old wood	Leaf: bronze to purple-red
S; symmetrical	Seed; difficult from cuttings	Little needed; will not grow from needleless wood; can pinch back young growth	
S; most soils with good drainage; protect from winter sun; poisonous foliage, bark, and seeds; male/female; good for hedging	Seed; hardwood cuttings taken after hard frost	Little needed; can be pruned and sheared as hedge	

VINES

The wonderful thing about vines is that they are both decorative and functional. Although they are not freestanding in the manner of shrubs, and are more often used to decorate walls and fences, vines have many uses in your garden. Grapevines grown over an arbor can provide delightful shaded sitting areas. A fragrant blossoming wisteria can mask an unsightly architectural feature, such as a chain link fence, bare wall, or storage shed. Or it can enhance a fine one, such as an iron balustrade or a stone chimney.

Vines can also be used to define boundaries, provided they are given some support. They can lend color and interest to your garden. Some have beautiful blossoms, like the hanging purple clusters of wisteria; others, like jasmine and sweet autumn clematis, have perfumed fragrances.

Still others have decorative fruits or seedpods, such as the unusual pods of the balloon vine or the bright orange berries of bittersweet. If chosen and planted with care, a vine can perform several functions with a minimum of maintenance.

Vines are not only versatile but also vigorous, fast-growing, and relatively pest-free. However, you should be aware that these advantages can turn into disadvantages if you plant a vine in the wrong place. Because they are so vigorous and fast-growing, they can get out of hand, competing with and smothering other plants, even tearing shingles from the side of the house!

SELECTING VINES

When choosing what vines to grow in your garden, you need to take into account several things: the availability of supporting walls or other structures, and their relative exposure; the amount of coverage required (or desired); and the importance to you of having year-round (evergreen) foliage, or of having fragrant or nonfragrant flowers.

Growth Pattern

The main characteristic of vines is their ability to grow, and then some. One of your first considerations in choosing a vine should be to match available support structures to the vine's climbing style.

Basically, vines are plants whose long stems are structurally so weak that they must trail, creep along the ground (as ground cover), or rely on some means of support to climb successfully. Vines most suitable for ground cover are featured in the next chapter.

All true vines grow by fastening to their support in one of several ways. Most are grasping (self-clinging), of which there are several kinds. The largest group consists of *twining* vines, such as morning glories. They simply go around and around the nearest vertical support, guided by their sensitive growing tips. Miraculously, they twine only around vertical supports!

Another group of grasping vines, including the sweet pea, clings to supports by means of *tendrils,* which grow from the stem opposite the leaves. These become strong enough to support the vine and also act as an elastic shock absorber that protects the vine in strong winds.

Still another group is vines that adhere by means of small adhesive discs that attach to flat surfaces like walls where other vines cannot grip. Boston ivy on the walls of college buildings belongs in this category of *suction* vines.

Other vines are *rooting* vines that produce clusters of small roots along the stem as they grow. English ivy is one such vine that doesn't need any type of trellis or artificial support, only a rough vertical surface like a brick wall.

A. Morning glory, a twining vine
B. Sweet pea, a tendril climber
C. Ivy, a rooting vine

A   B   C

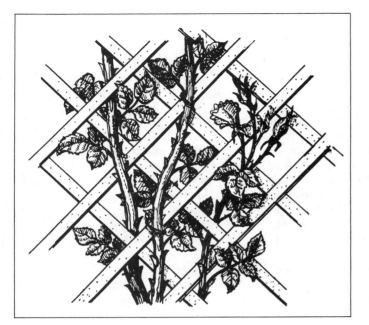

Roses are a leaning vine, requiring support on their climb upward.

Some vines are not true vines, but lean up against, or are tied to, a trellis or support. Rambler or climbing roses are a good example of *leaning* vines. Their thorns may hold them in place, but some means of fastening them upright is often necessary. Even some groundcover plants may develop long runners or grow upright if a convenient woven wire, chicken wire, or lattice trellis lets them weave among the supports.

Unlike shrubs, which are often very slow growing, many vines are fast growers, especially the annuals grown in the North. Because of the shorter growing season and the competition for light before the dense shade of summer arrives, they can grow several inches a day, up to a maximum of 30 or 40 feet. In fact, some gardeners swear that if they look closely, they can see the tendrils on some vines actually moving before their eyes. Those skeptics among us might suggest that they have read *Jack and the Beanstalk* one too many times!

Vines are adaptable to climate and weather conditions. The moonflower, a variety of the morning glory, grows as an annual in Zones 3 to 8 but becomes a perennial in Zones 9 and 10. In other cases, the most common variety of a species will be an annual, but other varieties will grow as perennials. It all depends on the part of the country in which you plant them.

Foliage, Flower, and Fragrance

Almost all vines are deciduous. Few are truly evergreen, holding their leaves year-round. Vines that are evergreen in warmer climates may drop their leaves when grown farther north. In Zones 5 through 7, only a few remain evergreen. One that does is English ivy, which can be grown with varying success as far north as the coast of Maine (although this far north, it would probably grow better as a ground cover). A good selection of vines that are evergreen in the South (including clematis, climbing hydrangea, and Japanese wisteria) can be grown in more northern zones, but they will drop their leaves in the winter.

Although this change from evergreen to deciduous is often attributed to the cold, it may be caused by the drying effects of winter sun and wind. Leaves lose moisture that the frozen roots are unable to replace and they finally die and drop off. For this reason, in colder areas you should plant evergreen vines where they will receive the least exposure to winter sun and wind.

For colorful fall foliage, choose a vine like bittersweet, which has showy golden-yellow leaves in autumn as well as colorful orange-red berries. Varieties of the creeper vine, such as Virginia creeper and Boston ivy, have rich scarlet and yellow-orange foliage, respectively. Generally, those vines grown in temperate climates display a smaller range of colors, and those in subtropical to tropical zones offer a greater range of sharper, fiery colors.

In addition, a good many are annuals that must be replaced each year. Typical of this category is cathedral bells *(Cobaea scandeas),* a vine that has a long blooming season and vigorous growth. Others in this group include the sweet pea *(Lathyrus),* a delicate plant that is hard to grow in many areas.

As mentioned earlier, grapevines in all varieties make excellent arbor plants, providing shade as well as delicious fruit. Wisteria also falls into this category; however, if left unchecked on building walls, its twining stems have been known to tear away wooden shingles and even separate bricks. In the Deep South, bougainvillea is preferred as the traditional porch decoration.

For climbing walls of buildings, vines with suction cups are your best bet. Boston ivy is the classic wall vine. To show off a bold or rough surface, choose vines with small leaves, such as a glossy winter creeper, which will accentuate the rustic effect of a fieldstone wall. Conversely, a smooth or fine-textured surface will be enhanced with a shiny large-leaved vine like Boston ivy.

Finally, many vines have magnificent fragrances—multiplied by the large number of flowers—a quality that is often desirable in vines that climb the walls of buildings, surrounding its windows. Wisteria is popular for its delicate fragrance, but others, like clematis, common white jasmine, and the cinnamon vine, are also popular.

Buying and Planting Vines

As a general rule, vines that survive in a cooler zone will do even better farther south. Many grow more vigorously as the climate becomes warmer. The list of vines you can grow increases greatly in the warmer zones of 9 and 10 and includes the whole spectrum of tropical vines, such as jasmine, passionflower, and bougainvillea, to name a few.

You can buy perennial vines from a retail nursery or by mail order. Both sell them either in pots or bare-rooted, depending on the season and plant.

On the whole, most vines need full sun to grow well, although Dutchman's pipe and Virginia creeper grow very well in the shade. Some, like the rampantly invasive kudzu grown in the South, can do well in both exposures. But though they may grow well in a partially shaded area, vines such as bittersweet and the cinnamon vine may not produce as many blossoms or as much fruit as they would in full sun.

Careful preparation of the planting bed is essential for all vines. Most grow well in soil that retains a moderate amount of moisture but drains well. Organic matter added to your soil will help in the extreme conditions of heavy clay or sand. Also, vines tend to grow in mildly acidic to slightly alkaline soils. However, if you plant them too close to the wall of your house, you may find that the lime from the foundation will affect them adversely. Adding peat moss or sulfur will acidify soil that is too alkaline.

When you are ready to plant, dig a hole wide enough and deep enough to bury the vine at the same depth at which it was previously planted. Before positioning the plant, mix the light-colored subsoil and richer topsoil you have dug up with one part organic matter to two parts of soil. By doing this in the beginning, your vines shouldn't need any fertilizer at this time.

However, when the soil is very light and sandy, some vines such as clematis will do better if they are set 2 to 4 inches *below* their previous depth. As with shrubs, make a 1- to 2-inch-wide depression around the plant and gently fill this small basin with water.

RECOMMENDED VINES

COMMON NAME (BOTANICAL NAME)	ZONES	TYPE	GROWTH HABITS/ HEIGHT	FLOWERS OR FRUIT OF INTEREST	SEASON OF BLOOM OF FRUITING	COLORS	EXPOSURE
BALLOON VINE (Cardiospermum halicacabum)	4–9	A	T/to 10'+	Flowers and seedpods	Summer to fall	W	FS
AMERICAN BITTERSWEET (Celastrus scadens)	3–9	D	T/20–40'	Orange berries	Fall		FS/PS
Oriental bittersweet (C. orbiculatus)	5–9	D	to 20'	Orange berries	Fall		FS/PS
BOUGAINVILLEA (Bougainvillea)	9–11	E	to 40'	Flowers	All year	PPi	FS
CATHEDRAL BELLS (Cobaea scandens)	3–8	A	C to 25'	Flowers	Early summer to mid-fall	P	FS
CHALICE VINE (Solandra grandiflora)	9–11	E	L to 20'	Flowers and red berries	Early spring to summer	Y	S/PS
CINNAMON VINE (Dioscorea batatas)	5–11	P	T/to 10'	Flowers	Late summer	W	FS/PS
JACKMAN CLEMATIS (Clematis jackmanii)	5–9	P	T/to 12'	Flowers and seedpods	Summer	all	PS
Oriental clematis (C. orientalis)	5–9	P	10–20'	Flowers and seedpods	Fall	Y	PS
Sweet autumn clematis (C. paniculata)	5 9	P	to 30'	Flowers and seedpods	Late summer	W	PS
VIRGINIA CREEPER (Parthenocissus quinquefolia)	3–9	D	T, S/to 60'	Dark blue berries	Fall		S/PS
Boston ivy (P. tricuspidata)	5–8	D	to 60'	Dark blue berries	Fall		S/PS
CROSSVINE (Bignonia)	7–11	E	T, S/to 60'	Flowers and seedpods	Late spring to fall	YO	FS/PS
DUTCHMAN'S PIPE (Aristolochia durior)	5–8	P	T/20–30'	Flowers	Spring	Y	PS/FS
Calico flower (A. elegans)	9–11	P	to 10'	Flowers	Summer	WP	PS/FS

KEY TO ABBREVIATIONS

Type		Growth Habits		Exposure		Growth Rate
A=annual	E=evergreen	C=climbing	S=suction	S=sun	FS=full sun	M=moderate
P=perennial		L=leaning	T=twining	PS=part shade		R=rapid
D=deciduous		R=rooting		Sh=shade		S=slow

GROWTH RATE, REQUIREMENTS, AND CHARACTERISTICS	PROPAGATION	CLIMBING METHOD	PRUNING	FALL FOLIAGE/FRUIT
R; well-drained soil; needs wind protection; tendrils	Seed	Tendrils		Fruit: decorative pods
R; needs support; m/f plants; good soil; invasive	Seed; softwood cuttings, July; division of suckers; root cuttings	Twining		Leaf: yellow Fruit: yellow-orange inside w/crimson seeds
M; fragrant blossoms; well-drained soil; climbing; dense w/many flowers	Stem cuttings, July; air layering; ground layering	Twining, needs ties	Deadhead; to control size, after bloom shorten laterals or cut back to main stems; keep some younger stems	
R; moist, well-drained soil; needs support	Seed	Tendril	Pinch back often	
R; moist, well-drained soil; needs support	Cuttings of firm, young shoots; ground layering	Needs support	Prune in spring	
R; moist, well-drained soil; needs support; cinnamon-scented flowers	Seed; pieces of tuberous root; cuttings	Twining		
R; moist, well-drained soil; needs light support; some with fragrant flowers	Seed; cuttings: take single-node cuttings when tight flower buds develop, or semihardwood later	Twining	Cut back overgrown plants; hybrids flower on new wood; cut back in late winter to 12" above ground; trim others lightly after bloom	
R; tolerates wind, heat, drought; creates dense cover; m/f plants; moist, humus-rich soil	Cuttings of underground stems, seeds	Twining, stem climbing		
R; most soils; clings to brick	Seed; softwood cuttings, June–Aug.	Tendrils	As for bougainvillea	Leaf: dense yellow-orange to crimson-red
M; any well-drained soil; makes good screen	Seed; ground layering, semihardwood cuttings	Tendrils	Prune in early spring	

Continued

RECOMMENDED VINES *(Continued)*

COMMON NAME (BOTANICAL NAME)	ZONES	TYPE	GROWTH HABITS/ HEIGHT	FLOWERS OR FRUIT OF INTEREST	SEASON OF BLOOM OF FRUITING	COLORS	EXPOSURE
ENGLISH IVY (Hedera helix)	6–9	E	R/to 100'	Purple berries	Fall		PS/FS
Algerian ivy (H. canariensis)	9–11	E	R/to 100'	Purple berries	Fall		PS/FS
FOX GRAPE (Vitis labrusca)	5–9	D	T, S/50–90'	Purple fruit	Summer		FS
Riverbank grape (V. riparia)	3–9	D	T, S/50–90'	Purple fruit	Summer		FS
Concord grape (V. labrusca)		D	T, S/50–90'	Purple fruit	Summer		FS
HALL'S HONEYSUCKLE (Lonicera japonica)	5–9	E/D	T/to 15'	Flowers	Summer	W	S/PS
Goldflame honeysuckle (L. heckrotti)	5–9	E/D	to 15'	Flowers	Summer	YR	S/PS
COMMON HOP VINE (Humulus lupulus)	4–10	P	T/20–35'	Thin cones	Summer		FS/PS
Japanese hop vine (H. japonicus)	all	A	to 25'				FS/PS
HYACINTH BEAN (Dolichos lablab)	3–8	A	T/10–30'	Flowers	Summer	WP	FS
CLIMBING HYDRANGEA (Hydrangea anomala petiolaris)	5–8	D	R/to 40'	Flowers	Summer	W	FS/PS
SCENTED STAR JASMINE (Jasminum floridum)	8–11	E	T, L/20–30'	Flowers	Spring/summer	Y	FS/PS
Common white jasmine (J. officinale)	7–11	E/D	to 20'	Flowers	Spring/summer	W	FS/PS
MORNING GLORY (Ipomoea purpurea)	3–11	A	T/to 20'	Flowers	Summer	WRPPi	FS/PS
Moonflower (I. alba)	3–11	A/P	to 40'	Flowers	Mid-summer	W	FS/PS
PASSIONFLOWER (Passiflora incarnata)	8–11	E	over 15'	Flowers	Summer	RPB	FS

KEY TO ABBREVIATIONS

Type		Growth Habits			Exposure			Growth Rate
A = annual	E = evergreen	C = climbing		S = suction	S = sun		FS = full sun	M = moderate
P = perennial		L = leaning		T = twining	PS = part shade			R = rapid
D = deciduous		R = rooting			Sh = shade			S = slow

GROWTH RATE, REQUIREMENTS, AND CHARACTERISTICS	PROPAGATION	CLIMBING METHOD	PRUNING	FALL FOLIAGE/FRUIT
R; well-drained soil; tolerates city air; flower malodorous	Seed; division; cuttings, July	Twining	Will stand heavy pruning; prune in winter	
M; mulch in spring; loam w/peat moss; tolerates shade; good for topiary	Seed; cuttings any time	Rootlike holdfasts	Little needed; in spring	
R; moist, well-drained, alkaline soil; fruit edible, good for jelly/wine	Seed; hardwood cuttings	Tendril	Prune fall/spring; cut back new growth to two-bud spurs in fall (there are numerous other training systems for grapes)	Leaf: red, orange, purple Fruit: purple (edible)
R; fragrant flowers; dense foliage; invasive growth	Seed; softwood cuttings June–Aug; soil layering; root division	Twining	As for bougainvillea	Fruit: black berry Aug.–Oct.
R; well-drained soil; doesn't transplant well; needs support	Seed	Twining, needs support		
M; tolerates varied soils; tiered branches; fragrant flowers	Seed	Aerial rootlets	Can be pruned severely in fall or early spring	
M; light, well-drained soil; fertilize monthly; fragrant	Seed; cuttings any time	Shrublike climbing stems	Occasional, to maintain shape	
R; very distinct large flowers; humus-rich soil	Seed (can be difficult); cuttings, Sept.; root division	Tendrils	To control size, cut back to 2 or 3 buds on last year's shoots	Fruit: yellow-green (edible)
R; any well-drained soil; flowers open in the a.m., close by noon	Seed	Twining		

Continued

RECOMMENDED VINES *(Continued)*

COMMON NAME (BOTANICAL NAME)	ZONES	TYPE	GROWTH HABITS/ HEIGHT	FLOWERS OR FRUIT OF INTEREST	SEASON OF BLOOM OF FRUITING	COLORS	EXPOSURE
SWEET PEA *(Lathyrus odoratus)*	5–9	A	T/to 6'	Flowers	Summer	RBP	FS
Beach pea *(L. japonicus)*	5–9	P	to 9'	Flowers	Summer	P	FS
WINTERCREEPER *(Euonymus fortunei)*	5–8	E	R/to 40'	Orange berries	Fall		FS/PS
WISTERIA *(Wisteria floribunda)*	6–10	D	T/25–30'	Flowers	Summer	P	FS
Chinese wisteria *(W. sinensis)*	6–10	D	to 50'	Flowers	Late spring	BP	FS

KEY TO ABBREVIATIONS

Type		Growth Habits		Exposure		Growth Rate
A = annual	E = evergreen	C = climbing	S = suction	S = sun	FS = full sun	M = moderate
P = perennial		L = leaning	T = twining	PS = part shade		R = rapid
D = deciduous		R = rooting		Sh = shade		S = slow

When planting vines to cover a specific area, you should not plant more than one plant to every foot, thus preventing vines from strangling one another as they quickly mature.

Since many vines are annuals, they can be started from seeds. Like other annuals, you may wish to start them indoors in peat pots to get an early start—especially for late bloomers like balloon vines.

Lastly, woody vines such as Boston ivy can be propagated from stem cuttings taken in early summer. These can be rooted in a plastic-covered pot of vermiculite or perlite placed on the windowsill in partial shade.

MAINTENANCE

Watering and mulching are beneficial to all vines. They are usually deep-rooted and need a thorough soaking every week to ten days during the growing season. Vines also benefit from periodic hosing of their foliage to keep down insects and grime. This is best done in the morning. Mulching will help reduce watering needs and keep roots cool and moist.

Winter protection is not generally needed except, perhaps, for climbing roses. They can be protected by laying the stems on the ground and covering them with soil.

Vines should be pruned starting at the planting stage. Remove any broken stems or roots. If you purchased the plant bare-rooted, trim at least one-third of the top growth after planting to compensate for root loss when the plant was dug up.

In addition, most perennial woody vines require pruning once a year in late winter or early spring to give the new growth ample time to mature before the next winter. Leafy vines, on the other hand, can be pruned whenever necessary. Flowering vines need to be

GROWTH RATE, REQUIREMENTS, AND CHARACTERISTICS	PROPAGATION	CLIMBING METHOD	PRUNING	FALL FOLIAGE/FRUIT
R; hard to grow; cool, moist, humus-rich, alkaline soil; fragrant flowers; needs support	Seed (though difficult)	Needs support tendril		
M; tolerates varied soils	Seed; cuttings any time	Clinging runners		Fruit: pink
M; fragrant blossoms; well-drained loam	Seed; cuttings, July	Twining	Cut back shoots in summer; in winter can cut shoots to 2 or 3 buds from base	Fruit: pods

pruned only after they flower, since many, such as wisteria, form their buds the previous summer.

Some vines also need to be trained to their supports. To do this, use a soft, flexible tie. Suction or clinging vines with rootlets or discs should not be trained against a wooden surface, such as clapboard or shingle, since they keep wood moist and tend to cause rot. Instead, choose vines with tendrils or a twining habit that can be trained on a trellis that stands a few feet from the surface.

GROUND COVERS

I t is useful as well as beautiful to plant expanses of your home landscape with a ground cover, in a way that replaces part or all of a grass lawn. In fact, the grass lawn itself (covered separately in Chapter 15) is the simplest ground cover, for ground cover is the most horizontal level of foliage in the landscape. The plants chosen for a dense, massed planting of ground cover may be low-growing perennial herbs such as pachysandra or ferns, evergreen perennial vines such as English ivy or periwinkle, or low-growing shrubs such as creeping juniper or dwarf cotoneaster. Be especially careful when choosing shrubs—select species and cultivars with a prostrate habit, not their close relatives that grow tall.

Groundcover plants are used in quantity to anchor and decorate the bare earth. Like living mulch, they help trees and shrubs grow better by keeping the soil moist and cool. They need only minimal upkeep once they are established—less than lawn grass, which must be mowed and fertilized often. The most effective groundcover plants are perennial, evergreen or nearly so, sturdy, and pest resistant. They spread horizontally, fill the ground so densely that weeds are crowded out, usually are propagated with ease, and stay low or at a uniform height without heavy pruning. Some will tolerate being walked on, but none of the many popular types can bear heavy recreational traffic. Few ground covers have showy flowers, but some do, either briefly or for many weeks each year. Groundcover plants are often utilized in difficult spots where lawns do not thrive—on steep slopes, in wet or dry areas, and in deep shade under trees.

Plants used as ground covers may also be used in flower beds or for other garden purposes. For instance, hostas are popular in flower borders, so the various cultivars and species are discussed more completely in its entry on pages 285–87. However, if used in masses, hostas serve as excellent ground covers, too. This is also true of ajuga, astilbe, bergenia, basket-of-gold, daylilies, phlox, yarrow, and others. Several herbs (thyme and sweet woodruff, for instance) are very popular as ground cover, for they make low, dense, matlike growth. Unsupported annual and perennial vines such as morning glory, clematis, nasturtium, thunbergia, and ivy geranium may serve as temporary or permanent ground cover, though they are usually used for other purposes. Even strawberries will work as ground cover, providing evergreen or nearly evergreen leaves, showy flowers, and edible fruit, but remember that they need more cultivation and care than the more usual ground-cover plants. Any low-growing plant that grows densely may be used as ground cover— literally, to cover the ground. The many plant choices offer you an array of colors, textures, sizes, functions, and forms to work with.

PLACEMENT

The most obvious site for a groundcover planting is any part of your landscape where other plants, especially lawn grasses, do not grow well. Another sensible area to cover is any spot that is difficult or tiresome to mow or maintain, or is subject to erosion. You can fill corners, rough terrain, and other spots with ground cover, leaving a smaller oval area of grass to mow very quickly, or use ground cover in combination with paved walks and living areas such as decks and terraces to eliminate grass and mowing altogether.

A less obvious spot to plant with ground cover is an area that is not a problem but would look better planted with the texture and color of groundcover plants. Ground covers are attractive when used as transition areas between the lawn and foundation plantings or shrubs. They can add subtle interest to an area that is too plain, or replace a mixed bed that looks too fussy or busy.

Once you have the general area to be covered in mind, refine it and give it shape. For instance, if you plan to use ground cover in a bare area under a shade tree, bring the edge of the groundcover bed out parallel to the outer edge of the tree's canopy, or nearly so—do not make a tiny circle around the tree trunk, as it will look inadequate. If there is a problem area next to the house, and the sidewalk is a few feet away, completely fill the space between them with ground cover, and consider adding a corresponding area of ground cover on the other side of the walk in addition. Use ground cover expansively, not in meager strips or dots. Plot the design out on paper if you can. Extend and fill in the areas of ground cover so that they give a finished look to the landscape.

SELECTION

A great-looking ground cover is one that thrives naturally in the kind of environment you give it—soil type, moisture, climate, exposure, etc. No matter how difficult or unusual the spot, some kind of ground cover can grow there. Many native plants are excellent, carefree ground covers, but so are some of the recent arrivals. The table of ground covers on pages 602–11 shows the attributes and needs of different species. Narrow the field by eliminating the types that are not suited to the growing conditions in your site, and then select from among the others. Try to find plants that will not be in the top or bottom of their hardiness range, for they may be only marginally hardy in your site. Although soil pH can be altered, you will save yourself work if you choose a plant that grows in the pH soil you have. Fortunately, most ground covers for areas with cold winters will grow in neutral to somewhat acidic soil—the prevailing conditions.

RECOMMENDED GROUND COVERS

COMMON NAME BOTANICAL NAME	ZONES	TYPE	EXPOSURE	SOIL
Asparagus fern (Asparagus densiflorus 'Sprengeri')	9–11	T/HP ES	FS/PS	Dry to moist, well drained
Bearberry (Arctostaphylos uva-ursi)	2–6	H/HP D	FS/PS	Well drained, acidic, salt tolerant
Bergenia (Bergenia cordifolia; Bergenia hybrids) (See pages 195–97 in Flowers)	3–9	H/HP D/E	S/PS S	Moist, rich, well drained
Bugleweed (Ajuga reptans) (See page 165 in Flowers)	4–9	H/HP D/ES	PS, FS	Any, prefers rich, moist
Chamomile, Russian chamomile (Chamaemelum nobile)	3–9	H/HP D/ES	FS/PS	Good, moist
Cinquefoil (Potentilla species)	4–8	H Shrub D	FS/PS	Rich, well drained
Cotoneaster (Cotoneaster prostrate species, e.g., C. adpressus and C. horizontalis)	5–9	H Shrub D	FS/PS	Average to rich, well drained
Crown vetch (Coronilla varia)	3–9	H/HP D	FS/PS	Poor to average, pH 6.5 to 7
Deutzia (Deutzia gracilis)	6–9	H Shrub D	FS/PS	Average, moist

KEY TO ABBREVIATIONS

Type
H = hardy
T = tender
HP = herbaceous perennial
D = deciduous
E = evergreen
ES = evergreen in South (Zones 9–11)

Exposure
FS = full sun
PS = part shade
S = sun
Sh = shade

DESCRIPTION	PLANTING RECOMMENDATIONS
3' spreading, arched plumes of airy green foliage, small white flowers, red berries, tuberous roots.	Plant 10 to 20" apart any time in mild weather, especially spring after frost. Division is easiest when new growth begins in spring. Prune for neatness at any time, removing yellowed foliage.
Creeping, low, evergreen, viny plants with small, glossy oval leaves, pink or white flowers, lasting red berries.	Plant 3 to 4' apart, ideally in late winter while plants are dormant and soil frozen, though potted plants may be planted in spring. Divide in late winter while dormant. Cuttings may be taken late fall through winter for growth in spring. Prune in late fall or winter.
Fleshy, round leaves a foot or two tall make sturdy mats of foliage, bear spires of white, pink, or lavender flowers.	Set plants 10 to 20" apart, preferably in early spring before frost ends. Divide and take cuttings in early spring, too. Remove damaged leaves and spent flowers whenever necessary.
Fast-creeping, stoloniferous creeping plants with low rosettes of oval leaves, spires of blue, white, or pink flowers.	Set plants 6" or more apart in spring or fall, or whenever weather is cool and moist. Divide by moving offshoots (which are basal rosettes on stolons) in fall or spring. Remove unsightly foliage whenever necessary.
Delicate, 1' plants with many branches, finely divided foliage, yellow and white daisylike flowers ½" wide in summer.	Sow seedlings indoors in flats in late winter and set out plants 3" apart a week or two before last expected frost, after hardening them off. Divide and take cuttings in early spring when new growth begins. Shear plants for neatness by mowing like grass.
2' bushy plants (many cultivars) have strawberrylike foliage and yellow, cream, or red flowers about an inch wide.	Plant spring through fall 1 to 3' apart, depending on species. Divide herbaceous types in spring. Take hardwood cuttings of shrubs in fall. Do major pruning in fall, winter, or spring, but clip for neatness whenever necessary.
Tall or low-growing cultivars have small, shiny oval leaves, red berries, and red leaves in fall. Deciduous.	Plant in spring or fall 3' or more apart, for most types. Spring is preferred. Take cuttings of half-ripened wood in late summer. Do major pruning in fall through spring, but clip for neatness whenever necessary.
2' tall, spreading plants have pink blooms from June to frost, green leaves. Roots anchor soil though leaves die in winter.	Plant crowns 2' apart in spring. Divide clumps in spring when new growth begins, rather than take cuttings. Remove browned foliage in late fall or winter, before growth resumes in spring, for neatness, if you wish.
Low, wide deciduous shrubs 2 to 4' tall, have slim green leaves and are covered with showy sprays of white flowers in May.	Plant 3 to 4' apart in spring. Divide in spring if plants have multiple rooted stems. Take softwood cuttings and tip layers in late spring or hardwood cuttings in late summer. Prune after flowering.

Continued

RECOMMENDED GROUND COVERS *(Continued)*

COMMON NAME BOTANICAL NAME	ZONES	TYPE	EXPOSURE	SOIL
Epimedium (*Epimedium* species)	4–8	H/HP D	PS/Sh	Humus-rich, moist, pH 5 to 6
Ferns (Several genera, many species, e.g., *Dryopteris spinulosa, Adiantum pedatum, Athyrium filix-femina, Osmunda cinnamomea*)	All (zones vary with the species)	H or T/HP D/E	PS (most)	Moist, rich, loamy
Foamflower (*Tiarella cordifolia*)	3–8	H/HP D	PS	Rich, moist, loamy
Ginger, European wild (*Asarum europaeum*)	4–8	H/HP D	PS/Sh	Rich, moist, loamy
Golden star (*Chrysogonum virginianum*)	5–9	H/HP D	FS/PS	Rich, moist, loamy
Goutweed, Bishop's weed (*Aegopodium podagraria* 'Variegatum')	3–9	H/HP D	FS/PS	Any
Heather, Heath (*Erica* species, e.g., *E. carnea, E. vagans*)	3–7, but this varies	H Shrub E	FS	Moist, acid
Heather, Scotch (*Calluna vulgaris*)	5–8	H Shrub E	FS	Well drained, sandy
Hosta (*Hosta* species) (See pages 285–87 in Flowers)	3–9	H/HP D	PS/Sh	Light to heavy, rich, damp to well drained, neutral to slightly acidic

KEY TO
ABBREVIATIONS

Type
H = hardy
T = tender
HP = herbaceous
  perennial
D = deciduous
E = evergreen
ES = evergreen
  in South
  (Zones 9–11)

Exposure
FS = full sun
PS = part shade
S = sun
Sh = shade

DESCRIPTION	PLANTING RECOMMENDATIONS
Fernlike leaves in sprays 1' tall are nearly evergreen. In spring, plants bear 6 to 8" sprays of yellow, pink, or red flowers.	Plant 10 to 20" apart in early spring before frost ends. Divide rhizomes in early spring. Remove browned foliage (for neatness) or leave it in place to mark location.
From ½ to over 4' tall, ferns vary in size, texture, and color. A few types are evergreen. Most spread thickly with runners.	Plant dormant plants with bare roots in spring before frost ends. Potted plants may be set in at any time if weather is cool and moist. Space plants as far apart as they are tall for most species. Do not set plants in too deeply. Divide plants in early spring before frost ends, when new growth begins. Remove browned foliage in late spring after danger of hard frost ends.
Semi-evergreen leafy plants stay low, bear delicate sprays of white flowers in spring.	Plant 10 to 20" apart, preferably in early spring. Divide in early spring. Remove browned foliage and spent flowers if you wish.
Shiny, round evergreen leaves about 3" wide make an attractive low cover. Flowers are brownish and inconspicuous.	Plant 1' apart in spring. If crowded, divide rhizomes in midspring when new growth begins (later than most other woodland plants). Remove browned foliage if you wish.
Creeping, low plants have oval, scalloped leaves and daisylike yellow flowers summer to fall. This U.S. native spreads rapidly.	Plant 1' apart in spring before or after last frost. Divide in early spring when new growth begins. Remove spent foliage if you wish.
A silver edge makes leaves of this cultivar attractive, though invasive. Foliage 6" tall bears sprays of white flowers on 14" stems.	Plant 1' apart in spring or fall where its weediness is not a problem. Plants spread vigorously and are hard to eradicate. Divide plants in spring or fall. Remove spent foliage and flowers for neatness.
1 to 2', low shrubs with small leaves bloom in spring or fall, white, rose, or purple. Foliage is colorful on some types.	Plant 1½ to 3' apart, preferably in early spring. Take tip cuttings in summer for outdoor planting or in winter for rooting indoors. Trim for neatness after flowering. Do not try to grow this in areas with hot summers in the mid-90's (F).
Low-growing shrubs form spreading mats of foliage. Leaves are small, plants bear masses of tiny white, rose, or purple flowers.	Plant 1 to 3' apart in early spring. Take tip cuttings in summer for outdoor planting or in winter for rooting indoors. Trim for neatness. In snowless areas, mulch in winter with pine boughs but remove in early spring. Trim for neatness whenever necessary. Plants tolerate salt air.
Basal rosettes of ovoid, pointed, deciduous leaves may be solid green or touched with white or yellow. Plants flower in summer, sizes vary.	Plant 10" to 3' apart, preferably in spring when new growth begins. Divide in spring or fall, using a sharp knife to cut through woody roots before digging. Remove the previous year's foliage in spring when new growth begins, or earlier for neatness.

Continued

RECOMMENDED GROUND COVERS *(Continued)*

COMMON NAME BOTANICAL NAME	ZONES	TYPE	EXPOSURE	SOIL
Ivy, English *(Hedera helix)*	3–10	H Vine E	PS/Sh	Any
Juniper, Creeping *(Juniperus, prostrate species such as J. sabina 'Forest,' J. conferta, J. chinensis, J. scopulorum)*	3–10	H Shrub E	FS/PS	Fertile, rich, well drained, neutral to acidic
Lady's mantle *(Alchemilla mollis)* (See pages 297–98 in Flowers)	3–8	H/HP D	FS/PS	Rich, moist
Lamium *(Lamium maculatum)*	4–9	H/HP E	PS/Sh	Rich, moist, loamy
Lawn leaf *(Dichondra micrantha)*	9–10	T/HP ES	FS/PS	Well drained
Lily of the valley *(Convallaria majalis)*	3–9	H/HP D	FS/PS	Rich, loamy, moist
Lilyturf *(Liriope muscari)*	6–9	H/HP D/ES	FS/PS	Any
Lilyturf, Creeping *(Liriope spicata)*	6–9	H/HP D/ES	FS/PS	Any
Mazus *(Mazus reptans)*	5–9	H/HP D/ES	PS, FS	Rich, moist

KEY TO ABBREVIATIONS

Type
H = hardy
T = tender
HP = herbaceous
   perennial
D = deciduous
E = evergreen
ES = evergreen
   in South
   (Zones 9–11)

Exposure
FS = full sun
PS = part shade
S = sun
Sh = shade

DESCRIPTION	PLANTING RECOMMENDATIONS
Evergreen, climbing, woody vines with lobed green or green-and-white leaves cover ground densely. Darker cultivars are more vigorous.	In spring or fall, plant 6" to 2' apart, depending on size of plant or cuttings—small rooted or unrooted cuttings are set closer than mature plants. Divide plants and take cuttings in spring or fall, or whenever weather is moist and mild. Trim for shape several times a year if needed, at any time.
Groundcover junipers have a prostrate habit. Densely branched plants often are bluish green, with small needles.	Plant 3 to 6' apart in spring, summer, or fall. Take cuttings in fall on new wood with a ½" bit of old wood at the base. Prune in spring or fall.
Round, fanlike, silvery green leaves up to 6" wide appear in spring, followed by sprays of chartreuse flowers in summer.	Plant 1' apart in spring at about the time of the last frost. Divide in spring when new growth begins. Remove spent flowers and foliage for neatness.
Textured, scalloped leaves touched with silver are evergreen on vinelike stems. Spires of white flowers appear in late spring.	Plant 6 to 20" apart, depending on size of cuttings or clumps, preferably in spring. Summer and fall are also good if weather is mild and moist. Divide at any time, especially spring and fall. Take tip layers and cuttings in spring. Trim for neatness whenever necessary.
Creeping plants have ½" kidney-shaped leaves of whitish green and minute flowers. Plants are related to morning glories.	Plant 6 to 20" apart, depending on size of cuttings or clumps, in winter or early spring. Divide in winter or spring, and take cuttings during wet, cool seasons. Prune as needed at any time. Plants may be walked on moderately.
Ovoid, pointed leaves 8 to 12" tall surround stems bearing a column of tiny white or pink flowers in spring. Foliage lasts through fall.	Plant 8 to 12" apart, preferably in midspring a few weeks before frost ends, while in pip stage, or later if plants are in pots, not bare rooted. Divide in early spring or late fall. Remove spent foliage for neatness, or leave it on plants through the winter to mark location.
2' straplike, grasslike leaves grow thickly. Spires of pale lilac flowers something like grape hyacinths appear in summer.	Plant 12" or more apart in spring in most areas, or any time during moist weather in Zone 9. Divide by separating and replanting stoloniferous roots. Trim browned ends if damaged in winter, and remove spent flowers.
Under 1' tall, the thin grasslike leaves make a deep green mat of foliage. Small spires of white or violet flowers bloom in summer.	Plant 6 to 16" apart any time, especially spring. Divide rhizomes in spring or any time in moist weather that is not too hot. Trim browned leaves if necessary (rarely).
Tiny, creeping plants under 3" tall have multitudes of purple or white orchidlike flowers ½" long in late spring.	Set clumps 4 to 20" apart or wherever needed between flagstones. They spread rapidly. Plant and divide from spring to fall in mild, moist weather. Trimming is seldom or never needed.

Continued

RECOMMENDED GROUND COVERS (Continued)

COMMON NAME BOTANICAL NAME	ZONES	TYPE	EXPOSURE	SOIL
Mondo grass (Ophiopogon japonicus)	7–10	H/HP D/ES	FS/PS	Any
Moss pink (Phlox subulata)	2–9	H/HP E, leaves discolor in summer	FS	Well drained, sandy
Pachysandra, Japanese spurge (Pachysandra terminalis)	3–9	H/HP E	PS/Sh	Average to good
Phlox, Creeping (Phlox stolonifera) (See pages 338–39 in Flowers)	4–8	H/HP D	PS/Sh	Loamy, well drained
Phlox, Mountain (Phlox divaricata) (See page 338 in Flowers)	3–8	H/HP D	PS/Sh	Loamy, well drained, neutral to acidic
Plumbago (Ceratostigma plumbaginoides)	5–9	H/HP D/ES	FS/PS	Any
Pussytoes (Antennaria dioica)	2–8	H/HP D	FS	Well drained
Rock cress (Arabis caucasica)	3–7	H/HP D	FS	Moist, well drained
Sedum, Stone crop (Sedum, prostrate species, e.g., S. spurium 'Dragon's Blood,' S. acre, S. album, S. spathulifolium)	3–9 (most)	H/HP D/E	FS/PS	Well drained

KEY TO ABBREVIATIONS

Type
H = hardy
T = tender
HP = herbaceous perennial
D = deciduous
E = evergreen
ES = evergreen in South (Zones 9–11)

Exposure
FS = full sun
PS = part shade
S = sun
Sh = shade

DESCRIPTION	PLANTING RECOMMENDATIONS
Evergreen in Zones 9 and 10, grassy, straplike leaves 8 to 18" tall arch gracefully.	Plant 6 to 24" apart at any time, especially spring. Divide in spring or summer during moist weather between 45° and 90°F. Trim for neatness whenever necessary.
Low, evergreen mats of foliage bear a dense layer of fragrant starlike, white, rose, or violet-blue flowers in spring.	Plant clumps 12 to 24" apart, depending on their size. The best time is in spring before or during bloom. Divide just after blooming ends. Take cuttings in spring or early fall. Trim off browned patches that fail to leaf out with the rest of the plant in spring.
Creeping, evergreen plants grow 8 to 12" tall with rosettes of scalloped leaves on short stems and small white flowers in spring.	Plant clumps or rooted cuttings 8 to 24" apart, depending on their size and how quickly you need coverage. Spring and fall are the best times to plant, divide, and take cuttings. Trim off leaves with brown patches and excess growth in spring.
Stoloniferous, creeping plants stay low and spread quickly. Showy 8" stalks of white, purple, or blue flowers bloom in spring.	Plant 10 to 20" apart any time in spring or fall. Divide in spring before or after bloom. Take cuttings any time from spring through fall. Shear spent flowers for neatness or leave them on to allow plants to self-sow.
Creeping, matlike evergreen foliage bears a thick cover of blue, white, or violet flowers in 3" balls on 10" stems in spring.	Plant 10 to 20" apart any time in spring or fall. Divide in spring. Take cuttings in spring or early fall. Shear off spent flowers if you wish, or allow plants to self-sow. Trim foliage for neatness any time it is needed.
Creeping plants form dense mats 18" in diameter, 4" tall. Blue flowers 6 to 10" tall are profuse in summer and fall, foliage reddens.	Plant 18 to 24" apart at any time from spring through fall. Divide in spring. Take cuttings in either spring or fall. Trim for neatness at any time, if needed.
Oval, silvery leaves are covered with fine white hairs on low, creeping plants. 6" woolly stems bear toelike flowers in spring.	Plant clumps or rooted cuttings 8 to 20" apart depending on their size. Plant and divide in spring. Shear spent flowers if they become unsightly.
Low, creeping plants form 1' mounds covered with white, pink, or purple flowers in spring.	Plant clumps 10 to 20" apart in spring. Divide them in early spring or fall. Take cuttings from new growth in spring or from old growth in summer. Trim for neatness at any time.
Smaller or larger fleshy leaves are nearly evergreen, in various shapes. Bunches of starlike flowers are white, yellow, pink, or red.	Plant 4 to 24" apart, depending on size of clump and growth habit of species. Plant and divide in spring. Take cuttings in spring or fall. Sedums will root from stems (stem cuttings or layers) laid on the ground horizontally and covered with soil an inch deep. Trim for neatness as needed.

Continued

RECOMMENDED GROUND COVERS *(Continued)*

COMMON NAME BOTANICAL NAME	ZONES	TYPE	EXPOSURE	SOIL
Strawberry *(Fragaria* species) (See also pages 563–66 in Fruits)	3–10	H/HP E	FS/PS	Well drained to moist
Sweet woodruff *(Galium odoratum,* formerly *Asperula odorata)*	4–8	H/HP D	PS/Sh	Loamy, moist
Thyme, prostrate species (Creeping, woolly, or mother-of-thyme) *(Thymus* species)	3–9 (most types)	H/HP D/ES	FS	Well drained
Vinca vine *(Vinca major)*	6–9	H/HP Vine E	PS, FS	Loamy
Vinca, Myrtle, Periwinkle *(Vinca minor)*	4–9	H/HP Vine E	PS, FS	Loamy, average to rich
Wintercreeper *(Euonymus,* trailing species, e.g., *E. fortunei)*	5–9 (variegated cultivars not as hardy)	H Shrub or vine E	FS/PS	Well drained
Yarrow, Woolly *(Achillea tomentosa)*	3–8	H/HP D	FS/PS	Loamy, well drained
Yellow dead nettle, Yellow archangel *(Lamiastrum galeobdolon)*	4–9	H/HP E	PS/Sh	Any

KEY TO ABBREVIATIONS

Type
H = hardy
T = tender
HP = herbaceous perennial
D = deciduous
E = evergreen
ES = evergreen in South (Zones 9–11)

Exposure
FS = full sun
PS = part shade
S = sun
Sh = shade

Other factors in your decision are either practical or aesthetic. There are many choices: Do you prefer plants that are flowering or nonflowering, deciduous or evergreen, short or tall, woody, viny, or herbaceous, colorful or plain? Will you combine plants or stay with one variety? Combinations are tricky, for most ground covers are invasive, and you do not want to make future work for yourself weeding one type out of another. However, a good combination can look very interesting. A deciduous ground cover with showy blooms, like

DESCRIPTION	PLANTING RECOMMENDATIONS
Evergreen plants with runners form rosettes of 3-part, toothed leaves 6 to 8" tall, plus bunches of white flowers and edible red berries.	Plant 4 to 12" apart in fall or early spring. Divide or move rooted offshoots (on stolons) in spring or fall every year. Trim for neatness. Discard any unhealthy-looking plants in the trash, not in the compost pile.
6" ferny, green deciduous plants have fluffy sprays of petite white flowers in spring. Plants grow in clumps with shallow, matlike roots.	Plant 4 to 16" apart in late fall or early spring. Divide at the same times. Cuttings from roots will take root in early spring. Trim for neatness if necessary.
Sturdy, low-growing mats of foliage may be evergreen with tiny, aromatic leaves, plain, woolly, or bicolored, and pink or white blooms.	Plant 1 to 2' apart in spring or fall. Divide in spring, preferably, or in fall, and take cuttings at the same time. Trim or shape for neatness at any time.
Heart-shaped or oval 2" leaves (larger than *V. minor*) have margins of white or yellow, on viny stems with small blue flowers.	Plant 6 to 20" apart, depending on size of cuttings or clumps. Plant, divide, and take cuttings in spring or fall or at any time in mild weather. Trim and shape for neatness at any time, especially early spring just before plants bloom.
Oval evergreen leaves on viny stems make a thick ground cover with small blue or white tubular flowers in spring.	Plant 6 to 20" apart, depending on size of cuttings or clumps. Plant, divide, and take cuttings in spring or fall, or at any time in mild weather. Trim and shape for neatness at any time.
Green, green-and-white, or green-and-gold evergreen leaves about 1½" long cover dense, low, viny plants. Species vary in shape.	Plant mature plants 3' apart or more, small rooted cuttings 1' apart, in spring or fall. Divide and take cuttings in spring or fall—they root readily. Prune for shape at any time, especially spring.
Though not evergreen, sturdy plants with ferny green foliage hold ground well. In bloom all summer, they are 1' tall with yellow flowers.	Plant 10 to 20" apart, preferably at any time in spring. Divide and take cuttings from early spring to midspring, before and after chance of frost ends. Trim browned foliage for neatness if necessary.
Bright silver markings distinguish ivylike leaves on viny stems. The evergreen plants bear yellow, salvialike flowers in spring.	Plant 6 to 20" apart, depending on size of clump or rooted cutting. Plant, divide, and take cuttings at any time in mild, moist weather, especially in spring and fall. Trim for neatness at any time, usually several times a year.

foamflower, can be combined with an evergreen ground cover such as periwinkle. Study good-looking landscapes in your region for ideas. A shady slope planted with a mixture of ferns, sweet woodruff, astilbe, and woodland phlox looks colorful and romantic; the same area planted with English ivy looks dark and formal.

Sometimes bulbs or other flowering plants are combined or interplanted with ground cover. This is more suitable for some ground covers than others. Two of the most popular groundcover plants, ivy and pachysandra, eventually grow so densely that an underplanting of bulbs would be killed in two or three years, and annual flowers would be squeezed out immediately. However, periwinkle (also known as vinca) makes a thinner cover over the ground. It combines well with spring bulbs such as crocus, daffodils, wood hyacinths, and grape hyacinths. Tulips and Dutch hyacinths suffer more from competition, so they should not be used this way in a permanent planting.

After the bulbs bloom, their foliage can be tucked below the vines during that awkward ripening period. The combination of blue grape hyacinths and blue-flowered periwinkle is quite striking, for they bloom simultaneously for over a month in Zones 5 to 8. Another outstanding combination is true lilies, such as Asiatic or tiger lilies, with ferns. The ferns cover the lower part of the lily foliage and remain attractive after the lilies fade.

Purchasing Ground Cover

It takes many plants to start an area of ground cover. Small cuttings of some types are spaced about 6 inches apart in all directions—requiring forty-nine plants per square yard. Longer vines, larger plants, or thicker clumps are spaced farther apart. You can have ground cover put in for you by landscapers or do it yourself. To get plants, purchase rooted cuttings or plantlets by the flat at nurseries, purchase plants by mail, or propagate plants yourself from ground covers on your property or donations from others. The most popular groundcover plants are quick to multiply, taking root from cuttings in just a few weeks. As they grow, the spaces between the plants fill, and in another year or two the planting will be dense enough to yield starter plants for other beds. Beds of viny ground covers such as ivy and vinca (myrtle) need trimming several times a year—the trimmings may be rooted and used to enlarge beds or start new colonies. Thinnings pulled from overcrowded pachysandra beds usually have roots and can be put to use in new or expanded beds immediately.

Whether the plants are purchased or donated, start with healthy ones. Look for strong leaf growth, few blemishes, good color, and well-developed roots.

It takes one to three years for new beds of ground cover to become thickly established, so choosing an affordable variety speeds things along by permitting you enough plants for a strong beginning. In addition, you can propagate a plentiful stock of rarer plants for future beds without much expenditure. Clumped herbaceous plants such as sedum, phlox, and sweet woodruff may be divided in spring for a large number of starter plants.

PLANTING

In northern and central zones (3 to 7), early spring, while daffodils and tulips are in bloom, is the best time to start new beds of ground cover. In the South (Zones 8 to 10), fall and winter are preferred for most types, but a rainy season is also good. Plants set in during damp, mild weather will take hold quickly.

To begin, single dig the area for the groundcover bed, as described on page 53, removing grass and weeds and incorporating soil amendments such as compost, leaf mold, fertilizer, peat moss, and lime, as needed. Compost and peat moss make the soil more water retentive. Try not to be too ambitious—do a moderately sized area so you can gauge the effort involved. You may want to do the work in stages. If your soil is exceptionally good, you can limit digging—dig just enough to permit plants to be placed at the right depth—and cover a lot of ground in a short time.

Set in the cuttings or plants evenly, 6 to 12 or more inches apart, depending on the variety, at the same depth as, or a little deeper than, they were growing in containers. The following table of ground covers gives the cultural requirements of the main types. Tuck in small plants with a trowel or dibble stick, but use a spade to make holes for shrubs. Water the new bed immediately. Add a 1- to 2-inch mulch of bark chips, compost, or shredded leaves to help conserve moisture and keep roots cool.

You can root tip cuttings (see pages 123–24) of some groundcover plants (ivy, pachysandra, vinca, deutzia, and lamium, for example) directly in the new bed if you can provide four to eight weeks of shady, cool, moist conditions and well-prepared soil. In drier areas or sandy soil, cover the cuttings with a layer of hay or burlap for extra protection while they root, or root them before planting—tip cuttings of most vines root quickly in soil or water.

MAINTENANCE

Though the installation of a bed of ground cover can be laborious, maintenance is not. Keep the new bed well watered for the first few weeks, never letting the surface of the soil dry out. After roots take hold, decrease watering, but do not let the soil get dry an inch below the surface. Until the growth thickens enough to cover the surface of the soil, you will have to weed the bed every few weeks, though mulching helps cut the need for weeding. If soil is poor, apply additional fertilizer lightly.

After the plants become established and growth thickens, continuing care is minimal. In poor soil, fertilize the bed two or three times a year or use a timed-release fertilizer product. In good soil, a single application of fertilizer (in spring in Zones 3 to 7, in fall in Zones 8 to 10) will be adequate. Use a flower fertilizer (such as 5-10-10, high in phosphorus and potassium) for blooming ground covers, and a grass fertilizer (such as 6-6-6) with a high proportion of nitrogen for nonblooming, leafy ground covers. Some areas, and some very rugged ground covers, need no extra fertilizer. Crown vetch, a legume, helps build soil fertility. Since it spreads wildly and is not evergreen, it is often used on large slopes in places that are hard to tend, such as near highways.

If plant growth lacks vigor, but is otherwise healthy, more fertilizer or a topdressing of compost may help. Reposition plants if growth is too uneven. If dust from a road makes leaves look dull, just hose them off from time to time.

Most ground covers are fairly insect resistant, but sometimes they shelter slugs and caterpillars during the day. The pests creep out at night to attack garden plants near and far. You can prevent this by dusting the groundcover bed with diatomaceous earth (its microscopic but sharp pieces pierce the insects' tender skins and kill them). Occasional sprays of insecticidal soap also help to kill pests or send them elsewhere. Rotenone and pyrethrum can be used to combat most insect problems.

Fewer weeds find a roothold as the ground cover thickens, but there are always a few that do, so keep pulling them out. Keep the edge of the bed neatly trimmed. Ivy, in particular, sends long runners out beyond the edge of the groundcover bed, so you will have to trim it several times a year. The unrooted pieces can be planted 6 to 8 inches deep wherever the bed seems to grow too thinly. Flowering ground covers may be sheared after blooming for neatness, if you wish, or left to go to seed for self-sowing of new plants. A healthy, well-chosen bed of ground cover is the most carefree thing you can plant.

ORNAMENTAL GRASSES

In sunny or partially shaded areas where you would like to have a lively, natural-looking, and easily cared for landscape, ornamental grasses are ideal. Without needing much space or soil, they add height and interest elegantly. Their size distinguishes them from low-growing lawn grasses (see Chapter 16). In the wild, grasses and their near-relatives fill open spaces with their rugged, slender leaves and waving seed plumes, rustling in the slightest breeze. Some, like sea oats, anchor the soil and reclaim sandy areas near the ocean, and others inland help to prevent erosion of soil that otherwise would be caused by wind or water—the prairie grasses, for instance. Grasses are just as useful and even more ornamental in our gardens and meadows, alone or combined with other plants. They change their color and form with the seasons, and most hold their seed heads or plumes through winter for long-lasting landscape impact. In addition, the long-stemmed seed clusters are highly valued in fresh or dried floral arrangements and wreaths—some types are grown just for this purpose, but most have several uses.

TYPES OF GRASSES

Ornamental grasses may be annuals or perennials. The annuals are grown from seed each year for temporary, seasonal plantings, and the perennials are a more permanent addition to the landscape. They often spread with creeping roots called rhizomes or stolons, growing into large stands or clumps. Plants usually have many feeder roots that form a dense matted layer in soil—the sod. Some varieties are adapted for growing in wetlands, even in salty or brackish water. There are three main groups of grasslike plants: the true grasses, the sedges, and the rushes.

TRUE GRASSES AND BAMBOOS (GRAMINEAE). Members of this broad and varied group of plants characteristically have narrow leaves with parallel veins and small inconspicuous flowers in summer, ripening into seeds later in the year. The stems are usually round and hollow except where the joints occur (as on a piece of bamboo). Each leaf has a slitted lower portion called a sheath which wraps around the stem. The flowers often grow in straight, dense spikes, but sometimes in showy arched plumes, which often last well into the winter. In some types, silvery hairs are attached to the seeds. Roots are dense and fibrous. Most true grasses thrive in sunny spots with dry soil, but their need for shade and water varies with the species. Many of the grasses found or grown in the United States were brought here from other countries, but the majority are native. Usually, the seeds of grasses are packed with protein—corn, wheat, oats, rye, millet, and rice are good examples. Grasses may be low and neat, like Kentucky bluegrass, which is used for lawns, or tall and showy, like pampas grass, which grows up to 14 feet tall. Many grasses are taller than that: For instance, some types of bamboo are treelike in height.

SEDGES (CYPERACEAE). Sedges have linear, parallel leaves and look very much like grasses, but usually their stems are solid and somewhat triangular in cross section, not round. They do not have joints, and the sheaths of the linear leaves are not slit. This group of plants often but not always grows in cold, wet places. Flowers are whorled or in spirals on the stems, or on many stemlets branching from the stem end. Most sedges found in the wild in the United States are native plants.

RUSHES (JUNCACEAE). Rushes also have linear leaves with parallel veins, but the stems are hollow and the small flowers have a shape something like a miniature lily. The fruit, which stays on the plant for many months, is usually a capsule filled with seeds, and grows in different kinds of clusters and bunches, some of which are strikingly lovely. Like sedges, rushes often grow in cold, wet places.

USING ORNAMENTAL GRASSES

In landscapes, grasses and grasslike plants are used to solve problems caused by difficult sites (too wet, too dry, sloping, infertile, too sunny, etc.) as well as for their unusual visual effect. You may want to place clumps of ornamental grasses in the landscape either in masses of the same kind planted closely together or as individual accent plants (like shrubs) in mixed borders. They look particularly appropriate planted in broad sweeps near modern homes and buildings, in place of lawn or ground cover. They are used in meadows, too, where they help crowd out weeds but, like wildflowers, need little care.

Bamboo and some of the other perennial grasses can be terribly invasive, so the best use for them is either in open places where they have room to spread, as tall ground covers in island beds surrounded by lawn grass or pavement, or else as accent plants confined to pots or other containers. The container, making an invisible barrier, can be plunged into the soil. Plants are kept within bounds either by the physical limit of the soil or barrier, or by mowing around the bed. Mowing alone, however, is not enough to inhibit the larger, woodier types of bamboo.

In fresh or dried floral arrangements, the feathery seed heads of most grasses are light-weight and graceful, yet showy. A number of kinds are grown for their different shapes and colors—the most popular of these are included in the table of grasses on pages 618–23. The small annual types make an attractive addition to flower borders, where they can be planted in large groups, then cut and harvested as needed. Any grass, annual or perennial, may be dried for bouquets. Cut the plumes as soon as they are barely mature, but before they begin to age or shatter. They will fluff out a little more as they dry. Handle them like other everlastings, hanging them upside down in bunches indoors until all the moisture has evaporated and stems are firm.

The accompanying table will help you identify grasses that suit your purposes and find the ones that will grow most successfully in the soil, climate, and exposure of your growing sites.

PURCHASING GRASSES

Plants and seeds of ornamental grasses are sold in local nurseries and garden supply stores and by specialty nurseries and seed companies with mail-order catalogs. In most areas, the selection is much greater from the catalogs; however, good local nurseries will carry popular types suited to your climate. In addition, sometimes plants and seeds are available from botanical gardens, arboreta, plant societies, and garden club plant sales. Do not dig up wild plants without permission from the owner, and do not disturb endangered or protected species, such as sea oats.

Early spring is a good time to buy, move, and set in plants, for they will have time to establish themselves in your site before they bloom. In nurseries, grasses are usually sold in containers. Look for firm soil, which shows that the plants have either been grown in or are already well established in the containers. Freshly dug-up plants put into containers have just had a shock to their roots; another change so soon (when you plant them at home) may slow their growth temporarily. Look for strong plants with new shoots coming up from the base, showing that the plants are alive and healthy.

PLANTING

Grasses are easy to grow and fairly similar to one another in their culture. Most types thrive in dry soil of average quality, a pH near neutral, and bright sunshine. Most of the exceptions are water plants, often able to grow in swampy or seaside conditions. Perennial grasses are stable and long-lasting in the garden or landscape, so take care to acquire plants of highest quality.

For most grasses, enrich soil moderately before planting (except those that will grow in water). Add lime to raise the pH if necessary, especially if it is below 6, although this varies with the type of grass you are planting. Most grasses are not too particular about the pH, but some of the western and southern U.S. grasses are adapted for an alkaline soil with a pH above 7. Dig the planting holes a little larger than the root balls, and set in plants at the same depth at which they grew, at the recommended spacing of a foot or more apart. Reeds, rushes, and sedges for tidal wetlands may be set into the sand or mud most easily at low tide. In the tideless shorelines of ponds, you may have to wade into the water in order to plant at the right depth—the recommended amount or about the amount the plants were growing in. Being invasive, they will spread farther into the water by themselves.

Back on land, water new plants for several weeks to help them become established. Ornamental grasses are strong and self-reliant, and most will need very little care after this period. When flowers appear, leave them alone to ripen, for they grow into the most decorative part of the plant. Many ornamental grasses retain the flower heads, stalks, and leaves through the winter, bleached to a lovely ivory. At the end of winter or when plants stop looking attractive in the late fall, shear them down to a foot or so above the base, so new shoots will have room to grow in spring. The smallest species may be cut down closer to the ground. In tropical areas, bamboo and other grasses may be evergreen; if so, they will not need to be cut down unless you wish to control their size this way.

After plants are established, no fertilizer will be needed in places where the soil is naturally rich. In poorer soils, use an all-purpose, slow- or timed-release fertilizer two to four times a year, according to product directions, but apply it lightly compared to the amount you would use on most flowering plants and vegetables. The most critical times for fertilizer are in early spring when growth begins and in warmer weather when seed heads are forming. If your grass blooms poorly, try using fertilizer with higher phosphorus and potassium (5-10-10, for instance). In northern states with rich but acid soils, a spring dose of lime and high-nitrogen fertilizer will "wake up" your grasses.

PROPAGATION

SEED. Grasses are grown from seed in the same way as other annuals and perennials (see pages 64–72). Most types germinate in about three weeks and are ready to transplant in another six to eight weeks. It is a good idea to grow each seed in its own small pot or six-pack pocket, or else widely spaced (6 or more inches apart) if sowing directly in the ground. Otherwise, the plants become too hard to separate because the dense, fibrous roots mat together. Shift them to larger pots or their outdoor places before they become pot-bound.

Annuals. Annual grasses have different degrees of cold hardiness, though all types die at the end of the season, when hard frost arrives. The group known as *hardy annuals,* like peas and lettuce, may be planted outdoors before the danger of frost ends, for they are especially frost-tolerant during their seed and seedling stages. They may also be planted after the danger of frost passes if the weather is not too hot—frequently over 85°F. *Half-hardy annuals* tolerate cool temperatures in the low 30's but are killed by frost. *Tender annuals* grow only during warm weather and may be killed or set back by the lightest frost, or, in some cases, cold weather in the low 30's.

In zones north of 6, where summers are short and winters are cold, start all kinds of annual grasses indoors in March for an early start on the season, and then transplant them to the garden when the weather improves. This way you can be sure they will bloom before freezing weather returns. In areas with warmer climates, you can plant any type indoors in March or April. Hardy annuals may be planted outdoors in early spring, half-hardy types outdoors in late spring, and tender types as soon as the danger of frost passes. In Zones 9 to 11, November through January are the best months to plant annual grass seeds because the seedlings do best in moderate, not hot weather.

RECOMMENDED ORNAMENTAL GRASSES

NAME	PLANT TYPE	ZONES	SPACING	DESCRIPTION
Agropyron smithii Western wheatgrass	Hardy perennial grass	8–9	10–24"	2'-tall clumps of blue grass that turn beige during drought. Seed heads also turn beige as they mature.
Agrostis nebulosa Cloud grass	Hardy annual grass	All	12–18"	1'- to 1½'-tall grass with delicate spraylike seed heads. Leaves and seeds ripen from green to beige. '
Andropogon gerardii Big and little bluestem	Hardy perennial grass	4–8	1–2'	4'- to 7'-tall grasses with silky tufts along stems. Green plants turn orange in fall, look good in winter.
Arundo donax Giant reed grass	Hardy perennial grass	7–11	2–6'	When plumes of flowers appear in fall, plants reach up to 14'.
Avena sterilis Animated oats	Hardy annual grass	All	2'	3'-tall green-leaved plants have bristled seed clusters that turn tan when dry.
Briza maxima *Briza minima* Quaking grass	Hardy annual grass	All	1–2'	2'-tall green plants bear fluffy panicles of small or large seed heads, each on a threadlike stalk, which turns ivory-white when mature.
Carex morrowii 'Variegata' Japanese sedge	Hardy perennial sedge	5–9	2'	Summer-blooming plants 1' tall form low, tufted green-and-white mounds of curving blades. Flowers are inconspicuous.
Coix lachryma-jobi Job's tears	Half-hardy annual grass	All	2'	2'- to 4'-tall green plants with arching stems that bear hard, gray, beadlike seeds. Seeds are green or yellow until they mature.
Cortaderia selloana Pampas grass	Hardy perennial grass	7–11	8–10'	Huge plumes crown plants 10 to 14' tall, lasting many months outdoors, years indoors.
Cymbopogon citratus Lemongrass	Tender perennial grass	9–11	4–5'	Aromatic green 6' grass grows in graceful clumps.
Cyperus papyrus Papyrus	Tender perennial sedge	9–11	2–6'	Rhizome-rooted rushlike plants up to 8' tall with raylike, drooping flower heads.
Eragrostis species Love grass	Hardy annual grass	All	15–24"	2'- to 3'-tall deep green grass with enormous light, airy, purplish seed heads with descending branchlets.

PLANTING RECOMMENDATIONS	USES	SOIL PREFERENCE
Sow seeds in tilled soil, in full sun in fall or spring. Remove last year's leaves if you wish.	Reclamation of meadows in dry areas. It forms sod.	Well drained, average
Sow seeds early indoors or in spring outdoors in full sun or partial shade.	Flower beds, floral arrangements	Well drained, average
Plant in full sun; cut down past year's growth in early spring.	Meadows, natural landscaping, floral arrangements	Well drained, average
Plant in full sun. Remove the previous year's growth if it is unsightly. Mulch in Zones 7 and 8 in winter.	Erosion control, musical reeds, floral arrangements, waterside gardens	Average to moist
Sow seeds early indoors or outdoors in spring in full sun.	Large floral arrangements	Well drained, average
Sow seeds early indoors or outdoors in spring in full sun.	Floral arrangements, flower beds	Well drained, average
Plant in partial shade. Remove leaves from last year's growth if you wish.	Weed-resistant ground cover	Moist
Sow seeds early indoors or outdoors when weather is warm in full sun or partial shade.	Beads, flower beds, floral arrangements	Well drained, average
Plant in spring in full sun. Cut down leaves from the previous year when new growth begins.	Landscaping, floral arrangements	Well drained, average
Plant in full sun or partial shade. Remove aged leaves if they are unsightly.	Landscaping, containers, home remedies (e.g., insect repellent)	Average
Plant in full sun. Remove aged leaves if they are unsightly. Plants are often set into shallow water 1 to 2' deep.	Water gardens, containers	Damp or wet (freshwater ponds)
Sow seeds early indoors or outdoors in spring in full sun.	Floral arrangements, flower beds	Well drained, average

KEY TO DEFINITIONS

Full sun means at least 8 hours of bright sunlight per day.

Partial shade means 6 to 8 hours of bright or filtered sunlight per day.

Hardy annuals tolerate light frost, especially in their seed and seedling stages.

Half-hardy annuals tolerate cool weather in the 30's (F), but may be killed by frost.

Tender annuals are killed by frost and sometimes harmed by cool weather in the low 30's (F).

Hardy perennials tolerate frost. Their hardiness, which varies, is indicated under **Zone** in this chart.

Tender perennials are tropical plants, killed by frost.

Continued

RECOMMENDED ORNAMENTAL GRASSES *(Continued)*

NAME	PLANT TYPE	ZONES	SPACING	DESCRIPTION
Erianthus ravennae Ravenna grass	Hardy perennial grass	5–9	8–10'	9 to 14' tall when in bloom, this has 3'-tall erect seed heads on strong stems; lasts into winter. Leaves are green; flowers tan.
Festuca ovina glauca Blue fescue	Hardy perennial grass	4–9	8–12"	Bluish-white 1' grass grows in small tufts. Wiry stems bloom in late summer and last through winter, turning ivory.
Hordeum jubatum Squirrel's tail grass	Hardy annual grass	All	12"	1½' green plants have 3" cylindrical wheatlike seedpods bearing long, silky hairs, gold to silver-gray.
Imperata cylindrica rubrum Japanese blood grass	Hardy perennial grass	5–9	12–18"	1 to 2' clumps have blades that come up green and turn bright red in summer, keep color in fall.
Koeleria glauca Blue meadow grass	Hardy perennial grass	4–9	12–18"	2' clump-forming, intensely blue grass bears pendant flower sprays, green and dense, aging to tan.
Lagurus ovatus Hare's tail grass	Hardy annual grass	All		1½' plants bear downy green leaves and long stems topped by 1½" furry, conical heads. Leaves and seed heads gradually turn ivory.
Liriope species Border grass, Lilyturf (Liliaceae)	Hardy perennial	5–11	6–15"	Rhizome-rooted ½ to 1½' plants have straplike green or green-and-white leaves, evergreen in South, lilac or white flowers in plumes.
Miscanthus sinensis Japanese silver grass	Hardy perennial grass	4–9	8–10'	Rhizome-rooted green, green-and-white, or green-and-yellow variegated plants grow up to 10' tall, form wide clumps with huge curved tan plumes, last all winter.
Molinia caerulea Purple moor grass	Hardy perennial grass	5–9	4'	4'- to 6'-tall clumps of green or green-and-white leaves bear 6 to 8' purplish-brown blooms on slender spikes.
Oryzopsis hymenoides Ricegrass, Mountain rice	Hardy perennial grass	8–9	1'	In bunches this green grass with curling fronds grows 1 to 2' tall, with beautiful branched seed heads above it. It bleaches to beige in winter or drought.
Panicum virgatum Red switch grass	Hardy perennial grass	3–11	1'	Upright 3 to 5' clumps of green or brown grass turn red-orange; arched brown seed heads last well in winter.

PLANTING RECOMMENDATIONS	USES	SOIL PREFERENCE
Plant in full sun or light shade. Remove aged leaves if they are unsightly.	Floral arrangements, landscaping	Rich, moist
Plant in full sun. Remove leaves from the previous year when new growth begins.	Weed-resistant ground cover, rock gardens, dunes	Well drained, average
Sow seeds early indoors or outdoors in spring in full sun.	Floral arrangements, flower beds	Well drained, average
Plant in full sun or partial shade. Cut back last year's growth in early spring.	Landscaping, herbaceous borders	Rich
Plant in full sun.	Meadows, landscaping, floral arrangements	Well drained, average
Sow seeds early indoors or outdoors in spring in full sun. Easy to grow.	Floral arrangements, flower beds	Well drained, average
Plant in full sun or partial shade. Remove aged leaves if they are unsightly.	Rugged ground cover	Well drained, average; does well in sandy soil
Plant in full sun. Cut down past year's growth in spring.	Landscaping, floral arrangements	Well drained, average
Plant in full sun or partial shade. Remove aged leaves if they are unsightly.	Landscaping, floral arrangements	Well drained, average; tolerates acidic soil
Plant in full sun. Plants tolerate drought.	Floral arrangements, landscaping, meadows, bird food, rock gardens	Sandy, dry, alkaline
Plant in full sun; cut back past year's foliage in early spring.	Landscaping, floral arrangements, seaside plantings	Well drained, average

Continued

KEY TO DEFINITIONS

Full sun means at least 8 hours of bright sunlight per day.

Partial shade means 6 to 8 hours of bright or filtered sunlight per day.

Hardy annuals tolerate light frost, especially in their seed and seedling stages.

Half-hardy annuals tolerate cool weather in the 30's (F), but may be killed by frost.

Tender annuals are killed by frost and sometimes harmed by cool weather in the low 30's (F).

Hardy perennials tolerate frost. Their hardiness, which varies, is indicated under **Zone** in this chart.

Tender perennials are tropical plants, killed by frost.

RECOMMENDED ORNAMENTAL GRASSES *(Continued)*

NAME	PLANT TYPE	ZONES	SPACING	DESCRIPTION
Pennisetum alopecuroides Fountain grass	Hardy perennial grass	6–9	3–5'	Green plants 3 to 6' tall (in bloom), with long, narrow, furry pink or white flower plumes that are showy summer through fall.
Pennisetum villosum Feathertop	Half-hardy annual grass	All	2'	Creamy white cylindrical 5" plumes rise above 2' plants with green leaves.
Phalaris arundinacea 'Picta' Ribbon grass, Gardener's garters	Hardy perennial grass	All	2'	2' striped green-and-white plants with ¾" leaves; spread rapidly. Flowers are green and not conspicuous.
Phragmites australis Reed grass	Hardy perennial reed	4–9	8–10'	12'- to 19'-tall green plants grow in most parts of the world, carrying large brown plumes of flowers summer to winter.
Setaria italica Foxtail grass	Half-hardy annual grass	All	2–3'	3'-tall green plants bear 5" cylindrical, red-gold seed heads covered with long furlike bristles.
Sorghastrum nutans Indian grass	Hardy perennial grass	5–9	2–4'	2'- to 9'-tall blue-green foliage turns orange in autumn; lasts well in winter.
Spodiopogon sibericus Silver spike grass	Hardy annual grass	All	2–3'	3'- to 4'-tall green plants have silvery foliage and rose flowers on erect stalks in late summer.
Stipa gigantea Giant feather grass	Hardy perennial grass	5–9	4–5'	6'-tall green plants form spreading clumps bearing huge, airy flower heads, first purple on green, then golden.
Triticum spelta Spelt wheat	Hardy annual grass	All	2'	2' green foliage bears tall green spikes of wheat with long bristles; seed heads turn golden when ripe.
Typha latifolia Cattail (Typhaceae)	Hardy perennial	4–9	3–4'	7'- to 9'-tall green plants that have straplike leaves and bear distinctive brown cigarlike flowers in summer and fall.
Uniola paniculata Sea oats	Tender perennial grass	7–11	2–3'	4' rhizome-rooted green plants have linear, fibrous leaves and arching tan seed heads.
Zea mays Ornamental corn	Tender annual grass	All	2–4'	3'- to 8'-tall large-leaved, tasseled plants produce multicolored ears of corn; multicolored foliage in some.

PLANTING RECOMMENDATIONS	USES	SOIL PREFERENCE
Plant in full sun; cut back past year's foliage in early spring.	Landscaping, floral arrangements	Well drained, rich
Sow seeds early indoors or in late spring outdoors in full sun.	Floral arrangements, bedding, and containers	Well drained, average
Plant in full sun or partial shade. Remove aged leaves if they are unsightly.	Ground cover (invasive), dune grass	Wet or dry
Plant in full sun. Remove last year's growth if it is unsightly.	Waterside or boggy wild gardens. Also good for seaside dunes.	Marshy, moist
Sow seeds early indoors or in late spring outdoors in full sun or partial shade.	Floral arrangements, flower beds. Plants become noxious weeds in some areas.	Good, well drained
Plant in full sun; cut back past year's growth in early spring.	Prairie or meadow restoration, floral arrangements	Well drained, average
Plant in full sun or shade.	Landscaping in problem soils and exposures	Wet or dry
Plant in full sun; cut down past year's growth in early spring.	Landscaping, floral arrangements	Well drained, average
Sow seeds in early spring; water if dry.	Floral arrangements, livestock food	Any well-drained soil
Plant in full sun in fresh or brackish water up to 3' deep. Cut down past year's growth in early spring, if you wish.	Natural water gardens, seaside plantings	Marshy, moist sites; brackish water tolerated
Plant in full sun or partial shade. Do not walk on plants. Do not remove aged foliage.	Beach restoration for stabilization of dunes. Plants protected by law.	Sand, near salt water
Sow seeds in full sun.	Decorative ears of corn for seasonal arrangements	Well drained, rich

Several less common cool-season grasses are described in the table on pages 628–31, along with the growing conditions they prefer. However, most northern gardeners choose Kentucky bluegrass, perennial rye, and fine fescue since improved varieties of these three species are widely available, and the grasses themselves are superior to other cool-season species.

TRANSITIONAL-ZONE GRASSES

The transitional zone stretches across the country's midsection from the Mid-Atlantic states westward to central California. Twenty years ago grass breeders began developing improved varieties of tall fescue *(Festuca arundinacea)*, which has proven to be a desirable grass for the transitional zone.

Cool-season grasses like bluegrass will also grow in the transitional zone, as will grasses best adapted in warmer climates, such as Bermuda grass. However, they require frequent irrigation when grown in the transitional zone, which can be a problem in some water-restrictive states. Since they remain dormant for several months each year, they are easily invaded by weeds. Yet bluegrass remains a good choice in cool exposures within the transitional zone, and Bermuda or zoysia work well in full sun. These three grasses are creeping types, so they have a more luxurious look and feel than tall fescue, which has a tufting habit. However, tall fescue's superiority lies in its ability to adapt to shade or sun, and its excellent resistance to drought and disease—which is probably why improved varieties of tall fescues are now the leading grasses planted from seed in the transitional zone.

WARM-SEASON GRASSES

These grasses thrive in hot weather and become dormant when temperatures consistently drop below 55°F. The most vigorous grower among the leading warm-season grasses is Bermuda *(Cynodon dactylon)*. Although older varieties of this creeping grass grew so enthusiastically that they were difficult to control, the newer improved ones are much more cooperative about staying out of beds and borders. Unfortunately, the updated Bermudas recommended by extension agents cannot be propagated from seed, so new Bermuda lawns must be plugged, sprigged, or planted from sod.

In many areas, Bermuda is overseeded with annual or perennial ryegrass in the early fall, just as the Bermuda becomes dormant. The ryegrass provides vibrant green color through the winter months and dies in spring (following close mowing), just as the Bermuda begins to green up in late spring.

Like Bermuda, centipede grass *(Eremochloa ophiuroides)* spreads rapidly by producing numerous wiry stolons, or stems. Although centipede does not have the refined appearance of other grasses (it has coarser blades and lacks a deep green color), it is increasingly popular since it grows well in poor soils and requires very little maintenance.

Zoysia *(Zoysia japonica)* is perhaps the lushest of the warm-season grasses, but it requires frequent mowing and supplemental water during droughts. Germination rates are extremely low when zoysia is planted from seed, and zoysia sod is quite expensive. However, zoysia remains a good choice for small, closely managed areas where superior quality is a high priority.

Bermuda requires full sun, and centipede and zoysia tolerate only a little shade, but there is a good grass for warm, shady areas. St. Augustine *(Stenotaphrum secundatum)* develops into a lovely, deep green lawn in speckled shade. No varieties have been developed that have proven hardy in climates where hard freezes are frequent, but several pest- and disease-resistant St. Augustine varieties have emerged from breeding programs in Florida.

Several other less common lawn grasses are described in the table on pages 628–31. The advice of your local extension agent, who has extensive knowledge of the soil types and idiosyncrasies of weather in your area, can be of tremendous value when choosing the right grass for your lawn.

BASIC LAWN MAINTENANCE

Lawn grasses can successfully resist weeds, insects, diseases, and weather-related stresses if they are healthy and vital. Other lawn problems, like excessive thatch buildup, also can be prevented with proper lawn care.

FERTILIZING. With the exception of centipede grass, lawns should be fertilized at least twice a year with a mild, nonburning fertilizer. Washed-out drab color and slow growth are typical symptoms of underfertilized lawns. Lawn grasses respond well to moderate applications of chemical fertilizers such as 12-4-8, or pulverized organic fertilizers that can be applied with a spreader. Use a fertilizer spreader (which you can rent) to apply lawn fertilizers in order to assure even distribution. A fertilized lawn should be watered after application.

Timing is more important than the fertilizer you choose. Lawn grasses should be fertilized to match their periods of active growth. In cool-season areas where grasses grow most vigorously in spring and fall, fertilize once in midspring, and two times in fall. In transitional areas, fertilize cool-season grasses like tall fescue in May, September, and November. Warm-season grasses should be fed in May and late July. As previously mentioned, centipede grass finds heavy doses of fertilizer distasteful, and the yellowing of centipede is more often a sign of iron deficiency than a symptom of substandard soil fertility.

Apply lawn fertilizers just before a rain whenever possible, or water thoroughly after application to wash the fertilizer into the root zone of the turf. Undissolved granular fertilizer left sitting on the grass for more than a few minutes may cause chemical burning of the grass's foliage and/or its shallow roots, evidenced by the sudden appearance of dry, brown spots on leaves and patches in the turf.

MOWING. The purpose of mowing is threefold. Mowing encourages grass to grow diagonally instead of vertically, resulting in a thicker, more resilient turf. Mowing also helps limit the production of unwanted grass seed. Seed heads are considered unsightly in turfgrass culture, and seed heads produced by centipede are also uncomfortable underfoot. Finally, frequent mowing helps control the proliferation of weeds, which seldom thrive when their tops are regularly mowed off.

RECOMMENDED LAWN GRASSES

NAME	ZONES	TYPE	SOIL	pH	EXPOSURE
Agrostis canina/ Velvet bentgrass *A. tenuis/* Colonial bentgrass	1 to 4 (cool season)	Creeping	Moist soils with high organic matter content	5 to 7	Full to almost-full sun
Axonopus affinis/ Carpet grass	9 and 11 (warm season)	Creeping	Sandy, wet, acidic soils	4.5 to 5.5	Full sun to part shade
Buchloe dactyloides/ Buffalo grass	Western parts of Zones 4 and 5 (warm season)	Creeping	Any soil in dry, semi-arid climates	6 to 7.5	Full sun, or slight shade from small trees Requires dry climate.
Cynodon dactylon sp./Bermuda grass	6 to 11 (warm season)	Creeping	Well drained	5 to 7. Some varieties are specially adapted to saline and alkaline conditions.	Full sun Bermuda will not grow in heavy shade.
Eremochloa ophiuroides/ Centipede grass	8 to 11 (warm season)	Creeping	Any well-drained soil of low to moderate fertility	4.5 to 6	Full to almost-full sun
Festuca arundinacea/ Tall fescue	5 to 7 (transitional)	Tufting	Any well-drained soil	5.5 to 7.5	Full sun to moderate shade
Festuca ovina/ Hard Fescue	1 to 5 (cool season)	Tufting	Well-drained soils of low to moderate fertility	6 to 7	Full sun

CHARACTERISTICS	PLANTING TIMES AND SEEDING RATES	MOWING HEIGHT	SPECIES COMBINATIONS
These two older lawn grasses form a thick, fine-textured turf, but require exact mowing and fertilization, with low tolerance for drought.	Sow 2 pounds of seed per 1000 square feet in early fall or early spring.	.5 to 1 inch	Too aggressive to mix with other grasses
A coarse, low-maintenance grass for difficult sites. Carpet grass has low tolerance for hard freezes and requires frequent mowing when seed heads are present.	Plant in May and June, sowing 1 to 3 pounds of seed per 1000 square feet.	1 to 2 inches	None
A special grass for dry places where more refined species often fail.	Plant 1 to 2 pounds of seed per 1000 square feet in April or May, which is also the best time to plant sod.	1.5 to 2.5 inches	None
A vigorous, spreading grass that responds well to frequent mowing and regular fertilization. Highly resistant to drought and summer weeds.	The rare improved Bermudas that can be propagated from seed may be sown at 2 pounds of hulled seed per 1000 square feet. Bermuda sod shows fast, active growth when planted in early summer.	1 to 1.5 inches	None, other than use of annual ryegrass for winter color
Spreading grass grows well with little care, and becomes brown and dormant in winter. May be oversown with annual rye for improved off-season color.	Only ½ pound of tiny centipede seed is needed to plant 1000 square feet, or you can buy 3 bushels of sprigs (pieces of shredded sod). Plant either seed or sprigs in May or June.	1 to 1.5 inches	None, other than annual ryegrass for improved winter color
Leaves are slightly coarse and medium green in color, but this grass has brief periods of dormancy and remains green most of the year. Low maintenance requirements.	Sow 6 to 8 pounds per 1000 square feet. Early-fall planting is preferred, but this grass also can be sown in early spring.	2 to 3 inches	Perennial ryegrass in small amounts improves cold tolerance
Stiff, needlelike leaves that grow slowly and require less mowing.	Sow at least 5 pounds per 1000 square feet in early fall, and fill in sparse places with additional seed the following March.	1.5 to 2 inches	None

Continued

RECOMMENDED LAWN GRASSES *(Continued)*

NAME	ZONES	TYPE	SOIL	pH	EXPOSURE
Festuca rubra/ Fine fescue	2 to 6 (cool season)	Creeping	Well-drained, slightly acidic soil	5.5 to 7	Full sun to moderate shade in cool climates; often blended with bluegrass to give the turf increased shade tolerance
Lolium multiflorum/ Annual ryegrass	2 to 9 (cool season)	Tufting	Any soil	5 to 7.5	Full sun to part shade
Lolium perenne/ Perennial ryegrass	4 to 6 (cool season)	Tufting to semicreeping	Any well-drained soil	5.5 to 7	Full sun to part shade
Poa pratensis/ Bluegrass, Kentucky bluegrass	2 to 6, and parts of Zone 7 (cool season)	Creeping	Well-drained, loamy soils	6 to 7.5	Full to almost-full sun in cool climates, and sun or light shade in warm temperate climates
Stenotaphrum secundatum/ St. Augustine	9 and 11, and parts of Zone 8 (warm season)	Creeping	Sandy soils with good fertility	6 to 8	Sun or shade
Zoysia spp./ Zoysia grass	6 to 9 (warm season)	Creeping	Fertile, well-drained, sandy soil	5 to 7	Full to almost-full sun

CHARACTERISTICS	PLANTING TIMES AND SEEDING RATES	MOWING HEIGHT	SPECIES COMBINATIONS
Fine leaves are stiff, and spreading is very slow, sometimes resulting in tufted appearance.	Sow 5 pounds per 1000 square feet in early spring or early fall. Use same rate for fine fescue/bluegrass mixtures.1.5 to 2 inches	Bluegrass (in shade); imparts smooth texture to lawns composed primarily of perennial ryegrass.	
Fast growing and hardy, annual rye can be seeded lightly over almost any turf in fall for improved winter color.	When planting over dormant warm-season grasses, sow 5 pounds per 1000 square feet from mid-September to early November. For temporary winter cover crop in bare soil, sow 10 pounds per 1000 square feet.	1 to 2 inches	May be sown over Bermuda or centipede for improved winter color
This grass becomes a cool-season annual where summers are hot. Excellent color and fast growth make it a valuable addition to many cool-season seed mixtures.	Plant 4 to 6 pounds per 1000 square feet in early spring or early fall.	1 to 2 inches	Fine fescue to improve texture, tall fescue to improve heat tolerance
Dark, dense grass with excellent texture and appearance; responds to drought by becoming dormant.	Sow 2 pounds of improved, mixed varieties per 1000 square feet in September or April. Sod can be planted any time the ground is not frozen, but early-summer and early-fall sodding results in fast, vigorous growth.	2 to 3 inches	Fine fescue improves shade tolerance; perennial rye aids fast establishment of turf when seeded
Coarse texture is offset by deep green color and vigorous growth. High fertilization requirments, and any stress increases risk of problems with insects and diseases.	Plant in May and June, and August if rain is plentiful. St. Augustine is propagated vegetatively and must be purchased as sod or sprigs. Pieces of sod may be cut into 4-inch-square plugs and planted in bare spots or existing grass.	1.5 to 2.5 inches	None
Thick, stiff, fine-textured grass well suited to high visibility areas. Above-average maintenance requirements, and susceptible to weed invasion if not kept in optimum condition.	Plant sod from late spring to midsummer. When strip-sodded, or when sprigs or plugs are used, zoysia may take 2 years to develop into an attractive lawn. Seed has a low germination potential and is very expensive.	.5 to 1.5 inches	None

The recommended mowing height varies with grass species, from ½ to 1 inch (above the soil line) for Bermuda and zoysia, to 2 to 3 inches for tall fescue, bluegrass, and most cool-season grass mixtures. The general idea is to remove top growth so that light can penetrate the turf while leaving the grasses' crowns, or basal growing tips, undisturbed.

Light layers of grass clippings may be left on the lawn to decompose naturally. Soil that is kept biologically active quickly "digests" the clippings. However, thick mats of grass clippings are best raked up and used as mulch around cultivated plants. If left on the lawn too long, the grass beneath the clippings will stop growing from simple light deprivation, and diseases may proliferate under the clumps of clippings.

Besides mowing, edges of the lawn that border sidewalks, driveways, and permanently mulched landscape plants should be trimmed or manicured. Modern edge-trimming machines make this easy work. If you maintain such edges by hand, try to time the job so that it coincides with a season when your grass will be growing slowly—midsummer for cool-season grasses, or late summer to fall in warmer climates.

WATERING. As long as they are in an active, nondormant phase of growth, grasses develop new foliage within hours after they are watered. Like other plants, grasses develop deepest root systems when they are thoroughly soaked once or twice a week. Frequent shallow watering can lead to a thin, thatchy turf. To measure how much water your lawn is receiving from a sprinkler, place a shallow, straight-sided container about the size of a cake pan on the area being watered. When ½ to 1 inch of water has accumulated in the container, the grass receiving the water has had enough.

WEED CONTROL. The most common and frustrating lawn problems involve weeds. Weeds often invade while the grass is dormant. Plus, many common weeds, like dandelion and nut grass, have huge, persistent roots that enable them to grow back even after their tops have been removed. Herbicides are available that will kill many lawn weeds. When using lawn herbicides, always wear the protective equipment recommended on the product's label, and keep pets and children away from the treated area for two days. Where weeds occur only in small patches, it is often simpler to dig them out with a small spade, and restore the area with seed or sod that matches the rest of your lawn. Weeds that resist chemical attack will need to have their roots dug out by hand (see pages 106–107 for more information on controlling weeds). When weeds are present only as isolated plants, maintain your lawn's quality by going on weed patrol twice a year, removing alien invaders with a chop from the sharpest corner of your hoe. Written information on identification and control of weeds common in your area is often available through local extension agents.

PLANTING A NEW LAWN

If no lawn exists and you are starting from bare soil, or if weeds cover more than half of the lawn's area, a total renovation is in order. Depending on the grass you will be planting and how much you are willing to spend, you can begin with either sod or seed. Sod (slabs or rolls of live turf with ½ inch of soil still attached to the roots) is more expensive, but it goes down fast and can be lightly trod upon almost immediately. Seed is considerably cheaper, but newly seeded lawns require a few weeks to develop to the point where they can withstand moderate wear without risk of damage.

Specific planting times for each grass variety can be found in the table on pages 628–31, but in general, plant warm-season grasses in early summer, and cool-season and transitional grasses in early fall.

PREPARING THE SOIL. Both seeding and sodding should be immediately preceded by a thorough preparation of the site to be planted. Test the soil for proper acidity, and add lime if the soil is too acid for the grass you have chosen. (For further discussion of soil testing, see page 48.) Remove patches of weeds and old grass with a sharp spade, slicing horizontally just below the soil surface. It is especially important to prepare the area equally well, regardless of whether it is to be seeded or planted from sod.

Where the soil is thin sand, heavy with rocks, or compacted clay, add plenty of organic soil amendments such as compost, well-rotted manure, or leaf mold, and till it in thoroughly. Fill in low places or ripples in the surface with quality topsoil.

Cultivate with a Rototiller until the soil is fine and crumbly. On the last pass with the tiller, work in a moderate application of fertilizer. Finally, rake until the site is as level as possible.

SEEDING of small areas can be done by hand, but it is a good idea to rent or borrow a mechanical seeder when planting large spaces. A seeder will help distribute the seed more evenly than you can by hand. Seeding rates vary with the species being planted, from less than ½ pound of centipede grass seed per 1000 square feet to 8 pounds of tall fescue for the same area. Approximate seeding rates are included in the table on pages 628–31.

After the seed is spread, rake it in lightly, and walk over the area to help firm in the seeds. While walking, shake a light layer of weed-free hay over the seeded area to help hold the soil in place. Use about two bales per 1000 square feet. Finally, set up a sprinkler so you can turn it on twice a day, or as often as needed to ensure constant soil moisture while the seeds are germinating—usually up to fourteen days.

When planting grass mixtures that include annual or perennial rye, mow the area about ten days after the first grasses appear. This helps keep the vigorous ryes from shading out the other seedlings in the mixture, which tend to germinate more slowly than the ryegrasses. With all grasses, mowing should begin at the desired height as soon as possible.

SODDING requires quite a bit of heavy lifting and bending, but the reward is an instant swath of green. The work goes much faster when two people work together. Sod comes in straight-edged strips of variable width. When arranging to buy sod, freshness should be a major consideration. Sod should be laid as soon as possible following delivery. Storing fresh-cut sod in the sun for only a few hours may result in a dramatic loss of vigor.

If the area being planted slopes, always run the strips of sod lengthwise across the slope to prevent possible erosion between the strips. Begin laying the strips along any straight edge, and plant the sod pieces end to end, in a long strip, before starting on the next row. In the next and succeeding rows, stagger the edges of the sod pieces so that the seams between strips in one row never meet the seams in the next one.

Trim off the ends with a sharp spade. To keep the soil uncompacted and your shoes free of mud, stand on a broad board placed over the planted sod when planting adjoining rows.

The board will also help press down the sod so its roots will be in firm contact with the soil.

After the sod is planted, sweep it clean with a broom, and deposit soil and other debris into the seams between the sod pieces. Water thoroughly until the entire lawn is well soaked, and once a day thereafter during periods of dry weather. Seams between sod pieces should disappear within two months. Sodded lawns can withstand light wear after three weeks, and tolerate normal wear after six weeks.

IMPROVING AN ESTABLISHED LAWN

If you are not satisfied with your present lawn, you can partially renovate the space and start enjoying a new lawn in a matter of weeks.

The most common problem in existing lawns is from thatch. In older lawns made up of creeping grasses (especially bluegrass, Bermuda, and zoysia), dead stolons (creeping stems) and roots may accumulate into a thick layer of thatch, which leads to a lackluster, washed-out appearance. By removing the thatch, you make it possible for the grass plants to root more firmly in the soil. Dethatching also helps to eliminate potential problems with diseases and insects that thrive in dead plant material.

Machines designed to remove thatch can often be rented from appliance rental stores. Terminology varies—a power rake, dethatcher, or vertical mower is what to ask for when planning to do the dethatching yourself. Or you can contract to have the work done by a landscaper.

After the thatch is removed, the lawn can be fertilized and allowed to regenerate on its own, or it may be overseeded (seeded at half the normal rate) with updated varieties, a common practice with Kentucky bluegrass. Of course, you cannot overseed a grass that is difficult to propagate that way, like zoysia or improved Bermuda. However, overseeding after dethatching is an excellent way to introduce improved varieties into Kentucky bluegrass or mixed-species lawns.

Where weeds grow in patches, the affected area can be repaired easily. Dig out the weeds with a shovel, and rake the area vigorously. Replant the plot with seed that matches the rest of your lawn, or with small pieces of sod taken from another part of your yard. When replanting small areas, remember that cultivated soil will sink down as it compacts. To make sure your renovated patches don't become little sinkholes, add topsoil if needed to raise the soil line about 1 inch higher than that of adjoining turf.

SOURCES OF SUPPLY

Most companies carry more than one category of seed or plant material, but are listed here under specific headings to facilitate the gardener's search for a particular seed or plant. All sources are mail order; call or write for their catalogs.

Bulbs

Bundles of Bulbs
112 Green Springs Valley Rd.
Owings Mills, MD 21117
(301) 363-1371

Jan de Graaff Oregon Bulb Farms
14071 N.E. Arndt Rd.
Aurora, OR 97002
(503) 226-7425

McLure & Zimmerman
1422 W. Thorndale
Chicago, IL 60660
(312) 274-0113

Messelaar Bulb Company
P.O. Box 269
County Rd., Rt. 150
Ipswich, MA 01938
(508) 356-3737

Quality Dutch Bulbs
P.O. Box 225
50 Lake Dr.
Hillsdale, NJ 07642
(201) 391-6586

John Scheepers, Inc.
R.D. 6, Phillipsburg Rd.
Middletown, NY 10940
(914) 342-3727

TyTy Plantation
P.O. Box 159
TyTy, GA 31795
(912) 386-8400

K. Van Bourgondien & Sons, Inc.
P.O. Box A
245 Farmingdale Rd.
Babylon, NY 11702
(800) 645-5830

Vandenberg
3 Black Meadow Rd.
Chester, NY 10918
(914) 469-2633

Veldheer Tulip Gardens
12755 Quincy St.
Holland, MI 49424
(616) 399-1900

Mary Walker Bulb Company
P.O. Box 256
Omega, GA 31775
(912) 386-1919

Flowers

Bluestone Perennials
7211 Middle Ridge Rd.
Madison, OH 44057
(216) 428-7535
plants

Lee Bristol Nursery
Rt. 55, P.O. Box 5
Gaylordsville, CT 06755-0005
(203) 354-6951
daylily plants

W. Atlee Burpee Company
300 Park Ave.
Warminster, PA 18974
(215) 674-4900
plants and seeds

The Country Garden
Rt. 2, Box 455-A
Crivitz, WI 54114
(715) 757-2045
plants and seeds

Crownsville Nursery
P.O. Box 797
1241 Generals Hwy.
Crownsville, MD 21032
(301) 923-2212
plants

Henry Field Seed & Nursery Company
407 Sycamore St.
Shenandoah, IA 51602
(712) 246-2011
plants and seeds

Johnny's Selected Seeds
Foss Hill Rd.
Albion, ME 04910
(207) 437-9294
seeds

J. W. Jung Seed Company
335 S. High St.
Randolph, WI 53957
(414) 326-3121
plants and seeds

Kelly Nurseries of Dansville, Inc.
19 Maple St.
Dansville, NY 14437
(800) 828-6977
plants

Orol Ledden & Sons
P.O. Box 7
Center & Atlantic Aves.
Sewell, NJ 08080-0007
(609) 468-1000
seeds

Ann Mann's Orchids
9045 Ron-Dn Ln.
Windermere, FL 32786
(305) 876-2625
plants

Milaeger's Gardens
4838 Douglas Ave.
Racine, WI 53402-2498
(414) 639-2371
plants

Park Seed Company, Inc.
P.O. Box 46
Hwy. 254, N.
Greenwood, SC 29648-0046
(803) 223-7333
plants and seeds

Pinetree Garden Seeds
Rt. 100, N.
New Gloucester, ME 04260
(206) 926-3400
seeds

Thompson & Morgan
P.O. Box 1308
Farraday & Gramme Aves.
Jackson, NJ 08527
(800) 367-7333
seeds

We-Du Nurseries
Rt. 5, Box 724
Marion, NC 28752
(704) 738-8300
plants

Fruits

Bear Creek Nursery
P.O. Box 411
Bear Creek Rd.
Northport, WA 99157-0411
plants

Brittingham Plant Farms
P.O. Box 2538
Salisbury, MD 21801
(301) 749-5153
plants

Hastings
P.O. Box 4274
Atlanta, GA 30302-4274
(800) 334-1771
plants

Makielski Berry Farm & Nursery
7130 Platt Rd.
Ypsilanti, MI 48197
(313) 434-3673
plants

J. E. Miller Nurseries, Inc.
5060 W. Lake Rd.
Canandaigua, NY 14424
(800) 828-9630
plants

New York State Fruit Testing Cooperative
  Association
P.O. Box 462
Geneva, NY 14456
(315) 787-2205
plants

Pacific Berry Works
P.O. Box 54
963 Thomas Rd.
Bow, WA 98232
(206) 757-4385
plants

Raintree Nursery
391 Butts Rd.
Morton, WA 98356
(206) 496-5410
plants

St. Lawrence Nurseries
R.D. 2
Rt. 345, Potsdam-Madrid Rd.
Potsdam, NY 13676
(315) 265-6739
plants

Stark Brothers Nurseries & Orchards
  Company
Hwy. 54, W.
Louisiana, MO 63353-0010
(800) 325-4180
plants

Whistling Wings Farm, Inc.
427 West St.
Biddeford, ME 04005
(207) 282-1146
plants

Ground Covers

Conley's Garden Center
Boothbay Harbor, ME 04538
(207) 633-5020
plants and seeds

Ernst Crownvetch Farms
R.D. 5, Box 806
Meadville, PA 16335
(814) 425-7276

Garden Place
P.O. Box 388
6780 Heisley Rd.
Mentor, OH 44061-0388
(216) 255-3705
plants

Gilson Gardens
P.O. Box 277
U.S. Rt. 20
Perry, OH 44081
plants

Native Gardens
Rt. 1, Box 494
Greenback, TN 37742
(615) 856-3350
plants and seeds

Plants of the Wild
P.O. Box 866
Willard Field
Tekoa, WA 99033
seeds

Herbs

Abundant Life Seed Foundation
P.O. Box 771
Port Townsend, WA 98368
(206) 385-5660
seeds

Casa Yerba Gardens
3459 Days Creek Rd.
Days Creek, OR 97429
(503) 825-3534
seeds

Catnip Acres Farm
67 Christian St.
Oxford, CT 06483-1224
(203) 888-5649
seeds

Halcyon Gardens
P.O. Box 124
Gibsonia, PA 15044
(412) 443-5544
seeds

Herb Gathering, Inc.
5742 Kenwood Ave.
Kansas City, MO 64110
(816) 523-2653
seeds

The Herbfarm
32804 Issaquah-Fall City Rd.
Fall City, WA 98024
(206) 784-2222
plants

Meadowbrook Herb Garden
Rt. 138
Wyoming, RI 02898
(401) 539-7603
seeds

Nichols Garden Nursery, Inc.
1190 N. Pacific Hwy.
Albany, OR 97321
(503) 928-9280
seeds

The Rosemary House
120 S. Market St.
Mechanicsburg, PA 17055
(717) 697-5111
plants and seeds

Sandy Mush Herb Nursery
Rt. 2, Surrett Cove Rd.
Leicester, NC 28748
(704) 683-2014
plants and seeds

Well-Sweep Herb Farm
317 Mount Bethel Rd.
Port Murray, NJ 07865
(201) 852-5390
plants

Ornamental Grasses

Applewood Seed Company
P.O. Box 10761, Edgemont Station
Golden, CO 80002
(303) 431-6283
seeds

Kurt Bluemel, Inc.
2740 Greene Ln.
Baldwin, MD 21013
(301) 557-7229
plants

Carter Seeds
475 Mar Vista Dr.
Vista, CA 92083
(629) 724-5931
seeds

Hortica Gardens
P.O. Box 308
Placerville, CA 95667
(916) 622-7089
plants and seeds

Stallings Exotic Nursery
910 Encinitas Blvd.
Encinitas, CA 92024
(619) 753-3079
plants

Andre Viette Farm & Nursery
Rt. 1, Box 16
State Rt. 608
Fisherville, VA 22939
(703) 943-2315
plants

Shrubs

Forestfarm
990 Tetherow Rd.
Williams, OR 97544
(503) 846-6963
plants

Gardens of the Blue Ridge
P.O. Box 10
U.S. 221, N.
Pineola, NC 28662
(704) 733-2417
plants

Heritage Rose Gardens
16831 Mitchell Creek Dr.
Fort Bragg, CA 95437
(707) 984-6959
roses

Little Valley Farm
R.R. 1, Box 287
Richland Center, WI 53581
(608) 538-3180
plants

Pacific Tree Farms
4301 Lynwood Dr.
Chula Vista, CA 92010
(619) 422-2400
plants

Roses of Yesterday & Today
802 Brown's Valley Rd.
Watsonville, CA 95076-0398
(408) 724-3537
roses

Wayside Gardens
P.O. Box 1
Hodges, SC 29695-0001
(800) 845-1124
plants

Weston Nurseries
Rt. 135
Hopkinton, MA 01748-0186
(508) 435-3414
plants

White Flower Farm
Rt. 63
Litchfield, CT 06759-0050
(203) 567-0801
plants

Woodlanders, Inc.
1128 Colleton Ave.
Aiken, SC 29801
(803) 648-7522
plants

Vegetables

Comstock, Ferre & Company
P.O. Box 125
263 Main St.
Wethersfield, CT 06109
seeds

The Cook's Garden
P.O. Box 65
Moffits Bridge
Londonderry, VT 05148
(802) 824-3400
seeds

Farmer Seed & Nursery
P.O. Box 129
818 N.W. Fourth St.
Faribault, MN 55021
(507) 334-1623
plants and seeds

Harris Seeds
3670 Buffalo Rd.
Rochester, NY 14624
(716) 594-9411
plants and seeds

High Altitude Gardens
P.O. Box 4238
620 Sun Valley Rd.
Ketchum, ID 83340
(208) 726-3221
seeds

Ed Hume Seeds, Inc.
P.O. Box 1450
Kent, WA 98035
(206) 859-1110
seeds

Le Jardin du Gourmet
P.O. Box 44
West Danville, VT 05873-0044
(802) 684-2201
seeds

Le Marche Seeds International
P.O. Box 190
Dixon, CA 95620
(916) 678-9244
seeds

Liberty Seed Company
P.O. Box 806
128 First Dr., S.E.
New Philadelphia, OH 44663
(216) 364-1611
seeds

Plants of the Southwest
1812 Second St.
Santa Fe, NM 87501
(505) 983-1548
seeds

Seeds Blum
Idaho City Stage
Boise, ID 83706
(208) 343-2202
seeds

Shepherd's Garden Seeds
6116 Hwy. 9
Felton, CA 95018
(408) 335-5400
seeds

Southern Exposure Seed Exchange
P.O. Box 158
North Garden, VA 22959
seeds

Stokes Seed Company
P.O. Box 548
Buffalo, NY 14240
(716) 688-4300
seeds

Sunrise Oriental Seed Company
P.O. Box 10058
Elmwood, CT 06110-0058
seeds

Tomato Growers Supply Company
P.O. Box 2237
Fort Myers, FL 33902
(813) 332-4157
seeds

Vines

Angelwood Nursery
12839 McKee School Rd.
Woodburn, OR 97071
(503) 634-2233
plants

Clifford's Perennial & Vine
Rt. 2, Box 320
East Troy, WI 53120
(414) 642-7156
plants

The Fragrant Path
P.O. Box 328
Fort Calhoun, NE 68023
seeds

J. L. Hudson, Seedsman
P.O. Box 1058
Redwood City, CA 94064
seeds

The Plant Kingdom
P.O. Box 7273
Lincoln Acres, CA 92047
(619) 267-1991
plants

Woodlanders, Inc.
1128 Colleton Ave.
Aiken, SC 29801
(803) 648-7522
plants

Equipment and Garden Products

Alsto's Handy Helpers
P.O. Box 1267
Rt. 150, E.
Galesburg, IL 61401
(800) 447-8192

Brookstone Company
127 Vose Farm Rd.
Peterborough, NH 03458
(603) 924-7181

Gardener's Eden
P.O. Box 737
San Francisco, CA 94120-7307
(415) 428-9292

Gardener's Supply Company
128 Intervale Rd.
Burlington, VT 05401
(802) 863-1700

Mellinger's Inc.
2310 W. South Range Rd.
North Lima, OH 44452
(800) 321-7444

The Natural Gardening Company
27 Rutherford Ave.
San Anselmo, CA 94960
(415) 456-5060

Necessary Trading Company
P.O. Box 305
626 Main St.
New Castle, VA 24127
(703) 864-5103

Ringer Research
9959 Valley View Rd.
Eden Prairie, MN 55344-3585
(612) 941-4180

Smith & Hawken
25 Corte Madera
Mill Valley, CA 94941
(415) 383-6399

Warnico/USA, Inc.
59 Rutter St.
Rochester, NY 14610
(800) 537-8007 (NY)
(800) 451-1118 (US)

INDEX

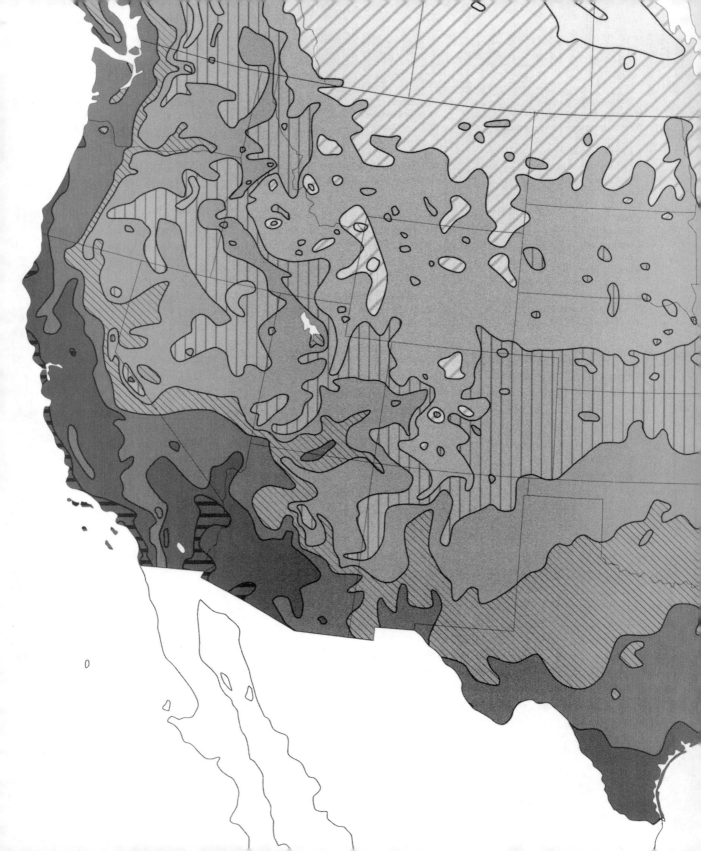

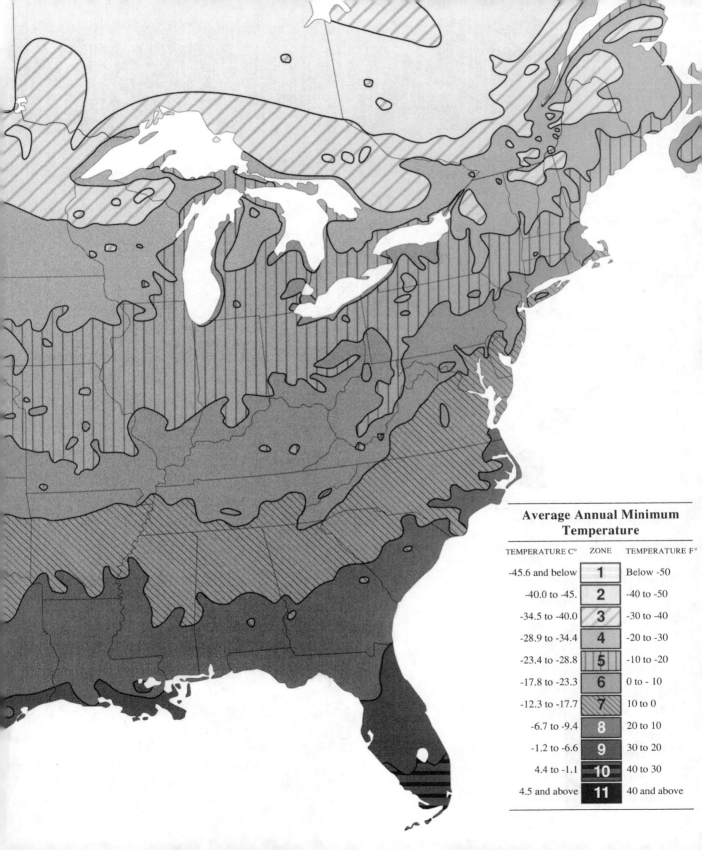

Average Annual Minimum Temperature

TEMPERATURE C°	ZONE	TEMPERATURE F°
-45.6 and below	1	Below -50
-40.0 to -45.	2	-40 to -50
-34.5 to -40.0	3	-30 to -40
-28.9 to -34.4	4	-20 to -30
-23.4 to -28.8	5	-10 to -20
-17.8 to -23.3	6	0 to -10
-12.3 to -17.7	7	10 to 0
-6.7 to -9.4	8	20 to 10
-1.2 to -6.6	9	30 to 20
4.4 to -1.1	10	40 to 30
4.5 and above	11	40 and above

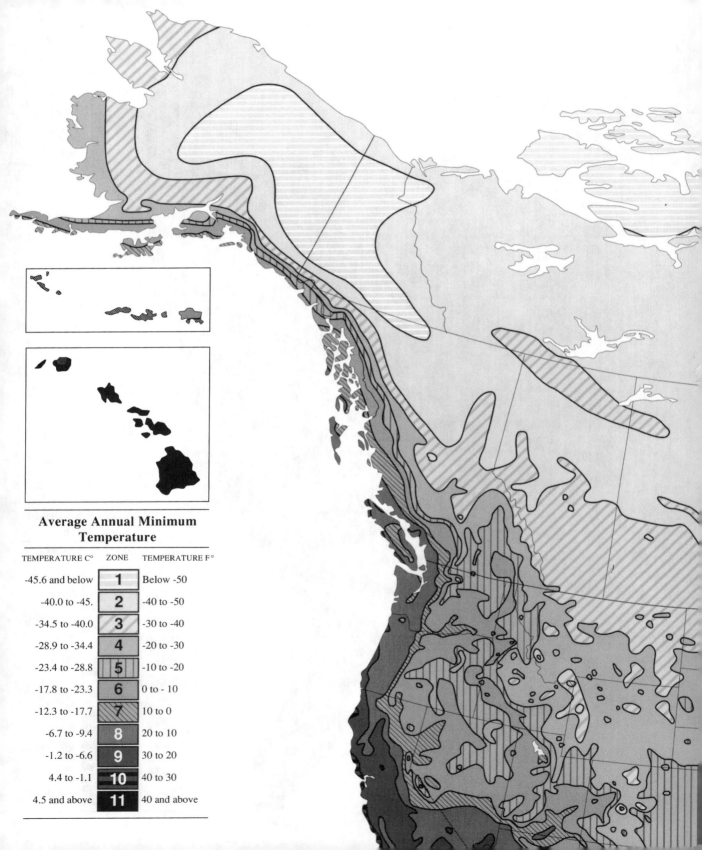

Average Annual Minimum Temperature

TEMPERATURE C°	ZONE	TEMPERATURE F°
-45.6 and below	1	Below -50
-40.0 to -45.	2	-40 to -50
-34.5 to -40.0	3	-30 to -40
-28.9 to -34.4	4	-20 to -30
-23.4 to -28.8	5	-10 to -20
-17.8 to -23.3	6	0 to -10
-12.3 to -17.7	7	10 to 0
-6.7 to -9.4	8	20 to 10
-1.2 to -6.6	9	30 to 20
4.4 to -1.1	10	40 to 30
4.5 and above	11	40 and above